Digitalization of Islamic Finance

Muhammad Ridhwan Ab. Aziz
Universiti Sains Islam Malaysia, Malaysia

Fuadah Johari
Universiti Sains Islam Malaysia, Malaysia

Ahmad Rafiki
Universitas Medan Area, Indonesia

IGI Global
Scientific Publishing
Publishing Tomorrow's Research Today

Vice President of Editorial | Melissa Wagner
Managing Editor of Acquisitions | Mikaela Felty
Managing Editor of Book Development | Jocelynn Hessler
Production Manager | Mike Brehm
Cover Design | Phillip Shickler

Published in the United States of America by
IGI Global Scientific Publishing
701 East Chocolate Avenue
Hershey, PA, 17033, USA
Tel: 717-533-8845
Fax: 717-533-8661
Website: https://www.igi-global.com E-mail: cust@igi-global.com

Library of Congress Cataloging-in-Publication Data

Names: Muhammad Ridhwan Ab. Aziz, editor. | Fuadah Johari, editor. | Rafiki, Ahmad, 1981- editor.
Title: Digitalization of Islamic finance / edited by Muhammad Ridhwan Ab. Aziz, Fuadah Johari, Ahmad Rafiki.
Description: Hershey, PA : IGI Global Scientific Publishing, [2025] | Includes bibliographical references and index. | Summary: "This book aims to provide relevant theoretical frameworks and the latest empirical research findings in the area to promote inclusive and sustainable financial systems aligned with Islamic principles and to support the achievement of the Sustainable Development Goals (SDGs)"-- Provided by publisher.
Identifiers: LCCN 2024048798 (print) | LCCN 2024048799 (ebook) | ISBN 9798369356531 (hardcover) | ISBN 9798369356548 (paperback) | ISBN 9798369356555 (ebook)
Subjects: LCSH: Finance--Religious aspects--Islam. | Finance--Technological innovations.
Classification: LCC BP190.5.F56 D54 2025 (print) | LCC BP190.5.F56 (ebook) | DDC 297.2/72--dc23/eng/20250111
LC record available at https://lccn.loc.gov/2024048798
LC ebook record available at https://lccn.loc.gov/2024048799

British Cataloguing in Publication Data
A Cataloguing in Publication record for this book is available from the British Library.

Table of Contents

Detailed Table of Contents

This chapter examines the impact of digital technologies on Islamic finance, focusing on Maqasid Al-Shariah and Maslahah. Technologies like blockchain and AI are transforming Islamic financial services. These advancements improve accessibility, efficiency, and adherence to Shariah principles. They also support Sustainable Development Goals (SDGs), such as reducing poverty, enhancing education, and promoting environmental sustainability. The integration of digital solutions in Islamic finance fosters ethical growth and inclusive development. This chapter provides valuable insights for policymakers and financial institutions looking to leverage digital innovations to achieve ethical and sustainable financial practices.

Participation banking in Turkey is a system that has been an alternative to conventional banking Although participation banking in Turkey has encountered many challenges thanks to the digitalization process, they could be able to reduce costs, increase revenues, ensure innovation, and respond to customer needs more quickly and effectively, in other words, they have strengthened their position in the financial sector and have managed to become an important alternative to conventional banks. The main goal of this study is to examine the development of participation banking in Turkey and to examine the performance of participation banks in the digital transformation process. It is revealed with the study that, efforts to increase product diversity, developing tools that can respond to customer needs more easily and quickly, informing the public (especially young population) accurately about participation banking, and increasing financial and digital literacy in the country may be the practices that will pave the way for participation banks in the digital transformation process.

This chapter explores the transformative potential of financial technology (FinTech) in the context of Islamic inheritance, offering innovative solutions to address the complexities and challenges inherent in the traditional practices. By integrating FinTech with Islamic principles, this research aims to enhance efficiency, transparency, and accessibility in the management and distribution of Islamic inheritance. Through qualitative analysis, the chapter examines various FinTech applications, such as blockchain, smart contracts, and digital platforms. The chapter also identifies the benefits and potential challenges associated with the adoption of FinTech in Islamic inheritance processes. The findings suggest that FinTech innovations can significantly streamline inheritance procedures, reduce disputes, and ensure equitable distribution among heirs, thereby aligning with the ethical and legal standards of Islamic jurisprudence.

Within the rapidly changing world of finance, Islamic finance is a unique sector with fundamentally ethical and Shariah-compliant processes at its core. A new age of innovation and accessibility in the financial industry has been brought about by the rise of Financial Technology, or Fintech. This chapter explores the intersection of Fintech, Blockchain, and Islamic finance and shows how these developments have revolutionized the market. The chapter seeks to offer a thorough analysis of the three main ways that Fintech—Digitalization, Development, and Disruption—is changing Islamic finance. It examines the current digital revolution in Islamic finance, investments, wealth management, insurance (takaful), and real-world examples and case studies. The book also investigates the development of Shariah-compliant Fintech solutions, or Shariahtech, and the regulatory frameworks supporting their growth.

Malaysia's rapidly growing Islamic finance industry is currently transitioning into the digitalization era. This shift underscores the importance of integrating digital tools and platforms to promote financial literacy and education. The chapter emphasizes the need to provide individuals with the necessary knowledge and skills to navigate the digital financial landscape, particularly in understanding Islamic financial products. It also highlights the significance of both formal and informal digital educational platforms in disseminating Islamic financial knowledge. Furthermore, the chapter stresses the comprehensive focus required for Islamic financial education across formal and informal settings, given the impact of the digital revolution on the financial services industry. By addressing the digital challenges faced by learners and educators and proposing solutions to bridge the gap between traditional and modern approaches, this chapter provides valuable insights for stakeholders in the Islamic finance and education sectors.

Legal certainty and investment are closely intertwined in Islamic economic frameworks, particularly in Indonesia. Legal certainty, defined as the clarity of norms, serves as a guide and protection for justice seekers. Investment involves capital accumulation, knowledge transfer, job creation and development of disadvantaged areas, necessitating a stable legal environment. The government recognizes the crucial link between legal certainty and investment, addressing various issues like the environment, employment, and socio-cultural aspects. From an Islamic law perspective, legal certainty is fundamental and hinted at in the Al Quran, forming the basis for asset development through investment. the holistic view of investment in Islam encompasses material and spiritual dimensions, emphasizing honesty, halal and haram principles, and social responsibilities. By ensuring legal certainty, policymakers can create a conducive environment for investors, fostering economic growth and national development.

The advancement of the current technology has totally changed the banking and financial services. Financial institution has been urged to react to the changes in order to provide a better service and product to the customers as well as to the underserved people. Throughout the development of digital banking, it will help many people to access the banking services in improving their socio-economic. However, the model of Shariah compliant digital banking is compulsory in order to achieve Maqasid al-Shariah for financial inclusion. The objective of this study is aimed to develop integrated model of Islamic digital banking based on Maqasid al-Shariah for financial Inclusion. Research methodology that has been applied is qualitative approach in which this research is conducted verification model with the experts. The selection of the experts is based on digital banking field and Shariah background. A general finding shows that, the integrated model is viable to be implemented in line with the current development of digital era.

This research aims to assess public attitudes towards a novel investing approach known as Islamic securities crowdsourcing, drawing on established context. Researchers employed the Unified Theory of Acceptance and Use of Technology (UTAUT) methodology to maintain this viewpoint. This research is based on the integrated UTAUT. The data were analyzed using multiple linear regression models in SPSS. The primary findings indicate that Performance Expectancy, Social Influence, and Facilitating Conditions strongly influence an individual's inclination to invest in securities crowdsourcing. Effort Expectancy does not significantly influence the decision to invest in stocks crowdsourcing. The results indicate that cooperation between the government and securities crowdfunding institutions is essential for establishing a well-organized investment environment and enhancing sharia financial literacy. This study enhances sharia financial literacy in securities crowdfunding and offers an overview of these institutions in the advancement of securities crowdfunding.

Due to the increasing use of e-wallets, it is crucial to evaluate their compliance with Shariah to meet the needs of Muslim customers in line with Islamic principles. This chapter seeks to offer understanding of maqasid al-Shariah in the context of e-wallet usage and financial well-being. In connection with this, the development of financial technology will expand the capabilities and services of e-wallets beyond being just a basic payment tool. This expansion includes multiple funding sources, such as credit cards, buy now, pay later (BNPL), and short-term loans. These multi-sourcing fundings may trigger expenditure, aid, or impede financial well-being. Therefore, a user's spending behaviour can affect the e-wallet usage and their financial well-being. Understanding the results of this research would partly contribute to the general knowledge of Islamic finance and fintech, with the intention of developing Shariah-compliant digital financial solutions suited to the needs of Muslims all over the world.

The research aims at analyzing the correlation between the accumulation of Non-Performing Assets (NPAs) in the private sector banks (ICICI, HDFC, Kotak Mahindra, Federal, Axis Bank) and the economic development of the Indian economy. An analysis of the correlation between NPAs of various private sector banks with annual Gross Domestic Product (GDP), Interest rates, Inflation rates, Unemployment rates. The purpose of this study is to investigate the relationship between various economic variables and the increase in NPA, particularly during a period when the economy is recovering from the COVID-19-induced stagnation in economic activities leading to an increase in inflation rates.

Sadaqa is a charitable donation encouraged by Islam. It is donated to the marginalized society or for community empowerment initiatives. The instrument can be deployed for inclusivity-motive projects. Empirical evidences on the programmes are well-documented. Islamic Banking Industry (IBI) has shown to be successful in the commercial sector but less pro-active in the welfare sector. The introduction of Sustainable Development Goals agenda and Value Based Intermediation (VBI) has inspired IBI to proactively embark on social empowerment initiatives positioning IBI in the inclusivity initiatives. Case study on Sadaqa House initiative by Bank Islam Malaysia Berhad showcasing how sadaqa can be harnessed and contribute to inclusivity programmes. Malaysia's Islamic Finance sector is progressive with a top-down agenda by the regulatory bodies. Bank Negara Malaysia's VBI, Malaysia International Islamic Finance Centre (MIFC) Leadership Council's Position Paper and other initiatives proof the progressiveness of IBI. This includes Sadaqa House's blended financing instruments.

Waqf-driven Inclusive Prosperity: Exploring the Intersection of Islamic Finance, Fintech, and Sustainable Development Goals (SDGs) examines how fintech innovations and AI-driven tools are advancing waqf management to foster inclusive economic growth and support the SDGs. The chapter explores the Waqf Analytics Platform for predictive analytics, resource optimization, and impact assessment, alongside fintech advancements such as AI-based fundraising, smart contracts, and digital platforms. It addresses challenges like data privacy, Shariah compliance, and implementation costs, and identifies future research opportunities, including Shariah-compliant AI algorithms and AI blockchain integration. The chapter offers insights into how these technologies can drive waqf initiatives and contribute to sustainable development.

The digital age is transforming Waqf institutions, enabling new opportunities for cooperation and co-creation. This chapter explores how digital information-sharing initiatives promote co-creation by enhancing information exchange efficiency. By leveraging digital platforms and tools, Waqf institutions can foster collaboration among stakeholders like donors, beneficiaries, and community members. This open information sharing improves engagement, accountability, and trust. The chapter, based on research from 2013-2023, covers digital tools, effective dissemination, and overcoming challenges, with case studies and some examples. It also identifies risks and provides solutions, highlighting future opportunities for Waqf institutions.

Preface

The rapid digital transformation across the global financial landscape is reshaping Islamic finance, offering both opportunities and challenges in equal manner. The convergence of technology and Islamic finance is sparking new discussions, and innovation is now a driving force behind efforts to create inclusive, accessible, and resilient financial systems that align with Islamic principles and Maqasid al-Shariah. As editors, we present this book, *Digitalization of Islamic Finance*, as a comprehensive exploration into how digital tools and platforms are reimagining Islamic finance in an era of heightened digital and economic connectivity.

In recent years, nations like Malaysia have taken significant strides to advance Islamic fintech and the broader digital economy to cater to the growing demand for Shariah-compliant financial products and services. Technology-driven solutions, including blockchain and other disruptive innovations, are being considered as means to enhance inclusivity, efficiency, and transparency within the industry. However, the transition from conventional to Islamic finance models is not without its hurdles. Operational complexities and the lack of standardization in Islamic financial instruments remain significant obstacles. The need for a unified approach to Islamic finance continues to be a subject of discussion and harmonization, with calls for further development to address efficiency gaps and maximize impact.

This book aims to provide a robust theoretical and practical foundation alongside the latest empirical research to encourage the sustainable growth of Islamic finance and its alignment with the Sustainable Development Goals (SDGs). Topics covered include improving the efficiency of financial services through technology, the importance of standardizing Shariah-compliant instruments, and strategies for increasing awareness and engagement among stakeholders. We believe that, through such insights, readers will come to appreciate the strategic role of technology in propelling Islamic finance forward.

Our intended audience spans a broad spectrum of professionals engaged in both Islamic finance and information technology, including practitioners, academics, students, entrepreneurs, and policymakers. Whether the reader is an experienced professional seeking to deepen their expertise or a student new to the field, this volume serves as both a guide and a source of inspiration for future developments in Islamic finance.

We hope this book fosters greater collaboration among Islamic finance institutions, policymakers, and technology providers, ultimately facilitating further expansion of Islamic finance on a global scale.

Organization of the Book

In *Chapter 1: Digital Frontiers in Islamic Finance: Advancing SDGs through Maqasid and Maslahah*, the authors delve into the transformative role of digital technologies in Islamic finance. They emphasize how tools such as blockchain and AI not only streamline financial processes but also ensure compliance with Maqasid Al-Shariah and Maslahah, fostering accessibility, efficiency, and ethical integrity. This chapter highlights the alignment of these digital advances with the Sustainable Development Goals (SDGs), underscoring Islamic finance's potential to alleviate poverty, promote education, and contribute to environmental sustainability. The authors provide a strategic overview for policymakers and financial institutions on leveraging digital innovations to uphold ethical finance while promoting inclusive growth.

Chapter 2: An Evaluation on the Development and Digitalization Performance of Participation Banking in Turkey examines the evolution of participation banking in Turkey as a viable alternative to conventional banking. Despite challenges, the chapter reveals how digitalization has enabled these banks to lower costs, boost revenues, and respond more effectively to customer needs. It proposes that strategies like diversifying products, enhancing public awareness, especially among younger populations, and improving financial and digital literacy will strengthen participation banks' positions within Turkey's financial sector, driving broader adoption and effectiveness in the digital age.

In *Chapter 3: Innovative Solutions: FinTech Transformations in Islamic Inheritance*, the authors explore how FinTech can address complexities in Islamic inheritance practices. The chapter discusses integrating technologies like blockchain and smart contracts to enhance transparency, efficiency, and accessibility. Through qualitative analysis, the authors show how these FinTech applications can streamline inheritance processes, reduce disputes, and ensure equitable distribution, aligning with Islamic legal and ethical standards. This chapter offers crucial insights into how FinTech can modernize inheritance management in an ethically sound manner.

Chapter 4: Islamic Finance, Islamic Fintech, and Digital Currency in the Digital Transformation Era: The Role of Blockchain Technology in Industry 4.0 explores the convergence of FinTech, blockchain, and Islamic finance, highlighting their disruptive influence on the financial sector. The authors discuss how digital transformation, development, and disruption impact key areas such as investments, wealth management, and Takaful (Islamic insurance), while offering real-world case studies. The chapter also introduces Shariah-compliant FinTech solutions, or "Shariahtech," and the regulatory frameworks supporting this evolution, presenting a comprehensive view of digital finance in the Islamic context.

In *Chapter 5: Digital Dilemmas and Solutions: Addressing Financial Challenges and Exploring Islamic Financial Educational Platforms*, the authors address Malaysia's Islamic finance sector's transition to digital platforms, focusing on financial literacy and education. This chapter stresses the importance of equipping individuals with the skills necessary to navigate the digital financial landscape, especially within Islamic finance. By exploring formal and informal educational platforms, the authors offer solutions for bridging traditional and digital financial education, enhancing literacy, and helping stakeholders adapt to digital challenges.

Chapter 6: Elevating Investment Confidence: The Imperative of Legal Certainty in Islamic Economic Framework emphasizes the link between legal certainty and investment confidence within Indonesia's Islamic economic framework. The chapter explores how clear legal norms protect investors and facilitate economic growth, aligned with Islamic law's emphasis on justice and ethical principles. Through this lens, the authors advocate for policies that bolster legal clarity, ultimately creating a stable environment conducive to sustainable development.

Chapter 7: Integrated Model of Islamic Digital Banking for Financial Inclusion Based on Maqasid Al-Shariah presents a framework for a Shariah-compliant digital banking model aimed at advancing financial inclusion. Utilizing qualitative research, the chapter details an integrated approach that leverages digital tools to improve socio-economic access and provide services tailored to underserved populations. The chapter's findings underscore the viability of this model for achieving Maqasid Al-Shariah goals in today's digital economy.

Chapter 8: Exploring Public Perceptions of Sharia Securities Crowdfunding: A Case Study from Indonesia, evaluates public attitudes toward Islamic securities crowdfunding in Indonesia. Using the UTAUT model and regression analysis, the chapter reveals that performance expectations, social influence, and facilitating conditions significantly affect individuals' willingness to invest. The authors advocate for collaboration between government and crowdfunding institutions to improve financial literacy and create a supportive investment environment, enhancing public understanding of sharia-compliant crowdfunding.

In *Chapter 9: Unleashing the E-Wallet Enchantment: A Journey Through Maqasid al-Shariah*, the authors explore the rise of e-wallets and their compliance with Shariah principles. The chapter examines how digital financial tools impact users' financial well-being, discussing expanded services like credit options that may influence spending behaviors. The authors highlight the significance of designing Shariah-compliant e-wallet solutions that align with Muslim consumers' ethical requirements, presenting a pathway to responsible digital finance.

Chapter 10: Empirical Study on Relationship between Macro Economic Variables and Non-Performing Assets in Private Banks investigates the influence of macroeconomic factors on non-performing assets (NPAs) in Indian private banks. The chapter provides an analysis of variables like GDP, interest rates, inflation, and unemployment on NPAs, particularly in the wake of economic slowdowns. Verma's findings offer valuable insights for understanding and managing NPAs, relevant for policymakers and financial institutions in a post-COVID-19 context.

Chapter 11: Harnessing Sadaqa to Achieve Inclusivity and Progressiveness of Islamic Banking, examines the role of Sadaqa (charitable donations) in promoting inclusivity within Islamic banking. The chapter showcases Malaysia's Sadaqa House initiative, highlighting how such programs can empower marginalized communities while aligning with Sustainable Development Goals. This case study underscores the Islamic banking sector's potential to balance commercial success with social responsibility, supported by national agendas and regulatory frameworks.

Chapter 12: Waqf-driven Inclusive Prosperity: Exploring the Intersection of Islamic Finance, Fintech, and Sustainable Development Goals discusses the integration of FinTech and AI tools in waqf (charitable endowment) management. The chapter details innovations such as the Waqf Analytics Platform, which enhances efficiency and impact assessment. By addressing Shariah compliance and data privacy, the chapter outlines opportunities for future research in AI applications, showcasing how waqf can support economic inclusion and the SDGs.

Finally, *Chapter 13: Enhancing Co-Creation in Waqf Institutions with Sharing Information Initiatives in the Digital Era* examines the transformative potential of digital information-sharing in waqf institutions. The chapter discusses how digital platforms facilitate transparency, accountability, and engagement among stakeholders, fostering collaborative efforts. By detailing the benefits and challenges of digital information sharing, this chapter provides valuable insights into how waqf institutions can leverage technology for improved stakeholder cooperation and social impact.

CONCLUSION

In closing, this book, *Digitalization of Islamic Finance*, presents a comprehensive exploration of the transformative power of digital technologies within the field of Islamic finance. Each chapter offers unique insights into how FinTech, AI, blockchain, and digital education platforms are reshaping traditional finance, fostering ethical growth, and advancing financial inclusivity in line with Islamic principles and Maqasid al-Shariah. Through practical case studies, policy analysis, and empirical research, the contributors highlight the potential of these innovations to not only streamline financial practices but also to empower communities, reduce inequalities, and support sustainable development goals.

As editors, we are inspired by the diversity of perspectives and depth of expertise shared by our contributing authors. They underscore the vital role that Maqasid al-Shariah and Maslahah play in shaping ethical financial frameworks, which prioritize transparency, inclusivity, and community welfare. Together, these insights provide a roadmap for academics, practitioners, and policymakers eager to embrace digital advancements in Islamic finance while maintaining strong adherence to Shariah-compliant values.

Our hope is that this volume will inspire continued exploration, innovation, and collaboration among stakeholders in Islamic finance, guiding the development of robust digital solutions that not only meet the financial needs of today but also align with the holistic aspirations for a just and prosperous future. As we embark on this journey into the evolving landscape of Islamic finance, let us carry forward the commitment to creating accessible, transparent, and socially responsible Islamic financial systems for all.

Chapter 1
Digital Frontiers in Islamic Finance Advancing SDGs Through Maqasid and Maslahah

Kamarudin Othman
Universiti Teknologi MARA, Malaysia

Muhammad Zarunnaim Haji Wahab
https://orcid.org/0000-0002-2016-7372
Universiti Teknologi MARA, Malaysia

Mohd Shahid Azmi Mohd Saufi
https://orcid.org/0009-0003-5528-475X
Universiti Teknologi MARA, Malaysia

ABSTRACT

This chapter examines the impact of digital technologies on Islamic finance, focusing on Maqasid Al-Shariah and Maslahah. Technologies like blockchain and AI are transforming Islamic financial services. These advancements improve accessibility, efficiency, and adherence to Shariah principles. They also support Sustainable Development Goals (SDGs), such as reducing poverty, enhancing education, and promoting environmental sustainability. The integration of digital solutions in Islamic finance fosters ethical growth and inclusive development. This chapter provides valuable insights for policymakers and financial institutions looking to leverage digital innovations to achieve ethical and sustainable financial practices.

DOI: 10.4018/979-8-3693-5653-1.ch001

INTRODUCTION

In today's global economy, where financial inclusion and sustainable development are pressing concerns, Islamic finance has emerged as an ethically driven system rooted in Shariah principles, offering unique solutions that align closely with global development goals, particularly the SDGs (Trimulato et al., 2022). This chapter explores how Islamic finance, historically grounded in trade financing, has evolved into a comprehensive financial system that adheres to ethical and moral guidelines, addressing issues such as poverty alleviation, economic inclusivity, and ethical investment. Core principles of Islamic finance such as risk-sharing, the prohibition of interest (riba), and the avoidance of speculative activities (gharar) are designed to promote fairness and prevent exploitation. These tenets distinguish Islamic finance from conventional systems, positioning it as a viable, socially responsible alternative within the global financial landscape (Yunus et al., 2018).

Despite this solid ethical foundation and historical significance, Islamic finance faces several modern challenges, including limited financial inclusion, the need for transparency, and rising demands for sustainable practices. These challenges are further intensified by the necessity to meet global development objectives, as outlined by the SDGs. Integrating digital frontier technologies presents a promising path forward, enabling Islamic finance to reach underserved communities, improve regulatory compliance, and strengthen its ethical practices. By adopting these technologies, Islamic finance can bridge critical gaps in inclusivity and transparency, effectively aligning itself with both the ethical imperatives of Shariah and the global sustainability agenda.

Figure 1. Islamic finance assets growth 2021-2027, USD billion (London Stock Exchange Group, 2023)

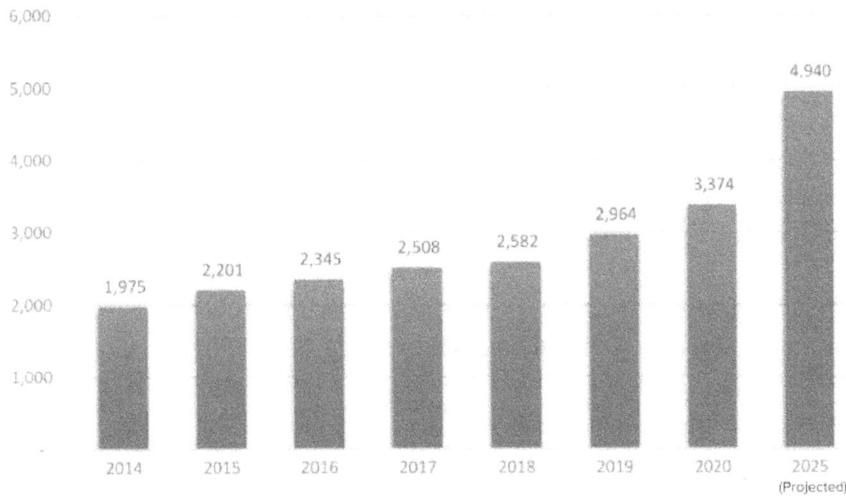

In recent years, Islamic finance has seen remarkable expansion, particularly in regions with large Muslim populations such as the Middle East, Southeast Asia, and parts of Africa. Its successful integration into the global financial ecosystem demonstrates the scalability of its practices and broad appeal, grounded in ethical principles that resonate with both Islamic and non-Islamic communities. The Islamic Financial Development Report 2023 underscores this growth, noting an increase in Islamic finance assets from USD 2,409 billion in 2016 to USD 4,508 billion in 2022, with projections nearing USD 6,667 billion by 2027, as shown in Figure 1.

The digital age has ushered in transformative changes across sectors, and Islamic finance is no exception. The sector's transition from traditional methods to digital platforms marks a critical evolution, particularly with the adoption of technologies like blockchain and smart contracts. This shift from Islamic fintech to a digital Islamic finance ecosystem not only reflects technological advancement but also signifies a deeper integration of these technologies with Shariah principles. Tools such as mobile applications, blockchain, peer-to-peer (P2P) platforms, and artificial intelligence enhance the accessibility, efficiency, and Shariah compliance of financial services.

Moreover, Islamic finance's focus on ethical financing, community welfare, and environmental stewardship closely aligns with the SDGs. Initiatives such as Islamic microfinance have been instrumental in serving underserved communities, promoting entrepreneurship, and empowering grassroots economic development, thereby actively contributing to poverty alleviation and economic growth.

This chapter aims to explore how digital technologies in Islamic finance can further the SDGs by examining these advancements through the lens of Maqasid (objectives of Shariah) and Maslahah (public interest). By exploring these applications and their potential impacts, this study seeks to provide stakeholders with valuable insights into emerging trends within Islamic finance as the world increasingly shifts toward a digital ecosystem.

THE EVOLUTION OF ISLAMIC FINTECH TO DIGITAL FRONTIERS

In today's rapidly advancing technological landscape, the term "digital frontier" refers to the continuously expanding and evolving boundaries of digital innovation. It encompasses pioneering technologies and trends that are reshaping how individuals, businesses, and industries operate. In the context of Islamic finance, digital frontiers signify not only the adoption of transformative technologies such as artificial intelligence (AI), blockchain, big data, and machine learning but also their integration in ways that respect Shariah principles. This integration ensures that technological advancements remain efficient and impactful while adhering to the ethical and socio-economic objectives outlined by Maqasid Al-Shariah (the objectives of Islamic law).

The concept of digital frontiers in Islamic finance builds upon the foundations laid by Islamic fintech and Digital Islamic Finance, emphasizing Shariah-compliant innovations that prioritize transparency, inclusivity, and social justice. Through this approach, Islamic finance is well-positioned to address global socio-economic challenges without compromising its ethical commitments. The responsible implementation of advanced technologies empowers Islamic finance to support sustainable development, develop innovative financial models, and address complex issues on a global scale, marking a significant evolution in the field.

This chapter addresses a crucial gap in the current evolution of Islamic finance: the limited application of digital frontier technologies to meet pressing global needs. While Islamic fintech has shown substantial growth, the full potential of advanced technologies such as AI, blockchain, and big data remains untapped. Embracing these technologies is essential for Islamic finance to realize its role as a tool for inclusive, ethical, and sustainable development. By advancing into these digital frontiers, Islamic finance can enhance transparency, broaden its reach to underserved communities, and more effectively align with the Sustainable Development Goals (SDGs), establishing itself as a globally impactful alternative to conventional financial systems.

Table 1 provides a structured comparison between three stages in the evolution of technology within the Islamic finance sector: Islamic fintech, digital Islamic finance, and digital frontiers in Islamic finance. Each of these categories represents a progressive step in integrating technology with Shariah-compliant financial services, distinguished by unique features, objectives, and technological applications.

Table 1. The evolution of Islamic fintech to digital frontiers

Aspect	Islamic Fintech	Digital Islamic Finance	Digital Frontiers in Islamic Finance
Definition	Use of innovative technology to create and support financial services adhering to Islamic law.	Digitization of existing Islamic financial services to improve their delivery and efficiency.	Explores new areas and utilizes cutting-edge technologies to push the boundaries of what's possible in Islamic finance.
Focus	Innovation and development of new tech-based products that are Shariah-compliant.	Integration of digital technologies into traditional Islamic financial operations and systems.	Emphasis on pioneering technologies and methodologies that may redefine or significantly evolve the Islamic finance industry.
Technologies Involved	Mobile apps, blockchain, P2P platforms, artificial intelligence for Shariah-compliant transactions.	Online banking systems, digital platforms for Takaful, Sukuk trading platforms.	Advanced technologies such as big data, AI, machine learning, and blockchain to explore new financial products and services.
Objective	To enhance accessibility, efficiency, and compliance of financial services with Islamic principles.	To convert traditional Islamic financial services into more user-friendly and efficient digital formats.	To innovate and experiment with new models and services that can expand the scope of Islamic finance.
Examples	Shariah-compliant mobile banking, Islamic robo-advisors, blockchain-based halal investment platforms.	Digitized processes for applying for and managing Islamic loans, online platforms for managing Takaful policies, digital issuance and management of Sukuk.	Development of AI-driven Shariah-compliant investment strategies, blockchain for Islamic charitable donations (Zakat), virtual reality for Hajj savings.

Source: Self-construct

Islamic Fintech

Islamic Fintech is a fast-evolving field that blends financial technology with the requirements of Islamic law (Shariah) to provide compliant financial services (Shaikh et al., 2020). Its primary aim is to innovate within the realm of financial services, ensuring that these solutions adhere strictly to Islamic principles like the prohibition of interest (riba) and speculative transactions (gharar) (Saba et al., 2019). Islamic Fintech places a strong emphasis on developing new, tech-based products that address the unique needs of users who seek Shariah-compliant financial options.

This sector encompasses technologies like mobile applications, blockchain, peer-to-peer (P2P) lending platforms, and artificial intelligence to verify and facilitate halal (permissible) transactions.

For example, mobile banking applications that operate on Shariah-compliant principles have gained traction, providing users with accessible banking that avoids interest-based income and operates within Islamic ethical standards. Additionally, Islamic robo-advisors, which use algorithms to offer investment advice, are designed to recommend portfolios that exclude industries prohibited in Islamic finance, such as those involving alcohol or gambling. Blockchain technology is also prominent within Islamic Fintech, particularly in areas like halal investment platforms, where transparency and trust are essential. By leveraging these technologies, Islamic Fintech enhances accessibility and provides efficient solutions that align with religious values.

Digital Islamic Finance

Digital Islamic Finance is focused on the digitization of traditional Islamic financial services, aiming to improve delivery and efficiency without changing the core structure of these services. Unlike Islamic Fintech, which creates new solutions, Digital Islamic Finance focuses on enhancing existing Islamic finance products by making them more user-friendly through digital platforms. For instance, digital banking solutions tailored to Islamic finance rules allow users to open accounts, apply for Islamic loans, or invest in Takaful (Islamic insurance) products entirely online. The digitization of these processes allows institutions to streamline services, offering quicker, more efficient transactions for clients while still meeting all Shariah compliance requirements (Alam et al., 2019).

In practice, digital platforms have made it possible for users to manage their Takaful policies or trade in Sukuk (Islamic bonds) through online trading platforms. This digital shift makes it easier for users to interact with Islamic financial institutions from anywhere, enhancing the reach and convenience of traditional Islamic banking and insurance services. By transitioning to online systems, Digital Islamic Finance also reduces administrative costs and processing times, creating a more agile and responsive financial sector. Overall, Digital Islamic Finance does not seek to revolutionize Islamic financial products but rather aims to modernize them to align with the digital expectations of today's consumers.

Digital Frontiers in Islamic Finance

Digital Frontiers in Islamic Finance represents the most advanced segment of Islamic finance technology, incorporating cutting-edge innovations to redefine what is possible within the sector. This area explores new technological frontiers like big data, artificial intelligence, machine learning, and blockchain to design next-generation financial products and services (Bughin et al.,2017). The objective is to push the boundaries of Islamic finance by creating novel financial models and services that expand beyond traditional limitations, offering unique options for Shariah-compliant finance. For instance, AI-driven investment strategies tailored to Shariah compliance can provide personalized, ethical investment plans, adapting to market trends while excluding prohibited sectors.

Another example is the use of blockchain for Zakat (charitable donations), where this technology ensures transparent and efficient donation processes by recording each transaction on a public ledger. This level of transparency and traceability helps address concerns about how Zakat funds are distributed and utilized, which is important for compliance and ethical considerations. Additionally, virtual reality (VR) is beginning to be explored as a tool for financial education, such as creating VR-based savings programs for Hajj (the annual pilgrimage to Mecca), providing an immersive experience that helps users better understand and manage their savings. Digital Frontiers in Islamic Finance, therefore, represents a bold step towards transforming the Islamic finance sector, not only keeping pace with global financial innovation but also expanding the industry's scope to offer broader, more diversified options that remain true to Islamic principles.

OVERVIEW OF *MAQASID AL-SHARIAH* AND *MASLAHAH*

Maqasid (plural) is an Arabic term derived from the root word "maqsad," meaning justice, balance, straightness of a path, and a direction to achieve goals. Shariah refers to a collection of rules, values, and guidelines that regulate every aspect of human life, encompassing principles that cover various aspects such as beliefs, the relationship between humans and the Creator, morality, ethics, and more. Therefore, Maqasid Al-Shariah can be defined as the highest objectives of Islamic principles, serving as a foundational framework guiding the ethical and operational standards of Islamic finance (Javed et al., 2022). These objectives aim to safeguard five essential aspects of life: religion, life, intellect, progeny, and wealth, which are crucial in shaping the ethical landscape of Islamic finance.

The principles of Maqasid Al-Shariah underscore the preservation and promotion of fundamental values, which are crucial in shaping the ethical landscape of Islamic finance. Meanwhile, Maslahah, often translated as 'public welfare' or 'benefit,' plays a crucial role in Islamic jurisprudence, particularly in areas where explicit scriptural guidance may not exist (Choudhury et al., 2019). This concept ensures that Islamic finance remains responsive to the changing needs of society while being firmly rooted in the pursuit of communal benefit and justice.

The main objectives of Shariah are to create a stable and strong society and to promote the orderly functioning of its affairs by attaining comprehensive welfare and preventing evil. Thus, anything that works to improve society, provides a conducive atmosphere for social welfare, and eliminates societal harm can be considered as achieving Shariah objectives. The Quran and Hadith are replete with references that underscore the importance of these objectives. For instance, the preservation of wealth is directly addressed in the prohibition of riba (usury) as stated in the Quran: "Those who consume interest cannot stand [on the Day of Resurrection] except as one stands who is being beaten by Satan into insanity" (Surah Al-Baqarah 2:275). This prohibition supports the objective of protecting wealth by discouraging exploitative financial practices.

Imam Malik is a scholar who accepted maslahah as a source of Shariah and a significant secondary reference compared to other major Sunni schools of Islamic Jurisprudence. He uses the term al-masalih al-mursalah because of the differentiated atmosphere or 'Urf in the Muslim state, which can solve many problems, especially in terms of Islamic finance issues. Indirectly, it can protect and preserve wealth as a part of Maqasid Al-Shariah.

The application of maslahah is evident in the development of financial products that meet the community's needs without compromising Islamic ethical standards. For example, Islamic microfinance models that provide interest-free loans support the maslahah of economic empowerment and poverty alleviation, aligning with the Prophet Muhammad's teachings: "The best of people are those who are most beneficial to people" (Al-Mu'jam Al-Awsat 5787) and the Quranic injunction to establish justice and prevent societal harm (Surah An-Nisa 4:58).

DIGITAL INTEGRATION IN ISLAMIC FINANCE AND CONTRIBUTION TO SDGS

Digital frontiers represent the next evolutionary phase for Islamic finance, advancing beyond fintech and basic digital finance to fully embrace disruptive technologies that fulfill Maqasid Al-Shariah at scale. Building on the foundations laid by Islamic fintech, digital frontiers incorporate groundbreaking innovations like blockchain and artificial intelligence (AI) to drive Shariah compliance and address pressing global needs. For instance, blockchain's capacity for secure, transparent, and decentralized transactions upholds Shariah's emphasis on fairness and trust, while AI-driven solutions optimize Islamic financial services for broader accessibility and efficiency. This transition to digital frontiers is essential for Islamic finance to not only compete with conventional systems but also to lead in providing ethical, sustainable solutions worldwide.

By promoting Maqasid values such as the preservation of religion, life, intellect, progeny, and wealth, these technologies shape the ethical landscape of Islamic finance. Blockchain and AI enhance transparency, lower transaction costs, and expand access to financial services, directly supporting SDGs, such as Quality Education (SDG 4) through Shariah-compliant educational financing, and Affordable and Clean Energy (SDG 7) by enabling investments in sustainable energy projects. Through the strategic integration of these principles, digital Islamic finance can meaningfully contribute to the SDGs while remaining steadfast in Islamic ethical standards, establishing itself as a socially responsible and forward-looking alternative in the global financial ecosystem (Trimulato et al., 2022).

The evolution of Maqasid Al-Shariah through centuries of interpretation by Islamic jurists and scholars provides a rich historical context that informs the current application of digital technologies in Islamic finance. This historical perspective ensures that the integration of modern innovations like blockchain and artificial intelligence does not deviate from the foundational principles of Shariah law. The application of these technologies in Islamic finance, such as the use of blockchain for transparent record-keeping and smart contracts for automating profit-sharing agreements, demonstrates the potential to significantly enhance ethical conduct and justice within financial transactions. Such technologies not only align with the Maqasid objectives of preserving wealth and promoting prosperity but also help reduce dependency on intermediaries, thereby decreasing the potential for unethical practices.

In the realm of contemporary Islamic finance, the principle of Maslahah or public welfare plays a pivotal role in shaping financial products and practices. Islamic financial institutions, by prioritizing Maslahah, ensure that their operations enhance public welfare and adhere to Shariah principles. This is evident in the development of products like Islamic microfinance and investment in sustainable projects, which are structured around the needs of the community and the broader societal good. The integration of digital technologies further enhances this focus on public welfare by enabling the creation of innovative financial solutions such as Shariah-compliant crowdfunding platforms and digital payment solutions, which expand access to financial services and meet the diverse needs of the Muslim community.

The use of advanced digital tools such as robo-advisors and algorithmic trading platforms also illustrates a significant shift towards aligning investment decisions with the Maqasid principles. These tools employ ethical screens that ensure investments are made in accordance with Shariah-compliant criteria and socially responsible investing principles. The deployment of artificial intelligence in areas like risk assessment and fraud detection not only enhances the operational efficiency of Islamic banks but also reinforces the ethical expectations inherent in Islamic finance. This alignment with both the principles of Maslahah and the objectives of Maqasid Al-Shariah underscores the potential of digital technologies to contribute positively to the ethical and sustainable progression of Islamic finance.

Despite these advancements, the integration of digital solutions in Islamic finance is accompanied by substantial challenges and ethical considerations. Ensuring that digital solutions comply with Shariah principles requires a sophisticated understanding of both the technological aspects and the ethical imperatives of Islamic finance. Issues such as the potential for gharar in algorithm-driven decisions, the use of data in compliance with ethical norms, and the overarching need to maintain transparency and justice in all transactions are critical considerations that must be addressed. Moreover, the rapid evolution of digital technologies poses a continuous challenge in maintaining their alignment with the ethical and social objectives of Islamic finance, necessitating ongoing vigilance and adaptation.

Furthermore, the sector faces internal resistance towards the adoption of digital innovations, often due to concerns about the preservation of traditional values and the potential displacement of established financial practices. Overcoming this resistance requires a balanced approach that respects cultural and ethical sensitivities while also demonstrating the benefits that digital solutions can offer in terms of enhancing the ethical and inclusive dimensions of Islamic finance. The commitment to advancing Maqasid Al-Shariah and Maslahah through digital integration highlights the potential of technology to not only meet contemporary needs but also to contribute to the sustainable and inclusive growth of the financial sector, aligning with global development goals.

SUSTAINABLE DEVELOPMENT GOALS (SDGS)

The SDGs are a set of 17 interlinked global goals designed to be a "blueprint to achieve a better and more sustainable future for all (Figure 2)." They were set in 2015 by the United Nations General Assembly and are intended to be achieved by the year 2030 (United Nations, 2015). These goals cover social, economic, and environmental development issues.

The concept of the SDGs is to protect people and the planet, ensuring prosperity, peace, and partnership by focusing on 17 goals, 169 targets, and more than 230 indicators. In the context of Islamic finance, the SDGs concept has shifted managers' and stakeholders' perspectives from addressing issues at the company level to considering global concerns. Recent studies have revealed that institutional investors are increasingly trying to understand the relevance of the SDGs to their work, and companies are beginning to integrate the SDGs into their corporate strategies.

Figure 2. Goals of SDGs (United Nations, 2015)

ADVANCING SDGS WITH MAQASID AND MASLAHAH IN DIGITAL ISLAMIC FINANCE

The principles of Maqasid Al-Shariah, which aim to preserve religion, life, intellect, lineage, and wealth, align closely with the broader objectives of sustainable development as outlined in the United Nations' SDGs. The integration of these principles into financial practices makes digital Islamic finance a critical player in global efforts towards sustainable development. Relating digital Islamic finance to the SDGs, one can observe a natural synergy between the two.

The objectives of the SDGs concept clearly illustrate a socially responsible tool that aligns with the Islamic concepts of Maqasid Shariah and Maslahah. Key issues such as no poverty, zero hunger, the improvement of quality of life, and the promotion of quality education are closely related to the Dharruriyat (necessities) of Maqasid Shariah. Furthermore, the SDGs concept emphasizes principles that promote socio-economic fairness, the avoidance of harm, and support for ethical and moral behavior, which are inherently aligned with Islamic values.

Commonalities between Maqasid Shariah and SDGs:

6.1.1 **Preservation of Life**: Maqasid Shariah holds the preservation of life as a fundamental objective, a principle closely tied to SDG 3: Good Health and Well-being. Islamic finance supports initiatives that enhance access to healthcare and improve health outcomes, ensuring that communities can thrive. Through funding healthcare infrastructure, supporting medical research, or providing affordable healthcare financing, Islamic finance contributes to better health and well-being, which are essential for a prosperous society.

6.1.2 **Improvement of Quality of Life**: The commitment to improving quality of life is central to both the SDGs and Maqasid Shariah. Goals such as SDG 1: No Poverty and SDG 4: Quality Education echo this intent. Islamic finance can play a transformative role in reducing poverty and promoting education. For example, financing mechanisms like Sukuk (Islamic bonds) can be issued to fund social welfare projects, including poverty alleviation programs and educational facilities. By channeling funds toward community development and providing educational opportunities, Islamic finance helps uplift communities and directly contributes to poverty reduction and enhanced quality of life.

6.1.3 **Preservation and Promotion of a Healthy Mind/Intellect**: Education, innovation, and intellectual growth are pillars of Maqasid Shariah, aligning closely with SDG 9: Industry, Innovation, and Infrastructure. This SDG supports investment in infrastructure and innovation, which are crucial for intellectual and societal advancement. Islamic finance can drive progress by funding research and development projects that prioritize ethical and socially beneficial innovations. This focus not only strengthens individual intellectual growth but also empowers communities with knowledge, contributing to a well-rounded and educated society.

6.1.4 **Socio-Economic Fairness**: A cornerstone of Islamic finance is the promotion of socio-economic equity, which is reflected in SDG 8: Decent Work and Economic Growth and SDG 10: Reduced Inequalities. These SDGs aim to create fair economic opportunities and reduce disparities among individuals. Islamic finance supports inclusive growth and decent employment by promoting ethical investment and prohibiting exploitative practices. By providing fair access to financing and supporting equitable business practices, Islamic finance helps ensure that economic growth benefits all segments of society, contributing to social equity and justice.

6.1.5 **Avoidance of Harm**: In Islam, the concept of Darar (harm) mandates that actions should not harm others or the environment. This aligns closely with SDG 13: Climate Action, which seeks to combat climate change and its impacts. Islamic finance encourages investments in sustainable, environmentally friendly projects that minimize harm to the planet. For instance, green Sukuk can be issued to fund renewable energy projects, supporting environmental preservation and ensuring that economic activities contribute to long-term sustainability without compromising the health of the planet.

6.1.6 **Ethical and Moral Behavior**: Islamic finance is governed by strict ethical guidelines, mandating honesty, transparency, and fairness in all dealings. These principles align with SDG 16: Peace, Justice, and Strong Institutions, which promotes just, inclusive, and accountable institutions. Islamic finance's commitment to ethical practices discourages corruption and ensures transparency, fostering trust within the financial system. By upholding these values, Islamic finance contributes to the creation of fair and strong institutions that are essential for sustainable peace and justice.

By integrating the SDGs with Maqasid Shariah and Maslahah, digital Islamic finance can provide a robust framework for promoting global development that is both ethical and effective. This synergy not only supports the achievement of SDG objectives but also ensures that these efforts are rooted in justice, equity, and the greater good of humanity.

Digital Islamic finance represents a confluence of traditional Islamic financial principles and modern digital technology. By aligning financial activities with the ethical frameworks of Maqasid Al-Shariah and Maslahah (principles like transparency, fairness, and social welfare), digital Islamic finance can significantly contribute to achieving the SDGs. These goals aim to address global challenges such as poverty, inequality, climate change, environmental degradation, peace, and justice. Digital Islamic finance leverages technology to provide financial services in accordance with Islamic principles such as the prohibition of interest (riba) and uncertainty (gharar). The integration of digital technology allows for greater financial inclusion, efficiency, and accessibility while ensuring adherence to Islamic ethical standards. This innovative approach not only fosters economic growth and stability within Muslim-majority countries but also promotes ethical and socially responsible financial practices globally.

Furthermore, the alignment of digital Islamic finance with Maqasid Al-Shariah, Maslahah, and SDGs underscores its potential to address complex socio-economic challenges. For instance, by promoting financial inclusion and fair wealth distribution, digital Islamic finance can directly contribute to the SDG of reducing poverty and inequality. Additionally, the emphasis on ethical investment and risk-sharing mechanisms aligns with the SDGs' focus on sustainable economic development and environmental conservation.

In this context, the development of digital Islamic finance platforms and products tailored to the specific needs of underserved communities can play a pivotal role in achieving the SDGs. By targeting areas such as affordable housing, microfinance, and SME financing, digital Islamic finance can address fundamental development needs and contribute to the overarching goal of sustainable global development. The integration of digital Islamic finance with the SDGs presents a compelling opportunity to combine faith-based principles with innovative technological solutions in pursuit of a more inclusive, equitable, and sustainable global financial system.

CONTRIBUTION OF DIGITAL ISLAMIC FINANCE TO SPECIFIC SDGS

7.1 **SDG 1 (No Poverty)**: Digital Islamic finance plays a significant role in poverty alleviation through innovative solutions like Islamic microfinance and digital zakat (almsgiving) platforms. These products provide accessible financial services to economically disadvantaged groups, particularly those underserved by traditional banking. Digital zakat platforms ensure a more equitable distribution of resources by simplifying the collection and distribution of zakat funds, while Islamic microfinance provides small-scale funding to those who might not otherwise qualify, empowering individuals to start businesses, support families, and work toward financial independence. By targeting the underserved and emphasizing financial inclusion, these platforms help lift individuals out of poverty.

7.2 **SDG 3 (Good Health and Well-being)**: Islamic finance, through digital platforms, can support healthcare initiatives that improve access to affordable and quality healthcare services. For example, digital Islamic financing solutions can be used to fund hospitals, clinics, and health outreach programs in underserved regions, facilitating community well-being. Additionally, crowdfunding platforms compliant with Shariah law can be used to fund medical research and healthcare programs, ensuring that critical health services reach communities in need. By supporting affordable healthcare access, digital Islamic finance contributes to improved health outcomes and overall well-being, essential components for thriving communities.

7.3 **SDG 4 (Quality Education)**: Digital Islamic finance enhances access to quality education by funding scholarships, supporting educational institutions, and promoting online knowledge-sharing platforms. Crowdfunding or waqf (endowment) platforms can be utilized to provide scholarships and financial aid to students from low-income families, enabling them to pursue quality education. Furthermore, Islamic finance supports building educational infrastructure, ensuring that schools and institutions in marginalized areas have access to necessary resources. Through these initiatives, digital Islamic finance helps break the cycle of poverty, empowering individuals with knowledge and skills for sustainable growth.

7.4 **SDG 5 (Gender Equality)**: Digital Islamic finance promotes gender equality by enhancing women's financial independence through accessible and inclusive financial services. Women often face barriers to traditional banking, but digital platforms offer a more accessible alternative, enabling them to engage in income-generating activities and take control of their financial well-being. Products like Islamic microloans, digital savings platforms, and women-centric crowdfunding initiatives can empower women, especially in developing countries, to participate in the economy. This support helps bridge gender gaps in financial services, promoting economic independence and equal opportunity.

7.5 **SDG 7 (Affordable and Clean Energy)**: Digital Islamic finance can facilitate investments in renewable energy projects through Shariah-compliant financial products, such as green Sukuk (Islamic bonds). Green Sukuk can be issued to fund solar, wind, and other clean energy projects, promoting affordable and sustainable energy solutions. These projects align with Islamic principles of environmental stewardship and sustainability. By investing in clean energy, Islamic finance contributes to reducing carbon emissions and promotes energy solutions that are both affordable and environmentally responsible, advancing sustainable development in alignment with Shariah law.

7.6 **SDG 8 (Decent Work and Economic Growth)**: Digital Islamic finance contributes to inclusive economic growth by supporting Shariah-compliant crowdfunding platforms and financing for small and medium-sized enterprises (SMEs). These platforms enable individuals to invest in startups and small businesses, fostering job creation and economic resilience. Islamic finance's principles of risk-sharing and prohibition of speculation encourage financial stability, creating a more inclusive growth environment. As SMEs are crucial for job creation, especially in emerging economies, digital Islamic finance helps sustain productive employment and a resilient economy, supporting SDG 8's goal of decent work for all.

7.7 **SDG 9 (Industry Innovation and Infrastructure)**: Digital Islamic finance channels investments into sustainable infrastructure, such as renewable energy, green buildings, and efficient transportation systems. Through digital platforms, Islamic finance supports sustainable industrialization by providing financing options for projects that align with Shariah principles. Additionally, blockchain-based Islamic finance products, fintech solutions for zakat and waqf management, and Shariah-compliant digital payment systems represent innovative financial services that contribute to SDG 9. These advancements not only modernize infrastructure but also set the stage for sustainable development across industries.

7.8 **SDG 10 (Reduced Inequalities)**: By promoting financial inclusion, digital Islamic finance helps reduce inequalities within and among countries. Digital banking and payment systems extend financial services to marginalized and rural communities, giving them access to secure banking, credit, and insurance. Islamic finance's emphasis on ethical transactions and social equity ensures that these services reach those who are most in need, reducing income and opportunity disparities. This focus on inclusivity contributes to a more equitable financial system, enabling fairer economic growth and reducing global inequality.

7.9 **SDG 13 (Climate Action)**: Environmental sustainability is integral to Islamic finance principles, which emphasize the avoidance of harm. Digital Islamic finance supports climate action by funding projects that promote climate resilience, reduce carbon emissions, and preserve natural resources. For instance, green Sukuk can be utilized to finance reforestation, renewable energy installations, and clean water initiatives. These investments help mitigate environmental impacts, supporting a sustainable future and reducing ecological footprints. Through such actions, digital Islamic finance actively contributes to climate action, aligning with the Islamic mandate to protect the planet.

7.10 **SDG 16 (Peace, Justice and Strong Institutions)**: Adhering to principles of fairness, transparency, and ethical conduct, digital Islamic finance fosters trust and integrity within financial institutions. By mandating transparency and honesty, Islamic finance discourages unethical practices, ensuring that all transactions are conducted justly. This aligns with SDG 16, which promotes strong institutions, peace, and justice. Ethical governance practices in digital Islamic finance contribute to building resilient financial institutions that operate transparently, ensuring stability and trustworthiness, which are essential for peaceful and just societies.

THE PRINCIPLES DIGITAL FRONTIER ISLAMIC FINANCE AND SDG FRAMEWORKS

The framework illustrated in Figure 3 integrates Maqasid Shariah (the objectives of Islamic law) with the Sustainable Development Goals (SDGs), showing how Islamic ethical principles can support sustainable development. This framework centers on three core Islamic principles: Falah (ultimate success), Maslahah (public interest), and the levels of Maqasid Shariah (objectives of Islamic law). It demonstrates that the Islamic view of success and ethical responsibility aligns with the global goals set out in the SDGs. This alignment offers a way to conceptualize Islamic finance that is not only compliant with Shariah but also promotes sustainable development outcomes.

Figure 3. The principles of digital frontier Islamic finance and SDG frameworks (Modified from Nugroho, Hidayah & Badawi, 2018)

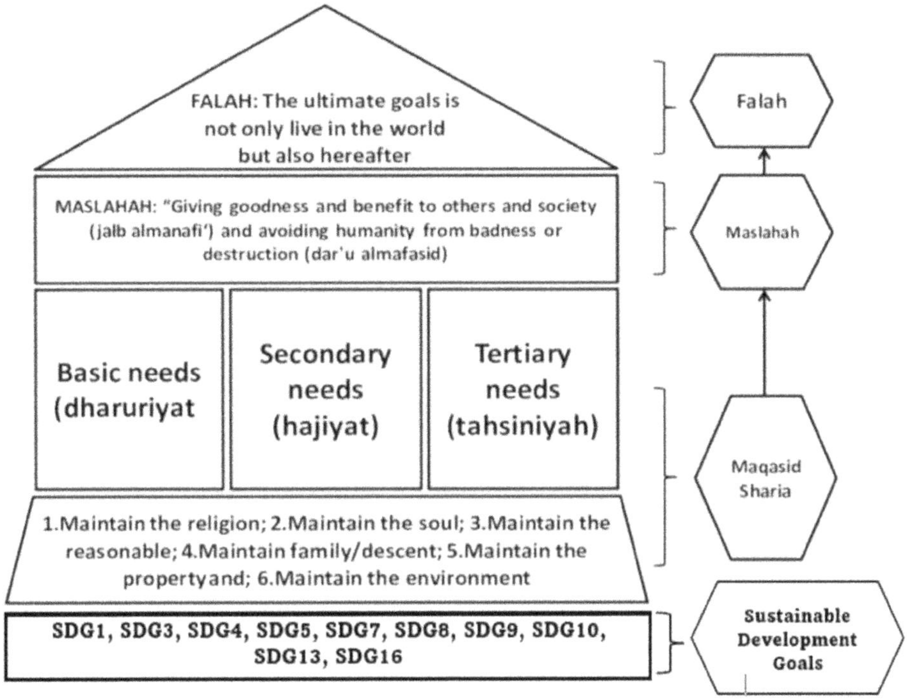

The explanation of the framework is as follows:

Falah: The Ultimate Goal

Falah, or ultimate success, represents the highest aspiration in Islamic ethics, embodying both material prosperity and spiritual fulfillment, with implications for both this world and the hereafter. In Islamic finance, Falah extends beyond individual wealth, aiming for a collective sense of well-being that upholds social justice, equity, and community welfare. It encompasses a broader definition of success that aligns well with the Sustainable Development Goals (SDGs), which aim for an inclusive and sustainable future. By pursuing Falah, Islamic finance aims to build a financial system that is not only profitable but also contributes positively to society, reflecting the ethical pursuit of balanced, holistic prosperity. This aspect of the framework emphasizes that true success is not limited to material gains but involves moral and social responsibilities that enhance societal welfare, mirroring the SDGs' vision of global peace, prosperity, and sustainability.

Maslahah: Public Interest

Maslahah, meaning public interest or social welfare, is a principle in Islamic ethics that emphasizes actions that bring benefit to society and minimize harm. In this framework, Maslahah serves as the foundation for financial activities in Islamic finance, encouraging the development of products and practices that prioritize social good over mere profitability. The alignment with SDGs becomes evident here, as both frameworks focus on addressing issues like poverty, inequality, and environmental sustainability. For instance, Maslahah justifies the prohibition of interest (riba) and speculative transactions (gharar) in Islamic finance, as these practices can lead to social inequities and economic instability. By centering on Maslahah, Islamic finance promotes a financial system that is accountable, equitable, and committed to ethical investment, ensuring that financial growth also leads to social development and the upliftment of communities.

Maqasid Shariah: The Objectives of Islamic Law

Maqasid Shariah outlines the objectives of Islamic law, structured around fulfilling the essential needs of humanity in a way that promotes both individual and societal welfare. It is divided into three levels of needs: Dharuriyat (basic needs), Hajiyat (secondary needs), and Tahsinat (tertiary needs). The Dharuriyat level focuses on fundamental requirements for survival and dignity, such as maintaining religion, life, intellect, family, property, and the environment. Islamic finance can address these needs by ensuring access to essential services and promoting financial inclusion for marginalized groups, aligning with SDGs like poverty alleviation (SDG 1) and health and well-being (SDG 3). The Hajiyat level encompasses needs that ease hardship, like providing interest-free loans (qard al-hasan) or profit-sharing investment options, which aligns with SDGs focused on economic resilience and decent work (SDG 8). Finally, Tahsinat relates to enhancements that bring moral value to life, supporting ethical and environmental initiatives that promote community welfare. This level reflects SDG goals such as responsible consumption and production (SDG 12) and climate action (SDG 13).

Linking Maqasid Shariah and SDGs

The framework demonstrates a strong alignment between Maqasid Shariah and the SDGs by connecting Islamic finance's objectives to the global goals of sustainable development. Each aspect of Maqasid Shariah corresponds with specific SDGs. For example, preserving religion aligns with promoting peace, justice, and strong institutions (SDG 16), while maintaining life supports goals like health and well-being (SDG 3). Similarly, fostering education aligns with SDG 4 (Quality Education), while ensuring economic equity aligns with SDG 8 (Decent Work and Economic Growth) and SDG 10 (Reduced Inequalities). Islamic finance also emphasizes environmental stewardship, aligning with SDG 13 (Climate Action). Through this alignment, the framework provides a structured pathway for Islamic finance to advance social, economic, and environmental objectives that are also the focus of the SDGs. By addressing these needs holistically, Islamic finance can create financial solutions that serve both individual and societal well-being, supporting sustainable development and promoting ethical practices that benefit humanity at large.

Overall, the integration of Maqasid Shariah with the SDG framework highlights the potential for Islamic finance to play a significant role in achieving sustainable development goals. This framework guides digital Islamic finance to create products and services that not only adhere to Shariah but also have tangible positive impacts on society and the environment. By prioritizing Maslahah and striving for Falah, Islamic finance bridges ethical values with practical solutions, offering a model that fosters welfare and social justice while addressing pressing global challenges. This integration enables Islamic finance to contribute meaningfully to economic development, reduce inequalities, and protect the environment, thereby aligning with the broader objectives of the SDGs and promoting a fairer, more resilient, and sustainable global economy.

CHALLENGES, OPPORTUNITIES, AND FUTURE DIRECTIONS FOR DIGITAL ISLAMIC FINANCE

Challenges

Digital Islamic finance faces a range of challenges, with regulatory hurdles being one of the most prominent. Different countries have varying regulatory frameworks for Islamic finance, and this diversity complicates the implementation of standardized digital Islamic finance products. Without a unified global framework, inconsistencies can arise, leading to fragmented and often conflicting regulations across borders. For instance, a digital Islamic finance product approved in one country may not be compliant in another due to differences in regulatory standards. This lack of regulatory cohesion hampers the potential for seamless, cross-border Islamic finance solutions and can pose additional compliance and operational challenges for financial institutions.

Technological adoption also presents significant challenges, particularly in regions where the necessary infrastructure is lacking. Many developing countries have limited access to advanced technology, which restricts the reach and effectiveness of digital Islamic finance solutions. This lack of infrastructure impacts everything from internet connectivity to mobile access, making it difficult for digital Islamic finance products to achieve widespread adoption. Additionally, traditional financial institutions and customers may be resistant to the transition to digital platforms. Established institutions often operate on legacy systems that can be costly and time-consuming to update, while customers may be wary of adopting new technologies, especially if they are not accustomed to digital banking. This resistance slows down the broader adoption of digital Islamic finance solutions, limiting their potential impact.

Another critical challenge is ensuring Shariah compliance in digital finance. Unlike conventional financial products, Islamic finance requires adherence to Shariah principles, which prohibit interest, excessive uncertainty, and unethical investments. Ensuring that digital financial products comply with these principles requires continuous oversight by Shariah boards. Each product or service must be reviewed and certified as Shariah-compliant, which is a complex and ongoing process. Developing innovative digital instruments that both meet Shariah requirements and address modern financial needs is also challenging, as these instruments must carefully balance compliance with flexibility and functionality to appeal to a diverse user base.

Awareness and education are essential to the growth of digital Islamic finance, yet limited awareness among potential users and stakeholders poses a challenge. Many people, even in predominantly Muslim countries, may not be familiar with the benefits and principles of digital Islamic finance, leading to slower adoption rates. Stakeholders such as banks, financial institutions, and fintech companies may also lack a comprehensive understanding of how digital Islamic finance works. Educational initiatives are necessary to bridge this knowledge gap and promote digital Islamic finance's benefits to a broader audience. By increasing awareness and providing training, these initiatives can help build trust and understanding, encouraging both individuals and institutions to adopt digital Islamic finance solutions.

Finally, financial inclusion remains a significant challenge, especially in remote or underserved areas. Digital Islamic finance aims to reach unbanked and underbanked populations, offering them access to financial services they might not otherwise have. However, infrastructure and connectivity issues can make it difficult to achieve this goal. In remote regions, limited internet access and low smartphone penetration create barriers to using digital financial services. Additionally, to be truly inclusive, digital finance solutions must be accessible and user-friendly for all demographics, including older adults and those who may not be technologically literate. Addressing these barriers is essential to ensuring that digital Islamic finance can reach its full potential and provide equitable financial services to all.

Opportunities

Digital Islamic finance offers numerous opportunities to innovate, expand financial inclusion, build impactful partnerships, promote sustainable investments, and leverage advanced technologies. One key area is the creation of innovative financial products. With tools like blockchain-based smart contracts, Islamic crowdfunding platforms, and digital wallets, digital Islamic finance can provide Shariah-compliant solutions that meet diverse financial needs while adhering to Islamic principles. For example, blockchain can be used to create transparent, immutable smart contracts that ensure compliance with Shariah while automating transactions and minimizing operational risks. Furthermore, Islamic crowdfunding platforms provide new opportunities for community-based investment, allowing individuals to fund and support projects that are ethical and beneficial. These products also open up Shariah-compliant investment opportunities that align with the Sustainable Development Goals (SDGs), addressing global challenges such as poverty and inequality while offering returns on investment.

Enhanced financial inclusion is another significant opportunity that digital Islamic finance provides. By expanding access to financial services through mobile banking and microfinance solutions, digital Islamic finance can bring essential services to underserved and unbanked populations. Mobile banking enables people in remote areas to access savings, transfers, and loans, while microfinance offers tailored financial products to low-income individuals and small businesses. These services are particularly impactful for women and small businesses, as they can offer the financial independence and support needed to contribute to economic growth and stability. By designing products that cater to the unique needs of women entrepreneurs and small business owners, digital Islamic finance can empower these groups, helping bridge financial inclusion gaps and fostering more resilient communities.

Partnerships and collaborations with international organizations, fintech companies, and governmental bodies are essential to furthering the reach and impact of digital Islamic finance. By working with these entities, digital Islamic finance can promote the development of infrastructure projects that contribute to the SDGs. Collaborations with fintech companies, for instance, can bring the latest technological solutions to Islamic finance, enhancing operational efficiency and customer accessibility. Similarly, partnerships with government bodies can provide the necessary regulatory support to ensure that Islamic finance products align with both national regulations and Shariah principles. These partnerships help standardize practices, create new infrastructure for digital finance, and encourage the global adoption of Islamic finance.

In line with global concerns for ethical investing, digital Islamic finance is also well-positioned to support sustainable investments. By promoting green and sustainable projects that align with both Maqasid Shariah and SDGs, Islamic finance can attract socially responsible investors who seek to make a positive impact. Green Sukuk, for example, can be issued to fund renewable energy projects, which address both environmental goals and Islamic principles of stewardship. By channeling investments toward projects that reduce carbon emissions, improve community well-being, and protect the environment, digital Islamic finance can meet the growing demand for ethical investments while aligning with broader environmental objectives.

Finally, technological advancements offer an unprecedented opportunity to enhance the transparency, efficiency, and security of digital Islamic finance. Technologies such as artificial intelligence (AI), big data, and blockchain enable more accurate data analysis, improve fraud prevention, and facilitate secure cross-border transactions. Blockchain, for example, allows for transparent, traceable transactions that can be crucial in maintaining Shariah compliance. Additionally, AI can personalize customer experience and streamline operations, making financial services more accessible and efficient. These technological solutions also enable the development of platforms that support global financial integration, connecting investors, institutions, and markets across borders, and expanding the reach and potential of Islamic finance.

Future Directions

To advance digital Islamic finance, several future directions are essential, focusing on standardization, education, innovation, alignment with sustainable development goals (SDGs), and global integration. Standardization and regulation are crucial, as they provide a unified regulatory framework to ensure consistency and Shariah compliance across different jurisdictions. Currently, the diversity of regulatory standards across countries can hinder the seamless adoption of digital Islamic finance, making the development of an internationally recognized regulatory framework a priority. Establishing international standards for Shariah compliance in digital finance would help streamline operations, build trust, and ensure that digital Islamic finance products are universally compliant, regardless of where they are offered.

Another vital area is education and awareness. Many individuals and institutions still lack a clear understanding of digital Islamic finance, its principles, and its benefits. To bridge this gap, educational campaigns can promote awareness of digital Islamic finance and highlight how it aligns with ethical financial practices and economic empowerment. Additionally, offering training and resources for financial institutions and stakeholders can facilitate a smoother transition to digital platforms, equipping them with the knowledge and skills necessary to integrate Shariah-compliant digital finance into their operations. By improving general awareness and understanding, the industry can attract a larger customer base and increase trust and adoption rates.

Innovation and research are also critical in keeping digital Islamic finance relevant and responsive to modern needs. Investing in research and development (R&D) enables the creation of new, Shariah-compliant financial products that address emerging challenges and meet the evolving demands of consumers. For instance, products that cater to the growing demand for digital payment solutions, sustainable investment products, and blockchain-based financial services all require continuous innovation. Collaborations between academia and industry can drive these efforts, combining academic expertise with practical insights to develop pioneering solutions that push the boundaries of digital Islamic finance.

A strong focus on the SDGs helps align digital Islamic finance with global sustainable development priorities. By designing financial products and services that contribute to goals such as poverty reduction, environmental sustainability, and inclusive economic growth, digital Islamic finance can make a meaningful impact beyond profit. For instance, developing green Sukuk and other sustainable investment instruments helps attract investors focused on social and environmental outcomes. Additionally, setting up systems to monitor and measure the impact of digital Islamic finance initiatives on achieving SDGs would provide valuable feedback, helping refine approaches and demonstrate the real-world benefits of Islamic finance in supporting sustainable development.

Finally, global integration is essential to create a cohesive digital Islamic finance ecosystem that facilitates cross-border collaboration. By fostering relationships among institutions, governments, and fintech companies worldwide, digital Islamic finance can build a more connected financial network that extends its reach across regions. Supporting the adoption of digital Islamic finance in emerging markets is particularly important, as it can promote economic growth and development in areas that stand to benefit the most from inclusive financial solutions. As a result, global integration not only enhances accessibility but also strengthens the role of digital Islamic finance on a worldwide scale, making it a viable option for investors, businesses, and individuals across different economies.

CONCLUSION

In conclusion, digital frontiers in Islamic finance hold substantial promise for advancing global socio-economic goals, particularly through alignment with the Sustainable Development Goals (SDGs) and core Islamic values of Maqasid Shariah and Maslahah. The integration of transformative technologies such as blockchain, artificial intelligence, and big data within Islamic finance has enabled the development of transparent, ethical, and inclusive financial solutions. These advancements have the potential to address key issues in financial inclusion, ethical investing, and sustainable development, effectively positioning Islamic finance as a socially responsible alternative within the global financial landscape. However, the journey towards fully realizing these digital frontiers is accompanied by notable challenges, including diverse regulatory environments, the complexity of ensuring Shariah compliance in digital solutions, limited technological infrastructure in some regions, and low awareness among potential users and stakeholders.

To address these challenges and capitalize on emerging opportunities, several recommendations for stakeholders in Islamic finance are crucial. Regulatory bodies and international organizations should work collaboratively to establish a unified regulatory framework that standardizes Shariah compliance across borders. This global standardization will ease the cross-border flow of digital Islamic finance products, ensuring consistency and fostering investor confidence. Financial institutions and fintech companies should prioritize education and awareness programs to bridge knowledge gaps and increase acceptance of digital Islamic finance. By raising awareness of its benefits and ethical foundations, these initiatives can foster a broader adoption of digital Islamic finance solutions among diverse populations. Additionally, partnerships between academic institutions, industry players, and government bodies are essential to drive innovation and tailor financial products that meet modern needs while adhering to Islamic principles.

Despite its progress, digital Islamic finance still faces limitations, particularly in the areas of technological infrastructure and user adoption. Future studies should investigate solutions for increasing access in underserved regions, assessing how to make digital platforms more inclusive and accessible to unbanked populations. Research on consumer behavior, including factors that influence the acceptance of digital Islamic finance, would also help develop strategies to overcome resistance from traditional customers and institutions. Furthermore, as new technologies evolve, continuous research into Shariah-compliant applications of emerging technologies like machine learning and decentralized finance (DeFi) will be necessary to ensure alignment with Islamic ethical standards.

In summary, by addressing regulatory, technological, and educational challenges, and through active collaboration and research, digital Islamic finance can become a cornerstone of an ethical and sustainable global economy. Continued efforts to integrate Maqasid Shariah with the SDGs in digital finance will create innovative and impactful financial solutions, empowering Islamic finance to contribute meaningfully to poverty reduction, environmental protection, and equitable economic growth. As this field expands, future studies and regulatory guidance will be essential to sustain momentum, further bridging the gap between Islamic finance principles and modern financial technology to foster a more inclusive and responsible global financial system.

REFERENCES

Alam, N., Gupta, L., & Zameni, A. (2019). Digitalization and disruption in the financial sector. In *Fintech and Islamic finance* (pp. 1–22). Palgrave Macmillan., DOI: 10.1007/978-3-030-24666-2_1

Bughin, J., Hazan, E., Ramaswamy, S., Chui, M., Allas, T., Dahlström, P., Henke, N., & Trench, M. (2017). Artificial intelligence: The next digital frontier? McKinsey Global Institute. https://www.mckinsey.com/mgi

Choudhury, M. A., Hossain, M. S., & Mohammad, M. T. (2019). Islamic finance instruments for promoting long-run investment in the light of the well-being criterion (maslaha). *Journal of Islamic Accounting and Business Research*, 10(2), 315–339. DOI: 10.1108/JIABR-11-2016-0133

Erba, D. M. F., & Nofrianto, N. (2022). Implementation of Maqashid Syariah in Sharia Business Transactions. *Al-Falah: Journal of Islamic Economics*, 7(1), 125–139. DOI: 10.29240/alfalah.v7i1.3703

Harahap, M. A., & Harahap, I. (2023). Measuring Muslim Welfare: A Falah-Based Index. *Jurnal Ekonomi dan Keuangan Islam, 12*(2), 478-499. https://doi.org/DOI: 10.22373/share.v12i2.19191

Haridan, N. M., Hassan, A. F. S., Shah, S. M., & Mustafa, H. (2023). Financial innovation in Islamic banks: Evidence on the interaction between Shariah board and FinTech. *Journal of Islamic Accounting and Business Research*, 14(6), 911–930. DOI: 10.1108/JIABR-11-2022-0305

Hegre, H., Petrova, K., & Uexkull, N. V. (2020). Synergies and Trade-Offs in Reaching the Sustainable Development Goals. *Sustainability (Basel)*, 12(8729), 1–24. DOI: 10.3390/su12208729

Javed, M. M., Ayaz, M., & Kalim, R. (2022). Examining the influence of Maqāsid al-Sharīʿah orientation on financial performance of Islamic banks: Evidence from Pakistan. *Journal of Islamic Business and Management*, 12(2), 181–197. DOI: 10.26501/jibm/2022.1202-004

LSEG. (2023). *Islamic Finance Development Report 2023: Navigating Uncertainty*. London Stock Exchange Group. (accessed 25 October 2024) https://solutions.lseg.com/IslamicFinance_ICD_LSEG

Nugroho, L., Hidayah, N., & Badawi, A. (2018). The Islamic Banking Asset Quality: Does Financing Segmentation Matter? (Indonesia Evidence). *Mediterranean Journal of Social Sciences*, 9(5), 235–245. DOI: 10.2478/mjss-2018-0154

Saba, I., Kouser, R., & Chaudhry, I. S. (2019).. . *Fintech and Islamic Finance-challenges and Opportunities.*, 5(4), 581–590. DOI: 10.26710/reads.v5i4.887

Shah, H. S., & Susilo, A. (2022). E-Commerce on the Study of Maslahah Mursalah (A Review from an Islamic Economic Perspective). *Tasharruf: Journal Economics and Business of Islam*, 7(1), 17–28. DOI: 10.30984/tjebi.v7i1.1944

Shaikh, I M., Qureshi, M A., Noordin, K., Shaikh, J M., Khan, A., & Shahbaz, M S. (2020). Acceptance of Islamic financial technology (FinTech) banking services by Malaysian users: an extension of technology acceptance model. Emerald Publishing Limited, 22(3), 367-383. https://doi.org/DOI: 10.1108/FS-12-2019-0105

Trimulato, N., Nafis, M. C., & Amalia, E. (2022). The role of Sharia fintech in supporting the Sustainable Development Goals (SDGs) program. *Jurnal Ilmiah Ekonomi Islam*, 8(1), 251–259. DOI: 10.29040/jiei.v8i1.3911

Trimulato, T., Nafis, M. C., & Amalia, E. (2022). The Role of Sharia Fintech in Supporting the Sustainable Development Goals Program (SDGs). *Jurnal Ilmiah Ekonomi Islam*, 8(1), 251–259. DOI: 10.29040/jiei.v8i1.3911

United Nations. (2015). *The UN Sustainable Development Goals.* United Nations. Available at (accessed 25 October 2024): https://www.un.org/sustainabledevelopment/summit/

Yunus, S. M., Kamaruddin, Z., & Embong, R. (2018). The Concept of Islamic Banking from the Islamic Worldview. *International Journal of Academic Research in Business & Social Sciences*, 8(11). Advance online publication. DOI: 10.6007/IJARBSS/v8-i11/4928

Chapter 2
An Evaluation on the Development and Digitalization Performance of Participation Banking in Turkey

Yasemin Tekiner
Ondokuz Mayıs University, Turkey

H. Işil Alkan
Ondokuz Mayıs University, Turkey

ABSTRACT

Participation banking in Turkey is a system that has been an alternative to conventional banking Although participation banking in Turkey has encountered many challenges thanks to the digitalization process, they could be able to reduce costs, increase revenues, ensure innovation, and respond to customer needs more quickly and effectively, in other words, they have strengthened their position in the financial sector and have managed to become an important alternative to conventional banks. The main goal of this study is to examine the development of participation banking in Turkey and to examine the performance of participation banks in the digital transformation process. It is revealed with the study that, efforts to increase product diversity, developing tools that can respond to customer needs more easily and quickly, informing the public (especially young population) accurately about participation banking, and increasing financial and digital literacy in the country

DOI: 10.4018/979-8-3693-5653-1.ch002

may be the practices that will pave the way for participation banks in the digital transformation process.

INTRODUCTION

Participation banking system, which aims to provide services to the interest-sensitive Muslim population with unique methods different from conventional banking, is a system that injects the idle funds kept under the pillow in order to stay away from interest into the real economy. As it is known, insufficient savings in developing countries such as Türkiye is one of the main factors that negatively affects economic functioning and growth. Considering the density of the interest-sensitive Muslim population in Türkiye, it becomes clear that the amount of unregistered funds in the Turkish economy is actually considerable. At this point, the importance of participation banks for the economy emerges; the participation banking system incorporates unregistered, under-the-pillow savings into the real economic system through fund collection and fund disbursement channels that work mostly on the axis of profit-loss sharing, improves the banking system and the real economy, and makes a significant contribution to budget revenues by paying taxes. On the other hand, considering that the labor market in Türkiye does not create enough employment, participation banks also increase their employment capacity through the employees they employ. Participation banks in Türkiye first operated under the name of "Special Financial Institutions" in the 1980s, and these institutions later acquired the status of "bank" thanks to the Banking Law No. 5411 enacted in 2005. With the Banking Law No. 5411, participation banks both gained the status of "Bank" and the funds they collect were taken under the guarantee of the Savings Deposit Insurance Fund (SDIF). Considering the development in the sector share of participation banks over the years and the increasing trend in the funds collected and disbursed by these banks, it can be stated that the participation banking sector has developed significantly and its contribution to the economy has increased significantly, especially in recent decades.

As is known, the world has been rapidly digitalizing in recent years and the banking sector stands out as one of the rapidly digitalizing sectors. Digitalisation has rapidly transformed the banking sector by significantly reducing costs, increasing revenues and rapidly meeting customer expectations. Banks, which previously provided services to their customers only through their branches during working hours, have become able to provide services to their customers without any time limit thanks to various digital channels. The spread of the internet and the increase in smartphone usage rates have paved the way for the rapid digitalization of the banking sector, and banks have given great importance to digital banking with the desire to reduce costs, increase efficiency and profitability, and respond to customers' needs more and faster. Participation Banks, which have been developing rapidly in the banking sector in Türkiye in recent years, have also tried to adapt to the relevant transformation process and have significantly improved their activities in the field of digital banking in recent years. The Covid 19 pandemic process has accelerated digitalisation in participation banking, just like in conventional banks. It should be noted that the number and transaction volumes of participation banks have increased significantly in Türkiye in recent years, and branchless banks that provide services only through digital channels have started to operate within the scope of this banking. In other words, digital transformation has significantly transformed not only conventional banks but also participation banks in Türkiye, as the first digital (branchless) bank to start operations in the country was a participation bank. The digital transformation process, which has significantly affected and transformed both conventional and participation banking, has also brought significant advantages and disadvantages. The aim of this study is to examine the development of participation banking in Türkiye and to investigate the digitalization performance of the relevant sector. In this framework, this chapter firstly explains the development of participation banking in Türkiye, and then examines the performance of participation banking in the digitalisation process with the help of data from the Banks Association of Türkiye and the Participation Banks Association of Türkiye. The other section of the study attempts to examine the advantages and disadvantages of the digitalisation process on participation banking. In this section, not only the advantages of digital transformation are emphasised, but also the measures to be taken in order to eliminate the problems arising from the related process are discussed. In the concluding section of the study, both the findings are briefly presented and policy recommendations that should be implemented for the further development of participation banking in Türkiye are tried to be revealed.

Development of Participation Banking in Türkiye

From the proclamation of the republic until the 1980s, the financial system in Türkiye operated through conventional banks. On the other hand, Muslims constitute a significant portion of the population in Türkiye and a legal system that operates on the principle of non-interest has always been desired by those who are against interest. With the 1980s, liberalisation and deregulation movements emerged in the Turkish economy and capital insufficiency became one of the main problems in economic functioning. Due to the lack of capital, the Turkish economy was directed towards the Middle Eastern countries and the institutions providing interest-free financial services in these countries attracted attention. This system, which has been operating effectively in the world since the 1970s, attracted the attention of the then

Prime Minister Bülent Ulusu and was brought to the agenda in Türkiye. The new financial system, which operates on the principle of non-interest, was given a legal basis in Türkiye with the Decree Law No. 837506 enacted in 1983 during the Prime Ministry of Turgut Özal and the Presidency of Kenan Evren. Considering the fact that the relevant system has been active in the world since the 1970s, it is understood that its entry into Türkiye was relatively late. These institutions were first named as "Private Financial Institutions" due to the thought that the concepts of Islamic Finance or Islamic Bank may be contrary to the principle of secularism (Özulucan & Deran, 2009, p. 91). However, since the Private Finance Institutions faced different problems such as reliability, transactionability and recognition problems in both local and global markets, the name of these institutions was changed with the Banking Law enacted in 2005 and these institutions were named as "Participation Bank" (Özsoy, 1999, p. 22).

The Private Finance Institutions, which gained full legal status in 1985, were able to attain the name of "Bank" on the occasion of the Banking Law No. 5411, which was put into effect in 2005. Therefore, while the period until 2005 can be referred to as the establishment period of Participation Banking, the period after 2005 can also be referred to as the development and expansion period of Participation Banking (Özulucan and Özdemir, 2010, p. 15). With the Banking Law No. 5411, the funds to be collected within the framework of Participation Banking were taken under the guarantee of the Savings Deposit Insurance Fund (SDIF), and the transfer of the Participation Banks that could not continue their activities to the SDIF was also stipulated by the relevant law, so the relevant law is a very important cornerstone in the development of Participation Banking in Türkiye (Nacar, 2007, p.16).

When the pioneering Private Finance Institutions established in Türkiye in the historical process are analysed, it is observed that the pioneering institutions are Albaraka Türk Finans Kurumu A.Ş. and Faisal Finans Kurumu A.Ş., which were established with foreign capital in 1985. Established in 1989 with foreign capital, Kuveyt Türk Evkaf Finans Kurumu A.Ş. is another institution. Anadolu Finans Kurumu A.Ş., which was established in 1991, was the first private financial institution in Türkiye to start operations with domestic capital. This institution, which was established with domestic capital, was followed by İhlas Finans Kurumu A.Ş. in 1995 and Asya Finans Kurumu A.Ş. in 1996. In 2001, the financial crisis led to the bankruptcy of İhlas Finans Kurumu A.Ş. In 2001, the Ülker Group took over Faisal Finans Kurumu A.Ş. and changed its name to Family Finans Kurumu A.Ş. In 2005, a new merger took place and it was decided that Family Finans Kurumu A.Ş. and Anadolu Finans Kurumu A.Ş. would continue their activities under the roof of Türkiye Finans Katılım Bankası (Sümer & Onan, 2015, pp. 299-300). In 2014, Ziraat Participation Bank was established with a capital size of TL 675 million with the permission of the Banking Regulation and Supervision Agency (BRSA) and financed by the Treasury, and the relevant institution gained an important place in the Participation Banking system (Ziraat Participation, 2023). In 2015, Vakıf Bank Participation Bank was established as a joint stock company, and the Bank took its place in the participation banking system on 24 February 2016 by obtaining an operating permit from the BRSA in 2016 (Vakıf Participation, 2023). In 2018, it was decided that Emlak Bank of Türkiye, which dates back to 1926, would re-establish itself as a participation bank under the name of Emlak Participation Bank of Türkiye, and the Bank obtained an operating licence in 2019 and started to serve (Emlak Participation, 2023).

Private capital participation banks with branches operating in Türkiye are Albaraka Türk Participation Bank Inc., Türkiye Finans Participation Bank Inc. and Kuveyt Türk Participation Bank Inc. Emlak Participation, Ziraat Participation and Vakıf Participation are participation banks with public capital. As of February 2024, participation banks in Türkiye have a total of 1,465 branches and nearly 20,000 employees (TKBB, 2024) (Table 1).

Table 1. Participation banks having branches in Türkiye (February 2024)

Name of the Bank	Number of Branches
Al Baraka	225
Kuveyt Türk	445
Emlak Katılım	104
Türkiye Finans	305
Vakıf Katılım	196
Ziraat Katılım	190

Kaynak: TKBB, 2024

Apart from the relevant banks with branches, TOM Bank and Hayat Finans have taken their place in the sector as digital banks that received the operating licence from the Banking Regulation and Supervision Agency in 2023 and started operating. Hayat Finans, Türkiye 's first branchless digital bank, stands out as a bank with 100% Turkish capital. Hayat Finans provides services through Hayat Finans Mobile application and internet banking with its technological infrastructure. The bank aims to offer new generation banking services in addition to basic banking services such as Commercial Banking, SME Banking, Retail Banking, Treasury Transactions, Investment Banking and Private Banking (Hayat Finans, 2024a). Tom Bank, Türkiye 's first digital retail bank to obtain an operating licence from the BRSA, was established in partnership with Dubai Islamic Bank, one of the largest banking groups in the United Arab Emirates (Tom Bank, 2024). The two banks mentioned above are newly operational banks in Türkiye and are important milestones in the acceleration of digitalisation both in the banking sector in general and in participation banking in particular. Therefore, as of 2024, a total of eight banks are operating in the Participation Banking sector.

When the functioning of participation banking in Türkiye is examined, it is observed that "Murabaha" and "Musaraka" methods come to the fore in this system. Murabaha method is a method in which a good is purchased from the seller in advance and sold to the customer on a deferred basis. In the Musharaka method, both parties participate in the capital or both labour and capital through a partnership contract. One of the objectives of participation banks is to try to finance long-term transactions with short-term funds (Hazıroğlu, 2004, pp. 40-60).

Article 3 of the Banking Law No. 5411 defines participation banks and deposit banks as follows;

"Participation banks: Institutions whose main business is to collect funds and grant loans through special current accounts and participation accounts within the scope of this Law and foreign branches of these institutions established in Türkiye " (Banking Law, 2005).

"Deposit Banks: Institutions that accept deposits and provide credit services in their own name and on their own account within the scope of this law and loans, and operate on the principle of serving the interests of individuals, and the branches of these foreign institutions established in Türkiye " (Banking Law, 2005).

As stated in these definitions, deposit banks can collect "deposits" and participation banks can collect "funds". Banking Law No. 5411 underlines that Participation Banks cannot collect deposits and can only collect funds. Therefore, Participation Banks, which cannot collect deposits, can collect funds through two methods. The first one is to collect funds by using special current accounts and the other one is to collect funds by using participation accounts (Banking Law, 2005).

Special current accounts are demand deposit accounts that allow interest-sensitive savers to withdraw all or part of their savings at any time. Thanks to these accounts, savers can ensure the security of their savings and can access them whenever they want (Takan, 2002, p.7). Other main features of special current accounts are that they can be opened in foreign currency or TL, they are within the scope of the Savings Deposit Insurance Fund (SDIF), they can be used as a source of funds in lending transactions, they cannot be used in escrow or real estate trade, and they can only be used in financing activities to third parties (Emiroğlu, 2019, pp. 56-57). Unlike special current accounts, participation accounts are time deposit accounts. Participation accounts do not promise a return to the fund owner, nor do they guarantee the repayment of the principal to the account owner. Through these accounts, the fund owner becomes a partner with the bank in the profit or loss that may arise from the fund (Kaçmaz, 2009, p.3). These accounts offer an interest-free earning opportunity to the account holders over the inflation rate, especially during inflation periods, so that the funds held by these account holders will not be depreciated due to inflation, and even if the amount is not clear, a gain proportional to inflation will be provided (Gökalp, 1993, p.91). Participation accounts that can be opened on behalf of real persons and legal entities are, as mentioned before, time deposit accounts, and the maturities of the relevant accounts can be created in 5 different maturities: 1 month, 3 months, 6 months, 1 year and longer than 1 year (Tok, 2006, p. 48). The Banking Regulation and Supervision Agency (BRSA) categorised the fund allocation methods of participation banks with the regulation issued in 2006. According to the relevant classification, participation banks can provide funds in the forms of corporate financing support, individual financing support, profit-loss sharing investment, financial leasing, documentary financing against goods and joint investments (BRSA, 2006).

It should also be underlined that Participation Banks in Türkiye have encountered various challenges in the development process. The first is the 2008 Global Crisis. As is known, the crisis affected all banks in the sector, and it can be stated that Participation Banks were relatively less affected by the crisis. The main reason for this situation is that risk sharing is essential in the functioning of Participation Banking. In addition, since Participation Banks generally base their financing on a real asset and are fully collateralised, they have been significantly protected from the crisis (Sarıdoğan, 2020, pp. 145-155). Another adversity faced by participation banks is the seizure of Asya Finans by the SDIF in 2015 and the 15 July coup attempt in 2016. The fact that Asya Finans was a participation bank and its transfer to the SDIF caused the public to approach participation banks with scepticism, and the coup attempt put forward by the related community structure in the following year increased the public's uneasiness towards participation banking. In fact, the share of participation banks' assets in the sector declined from 5.2% in 2014 to 4.78% in 2016. In 2017, although a recovery trend was observed, the values of 2015 could not be achieved. However, in 2018, the share of participation banks' assets in the sector reached 5.15%, which was the 2015 value (TKBB, 2024). In addition to macroeconomic and political problems, there are other problems that hinder the development of participation banking in Türkiye. The first of these is the problem of recognition. The functioning of participation banks is often seen to be the same as conventional banking, and the differences in fund utilisation methods in participation banking are not sufficiently known by the public. This situation leads to the problem of awareness (Çürük, 2013,p. 52). Product diversity in participation banking is low, this leads to product inadequacy and capital insufficiency. While conventional banks can solve the capital shortage problem by obtaining interest-bearing loans from the Central Bank or other institutions, participation banks cannot easily overcome this problem since they have interest-free operations. The lack of a common market and accounting standard among Islamic banks leads to different recording of transactions carried out in different banks. This situation prevents unity in practice (Hazıroğlu, 2016, pp. 119-132). Another important problem faced by participation banking is the problem of asymmetric information. Participation banking and its functioning are not sufficiently known in the society. It is known that even the theological community, which constantly guides the society by issuing fatwas, does not have much information about the system. Since the theological community does not have accurate and complete information about the system, it may issue negative fatwas about the system from time to time (Aktepe, 2014, p. 90).

According to the data of the Participation Banks Association of Türkiye, the sector share of total assets of participation banks was 8.64% as of November 2023. Although the sector share of participation banks showed a downward trend compared to the previous year due to the seizure of Asya Finans by the SDIF in 2015 and the coup attempt in 2016, it has been on an upward trend since 2018 (Figure 1).

Figure 1. Sector share of participation banking by years (%) (TKBB, 2024)

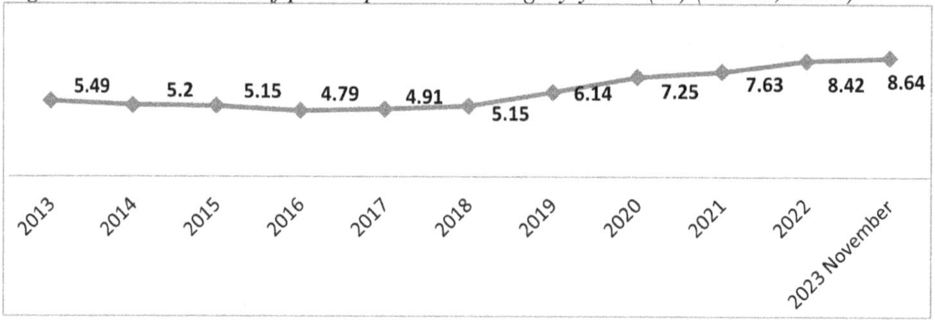

As of November 2023, the sector share of funds collected by Participation Banks was 10.09%, and it can be stated that the funds collected have been on an upward trend since 2013 (TKBB, 2024). Especially in 2020, the funds collected by Participation Banks increased significantly compared to the previous year. The same upward trend continued in the following years. As can be seen in Figure 2, the PBAT data reveal that the funds collected by the Participation Banking system have shown significant development especially in the last five years (Figure 2).

Figure 2. Development of funds collected by participation banks (TL million) (2013-2023) (TKBB, 2024)

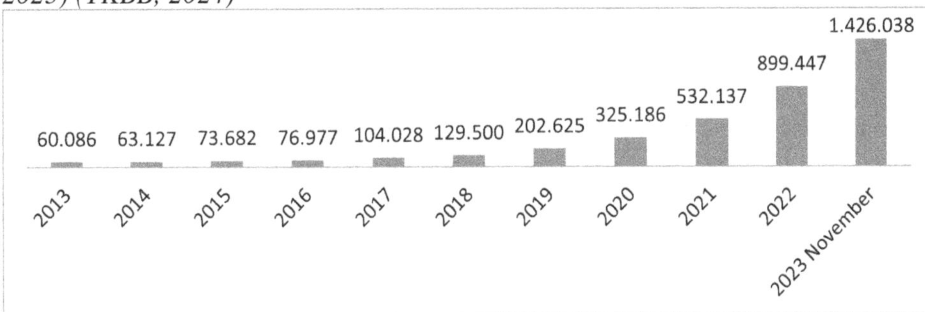

As of November 2023, the sector share of funds disbursed by Participation Banks was 7.7%. Since 2019, it can be seen in Figure 3 that the funds disbursed by Participation Banks have shown a significant upward trend (Figure 3).

Figure 3. Development of funds allocated by participation banks (TL million) (2013-2023) (TKBB, 2024)

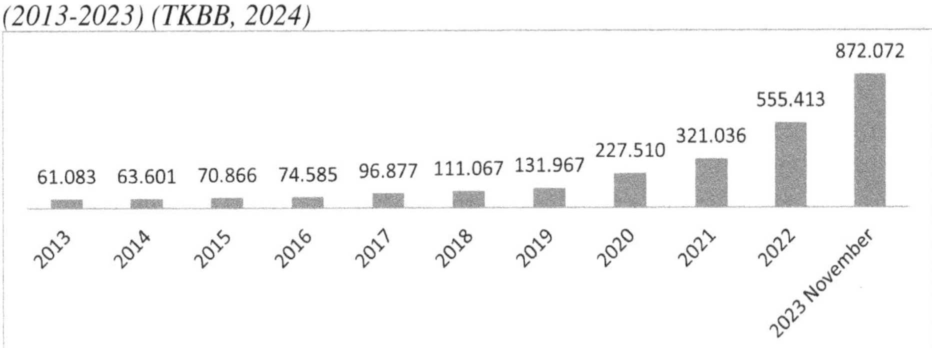

In conclusion, considering the development in the sector share of Participation Banks over the years and the upward trend in the funds collected and utilised by these banks, it can be stated that the Participation Banking sector has developed significantly in recent years and its contribution to the economy has increased significantly. Considering that the Participation Banks employed approximately 20,000 personnel as of the end of 2023, it is understood that these banks also contribute to the development of the employment capacity of the country.

Digitalization Performance of Participation Banking in Türkiye

In the 21st century, which will also be called the age of technology, financial services have been significantly affected by technological developments and the banking system has experienced a digital transformation. With the digital transformation, it has become possible to perform many banking transactions without leaving home, and it has provided significant convenience for bank customers to carry out financial transactions without space and time constraints. While digitalisation has reduced costs for the banking sector, it has also increased competition among banks. In order to reduce costs, increase revenues and respond to the rapidly changing needs of customers, banks have focused on technology investments in the relevant process. Forecasts for transaction costs in banking have led to a great emphasis on digital banking applications. According to a research, transaction costs are calculated as 4.3 USD for branch banking, 1.3 USD for telephone banking, 0.2 USD for internet banking and 0.1 USD for mobile banking. Therefore, branch banking is 43 times more costly than mobile banking (Bayrakdaroğlu, 2016, p.31). Competitive advantage, rapid response to customer needs, profitability, new customer acquisition, maintaining customer loyalty, and new revenue opportunities are the factors that encourage digitalisation in the banking sector (TSDG, 2016, pp.44-45). Banks, which were previously able to reach their customers only through their branches, have started to use alternative distribution channels with the help of information technologies. In this framework, firstly, branchless and unstaffed banking services were provided through ATMs, and then new distribution channels were used through telephone banking, internet banking and mobile banking. With the widespread use of smart phones, mobile banking applications have come to the forefront. Mobile banking has also eliminated the location and space problems experienced in internet banking (Ustaömer ve Bakırtaş, 2019, p.11). When the development of digital applications in banking in Türkiye is analysed, it is observed that the pioneer bank in this field is Türkiye İş Bankası. Internet banking, one of the most important elements of digital banking in Türkiye, was first launched by Türkiye İş Bankası in 1992. Internet banking has enabled all kinds of money transfer, investment, credit, credit card, invoice and various payment transactions to be carried out easily and rapidly. Nowadays, mobile banking has become the centre of digital banking with the recent developments in internet infrastructure and the widespread use of smartphones and tablets (TBB, 2022). The first mobile banking application (İşcep) in Türkiye was also launched by Türkiye İş Bankası in 2007 (İsbank, 2024a). Both internet banking and mobile banking have reached a significant number of bank customers in the country, and the banking sector has stepped into a new era with digitalisation. In this context, the advantages offered by digital banking to the customer are very diverse. With the rapid spread of digital banking, it has become possible to save time, and almost all transactions that can be physically performed in banks can be completed from the customer's location without the obligation to go to the bank. Digitalisation has eliminated the obligation to wait for the working hours of physically serving banks, and customers have the opportunity to perform many transactions at any time. Internet banking and mobile banking applications have provided customers with the opportunity to perform many banking transactions without paying costs and commissions. The related applications provided the customer with the opportunity to control all their accounts at any time they needed. Customers were able to create virtual cards linked to their accounts or credit cards and thus complete their online shopping with higher security. In addition to the advantages of these applications, there are also disadvantages. Short-term access problems may occur due to service updates. Internet connection and smart devices are required to use digital banking services. A problem in the device or internet connection prevents access to the relevant services (Hayat Finans, 2024b).

An important process that led to significant digitalisation of the banking operations in Türkiye is the Covid 19 pandemic process. In the Covid-19 pandemic, the banking sector differentiated from all sectors and came to the forefront with the intensive use of digital channels. Since Covid-19 is a contagious disease, contactlessness has gained importance and digitalisation has become strategic in this context. The number of active digital banking customers in Türkiye increased by 11.39% in September 2020 compared to March 2020. Since March 2020, all digital banking channels have been actively used in the banking sector in Türkiye and the negative impact of the pandemic on the banking sector has been relatively reduced. The widespread use of credit cards and the increase in online shopping during the pandemic also increased the transaction volume of the banking sector. Considering the increase in transaction volume and the number of active customers, it is evident that the banking sector in Türkiye is not one of the sectors caught unprepared for the pandemic (Beybur&Çetinkaya 2020, pp.159-161). According to data from 28 member banks of the Banks Association of Türkiye (providing conventional banking services), the number of active digital banking customers reached 100 million as of March 2023. Of this number, 87.5 per cent of them have only made mobile banking transactions, 2 per cent have only made internet banking transactions and the remaining 11.5 per cent have made both mobile banking and internet banking transactions. When active retail digital banking customers are analysed according to their gender and age groups, it is determined that 66% of these customers are male and 34% are female. In the distribution of the age groups of the relevant customers, the 36-55 age group ranks first, the 26-35 age group ranks second and the 18-25 age group ranks third (TBB, 2023).

The main technologies used within the framework of digital transformation in the banking sector and their benefits are as follows:

- ***Blockchain:*** It is a prominent technology in ensuring the security of data. It can be described as a kind of virtual ledger technology. Thanks to this technology, all transactions are recorded, all transactions are controlled and monitored. Only authorised members can access this system. Many banking transactions can be done securely by the help of this technology such as smart contract system, corporate and commercial loan utilisation and international money transfer (Denizbank, 2024).
- ***Artificial intelligence (AI):*** It operates on the principle of collecting and analysing data, collects different types of data in banking, analyses the preferences and needs of customers in a fast and detailed manner, and enables the personalisation of products and services. Applications such as voice mobile assistants are among the most popular AI banking products (GarantiBBVA, 2020).
- ***Open Banking***: Open Banking is the sharing of banking data with third party banks and institutions through interfaces and with the consent of customers. In this way, new products and services can be developed. The ability to view all accounts in a single bank is an example of open banking. It stands out as a method that saves time and accelerates transactions (Ziraat, 2024).
- ***Big Data:*** It is a set of meaningful data resulting from the processing and evaluation of various data about users by some software and companies based on any transaction made on the Internet (İsbank, 2024b). Thanks to big data, banks can analyse their customers' behaviour in more depth and become more competent in many different areas such as cross-selling products, risk management and dealing with financial crimes (Srivastava& Gopalkrishnan, 2015, p. 643).
- ***The Internet of Things:*** It is a technology that enables devices used in daily life to communicate via the Internet. This technology can be used in many areas of life, facilitates financial transactions in the banking sector, enables many transactions to be carried out remotely without the need to go to the branch, and enables making the right investment and obtaining maximum profit from investments (Kuveytturk, 2024).

While the digitalisation process developed rapidly in recent decades, the rapidly developing participation banking sector in Türkiye also received its share from the relevant process. The rapid progress of conventional banks in the field of digital banking has necessitated the adaptation of participation banks to the relevant process and thus participation banks have accelerated their adaptation processes. Digital transformation has come to the fore as an important tool in competition with conventional banks. Thanks to this process, the problems related to the access of customers to the interest-free banking system have been eliminated to a great extent and the way for participation banking has been paved (Yıldırım and Yıldırım, 2022). In this framework, both conventional banks and participation banks in Türkiye have intensively adapted to the digital transformation technologies mentioned in the previous paragraph. In a study, digital applications in six participation banks (Albaraka Türk, Kuveyt Türk, Türkiye Emlak Katılım, Ziraat Katılım, Vakıf Katılım, Türkiye Finans Katılım) were analysed by content analysis method in Türkiye. According to the findings of the study, innovative digital applications of participation banks include the use of technology such as artificial ıntelligence etc. It has been observed with the study that these practices create brand value, enable better communication with customers, meet customer expectations, increase performance and productivity, save time, increase competitiveness and increase the number of customers (Tekin, 2020).

Participation banks in Türkiye have largely taken their place in the digital world through mobile banking and internet banking channels since 2000's. When the applications used by digitally active customers in participation banking are analysed, it is seen that mobile banking applications have the highest share today (Figure 4). When the transaction volume by channels is investigated, it is observed that the volume is 2,5 trillion TL in mobile banking and 751 billion in internet banking as of 2023Q4 (TKBB,2024).

Figure 4. Channels used by digitally active customers of participation banks; 2023 Q4 (TKBB, 2024)

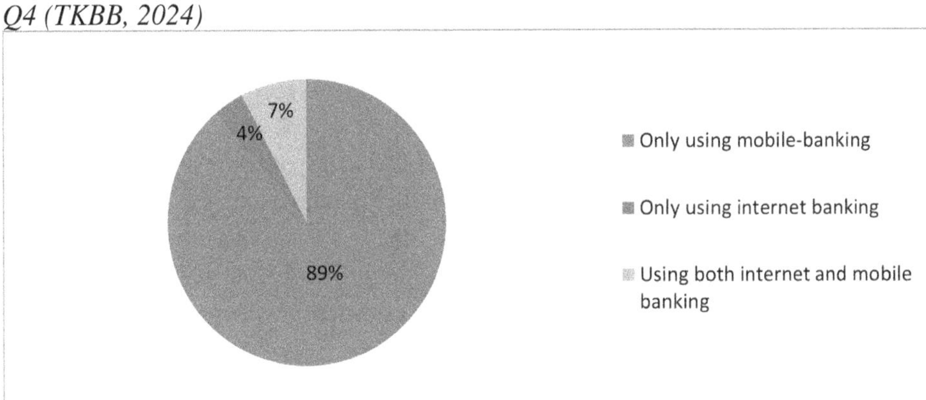

An analysis of the number of transactions in digital banking by customer segments for the period 2023Q4 reveals that retail customers account for 78% of transactions, while corporate customers account for 22% . On the other hand, when classified according to transaction volume, it is seen that the transaction volume of retail customers is 36% and the transaction volume of corporate customers is 64%. When the distribution of number of transactions is investigated as of 2023Q4, it is observed that the highest share belongs to financial transactions money transfers (65%). The share of non-financial transactions is 14%, share of financial transactions payments 10%, share of financial transactions investment transactions 6% and credit card transactions 5% (TKBB,2024) .

When the distribution of customers using digital banking in Türkiye is analysed according to their place of residence, the top five cities are Istanbul, Ankara, Konya, Bursa and Kocaeli. It is noticed that participation banking customers residing in foreign countries also use digital channels extensively (Figure 5).

Figure 5. Number of active digital banking customers of participation banks by province; 2023 Q4 (TKBB, 2024)

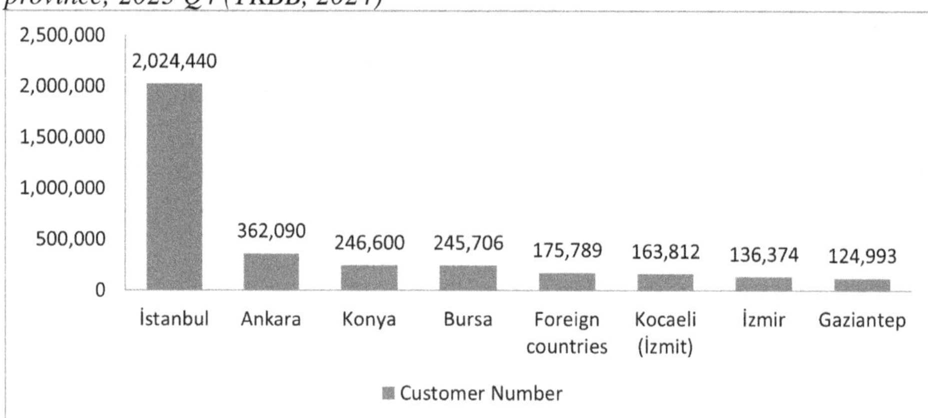

As mentioned in the previous section, the Covid 19 pandemic accelerated the digitalisation of the banking sector in Türkiye. In the relevant process, participation banks, just like conventional banks, have become more active in the digital world. Table 2 shows that the Covid-19 pandemic, which has affected Türkiye since early 2020, increased the number of customers and transaction volume of participation banking in the period between 2020-2023. Therefore, it can be stated that the Covid 19 pandemic paved the way for the development of participation banks through the intensive use of digital channels.

Table 2. Number of digital customers, total volume and number of transactions in digital participation banking

Period	Number of Active Digital Customers	Total Volume of Transactions	Total Number of Transactions
2020 Q1	2,6 million	331,7 billion TL	54,8 million
2020 Q4	3,3 million	593,7 billion TL	103,5 million
2021 Q1	3,5 million	573,3 billion TL	106,5 million
2021 Q4	4 million	1 trillion TL	135,6 million
2022 Q1	4,2 million	937,6 billion TL	148,8 million
2022 Q4	4,7 million	2,9 trillion TL	125,5 million
2023 Q1	4,8 million	2,1 trillion TL	112,8 million
2023 Q4	5,4 million	3,2 trillion TL	137,8 million

Source: TKBB, 2024

Different studies in the literature confirm that digital transformation positively affected customer satisfaction, transaction volume and financial performance of participation banking in Türkiye. According to a study examining the impact of digital applications (such as internet banking and mobile banking) on return on equity and return on assets in participation banks, it is revealed that increasing the online banking transaction volume of participation banks increases asset profitability. Moreover, it is asserted that the increase in the number of mobile banking customers and the increase in the number of mobile banking transactions significantly increases the asset profitability of these banks. Another finding of the same study is that when participation banks increase the number of mobile banking customers and transaction volume, they also increase their return on equity (Ahmetoğulları, 2023). According to another study, the profitability of participation banks was not adversely affected by the Covid 19 pandemic, and when a comparison was made by comparing the profit and loss statements of each quarter of 2019 with the profit and loss statements of each quarter of 2020, it was found that the profitability of participation banks increased after the onset of the pandemic (Yurttadur, 2021). A recent study investigated the impacts of financial technology applications such as internet banking and mobile banking on the financial performance of participation banks in Türkiye with quarterly data for the period 2020-2022 and revealed that internet banking, mobile banking, digital banking and the number of ATMs have a significant effect on the return on assets and return on equity of the relevant banks (Çalış, 2023). A different research also asserted that the innovative digital applications of participation banks have positive impacts on customer satisfaction, performance and efficiency of the stated banks (Tekin, 2020). According to the Participation Banking Digital Research Report (which was conducted in Türkiye), the ease and usability of the services offered digitally significantly affect the preferences of 64% of participation banking customers. Nearly half (43%) of participation banking customers state that they would switch to a bank that offers easier, usable and comprehensive digital services. It is asserted with the research that Participation Banking customers use the "Smart Assistant" application much more than conventional bank customers. Additonally, especially the young population has insufficient knowledge about participation banking and the services it offers (TKBB, 2021).

As it is known, customer acquisition is one of the prominent targets of all banks. As emphasised in the previous paragraphs, one of the most prominent problems of participation banking is the problem of awareness. TKBB data show that the intensive use of digital channels in participation banking has led to a significant increase in remote customer acquisition. According to current data, the number of customers acquired through remote customer acquisition is 832,054. When the monthly data for the last three years are analysed, it is observed that remote customer acquisition is on an upward trend (TKBB,2024). The spread of open banking applications is one of the factors accelerating digitalisation in the banking sector. Today, three of the 16 banks that are account service providers (AISP - Account Information Service Provider) on the Open Banking national platform are participation banks, namely Albaraka Türk Participation Bank, Kuveyt Türk Participation Bank and Ziraat Participation Bank. In addition, two of the 15 banks with authorised payment system (PISP - Payment Initiation Service Provider) status are Albaraka Türk Participation Bank and Kuveyt Türk Participation Bank (Katılımfinans, 2024).

An Overview of the Advantages and Disadvantages of Digital Transformation to Participation Banks in Türkiye (Measures to be Taken for the Healthy Functioning of Participation Banks)

In the previous section, the advantages faced by banks and customers in the banking sector with digitalization were mentioned. From the customers' point of view, some of these advantages were as follows; speed, saving time, having opportunity to carry out transactions in any environment (which they could only carry out in bank branches previously) regardless of their location, the freedom to perform many transactions at any time, the ability to carry out many banking transactions without paying commissions and fees, the ability to perform transactions without any time restriction and the ability to shop online especially thanks to virtual cards

(Bayrakdaroğlu, 2016; Ustaömer ve Bakırtaş, 2019; TSDG, 2016; Hayat Finans, 2024b) . The advantages of the digitalization process for banks were as follows; carrying out financial transactions without space and time constraints, reducing costs, increasing competition, new revenue opportunities and increasing revenues, responding to the rapidly changing needs of customers, increasing profitability, new customer acquisition and maintaining customer loyalty (Bayrakdaroğlu, 2016; Tekin, 2023; Çalış, 2023; TSDG, 2016).

Although developments in financial technology offer various advantages to all banks that continue their activities and also the customers, rapidly developing technologies also create disadvantages. According to a study on banks in Türkiye, the disadvantages of digital transformation in the banking sector are risks related to security, weakening of customer relations, reduction in the number of employees in the banking sector as digitalisation leads to a decrease in the number of branches and employees, and the resulting unemployment (Karyağdı, 2022, p.865). Customers' computers, smartphones and tablets can be exposed to malware in various ways. Fake e-mail links sent to customers, advertisement links on social media and websites, links sent to customers via SMS that create the perception of being sent by the bank, fake page links encountered in search engines, fake banking applications downloaded from application markets, various networks that are in use without a password and whose security is not sure are the risks that customers may encounter througout the digitalization process.

In this framework, we have to emphasise that cyber risks are one of the leading risks that highly increase with the digitalisation in the banking sector. According to international data, the sector most targeted by cyber attacks in 2023 is first the manufacturing sector and second the finance sector (Statista, 2023). With digitalisation, information stored in digital systems becomes the main target of cyber criminals and this situation poses a great risk for the banking sector. Managing cyber threats in the banking sector is challenging because these threats have a constantly evolving and renewed nature. The costs of a cyber attack on a financial institution are measured in millions of dollars. Moreover, cyber attacks not only cause financial losses but also reputational damage and legal liabilities. In order to eliminate these risks, banks have to invest more in cyber security measures like firewalls and detection systems. Investments in these fields should be continuous, not one-time, because constantly developing technology can create a different threat every day. To deal with cyber risks, banks need to be able to significantly improve their risk management frameworks. The first step in this context is risk identification. Since banks may face internal risks such as employee errors, system failures, and external risks such as cyber attacks and malwares, it is important to identify these risks. After identifying risks, banks should also consider the effectiveness of cyber security measures and be able to diagnose gaps and vulnerabilities that may occur in this area. Hence, risk assesment is another important fact after risk identification. In order to be protected from negative situations during the digitalization process, banks should develop a risk mitigation plan based on risk assessment, thus reducing the possibility and effects of cyber incidents. Technical controls, development of security policies, training of personnel and sudden response plans are the prominent activities at this stage. Banks should establish a process to monitor cyber risks and the effectiveness of risk mitigation measures should be monitored regularly. In this process, evaluation of the bank's cyber security posture, vulnerability scanning, incident reporting and analysis are the procedures that need to be performed. Risk reporting and effective risk management is a very important step in this context. Moreover, regulatory authorities in countries also have duties to undertake to manage cyber risks. Federal Financial Institutions Examination Council and New York State Department of Financial Services in United States, General Data Protection Regulation and European Banking Authority in the European Union and Monetary Authority of Singapore are the main institutions that have taken important steps in this field (Vierescu&Toader, 2023, p.713-714). Therefore, banks have to invest in cyber security measures, partner with cyber security companies or work with cyber security experts constantly, perform risk assesment and risk management effectively in order to protect themselves from cyber threats in the digitalisation process. Staying away from cyber risks in the financial sector, where cyber attacks are rapidly increasing, is not something that can only be achieved by the efforts of financial institutions. Regulatory authorities also have a lot of work to do in this field. Regulatory authorities in certain countries around the world pave the way for safer operation of financial systems with various regulations in the digital era. Legal regulations in this field are very important for the healthy functioning of the financial system. However, there is a lack of legal infrastructure in Türkiye. There is no specific cyber security law in Türkiye. There is a need for a comprehensive law in the field of cyber security in the country. A comprehensive law regarding cyber security should come into force in the country as soon as possible, and after the relevant law comes into force, each critical area should be protected against cyber threats with different legal regulations (Karasoy&Babaoğlu, 2021, p.151). The banking system can be considered one of the leading critical areas. According to the findings announced by Kaspersky, Türkiye is one of the regions where cyber threats are most concentrated in 2023. The rapid increase in cyber threats targeting Türkiye reveals the necessity of the spread of cyber security measures and the rapid development of an infrastructure for this subject. A Kaspersky employee underlines that the widespread availability of artificial intelligence will lead to various security vulnerabilities, especially on mobile devices, and will increase hacking activities (Sabah, 2023).

On the other hand, in adapting to financial technologies, it should be emphasised that banks operating in developing countries do not operate under the same conditions as banks operating in developed countries. There are structural features that significantly affect digitalisation in emerging countries. Low income and low financial literacy levels, weak technological infrastructure, undeveloped technology ecosystem and low penetration of formal financial services are notable features impacting on the digitalisation in emerging countries (IFC, 2017). Therefore, in order for participation banking to adapt to digital transformation in a developing country like Türkiye, an improvement in the aforementioned qualities is essential. This situation is very important not only for participation banking but also for conventional banking in Türkiye.

Studies covering different countries underline that banks, especially those operating in high-income economies, have assumed the role of 'digital leader' to a significant extent, have an important digital infrastructure, as well as a strong legal system, thereby increasing their competitiveness. However, this is not the case for every bank. Even in high-income economies, some banks fail to become 'digital leaders' in the long term, have difficulty in adopting new technologies due to the established consumer behaviour that prefers old technologies, and continue their activities with less active fintechs (Liu, 2021, p.2). Therefore, it should be underlined that adaptation to new technologies requires not only a strong financial structure, but also a consumer group that can quickly adapt to new technologies. To be effective in the digitalization process, participation banks need technological investments to create digital infrastructure and use new technologies. Today, technology is developing rapidly and conventional banks make significant investments in the relevant field, it is thought that small and medium-sized participation banks may have difficulties in adapting to technology. Therefore, participation banks in Türkiye can be further supported financially regarding the technological investments and infrastructure. Moreover, participation banks should educate their customers to increase the use of digital channels. Although this will cause the training costs of participation banks to increase, it should be taken into consideration that the training is necessary considering the benefits it will bring in the long term. As emphasized in the previous paragraphs, especially the young population in Türkiye does not have enough information about participation banking and the services it offers (TKBB, 2021). Since Türkiye is a country with a large young population, raising the awareness of the young population in this field is very important for the development of participation banking. On the other hand, as it is known, it is easier for the young population to adapt to digital applications. For this reason, training activities, especially for young customers, should be accelerated even though they require a certain cost, and state support should be provided in this field if necessary.

Additionally, as Yıldırım and Yıldırım (2022, p.82) stated in their study, digital banking applications of participation banks should be differentiated for different customer types. For example, separate adaptations should be provided for individual customers and for corporate customers. Digital banking should be planned separately for internet banking and mobile banking. Considering that mobile banking is used more than internet banking, it is very important that mobile applications are developed and installed to be suitable for every phone model. As it is known, Islamic finance is subject to its own regulations and principles. In this case, as stated by Yıldırım and Yıldırım (2022, p.82), the content of e-transactions or e-services should also be in compliance with the relevant principles. Technological solutions compatible with these principles may also create additional costs. Cyber security applications stand out as applications that protect financial institutions and their customers from attacks and dangers. Therefore, it is inevitable for participation banks to take extra security measures during the intensifying digitalization process. These practices may also cause additional financial burdens. Finally, since participation banks are in an increasing competitive relationship with traditional banks, they have to develop innovative products. This may increase their financial burden. Therefore, relevant banks may need to be supported in the stated fields as well. On the other hand, participation banking in Türkiye is a relatively new field of economic activity that has developed mostly in the last twenty years, and it is known that the opportunities available to participation banking in the digital transformation process are not equal to those of conventional banks. In this context, participation banks' efforts to adapt to digital transformation should be supported by the state and should not be left solely to their own initiative. Investing in and maintaining cyber technology is a high-cost business. Considering the scale size of participation banks in Türkiye and their share in the banking system, it is obvious that these banks cannot invest in cyber security as much as conventional banks with high capital and high profits. On issues such as effective risk management and risk reporting, senior officials of participation banking should be subjected to periodic training, if necessary, by experts working in conventional banks and should be constantly informed in this field. The Banking Regulation and Supervision Agency, the Banks Association of Türkiye and the Participation Banks Association of Türkiye, which are the leading authorities in the banking sector in Türkiye, should undertake joint work to improve cyber security in both conventional and participation banks. For the healthy and safe functioning of the banking system in Türkiye, participation banks should not be left to their own resources and should be supported by the related institutions in the field of cyber security.

CONCLUSION

In Türkiye, economic liberalisation or in other words liberalisation movements emerged in the 1980s and the interest in interest-free financial institutions developed in coordination with these liberalisation movements. Interest-free financial institutions gained a legal framework in 1985 and continued their activities under the name of "Financial Institution" until 2005. The Banking Law No. 5411, which entered into force in 2005, gave the name "Bank" to the relevant institutions and the relevant institutions have continued their activities under the name of "Participation Bank" since 2005. Today, nine banks, including two digital banks, operate in the participation banking system, which has developed significantly in Türkiye in recent years. As revealed by the data of the TKBB, the funds collected and disbursed by these banks have increased significantly in the last two decades, and these institutions have played an important role in integrating the funds of the interest-sensitive sector into the real economy. The interest-sensitive Muslim population in Türkiye is notable, thus the mission of participation banking in the Turkish economy is significant. The Turkish economy, one of the largest economies in the world, is a country with macroeconomic problems such as the informal economy, inadequate employment, and the inability to include under-pillow funds in the economy. Therefore, the participation banking system, which includes idle funds into the economy, reduces the informal economy and makes a significant contribution to the labor market with approximately 20,000 employees, is very important for Türkiye. On the other hand, it should be underlined that the majority of the population in Türkiye is Muslim and a significant part of it is sensitive to interest. While participation banks in Türkiye developed since 2000s, they were also significantly affected by the digital transformation that emerged in the banking sector and tried to adapt the technologies that emerged with the relevant transformation to their operations. Digital transformation has come to the fore in participation banking's competition with conventional banks, and it has become easier for customers to access interest-sensitive banking. As TKBB data reveals, the Covid 19 pandemic, where restrictions and contactlessness are at the forefront, has significantly increased the number of active digital customers, total number of transactions and volume in the participation banking system. Studies in the literature shows that the intensive use of digital applications since the early 2020s not only increases the number of customers and transaction volume, but also increases customer satisfaction and financial performance of these banks (Ahmetoğulları, 2023; Çalış, 2023; Yurttadur, 2021; Tekin 2020). Two digital banks (Hayat Finans and TOM Bank) that have recently been introduced to the banking sector within the framework of participation banking show that participation banking has made significant progress towards digitalization. Despite all this, the share of participation banking in total banking is limited and should be improved. Increasing the market share of participation banks across the country will also increase fintech cooperation opportunities. In the development process of participation banking, the correct use of digital transformation tools will both ensure the growth of the relevant sector and increase customer satisfaction and profitability. In this sense, it is crucial for participation banks to increase product diversity and implement easy applications that customers can adapt to more easily. Türkiye is a country with a large young population. On the other hand, according to the Participation Banking Digital Research Report, the young population's knowledge of participation banking in the country is quite insufficient. In this context, the young population should be informed about the operation of participation banking and digital banking applications. The relevant report also reveals that customer acquisition and deepening opportunities will increase with the development of digital services in participation banking. Therefore, digitalization can help eliminate the "awareness" problem, which is one of the main problems of participation banking. Moreover, improving financial literacy and digital literacy throughout the country and informing the population accurately about participation banking within this framework will make a significant contribution to the development of participation banking.

As emphasised in the previous sections, digital transformation has caused the banking system to face both various advantages and disadvantages. Various advantages such as saving time for the customer, speed in transactions, the ability to perform banking transactions in any environment, exemption from various commissions and fees, and the opportunity to make online shopping thanks to virtual cards are positive developments that stand out on the customer side. Reduced costs, new revenue opportunities, increased bank revenues and profitability, easier and increased access to new customers, increased customer loyalty and increased competitiveness are the advantages standing out on the banking sector side. However, with fast digitalization process, both banks and their customers may face significant disadvantages. The main disadvantages are the weakening of customer relations, the decrease in employment and increase in unemployment in the relevant sector with the increase in branchless banking, the emerging security vulnerabilities, becoming the target of cyber attacks, weakness in risk reporting and the lack of effective risk management. Inadequacy in the legal legislation on the subject is also one of the important disadvantages. Each country has a different capacity to cope with these disadvantages brought about by digital transformation. While developed countries can make significant investments in this field of cyber security and secure themselves in this field, there is sufficient investment in this field in many developing countries. Türkiye, being one of the twenty biggest economies in the world according to World Bank classification as of 2023 (WB, 2023) has a complex financial system. On the other hand, Türkiye is one of the countries that cannot adequately take the necessary security measures in the digitalization process. The legal legislation in this field is insufficient in the country, and the country does not have a cyber security law. In this context, a comprehensive cyber security law should be prepared in the country and come into force as soon as possible. Since digital transformation significantly affects every field in the country, from health to industry, from finance to education, a comprehensive law will secure not only the financial field but also the transactions in many areas in the country. Moreover, the main targets of cyber attacks in the world is the financial sector, and Türkiye has been one of the countries that have been targeted by cyber attacks in recent years. As mentioned before, cyber security applications are quite costly and need to be constantly maintained and improved. It is obvious that participation banks, which have a limited asset size and a limited share in the banking sector compared to conventional banks, cannot compete with large conventional banks that operate with high profits in investing in cyber security. Therefore, participation banking, which manages to incorporate unregistered, under-the-pillow savings into the real economic system through fund collection and fund disbursement channels, improves the banking system and the real economy, and makes a significant contribution to budget revenues by paying taxes, increase the employment capacity of the country through the employees they employ in the country in this context, should be supported by the state, especially in the field of cyber security. It is obvious that a participation banking system that manages to adapt to the digital transformation process and operates securely will make positive contributions to the general banking sector in Türkiye.

AUTHOR'S NOTE

This study is the expanded version of M.S. Thesis of Yasemin Tekiner (The development of participation banking in Türkiye and its comparison with conventional banking based on selected indicators) which has been accepted by Ondokuz Mayıs University Postgraduate Education Institute/ Türkiye as of 2023.

REFERENCES

Ahmetoğulları, K. (2023). The role of digitalisation in the financial performance of the participation banking sector. In Yücel, R., Ayyıldız, Y., & Er, H. (Eds.), *Innovations Brought by Digitalisation to the Finance Sector*. Özgür Yayın Dağıtım. (In Turkish)

Aktepe, İ. E. (2014). *Participation banking with questions*. TKBB.

Banking Law. (2005). Law Number: 5411. https://www.mevzuat.gov.tr/mevzuatmetin/1.5.5411.pdf

Bayrakdaroğlu, A. (2016). Development of electronic banking after the crisis. In Gündoğdu, A. (Ed.), *Fundamentals of Banking in the Light of Developments After the Global Crisis*. Nobel Publishing. (In Turkish)

Beybur, M., & Çetinkaya, M. (2020). The impact of covid-19 pandemic on usage of digital banking products and services in Turkey. [In Turkish]. *International Journal of Western Black Sea Socialand Humanities Sciences*, 4(2), 148–163. DOI: 10.46452/baksoder.829078

BRSA. (2006). Banking Regulation and Supervision Agency. Regulation on Credit Transactions of Banks. https://www.resmigazete.gov.tr/eskiler/2006/11/20061101-13.htm

Çalış, N. (2023). The effect of digital banking applications on profitability: An application on participation banking sector. In Dündar, Ö. (Ed.), *Theory, Practice and Current Debates in Economics and Administrative Sciences*. Gazi Bookshop. (In Turkish)

Çürük, S. (2013). The development of İslamic finance in Turkey, existing problems and recommendations. *Doctoral Thesis. Selçuk University Institute of Social Sciences, Department of Business Administration,* Konya (In Turkish).

Denizbank, 2024. How Safe Is Your Data: Blockchain Technology https://www.denizbank.com/blog/dijital-dunya/verileriniz-ne-kadar-guvende-blockchain-teknolojisi-105489#:~:text=Farkl%C4%B1%20bloklar%C4%B1n%20bir%20araya%20gelmesinden,payla%C5%9F%C4%B1ml%C4%B1%20bir%20defter%20olarak%20d%C3%BC%C5%9F%C3%BCn%C3%BClebilir

Emiroğlu, O. (2019). Participation and the importance of the banking in Turkey. *Unpublished Master Thesis. Kastamonu University, Institute of Social Sciences, Department of Economics,* Kastamonu (In Turkish).

Emlak Participation. (2023). History of Emlak katılım_https://www.emlakkatilim.com.tr/tr/hakkimizda/tarihce

Garanti, B. B. V. A. (2020). The new hero of the financial sector: Artificial intelligence_https://www.garantibbva.com.tr/blog/yapay-zeka

Garanti, B. B. V. A. (2024). Possible Dangers in Digital Banking_https://www.garantibbva.com.tr/dijital-bankacilik/olasi-tehlikeler

Gökalp, M. F. ve Güngör, T. (1993*). Economic structure of Islamic society, Istanbul: Fey Foundation Publications(In Turkish).*

Hayat Finans. (2024a). About us_https://www.hayatfinans.com.tr/hakkimizda

Hayat Finans. (2024b). Advantages and disadvantages of mobile banking applications_https://www.hayatfinans.com.tr/mobil-bankacilik-uygulamalarinin-avantajlari-ve-dezavantajlari

Hazıroğlu, T. (2004). *Private financial institutions or participation banking*. Yeni Şafak. (In Turkish)

Hazıroğlu, T. (2016). The emergence and conceptual importance of the participation banking idea in Turkey. [İEFD]. *Journal of Islamic Economics and Finance*, 2(1), 119–132. https://dergipark.org.tr/tr/pub/jief/issue/24515/259788

IFC. 2017. Digital Financial Services: Challenges and Opportunities for Emerging Market Banks, International Finance Corporation, World Bank Group._https://openknowledge.worldbank.org/server/api/core/bitstreams/f10918de-9755-58ac-9350-1cc944dfb94f/content

İsbank. 2024a. World's Best Mobile Banking Application 'İşCep'_https://www.isbank.com.tr/bankamizi-taniyin/dunyanin-en-iyi-mobil-bankacilik-uygulamasi-iscep

İsbank. 2024b. What is Big Data?_https://www.isbank.com.tr/blog/big-data-buyuk-veri-nedir

Kaçmaz, A. (2009). *The development of participation banks in the Turkish banking sector between 2005-2008. Unpublished Master's Project*. Fatih University, Institute of Social Sciences. (In Turkish)

Karasoy, H. A., & Babaoğlu, P. (2021). Cyber security in Turkey: Legal and institutional infrastructure. Legislative (Yasama) [In Turkish]. *Journal*, (44), 123–155.

Karyağdı Güngör, N. (2022). Effects of Digital Transformation on Efficiency in the Banking Sector: A Qualitative Study in the TRB2 Region. [In Turkish]. *Kahramanmaraş Sütçü İmam University Social Sciences Journal*, 19(2), 852–870. DOI: 10.33437/ksusbd.990218

Katılımfinans. (2024). Digitalisation Highlights in the Turkish Participation Banking Sector https://katilimfinans.com.tr/finansal-raporlar/turk-katilim-bankaciligi-sektorunde-dijitallesmede-one-cikanlar-h14522.html

Kuveyttürk. 2024. How Will the Internet of Things Change Our Lives? https://www.kuveytturk.com.tr/blog/teknoloji/nesnelerin-interneti-hayatimizi-nasil-degistirecek

Liu, E. X. (2021). Stay Competitive in the Digital Age: The Future of Banks, IMF Working Paper, WP/21/46. https://www.imf.org/-/media/Files/Publications/WP/2021/English/wpiea2021046-print-pdf.ashx

Nacar, Y. (2007). *Participation banks and financial solutions*. Istanbul Chamber of Commerce.

Özsoy, İ. (1999). *Special finance institutions*. Asya Finans Institution Publication.

Özulucan, A., & Deran, A. (2009). The Comparison of Participation Banking and Traditional Banking on the Perspective of Banking Services and Accounting Applications. [In Turkish]. *Mustafa Kemal University Journal of Social Sciences Institute*, 6(11), 85–108.

Özulucan, A., & Özdemir, S. F. (2010). *Participation Banking*. Türkmen Kitabevi.

Sabah, 2023. Türkiye becomes world's most cyber targeted region in 2023 https://www.dailysabah.com/turkiye/turkiye-becomes-worlds-most-cyber-targeted-region-in-2023/news

Sarıdoğan, H. Ö. (2020). The factors affecting the performance of the partipacition banks: A dynamic panel data analysis in the context of the global crisis. [In Turkish]. *Bartın University Journal of Economics and Administrative Sciences*, 11(21), 148–167.

Srivastava, U., & Gopalkrishnan, S. (2015). Impact of big data analytics on banking sector: Learning for Indian banks. *Procedia Computer Science*, 50, 643–652. DOI: 10.1016/j.procs.2015.04.098

Statista, 2023. Distribution of cyberattacks across worldwide industries in 2023 https://www.statista.com/statistics/1315805/cyber-attacks-top-industries-worldwide/

Sümer, G. & ONAN, F. (2015). Emergence of participation banking in the world,developing period of participation banking in Turkey and difference versus conventional banking sector. [In Turkish]. *Gazi University Journal of Faculty of Economics and Administrative Sciences*, 17(3), 296–308.

Takan, M. (2002). *Banking theory, practice and method.* Nobel Kitabevi. (In Turkish)

TBB. (2022). Digital Journeys of Banks and Studies of the Banks Association of Turkey https://www.tbb.org.tr/Content/Upload/tos/Dijital%20Yolculuk.pdf

TBB. (2023). Digital, Internet and Mobile Banking Statistics, March 2023, Banks Association of Turkey https://www.tbb.org.tr/Content/Upload/istatistikiraporlar/ekler/4057/Dijital-Internet-Mobil_Bankacilik_Istatistikleri-Mart_2023.pdf

Tekin, Z. (2020). Innovative and digital solutions in participation banking: A model proposal for Turkey, Turkish Studies-Economics, Finance, Politics. https://www.researchgate.net/profile/Zeliha-Tekin/publication/344467452_Katilim_Bankaciliginda_Inovatif_ve_Dijital_Cozumler_Turkiye_Icin_Bir_Model_Onerisi_Innovative_and_Digital_Solutions_in_Participation_Banking_A_Model_Proposal_for_Turkey/links/5f7a1f9ea6fdcc00865723d7/Katilim-Bankaciliginda-Inovatif-ve-Dijital-Coezuemler-Tuerkiye-Icin-Bir-Model-Oenerisi-Innovative-and-Digital-Solutions-in-Participation-Banking-A-Model-Proposal-for-Turkey.pdf

TKBB. (2021). Participation Banking Digital. *Research Reports (Montgomery)*, 2021, •••. https://yonetim.tkbb.org.tr/upload/KATILIM%20BANKACILI%C4%9EI%20D%C4%B0J%C4%B0TAL%20ARA%C5%9ETIRMA%20RAPORU%202021.pdf

TKBB. (2024). Banking and Sector Information Participation Banks Association of Turkey https://www.tkbb.org.tr/veripetegi

Tok, A. (2006). Fund collection and utilisation transactions of participation banks and classical banking transactions in Turkish law. *Published Master Thesis.* Marmara University, Institute of Social Sciences, Department of Law, Istanbul (In Turkish).

TOM BANK. (2024). About Us. https://www.tombank.com.tr/index.html

TSDG. (2016). TÜSİAD, Samsung Türkiye, Deloitte Türkiye, GFK Türkiye, "CEO Perspective on Digital Change in Turkey" https://www2.deloitte.com/content/dam/Deloitte/tr/Documents/technologymedia-telecommunications/turkiyedeki-dijital-degisime-CEO-bakisi.pdf

Ustaömer, K., & Bakırtaş, T. (2019). Case of Digitalization in Turkish Banking Sector. *Journal of Economy* [In Turkish]. *Business and Management*, 3(1), 1–24.

Vakıf Participation. (2023). Know Vakıf Katılım. https://www.vakifkatilim.com.tr/tr/hakkimizda

Vierescu, E. M., & Toader, C. I. (2023). The Impact of Digitalisation and Cyber Risks on the Banking Sector, *The 6th International Conference on Economics and Social Sciences Geopolitical Perspectives and Technological Challenges for Sustainable Growth in the 21st Century,* June 15-16, 2023, Bucharest University of Economic Studies, Romania.

WB. 2023. World Bank Data https://data.worldbank.org/

Yıldırım, S., & Yıldırım, D. Ç. (2022). Digital transformation and adaptation in Islamic banking sector: A case of Turkey. [In Turkish]. *Journal of Kapanalti Accounting Finance Economics*, (1), 73–84.

Yurttadur, M. (2021). The effects of the covid 19 pandemic on the profitability of participation banks. [In Turkish]. *Nevşehir Hacı Bektaş Veli University Journal of ISS*, 11(4), 2285–2297. DOI: 10.30783/nevsosbilen.1009126

Ziraat, (2024). Open Banking https://www.ziraatbank.com.tr/tr/dijital-bankacilik/acik-bankacilik#:~:text=A%C3%A7%C4%B1k%20Bankac%C4%B1l%C4%B1k%20Nedir%3F,i%C5%9F%20modeline%20A%C3%A7%C4%B1k%20Bankac%C4%B1l%C4%B1k%20denilmektedir

Ziraat Participation. (2023). Ziraat Participation Corporate Information https://www.ziraatkatilim.com.tr/bizi-taniyin/kurumsal-bilgiler/ziraat-katilim-hakkinda

Chapter 3
Innovative Solutions:
Fintech Transformations in Islamic Inheritance

Norhazlina Ibrahim
https://orcid.org/0000-0003-1044-6463
Universiti Sains Islam Malaysia, Malaysia

Khairatun Hisan Idris Shazali
United Nations Institute for Training and Research International University, Malaysia

ABSTRACT

This chapter explores the transformative potential of financial technology (FinTech) in the context of Islamic inheritance, offering innovative solutions to address the complexities and challenges inherent in the traditional practices. By integrating FinTech with Islamic principles, this research aims to enhance efficiency, transparency, and accessibility in the management and distribution of Islamic inheritance. Through qualitative analysis, the chapter examines various FinTech applications, such as blockchain, smart contracts, and digital platforms. The chapter also identifies the benefits and potential challenges associated with the adoption of FinTech in Islamic inheritance processes. The findings suggest that FinTech innovations can significantly streamline inheritance procedures, reduce disputes, and ensure equitable distribution among heirs, thereby aligning with the ethical and legal standards of Islamic jurisprudence.

DOI: 10.4018/979-8-3693-5653-1.ch003

INTRODUCTION

In Islam, wealth is a valuable blessing granted by God to humanity, intended not only for material sustenance and success but also as a means of achieving eternal salvation in the hereafter. One of the primary goals of *Shariah* (*Maqasid Shariah*) is the protection of wealth. Islam provides Muslims with clear guidelines on how to manage wealth under all circumstances. For Muslims, any wealth management process must comply with *Shariah* law. Throughout life, individuals may go through some or all of the five phases of wealth management. The first phase, wealth creation, begins with earning income. A portion of this income is then invested in *Shariah*-compliant vehicles during the wealth accumulation phase, ensuring avoidance of interest, gambling, gharar, and haram elements. Wealth protection is another critical phase, safeguarding assets against unexpected losses through means such as takaful (Islamic insurance), which provides compensation for incidents like accidents, death, critical illness, and lawsuits. The fourth phase, wealth purification, includes two key aspects: fulfilling religious obligations, such as *zakat, sadaqah*, and *waqf* and purifying wealth that may be non-compliant with *Shariah*, like income from gambling or interest-based activities. The final phase, wealth distribution, takes place after death, with assets distributed according to faraid (Islamic inheritance law) after deducting funeral expenses, debts, and other obligations.

Numerous studies have explored various issues across all these phases; however, the wealth distribution phase remains the most controversial and unresolved. Planning for asset and wealth distribution to future generations is essential, using tools such as wills, trusts, and other estate planning strategies to ensure the heirs' wishes are fulfilled while minimizing estate taxes and potential disputes. Nasrul et al. (2021) has revealed that Malaysia and Indonesia share similar issues and problems influencing inheritance practices. Malaysia has been facing the challenge of unclaimed assets among Muslims for more than two decades. This issue has been explored in numerous studies dating back to 2001 (Noordin et al., 2012; Shafie et al.2014, 2016; Zulkifli & Ahmad, 2016; Kamarudin et al., 2019; Ibrahim et al., 2024a). Despite ongoing efforts to resolve this concern, the amount of unclaimed assets has increased substantially over time, underscoring the need for more effective estate planning and greater awareness within the Muslim community.

ISSUES IN ISLAMIC INHERITANCE

Even though Islam taught the believers the important of estate planning, the issue of frozen assets has been a great concern in many countries (Nasrul et al., 2021). There are multiple reasons account for this occurrence and are further discussed accordingly.

Ignorance, Lack of Knowledge and Disputes Among Heirs

Islamic inheritance in faces numerous, deeply rooted challenges that impact the effectiveness and efficiency of the distribution process. Studies by Abd Rahman et al. (2017) and Noordin et al. (2012) reveal various dimensions of these challenges, underscoring that the majority of issues stem from the heirs' significant misunderstanding of inheritance processes, as well as their limited knowledge of the relevant laws and procedures. This gap in understanding often leads to incorrect assumptions or mistaken steps, which, in turn, cause delays and additional complications in accessing their rightful shares. Additionally, many heirs are unaware of the precise legal requirements for inheritance claims, such as document preparation, application deadlines, and specific procedural steps dictated by Islamic law (*Faraid*) (Wajis et al., 2018). As a result, estates often remain unsettled, and assets are left unclaimed for extended periods. The lack of knowledge also means that heirs may not recognize their rights under Islamic law, leading to cases where rightful beneficiaries are left out or where disputes arise due to misunderstandings over asset division.

The issue is further exacerbated by a general lack of public awareness and education surrounding Islamic inheritance laws and the procedures required to enforce them. For example, while there are provisions within Islamic law to ensure fair distribution among beneficiaries, many heirs are unaware of these rights or how to initiate claims. Moreover, the complexity of the legal language and the multitude of required steps intimidate many heirs, particularly those unfamiliar with formal legal processes. Disputes among heirs can also result in overlapping deaths across successive generations, further complicating inheritance distribution and prolonging the settlement process (Sulong, 2011).

This lack of accessibility to clear information hinders beneficiaries, who may rely on informal advice or incomplete guidance, ultimately complicating an already complex process. This need for greater public education and awareness suggests a critical opportunity for institutions to streamline processes and provide clearer, more accessible resources on inheritance law. Improved education initiatives could help heirs better understand their rights and responsibilities, leading to smoother inheritance claims and helping prevent assets from becoming unclaimed or underutilized.

Incomplete Documents

One of the significant challenges in estate settlement is when heirs fail to provide a comprehensive set of documents required for the inheritance process. This can result from a lack of awareness about which documents are essential, difficulties in obtaining them, or simply not understanding the legal requirements (Shafie et. al., 2016, Zulkifli & Ahmad, 2016). In Malaysia, required documents often include identification details, proof of kinship, and verification of legal rights, depending on the estate's complexity. Missing paperwork delays the process, leading to additional bureaucratic back-and-forth that can take weeks or even months to resolve. Identifying legitimate heirs and beneficiaries is a complex process, especially in cases where family structures are intricate or when potential claimants are unknown. Verifying heirs requires confirmation of relationships, including proof of marriage, birth certificates, and other documentation to establish eligibility.

Challenges also arise in cases involving polygamous marriages or informal guardianships, which are more common in some communities. Misidentifying beneficiaries can lead to disputes among family members, potentially resulting in legal battles that further slowdown the estate settlement (Afiqah & Sabit, 2021). Critical documents such as birth, death, marriage, adoption, and conversion certificates are necessary to establish an heir's identity and relationship with the deceased. Loss or misplacement of these records creates substantial hurdles, as these documents are foundational to the claim process. In some cases, locating replacements can be difficult, especially for older documents or when records were not meticulously maintained. Without these documents, proving entitlement becomes challenging, leaving heirs in a limbo where they may not be able to assert their rights or access inherited assets.

Lengthy Processes

Another significant issue lies in the inheritance processes themselves, which are often drawn-out and complex. Many have criticized these agencies for the overly complicated and slow procedures involved (Abdullah et al., 2021; Abd Rahman et al., 2017). The bureaucratic nature of these processes typically results in extended waiting times, making the experience cumbersome for heirs. Such inefficiencies can lead to frustration and discouragement, often resulting in further delays and even leaving assets unclaimed (Sulong, 2011). However, these delays are not always due to the organizations alone. In some instances, the heirs themselves contribute to the delays, whether due to missing beneficiaries, false claims, or dishonest identification of heirs. Fraudulent cases, such as duplicate certifications and counterfeit documents, also complicate the inheritance process and increase the risk of further disputes.

Regulation and Legal

Most existing studies have primarily focused on the challenges that heirs encounter at different stages of the inheritance process. One of the foremost challenges is navigating the legal system, which can be complex and daunting. Heirs often find themselves confronted with intricate legal terminology and procedures that can be overwhelming, particularly for those who lack prior legal knowledge or experience (Kamarudin et al., 2019). This complexity can lead to confusion and missteps, delaying the overall process of claiming their inheritance.

Additionally, the financial burden associated with legal proceedings can be significant. The costs of hiring legal counsel, filing fees, and other expenses can accumulate quickly, placing a strain on heirs who may already be dealing with the emotional weight of loss. Many heirs are unprepared for these costs, and this unexpected financial pressure can create further stress and may even deter some from pursuing their rightful claims altogether.

The majority of existing studies have primarily focused on the challenges experienced by heirs during various stages of the inheritance process. These challenges include difficulties in navigating the legal system, the high costs associated with legal proceedings, and the emotional strain of dealing with inheritance matters during a period of grief (Ibrahim et al., 2024b). The complexity of the legal requirements and the necessity for multiple documents and certifications add to the burden faced by heirs. Lastly The storage of documents also poses a problem, contributing to the inefficiency and complexity of the inheritance system.

Multiple Jurisdictions

The estate claim process for heirs is particularly challenging due to the involvement of multiple organisations, each governing different aspects of inheritance law. For instance in Malaysia, these include bodies such as the Civil Courts, the Syariah Court (for Muslim estates), the Land Office, and the Amanah Raya (Public Trustee). Heirs often face confusion navigating through these multiple jurisdictions, each with its own set of rules and regulations that vary based on factors such as the religion of the deceased, the type of assets, and the amount in question (Fokri et al., 2021). This decentralization leads to a lack of clear guidance, as these bodies often provide inconsistent information, creating further frustration for heirs who may not be well-versed in legal intricacies. Additionally, since information is not centralized, heirs have to spend more time and resources to coordinate between these organizations. Nasrul et al. (2022) highlights that these conflicting regulations and unaligned procedures create obstacles that delay the inheritance process, often prolonging the settlement of estates for years. This inefficient and fragmented process underscores the need for a more streamlined, integrated approach to estate management.

While numerous solutions have been proposed to address these issues, one promising alternative is the use of financial technology (FinTech). Innovative solutions provided by FinTech could offer several advantages in solving the problems associated with Islamic inheritance in Malaysia.

RESEARCH METHODOLOGY

Thus, this chapter aims to conduct a comprehensive review of the current literature regarding the application of FinTech in the realm of Islamic inheritance. By identifying and addressing existing gaps in the literature, this chapter seeks to provide valuable insights into how financial technology can be leveraged to improve and streamline inheritance processes within Islamic law. To achieve this, the chapter employs qualitative analysis through a thorough content analysis of relevant literature. This analysis focuses on several key areas: the various applications of FinTech in Islamic inheritance, the benefits that arise from integrating FinTech solutions, and the challenges that organizations face when implementing these technologies in Islamic inheritance. Data and information for this chapter are collected from a variety of reputable sources, including academic journals, industry reports, and authoritative websites. This diverse range of sources ensures a well-rounded perspective on the subject, allowing for a more comprehensive understanding of the intersection between FinTech and Islamic inheritance.

The issues and themes identified in this chapter are intended to contribute new knowledge and insights that can guide future research and practice in the field. Additionally, the chapter seeks to highlight potential loopholes in the current system that FinTech could address, providing practical solutions that could enhance the efficiency and effectiveness of inheritance management.

RESULTS AND DISCUSSIONS

Various application of FinTech in Islamic Inheritance

In recent years, the convergence of financial technology (FinTech) and Islamic finance has ushered in transformative changes in various aspects of wealth management and financial transactions. One area where FinTech is making significant strides is in the domain of Islamic inheritance. This chapter delves into the application of FinTech in streamlining the Islamic inheritance process, addressing unique challenges, and reaping the benefits of technological advancements. FinTech solutions tailored for Islamic inheritance encompass a range of innovative tools and platforms designed to facilitate efficient, transparent, and Sharia-compliant distribution of estates. Include examples of FinTech tools or platforms currently utilized or underutilized or under development for managing Islamic inheritance. Several FinTech platforms and initiatives have emerged to address the specific needs of Islamic inheritance, including:

Digital Wills

Digital platforms allow individuals to create and manage their wills online, ensuring that asset distribution aligns with Islamic laws and principles. These platforms offer templates, legal guidance, and secure storage for will documents. Several institutions have launched online will services, including As-Salihin Trustee Berhad, Wasiyyah Shoppe Berhad, Amanah Raya Berhad, and MyAngkasa Berhad (Nordin and Ahmad, 2023). Additionally, the recent introduction of the Koha Islamic Digital Platform provides a wide range of services, including digital will writing, faraid calculation, power of attorney, trust arrangements, financial planning, and legal services. https://inceif.edu.my/launch-of-koha-islamic-digital-platform-by-minister-in-the-prime-ministers-department-religious-affairs/

Smart Contract

Smart contract is a self-executing digital contract with the terms of the agreement directly written into code (Mat Rahim et al., 2018). Smart contracts run on blockchain platforms and automatically enforce and execute the terms of an agreement when predetermined conditions are met. They are decentralized, meaning they do not rely on intermediaries, and are tamper-proof, providing security and transparency. mart contracts have various applications beyond cryptocurrency. They can be used in finance, supply chain management, insurance (automated claims), wealth management, and even legal agreements. Smart contracts are currently being developed on Bitcoin and other cryptocurrency platforms. Smart contract could be used in will creation. By removing intermediaries and automating processes, smart contracts create efficiencies, reduce costs, and open up new possibilities across industries (Mohamed, 2017). Fokri (2021) proposed possible smart contract as in Figure 1.

Figure 1. Application of smart contract in Inheritance property distribution (Fokri et al, 2021)

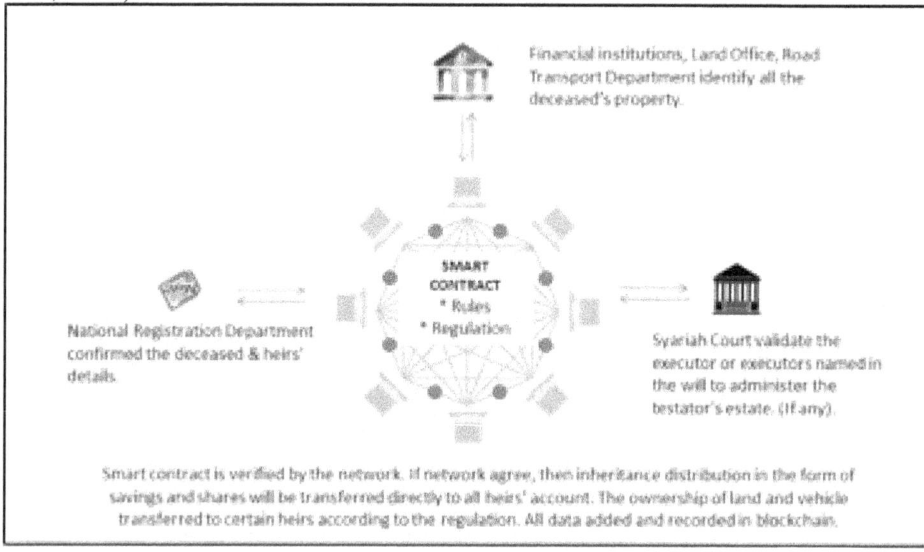

As these applications grow, so do the advancements in smart contract security and scalability, which are critical to supporting larger-scale implementations.

Blockchain-based Asset Distribution

Blockchain technology offers immutable and transparent records of asset ownership and transactions, which can be leveraged to automate asset distribution in Islamic inheritance. Smart contracts deployed on blockchain networks can execute inheritance instructions automatically upon predefined conditions (Mohanta et al., 2018; Karamitsos, 2018; Mukhopadhyay, 2018).

To address this problem, implementing this technology from the very start, which begins from the inheritance property distribution process right after a death occurs. The implementation of this technology requires the use of a database system that is similar across all the interested parties involved, such as the National Registration Department (JPN), High Courts, Land Office, Land Transport Department (JPJ) and other financial institutions. (TSS) (Fokri et al., 2021). They further elaborated on how block chained can be applied in the process.

Firstly, the heir is required to notify the National Registration Department (JPN) of the decedent's death by submitting the Death Registration or Burial Permit. Subsequently, the JPN will verify the details of both the deceased and the heir. In cases where a will exists, the High Court will validate the names specified within it. Prior to the development of a smart contract for the distribution of inheritance assets, relevant agencies should secure data on a blockchain platform. For instance, if the JPN confirms that the deceased was a Muslim, the distribution of inheritance will proceed in accordance with Islamic law, specifically the principles of *Faraid*, with the stipulation that the will may allocate no more than one-third of the total estate. The smart contract will be validated by the blockchain network, and once certification is obtained, the total value of the estate will be distributed among the heirs in compliance with legal requirements. Financial assets, such as shares and cash, will be transferred directly to the heir's account, while the ownership of vehicles and real estate will be formally assigned to the new owner. The most current information will be updated and maintained within the blockchain as in Figure 2.

Figure 2. Conceptual framework of blockchain technology in estate distribution (Safina (2021) and Anuar et al. (2022))

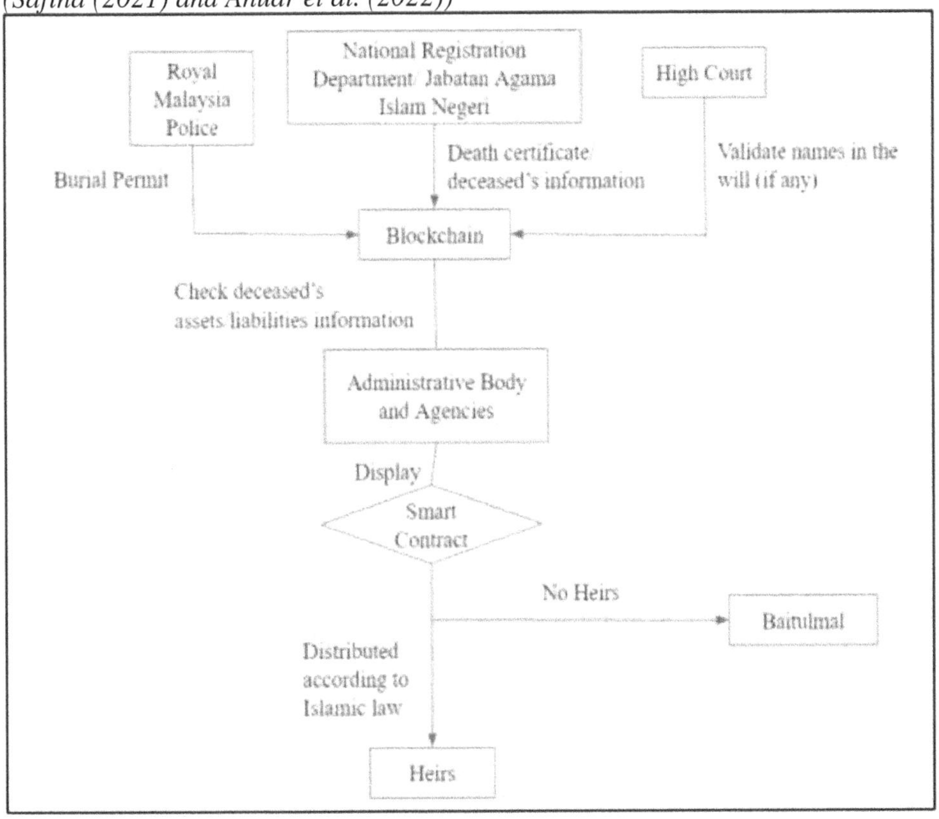

Blockchain technology could potentially impact the inheritance process based on trends up to the creation of digital tokens representing assets. In the context of inheritance, physical assets like real estate or art collections can be tokenized, making it easier to divide them among heirs (Nordin and Ahmad, 2023). These digital tokens can be securely and transparently transferred to the rightful heirs. Additionally, smart contracts are self-executing contracts with the terms of the agreement directly written into code. They can automatically execute actions when predefined conditions are met. In inheritance, smart contracts could be used to automate the distribution of assets based on a set of rules specified in the contract. This can reduce the need for intermediaries and legal disputes (Anuar et al., 2022).

The industry can benefit immensely by incorporating such a shared ledger system as it would not just help in automating processes but would also reduce compliance errors. The historical record of all transactions that have taken place and all documents that have been shared can be used as evidence that the institutions have acted in accordance with the guidelines placed by regulators. Seamless integration among agencies is critical to ensure the process is as swift as possible, avoiding delays as in Figure 2. Advancing the system allows the organisation to connect with heirs, and different agencies more quickly and efficiently, reducing complaints and grievances about the processes. This improvement would help address delays in resolving small inheritance cases by enabling better monitoring through the system.

Automated Inheritance Management Platforms

FinTech platforms equipped with algorithms and artificial intelligence capabilities streamline the inheritance management process by automating tasks such as asset valuation, calculation of shares, and distribution among heirs. These platforms ensure accuracy, reduce administrative burden, and minimize the risk of errors or disputes. that calculates shares and distributes assets among heirs in accordance with Islamic law. The platform employs algorithms to handle complex inheritance structures and generate comprehensive reports for stakeholders.

Furthermore, the implementation of automated systems can enhance the accuracy and reliability of legal document preparation. Automation tools can assist in generating standard documents by pre-filling templates with necessary information, reducing the likelihood of errors that often occur during manual entry. This not only saves time but also ensures compliance with legal requirements, thereby reducing the risk of disputes or complications in the inheritance process. Currently, there is no platform available specifically for Islamic inheritance, but the new MyLand system could serve as a foundation for its development. Although MyLand is not fully automated, it represents an initial step toward creating a fully automated system. MyLand is an instrument of estate distribution management. It is a new system that was transmitted from MyeTaPP. It was designed to facilitate the management of federal land and Bahagian Pembahagian Pusaka (BPP) at Jabatan Ketua Pengarah Tanah dan Galian Persekutuan (JKPTG) in Malaysia. Thus, it is to improve the administration of land and estate management by providing better services to the users by enhancing the efficiency and effectiveness of estate distribution management.

Digitalization of the Process

Digital technologies and automation present a transformative opportunity for organizations involved in the inheritance process by facilitating the digitization of documents, records, and procedures within the industry. As these organizations adopt digital solutions, they can significantly enhance the efficiency and effectiveness of their operations. The digitization process can streamline the creation and storage of essential legal documents such as wills, trusts, and other inheritance-related paperwork (Nordin and Ahmad, 2023). Traditionally, these documents have been created, managed, and stored in physical formats, which often leads to challenges related to accessibility, security, and the potential for loss or damage. By transitioning to digital formats, organizations can ensure that these critical documents are not only more secure but also easily retrievable and manageable. For example, digital storage solutions can employ advanced encryption and cybersecurity measures to protect sensitive information from unauthorized access. The potential for online wills and trusts is particularly noteworthy in this context.

By leveraging digital platforms, individuals can create, modify, and store their wills and trusts online, making the process more accessible and user-friendly. This convenience encourages more people to engage in estate planning, ultimately leading to a higher number of legally binding documents being created and stored securely. Online services can offer guided processes that educate users on the requirements and implications of their choices, helping to demystify the legal intricacies of inheritance planning.

In summary, the adoption of digital technologies and automation in the inheritance process holds immense potential for improving organizational efficiency and enhancing the overall experience for users. By streamlining the creation and storage of wills, trusts, and other legal documents, organizations can provide a more effective service, ultimately contributing to a more organized and transparent inheritance system

Web Based Expert System

A **web-based expert system** is a computer program that uses artificial intelligence techniques to emulate the decision-making ability of a human expert in a specific domain. Web-based expert systems leverage the power of artificial intelligence to deliver expert-level knowledge and support across various domains, enhancing decision-making processes and providing users with valuable insights. Their accessibility and adaptability make them increasingly valuable in today's digital landscape. They are still intended to address complex problems by inferring knowledge, similar to the way a human expert would. Expert systems are applied to a variety of issues, including decision-making, financial planning, disease diagnosis, and matters related to Islamic law, such as the calculation of *Zakat* and *Faraid*, which all necessitate human experience.

E-*Faraid*Tanah is one of the automated inheritance management platforms that calculates shares and distributes assets among heirs in accordance with Islamic law. The platform employs algorithms to handle complex inheritance structures and generate comprehensive reports for stakeholders (Saad & Rasli, 2022; Nafed, 2009). Furthermore, MAIS has introduced the MAIS e-*Faraid* System, marking a significant paradigm shift. This pioneering system, developed by the State Islamic Religious Council, includes (1) Online estate management services (2) A *Faraid* calculation tool (3) File management and reporting capabilities for managing officers (Saad & Rasli, 2022). Other websites that provide *faraid* calculation are Kalkulator *Faraid*[1], Kalkulator Pembahagian *Faraid*[2] and *Faraid* Calculator as-Salihin[3].

Robo Advisor

A robo-advisor for Islamic inheritance could serve as an automated tool that helps Muslims navigate the complexities of Islamic estate planning, ensuring *Shariah* compliance in the distribution of assets (Fazmi, 2019). Robo advisor has been widely used in Islamic investment platform. It helps investors manage their portfolios according to *Shariah*-compliant principles. It uses algorithms to offer low-cost, personalized investment advice, while strictly avoiding interest, gambling, excessive uncertainty (gharar), and investments in industries forbidden in Islam (e.g., alcohol, gambling, pork) (Gazali et al., 2020). Some existing platforms offer Islamic robo-advisory services, such as Wahed Invest, Sarwa (with a halal option), and ShariaPortfolio. These platforms help users invest in *Shariah*-compliant portfolios that align with their financial and ethical goals.

Wahed Invest initially launched as an Islamic robo-advisor in the United States, providing *Shariah*-compliant investment options for Muslim investors (Abdullah et al., 2022). By 2017, it had expanded its services to over 100 countries worldwide, marking its rapid global growth. Shortly after Wahed's launch, the Farringdon Group, a financial services company based in Kuala Lumpur, introduced Asia's first *Shariah*-compliant robo-advisor named Algebra (Global Islamic Finance Report, 2017).. This platform offers automated portfolio management and is accessible to investors globally, requiring a minimum investment of USD 200 per month. Through Algebra, clients can select from a range of funds included in its Islamic Master Select Portfolio, ensuring that their investments align with Islamic principles (Rahman, 2019).

IRSHAD, which stands for "Intelligent Robo *Shariah* Advisor," is a digital platform designed to provide automated financial advice and investment management solutions in accordance with *Shariah* principles. Another module of IRSHAD focuses on Islamic wills and inheritance. It provides guidance for Muslims on distributing their wealth and assets according to *Shariah* principles. This is especially valuable for those living in Muslim-minority countries, where inheritance laws do not follow *Shariah*. In such places, having a *Shariah*-compliant will is crucial; otherwise, the assets of a deceased Muslim will be distributed according to local laws rather than Islamic guidelines (Obaidullah 2021)..

Table 1. Overview of research on fintech applications in Islamic inheritance

No	Authors (year)	Digital Will	Smart contract	Blockchain	Digitalization	Robo Advisor	Web Based/ *Faraid* Tech
1	Nordin and Ahmad (2023)	/		/	/		/
2	Mat Rahim et al. (2018)		/			/	
3	Fokri et al. (2021)		/	/			
4	Nafed, 2009.						/
5	Saad and Rasli (2022)						/
6	Anuar et al. (2022)			/			
7	Safina (2021)			/			
8	Gazali et al. (2020)					/	
9	Abdullah et al (2021)					/	/

Benefits of Integrating FinTech into Islamic Inheritance

The integration of FinTech into the Islamic inheritance process offers several compelling benefits:

Efficiency

FinTech solutions automate manual processes, reducing the time and effort required for estate administration. Digital platforms enable seamless collaboration among stakeholders, streamlining communication and document management. Absolutely, researching the accurate determination of the true value of unclaimed assets is a significant and valuable endeavor. Overall, research into this area can lead to improved asset management processes, reduce uncertainties, and protect the interests of heirs and claimants, as well as enhance the overall efficiency and fairness of the inheritance process.

Accuracy

Automated calculations and digital records minimize the risk of errors in asset valuation and distribution, ensuring that heirs receive their rightful shares in accordance with Islamic law. Absolutely, researching the accurate determination of the true value of unclaimed assets is a significant and valuable endeavor. Overall, research into this area can lead to improved asset management processes, reduce uncertainties, and protect the interests of heirs and claimants, as well as enhance the overall efficiency and fairness of the inheritance process.

Reduce Cost

As previously mentioned, smart contract with the support by the blockchain technology can reduce the cost by eliminating the involvement of middlemen or intermediaries, thus, it will speed up the estate distribution process and to be utilized by the rightful heirs (Fokri et. al, 2021).

Reduce Disputes

As mentioned above, blockchain technology allows for the storage and recording of data and transactions linked to inheritance, including asset ownership and distribution. This includes the ability to record and save information. Consequently, this makes all transfers available to all parties involved and allows them to verify them. In addition to ensuring that the distribution process is fair and conducted in accordance with the principles of Shariah, this has the ability to prevent claims of misappropriation or fraud from occurring.

Contracts or records that are saved on blockchains, as stated by Mohamed (2017), have the potential to eliminate the need for intermediaries through the provision of trust in the system, which in turn can reduce the number of disputes that occur.

Promote Financial Inclusions

The preceding discussion on blockchain illustrates that the application of fintech can significantly improve financial inclusion in the context of Islamic inheritance. Fintech can markedly improve access to financial services related to Islamic inheritance. It achieves this by offering accessible, economical, and informative tools. This is especially important for persons who may have previously been deprived of these services.

Employing fintech allows individuals to understand and manage their inheritance rights and responsibilities in accordance with Islamic law. This strategy streamlines the inheritance procedure for everyone, especially those from disadvantaged regions. It promotes equity in financial matters, guaranteeing that all persons possess an equal opportunity to manage their assets.

Compliance with Islamic Principles

FinTech solutions are designed to uphold Sharia principles of fairness, transparency, and adherence to legal requirements. By leveraging technology, inheritance processes can be conducted with greater integrity and accountability. Protecting the information and the data is an element of integrity which align with Islamic perspective.

Challenges and Limitations

Challenges or limitations associated with implementing FinTech solutions in Islamic inheritance and potential strategies for overcoming them. These include:

Shariah Compliance

Even though fintech is designed with the upholding of Shariah principles, it should be used by individuals who understand the context of Islamic law and the limits and possibilities of such technology. Therefore, the training of jurists and Islamic legal experts in using artificial intelligence will be an essential component in optimizing the benefits of this technology. Thus, the development of artificial intelligence in Islamic law must be carried out with an awareness of the challenges and a commitment to ensure that the values of Islamic law and the principles of justice are maintained (Karimullah, 2023).

Karimullah (2023) mentioned that there is debate about the extent to which artificial intelligence can replace the role of humans in the discovery process of Islamic law. He further discussed whether involvement of AI may reduce the role and involvement of Islamic scholars and scholars in the process of ijtihad. And AI can be an opportunity in the development of decision-making support tools for Islamic jurists where jurists can have faster and more accurate access to relevant Islamic legal information, thus enabling them to make legal decisions better and more efficiently. This can speed up the ijtihad process and help solve more complex legal issues. Furthermore, there are opportunities to expand access to Islamic legal services through digital platforms. With the help of technology, Islamic legal information can be disseminated more widely and more accessible to the public. For example, apps or websites that use artificial intelligence can provide Islamic legal advice tailored to an individual's question or regarding a specific situation, thereby assisting the individual in understanding and complying with Islamic law. However, Karimullah (2023) highlighted additional challenges requiring attention, specifically ethics and accountability. How can we ensure that artificial intelligence algorithms in Islamic law do not result in discriminatory or unfair decisions? And it is not easy to balance between technological efficiency and the sustainability of intellectual traditions in Islamic law. Therefore, to implement an AI that can discover Islamic law, it critically needs the collaboration between the Islamic jurists, computer scientists, and religious communities.

Cybersecurity

The adoption of artificial intelligence (AI) and machine learning (ML) expands the potential for cyber threats. Besides the conventional cyber threats arising from human or software failures, they are vulnerable to emerging threats. These threats concentrate on altering data at various points in their lifecycle to exploit the intrinsic constraints of the algorithms (Comiter, 2019). This manipulation enables attackers to avoid detection and causes the systems to make erroneous decisions while retrieving information. According to AlAjmi et. al (2021), ML models, given their complexity and potential impact on financial sector institutions, necessitate constant oversight to ensure consistent detection and prompt management of such attacks. Besides the typical cybersecurity concerns, specific cyber threats to AI/ML can be categorized into three distinct types: "data poisoning," which causes the AI to incorrectly learn to recognize information; "input attacks," which allow attackers to perturb data inputs and mislead AI systems during operations; and model inversion attacks, which aim to recover training and input data or the model itself (Karimullah, 2023). Attackers or hackers may intrude on data and information, including important documents. This could lead to the leakage or manipulation of private and confidential inheritance-related data.

Data Privacy

Debating on data privacy, fintech is often prioritize the data security and privacy. The secure digital vault could store important documents such as wills or wasiyyah, asset lists, heirs' information, ensuring sensitive information pertaining inheritance is protected. Furthermore, the accessibility that will be created only to authorized users will enhance the confidentiality of the data and information. However, it can be hack by the hackers or attackers. An example mentioned by AlAjmi et. al (2021), attackers could alter images with elements unperceivable to human vision, but which provoke AI/ML image recognition systems to mislabel the images. Corrupted systems could undermine the financial sector's capacity to accurately assess, price, and manage risks, which could lead to the buildup of unobserved systemic risks. Attackers could also acquire training data sets that contain sensitive financial and personal information (AlAjmi et. al, 2021). Furthermore, the use of AI in discovering Islamic law may involve collecting and analyzing sensitive individual personal data. Therefore, there needs to be strict measures in place to protect data privacy and ensure that personal data is not misused or misused in the legal discovery process. Mohd (2019) mentioned that among the elements of integrity in information security from Islamic perspective is confidentiality.

Nevertheless, it should be noted that the use of AI in the invention of Islamic law should not wholly replace humans' role. The jurists, religious scholars, and legal practitioners should remain integral to this process. AI should be considered an auxiliary tool to assist them in legal analysis and discovery.

Financial inclusion

According to Karimullah (2023), the social and cultural factors should be taken into consideration. There is a possibility that communities or groups that believe this technology does not align with their beliefs or traditions would oppose the use of artificial intelligence in the process of discovering Islamic law. He continued by emphasizing that there is a need of an effort to educate and communicate to the community the beneficial goals and benefits that may be achieved through the utilization of AI within the context of Islamic law. It should also be emphasized that the fintech industry suffers from a shortage of skilled Shariah consultants, which might be a barrier to the creation of solutions that are compliant with Shariah. It is possible that fintech solutions, in the absence of appropriate advice, could mistakenly deliver services that are not in accordance with Islamic values, so avoiding compliance.

Risk of embedded bias in Fintech Solution

The term "embedded bias" in fintech solutions denotes the unintentional prejudice that may emerge within systems, algorithms, or processes due to the foundational data, design, or assumptions established during the development phase. Embedded bias in fintech solutions for Islamic inheritance can provide several issues. If the data that is utilized for training algorithms is predominantly derived from a certain demographic or region, it is possible that it does not adequately reflect the experiences of all potential users (AlAjmi et. al 2021, as cited in Goodman and Flaxman, 2016). This can lead to solutions that do not adequately address the needs of underrepresented groups, which will in turn perpetuate injustice.

Another challenge that needs to be considered is the interpretation of Shariah principles. Different schools of thought (Mazhab) may interpret Islamic law differently, potentially leading to an unfair application of inheritance laws in fintech solutions, despite the Al-Quran and As-Sunnah clearly outlining the division of an estate and its distribution.

Consequently, developers must actively interact with varied communities, integrate comments, and consistently assess their algorithms and designs to mitigate or reduce bias. This approach will help in the development of solutions that are equitable, inclusive, and that cater to the requirements of all users.

CONCLUSION

The application of FinTech in the Islamic inheritance process holds immense promise for enhancing efficiency, accuracy, and compliance with Sharia principles. In summary, while the challenges associated with Islamic inheritance in Malaysia are significant, FinTech offers a promising avenue for addressing these issues, especially in reducing frozen assets. By leveraging several innovative digital solutions, it is possible to streamline processes, enhance document security, improve access to information, reduce fraud, and ensure efficient document storage. This could lead to a more efficient, transparent, and accessible inheritance system that better serves the needs of heirs. By harnessing innovative technologies and tailored solutions, stakeholders can navigate the complexities of estate distribution with greater ease and confidence, ensuring equitable outcomes for heirs while upholding the tenets of Islamic law.

REFERENCES

Abd Rahman, S., Yaakob, A., Fadzil, A., & Shaban, M. (2017). *Asset Distribution Among the Qualified Heirs Based on Islamic Inheritance Law*. Academy of Contemporary Islamic Studies.

Abdullah, M. M. I., Fariddudin, S. N. F. M., Muhamad, N. H. N., & Awang, A. B. (2021). Islamic estate planning in the industrial revolution 4.0 era: Issues and challenges. *Journal of Emerging Economies and Islamic Research*, 9(2), 40–56. DOI: 10.24191/jeeir.v9i2.12413

Abdullah, O., Shaharuddin, A., Wahid, M. A., & Harun, M. S. (2022). Artificial Intelligence (AI) Application In Islamic Finance: A Review Of Business Use Cases. In *The Seminar Antarabangsa Islam dan Sains (SAIS 2022).*

Afiqah, F. & Sabit, M. T. (2021). A Proposal for A Single Tribunal of Estate Distribution. *Jurnal Teknologi (Sciences & Engineering)*, 75(10), 1–16.

AlAjmi, K., Deodoro, J., Farias, A., Iskender, E. S., Mirestean, A. T., & Ravikumar, R. (2021). Powering the Digital Economy.

Anuar, S. B., Azmi, F. A. M., & Sidek, S. N. S. (2022). Exploring the potential and suggesting a new conceptual framework of blockchain technology in estate distribution. *International Journal of Advanced Research in Technology and Innovation*, 4(1), 35–43.

Comiter, M. (2019). Attacking artificial intelligence. *Belfer Center Paper*, 8, 2019–08.

Fazmi, F. (2019). Role of robo-advisors in Islamic financial institutions. Retrieved from https://journal.wahedinvest.com/role-of-robo-advisors-in-islamic-financial-institutions/

Fokri, W. N. I. W. M., Ali, E. M. T. E., Nordin, N., Chik, W. M. Y. W., Aziz, S. A., & Jusoh, A. J. M. (2021). The Unclaimed Inheritance Issues: A Solution Using Blockchain Technology. *Psychology (Savannah, Ga.)*, 58(1), 4709–4717. DOI: 10.17762/pae.v58i1.1630

Gazali, H. M., Jumadi, J., Ramlan, N. R., Abd Rahmat, N., Uzair, S. N. H. M., & Mohid, A. N. (2020). Application of artificial intelligence (AI) in islamic investments. *Journal of Islamic Finance*, 9(2), 70–77.

Global Islamic Finance Report. (2017). *Islamic Finance in the Digital Age*, 282–290.

Ibrahim, N., Ismail, M. N., Sapian, S. M., Ramli, A. M., & Shazali, K. H. I. (2024b). Navigating The Implications for Heirs: An Analysis of The Amendment to The Small Estate Act (Distribution) 1955. *Ulum Alamiyyah.*, 36(2), 118–126. DOI: 10.33102/uij.vol36no02.590

Ibrahim, N., Shazali, K. H. I., & Rusgianto, S. (2024a). A Systematic Literature Review of Islamic Inheritance in Malaysia. *Islāmiyyāt: International Journal of Islamic Studies*, 46(1), 113–131. DOI: 10.17576/islamiyyat-2024-4601-09

Kamarudin, M. K., Zaman, N., & Razak, R. M. (2019). Thematic Analysis on The Necessity of Hibah Law In Malaysia. *al-Qanatir. International Journal of Islamic Studies*, 16(1), 1–13.

Karamitsos, I., Papadaki, M., & Al-Balghuti, N. B. (2018). Design of the Blockchain Smart, Contract: A Use Case for Real Estate. *Journal of Informative Security*, 2018(9), 177–190. DOI: 10.4236/jis.2018.93013

Karimullah, S. S. (2023). The Application of Artificial Intelligence in Islamic Law Discovery. *Mutawasith: Jurnal Hukum Islam*, 6(2), 109–121.

Mat Rahim, S. R., Mohamad, Z. Z., Abu Bakar, J., Mohsin, F. H., & Md Isa, N. (2018). Artificial Intelligence, Smart Contract And Islamic Finance. *Asian Social Science*, 14(2), 145–154. DOI: 10.5539/ass.v14n2p145

Mohamed, H. (2017). Smart contracts in Islamic economic transactions. Retrieved from https://www.linkedin.com/pulse/smart-contracts-islamic-economic-transactions-hazik-mohamed/

Mohanta, B. K., Panda, S. S., & Jena, D. (2018). *An Overview of Smart Contract and Use cases in Blockchain Technology. 9th ICCCNT 2018. July 10-12*. Bengluru.

Mohd, K. B. (2019). The Integrity of Fintech In Information Security From Islamic Perspective. *Editorial board, 61.*

Mukhopadhyay, M. (2018). *Ethereum Smart Contract Development.* Packt Publishing Ltd.

Nafed, H. H. M. (2009) *Web Based Expert System for i-Faraid.* Masters thesis, Universiti Utara Malaysia.

Nasrul, M. A., Mohd Alam Shah, N. A., Abdul Hak, N., & Halim, A. H. (2022). Administration Of Estates: Resolution Of Disputes In Achieving Sustainability Among The Deceased's Family. *IIUM Law Journal*, 30(2), 253–279. DOI: 10.31436/iiumlj.v30i2.711

Nasrul, M. A. D., Manaf, Z. I. A., Syafril, S., & Fathurrohman, M. (2021). An Overview of the Inheritance Legal System in Malaysia and Indonesia: Issues Faced by Both Countries. *Journal of Shariah Law Research*, 6(2), 181–200.

Noordin, N., Shuib, A., Zainol, M., Azam, M., & Mohamed Adil, M. (2012). Review On Issues And Challenges In Islamic Inheritance Distribution In Malaysia. *OIDA International Journal of Sustainable Development*, 3, 27–38.

Nordin, S., & Ahmad, M. A. (2023). The internet of things and Islamic estate planning in the forth industry revolution (4ir) in Malaysia: Issues and challenges. [GBSE]. *Journal of Global Business and Social Entrepreneurship*, 9(27), 43–63.

Obaidullah, M. (2021). Promise of IRSHAD: The Intelligent Robo Shariah Advisor. IBFNet. https://conference.ibfnet.ie/2021/03/03/promise-of-irshad-the-intelligent -robo-shariah advisor/

Rahman, A. (2019). Opportunities and threats of Shariah-compliant robo advisory. the case of Wahed Invest. Retrieved October 15, 2019, from, https://www.grin.com/ document/540407

Saad, M. S. M., & Rasli, R. M. (2022). Web Based Expert System in Area & Land Value Calculation and Faraid Distribution. *International Journal of Artificial Intelligence*, 9(2), 83–89. DOI: 10.36079/lamintang.ijai-0902.468

Safina, Mohd Ali. (2021). Information Sharing and Search System to Ease Estate Distribution in Malaysia.

Shafie, F., Yusoff, W., Zahari, W., Abdullah, S., & al-Edrus, S. M. D. (2014). Islamic real estate management: Review on issues and challenges in managing inheritance property in Malaysia. Paper presented at the 7th International Real Estate Research Symposium 2014 (7th IRERS). Retrieved from https://www.inspen.gov.my/

Shafie, F., Yusoff, W., Zahari, W., & al-Edrus, S. M. D. (2016). *Factors of Failure and Delay in Islamic Inheritance Distribution in Malaysia, Conference IPERS*. INSPEN.

Sulong, J. (2011). *Pembaharuan Undang-undang Pentadbiran Pusaka Islam*. Penerbit Universiti Sains Malaysia.

Wajis, N. R. N. (2018). Mutalib, LA. Rahman, AA. Sahid, MM. Saleh, NSSN, Rusli, MHM. Ali, MM. Rab, MAA. Gunardi, S.Tagoranao, MS. Saleh, MAM. Hanafo, LHH. & Ahmad, AS. (2018) Harta Tidak Dituntut: Punca dan Kaedah Penyelesaiannya. *Malaysian Journal of Syariah and Law*, 7(June), 129–141. DOI: 10.12816/0051395

Zulkafli, B. N. A., & Ahmad, M. Y. (2016). Constraints and Solutions of Delayed Management of Muslim Immovable Property Management in Malaysia. *Islamiyyat-The International Journal of Islamic Studies*, 38(1), 53–63.

ENDNOTES

1 https://pewarisan.com/kalkulator-faraid/,

2 https://myland.gov.my/myland-adm/waris/WarisFaraidForm.xhtml

3 https://as-salihin.com/en/faraid-calculator/

Chapter 4
Islamic Finance, Islamic Fintech, and Digital Currency in the Digital Transformation Era:
The Role of Blockchain Technology in Industry 4.0

Mohammad Rashed Hasan Polas
Sonargaon University, Bangladesh

Nowshin Mahmood Tahiya
https://orcid.org/0009-0002-0542-6644
Shanghai University of Finance and Economics, China

Ahmed Imran Kabir
https://orcid.org/0000-0001-5442-0084
United International University, Bangladesh

Abu Saleh Md. Sohel-Uz-Zaman
United International University, Bangladesh

Rajib Biswas
Sonargaon University, Bangladesh

ABSTRACT

Within the rapidly changing world of finance, Islamic finance is a unique sector with fundamentally ethical and Shariah-compliant processes at its core. A new age of

DOI: 10.4018/979-8-3693-5653-1.ch004

innovation and accessibility in the financial industry has been brought about by the rise of Financial Technology, or Fintech. This chapter explores the intersection of Fintech, Blockchain, and Islamic finance and shows how these developments have revolutionized the market. The chapter seeks to offer a thorough analysis of the three main ways that Fintech—Digitalization, Development, and Disruption—is changing Islamic finance. It examines the current digital revolution in Islamic finance, investments, wealth management, insurance (takaful), and real-world examples and case studies. The book also investigates the development of Shariah-compliant Fintech solutions, or Shariahtech, and the regulatory frameworks supporting their growth.

INTRODUCTION

Islamic finance, a sector that has gained notable attention as an alternative to conventional financial systems, adheres to Shariah principles which emphasize ethical investments, profit-sharing, and the prohibition of interest (Hassan et al., 2022). Recently, the rapid evolution of financial technology (Fintech) has reshaped the financial services industry, delivering more efficient and accessible solutions to customers globally (Atif et al., 2021; Muryanto et al., 2022; Muhammad et al., 2024). Fintech's integration with Islamic finance has created promising opportunities for innovation, enabling more inclusive, Shariah-compliant financial products and services while also presenting new ethical and operational challenges. This convergence of Islamic finance and Fintech—Islamic Fintech—introduces pathways to expand financial inclusion, transparency, and cost efficiency for customers who seek alignment with Shariah principles (Qudah et al., 2023; Kusuma et al., 2024).

In the digital transformation era, blockchain technology emerges as a revolutionary tool, providing decentralized, transparent, and secure transaction mechanisms that align well with Islamic finance's foundational values. By enhancing integrity and transparency, blockchain technology facilitates innovations in Islamic Fintech, making it an essential focus for researchers and practitioners alike (Azizah, 2023). Despite these advances, the integration of Fintech and blockchain into Islamic finance raises several critical challenges, such as regulatory compliance, the need for international standardization, and stakeholder support (Khalil et al., 2022). The effective management of such innovations within Islamic finance requires a structured approach, yet, to date, there is a lack of established development processes and guidelines specific to Islamic Fintech.

Although Islamic Fintech and blockchain technology hold significant potential to reshape financial services, there remains a need to critically assess their impact on Islamic finance and the pathways for integrating digital currency within Shariah boundaries (Mohd Nor et al., 2021). Existing literature provides foundational insights into these intersections; however, gaps persist, particularly regarding frameworks that address compliance, governance, and international collaboration in Islamic Fintech.

This chapter aims to explore the evolving role of Islamic Fintech and blockchain in transforming Islamic finance within the digital economy. By examining the integration of Fintech, blockchain, and digital currency into Shariah-compliant financial systems, the chapter identifies key challenges, opportunities, and future directions for sustainable growth. This discussion is intended to guide readers through the complex landscape of Islamic finance in the digital age and to offer practical insights for navigating the technological, regulatory, and ethical dimensions of Islamic Fintech.

Digitalization and the Emergence of Islamic Fintech and Digital Currency in Islamic Finance

The digitalization of Islamic finance has brought about transformative changes, with the advent of Islamic Fintech and Islamic digital currency representing pivotal developments in this evolution. Rather than merely integrating existing financial systems with technology, Islamic Fintech and digital currencies have emerged as direct outcomes of digitalization, driven by the principles of Shariah compliance and ethical finance. These innovations have fundamentally reshaped financial products and services by introducing transparency, accessibility, and efficiency, aligning with the values and demands of modern consumers. Blockchain technology has further bolstered this shift, providing a decentralized, transparent framework that enhances the operational integrity of Islamic Fintech and digital currency platforms. Therefore, it is essential to recognize that Islamic Fintech and Islamic digital currency are not merely integrative components but are themselves unique byproducts of digital transformation within Islamic finance. This chapter aims to explore these developments, highlighting the new potential and challenges they bring to the Islamic finance landscape in the digital age.

Digital transformation has profoundly reshaped industries worldwide, and Islamic finance is no exception. Digitalization in Islamic finance has accelerated the development of innovative financial products and services tailored to meet Shariah principles, which emphasize ethical investment, social responsibility, and interest-free transactions. This transformation is not merely a matter of integrating technology into existing financial frameworks; rather, it has catalyzed the emergence of entirely new sectors within Islamic finance, most notably Islamic Fintech and Islamic digital currency.

Islamic Fintech emerged as a result of the push to create technology-driven, Shariah-compliant financial solutions that offer greater transparency, accessibility, and efficiency. By leveraging financial technologies, Islamic Fintech enables service providers to create inclusive financial products that reach unbanked populations while remaining compliant with Islamic principles. These services span a range of areas, including digital payments, peer-to-peer lending, and crowdfunding, which are adapted to respect the core tenets of Islamic finance. Unlike conventional Fintech, Islamic Fintech integrates principles of risk-sharing, ethical investing, and social welfare, addressing the unique demands of consumers seeking faith-based financial products.

Similarly, Islamic digital currency represents an innovative response to the digitalization of Islamic finance, aligning with the need for Shariah-compliant financial assets in a digitalized economy. Islamic digital currencies provide a transparent, decentralized, and secure alternative for transactions, drawing from blockchain technology to ensure compliance with ethical and religious standards. These digital assets aim to offer the same level of trust and ethical assurance as traditional Islamic financial products, while providing the flexibility and accessibility demanded by a modern, globalized economy.

Blockchain technology plays a pivotal role in both Islamic Fintech and Islamic digital currencies. Its decentralized structure and transparency align well with the values of Islamic finance, enabling the traceability and accountability of financial transactions. Blockchain's smart contract capabilities ensure adherence to agreed-upon terms, facilitating trust and reducing the need for intermediaries. By offering a secure and efficient foundation, blockchain supports the unique operational requirements of Islamic Fintech and digital currency, enhancing credibility while fostering innovation.

Through these advancements, digitalization has redefined what Islamic finance can achieve, extending its reach and making Shariah-compliant financial products more accessible to a broader audience. Islamic Fintech and digital currency are thus not simply integrated tools but represent the next evolution of Islamic finance, shaped by the principles of digital transformation and responding to the unique needs of modern consumers.

ISLAMIC FINANCE: PRINCIPLES AND PRACTICES

Islamic finance is based on Shariah law, which emphasizes ethical and socially responsible financial practices. Key principles include the prohibition of riba (interest), where any payment or receipt of interest is forbidden (Hassan et al., 2022). Instead, profit-and-loss sharing arrangements are encouraged, aligning with Shariah's focus on fair risk distribution. Another core concept is the avoidance of gharar (excessive uncertainty), meaning that high levels of speculation or ambiguity in transactions are avoided, ensuring transparency and stability in financial dealings. Islamic finance also mandates the exclusion of investments in haram (prohibited) industries, such as alcohol, gambling, and other sectors considered harmful or unethical (Kusuma et al., 2024). This requirement extends to all types of transactions, underscoring the ethical responsibility embedded in Shariah-compliant finance.

Risk-sharing is fundamental to Islamic finance, as it requires all parties involved in a financial transaction to share both risks and rewards, promoting an equitable distribution of outcomes. These principles manifest in different financing models, each tailored to meet Shariah standards. Murabaha, for example, is a cost-plus-profit arrangement where the seller discloses both costs and profits to the buyer, facilitating informed transactions. Mudaraba allows a partnership between a capital provider and an expert partner, with profits distributed as per prior agreement. Musharaka, a joint venture model, enables all partners to contribute capital and share both profits and losses. Similarly, Ijara represents an Islamic leasing model in which the owner leases an asset to a tenant in exchange for agreed-upon rental payments (Hassan et al., 2022).

These ethical foundations of Islamic finance align well with technological advancements, setting the stage for Islamic Fintech and Islamic digital currency within the broader digital transformation era. As these principles are integrated into modern technologies, they support transparent, inclusive, and Shariah-compliant financial solutions. Fintech applications and blockchain-powered digital currencies further reinforce these principles by enabling decentralized, transparent, and ethically driven transactions that adhere to Shariah law. In this digitalized context, Islamic finance can now reach a broader audience, providing accessible and efficient financial services that maintain its ethical standards. Through these digital tools, the essence of Islamic finance continues to evolve, expanding the scope of Shariah-compliant financial offerings while staying rooted in its core values.

ISLAMIC FINTECH: INNOVATING WITHIN ETHICAL BOUNDARIES

Islamic Fintech represents a convergence of financial technology and Islamic finance principles, offering new Shariah-compliant financial products and services that leverage digital tools to meet the needs of modern consumers (Alam et al., 2019). Rooted in the core values of Islamic finance—such as risk-sharing, ethical investment, and transparency—Islamic Fintech introduces platforms that support companies in raising funds under fair investment principles. Through digitalization, innovative Islamic Fintech services, such as peer-to-peer (P2P) lending, connect borrowers and lenders directly while adhering to Islamic guidelines on interest prohibition and risk-sharing (Muryanto et al., 2022). This form of lending exemplifies the way digital tools can reinforce Shariah-compliant finance by fostering inclusive, direct interactions between financial parties. Furthermore, digital advances like robo-advisors provide Sharia-compliant investment advice and portfolio management through automated systems, expanding access to ethical investments without compromising Islamic principles. Financial inclusion is another significant benefit, as Islamic Fintech broadens access to financial services for unbanked and underserved communities, particularly in Muslim-majority areas where Shariah adherence is essential.

Blockchain technology has furthered these advances by enabling a new layer of transparency and trust. Shariah-compliant smart contracts, powered by blockchain, uphold transparency, build user trust, and ensure compliance with Islamic rules. As part of this digital transformation, cryptocurrency and blockchain's decentralized nature provide a means of enhancing operating efficiencies and lowering costs for financial services, making them more accessible to a wider audience (Kusuma et al., 2024). Shariahtech, as this fusion of Islamic finance and technology is sometimes known, has not only transformed traditional financial services but also introduced new mechanisms, such as Islamic digital currency and smart contracts, that are uniquely shaped by Shariah values.

BLOCKCHAIN TECHNOLOGY: ENHANCING TRANSPARENCY AND EFFICIENCY

Blockchain technology serves as a transformative force within the realm of Islamic finance, creating new avenues for transparency, security, and efficiency in financial transactions. As a distributed ledger technology, blockchain operates across multiple computers without a central authority, relying instead on a network of nodes for decentralized governance (Ghode et al., 2020; Tariq, 2024). This decentralization is crucial in Islamic finance, where the principles of fairness and ethical governance align with the transparent nature of blockchain.

One of the standout features of blockchain is its transparency, as all transactions are recorded in a public ledger accessible to all participants. This characteristic enhances trust among stakeholders, which is a cornerstone of Islamic finance. Additionally, the use of encryption technology within blockchain ensures the integrity and security of transactions, addressing the Islamic finance principle of risk management and ethical oversight.

Immutability is another essential aspect of blockchain, as once a transaction is recorded, it cannot be altered or canceled. This quality is particularly relevant in the context of Islamic finance, where contract integrity is paramount. Smart contracts, which are self-executing contracts written directly into the program code, further exemplify the impact of blockchain on Islamic finance. These contracts facilitate automatic and transparent execution of agreements, aligning with Shariah principles of clarity and certainty in financial dealings.

Moreover, the rise of cryptocurrencies, such as Bitcoin and Ethereum, underpinned by blockchain technology, offers new opportunities for Islamic finance. While the use of digital currencies must be carefully assessed to ensure compliance with Shariah law, they represent a significant advancement in financial technology. Blockchain also enhances supply chain finance by increasing efficiency and transparency, allowing for precise tracking of transactions throughout the financial chain (Tariq, 2024).

Through these advancements, blockchain exemplifies the integration of technology into Islamic finance, leading to the emergence of innovative financial solutions such as Islamic digital currency and Shariah-compliant fintech services. This digitalization process not only modernizes traditional Islamic financial practices but also supports the development of a robust ecosystem where ethical finance can thrive in the digital age.

Digital Currency in Islamic Finance

The emergence of digital currencies, particularly cryptocurrencies, represents a significant development within Islamic finance, showcasing the impact of digitalization on traditional financial systems. Cryptocurrencies have garnered attention for their potential to transform the financial landscape, yet their relationship with Sharia law remains contentious among scholars. For cryptocurrencies to align with Islamic finance principles, the market must be asset-based and emphasize risk-sharing (Alam et al., 2019). These foundational principles are essential to creating a fair and equitable financial environment. Despite the innovative features of cryptocurrencies like Bitcoin, which operate without interest payments, certain activities within the crypto ecosystem—such as lending—can invoke concerns regarding riba (interest) and gharar (excessive uncertainty) in Islamic finance (Thaker et al., 2022). The inherent volatility of cryptocurrencies raises significant Sharia concerns, as drastic price fluctuations introduce high levels of uncertainty, potentially likening cryptocurrency trading to gambling—an activity prohibited under Islamic law. This ambiguity makes distinguishing between investment and speculation particularly challenging (Chong, 2021).

For digital currencies to achieve Sharia compliance, asset-backed validation becomes crucial. Some cryptocurrencies are better positioned within Islamic finance, especially those supported by physical assets, such as fixed-income products. Initiatives to develop Sharia-compliant cryptocurrencies, such as Islamic coins, are underway, aiming to ensure adherence to Islamic law. Blockchain technology plays a pivotal role in this evolution, providing the transparency and traceability needed to foster trust and mitigate concerns of jalari (deception) in financial transactions.

While traditional cryptocurrencies grapple with Sharia compliance, there is promising potential for developing digital currencies that align with Islamic principles.

To navigate this complex landscape, ongoing dialogue among experts, economists, and technologists is essential (Rabbani et al., 2022). This collaborative effort can guide the creation of digital currencies that not only innovate within the financial sector but also uphold the ethical standards of Islamic finance. The integration of digital currencies and blockchain into the Islamic finance framework signifies a transformative impact that has the potential to enhance financial inclusion and accessibility in Muslim-majority regions.

THE FUTURE OF ISLAMIC FINANCE, FINTECH, AND BLOCKCHAIN

The Importance of Islamic Finance

The financial sector is a crucial driver of growth and development for any country (Alshater et al., 2022). This sector encompasses various components, including money markets, capital markets, financial institutions, credit markets, microfinance, and both Islamic and non-Islamic insurance companies (Yasini & Yasini, 2019). Among these, Islamic finance has emerged as a prominent aspect globally, characterized by its adherence to Sharia law. Islamic finance encompasses financial activities rooted in principles such as profit and loss sharing and the prohibition of riba (interest), ensuring that both lenders and investors engage in ethical transactions (Atif et al., 2021). Unlike conventional finance, Islamic finance prohibits generating wealth solely from money; instead, it promotes legitimate, asset-based investments that avoid excessive risk and unethical businesses. This inclusive financial approach benefits all income levels, fostering social responsibility, altruism, and economic activity through shared risk and profit among fund users and providers.

As the financial landscape evolves, Islamic financial technology (Islamic fintech) continues to innovate by leveraging blockchain technology to develop new financial products and services. This integration of Islamic finance and fintech is essential for stimulating growth and enhancing compliance across the sector (Alam & Nazim, 2021). The collaboration between Islamic financial institutions, fintech companies, and blockchain technology paves the way for increased understanding and application of Islamic finance principles. Establishing clear guidelines for Islamic fintech and digital currencies is crucial to ensure compliance with Sharia law and secure financial transactions. Developing application standards and frameworks for Sharia compliance in fintech and blockchain applications will facilitate this process (Unal & Aysan, 2022).

The digital transformation era presents unprecedented opportunities for Islamic finance, fintech, and blockchain technology to reshape the financial landscape. By adhering to ethical standards and leveraging emerging technologies, these sectors can enhance financial accountability, increase transparency, and foster trust among users. As Islamic finance, fintech, and blockchain converge, encouraging collaboration becomes vital to address management challenges, stimulate innovation, and unlock their full potential. The future of finance is undeniably digital, and Islamic finance stands at the forefront of this transformative journey, showcasing the profound impact of digitalization on traditional financial practices. Concepts such as Shariahtech, smart contracts, and cryptocurrencies exemplify the significant transformations occurring within Islamic finance due to digitalization, paving the way for a more integrated and innovative financial ecosystem (Chong, 2021).

Evolution and Emergence of Financial Technology (Fintech)

Financial technology, commonly referred to as fintech, represents the intersection of finance and technology (Jalal et al., 2023). Over the last decade, fintech has experienced exponential growth, revolutionizing how financial services are delivered. While there is no universally accepted definition of fintech, the Financial Stability Board (FSB) of the Bank for International Settlements defines it as "technologically enabled financial innovation that could result in new business models, applications, processes, or products with an associated material effect on financial markets and institutions and the provision of financial services" (Sahabuddin et al., 2023). This evolving landscape has prompted both startups and traditional financial institutions to adopt fintech solutions to maintain competitive advantages in a rapidly changing market.

The evolution of fintech can be categorized into several distinct eras, each reflecting shifts in consumer behavior and technological advancements. The first era, spanning from 1886 to 1967, laid the groundwork for global financial services infrastructure. Key developments during this period included the establishment of the first transatlantic cable in 1866 and the introduction of Fedwire in 1918, enabling electronic fund transfers through telegraph and Morse code (Suryono et al., 2020). The second era, from 1967 to 2008, marked a significant transition from analog to digital finance. This phase began with the introduction of ATMs by Barclays in 1967 and saw the rise of innovations such as the NASDAQ (the world's first digital stock exchange) and SWIFT (Society for Worldwide Interbank Financial Telecommunications). The emergence of bank mainframe computers and the growth of online banking and digital payment systems, like PayPal, defined this era (Palmié et al., 2020).

Following the global financial crisis of 2008, a shift occurred characterized by a lack of trust in traditional banking systems and changes in regulations that allowed new providers to enter the market. This era saw the birth of numerous cryptocurrencies, including Bitcoin, Ethereum, Tether, and Dogecoin, as investors and consumers sought innovative financial products and services. This landscape prompted existing banks to rebrand themselves as startups, leveraging open banking and platforms like Treezor and Solarisbank to compete effectively. Thus, this period is aptly dubbed the "era of startups" (Alt et al., 2018).

The integration of fintech into the framework of Islamic finance further amplifies its significance. The rise of Shariah-compliant fintech solutions—such as Shariahtech, which aligns technological innovations with Islamic finance principles, and smart contracts that facilitate transparent and compliant transactions—illustrates the profound impact of digitalization on traditional financial practices. By providing new opportunities for asset-backed digital currencies and enhancing financial inclusivity, fintech is positioned to transform the Islamic financial landscape. As these sectors continue to evolve, collaboration among fintech developers, Islamic finance experts, and regulatory bodies will be crucial in harnessing the potential of these innovations, ensuring compliance with Sharia law, and fostering trust in the financial ecosystem. This dynamic interplay between fintech and Islamic finance exemplifies the transformative power of digitalization in the broader financial industry.

Blockchain Technology and Its Relevance in Finance

Blockchain technology, introduced by Satoshi Nakamoto with the advent of Bitcoin in 2009, represents a decentralized database mechanism for recording large-scale transactions securely and transparently (Yu et al., 2018; Javaid et al., 2022). This innovative approach to data management allows transactions to be recorded in blocks linked together in a secure chain, eliminating the need for intermediaries such as banks or financial institutions. The transparency afforded by blockchain, combined with its immutable nature, reduces compliance costs and accelerates data transfer processes (Pal et al., 2021). As a result, blockchain technology is increasingly recognized for its profound implications for the financial markets of various countries (Javaid et al., 2022).

In the context of Islamic finance, blockchain technology plays a crucial role in enhancing service delivery and compliance with Shariah principles. By facilitating the design of new financial service models, blockchain enables Islamic financial institutions to integrate resources efficiently, analyze customer needs in real-time, and adapt credit systems to better align with ethical standards (Polyviou et al., 2019). This alignment is vital in the Islamic financial landscape, where adherence to Shariah law is paramount.

The relevance of blockchain extends beyond operational improvements; it serves as a promising tool for financial innovation and economic development within a country's financial system (Yu et al., 2018). By adopting modern business strategies that leverage blockchain and information technology, financial institutions can achieve significant performance enhancements (Pal et al., 2021). For instance, the use of blockchain in Islamic finance can lead to the creation of Shariah-compliant crypto assets, allowing for greater transparency and accountability in financial transactions. Moreover, blockchain's decentralized and automated features are instrumental in combating financial crimes, such as money laundering and the financing of terrorism, which pose significant challenges to the integrity of financial systems (Yu et al., 2018). By providing a real-time, intermediary-free platform, blockchain empowers financial markets to gain a competitive advantage, as they can operate more effectively and securely (Javaid et al., 2022).

Therefore, the integration of blockchain technology into Islamic finance represents a pivotal development in the digitalization process. It not only enhances operational efficiency but also ensures compliance with Islamic principles through innovative solutions such as Shariahtech and smart contracts. The interplay between blockchain, digital currencies, and Islamic finance underscores the potential for transformative change within the financial sector, paving the way for a more transparent, accountable, and equitable financial landscape.

DIGITAL TRANSFORMATION IN ISLAMIC FINANCE

Digitalization of Traditional Islamic Financial Services

Islamic financial services adhere to the principles of Islamic Shariah, which prohibits interest-based transactions (Chong, 2021). These services encompass a variety of models, including Mudharabah (profit sharing), Musharakah (joint venture), Murabahah (cost-plus finance), Takaful (Islamic insurance), Sukuk (Islamic bonds), and Hawala (an international fund transfer system). The digital transformation of these traditional services through the adoption of financial technology (Fintech) has led to the emergence of Islamic Fintech, which aims to provide innovative digital solutions to common financial service challenges in compliance with Shariah principles (Banna et al., 2022). Islamic Fintech facilitates access to financial services for individuals across all socioeconomic levels, offering affordable and convenient solutions for products like Takaful, Sukuk, and payment systems (Rabbani et al., 2021). Examples of these Fintech solutions include the Cellfin and IBBL iSmart apps from Islami Bank Bangladesh PLC, as well as SJIBL NET from Shahjalal Islami

Bank PLC, which promote cashless transactions in line with Islamic regulations (Banna et al., 2022).

In the broader context of digital transformation, blockchain technology is playing a significant role in enhancing Islamic Fintech platforms. For instance, Singapore-based FINTERRA focuses on microfinance, wealth management, crowdfunding, and E-Wallet solutions that align with Islamic principles. Tazapay is another digital payment platform in Singapore that provides Shariah-compliant payment solutions (Qudah et al., 2023). In the United States, Zoya offers a platform that assists clients in accessing Shariah-compliant financial products and services, while Wahed Invest serves as a robo-advisory platform for investment solutions (Yudaruddin, 2023). Similarly, Alinma Bank in Saudi Arabia provides a variety of Shariah-based banking services through its digital platform, showcasing the integration of Fintech in traditional banking.

Additionally, a B2B microfinance platform named HAL CAPITAL operates in Kenya and Oman, offering Islamic rule-based financing solutions. Other noteworthy Islamic Fintech solutions include SalamWeb, HalalZilla in Malaysia, Amanah Finance in the UK, and Finocracy in the UAE (Rabbani et al., 2020). The integration of digital currencies and blockchain technology within Islamic finance not only enhances operational efficiency but also introduces new models like Shariahtech and smart contracts, which exemplify the impact of digitalization on Islamic financial services. This transformation not only broadens access to financial resources but also aligns modern financial practices with the ethical standards mandated by Islamic law, ultimately leading to a more inclusive and equitable financial system.

Role of Fintech in Enhancing Accessibility and Inclusivity in Islamic Finance

Islamic finance seeks to promote equality and prosperity within individuals and society as a whole. This objective is increasingly realized through the adoption of financial technology (Fintech), which employs innovative digital solutions to enhance social welfare and increase financial inclusion across various segments of society (Shofawati, 2023). By integrating Islamic principles with advanced technologies, Islamic Fintech plays a crucial role in ensuring sustainable development while enabling Shariah-compliant banks to capture their targeted market share (Oseni & Ali, 2019). A key beneficiary of Islamic Fintech is the microentrepreneur sector, where many individuals leverage mobile financial services to enhance their business models and increase their income potential (Jouti, 2021). Through mechanisms such as crowdfunding and peer-to-peer lending (P2PL), Fintech facilitates easier access to funding, fostering sustainable income generation for these entrepreneurs. Shariah-compliant P2PL services, in particular, contribute significantly to the financial inclusion of micro, small, and medium enterprises (MSMEs) by streamlining the financing application process and providing tailored digital financial services. Additionally, these platforms often collaborate with various business groups and digital ecosystems to enhance their reach and impact (Alshater et al., 2022).

Furthermore, Islamic Fintech extends its services to vulnerable populations, including marginalized communities, women, and individuals without bank accounts. This inclusivity is pivotal in transforming the economy into a digital ecosystem, allowing these groups to actively participate in financial activities and improving their economic prospects (Jouti, 2021). The digitalization process incorporates various concepts such as Shariahtech, smart contracts, and cryptocurrencies, all of which exemplify the impact of technology on Islamic finance. These advancements not only facilitate access to financial resources but also reinforce the ethical foundations of Islamic finance, aligning modern financial solutions with traditional principles.

Therefore, the integration of Fintech in Islamic finance is a transformative force that enhances accessibility and inclusivity. By providing innovative solutions and bridging gaps in financial access, Islamic Fintech contributes to a more equitable economic landscape, fostering a sustainable and inclusive digital economy that benefits all members of society.

Case Studies Illustrating Successful Digital Transformation in Islamic Finance Institutions

Case Study 1: Al Rajhi Bank's Digital Transformation

Al Rajhi Bank, one of the world's largest banks, has undergone significant changes to improve its services and customer experience. The company's digitalization initiatives include the launch of mobile banking applications, online banking services and integration of blockchain technology (Shehadeh et al., 2023). Mobile and Internet Banking Services Internet banking platform provides convenient banking services to customers. These platforms offer a variety of services such as account management, money transfers, payments and investment options, all of which comply with Shariah principles and transparency in its operations. For example, blockchain has been used to facilitate the issuance of Islamic products such as Islamic bonds (Sukuk). This leads to customer satisfaction and loyalty (Rashwan & Kassem, 2021).

Case Study 2: Dubai Islamic Bank's Digital Strategy

Dubai Islamic Bank (DIB) is a pioneer in Islamic finance and implements a comprehensive strategy to stay ahead in the competitive banking industry (Gulrez, 2021). The bank's initiatives focus on the use of fintech solutions to provide innovative and Shariah-compliant financial services, fostering innovation and creating new financial services. The lab works with fintech startups to explore new technologies such as artificial intelligence (AI), blockchain and big data analytics (Muhammad et al., 2024). Providing customers with secure and instant payment access. This wallet supports many features such as peer-to-peer purchases, bill payments, and online purchases. Products and financial services are profitable to meet changing needs. Increase growth in the financial sector (Shaikh et al., 2021).

Case Study 3: Ethis - Islamic Crowdfunding Platform

Ethis is a leading Islamic crowdfunding platform connecting investors with fair and Sharia-compliant investment opportunities. The platform uses blockchain technology to ensure transparency and security in its operations. All transactions are recorded on the blockchain, ensuring that the funds are used for their intended purpose. All investments are subject to strict Sharia evaluation to ensure compliance with Islamic law of democratization. This supports accounting and financial support (Pratiwi et al., 2023).

Case Study 4: HalalChain - Blockchain-Based Halal Supply Chain

HalalChain is a blockchain-based platform that ensures traceability and authenticity of halal products, including financial transactions. The platform focuses on using blockchain technology to provide transparency and trust to the halal market. To the entire production chain for consumption, this ensures that the product is halal certified and complies with Islamic standards in the law. Financial Services promotes financial integrity to ensure all transactions are Sharia compliant and transparent (Hew et al., 2020).

Case Study 5: Stellar and Islamic Development Bank (IsDB)

The Islamic Development Bank (IsDB) is partnering with the Stellar Development Foundation to explore blockchain-based solutions to improve financial inclusion and economic development in Muslim-majority countries (Kılıç & Türkan, 2023). Blockchain for financial computing: IsDB and Stellar are developing solutions through blockchain to provide financial services to the unbanked and unbanked. This includes the development of sharia-based microfinance solutions and remittance services. Blockchain-based solutions foster economic development by providing accessible and affordable financial services to provide energy to communities without utilities. The use of smart contracts increases users' trust by ensuring that financial transactions are transparent, secure and comply with Sharia principles (Humphrey, 2019).

SHARIAHTECH: FINTECH IN LINE WITH SHARIAH PRINCIPLES

Shariahtech and Its Importance in Islamic Finance

Shariahtech represents a significant advancement within the Islamic finance sector, emerging as a technologically enabled financial innovation that adheres to Shariah requirements. This development not only creates new service models, processes, applications, and products in financial markets and institutions but also enhances the operational efficiency and risk management of Islamic financial services (Alam et al., 2019). While Shariahtech shares similarities with traditional Fintech, its primary focus is on augmenting Islamic financial services, thereby addressing the growing demand for Shariah-compliant financial solutions.

The integration of technologies such as big data, blockchain, artificial intelligence (AI), and cloud computing in Shariahtech has a transformative impact on Islamic finance. For instance, AI applications in financial transactions, such as tawarruq, improve customer experiences and streamline operations (Hassan et al., 2021). By increasing access to Islamic finance for unbanked retail clients and micro, small, and medium enterprises (MSMEs), Shariahtech promotes financial inclusion and entrepreneurship, contributing to the sustainability of MSMEs. Moreover, it facilitates efficient remittance transfers, addressing social needs by enabling quick and secure money transfers from developed countries to developing nations, ultimately fostering economic development (Delle Foglie et al., 2021).

Shariah-compliant Fintech applications are proliferating across various sectors of Islamic finance, including banking, investment, insurance (takaful), wealth management, and robo-advisory services. Each of these sectors demonstrates the integration of modern financial technologies with Shariah principles derived from the Holy Qur'an and Sunnah.

Banking and Investment: Islamic banking leverages Shariah-compliant Fintech to enable fast, secure, and transparent transactions. The adoption of contactless payment methods and mobile banking services enhances customer convenience. For example, the application "Zilzar Life" facilitates halal transactions and has attracted a global user base (Akiyoshi, 2019). Additionally, Islamic banks, such as Maybank Islamic in Malaysia, provide digital banking services that encompass investing, financing, and savings while adhering to Shariah principles (Abaidoo & Agyapong, 2022).

Insurance (Takaful): The takaful industry, based on cooperative risk-sharing principles, is increasingly adopting Islamic Fintech solutions, often referred to as 'Insurtech' (Nazarov & Dhiraj, 2019). This integration enhances the effectiveness and user experience of takaful services through automated underwriting, customer support chatbots, and blockchain technology for claims processing. For instance, Noor Takaful in the UAE employs Insurtech to offer online services for its takaful products, while a Malaysian takaful operator provides services via a user-friendly mobile app to cater to underserved populations (Sa Khan et al., 2020).

Wealth Management and Robo-Advisory Services: Islamic wealth management encompasses Shariah-compliant portfolio management, investment guidance, and financial planning that aligns with Islamic principles (Bhatia et al., 2022). Robo-advisory services utilize algorithms to deliver investment solutions in Shariah-compliant assets. An example is Wahed Invest, which combines Islamic wealth management with robo-advisory services, fostering inclusivity by allowing a diverse range of individuals to engage in halal investments that reflect Islamic beliefs (Chong, 2021).

Therefore, Shariahtech is integral to the ongoing digital transformation within Islamic finance. By harnessing the potential of modern technologies and aligning them with Shariah principles, Shariahtech not only enhances the accessibility and efficiency of financial services but also promotes greater financial inclusion, entrepreneurship, and overall socio-economic development. The integration of these technologies, including smart contracts and cryptocurrency, further exemplifies the profound impact of digitalization on the Islamic finance landscape.

Regulatory Challenges and Opportunities in Shariahtech Adoption

The advent of Shariahtech has significantly enhanced the efficiency of Shariah-compliant operations within Islamic finance. However, it also introduces certain risks, particularly concerning Shariah compliance due to the use of digital technologies and platforms (Hamsin et al., 2023). As Islamic finance integrates innovative solutions such as smart contracts, cryptocurrency, and blockchain, the challenge lies in maintaining adherence to Shariah principles while leveraging these advanced technologies.

One of the primary obstacles to Shariahtech adoption is the customer experience. While tech-savvy individuals may find these digital solutions appealing, older demographics often struggle to navigate modern, digitized platforms. This disparity can hinder the broader acceptance of Shariah-compliant technologies (Oseni & Ali, 2019). Additionally, trust issues arise from a lack of understanding of these technologies. Misconceptions surrounding their operation and purpose lead some potential users to prefer traditional service methods, where they feel more secure (Khatoon et al., 2019). Cybersecurity also presents a significant challenge in the realm of Shariahtech. The automated nature of online transactions increases the vulnerability of sensitive information and digital assets to theft and fraud. Despite the transparency that Shariahtech offers, concerns regarding the safety of digital transactions remain prevalent (Pratiwi et al., 2023).

Nevertheless, the growth of Shariahtech signals the emergence of a vibrant digital Islamic finance landscape. This innovation is set to support the expansion of alternative finance models, digital assets, and digital payment systems, effectively shaping the future of Islamic finance. Opportunities abound within this sector, particularly in addressing pressing global issues such as poverty alleviation. The rising demand for ethical financial products among an increasingly tech-savvy Muslim population further reinforces the potential for Shariahtech (Rabbani et al., 2020). By fostering a better understanding of digital solutions and addressing trust and usability challenges, Shariahtech can significantly contribute to financial inclusion and enhance access to Islamic finance for marginalized communities.

Therefore, while regulatory challenges persist, the integration of Shariahtech within the broader context of Islamic finance and digitalization presents numerous opportunities for growth and innovation. By overcoming existing obstacles and harnessing the potential of emerging technologies, Shariahtech can effectively transform the Islamic finance landscape and meet the evolving needs of consumers.

BLOCKCHAIN AND FINTECH EVOLUTION

Historical Perspective on the Evolution of Blockchain

Blockchain technology represents a significant advancement in the provision of financial services, serving as the backbone of various digital innovations within the fintech landscape. The journey of blockchain began in 1976 with the release of a pivotal paper titled "New Directions in Cryptography," which laid the groundwork for distributed ledger technology (Khalil et al., 2022). Following this, Stuart Haber and Scott Stornetta introduced the concept of timestamping digital documents in their influential work, "How to Time-Stamp a Digital Document" (Griffiths, 2021). These early developments set the stage for the later emergence of digital currencies.

David Chaum's introduction of "Digital Currency" or "Electronic Cash" marked another milestone in this evolution. This concept was further advanced by Adam Back's "Hashcash" in 1997, which proposed a method for controlling spam emails, thereby hinting at potential applications in digital transactions (Locatelli et al., 2021). Subsequently, Wei Dai introduced the concept of "b-money," which facilitated peer-to-peer transactions without intermediaries.

The breakthrough came in 2008 when an anonymous entity known as Satoshi Nakamoto published a seminal paper titled "Bitcoin: A Peer-to-Peer Electronic Cash System" (Molla & Biru, 2023). This paper outlined a decentralized electronic payment system reliant on cryptographic principles, eliminating the need for a central authority. Nakamoto's work not only established the first cryptocurrency,

Bitcoin, but also introduced the concept of blockchain as a secure and transparent ledger for recording transactions.

With the launch of the Bitcoin network in early 2009 and the creation of the first bitcoins, blockchain technology entered its first generation, quickly gaining traction worldwide. Since then, many countries have embraced blockchain, seeking to reform various sectors, including finance, by enhancing efficiency and transparency (Nazarov & Dhiraj, 2019). The integration of blockchain within Islamic finance has introduced new dimensions, particularly through the development of Shariahtech, which employs blockchain to ensure compliance with Islamic principles while enhancing operational efficiency. This technology facilitates innovations such as smart contracts and cryptocurrency, which align with the ethical requirements of Islamic finance.

Therefore, the historical evolution of blockchain underscores its transformative impact on fintech and Islamic finance. By fostering secure, transparent, and efficient transactions, blockchain serves as a vital enabler of financial inclusion and accessibility in Islamic finance, paving the way for future innovations in the sector. As the digital landscape continues to evolve, the synergy between blockchain, Islamic fintech, and digital currencies promises to reshape the financial services industry, ensuring adherence to Shariah principles while embracing technological advancements.

Historical Perspective on the Evolution of Fintech

Fintech, a blend of "finance" and "technology," encompasses innovations aimed at enhancing the delivery and accessibility of financial services. Its evolution can be delineated into distinct phases, each characterized by technological advancements and shifts in consumer behavior (Hamsin et al., 2023). The origins of fintech can be traced back to the late 19th century with the invention of the telephone, which revolutionized the dissemination of financial information. The early 20th century saw the emergence of communication technologies like the telephone and telex, enhancing the speed and efficiency of money transactions (Griffiths, 2021).

The introduction of computers in financial institutions during the 1950s and 1960s laid the groundwork for modern fintech, automating tasks such as payroll and accounting (Ghode et al., 2020; Sahabuddin et al., 2023). The 1970s marked a pivotal shift with the advent of electronic funds transfer (EFT) and automatic teller machines (ATMs), significantly improving transaction convenience (Bhatia et al., 2022). Furthermore, the rise of credit and debit cards during this period contributed to the cashless economy, facilitating easier transactions. The late 1980s and early 1990s heralded the digital revolution in banking with the emergence of online banking services, enabling customers to manage their accounts from home (Ghode et al., 2020; Sahabuddin et al., 2023). The 1990s brought widespread internet use, revolutionizing financial services through online trading and payment systems like PayPal, which provided secure and convenient online transactions (Alam et al., 2019). Although the dot-com bubble burst in the early 2000s, it established a foundation for future digital finance growth.

The 2000s to 2010s saw the rise of mobile banking applications and peer-to-peer (P2P) lending platforms like LendingClub and Prosper, which connected borrowers directly to lenders, bypassing traditional financial institutions (Ghode et al., 2020; Sahabuddin et al., 2023). Social media platforms also began playing a crucial role in fintech, enabling financial institutions to engage with customers and market products effectively. The launch of Bitcoin in 2009 by the anonymous Satoshi Nakamoto marked the beginning of the cryptocurrency revolution, underpinned by blockchain technology, which ensures secure and transparent transaction recording (Erić, 2022). This era also saw the emergence of decentralized finance (DeFi), which offers financial services without intermediaries (Molla & Biru, 2023).

Looking ahead, artificial intelligence (AI) and machine learning are poised to play significant roles in fintech, providing insights, fraud detection, and personalized financial advice. DeFi represents a new frontier, enabling users to borrow, exchange, and invest without traditional interference. However, regulatory challenges remain as authorities seek to balance innovation with consumer protection. Ongoing efforts to enhance financial inclusion through mobile banking, digital wallets, and micro-finance platforms are vital to fintech's global expansion (Locatelli et al., 2021).

The evolution of fintech illustrates a transformative journey from early telecommunications to advanced digital technologies, significantly influencing financial services. Within this context, the integration of blockchain and cryptocurrencies into Islamic finance through Shariahtech illustrates the impact of digitalization on creating ethical financial solutions. Innovations like smart contracts and digital currencies not only align with Islamic principles but also enhance accessibility and efficiency in financial transactions. As fintech continues to evolve, the potential for AI, DeFi, and other innovations to further shape Islamic finance remains promising, paving the way for a more inclusive and technologically advanced financial landscape.

SMART CONTRACTS IN ISLAMIC FINANCE

Smart Contracts and Their Applications in Islamic Finance

A smart contract is a self-signed contract where the contract terms are written directly in the line of code. They are stored and replicated on the blockchain and automatically perform tasks when events are completed (Nienhaus, 2019). This automation reduces the need for intermediaries and increases efficiency and reliability. Islamic finance refers to the method by which businesses in the Muslim world, including banks and other financial institutions, raise capital in accordance with sharia law. The type of investment allowed by this law is also mentioned. The basic principles include prohibition of riba (interest), uncertainty (gharar) and investment in prohibited businesses (Rahim et al., 2019).

a. Islamic Finance Applications

Sukuk (Islamic Bonds): Smart contracts can be used for Sukuk issuance and management. They can comply with Sharia requirements by including these rules in the contract. Payment, income distribution and other activities for sukuk holders can be carried out in a completely transparent manner (Rahim et al., 2019).

Takaful (Islamic Insurance): Smart contracts can facilitate Takaful through risk sharing and sharing. Claims can be processed and paid according to predefined conditions, increasing reliability and efficiency (Shaikh et al., 2021).

Murabaha (Cost-plus Financing): In Murabaha transactions, smart contracts can manage the entire process, from the initial contract to the transfer of goods and payments. This may include verifying shipments and ensuring payments are made as promised (Shaikh et al., 2021).

Musharaka (Partnership): Smart contracts can manage the contract with the partner by sharing profits and losses, making it transparent and tracking the contract (Shaikh et al., 2021).

b. Potential benefits of smart contracts in increasing efficiency and transparency

Efficiency

Automation: Smart contracts eliminate the need for ledger work and reduce the time and effort required for financial transactions. This is especially beneficial for Islamic finance because transactions often require many steps and parties' compliance with Sharia law (Khatoon et al., 2019).

Cost Reduction: Smart contracts can reduce transaction costs by eliminating the middleman. This is very important in Islamic finance because it is fair to avoid excessive costs (Khatoon et al., 2019).

Speed: Transactions made through smart contracts are faster because they do not rely on manual intervention. This speed is useful for time-sensitive transactions such as Murabaha and Sukuk (Khatoon et al., 2019).

Transparency

Immutable Records: Blockchain technology ensures that a transaction cannot be changed once it is recorded. This transparency increases transparency, making it easier for businesses to be examined and identified for Sharia compliance (Omar et al., 2020).

Clear Terms and Conditions: Smart contracts reduce the possibility of misunderstandings and disputes by clarifying the terms and conditions of financial contracts in the rules Omar et al., 2020.

Real-Time Monitoring: Participants in a smart contract can instantly monitor the execution of the contract, increasing trust and accountability. This is especially important in Islamic finance, where trust and transparency are important (Omar et al., 2020).

Shariah Considerations in the Development and Implementation of Smart Contracts

9.2.1 Compliance with Shariah Principles

Prohibition of Riba (Interest): Smart contracts should ensure that no interest or fees are charged for transactions. This can be added to the contract code to reject provisions involving interest (Rahim et al., 2019).

Avoidance of Gharar (Uncertainty): Contracts must be clear and concise. Smart contracts can help reduce GALAR by clearly defining the terms and conditions of transactions in the rules, ensuring everyone understands their obligations and rights (Rabbani et al., 2021).

Halal Transactions: Smart contracts must ensure that assets and operations are halal (permissible). This may be regulated by a contract to prevent business involving illegal (prohibited) activities such as alcohol or gambling (Rabbani et al., 2021).

Ethical Considerations in Smart Contracts for Islamic Finance

As the digitalization of Islamic finance advances, particularly through the integration of smart contracts and blockchain technology, ethical considerations become increasingly critical. These innovations, part of the broader landscape of Islamic fintech, must align with the core values of fairness, transparency, and compliance with Sharia principles to enhance their impact on the financial ecosystem.

Fairness and Justice: One of the primary ethical imperatives in Islamic finance is ensuring fairness and justice among all parties involved. Smart contracts must incorporate provisions that guarantee equitable treatment, particularly regarding the distribution of profits and losses. By embedding fairness considerations directly into the contract's code, stakeholders can create a system that respects Islamic values and enhances trust among participants (Molla & Biru, 2023). This approach fosters a collaborative environment where all parties feel secure in their transactions.

Transparency and Accountability: Blockchain technology plays a pivotal role in promoting transparency and accountability in Islamic finance. The immutable nature of blockchain records ensures that all transactions are auditable, thereby reinforcing trust among stakeholders. This transparency aligns with the Islamic principle of accountability, as it facilitates scrutiny of transactions for Sharia compliance (Molla & Biru, 2023). As financial transactions become more visible, the potential for unethical behavior diminishes, creating a safer and more reliable financial environment.

Complexity of Shariah Compliance: Despite the benefits, ensuring that smart contracts comply with all aspects of Sharia law presents significant challenges. This complexity necessitates collaboration among Islamic scholars, legal experts, and technologists to create Sharia-compliant contracts. By working together, these experts can develop smart contracts that not only automate processes but also adhere to the ethical and legal standards set forth by Islamic finance (Locatelli et al., 2021). This collaborative approach is essential for fostering innovation while maintaining adherence to Sharia principles.

Regulatory and Legal Frameworks: The successful adoption of smart contracts in Islamic finance also depends on robust regulatory and legal frameworks. For the integration of blockchain and smart contracts to be effective, governments and regulatory bodies must create supportive environments that encourage innovation while protecting the rights of all parties involved (Locatelli et al., 2021). Establishing clear regulatory guidelines will facilitate trust and stability, essential for the widespread acceptance of these technologies in Islamic finance.

Interoperability and Standardization: Achieving widespread acceptance of smart contracts requires interoperability and standardization across various platforms and jurisdictions. This necessitates collaboration among industry stakeholders to establish unified standards and procedures (Molla & Biru, 2023). By creating a cohesive framework, the Islamic finance sector can ensure that smart contracts operate effectively across different contexts, enhancing their utility and reliability.

Smart contracts represent a transformative opportunity for Islamic finance, promising increased efficiency, transparency, and adherence to Sharia principles. However, realizing their full potential necessitates careful consideration of ethical principles, including fairness, transparency, and compliance. As digital transformation reshapes the financial landscape, the integration of smart contracts into Islamic finance can significantly influence the future of the economy. By addressing the challenges of compliance, regulation, and standardization, stakeholders can leverage these technological advancements to create an inclusive and ethical financial system that aligns with the values of Islamic finance.

ISLAMIC PERSPECTIVE ON CRYPTOCURRENCY

The rapid evolution of digital finance, particularly through the advent of cryptocurrencies, has ignited discussions within Islamic finance circles regarding their alignment with Sharia principles. Islamic finance is founded on ethical principles that prioritize justice, accountability, and transparency, prohibiting practices such as riba (interest), gharar (uncertainty), and maysir (gambling) (Khan, 2023). As the landscape of Islamic fintech continues to expand, understanding the implications of cryptocurrency in this context is essential.

Cryptocurrency, as a digital or virtual currency that utilizes encryption technology for security, was first introduced with Bitcoin in 2009. This was followed by the emergence of numerous other cryptocurrencies. Operating on a decentralized network based on blockchain technology, cryptocurrencies promise enhanced transparency, security, and the immutability of transactions (Rabbani et al., 2020). These characteristics position cryptocurrencies as significant players in the broader digital finance ecosystem, challenging traditional financial structures and opening new avenues for innovation within Islamic finance.

The debate surrounding the compatibility of cryptocurrencies with Sharia law has intensified among Islamic scholars. While some view cryptocurrencies as a legitimate means of generating profit, others raise concerns regarding their speculative nature and potential for misuse (Rabbani et al., 2021). Institutions like Egypt's Dar al-Ifta and Turkey's Religious Authority have expressed reservations, deeming cryptocurrencies impermissible due to their inherent risks and association with illicit activities. Conversely, scholars from Malaysia and Indonesia have adopted a more optimistic stance, recognizing the potential of cryptocurrencies to drive financial inclusion, enhance security, and promote ethical investments.

Benefits and Challenges of Cryptocurrency in Islamic Finance

The integration of cryptocurrencies into Islamic finance presents several benefits, including:

Financial Inclusion: Cryptocurrencies can provide access to financial services for unbanked populations, aligning with the Islamic ethos of supporting equitable economic participation.

Enhanced Security: The security features inherent in blockchain technology can mitigate risks associated with traditional financial systems, fostering trust among users.

Promotion of Ethical Investment: The transparency of blockchain transactions allows for greater scrutiny and accountability, enabling investors to make informed decisions that align with Sharia principles.

However, significant challenges also persist:

Risk and Volatility: The speculative nature of many cryptocurrencies can lead to significant financial risk, raising concerns about compliance with the Sharia prohibition against excessive uncertainty.

Regulatory Flexibility: The evolving regulatory landscape surrounding cryptocurrencies necessitates continuous adaptation by financial institutions and investors, creating challenges for ensuring Sharia compliance.

Facilitation of Crime: The potential for cryptocurrencies to be used in illegal activities remains a critical concern, underscoring the need for stringent regulatory measures.

As the integration of cryptocurrencies and Islamic finance continues to unfold, it is essential to balance the potential benefits of digital currency against the ethical and legal considerations outlined by Sharia law. Engaging in a comprehensive dialogue among scholars, financial institutions, and regulatory bodies will be crucial in navigating this complex landscape. By addressing the integration of cryptocurrencies as part of the broader impact of digitalization in Islamic finance, stakeholders can work towards creating a framework that aligns innovation with ethical principles, paving the way for a more inclusive and responsible financial future.

Compatibility of Cryptocurrency with Islamic Finance Principles

The rise of cryptocurrencies marks a significant shift in the landscape of finance, particularly within Islamic finance, which is governed by the principles of Sharia law. This digital transformation is evident in the integration of Islamic fintech, digital currencies, and blockchain technology, each contributing to a broader understanding of financial transactions in accordance with Islamic ethics.

Characteristics and Ethical Implications of Cryptocurrencies: Cryptocurrencies are defined by their decentralization, cryptographic security, and reliance on blockchain technology, setting them apart from traditional fiat currencies that are issued and regulated by central authorities. Despite the innovative potential of cryptocurrencies, concerns have arisen regarding gharar (uncertainty) (Shofawati, 2023). However, if used for legitimate transactions and investments, these digital assets can avoid the pitfalls of riba (interest) and gharar. It is essential to recognize that not all cryptocurrency applications are speculative; with appropriate regulations, their usage can be aligned with Islamic standards. The inherent immutability of blockchain enhances trust and reduces fraud, making cryptocurrencies suitable for legitimate purposes like business promotion and ethical investments, which can be deemed halal (Ayedh et al., 2021).

Ensuring Sharia Compliance: For crypto currencies to be classified as Sharia-compliant they must adhere to Islamic contract laws, which necessitate the exclusion of riba, gharar, and maysir (gambling) from their frameworks. The deployment of smart contracts—self-executing contracts with terms encoded in software—can bolster compliance by mitigating ambiguity and ensuring clarity in transactions (Alt et al., 2018). However, the existence of speculative cryptocurrencies poses challenges to achieving this compliance. In contrast, asset-backed cryptocurrencies, which are tied to tangible assets, offer a viable pathway to compliance by ensuring that profits are derived from shared resources (Ghode et al., 2020).

Opportunities for Islamic Banks and DeFi Platforms: Islamic banks can leverage cryptocurrencies to create Sharia-compliant financial products and services, providing investment solutions that align with Islamic principles. Utilizing decentralized finance (DeFi) platforms can enhance transparency and reduce costs while offering Sharia-compliant financial products such as Mudarabah (profit-sharing) and Ijara (leasing). To achieve this, robust governance and management systems are essential for upholding Sharia compliance, safeguarding investor interests, and mitigating risks associated with illicit activities (Erić, 2022).

Collaborative Efforts for Regulatory Frameworks: The successful integration of cryptocurrencies into Islamic finance necessitates collaboration between Islamic financial institutions and regulatory bodies. Developing comprehensive guidelines and standards will facilitate the responsible adoption of cryptocurrencies, ensuring alignment with Sharia principles. By fostering a collaborative environment, stakeholders can create a secure and compliant framework that encourages innovation while adhering to ethical standards.

The compatibility of cryptocurrencies with Islamic finance principles exemplifies the broader impact of digitalization on traditional financial system. By navigating the complexities of Sharia compliance and embracing technological advancements, Islamic finance can harness the potential of cryptocurrencies to enhance financial inclusion and ethical investment opportunities. Through careful regulation and collaborative efforts, the integration of cryptocurrencies can lead to a more transparent and resilient financial ecosystem aligned with Islamic values.

Case Studies on the Application of Cryptocurrency in Islamic Finance Contexts

Case Study 1: Islamic Crowdfunding Platforms

Islamic crowdfunding platforms such as Blossom Finance and Ethis use blockchain technology to facilitate Shariah-compliant investments. These platforms allow investors to finance projects that promote health and economic development, transparency and security through blockchain (Zain et al., 2019).

Study 2: Blockchain in Islamic Banking

Many Islamic banks have incorporated blockchain technology to improve their operations. For example, Al Hilal Bank in the UAE has increased transparency and reduced transaction times by using blockchain to issue Shariah-compliant bonds (Sukuk). Blockchain technology can improve processes, reduce costs and increase trust in the Islamic economy (Unal et al., 2022).

Case Study 3: Shariah-Compliant Cryptocurrencies

Many sharia-based cryptocurrencies have been developed in accordance with Islamic principles. An example of this is OneGram, a cryptocurrency backed by gold. Each OneGram coin is backed by one gram of gold, making it efficient and compliant with Islamic finance standards. Another example is the X8 currency, which is a stable currency backed by a number of fiat currencies and gold, ensuring stability and compliance with Sharia law (Aliyu et al., 2020).

Case Study 4: Islamic Fintech Startups

Many Islamic fintech companies are starting to leverage blockchain technology to provide new financial solutions. For example, HalalChain is a blockchain-based platform that provides traceability and transparency for halal products and services, including financial transactions. These initiatives are driving the digital revolution of Islamic finance by ensuring adherence to Islamic principles (Ali et al., 2019).

This case study highlights the potential of cryptocurrency and blockchain technology to revolutionize Islamic finance. These technologies can support accounting, business development and investment efficiency by increasing transparency, security and efficiency. Successful integration of cryptocurrencies into the Islamic financial environment can pave the way for integration and financial stability (Alam et al., 2019). Despite the challenges and concerns regarding predictability, flexibility and compliance with Sharia principles, the benefits of cryptocurrencies in improving the quality of accounting, transparency and efficiency are significant. China's future vision depends on the development of a strong administrative and management system that ensures compliance with Islamic laws (Atif et al., 2021). By adopting new technologies and partnering with stakeholders, Islamic finance can leverage the potential of cryptocurrencies to promote fair and inclusive financial solutions. Conducting research and discussion on Shariah-compliant cryptocurrencies, design Shariah-compliant cryptocurrencies and financial products, and work with regulators to develop guidelines and standards for the use of cryptocurrencies in Islamic finance makers. Application of cryptocurrencies in Islamic finance While Islamic finance presents challenges, it also offers opportunities for innovation and growth. Cryptocurrencies can play an important role in the digital transformation of Islamic finance by adhering to the ethical and social principles of Sharia law and deliver positive and inclusive financial benefits in the future (Alshater et al., 2022).

FUTURE TRENDS AND CHALLENGES IN ISLAMIC FINANCE, FINTECH, AND BLOCKCHAIN

The integration of Islamic finance principles with fintech and blockchain technologies represents a transformative opportunity in the financial landscape. Sharia-compliant finance, grounded in moral and ethical frameworks, now faces unique prospects and challenges as it intersects with the digital transformation of financial services. This section discusses emerging trends, management challenges, and offers recommendations for stakeholders to navigate this evolving landscape.

Emerging Trends

The expansion of digital banking is reshaping traditional financial services by increasing accessibility, convenience, and efficiency. Islamic digital banks, such as Germany's Insha and Al Rajhi Bank, are pioneering Sharia-compliant digital banking solutions, promoting financial inclusion, particularly in Muslim-majority regions (Hasan et al., 2020). These banks leverage technology to streamline services and extend access to underserved communities, adhering to Islamic values of social equity and economic justice.

Smart contracts, a key feature in blockchain technology, are transforming contract execution in Islamic finance. These self-executing contracts operate based on coded terms, providing transparency, reducing fraud risk, and building trust in financial transactions. Platforms like Tezos are actively developing Sharia-compliant smart contracts that facilitate seamless and secure transactions, aligning with Islamic finance's emphasis on accountability and ethical practices. The rise of crowdfunding and peer-to-peer (P2P) lending within Islamic finance also highlights the sector's adaptability to modern financial solutions. Platforms such as Ethis and Blossom Finance utilize blockchain technology to offer transparent and Sharia-compliant investment options. These platforms enable small and medium-sized enterprises (SMEs) to access capital, fostering business growth and economic development in alignment with Sharia principles (Yu et al., 2018).

The increasing acceptance of cryptocurrencies and stablecoins within Islamic finance is another notable trend. Sharia-compliant cryptocurrencies, such as OneGram (backed by physical gold) and the X8 currency (backed by a mix of fiat currency and gold), present a stable and ethical alternative to conventional currencies. These assets comply with Sharia requirements and provide investors with viable options in digital finance that align with Islamic values. Decentralized Finance (DeFi) is emerging as a groundbreaking ecosystem built on blockchain technology that offers financial services without traditional intermediaries. DeFi presents a unique challenge for Islamic finance due to Sharia compliance requirements. However, it also holds significant potential for the development of transparent, efficient, and accessible Sharia-compliant financial products, thus expanding opportunities for ethical finance (Yasini & Yasini, 2019).

Given the rapid advancements in digital finance, Islamic finance stakeholders should prioritize regulatory collaboration and develop guidelines to ensure the integration of blockchain and fintech within a Sharia-compliant framework. By focusing on transparent governance, robust risk management, and ethical alignment, stakeholders can cultivate a resilient ecosystem that enhances accessibility, fosters trust, and aligns with Islamic ethical standards. The intersection of Islamic finance with fintech and blockchain technology represents both a transformative shift and a challenge in achieving Sharia compliance within a rapidly digitalizing economy. As these trends continue to unfold, thoughtful integration and adherence to Islamic ethical principles will be crucial in advancing Sharia-compliant solutions that are both innovative and aligned with the moral tenets of Islamic finance.

Regulatory Challenges and Opportunities in the Digital Transformation

The digital transformation in Islamic finance brings about new regulatory challenges and opportunities that call for a balanced approach between Sharia compliance and fostering innovation. As financial services incorporate fintech and blockchain technology, regulators must align these innovations with Islamic principles, ensuring both the ethical integrity of financial products and consumer trust.

Establishing Standards and Compliance

Regulatory bodies such as the Accounting and Auditing Organization for Islamic Financial Institutions (AAOIFI) play a critical role in setting global standards for Sharia-compliant fintech and blockchain applications (Yudaruddin, 2023). Clear guidelines are needed to address how Islamic finance can incorporate blockchain for cross-border transactions, where differences in national regulations pose complex challenges. Ensuring both national and international Sharia compliance in blockchain transactions is fundamental to promoting Islamic finance globally, facilitating more accessible, transparent, and compliant services (Rahim et al., 2019).

Managing Cybersecurity and Fraud Risks

Digital transformation introduces risks unique to fintech and blockchain, including heightened cybersecurity threats and fraud vulnerabilities. To address these risks, regulators must implement stringent risk management frameworks to protect users and uphold financial integrity. Effective Know Your Customer (KYC) and Anti-Money Laundering (AML) measures are also essential to maintaining a secure Islamic finance ecosystem. Through regulatory oversight, consumer data and transaction integrity can be safeguarded, minimizing threats to both users and financial systems (Zain et al., 2019).

Enhancing Digital Literacy and Supporting Innovation

Successful adoption of digital solutions in Islamic finance also depends on digital literacy. A supportive regulatory environment is needed that fosters educational programs aimed at improving digital literacy for both individuals and businesses. This approach will enhance users' abilities to navigate digital financial services confidently and ethically, while understanding the benefits and responsibilities that come with these tools.

Aligning with Social and Ethical Objectives

Islamic finance, deeply rooted in social and ethical values, calls for regulations that emphasize health, welfare, and ethics. Regulatory bodies should encourage investment in social projects that align with Islamic finance principles, promoting fairness, ethical practices, and economic welfare within digital financial services. For instance, blockchain-based social finance projects can support welfare-driven financial markets, bridging digital innovation with Islamic ethical values (Shaikh et al., 2019).

The integration of fintech and blockchain in Islamic finance holds substantial promise, yet requires robust regulatory oversight to ensure compliance, security, and ethical alignment. By addressing challenges in standardization, risk management, and literacy, regulators can pave the way for an Islamic finance ecosystem that is both innovative and firmly rooted in Sharia principles.

RECOMMENDATIONS FOR POLICYMAKERS, PRACTITIONERS, AND RESEARCHERS

To navigate the complexities introduced by the digital transformation of Islamic finance, it is essential for stakeholders—including policymakers, practitioners, and researchers—to foster a regulatory and operational environment that balances Sharia compliance, innovation, and consumer protection. By addressing integration and impact, this section provides tailored recommendations to help advance Islamic finance in the fintech and blockchain era.

For Policymakers: Developing a Sharia-Compliant Regulatory Framework

Policymakers should focus on developing a regulatory framework that accommodates the unique characteristics of Islamic finance, fintech, and blockchain while aligning with Sharia principles. This framework must provide clear guidelines to support innovation without compromising Sharia law, ensuring that digital products and services maintain ethical integrity (Pratiwi et al., 2023). Policymakers should collaborate with international regulators to harmonize standards, facilitating cross-border transactions and fostering global growth in Islamic finance, which is increasingly important as digital finance becomes more interconnected. These collaborative efforts will empower individuals and businesses alike to access Islamic finance products, make informed financial decisions, and reinforce Islamic ethical standards.

For Financial Institutions: Embracing Fintech and Blockchain Innovations

Financial institutions must adopt fintech and blockchain technologies to enhance operational efficiency, transparency, and accessibility in Islamic finance. By investing in Sharia-compliant digital products and services, institutions can address evolving consumer demands while adhering to Islamic principles. This includes using smart contracts and cryptographic security in digital finance to promote trust and transparency. Additionally, implementing robust Know Your Customer (KYC) and Anti-Money Laundering (AML) protocols will further secure these services and maintain the integrity of funds, helping to align with Islamic finance ethics and consumer protection standards (Nienhaus, 2019). Furthermore, institutions should actively contribute to the development of industry best practices, which will support sustainable growth and encourage financial inclusion.

For Researchers: Advancing Knowledge and Innovation in Islamic Fintech

Researchers have a vital role in supporting the evolution of Shariah-compliant fintech and blockchain solutions. By studying the unique interactions between Islamic finance principles and emerging digital technologies, researchers can identify best practices and inform regulatory policies that uphold Islamic ethics (Nazarov & Dhiraj, 2019). It is essential to explore how blockchain, digital currencies, and smart contracts can be effectively integrated into the Islamic finance context, enabling a deeper understanding of their ethical implications. Research should also focus on developing frameworks and methodologies that ensure new technological applications comply with Sharia standards, fostering a sustainable and ethical Islamic finance ecosystem.

Establishing a Collaborative Platform for Innovation and Dialogue

Finally, creating platforms for discussion and exchange of ideas among policymakers, practitioners, and researchers will be critical to foster innovation in Islamic finance. Such collaboration will support a unified approach to managing digital finance challenges while staying aligned with Islamic ethics. By addressing regulatory issues, best practices, and emerging trends through collaborative discussions, stakeholders can accelerate the adoption of innovative, Sharia-compliant financial solutions, paving the way for a dynamic and ethical future in Islamic finance (Muhammad et al., 2024).

A concerted effort among policymakers, practitioners, and researchers is essential to leverage fintech and blockchain in Islamic finance effectively. Through regulatory clarity, institutional adoption of innovation, and rigorous research, stakeholders can ensure that Islamic finance continues to meet the needs of a digital economy while remaining true to its foundational principles.

CONCLUSION

The digital transformation of Islamic finance—driven by fintech innovations, blockchain technology, and digital currencies—offers a range of opportunities as well as unique challenges. Emerging tools such as smart contracts, Sharia-compliant cryptocurrencies, and digital marketplaces are reshaping Islamic financial services, creating a more integrated and accessible financial ecosystem. However, achieving sustainable growth in this sector requires carefully navigating Sharia compliance, addressing cross-border trade issues, strengthening risk management, and enhancing digital literacy (Muryanto et al., 2020).

To ensure Islamic finance meets the demands of this digital era, stakeholders must prioritize creating robust regulatory frameworks that harmonize with both Islamic ethics and modern technological advancements. By fostering innovation, protecting consumer interests, and conducting rigorous research, policymakers and practitioners can help integrate fintech and blockchain into Islamic finance in a way that upholds Sharia principles. This integration will not only enable financial inclusion and productive investment but will also contribute to broader economic development.

The successful merger of fintech and blockchain within Islamic finance will be essential for promoting a fair and efficient financial ecosystem aligned with Islamic ethics. As the global financial landscape continues to evolve, ongoing collaboration and innovation among stakeholders will be a key to addressing emerging challenges, thus unlocking the full potential of Islamic finance in the digital age (Omar et al., 2020).

REFERENCES

Abaidoo, R., & Agyapong, E. K. (2022). Banking industry stability and investment dynamics. *Journal of Financial Regulation and Compliance*, 30(2), 215–239. DOI: 10.1108/JFRC-06-2021-0049

Akiyoshi, F. (2019). Effects of separating commercial and investment banking: Evidence from the dissolution of a joint venture investment bank. *Journal of Financial Economics*, 134(3), 703–714. DOI: 10.1016/j.jfineco.2019.05.004

Alam, N., Gupta, L., Zameni, A., Alam, N., Gupta, L., & Zameni, A. (2019). Challenges and success factors for Islamic fintech. *Fintech and Islamic Finance: Digitalization, Development and Disruption*, 159-173.

Alam, N., Gupta, L., Zameni, A., Alam, N., Gupta, L., & Zameni, A. (2019). Cryptocurrency and Islamic finance. *Fintech and Islamic Finance: Digitalization, Development and Disruption*, 99-118.

Alam, N., Gupta, L., Zameni, A., Alam, N., Gupta, L., & Zameni, A. (2019). Emergence of Shariah-Tech and Its Landscape. *Fintech and Islamic Finance: Digitalization, Development and Disruption*, 63-79.

Alam, N., & Nazim, S. (2021). Fintech, digital currency and the future of Islamic finance. *Cham: Springer International Publishing, 257.*

Ali, H., Abdullah, R., & Zaini, M. Z. (2019). Fintech and its potential impact on Islamic banking and finance industry: A case study of Brunei Darussalam and Malaysia. [IJIEF]. *International Journal of Islamic Economics and Finance*, 2(1), 73–108. DOI: 10.18196/ijief.2116

Aliyu, A., Abu Bakar, K., Matsuda, G., Darwish, T. S., Abdullah, A. H., Ismail, A. S., & Yaacob, A. C. (2020). Review of some existing shariah-compliant cryptocurrency. *Journal of Contempory Islamic Studies*, 6(1), 22–43.

Alshater, M. M., Saba, I., Supriani, I., & Rabbani, M. R. (2022). Fintech in islamic finance literature: A review. *Heliyon*, 8(9), e10385. DOI: 10.1016/j.heliyon.2022.e10385 PMID: 36060472

Alt, R., Beck, R., & Smits, M. T. (2018). FinTech and the transformation of the financial industry. *Electronic Markets*, 28(3), 235–243. DOI: 10.1007/s12525-018-0310-9

Atif, M., Hassan, M. K., Rabbani, M. R., & Khan, S. (2021). Islamic FinTech: The digital transformation bringing sustainability to Islamic finance. In *COVID-19 and Islamic social finance* (pp. 91-103). Routledge.

Ayedh, A., Echchabi, A., Battour, M., & Omar, M. (2021). Malaysian Muslim investors' behaviour towards the blockchain-based Bitcoin cryptocurrency market. *Journal of Islamic Marketing*, 12(4), 690–704. DOI: 10.1108/JIMA-04-2019-0081

Azizah, S. N. (2023). The adoption of FinTech and the legal protection of the digital assets in Islamic/Sharia banking linked with economic development: A case of Indonesia. *The Journal of World Intellectual Property*, 26(1), 30–40. DOI: 10.1111/jwip.12257

Banna, H., Hassan, M. K., Ahmad, R., & Alam, M. R. (2022). Islamic banking stability amidst the COVID-19 pandemic: The role of digital financial inclusion. *International Journal of Islamic and Middle Eastern Finance and Management*, 15(2), 310–330. DOI: 10.1108/IMEFM-08-2020-0389

Bhatia, A., Chandani, A., Divekar, R., Mehta, M., & Vijay, N. (2022). Digital innovation in wealth management landscape: The moderating role of robo advisors in behavioural biases and investment decision-making. *International Journal of Innovation Science*, 14(3/4), 693–712. DOI: 10.1108/IJIS-10-2020-0245

Chong, F. H. L. (2021). Enhancing trust through digital Islamic finance and blockchain technology. *Qualitative Research in Financial Markets*, 13(3), 328–341. DOI: 10.1108/QRFM-05-2020-0076

Delle Foglie, A., Panetta, I. C., Boukrami, E., & Vento, G. (2021). The impact of the Blockchain technology on the global Sukuk industry: Smart contracts and asset tokenisation. *Technology Analysis and Strategic Management*, •••, 1–15. DOI: 10.1080/09537325.2021.1939000

Erić, D. (2022). Innovation and Fintech. In *Digitalization and the Future of Financial Services: Innovation and Impact of Digital Finance* (pp. 19–39). Springer International Publishing. DOI: 10.1007/978-3-031-11545-5_2

Ghode, D. J., Jain, R., Soni, G., Singh, S. K., & Yadav, V. (2020). Architecture to enhance transparency in supply chain management using blockchain technology. *Procedia Manufacturing*, 51, 1614–1620. DOI: 10.1016/j.promfg.2020.10.225

Griffiths, P. D. R. (2021). Fintech and its historical perspective. *The Palgrave Handbook of FinTech and Blockchain*, 19-50.

Gulrez, T. (2021). Strategic assessment of Islamic Fintech in GCC countries. *Fintech, digital currency and the future of Islamic finance: Strategic, regulatory and adoption issues in the Gulf Cooperation Council*, 223-241.

Gün, M. (2020). The path to fintech development research on Islamic finance in Turkey. In *Impact of Financial Technology (FinTech) on Islamic Finance and Financial Stability* (pp. 65-96). IGI Global.

Hamsin, M. K., Halim, A., Anggriawan, R., & Lutfiani, H. (2023). Sharia E-Wallet: The Issue of Sharia Compliance and Data Protection. *Al-Manahij: Jurnal Kajian Hukum Islam*, 17(1), 53–68. DOI: 10.24090/mnh.v17i1.7633

Hasan, R., Hassan, M. K., & Aliyu, S. (2020). Fintech and Islamic finance: Literature review and research agenda. [IJIEF]. *International Journal of Islamic Economics and Finance*, 3(1), 75–94. DOI: 10.18196/ijief.2122

Hassan, M. K., Jreisat, A., Rabbani, M. R., & Al-Mohamed, S. (2022). Islamic fintech and Bahrain: an opportunity for global financial services. *Fintech in Islamic financial institutions: Scope, challenges, and implications in Islamic finance*, 65-87.

Hassan, M. K., Muneeza, A., & Khan, A. (2021). Pandemic crisis, digitalization and social responsibility: an emerging role of Islamic economics and finance. *Islamic Finance and Sustainable Development: A Sustainable Economic Framework for Muslim and Non-Muslim Countries*, 35-53.

Hassan, M. K., Zulfikar, Z., Rabbani, M. R., & Atif, M. (2022). Fintech trends: Industry 4.0, Islamic fintech, and its digital transformation. In *FinTech in Islamic Financial Institutions: Scope, Challenges, and Implications in Islamic Finance* (pp. 113–130). Springer International Publishing. DOI: 10.1007/978-3-031-14941-2_6

Hew, J. J., Wong, L. W., Tan, G. W. H., Ooi, K. B., & Lin, B. (2020). The blockchain-based Halal traceability systems: A hype or reality? *Supply Chain Management*, 25(6), 863–879. DOI: 10.1108/SCM-01-2020-0044

Humphrey, C. (2019). 'Minilateral'development banks: What the rise of Africa's trade and development bank says about multilateral governance. *Development and Change*, 50(1), 164–190. DOI: 10.1111/dech.12467

Jalal, A., Al Mubarak, M., & Durani, F. (2023). Financial technology (fintech). In *Artificial Intelligence and Transforming Digital Marketing* (pp. 525–536). Springer Nature Switzerland.

Javaid, M., Haleem, A., Singh, R. P., Suman, R., & Khan, S. (2022). A review of Blockchain Technology applications for financial services. *BenchCouncil Transactions on Benchmarks. Standards and Evaluations*, 2(3), 100073.

Jouti, A. T. (2021). Islamic fintech and financial inclusion. *Islamic FinTech: Insights and Solutions*, 209-229.

Khalil, M., Khawaja, K. F., & Sarfraz, M. (2022). The adoption of blockchain technology in the financial sector during the era of fourth industrial revolution: A moderated mediated model. *Quality & Quantity*, 56(4), 2435–2452. DOI: 10.1007/s11135-021-01229-0

Khan, A., Hassan, M. K., Paltrinieri, A., Dreassi, A., & Bahoo, S. (2020). A bibliometric review of takaful literature. *International Review of Economics & Finance*, 69, 389–405. DOI: 10.1016/j.iref.2020.05.013

Khan, S. N. (2023). The legality of cryptocurrency from an Islamic perspective: A research note. *Journal of Islamic Accounting and Business Research*, 14(2), 289–294. DOI: 10.1108/JIABR-02-2022-0041

Khatoon, A., Verma, P., Southernwood, J., Massey, B., & Corcoran, P. (2019). Blockchain in energy efficiency: Potential applications and benefits. *Energies*, 12(17), 3317. DOI: 10.3390/en12173317

Kılıç, G., & Türkan, Y. (2023). The Emergence of Islamic Fintech and Its Applications. *International Journal of Islamic Economics and Finance Studies*, 9(2), 212–236.

Kusuma, K., Sheela, P., Panigrahi, R. R., & Shaikh, Z. H. (2024). Blockchain Technology and Islamic Finance: A Decade of Growth Trends. *Fintech Applications in Islamic Finance: AI, Machine Learning, and Blockchain Techniques*, 59-79.

Locatelli, R., Schena, C., & Tanda, A. (2021). A historical perspective on disruptive technologies. *Disruptive Technology in Banking and Finance: An International Perspective on FinTech*, 9-45.

Mohd Nor, S., Abdul-Majid, M., & Esrati, S. N. (2021). The role of blockchain technology in enhancing Islamic social finance: the case of Zakah management in Malaysia. *foresight, 23*(5), 509-527.

Molla, A., & Biru, A. (2023). The evolution of the Fintech entrepreneurial ecosystem in Africa: An exploratory study and model for future development. *Technological Forecasting and Social Change*, 186, 122123. DOI: 10.1016/j.techfore.2022.122123

Muhammad, A. M., Basha, M. B., & AlHafidh, G. (2024). Use of emerging social media platforms in reshaping the UAE Islamic banks' promotional strategies. *Journal of Islamic Marketing*, 15(2), 338–360. DOI: 10.1108/JIMA-01-2022-0015

Muryanto, Y. T., Kharisma, D. B., & Ciptorukmi Nugraheni, A. S. (2022). Prospects and challenges of Islamic fintech in Indonesia: A legal viewpoint. *International Journal of Law and Management*, 64(2), 239–252. DOI: 10.1108/IJLMA-07-2021-0162

Nazarov, I. I., & Dhiraj, N. S. (2019). A conceptual understanding and significance of takaful (Islamic insurance): History, concept, models and products. *International Journal for Innovation Education and Research*, 7(4), 280–298. DOI: 10.31686/ijier.vol7.iss4.1408

Nienhaus, V. (2019). Blockchain technologies and the prospects of smart contracts in Islamic finance. In *Fintech in Islamic Finance* (pp. 183–210). Routledge. DOI: 10.4324/9781351025584-13

Omar, I. A., Jayaraman, R., Salah, K., Simsekler, M. C. E., Yaqoob, I., & Ellahham, S. (2020). Ensuring protocol compliance and data transparency in clinical trials using Blockchain smart contracts. *BMC Medical Research Methodology*, 20(1), 1–17. DOI: 10.1186/s12874-020-01109-5 PMID: 32894068

Oseni, U. A., & Ali, S. N. (2019). Fintech in Islamic finance. In *Fintech in Islamic finance* (pp. 3–14). Routledge. DOI: 10.4324/9781351025584-1

Pal, A., Tiwari, C. K., & Behl, A. (2021). Blockchain technology in financial services: A comprehensive review of the literature. *Journal of Global Operations and Strategic Sourcing*, 14(1), 61–80. DOI: 10.1108/JGOSS-07-2020-0039

Palmié, M., Wincent, J., Parida, V., & Caglar, U. (2020). The evolution of the financial technology ecosystem: An introduction and agenda for future research on disruptive innovations in ecosystems. *Technological Forecasting and Social Change*, 151, 119779. DOI: 10.1016/j.techfore.2019.119779

Polyviou, A., Velanas, P., & Soldatos, J. (2019, October). Blockchain technology: financial sector applications beyond cryptocurrencies. In *Proceedings* (Vol. 28, No. 1, p. 7). MDPI. DOI: 10.3390/proceedings2019028007

Pratiwi, R. E., Meirani, N., Khumairah, K., Saharan, M. S., & Hassan, H. E. (2023). Crowdfunding: As an Alternative to Islamic Funding. *Journal of Business Studies and Management Review*, 6(2), 109–117. DOI: 10.22437/jbsmr.v6i2.24535

Qudah, H., Malahim, S., Airout, R., Alomari, M., Hamour, A. A., & Alqudah, M. (2023). Islamic finance in the era of financial technology: A bibliometric review of future trends. *International Journal of Financial Studies*, 11(2), 76. DOI: 10.3390/ijfs11020076

Rabbani, M. R., Abdulla, Y., Basahr, A., Khan, S., & Moh'd Ali, M. A. (2020, November). Embracing of Fintech in Islamic Finance in the post COVID era. In *2020 international conference on decision aid sciences and application (DASA)* (pp. 1230-1234). IEEE. DOI: 10.1109/DASA51403.2020.9317196

Rabbani, M. R., Abdulla, Y., Basahr, A., Khan, S., & Moh'd Ali, M. A. (2020, November). Embracing of Fintech in Islamic Finance in the post COVID era. In *2020 international conference on decision aid sciences and application (DASA)* (pp. 1230-1234). IEEE. DOI: 10.1109/DASA51403.2020.9317196

Rabbani, M. R., Bashar, A., Nawaz, N., Karim, S., Ali, M. A. M., Rahiman, H. U., & Alam, M. S. (2021). Exploring the role of islamic fintech in combating the aftershocks of covid-19: The open social innovation of the islamic financial system. *Journal of Open Innovation*, 7(2), 136. DOI: 10.3390/joitmc7020136

Rabbani, M. R., Bashar, A., Nawaz, N., Karim, S., Ali, M. A. M., Rahiman, H. U., & Alam, M. S. (2021). Exploring the role of islamic fintech in combating the aftershocks of covid-19: The open social innovation of the islamic financial system. *Journal of Open Innovation*, 7(2), 136. DOI: 10.3390/joitmc7020136

Rabbani, M. R., Hassan, M. K., Hudaefi, F. A., & Shaikh, Z. H. (2022). Islamic finance and cryptocurrency: a systematic review. *FinTech in Islamic Financial Institutions: Scope, Challenges, and Implications in Islamic Finance*, 279-306.

Rahim, N. F., Bakri, M. H., & Yahaya, S. N. (2019). Fintech and Shariah principles in smart contracts. In *FinTech as a disruptive technology for financial institutions* (pp. 207–220). IGI Global. DOI: 10.4018/978-1-5225-7805-5.ch009

Rahim, N. F., Bakri, M. H., & Yahaya, S. N. (2019). Fintech and Shariah principles in smart contracts. In *FinTech as a disruptive technology for financial institutions* (pp. 207–220). IGI Global. DOI: 10.4018/978-1-5225-7805-5.ch009

Rashwan, A. R. M. S., & Kassem, Z. A. E. A. (2021). The role of digital transformation in increasing the efficiency of banks' performance to enhance competitive advantage. In *The big data-driven digital economy: Artificial and computational intelligence* (pp. 325–335). Springer International Publishing. DOI: 10.1007/978-3-030-73057-4_25

Sahabuddin, M., Ahmad, A. U. F., & Islam, M. A. (2023). Emergence of Islamic Finance in the Fourth Industrial Revolution and COVID-19 Post-Pandemic Era. In *Islamic Finance, FinTech, and the Road to Sustainability: Reframing the Approach in the Post-Pandemic Era* (pp. 123–141). Springer International Publishing. DOI: 10.1007/978-3-031-13302-2_6

Sahabuddin, M., Sakib, M. N., Rahman, M. M., Jibir, A., Fahlevi, M., Aljuaid, M., & Grabowska, S. (2023). The evolution of FinTech in scientific research: A bibliometric analysis. *Sustainability (Basel)*, 15(9), 7176. DOI: 10.3390/su15097176

Shaikh, Z. H., Sarea, A., & Irfan, M. (2021, September). Islamic banking strategies in the world of Fintech: success story of Bahrain. In *The International Conference On Global Economic Revolutions* (pp. 97-104). Cham: Springer International Publishing.

Shehadeh, M., Almajali, D., Abu-AlSondos, I. A., Alkhwaldi, A. F., & Al-Gasaymeh, A. S. (2023, March). Digital transformation and its impact on operational efficiency and competitive advantage in Islamic banks. In *2023 International Conference on Business Analytics for Technology and Security (ICBATS)* (pp. 1-6). IEEE. DOI: 10.1109/ICBATS57792.2023.10111266

Shofawati, A. (2023). The Role of Islamic Fintech in Indonesia to Improve Financial Inclusion for Resolving SDGs. In *Artificial Intelligence, Fintech, and Financial Inclusion* (pp. 112-134). CRC Press. DOI: 10.1201/9781003125204-8

Suryono, R. R., Budi, I., & Purwandari, B. (2020). Challenges and trends of financial technology (Fintech): A systematic literature review. *Information (Basel)*, 11(12), 590. DOI: 10.3390/info11120590

Tariq, M. U. (2024). Revolutionizing health data management with blockchain technology: Enhancing security and efficiency in a digital era. In *Emerging Technologies for Health Literacy and Medical Practice* (pp. 153–175). IGI Global. DOI: 10.4018/979-8-3693-1214-8.ch008

Thaker, M. A. B. M. T., Khaliq, A. B., Thaker, H. B. M. T., Amin, M. F. B., & Pitchay, A. B. A. (2022). The potential role of fintech and digital currency for islamic green financing: toward an integrated model. In *Green digital finance and sustainable development goals* (pp. 287–308). Springer Nature Singapore. DOI: 10.1007/978-981-19-2662-4_14

Unal, I. M., & Aysan, A. F. (2022). Fintech, digitalization, and blockchain in Islamic finance: Retrospective investigation. *FinTech*, 1(4), 388–398. DOI: 10.3390/fintech1040029

Yasini, S., & Yasini, M. (2019). Current trends and future impacts of fintech in Islamic finance. In *FinTech in Islamic Finance* (pp. 327–335). Routledge. DOI: 10.4324/9781351025584-20

Yu, T., Lin, Z., & Tang, Q. (2018). Blockchain: The introduction and its application in financial accounting. *Journal of Corporate Accounting & Finance*, 29(4), 37–47. DOI: 10.1002/jcaf.22365

Yudaruddin, R. (2023). Financial technology and performance in Islamic and conventional banks. *Journal of Islamic Accounting and Business Research*, 14(1), 100–116. DOI: 10.1108/JIABR-03-2022-0070

Zain, N. R. M., Mahadi, N. F., & Noor, A. M. (2019). *The potential in reviving waqf through crowdfunding technology: the case study. Al-Shajarah: Journal of the International Institute of Islamic Thought and Civilization*. ISTAC.

Chapter 5
Digital Dilemmas and Solutions:
Addressing Financial Challenges and Exploring Islamic Educational Platforms

Nur Shuhada Kamarudin
https://orcid.org/0000-0002-3023-8920
Universiti Sains Islam Malaysia, Malaysia

Muhammad Zikry Hishamudin
https://orcid.org/0000-0003-0279-0563
Universiti Sains Islam Malaysia, Malaysia

ABSTRACT

Malaysia's rapidly growing Islamic finance industry is currently transitioning into the digitalization era. This shift underscores the importance of integrating digital tools and platforms to promote financial literacy and education. The chapter emphasizes the need to provide individuals with the necessary knowledge and skills to navigate the digital financial landscape, particularly in understanding Islamic financial products. It also highlights the significance of both formal and informal digital educational platforms in disseminating Islamic financial knowledge. Furthermore, the chapter stresses the comprehensive focus required for Islamic financial education across formal and informal settings, given the impact of the digital revolution on the financial services industry. By addressing the digital challenges faced by learners and educators and proposing solutions to bridge the gap between traditional and modern approaches, this chapter provides valuable insights for stakeholders in the Islamic finance and education sectors.

DOI: 10.4018/979-8-3693-5653-1.ch005

INTRODUCTION

Malaysia is a fast-growing country in the financial services industry, particularly as an Islamic finance hub. The use of technology in financial services is visible through Internet banking, financial apps, and Fintech. However, there is a need to focus on Islamic financial education, including understanding the digital landscape. Despite the complexity of Islamic financial products available in the market, individuals face challenges in understanding the digital products offered, highlighting the importance of financial education. Financial education is essential for individuals to gather information, develop skills, and build confidence to make sound financial decisions (Financial Education Network, 2019). In addition, financial education is a critical tool for individuals to enhance their financial knowledge and skills, ultimately empowering them to make informed financial decisions (Mishra, 2019). In addition to technological advancements, it's important to have widespread discussions about the digitalization of financial education. This expanded definition of financial education takes into account the digital impact. Digital financial education, also referred to as digital financial literacy (DFL), is an essential skill for individuals in the digital age. It empowers them to make informed financial decisions and navigate the complexities of digital financial services (Goel, 2024; Golden & Cordie, 2022; Lyons & Kass-Hanna, 2021; Morgan et al., 2019). Furthermore, this chapter on financial education will include a discussion of financial education from an Islamic perspective, incorporating Islamic digital financial education. Given the rapidly evolving digital landscape, it is crucial to address financial challenges and explore digital educational platforms within the context of Islamic finance. This chapter will delve into the digital challenges faced by learners and educators, emphasizing solutions to bridging the gap between traditional and modern approaches. Specifically, it will examine formal and informal digital platforms, each playing a distinct role in disseminating Islamic financial knowledge.

Keywords: Islamic Financial Education, Digital Platform, Islamic Digital Financial Literacy, Financial Well-Being, Islamic Finance

LITERATURE REVIEW

As the Islamic finance industry has already become one of the important industries established on the global stage, the need for comprehensive Islamic financial education has become increasingly crucial. The industry's growth and sustainability depend on a well-informed workforce and educated consumers. In Malaysia, as a leading hub for Islamic finance, it is important to ensure that Islamic financial education is a priority for Malaysians to be literate and informed about Islamic finance (Biplob & Abdullah, 2019). The advantages of the digitalization era, digital platforms help to accelerate the education process and provide information to the wider community in a short time.

Islamic Financial Education in Malaysia

Financial education can be a compulsory or optional subject in schools, and this varies from country to country. In Belgium, financial education is part of the secondary education curriculum. In Shanghai, China, financial concepts are taught as early as primary school (Salas-Velasco & Sánchez-Campillo, 2018). In Malaysia, subjects such as economics, household economics, business, and accounting principles are taught in primary and secondary schools as part of the curriculum, either directly or indirectly. Although these are elective subjects and not compulsory for every student, the Malaysian Ministry of Education has included basic financial elements in subjects such as Malay, English, Mathematics, Islamic Education, and Moral Education. Financial education content was explicitly included in the primary school Mathematics Standard-Based Curriculum and Assessment Document (DSKP) (M. Subramaniam et al., 2024). However, there is currently less focus on offering specific subjects in schools that particularly focus on Islamic financial education, despite general financial education being included in the subjects mentioned above. This differs from the approach to higher education in Malaysia. Several universities in Malaysia offer subjects related to Islamic finance, *Muamalat*, wealth management, and financial planning as part of formal education. Despite Malaysia being among the top countries in the Islamic finance industry, it could be argued that there is a need for a comprehensive focus on Islamic financial education in formal education.

Table 1. List of several examples of universities that offered Islamic finance courses

University/College	Course Name
Management and Science University (MSU)	Bachelor in Islamic Banking Honours
	Bachelor in Islamic Finance Hons
	Bachelor in Islamic Management (Hons)
Universiti Kuala Lumpur (UniKL)	Bachelor of Business Administration (Hons) in Islamic Finance
Universiti Tun Abdul Razak (UNIRAZAK)	Bachelor of Business Administration (Islamic Banking & Finance) (Honours)
International University of Malaya Wales (IUMW)	Bachelor of Business Administration Hons in Islamic Finance
UNITAR International University	Bachelor of Finance Islamic Finance Hons

continued on following page

Table 1. Continued

University/College	Course Name
University of Islamic Sciences Malaysia (USIM)	Bachelor of Islamic Banking and Finance with Honours
University of Malaysia Sabah (UMS)	Bachelor of Islamic Finance

Sources: Sources indicate data from universities' websites as of June 26, 2024

The Malaysia Islamic Finance Education Report (MIFER) from UUM Press in 2021 revealed that the majority of Islamic Finance and Banking education in Malaysia includes 36% associate degree programs, 25% undergraduate programs, 21% doctorate programs, and 18% master's programs. According to Haneef (2018), Islamic finance education in Malaysia is divided into approximately 32% Syariah and Law, 28% Islamic finance and banking, 17% Islamic economics, 14% Islamic management and marketing, and 9% Islamic accounting and governance. Despite this, a report estimated that there was a demand for 56,000 Islamic finance professionals in 2020 (Haneef, 2018). In 2015, it was estimated that around 13,000 graduates received degrees in Islamic finance from Malaysian universities, indicating a shortage of professionals in the field (Aslam Haneef, 2018).

Islamic financial education should encompass Islamic finance, financial planning, and wealth management elements. These areas involve cash flow and net worth planning, Islamic investment planning, Islamic risk management, tax and zakat planning, Islamic retirement planning, and Islamic legacy planning. By adhering to Shariah compliance requirements, individuals aim to achieve "al-falah" (success in this world and hereafter) while focusing on their financial goals. The main challenges in society regarding financial management include the inability to understand financial concepts and risks, which can lead to wrong decision-making and worsen someone's financial condition (Saputra et al., 2019). In addition, Islamic financial planning knowledge is crucial in Malaysia due to the complexity of Islamic banking products and services offered by various institutions, and it is considered vital because it provides knowledge and understanding of Islamic financial services institutions, products, and services offered (Yunus et al., 2017). The importance of financial education is significant, but not everyone has had the opportunity to learn about Islamic financial education through formal channels. Financial inclusion goes beyond just access to financial services; it also encompasses access to financial education. As Malaysia's financial industry continues to grow and move towards digitalization, new digital financial challenges are emerging.

Global Trends in Islamic Digital Finance

Recent studies underscore the worldwide expansion of Islamic fintech, reaching areas such as Western Europe and North America (Nagimova, 2022). This rapid growth is not merely a trend but reflects a broader acceptance and integration of Islamic financial principles into the global financial system. As countries around the world increasingly recognize the potential of Islamic finance, the sector has gained significant investments and plays an essential role in promoting financial inclusion, fostering the growth of small enterprises, and supporting the attainment of the United Nations Sustainable Development Goals (Alshater et al., 2022; Tlemsani et al., 2023). These developments highlight a paradigm shift, where financial systems are evolving to cater to diverse populations, including Muslims and non-Muslims alike, who seek ethical and responsible financial options. Nevertheless, obstacles remain, including regulatory challenges and a lack of financial literacy (Alshater et al., 2022). The regulatory landscape for Islamic fintech can be complex, as it often involves navigating between traditional banking regulations and the unique requirements of Shariah compliance. This complexity can deter potential investors and hinder the growth of Islamic fintech companies. Moreover, the lack of financial literacy, particularly concerning Islamic financial principles, poses a significant barrier. Many potential users of Islamic fintech are unfamiliar with its products, services, and underlying ethical principles, leading to skepticism and reluctance to engage with these financial offerings.

Addressing these challenges requires enhancing Islamic financial digital literacy, which enables users to engage more effectively with fintech platforms and better understand Shariah-compliant financial tools. By fostering digital literacy, stakeholders can empower individuals to make informed financial decisions, thereby promoting the use of Islamic fintech solutions. Educational initiatives and programs focused on Islamic finance principles can significantly bridge the knowledge gap and increase confidence in utilizing these services. These efforts are vital in building a user-friendly ecosystem that resonates with the ethical values of potential customers, making Islamic fintech a viable option for a broader audience. Islamic digital finance has also been making remarkable strides globally, utilizing technologies like blockchain, artificial intelligence (AI), and mobile banking to support the demands placed by today's financial ecosystems. This digital transformation is not only increasing the efficiency and accessibility of Islamic financial services but also ensuring compliance with Shariah principles. For instance, the integration of AI in Islamic finance has revolutionized credit assessments and fraud prevention. By leveraging AI algorithms, fintech companies can analyze vast amounts of data to assess creditworthiness more accurately, which enhances financial inclusion and stability (Ali & Khan, 2023). This is particularly important in regions where access to traditional banking services is limited, allowing individuals and small businesses to secure financing that aligns with their ethical beliefs.

In addition, Islamic fintech is progressively attracting a recent cohort of Muslims through the provision of Shariah-compliant financial products that are both morally sound and technologically sophisticated (Economist Impact, 2020). This advancement is crucial in meeting the financial requirements of the financially excluded demographic while fostering sustainable economic development. The appeal of these products lies not only in their compliance with Islamic principles but also in their ability to integrate seamlessly with users' lifestyles. Features such as user-friendly mobile applications and digital wallets have made it easier for individuals to manage their finances in accordance with their values. The need for education in Islamic digital financial literacy has grown over the years. With the increasing trend of digital finance, there is a growing need for awareness regarding Islamic finance principles and benefits. Studies indicate that increased financial literacy will result in considerable improvement in terms of financial inclusion and economic empowerment. Hassan (2023) highlighted that digital finance literacy programs focusing on Islamic finance principles can help reduce the knowledge gap and empower people to make appropriate financial decisions. These programs can take various forms, including workshops, online courses, and community outreach initiatives, targeting diverse demographics, including young adults, women, and underserved communities.

Furthermore, Qudah et al. (2023) analyze emerging trends in Islamic finance and financial technology, highlighting critical roles played by aspects such as financial inclusion and corporate governance. Improved digital financial literacy will, therefore, ensure access to the benefits of Islamic digital finance by as many people as possible and create a relatively inclusive and fair financial system. By equipping individuals with the knowledge and skills necessary to navigate the complexities of digital finance, stakeholders can cultivate a culture of financial literacy that permeates communities. This grassroots approach will enhance the overall financial resilience of individuals and promote economic stability in the long term. The rapid expansion of Islamic fintech, projected to reach $179 billion in OIC countries by 2026 (Dinar Standard, 2022), underscores the need for targeted financial literacy initiatives, particularly with the rise of blockchain, digital currencies, and other innovations (Glavina & Asmiatullin, 2023; Qadri & Malik, 2024). Blockchain technology, for example, is consistent with Islamic ethical principles due to its provision of transparency and accountability. However, users must thoroughly understand its applications, especially in domains such as privacy and security (Bashir, 2024). Education programs that interpret these technologies will not only empower users but also encourage broader adoption of Islamic fintech solutions.

Addressing gaps in digital literacy education can facilitate sound policymaking and foster a robust Islamic digital financial ecosystem. Policymakers must collaborate with educational institutions, fintech companies, and community organizations to design comprehensive literacy programs that address the unique needs of various populations. By fostering a deeper understanding of Islamic finance and digital tools, stakeholders can create an environment where individuals feel confident in their financial choices. This approach will ultimately lead to a more equitable financial landscape where everyone has the opportunity to thrive, regardless of their background or beliefs. In conclusion, the rise of Islamic fintech represents a significant opportunity to reshape the global financial landscape. By addressing regulatory challenges and promoting financial literacy, stakeholders can unlock the full potential of this burgeoning sector. As Islamic fintech continues to expand and innovate, it is essential to ensure that individuals are equipped with the knowledge and skills necessary to navigate this evolving space. Through targeted educational initiatives and collaboration among various stakeholders, the financial benefits of Islamic fintech can be accessible to a diverse range of individuals, fostering inclusivity and contributing to sustainable economic growth worldwide.

Digital Financial Challenges

According to previous studies, the digital finance sector faces various challenges. Kanapathipillai et al., (2023) and Mohsin et al., (2022), both highlight the need for improved cyber security and customer readiness, particularly in rural areas. Tokiran et al. (2021) and Sharizan et al. (2021) emphasize the importance of addressing digital divides, demographic factors, and the lack of financial literacy, particularly among the B40 group in rural areas. While digital services still encounter challenges in ensuring inclusiveness nationwide, there have been improvements. It's important to emphasize digital financial education and deliver it through digital platforms. In the long term, using technology in education was suggested can speed up the process of learning, and the intervention of technology in education was able to motivate modern students to be more focused in learning sessions (Zabir, 2018). However, when taking the factor of Malaysians coming from various demographics into consideration, it could be argued that learning using digital platforms requires knowledge, skill, and learning discipline (Ispriandina & Sutisna, 2019). Thus, it was suggested there is a need for more study and research to ensure the digital platform for Islamic financial education could be fully utilized by all Malaysians. Hence, the Malaysia government was also aware of the importance of digital platforms for financial education was already taken steps by introducing the National Strategy for Financial Literacy 2019 to 2023 (Financial Education Network, 2019) and then developing the Financial Sector Blueprint 2022 to 2026 (Bank Negara Malaysia,

2022) which both emphasize the use of the digital platform as an effective tool to literate Malaysian about financial education. Therefore, digital platforms are suggested to be the platform for Islamic financial education to increase Malaysian Islamic financial literacy.

Formal and Informal Digital Platform for Islamic Financial Education in Malaysia

According to Hishamudin et al. (2024), digital platforms for financial education can be categorized into two categories Formal and Informal digital platforms. The formal digital platform can be defined as a digital platform that is designed and developed specifically for financial education purposes while an Informal digital platform is defined as a digital platform that does not aim specifically at financial education but could be chosen by the users as one the platform for learning financial education. Figure 1 below shows the categories of formal and informal digital platforms that are suggested to be used for financial education.

Figure 1. Formal and informal digital platform for Islamic financial education in Malaysia

Formal Digital Platform

- MICRA (INCEIF)
- FIS E-Learning Portal (IFSB)
- Digital Learning (IBFIM)
- Online Course, Webinar and E-learning modules endourse by education institutions (currently there 28 University & College in Malaysia offering Islamic Finance Courses)

Informal Digital Platform

- Tiktok
- Youtube
- Facebook
- Instagram
- Twitter
- Telegram
- Reddit
- LinkedIn
- Blog

Formal digital platforms were suggested to be referred to as structured platforms developed specifically for education (Hishamudin et al., 2024). For instance, formal digital platforms used for education were including online courses webinars, and e-learning modules offered by universities and financial institutions. In Malaysia, formal digital platforms for Islamic finance could be found offered by courses in universities such as diplomas and degrees in Islamic finance and related. The courses or programs offered are designed to blend with theoretical and practical knowledge and are often recognized by accreditation bodies such as the Malaysian Qualifications Agency (MQA). In addition, for instance, organizations like the Islamic Banking and Finance Institute Malaysia (IBFIM) and the Chartered Institute of Islamic Finance Professionals (CIIF) provide professional certification courses and continuous professional development (CPD) programs through digital platforms. These certifications, such as the Certified Islamic Financial Planner (IFP) and Chartered Professional in Islamic Finance (CPIF), are highly valued in the industry, enhancing career prospects for professionals.

Moreover, Islamic financial institutions in Malaysia, also offer digital learning resources and webinars aimed at educating their employees and the public about Islamic finance products and services. These institutions often collaborate with academic and professional bodies to ensure the accuracy and relevance of the educational content. Table 2 below shows the formal digital platform that was developed with the help of financial institutions such as the International Centre for Education in Islamic Finance (INCEIF), Islamic Financial Service Board (IFSB), and Islamic Banking and Finance Institute Malaysia (IBFIM). The platforms developed are categorized into formal digital platforms for Islamic financial education as the purpose of development that is related to financial education.

In the other side, Informal digital platforms cover a wide range of non-accredited, community-driven educational resources. The use of digital media in education has the potential to improve academic outcomes and enhance the overall learning experience (Ramsurrun et al., 2024; Tazhenova et al., 2024). Through social media for instance, educators can create online communities, share resources, facilitate discussions, and provide instant feedback to enhance the learning process which also can promote collaboration, communication, and personalized learning experiences (Zdravkova & Basnarkov, 2022). It has been a crucial tool for communication, information sharing, and maintaining social connections during times of physical distancing and remote learning during pandemic Covid-19 previously (Sato et al., 2023) and is expected to continue playing a crucial role in education post-COVID (Nikolopoulou, 2023). Therefore, educators could be found extensively using social media platforms such as Facebook, TikTok, Instagram, and LinkedIn to share insights and updates on Islamic finance information.

Digital platforms are widely used nowadays, particularly by young adults. 96.8% of Malaysians reported by the Department of Statistics Malaysia (2021) have access to the internet. 99% use the internet to participate in social networks, and 89.4% use it to find information about goods or services. Concerning this report, Digital Malaysia 2022 globally stated that Malaysia is the 9th top country in the world most actively using digital platforms (Global Digital Insight, 2022). Other than that, as reported in 2020, 57.6% of digital users came from individuals between 20 to 35 years old and 9.3% were between 15 to 19 years old (Malaysian Communications and Multimedia Commission, 2020). In 2020, 86.7% of total users shared content on social media compared to group messaging, private messages, email, blogs, and forums (Malaysian Communications and Multimedia Commission, 2022). As for that, various types of informal digital platforms have been introduced and are regularly used by the community in Malaysia.

Figure 2. Top social media used by Malaysian young adults (Malaysian Communications and Multimedia Commission, 2022)

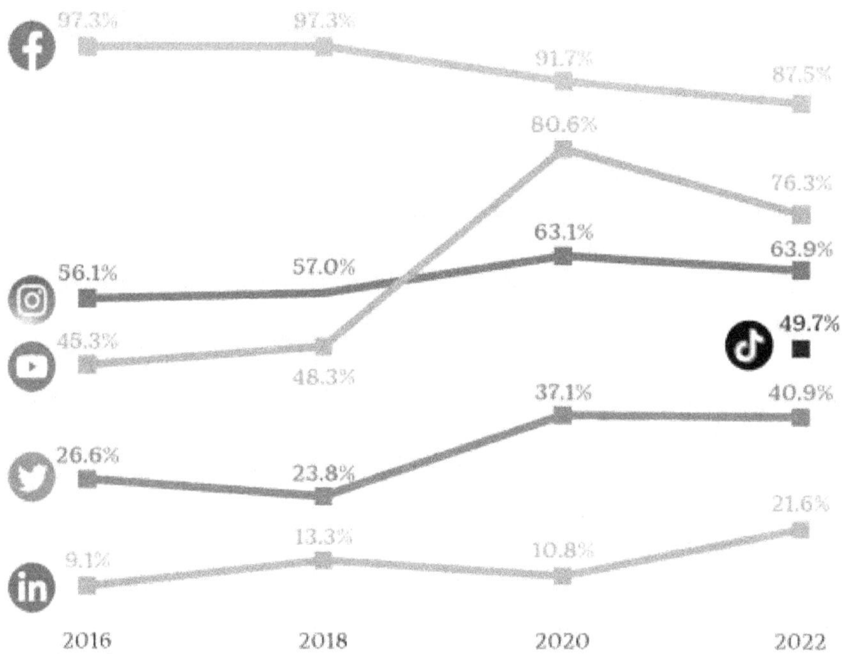

Figure 2 above shows the top social media used by Malaysians which was reported by Facebook has declined in percentage over the year from 97.3% of Malaysian users in 2016 decrease to 91.7% in 2020 and 87.5% in 2022. Next, Instagram and Twitter show the increasing statistics which started with 56.1% (Instagram) and 26.6% (Twitter) in 2016 increasing to 63.9% (Instagram) and 40.9% (Twitter) in 2022. Other than that, YouTube which started with only 45.3% in 2016 drastically increased to 80.6% in 2020 and currently declined to 76.3% in 2022. Afterwards, given the ever-increasing popularity of new social networking sites, LinkedIn shows a great percentage of growth which starts from just only 9.1% in 2016 to 21.6% in 2022. Lastly, TikTok demonstrated soaring performance in 2022 with a 49.7%

increase in popularity among Malaysians and was also suggested to affect the decrease of other social media such as YouTube and Facebook.

Furthermore, influential figures in Islamic finance utilize these channels to reach a broad audience, creating a community of learners who engage through comments, shares, and discussions. For example, TikTok and YouTube which are the platforms used for informal Islamic financial education, host numerous channels dedicated to the topic. Content varies from introductory videos explaining the basics of Islamic finance to detailed analyses of specific financial instruments. For example, the Channels "Islamic Finance Today" (@iftmagazine) and "Mufti Menk (@muftimenkofficial) attract thousands of viewers, leveraging the visual and auditory appeal of video content to enhance understanding and retention. Blogs such as "Islamic Finance News" (islamicfinancenews.com) and "Shariah Scholar"(muftiwp.gov.my/ms/) for instance, offer accessible articles that simplify complex concepts into easily understandable information. Besides, social media offers interactive discussion platforms. These platforms allow users to ask questions, share experiences, and provide peer-to-peer support. The informal nature of these discussions encourages participation from a wide audience, including those who may be hesitant to engage in more formal settings.

Table 2 below show the differential purpose between formal and informal digital platform.

Table 2. Formal and informal digital platform purpose of development

Formal Digital Platform	Purpose of Development
MICRA (INCEIF)	"To develop and nurture talent and experts in the Islamic financial services industry."
FIS E-Learning (IFSB)	"To facilitate training and personnel development in skill areas relevant to the effective supervision and regulation of the Islamic financial services industry."
Digital Learning (IBFIM)	"To be a global reference center for Islamic finance"
Informal Digital Platform	**Purpose of Development**
Tiktok	"To inspire creativity and bring joy."
Facebook	"To make the world more open and connected."
Youtube	"To give everyone a voice and show them the world."
Instagram	"Give people the power to build community and bring the world closer together."
Twitter	"To serve the public conversation."
Telegram	"To provide a secure means of communication that works everywhere on the planet."
LinkedIn	"To create economic opportunity for every member of the global workforce."

Sources: (Hishamudin et al., 2024)

METHODOLOGY

This study was conducted to achieve the research objective which is mainly to identify the digital tools of finance education. The research questions were listed and focused as below:

- How do young adults begin accessing Islamic finance education and knowledge?
- Are young adults interested in using digital platforms to learn about Islamic finance?
- Which educational platforms, formal or informal, do young individuals prefer for Islamic financial education?

To achieve the objective of this study, a survey was developed and used to collect data and answer the research questions. The research process began with identifying the problem, focusing on the financial decision-making processes of Malaysian young adults and their use of digital tools for financial education. Following this, clear objectives were developed, aiming to explore these behaviors and understand the adoption of digital financial education tools among this demographic. The study targeted young adults, defined as individuals aged 18-35, as this age group is at an early stage in financial independence and decision-making. Many young adults in this age group are not yet financially independent and may lack the experience to make sound financial decisions (Ansar et al., 2023; Sabri et al., 2023). Several definitions of "young adults" were considered for this study. The Association of Southeast Asian Nations (ASEAN) classifies youth as individuals aged 15-35, while the Malaysian Youth Policy 2015 defines youth as people between 18 and 30 (Islamic Development Bank, 2019). Additionally, the Department of Statistics Malaysia (DoSM) defines youth as those aged 15-24. However, this study adopted the young adult definition from previous research, which defines them as individuals aged 18-35 (Adzis et al., 2017; Loh et al., 2019; Petry, 2002; Yahya et al., 2021).

A questionnaire was then designed by adopting and adapting existing instruments from previous studies. It was distributed using a simple random sampling method via online platforms to ensure a broad and representative sample. In total, 311 responses were collected, but 21 respondents indicated no intention to use digital tools for financial education, leaving 290 valid responses for analysis. These data were analyzed using Microsoft Excel and SPSS software to provide descriptive insights and address the research questions. This comprehensive methodology ensured that the study provided meaningful insights into the financial behaviors of young adults in Malaysia, particularly regarding their approach to digital financial education. The descriptive analysis drew the conclusions, helping to understand how this age group engages with digital tools for financial education. The flow of this research process is visually represented in Figure 3, which outlines the steps from problem identification to conclusion.

Figure 3. Methodology of the study

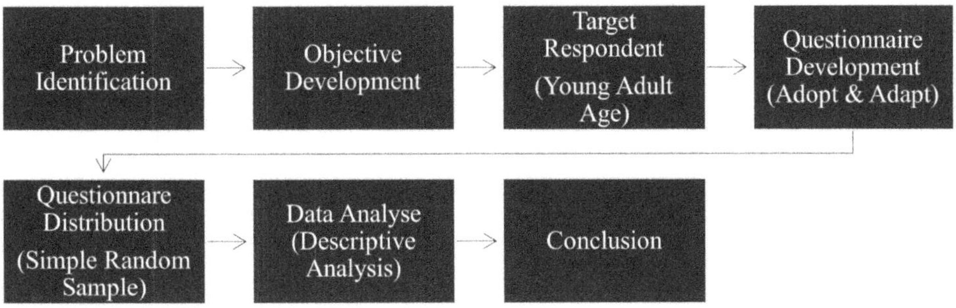

RESULT ANALYSIS

After the data was collected, it was properly processed in IBM-SPSS 25.0 before running the frequency analysis. Table 4 below shows the demographic of the respondents collected for this study which is 67% of respondents were female while in comparison 96 (33%) were male young adults. Aside from that, the highest number of respondents for this was between the ages of 18 and 20 (37%), and the second largest group was between the ages of 21 and 25 (35%). Next, 15% and 13% were between the ages of 26 to 30, and 31 to 35, respectively. Furthermore, just 6% of respondents were from high-income households earning more than RM10791, whereas the majority (55%) came from low-income families. Seventy-four (24%) respondents said their household income ranged from RM2501 to RM4850, while forty-two (15%) said it ranged from RM4851 to RM10790. Next, one hundred and twenty-eight (44%) respondents remained in Malaysia's center zone, forty-five (16%) in the north zone, fifty-five (19%) in the south zone, thirty-two (11%) in the east zone, and thirty (10%) in the western zone. The majority of this study's participants are degree graduates, accounting for 73% of the total. 15% have a diploma or skill certificate, 4% just have high school degrees, and the remaining 8% have a master's or doctorate in philosophy or comparable.

Table 4. Demographic of respondents

Option in questionnaire	Frequency	Percentage
Gender		
Male	96	33.1
Female	194	66.9
Age		
18 - 20	108	37.2
21 - 25	100	34.5
26 - 30	44	15.2
31 - 35	38	13.1
Household Income		
Less than RM2500	161	55.2
RM2501 - RM4850	70	24.1
RM4851 - RM10970	42	14.5
RM10971 and above	17	5.9
Residential Area		
Central Zone - Selangor, Kuala Lumpur dan Putrajaya	128	44.1
North Zone - Perlis, Kedah, Pulau Pinang dan Perak	45	15.5
South Zone - Johor, Negeri Sembilan dan Melaka	55	19.0
Western Zone - Labuan, Sabah dan Sarawak	32	11.0
East Zone - Pahang, Kelantan dan Terengganu	30	10.3
Education Level		
Secondary School	12	4.1
Skill Certificate / Diploma	42	14.5
Degree	212	73.1
Master / Doctor of Philosophy	24	8.3

Further subsection (4.1, 4.2, and 4.3) explains the findings according to the research objectives.

Education Resources for Islamic Finance

From the research conducted, the data was descriptively analyzed and interpreted as the following result below. First, this study presents the findings of young adult's access to education resources for Islamic finance in their early stages. Answering the first research question: How do young adults begin accessing Islamic finance education and knowledge? Thus, Table 5 and Figure 3 below show several resources which are parents, schools or universities, friends, social media, and financial courses. The result shows that most respondents begin learning their Islamic financial education at school or university, with 37% following social media (25%). Based on these findings, an educational institution in Malaysia was suggested to be the initial platform for finance education to reach the Malaysian younger generation. However, it was also 24% of respondents reported that their parents introduced Islamic finance education to them which was unexpectedly surprising. Parent was suggested to be the first teachers for most individuals and for the young generation since financial education also might be started at home. Very few admit attending financial courses to learn Islamic financial education, which was only 5%, which may be the fact that to attend the courses for finance education formally requires some cost. Lastly, the findings also show that only 8% of Malaysian young adults begin to get their financial education from friends. It could be suggested that the various social circle types might be one of the factors affecting this percentage of education resources for Islamic finance.

Table 5. Education resources for Islamic finance

I started getting my education in Islamic finance from: -	**Total %**
School / University	37.4
Social media	24.7
Parent	24.4
Friend	8.3
Financial Course	5.1
Total	100

Figure 4. Education resources for Islamic finance

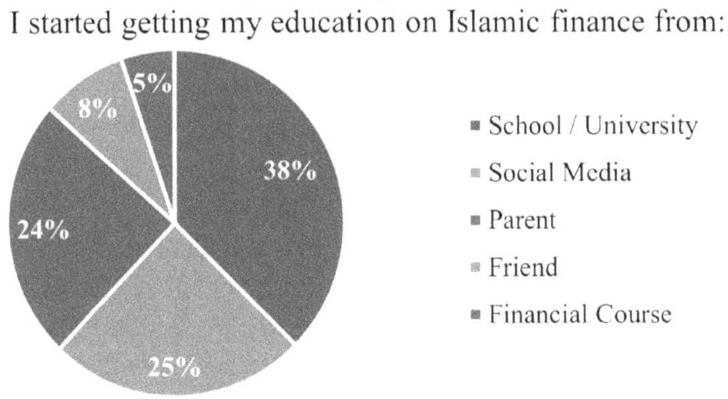

Financial knowledge, parental socialization, and peer influence significantly impact the saving behavior and financial well-being of young adults(Kadir et al., 2021; Mohamed, 2017). Primary school children in Malaysia demonstrate high financial literacy levels, with parents favoring interactive and engaging methods for teaching financial concepts (Murugiah et al., 2023). The frequency of observing and interacting with parents regarding finances positively correlates with the acquisition of financial knowledge and behavior, while peer influence primarily affects financial behavior (Mohamed, 2017). These findings emphasize the crucial roles of schools, teachers, and parental involvement in enhancing financial literacy (Murugiah et al., 2023). It was suggested that policymakers should focus on strategies to improve financial knowledge and maximize the influence of parents and peers to encourage better saving behavior and financial well-being among youth in emerging countries like Malaysia (Kadir et al., 2021). Interestingly, financial education can create spillover effects, with students transferring knowledge to their parents, especially when face-to-face interaction is frequent (Kallenos et al., 2024). Peer pressure significantly influences financial behavior (Mohammed Esmail Alekam et al., 2018). These findings highlight the complex interplay of factors affecting financial knowledge acquisition and behavior, emphasizing the importance of tailored financial education programs for different demographic groups. On the other hand, this study contributes to current findings to expand on Islamic financial knowledge. Most of the respondents mentioned that they first encountered Islamic financial knowledge during their time at school and university. As a result, it could be recommended that educational institutions prioritize including Islamic financial knowledge in their syllabus, courses, and activities, such as incorporating it into the curriculum. This would increase exposure and introduce this knowledge to the younger generation.

Intention to Use Digital Platforms for Islamic Financial Education

The respondents in this study were asked does they had the intention to use digital platforms to learn Islamic financial education to answer the second research question. Table 6 and Figure 4 below show young adults' intention to use digital platforms to learn Islamic financial knowledge. It was found that of the total of 311 young adults, 21 do not intend to use digital platforms for Islamic financial education. As a result. 93% of total young adults are found to have the intention to use digital platforms for Islamic finance education. These findings show that the young adult generation that lives in the digital era was ready to accept the changes in education from the traditional way to being digital that offered a wider range to reach people, less energy, time-consuming, and cost. Although previously, most respondents first learned about Islamic financial knowledge through schools or universities, they now prefer to acquire Islamic financial education through digital platforms. The findings of this study also were supported by a previous study by Ahmed & Mustafa, (2023) which investigated and found that digital platforms serve as alternative sources for acquiring Islamic knowledge, particularly among Muslim youth. The digitalization of Islamic economics and finance is gaining traction, particularly among Generation Z, who are highly engaged with digital technology (Nusaibah, 2023). This trend is reflected in the adoption of innovative teaching methods such as student-centered learning, project-based learning, and mind mapping in Islamic economics education (Beik & Arsyianti, 2021). Furthermore, e-learning platforms have shown promise in effectively transmitting Islamic values to students, addressing the declining role of family and community in character development (Syarif, 2020). These developments highlight the potential of digital technology to enhance Islamic financial education.

Table 6. Intention to use digital platforms for Islamic financial education

Do you want to use a digital platform to learn Islamic financial knowledge?	Frequency	%
Yes	290	93
No	21	7
Total	311	100

Figure 5. Intention to use digital platform to learn Islamic financial knowledge

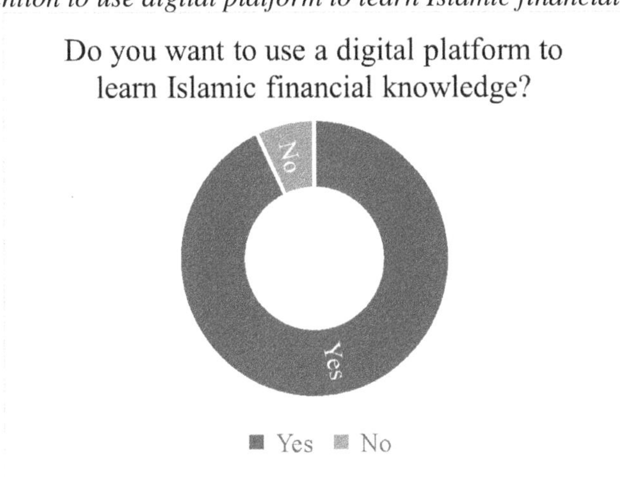

The Preference Platform between Formal and Informal

This study further answers the third research question: Which educational platforms, formal or informal, do young adults prefer for Islamic financial education? The findings showed that young adults mostly were unaware of the existence of official platforms and preferred to use informal digital platforms, as shown in Table 7 below. Malaysia's young adults in this study choose informal digital platforms such as Twitter, Instagram, YouTube, TikTok, and Facebook to learn about Islamic financial education. Thus, these findings support the previous findings that informal digital platforms are preferred over formal education platforms (Cooper et al., 2022). Table 7 and Figure 5 below show the outcome of the study where the preference platform of Malaysian young adults was informal rather than formal digital platform. The study shows that 97% of Malaysian young adults have used Informal digital platforms and only 29% have experience using formal digital platforms to learn Islamic finance.

Table 7. The preference platform between formal and informal

Digital Platform	Used (%)	Never (%)
Informal	97.3	2.7
Formal	29	71

Figure 6. The preference platform between formal and informal

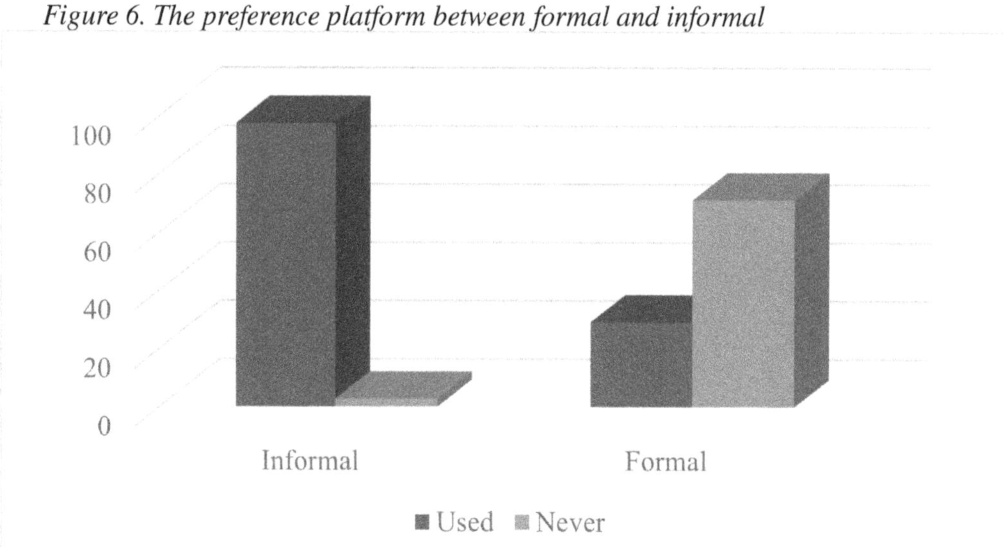

Figure 7 illustrate the use of websites for learning about Islamic finance. The majority of respondents (71%) have never utilized these platforms learning Islamic finance. Among the respondents, 10% have used AKPK Online Learning, 8% have engaged with IBFIM Digital Learning, 5% have accessed the FIS E-Learning Portal, 4% have used MICRA by INCEIF, and 3% have explored the uLearnMONEY website.

Figure 7. Formal platforms used by Malaysian young adults for Islamic financial education

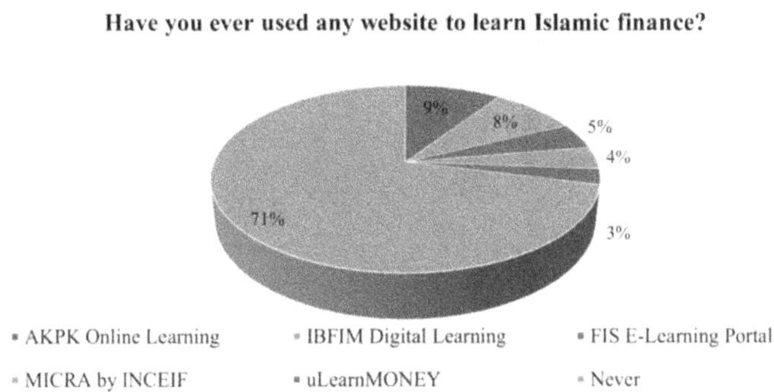

Furthermore, Figure 8 below shows the informal digital platform that is mostly reported used by Malaysian young adults in this study to learn Islamic finance which is on Twitter with 21% and the second most used on TikTok with 21%. Next is Instagram with 20% followed by YouTube 19% and Facebook 17% used by Malaysian young adults for Islamic financial education.

Figure 8. Informal platforms used by Malaysian young adults for Islamic financial education

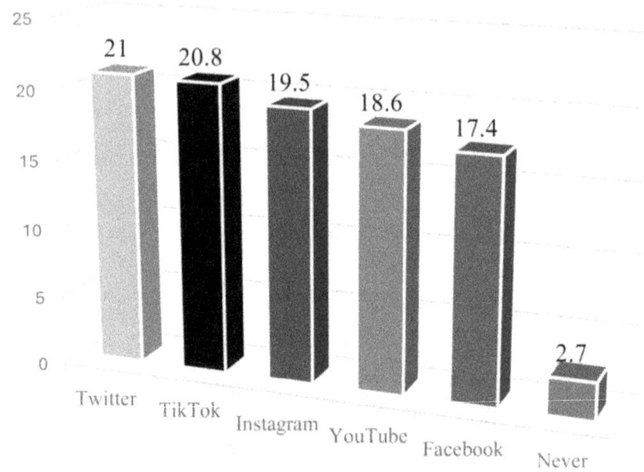

Although, in a previous section (2.3), it was reported that Facebook is one of the top social media platforms used by Malaysians (Malaysian Communications and Multimedia Commission, 2022), however, in this study, was found that when it comes to acquiring Islamic financial knowledge, young adults prefer to use Twitter, followed by TikTok. These social media platforms have a significant impact on this specific group in the Malaysian context. In Indonesia, several studies (Dayyan et al., 2023; Fahmi et al., 2023; Gunawan et al., 2020; Rachmat Riski et al., 2024) have shown that social media, particularly Instagram, greatly contributes to the learning of Islamic finance knowledge. Ahmed & Mustafa, (2023) noted a shift from traditional methods of acquiring Islamic knowledge to the use of online platforms and social media, particularly among Muslim youth. Social media influencers such as Ahmed Al Sayed have a significant influence on Muslim youth in the Arab world, as they conduct online Islamic education courses and attract large followers which then online platforms, including social media, help Muslim youth confirm their identity and satisfy their desire for Islamic knowledge (Ahmed & Mustafa, 2023). Susilawati et al., (2021) highlighted the need for utilizing social media for educational purposes and providing adequate supervision, aligning with the familiarity of Generation Z with this platform. Since influencers play an important role in delivering Islamic financial knowledge, individuals should identify the background of the influencer before deciding to accept their advice (Gunawan et al., 2020; Lutfi & Prihatiningrum, 2023).

It is important to prioritize Islamic financial knowledge as it involves an understanding of Shariah. However, it could be highlighted that young individuals should be cautious when learning about it through social media, ensuring the content is legitimate and factual. It is suggested to address the challenge of developing Shariah-based knowledge to prevent the spread of misinformation and misunderstandings in social media. This is important since previous studies (Dayyan et al., 2023; Sconti, 2022) have shown that social media significantly impacts individuals' decisions regarding Islamic finance and literacy, including their use of banking and financial products. In relation, also a need for a better understanding of the community for its development and adoption, especially in Islamic digital which can promote more financial inclusion (AB. Aziz, 2022). Other than that, it was suggested to look into the depth understanding on what the factor that contribute to the preference digital platform for Islamic financial Literacy (Hishamudin et al., 2025).

Government Initiatives and Possible Contributions to Enhancing Islamic Financial Literacy

Digital transformation in financial education within both formal and informal platforms could not have been addressed without the required technological infrastructure necessary for Islamic finance education to develop. This has been addressed in Malaysia through proactive government efforts to ensure that the technological infrastructure is highly developed across the country. The implementation of the JENDELA initiative exemplifies a joint endeavor that includes the Ministry of Communications and Multimedia Malaysia (KKMM), the Malaysian Communications and Multimedia Commission (MCMC), along with key communication service providers. Together, these organizations aim to improve the accessibility of broadband services and develop the necessary digital infrastructure essential for the widespread adoption of 5G technology. Recent studies emphasize the significance of JENDELA in the digital transformation of Malaysia (Abdullah et al., 2023).

Research conducted by MCMC (2022) emphasizes the critical importance of the JENDELA initiative in mitigating the digital divide in Malaysia, facilitating fair access to digital services throughout urban and rural areas. Furthermore, the collaborative endeavors involving KKMM, MCMC, and service providers are acknowledged as a commendable instance of successful public-private partnership in the enhancement of digital infrastructure (MCMC, 2022) . The integration has, therefore, become imperative to make sure that this digital economy does indeed remain all-inclusive and reaches all sections of society, particularly for those people who either prefer or need financial products that are ‘Sharia-compliant.’ In summary, the JENDELA Action Plan represents a critical element of Malaysia’s approach to digitalization, with the objective of establishing a robust digital infrastructure that promotes the nation's economic development and technological progress. Integrating Islamic digital financial literacy education into this initiative can facilitate the equitable distribution of the advantages associated with digitalization, making them available to all segments of society.

Way Forward for Policies Implementation

The National Financial Literacy Strategy 2019-2023 was introduced to bridge financial gaps across Malaysia to empower individuals with essential financial knowledge and tools to enhance their economic well-being. In response to the fast changes in the financial situation, the National Strategy emphasizes embedding financial education from an early age, providing access to necessary financial management resources, and promoting responsible financial behaviors. Furthermore, there is a need for a holistic approach to reach various demographic groups, which are young adults, working professionals, retirees, and vulnerable communities. Aside from that, by addressing important concerns such as low savings rates, high levels of household debt, and insufficient retirement planning, the strategy sees financial literacy as a significant aspect of national economic resilience, as well as a means of improving individual wealth. Also, by providing residents with knowledge and skills, this project seeks to develop a culture of financial responsibility consistent with long-term economic success. This research, therefore, suggested highlighting the strategy to emphasize Islamic digital financial literacy. As Malaysia is a global leader in Islamic finance, there is a need for a pulling factor to ensure that the majority of Malaysians understand Islamic financial principles. Given that Islamic finance operates on distinct ethical principles such as risk-sharing, the prohibition of interest (riba), and ethical investing, it is essential that financial literacy in Malaysia encompasses these values to meet the needs of the population, especially those interested in Shariah-compliant options. Thus, the strategy promotes the use of digital tools and platforms to educate the public on foundational Islamic financial concepts like zakat (almsgiving), waqf (endowment), and qard hasan (interest-free loans). Through digital resources, the initiative aims to make Islamic financial education more interactive and accessible, particularly for younger tech-savvy Malaysians, who are more likely to engage through digital platforms.

The Bank Negara Malaysia (BNM) Financial Sector Blueprint 2022-2026, which aligns with the National Financial Literacy Strategy, aims to make the financial industry more inclusive, resilient, and sustainable by focusing on digital transformation. The Blueprint acknowledges that digitalization is helping to achieve these objectives, particularly as the financial sector shows rapid transitions towards online platforms. Emphasizing digital literacy with financial literacy is critical to preventing growing gaps between financially and digitally literate people. By encouraging digital financial literacy, the blueprint hopes to guarantee that all Malaysians have the knowledge and skills to make safe financial decisions, particularly while using Shariah-compliant services. The Blueprint also emphasizes the importance of digital technologies in developing financial literacy; thus, this study provides insights into digital platforms for Islamic financial literacy. The Blueprint gives the public insight into various Islamic financial products, including Shariah-compliant savings accounts, investment options such as sukuk (Islamic bonds), and Takaful (Islamic insurance). With these tools, Malaysians can make well-informed decisions that are consistent with their financial goals and ethical convictions. Furthermore, the Blueprint uses fintech advances to promote Islamic banking by creating digital platforms that make it easier to obtain information, compare financial products, and interact securely. For instance, a digital platform that allows users to calculate zakat, learn about waqf projects, or apply for a qard hasan loan would make Islamic financial engagement more accessible and user-friendly.

The synergy between these policies could address a cohesive framework for advancing Islamic digital financial literacy. The National Financial Literacy Strategy lays a foundation of knowledge and tools for financial literacy. At the same time, the BNM Blueprint focuses on advancing the infrastructure and digital frameworks necessary to reach a broader audience. By combining financial education with digital accessibility, these policies democratize financial knowledge and support financial inclusion. Digital channels in financial education make learning about Islamic finance more convenient and engaging, allowing individuals to access resources, attend virtual workshops, and connect with financial experts. This approach is especially beneficial for younger generations who prefer digital mediums for learning over traditional settings. Numerous areas are significantly impacted by the National Financial Literacy Strategy and the BNM Blueprint working together. By guaranteeing that all Malaysians, irrespective of socioeconomic background, have access to financial knowledge and services, it first enhances financial inclusion. These initiatives give Malaysians, particularly Muslims, the tools they need to make financial decisions consistent with their faith by integrating Islamic finance into the digital platform for Islamic financial literacy. Second, because financial literacy encourages investing, saving, and budgeting, all of which support economic stability, these measures improve economic resilience. Third, by utilizing tools like zakat and waqf, the emphasis on Islamic finance supports sustainable development by advancing objectives like social welfare, poverty reduction, and community development. Lastly, by building trust in the financial system, these policies make financial services more transparent and trustworthy, especially for those who prioritize Sharia-compliant products.

Despite the all-encompassing strategy, putting these policies into practice presents difficulties. The digital gap is a major problem since not all Malaysians, especially those living in rural areas, have access to the digital tools required to take advantage of these resources. To fully benefit from Islamic digital financial literacy, ensuring everyone has access to digital resources is essential. Awareness and engagement are also barriers; financial literacy programs often struggle to attract participants, particularly if individuals do not see the content as directly relevant. Moreover, ensuring that digital financial platforms are Shariah-compliant requires collaboration with Islamic finance experts and regulatory bodies, adding complexity to developing fintech solutions. There are also gaps in foundational financial knowledge among Malaysians, which may complicate efforts to introduce Islamic finance concepts without first building basic financial literacy. As for addressing these challenges, several recommendations for future action are essential. First, to guarantee that resources for digital financial literacy reach rural areas, investments in digital infrastructure are required. Government-private sector collaborations may play a key role in enhancing digital literacy and internet access. Second, working with community organizations, Islamic banks, and religious establishments like mosques could increase knowledge and involvement, especially concerning Islamic finance ideas like qard hasan, zakat, and waqf. Third, information should be tailored to the needs of various groups; for example, elderly people, low-income families, and young adults may all need different approaches to financial literacy. Fourth, a monitoring and evaluation system can assist in determining how effective the methods are, enabling any necessary modifications based on data analysis and public input. Lastly, promoting private sector participation can help create a varied ecosystem of digital tools and financial literacy programs suited to the Malaysian market.

In conclusion, the National Financial Literacy Strategy 2019-2023 and the Bank Negara Malaysia Financial Sector Blueprint 2022-2026 were suggested to provide a comprehensive roadmap for advancing financial literacy in Malaysia. By emphasizing digital tools and focusing on Islamic finance, these policies address the unique needs of the Malaysian population while promoting financial inclusion, economic resilience, and sustainable development. Furthermore, with effective implementation, these policies can position Malaysia as a global leader in Islamic digital financial literacy, setting an example for other nations with similar cultural and financial landscapes. Malaysia is poised to create a financially literate, digitally connected, and economically resilient society through ongoing commitment and collaboration.

CONCLUSION

This study reveals that formal education, such as schools and universities, plays a significant role in acquiring Islamic financial knowledge among young adults. Formal education systems provide structured curricula that introduce students to essential concepts of Islamic finance, including the foundational principles of Shariah-compliant financial transactions, the importance of zakat (almsgiving), the concept of waqf (endowment), and the prohibition of riba (interest). By incorporating Islamic finance into their educational programs, institutions can equip young adults with the knowledge and skills to navigate the financial landscape effectively. This formal exposure lays the groundwork for more informed decision-making as these individuals transition into adulthood and encounter various financial products and services. In recent years, the rise of digital platforms has transformed how young adults access educational materials related to Islamic finance. The study explored the various digital sources utilized by young adults, revealing that they often rely on both formal and informal platforms. However, it was noted that there is a significant preference for informal platforms over formal ones when it comes to learning about Islamic finance. This preference underscores a broader trend where young adults gravitate toward sources that offer convenience, relatability, and an interactive learning experience. Informal platforms are often perceived as less intimidating, making it easier for users to engage with the content and ask questions. Among the informal platforms, social media sites such as Twitter and TikTok have emerged as the most popular choices for accessing Islamic financial education. These platforms allow users to consume bite-sized content that is easy to understand and share, creating an engaging environment for learning. The appeal of social media lies in its ability to present complex financial concepts in a simplified manner, often through visual aids, infographics, and short videos. This multimedia approach caters to the preferences of younger generations who prefer dynamic content over traditional textbooks or lectures. Moreover, social media platforms provide opportunities for peer-to-peer learning, enabling users to share experiences, insights, and advice, which can significantly enhance their understanding of Islamic finance.

Digital financial education also offers flexibility regarding time and pace, allowing learners to access information whenever and wherever they choose. This adaptability is particularly beneficial for young adults who may have busy schedules balancing studies, work, and social commitments. Additionally, online platforms can employ interactive and engaging methods, such as quizzes, simulations, and discussion forums, to enhance the learning experience. These interactive elements promote active participation, helping learners retain information more effectively. To further capitalize on the benefits of digital platforms, it is essential to facilitate open dialogue within these online communities. Platforms designed to enable users to ask questions, share experiences, and offer mutual support can create a more inclusive learning environment. Such informal spaces encourage broader participation, even from those who may feel reserved in more structured environments. This inclusivity is crucial for fostering community engagement and disseminating Islamic financial knowledge.

The study indicates that Malaysian young adults are particularly interested in utilizing digital tools as platforms for financial education, with a clear preference for informal digital sources. These findings provide valuable insights into the educational behaviors and preferences of young adults regarding Islamic finance education. Recognizing these trends can enable educators and policymakers to tailor their approaches to better align with the needs of this demographic. Furthermore, the increasing interest in digital platforms highlights significant opportunities for developing and improving online educational tools. These tools can increase accessibility and engagement, breaking down barriers that might prevent individuals from seeking financial education. However, it is essential to address the challenge of ensuring that the Islamic knowledge distributed on social media is legitimate and ethically sourced. Misinformation and lack of reliable content can hinder learning and lead to misconceptions about Islamic financial principles. Educators and policymakers must emphasize the importance of verifying information and creating a framework for assessing the credibility of digital resources. The impact of policies on the landscape of Islamic financial education cannot be overstated. The Malaysian government has made significant strides in promoting financial literacy through initiatives such as the National Financial Literacy Strategy and the Bank Negara Malaysia Financial Sector Blueprint. These policies aim to enhance financial literacy across various demographics, specifically focusing on digital financial education. By prioritizing integrating Islamic finance education into broader financial literacy initiatives, these policies create an environment conducive to the growth and dissemination of knowledge in this field.

Moreover, as the government and regulatory bodies increasingly recognize the importance of digital literacy, they can develop targeted programs and partnerships to support the use of digital platforms for Islamic finance education. Collaborations between educational institutions, financial organizations, and technology firms can create innovative tools and resources that cater to the unique needs of young adults. Additionally, leveraging insights from this study can help inform policy decisions and outreach efforts, ensuring that resources are effectively targeted to address the educational gaps in Islamic finance knowledge. In conclusion, this study provides a comprehensive understanding of the educational behaviors and preferences of young adults regarding Islamic finance education. It highlights the significant role that formal education plays in the initial acquisition of knowledge while also emphasizing the importance of informal digital platforms in fostering engagement and community learning. The findings suggest that educators and policymakers can leverage these insights to develop more effective and inclusive educational strategies that enhance financial literacy and empowerment among future generations. As digital tools continue to evolve, there is a pressing need to ensure that the information disseminated is legitimate and ethically sourced, fostering a knowledgeable and financially literate society. By focusing on these critical areas, Malaysia can be a leader in Islamic financial education, ultimately contributing to a more informed and empowered citizenry.

ACKNOWLEDGEMENT

This research is supported by the Ministry of Higher Education's Fundamental Research Grant Scheme (FRGS/1/2020/SS01/USIM/02/1).

REFERENCES

Abdullah, A., Mohd Zaidi, N. S., & Asar, A. K. (2023). Digital Wellbeing: Does It Matter in Malaysian Education? In *Industry Forward and Technology Transformation in Business and Entrepreneurship* (pp. 753-762).

Adzis, A. A., Bakar, J. A., & Shahar, H. K. (2017). Factors influencing young adults' debt in Malaysia. *The Journal of Business and Retail Management Research*, 12(1), 76–85. DOI: 10.24052/JBRMR/V12IS01/FIYADIM

Ahmed, E., & Mustafa, A.Esra Ahmed Abdulhalim Mustafa. (2023). The Thirst for Islamic Knowledge in the Digital Era. *Digital Muslim Review*, 1(1), 54–67. DOI: 10.32678/dmr.v1i1.12

Ali, S., & Khan, M. (2023). *The role of AI in enhancing Islamic finance*. SpringerLink. Retrieved from https://link.springer.com/chapter/10.1007/978-3-031-13302-2_11

Alshater, M. M., Saba, I., Supriani, I., & Rabbani, M. R. (2022). Fintech in islamic finance literature: A review. *Heliyon*, 8(9), e10385. DOI: 10.1016/j.heliyon.2022.e10385 PMID: 36060472

Ansar, R., Chekima, B., Lada, S., Lim, M. F., & Bouteraa, M. (2023). Determinants of personal financial management practices among Malaysian youth. *Asian Economic and Financial Review*, 13(12), 996–1007. DOI: 10.55493/5002.v13i12.4931

Aslam Haneef, M. (2018). Islamic Finance Education: Is There a Misallocation of Resources Between Curriculum and Academic Talent? *Islamic Banking and Finance Review*, 05(01), 58–67. DOI: 10.32350/ibfr.2018.05.04

Aziz, A. B. M. R. (2022). Digital Transformation Through Islamic Digital Banking For Financial Inclusion. *Proceeding of International Conference on Science and Technology*, 12–19. https://doi.org/https://doi.org/10.36378/internationalconferenceuniks.v0i0.2818

Bank Negara Malaysia (BNM). (2022). Financial Sector Blueprint 2022-2026. *The Central Bank of Malaysia*, 1–121. https://www.bnm.gov.my/documents/20124/5915429/fsb3_en_book.pdf%0Ahttps://www.bnm.gov.my/publications/fsb3

Bashir, M. S. (2024). Globalization, Digitalization, and Financial Inclusion in Islamic Banking. In Globalization, Digitalization, and Financial Inclusion in Islamic Banking (p. 37). DOI: 10.4018/979-8-3693-4111-7.ch012

Beik, I. S., & Arsyianti, L. D. (2021). Application of SCL, PBL, and MM In Teaching Islamic Economics And Finance. *Teaching and Research Methods for Islamic Economics and Finance*, 137–151. https://doi.org/http://dx.doi.org/10.4324/9781003252764-12

Biplob, H., & Abdullah, M. (2019). The importance of islamic financial literacy for muslims: a general review. *Islam & Civilisational Renewal, 10*(1).

Cooper, B. R., Concilla, A., Albrecht, J. M., Bhukhan, A., Laughter, M. R., Anderson, J. B., Rundle, C. W., Mceldrew, E. C., & Presley, C. L. (2022). *Social Media as a Medium for Dermatologic Education*. 103–109. DOI: 10.1007/s13671-022-00359-4

Dayyan, M., Prodi, M., Syariah, P., & Langsa, I. (2023). Analysis Sharia Financial Literacy of Kualasimpang City Community in The Digital Era. *Jurnal Ekonomi Syariah* [JESKaPe]. *Akuntansi Dan Perbankan*, 7(2), 134–146. DOI: 10.52490/jeskape.v7i2.1459

Department of Statistics Malaysia. (2021). *Ict Use and Access By Individuals and Households Survey Report 2021*. Issue April.

Fahmi, M., Warman, A. B., & Hayati, R. F. (2023). Literasi Hukum Ekonomi Syariah di Era Digital dan Kontribusinya bagi Penguatan Ekonomi Syariah di Indonesia (Studi terhadap Platform Instagram). *Al-Huquq: Journal of Indonesian Islamic Economic Law, 5*(1), 20–43. https://ejournal.iainmadura.ac.id/index.php/alhuquq/article/view/5729

Financial Education Network. (2019). *National Strategy for Financial Literacy 2019-2023*. Strategy.

Glavina, S. G., & Asmiatullin, R. R. (2023). Digital Currencies: Opportunities in Islamic Finance. Scientific and Educational Areas Under Modern Challenges, 128–135. DOI: 10.21661/r-560136

Global Digital Insight. (2022). *Digital 2022*. https://datareportal.com/reports/digital-2022-malaysia

Goel, I. (2024). Financial Education and Digitalisation: Analysis of Avenues. *Sachetas*, 3(1), 17–25. DOI: 10.55955/310003

Golden, W., & Cordie, L. (2022). Digital Financial Literacy. *Adult Literacy Education: The International Journal of Literacy, Language, and Numeracy*, 4(3), 20–26. DOI: 10.35847/WGolden.LCordie.4.3.20

Gunawan, M. R., Qurratu'ayuni Mustafa, M., Salsabil, N. Z., & Gunawan, M. R. (2020). The Effect of Social Media Content and Personal Background Performance on Financial Planning Awareness of Generation Z Muslim. *Ekonomi Islam Indonesia*, 2(2). Advance online publication. DOI: 10.58968/eii.v2i2.50

Hassan, R. (2023). *Digital finance literacy programs and their impact on financial inclusion. Journal of Islamic Accounting and Business Research.* Retrieved from https://www.emerald.com/insight/content/doi/10.1108/JIABR-03-2023-0092/full/html

Hishamudin, M. Z., Kamarudin, N. S., & Abdul Hadi, N. (2024). Formal and Informal Digital Platform for Islamic Financial Education. *Semarak International Journal of Islamic Studies and Culture*, 2(1), 18–28. DOI: 10.37934/sijisc.2.1.1828

Hishamudin, M. Z., Kamarudin, N. S., Hadi, N. A., & Ahmad, A. (2025). Intention to Use Digital Platforms for Islamic Financial Education in Malaysia: Structural Equation Model. *Journal of Advanced Research in Applied Sciences and Engineering Technology*, 49(1), 298–311. DOI: 10.37934/araset.49.1.298311

Impact, E. (2020). *Islamic fintech: Reaching a new generation.* Retrieved from https://impact.economist.com/perspectives/sites/default/files/eiu-diedc_article_2_26th_april_2020_0.pdf

Islamic Development Bank. (2019). *Country Youth Profile- Malaysia* (Issue February). https://www.jiasociety.org/content/10/6/148

Ispriandina, A., & Sutisna, M. (2019). Faktor-Faktor Penerimaan Teknologi Yang Memengaruhi Intensi Kontinuitas Penggunaan Mobile Wallet Di Kota Bandung. *Prosiding Industrial Research Workshop and National Seminar, 10*(1), 1046–1055. https://jurnal.polban.ac.id/ojs-3.1.2/proceeding/article/view/1462

Kadir, J. M. A., Shoukat, A., Naghavi, N., & Jamaluddin, A. A. (2021). The Saving Behavior in Emerging Country: The Role of Financial Knowledge, Peer Influence and Parent Socialization. *Pakistan Business Review, 22*(4). https://jmsnew.iobmresearch.com/index.php/pbr/article/view/396

Kallenos, T. L., Milidonis, A., Nishiotis, G. P., & Zenios, S. A. (2024). Financial Education and Spillover Effects. SSRN *Electronic Journal.* https://doi.org/DOI: 10.2139/SSRN.4094763

Kanapathipillai, K., Shari, A. N., Ajmain, M. F. B. M., & Rahman, N. S. B. A. (2023). Navigating The Digital Shift: How Acceptance Factors Shape Malaysia's Banking Evolution. *European Journal of Management and Marketing Studies*, 8(3). Advance online publication. DOI: 10.46827/ejmms.v8i3.1547

Loh, A. M., Peong, K. K. P., & Peong, K. K. P. (2019). Determinants of Personal Financial Literacy among Young Adults in Malaysian Accounting Firms. *GATR Global Journal of Business Social Sciences Review*, 7(1), 8–19. DOI: 10.35609/gjbssr.2019.7.1(2)

Lutfi, L., & Prihatiningrum, V. (2023). Social Media, Islamic Financial Literacy, and Islamic Banking Product Ownership: A Moderating Model. *EL DINAR: Jurnal Keuangan Dan Perbankan Syariah*, 11(1), 35–58. DOI: 10.18860/ed.v11i1.17803

Lyons, A., & Kass-Hanna, J. (2021). A Multidimensional Approach to Defining and Measuring Financial Literacy in the Digital Age. SSRN *Electronic Journal*. DOI: 10.4324/9781003025221-7

Malaysian Communications and Multimedia Commission. (2020). *Internet Users Survey*. https://www.mcmc.gov.my/skmmgovmy/media/General/pdf/IUS-2020-Report.pdf

Malaysian Communications and Multimedia Commission. (2022). Internet users survey. In *Malaysian Communications And Multimedia Commission*. https://www.mcmc.gov.my/skmmgovmy/media/General/pdf/Internet-Users-Survey-2018-(Infographic).pdf

Mishra, D. M. K. (2019). Financial Literacy and Education for Improving Financial Skills. SSRN *Electronic Journal*. https://doi.org/DOI: 10.2139/SSRN.3488670

Mohamed, N. A. (2017). Financial socialization: A cornerstone for young employees' financial well-being. *Reports on Economics and Finance*, 3, 15–35. DOI: 10.12988/ref.2017.711

Mohammed Esmail Alekam, J., & Salniza, Md. S., & Sanuri, Mohd. M. (. (2018). The Effect of Family, Peer, Behavior, Saving and Spending Behavior on Financial Literacy among Young Generations. *International Journal of Organizational Leadership*, 7(3), 309–323. DOI: 10.33844/ijol.2018.60258

Mohsin, M. I. A., Ahmad, R., & Chan, W. M. (2022). Exploring Digitalization of Malaysian Banking and Fintech Companies' Services from the Customer's Perspective. *International Journal of Management and Applied Research*, 9(2), 140–160. DOI: 10.18646/2056.92.22-007

Morgan, P., Huang, B., & Trinh, L. Q. (2019). The Need to Promote Digital Financial Literacy for the Digital Age. In *The Future of Work and Education for the Digital Age. In Realizing Education for All in the Digital Age*. https://www.adb.org/sites/default/files/publication/503706/adbi-realizing-education-all-digital-age.pdf#page=56

Murugiah, L., Ismail, R., Taib, H. M., Applanaidu, S. D., & Long, M. N. H. B. H. (2023). Children's understanding of financial literacy and parents' choice of financial knowledge learning methods in Malaysia. *MethodsX*, 11, 102383. Advance online publication. DOI: 10.1016/j.mex.2023.102383 PMID: 37767158

Nagimova, A. (2022). Islamic Fintech: Digitalization of Global Islamic Finance. *World Economy and International Relations*, 66(5), 50–58. DOI: 10.20542/0131-2227-2022-66-5-50-58

Negara Malaysia, B. (2019). *Commission Malaysia, S.* National Strategy for Financial Literacy.

Nikolopoulou, K. (2023). Digital Education in the Post-Covid Era: Challenges and Opportunities to Explore. *IFIP Advances in Information and Communication Technology, 685 AICT*, 3–14. DOI: 10.1007/978-3-031-43393-1_1

Nusaibah, umu. (2023). Digitalisasi Ekonomi Syariah di Kalangan Generasi Z Untuk Peningkatan Literasi Keuangan Syariah (Studi Kasus Mbanking BSI). *Musyarakah: Journal of Sharia Economic (MJSE), 12*(1), 12–22. DOI: 10.24269/mjse.v12i1.6695

Petry, N. M. (2002). A comparison of young, middle-aged, and older adult treatment-seeking pathological gamblers. *The Gerontologist*, 42(1), 92–99. DOI: 10.1093/geront/42.1.92 PMID: 11815703

Qadri, H. M.-D., & Malik, F. A. (2024). Emergence of Islamic Digital Economy. In Islamic Finance in the Modern Era (p. 14). DOI: 10.4324/9781003366751-2

Qudah, H., Malahim, S., Airout, R., Alomari, M., Hamour, A. A., & Alqudah, M. (2023). Islamic Finance in the Era of Financial Technology: A Bibliometric Review of Future Trends. *International Journal of Financial Studies*, 11(2), 76. DOI: 10.3390/ijfs11020076

Rachmat Riski, T., Sulistianingsih, H., Ekonomi Dan Bisnis, F., & Dharma Andalas, U. (2024). Literasi Keuangan, Media Sosial dan Perilaku investasi Instrument Keuangan Syariah Generasi Muda dikota Padang. *Jurnal Ekonomi Dan Bisnis Dharma Andalas*, 26(1), 176–189. DOI: 10.47233/jebd.v26i1.1244

Sabri, M. F., Anthony, M., Law, S. H., Rahim, H. A., Burhan, N. A. S., & Ithnin, M. (2023). Impact of financial behaviour on financial well-being: Evidence among young adults in Malaysia. *Journal of Financial Services Marketing*, 0123456789. Advance online publication. DOI: 10.1057/s41264-023-00234-8

Saputra, K. D., Rahmaastri, D. A., Setiawan, K., Suryani, D., & Purnama, Y. (2019). Mobile financial management application using google cloud vision API. *Procedia Computer Science*, 157, 596–604. DOI: 10.1016/j.procs.2019.09.019

Sato, S. N., Condes Moreno, E., Rubio-Zarapuz, A., Dalamitros, A. A., Yañez-Sepulveda, R., Tornero-Aguilera, J. F., & Clemente-Suárez, V. J. (2023). Navigating the New Normal: Adapting Online and Distance Learning in the Post-Pandemic Era. *Education Sciences 2024, Vol. 14, Page 19, 14*(1), 19. DOI: 10.3390/educsci14010019

Sconti, A. (2022). Digital vs. in-person financial education: What works best for Generation Z? *Journal of Economic Behavior & Organization*, 194, 300–318. DOI: 10.1016/j.jebo.2021.12.001

Sharizan, S., Redzuan, N. H., & Rosman, R. B. (2021). Issues and Challenges of Financial Inclusion Among Low-Income Earners In Rural Areas of Malaysia. *Turkish Journalof Islamic Economics, 8*(Special Issue), 278–299. https://www.tujise.org/content/6-issues/16-special-issue-06-2021/5-a2376/tuj2376.pdf

Standard, D. (2022). Global Islamic Fintech Report 2023. In *Global Islamic Fintech Report*. https://cdn.salaamgateway.com/special-coverage/islamic-fintech-2021/Global-Islamic-Fintech-Report-2021-Executive-Summary.pdf

Susilawati, S., & Chakim, A. Hambali, Muh., Islamy, M. I., & Rahmaniah, A. (2021). *The urgency of digital literacy for generation z in improving learning of islamic religious education*. https://digitalcommons.unl.edu/libphilprac/5143/?utm_source=digitalcommons.unl.edu%2Flibphilprac%2F5143&utm_medium=PDF&utm_campaign=PDFCoverPages

Syarif, S. (2020). Building plurality and unity for various religions in the digital era: Establishing Islamic values for Indonesian students. *Journal of Social Studies Education Research*, 11(2), 111–119. https://www.learntechlib.org/p/217571/

Tlemsani, I., Zaman, A., Hashim, M. M., & Matthews, R. (2023). Digitalization and sustainable development goals in emerging Islamic economies. *Journal of Islamic Accounting and Business Research*. Advance online publication. DOI: 10.1108/JIABR-03-2023-0092

Tokiran, N. S., Hussin, N., & Shahibi, M. S. (2021). Challenges in Implementation of Digital Culture Environment among Rural Community in Malaysia: An Overview. *Journal of Asian Scientific Research*, 11(3), 25–33. DOI: 10.18488/journal.2.2021.113.25.33

Yahya, F., Wilson, S., Sochos, A., Talib, A. T., Singh, S. S. D., Khiri, M. J. A., & Khan, A. (2021). Parent-Child Attachment and Romantic Relationship among Young Adults in Malaysia. [TURCOMAT]. *Turkish Journal of Computer and Mathematics Education*, 12(5), 1343–1352. DOI: 10.17762/turcomat.v12i5.2026

Yunus, S. M., Kamaruddin, Z., & Embong, R. (2017). Towards banking jurisprudence: Understanding Islamic banking products in Malaysia. *International Journal of Academic Research in Business & Social Sciences*, 7(8), 215–228. DOI: 10.6007/IJARBSS/v7-i8/3223

Zabir, A. (2018). Pengaruh Pemanfaatan Teknologi Pembelajaran Terhadap Motivasi Belajar Siswa SMPN 1 Lanrisang Kabupaten Pinrang. *Jurnal Azhari, 1*(1), 1–10. https://eprints.unm.ac.id/id/eprint/9823

Zdravkova, K., & Basnarkov, L. (Eds.). (2022). *ICT Innovations 2022. Reshaping the Future Towards a New Normal. 1740*. DOI: 10.1007/978-3-031-22792-9

Chapter 6
Elevating Investment Confidence:
The Imperative of Legal Certainty in Islamic Economic Framework

Andi Fariana
Perbanas Institute, Indonesia

Prameswara Samofa Nadya
https://orcid.org/0000-0002-9889-9469
Perbanas Institute, Indonesia

ABSTRACT

Legal certainty and investment are closely intertwined in Islamic economic frameworks, particularly in Indonesia. Legal certainty, defined as the clarity of norms, serves as a guide and protection for justice seekers. Investment involves capital accumulation, knowledge transfer, job creation and development of disadvantaged areas, necessitating a stable legal environment. The government recognizes the crucial link between legal certainty and investment, addressing various issues like the environment, employment, and socio-cultural aspects. From an Islamic law perspective, legal certainty is fundamental and hinted at in the Al Quran, forming the basis for asset development through investment. the holistic view of investment in Islam encompasses material and spiritual dimensions, emphasizing honesty, halal and haram principles, and social responsibilities. By ensuring legal certainty, policymakers can create a conducive environment for investors, fostering economic growth and national development.

DOI: 10.4018/979-8-3693-5653-1.ch006

INTRODUCTION

The role of investment is not only as an alternative for financing development but also as a tool to integrate into the global economy. Moreover, investment can produce a multiplayer effect on national economic development, because investment activities are not only about capital and goods transfer but also knowledge and human resources transfer (Sulistiawati, 2012:29-50), also expand employment opportunities, encourage non-oil and gas exports to generate foreign exchange, transfer technology, infrastructure building and developing underdeveloped areas (Yohani, 2019). Therefore, many countries, including Indonesia, have made investment activities part of the general implementation of their national economy. Investment provides a great opportunity to support the creation of jobs, namely decent jobs that contribute to the preservation or restoration of the environment, and in 2060, predicted that there will be an additional 1.8 million to 2.2 million jobs, consisting of three sectors: renewable energy, sustainable land and agricultural revitalization as well as the circular economy, even from January to December 2021, 1,207,893 Indonesian workers were recorded from 128,258 investment projects (Ikhwan, 2022).

The economic growth targets in the 2021-2023 period are 3.3%, 5.6%, and 6.0%, set by the Indonesian government need to be accompanied by various comprehensive policies such as policies in the health sector, monetary and fiscal policies as well as international cooperation (the Ministry of Finance of Republic Indonesia, 2022) which, of course, will have an impact on investment activities. Attracting investors is not easy. Serious, systematic, integrated, and consistent efforts are needed to instill confidence in investors to invest their capital. Before investing their capital, investors' considerations are often based on economic principles and analysis, which is how to generate profits from the capital and all the resources used. Therefore, investors will conduct a feasibility study on various aspects, this is including economic, political, and legal aspects before deciding to invest. This aims to ensure the security of the investment. regarding this situation, at least potential investors will consider aspects of economic opportunity (Christanti & Ariany, 2011), political stability and legal certainty, which seem to be an absolute requirement.

The government of the Republic of Indonesia supports the need for comfort in investment by enacting Law number 25 of 2007 which guarantees investors' rights in investing in the territory of the Republic of Indonesia (Presiden Republik Indonesia, 2007), and is complemented by Omnibus Law, Law number 11 of 2020 concerning Job Creation which aims to create a quality business and investment climate, after previously Indonesia had many regulations regarding the investment that did not benefit to investors (Pardede, 2023), issued a List of Investment Priorities in Presidential Decree number 10 of 2021, as well as establishing the Indonesia Investment Authority which aims to increase investor confidence that Indonesia has well-managed investment institutions. This has at least an impact on the investment realization of IDR 431.48 trillion or an increase of 15.24% compared to the same period in the previous year (Kementerian Investasi / BKPM, 2024).

In an Islamic perspective, investment is in line with several principles, namely collaboration to achieve a better life (Ministry of Religion of Republic of Indonesia, 2022, QS 5:2)(Abu Dawud, 1992), financial freedom (Bukhari, 2024), as well as self-preparing to uncertainty (Ministry of Religion of Republic of Indonesia, 2022, QS 59:18-19). This perspective is important considering that most of the Indonesia's population is Muslim (Central Bureau of Statistics, 2024), where Muslims have a crucial interest in avoiding prohibited things, in addition to following orders and choosing to do things that are permitted (Bukhari, 2024). In several aspects, there is government interference with investments permitted by Sharia, both in enforcing rules based on ulema fatwas (National Sharia Council - Indonesian Ulema Council, 2024), as well as preparing instruments that meet Sharia compliance (Indonesia Stock Exchange, 2019).

Of these aspects, legal certainty concerning investment will be the focus and this study, it is specifically studied from the perspective of Islamic economic law as part of the national legal system in Indonesia because similar studies have been widely studied, therefore this perspective of Islamic economic law will be explored more comprehensively, not only based on a search for statutory regulations as positive law but also from the perspective of Islamic law in looking at investment and how Islam views the concept of legal certainty or whether Islam views legal certainty as something that important. This is all aimed at making potential investors feel safe, comfortable, and confident that investment is a way to gain profits and blessings on assets. Besides that, this study can be input for policymakers so that they can produce policies that provide benefits for many parties. Choosing the theme of legal aspects of investment based on an Islamic perspective is our effort to show the support for digitalization in the Islamic financial sector, where investment is a part of the financial sector that is greatly impacted by digitalization. For this reason, we ensure that legal and fiqh support in investment is crucial.

Research Method

This research is normative-legal research with a statutory approach and a conceptual approach as well as a comparative approach which aims to produce arguments and concepts. This research was carried out by first collecting related legal materials followed by conducting a study of investment both in terms of meaning, form and statutory regulations as well as conducting a study of legal certainty and then conducting an analysis by comparing positive law with Islamic law on both concepts. So that, at the end, it becomes a part that strengthen the Islamic economic law framework.

Results and Discussions

Indonesia as a rule of law makes the issue of legal certainty an important matter because it has implications for several aspects of state life, and talking about legal certainty will not be separated from the issue of legal politics or it could be said that in legal politics legal certainty is also needed as is the case in the formation of an Islamic economic legal system (part of national law whose values come from Islamic law) makes legal politics a catalyst and the formation of an Islamic economic legal system also an effort to create legal certainty in the economic sector based on Islam and one of which aims to trigger investment in all Islamic economic sector as they are currently developing, for example in the halal tourism sector and its supporting industries, including in the creative industry sector with a very wide range of economic activities.

Legal certainty is one of the three basic values important in law, being a principle apart from justice and the benefit of the law, and legal certainty is a form of protection for justice seekers against arbitrariness. Van Apeldoorn stated that legal certainty has two sides, it can determine the law in concrete terms and legal security, which means that the party seeking justice wants to know what the law is in a particular matter before starting a case and providing protection for seekers of justice (Mertokusumo, 1993). It can even be said that legal certainty is the fruit of law enforcement, and the principle of legal certainty is equality before the law which demands the same treatment in resolving the same case and applying differently to different cases. The link between law enforcement and legal certainty is very strongly illustrated by the opinion of Prof. Hikmahanto Juwana who stated that there are five reasons why it is difficult to enforce the law in Indonesia because law enforcement officers are subject to suspicions and charges of corruption or bribery, the rise of the judicial mafia, the law seems to be able to be manipulated and even only favors those with high social status, weak law enforcement because of the loss of people's trust and an apathetic and scornful society that tends to carry out street justice processes (Juwana, 2006). This causes weak legal certainty and has an impact on the investment, this impression is reinforced by Mc. Cawley described the condition of legal certainty and investment in Indonesia as "Each regulation seems to create another regulation, so that at the end lower-level officials in regional offices and ports feel free –even have to—determine vague things by issuing their regulations." (Siregar: 2022)

This usually unsatisfactory situation is often laced with the tendency of senior officials to bypass all the red tape and slowness by granting exemptions from regulations or by making public decisions at will laws. When this happens, it is often unclear whether they express their statements or implement government regulations. This statement indicates weak law enforcement which gives the impression of a lack of legal certainty in the field of international business transactions, which are investment issues.

Legal certainty as described above is the same as the Islamic perspective which makes it an important principle. Legal certainty is implied as a principle that states that no act can be punished except for the existence of a legal force or statutory regulations that exist in advance and are enforced regarding that act, and talking about legal certainty will not be separated from the law that has been established ordained by Allah, namely, the guidelines are found in Al Quran. Regarding legal certainty in Islam, one of the verses related to this is as hinted at in the Al Quran "...and we will not punish until we send an Apostle." (QS 17:15). This principle is the principle of legal certainty which does not only apply in criminal law, but also applies in civil law and certain cases (Harjono, 1968). Several principles in Al Quran which contain the meaning of legal certainty:

It is permitted to you, on the night of the fasting month, is the approach to your wives. They are your clothes and you are their clothes. Allah knows that you cannot restrain your desires; but He turned to you and forgave you; so now associate with them, and seek what Allah Hath ordained for you, and eat and drink, until the white thread of dawn appear to you distinct from its black thread; then complete your fast till the night appears; but do not associate with your wives while you are in retreat in the mosques. Those are limit (set by) Allah...
(Al Quran Al Kareem 2:187)

Likewise

Talaq (which can be referred to) twice. After that, you can reconcile again in a peaceful way or divorce in a good way. It is not lawful for you to take back something that you have given them, unless both are afraid that they will not be able to carry out God's laws, then there is no sin on either of them regarding the payment given by the wife to redeem herself.
(Al Quran Al Kareem 2:187)

These verses are indeed in the context of family law but are from the verses revealed in one of the studies. This gives a signal of how Allah establishes laws and or customs that apply in society with clear provisions, namely permissible eating and drinking and husband and wife relations at specified times during the month of Ramadhan, as well as providing legal certainty for a wife who is divorced. The description of this example confirms that legal certainty in Islam is the principle that is the basis for implementing law enforcement and justice because the principle is the foundation. Apart from being a foundation for enforcing the law, legal certainty is also an important consideration in deciding to take legal action, not only in terms of family law but also in other legal aspects, including legal actions in terms of investment.

Investment means to plant or *istathmara* in Arabic, means to make fruitful, develop and increase in number (Antonio, 2017). Meanwhile, in terms of terms, investment is defined as investment or capital participation in a particular business sector whose business activities do not conflict with Islamic principles, both the object and the process (Arifin, 2019). Investment is related to developing capital for future purposes and the important thing that needs to be considered when investing is paying attention to sharia provisions because obeying Allah's commands and avoiding Allah's prohibitions is a form of submission and has the highest position in Islamic beliefs.

The government is also aware of the importance of investment and the various conditions that can link legal certainty with investment. in this regard, the government has also issued various policies. Legislation was also issued. Several search results showed that Law No. 25 of 2007 which replaced Law No. 1 of 1967 concerning Foreign Investment and Law No. 6 of 1968 concerning Domestic Investment. Law No. 25 of 2007 states that investment is all forms of investment activities, both by domestic investors and foreign investment to carry out business in the territory of the Republic of Indonesia (this definition of investment is repeated as confirmed in Presidential Regulation No. 10 of 2021 concerning Investment Business Sector). Meanwhile, article 1 Point 4 states that investment is an individual or business entity that makes investment which can be in the form of domestic investment and foreign investment. the important thing is also stated in Article 3 that investment is carried out based on the principles of: legal certainty, openness, accountability, equal treatment, and no distinction between countries of origin, togetherness, fair efficiency, sustainability, environmental awareness, independence and balance of progress and national economic unity. Regarding legal certainty, this is further emphasized by the mention in Article 4 paragraph (2) point b that the Government guarantees legal certainty, business certainty and business security for investors from the licensing process until the end of investment activities in accordance with the provisions of laws and regulations. (Law of the Republic of Indonesia Number 25 of 2007 concerning Capital Investment) The confirmation of these principles indicates that legal certainty is the main thing and indicates that investment is influenced by many aspects have to be the focus.

Investment activities are indeed complex and one law is not enough for the problem to be resolved because investment will be related to other legal issues such as tax law, employment law, land law, trade law and other legal fields. Thus, legal certainty should touch all areas of law, especially those related to investment in certain areas and Article 3 of Law No. 25 of 2007 places the principle of legal certainty at the top of the 10 principles of implementing investment in Indonesia. This principle is linked to the theory of Lawrence W. Friedman which emphasizes that the effectiveness of law enforcement (which implies the existence of legal certainty) depends on the legal system which consists of three subsystems, namely legal structure, legal substance and legal culture, but the basis of these three aspects is actually legal culture (Sudjana, 2019), then legal certainty in the implementation of investment is not only determined by the legal rules contained in the Law but also touches on other aspects, namely legal certainty in the structure of law enforcement and ultimately becomes a legal culture because of these three aspects, namely substance, enforcement law and legal culture are unity that can create legal certainty. This can be interpreted as meaning that by structuring regulations on investment as intended by the issuance of Law No. 11 of 2020 (Omnibus Law) which was passed on October 5, 2020, it will not necessarily provide legal certainty from a law enforcement perspective because investment growth is not only determined by structuring regulations but are also influenced by other factors (Asari, 2022). Moreover, with the issuance of the Constitutional Court (*MK*) Decision Number 91/PUU-XVIII/2020 which stated that Law Number 11 of 2020 was conditionally unconstitutional, but then the Government in Lieu of Law (*Perppu*) Number 2/2022 concerning Job Creation was issued, according to the Deputy Chairperson Commission IX of the House of Representatives is an inconsistency from the government because with the Supreme Court Decision Number 2 of 2022 the government should revise (improve) the substance of Law Number 11 of 2020 because in the consideration of the Constitutional Court decision it is stated that Law Number 11 of 2020 is formally flawed because of the procedures the formation of the Job Creation Law was not based on definite and standard methods and methods as well as appropriate standards. Later in its formation there were also changes in the writing of several substances after the joint agreement between House of Representative (*DPR*) and the President (Dewan Perwakilan Rakyat, 2023). The polemic regarding Law Number 11 of 2020 should still be prolonged and create legal uncertainty, especially in the investment sector, which is one of the substances of the law.

Apart from the Law on Investment, several laws and regulations relating to investment include Government Regulation Number 8 of 2007 concerning Government Investment, which clearly stated in Article 2 that investment carried out by the government is aimed not only at obtaining benefits in economic but also in social benefits, and/or other benefits which generally aim at economic growth to advance general welfare. Apart from that, to regulate more technical operations regarding capital investment, several Financial Services Authority Regulations (*POJK*) were issued. All of these laws and regulations are Positive Laws that must oversee the implementation of investment, while from the perspective of Islamic economic law, all of these laws become guidelines from investment activities because Islamic economic law is part of the national legal system which is a transformation of legal raw materials (in this case Islamic Law) that live and develop in society (the living law), in other words, Islamic economic law is the entirety of legal regulations and provisions relating to Islamic business practices, or in accordance with sharia in order to improve the welfare and benefit of mankind (Mardani, 2014).

Apart from the various statutory regulations above, based on the perspective of Islamic economic law, the fatwa of National Sharia Council-Indonesian Ulema Council (DSN-MUI) can also be used as a guideline and related to this, among others, Fatwa Number 40/DSN-MUI/2002 concerning Capital Markets and General Guidelines for the Application of Islamic Principles in the Capital Market Sector, Fatwa Number 38/DSN-MUI/X2022 concerning Interbank Investment Certificates (IMA Certificates), Fatwa Number 33/DSN-MUI/IX/2002 concerning Islamic Bonds *Mudharabah*, Fatwa Number 32/DSN-MUI/IX/2002 concerning Islamic Bonds. This DSN-MUI Fatwa, even though the statutory hierarchy approach is not included or part of statutory hierarchy in question, the DSN-MUI Fatwa influences national life because many DSN-MUI Fatwas have been transformed into various forms of statutory regulations (Fariana, 2017), because the fatwa becomes a vehicle that 'raises' the values of Islamic law that live and develop in society (The Living Law) which is ultimately processed by legal politics so that it becomes a national legal system that applies to the entire population of Indonesia because legal politics can be a catalyst positive, namely changing Islamic law, which is one of the living laws, into positive law.

Islam as a religion has comprehensive norms and teachings, like other religions, asking all its adherents to believe and be sheltered under Islam to practice Islam in full totality (*kaffah*) as mentioned in the Al Quran "O you who believe, enter the whole of Islam, and do not follow the steps of the devil. Indeed, Satan is a real enemy for you." (QS 2:208). Islam brought by the Prophet Muhammad includes teachings regarding faith, worship, *muamalah*, morals including very clear commands and prohibitions. Meanwhile, the *kaffah* in QS 2:208 indicates a call to all followers of the Islamic religion for all movements of their lives to be aimed at being completely devoted to Allah with all sincerity. On the other hand, the meaning of this verse is 'enter into all the teachings of Islam', therefore preach Islam and practice it totally, and it is not permissible to take one part and leave the other part (Ahmadji, 2016).

In relation to *kaffah*, this means that the issue of investment is also part of the issues regulated in Islamic teachings because it is related to the issue of *muamalah* which must be understood and implemented. The argument states that the original law of all forms of *muamalah* is that it is permissible to do it unless there is an argument that forbids it (Djazuli, 2010:10). Economics is a *muamalah* activity so this proposition is a strong foundation. In Islamic perspective, economics aims at prosperity, namely external prosperity accompanied by inner prosperity, worldly and spiritual pleasures, a balance between material and immaterial (Pradja, 2012).

Therefore, the source of law in economic activities is the Al Quran, Hadith, Ijma or even other sources of law as in other *muamalah* activities.

Islam recommends investment so that wealth does not circulate only in the hands of the rich, this is stated in Al Quran (QS 59:7). This investment will provide multi-effect benefits, namely the creation of business opportunities and jobs (Pardiansyah, 2017). The concept of investment aimed at Allah will have an extraordinary impact as hinted at in QS 2:261:

> *The parable of those who spend their wealth in the way of Allah is similar to a seed that grows seven ears. In each ear a hundred seeds. Allah multiplies (rewards) from whom He wills. And Allah is all-encompassing (His gifts) and all-knowing. (Al Quran Al Kareem 2:261)*

Likewise, investment is needed to prepare the next generation, this is hinted as QS 4:9: "And let fear to Allah those who would leave behind their weak children..." Investment is also needed because no one knows what will happen tomorrow (QS 31:34), therefore preparing and paying attention to what has been prepared for tomorrow is a must (QS 59:18).

Besides several verses in the Al Quran indicating the importance of investment, the Prophet's hadith also guides us to invest, namely in the form of the Prophet Muhammad's business activities recorded in history. Rasulullah Muhammad had been doing business from a young age and his main capital was trust (*al amin*). This trust made it easier to get investors, apart from honesty which created trust, Rasulullah's competence as a businessperson was beyond doubt, as evidenced by the establishment of markets and trading places throughout the Arabic Peninsula which show an understanding of the world of business and the economy (Sitepu, 2016). In addition to honesty and understanding of business, the Prophet was always guided by the halalness of the product or business activity (according to the sharia). The current phenomenon is that when social media influences society with information that depicts a successful life with all its luxuries, collecting wealth to live well has become a dream, so it is easy to be tempted to collect wealth in a quick way, namely under the guise of investment without paying attention to its halalness, even though the Prophet 14 centuries ago had predicted this with the words: "Later there will come to man a time when man will not care where he gets his wealth, whether from halal or haram (Bukhari, 1991, No. 2083).

Investment is a form of economic activity and Islam does not prohibit this activity. Based on the verses of the Al Quran above (QS 2:261), investment is specifically defined as giving *infaq* which can produce up to seven times the income. Therefore, investment from an Islamic perspective is certainly different from investment in a conventional perspective which is only oriented towards increasing capital, gaining passive profits and increasing assets, whereas from an Islamic perspective, investment has social implications because the profits obtained from the investment are not only intended for investors but there are also parts which is given to help others (social dimension), namely utilizing *infaq* or alms or zakat or other practices which begin with an agreement when the agreement is made or when the contract is carried out so that from the start all parties involved in the investment are aware of the obligations stipulated.

In Islamic investment, regarding investment products or instruments is very limited because investment in Islam does not allow investors to invest their capital in products that are contrary to the sharia because based on the hadith of the Prophet:

> *Indeed, what is halal is clear and what is haram is clear, between the two there are matters which doubtful. Most people do not know about this matter of doubt, whoever protects himself from matters of doubt will save his religion and self-respect. Whoever falls into syubhat (doubtful) matters will fall into what is haram." (Hadith narrated by Muslim, number 2996).*

Moreover, it should also be noted that in Islam, investment, or activities in the economic sector in whatever form are aimed at making a profit, a formula has been established since the contract, namely profit sharing, which means the distribution of profits in accordance with the sharia, including if losses occur, they will be borne jointly (Fitrianingsih, 2021).

Islam through Al Quran and the example of the Prophet (Hadith) reminds us to have a positive attitude towards wealth. The Prophet emphasized that wealth is a deposit that will be accounted for one day, wealth is life's jewellery that can be enjoyed without being excessive, wealth is a test of faith because it is closely related to how to obtain it and how to use it and wealth is a provision for worshiping Allah in a way. Carry out orders and make peace with fellow humans. These things are guidelines to believe in and guide in managing assets, developing, or investing them because there is potential for the use of assets that is oriented solely to fulfil human desires and egoism so that in responding to, acquiring, spending and developing assets they often exceed limits. Ethics and morals even violate reasonable values due to greed to maintain and develop or increase these assets (Antonio, 2010).

On this basis, the principles in investment need to be observed, including not seeking fortune in the haram business sector, both in terms of substance and process, and not using it for haram things, not tyrannizing or being tyrannized, having justice in the distribution of income, transactions are carried out on the basis of mutual consent without any coercion, there are no elements of *riba* (usury), *maysir* (gambling), *gharar* (obscurity), *tadlis* (fraud), *darar* (damage/disadvantage), and do not contain immorality. These principles provide an understanding that Islam encourages investment but there are limitations that must be considered so that Allah will be pleased and bring blessings (Pardiansyah, 2017).

Suggestion

This chapter includes an in-depth explanation of how important legal certainty is for investment to strengthen Islamic economic law, which is expected to become a reference for efforts to strengthen regulations and innovations in the field of sharia investment. apart from that, it is also expected that in the future, referring to the results of this research, new research can be produced that focuses on strengthening legal certainty in the realm of digital investment, both investments in the form of existing securities, as well as in cryptocurrencies, especially related to the sharia-compliant products and mechanism of investment.

CONCLUSION

Legal certainty and investment are two things that are interrelated and cannot be separated. Investment is strongly influenced by legal certainty, while on the other hand, investment is also related to many aspects, including environmental and labor issues. In the view of Islamic economic law, investment issues are part of managing assets and assets are important because searching for or collecting assets, utilizing them, and managing or developing them is obligatory just like other acts of worship. Investment from an Islamic economic perspective is not only a material problem but has an impact on life in the hereafter, therefore the elements of honesty, halalness and social function aspects are important aspects. Taking these things into account, in the context of developing and strengthening the Islamic economy in Indonesia, it is appropriate to pay attention to build a legal system that will provide support for investment growth, especially investment in Islamic economic sectors because this has the potential to contribute to National Development. Government support for investors which has become increasingly visible in the harmonization of regulations recently shows real seriousness in being able to create a healthy investment climate in Indonesia, but this support should always be in line with Islamic aspects in investment, as Law number 59 of 2024 has included strengthening Islamic economics and finance into the national long-term plan 2024-2029 (Presiden Republik Indonesia, 2024).

REFERENCES

Abu Dawud. (1992). *Sunan Abu Dawud*. https://www.alkhoirot.org/2018/04/terjemah-sunan-abu-dawud.html#english

Ahmadij. (2016), Islam Kaffah: Tinjauan Tafsir QS Al Baqarah: 208. Jurnal Syariati, 2(2).

Al Quran dan Terjemahannya. (n.d.). Departemen Agama Republik Indonesia.

Ali, M. D. (1993). Hukum Islam: Pengantar Ilmu Hukum dan Tata Hukum Islam di Indonesia. Jakarta: Raja Grafindo, h. 43

Anam, K., & Qomariyah, I. (2020). *Asas-asas Hukum Islam dalam Hukum Modern*. Jurnal Al-Maqashidi.

Andrianto, F. (2020), Kepastian Hukum Dalam Politik Hukum di Indonesia. Administrative Law Governance Journal, 3(1).

Antonio, M. S. (2010). *Bisnis dan Kewirausahaan, Ensiklopedia, Leadership & Manajemen Muhammad SAW "The Super Leader Super Manajer" Jilid 2*. Tazkia Publishing.

Antonio, M. S. (2017). *Muhammad SAW: The Super Leader Super Manager*. ProLM Centre & Tazkia Multimedia.

Arifin, Z. (2009), Dasar-dasar Manajemen Bank Syariah. (Tangerang: Azkia Publisher, h. 56. Asari, M. I. (n.d.). (2022), Omnibus Law Untuk Menata Regulasi Penanaman Modal. Retrieved from https://rechtsvinding.bphn.go.id

Bukhari. (2024). *Shahih Bukhari*. http://103.44.149.34/elib/assets/buku/Shahih_bukhari_muslim.pdf

Central Bureau of Statistics. (2024, May 17). *Religion in Indonesia, 2024*. https://samarindakota.bps.go.id/id/statistics-table/1/MzI0IzE=/agama-di-indonesia-2024.html

Christanti, N., & Mahastanti Ariany. (2011), Faktor-faktor Yang Dipertimbangkan Investor Dalam Melakukan Investasi. Jurnal Manajemen Teori dan Terapan Tahun, 4(3).

Djazuli, A. (2010), Kaidah-kaidah Fiqih: Kaidah Hukum Islam Dalam Menyelesaikan Masalah-masalah Yang Praktis, Jakarta: Kencana, h.10

Fariana, A. (2017), Urgensi Fatwa MUI dalam Pembangunan Sistem Hukum Ekonomi Islam di Indonesia. Al Ihkam Jurnal Hukum & Pranata Sosial, 12(1).

Fariana, A. (2021), Legal Politics as a Catalyst in Forming Sharia Economic Legal System in the Indonesia's New Order and Reform Era. Ijtihad: Jurnal Wacana Hukum Islam dan Kemanusiaan, 21(2).

Fatwa-Laman 11-DSN-MUI. (n.d.). Retrieved from https://dsnmui.or.id, diakses pada 5 April 2022

Fitrianingsih. (n.d.). Investasi dalam Islam: Hukum, Prinsip dan Jenisnya. Retrieved from https://www.qoala.app/2021

Harjono, A. (1968). *Hukum Islam: Keluasan dan Keadilannya*. Bulan Bintang.

Ikhwan, N. (2022), Makalah di dalam webinar series 22 Fakultas Ekonomi dan Bisnis Perbanas Institute bekerjasama dengan kementrian BKPM

Indonesia Stock Exchange. (2019). *Surat Berharga Syariah Negara*. https://idxislamic .idx.co.id/edukasi-pasar-modal-syariah/sukuk-negara/

Juwana, H. (2006), Pidato di dalam Dies Natalis ke 56 Universitas Indonesia Kementerian Investasi / BKPM. (2024). *Siaran Pers*. https://bkpm.go.id/id/info/siaran-pers/ rosan-realisasi-investasi-terus-bertumbuh-indonesia-konsisten-jalankan-hilirisasi

Kementrian Keuangan Republik Indonesia. (n.d.). Proyeksi Pertumbuhan Ekonomi Indonesia 2022 dan 2023 kuat. Retrieved Maret 2022, from fiskal.kemenkeu.go.id/ publikasi/siaran-pers-detil/364

Mardani. (2014), Hukum Bisnis Syariah. Jakarta: Prenada Media

Mertokusumo, S. (1993), Bab-bab tentang Penemuan Hukum. Bandung: Citra Aditya Bakti Ministry of Religion of Republic of Indonesia. (2022). *Al Quran Al Kareem*. https://quran.kemenag.go.id/

National Sharia Council - Indonesian Ulema Council. (2024). *Fatwa DSN-MUI*. DSN-MUI.

Pardede, M. (2023). DILEMA REFORMASI REGULASI HUKUM INVESTASI DALAM SISTEM HUKUM SIPIL DALAM PERSPEKTIF JAMINAN KEPASTIAN HUKUM PENANAMAN MODAL (Suatu Upaya Peningkatan Iklim Daya Saing dan Jaminan Kepastian Hukum Penanaman Modal). *Jurnal Penelitian Hukum De Jure*, 23(2), 231. DOI: 10.30641/dejure.2023.V23.231-244

Pardiansyah, E. (2017), Investasi dalam Perspektif Ekonomi Islam. Economica: Jurnal Bisnis dan Ekonomi Islam, 8(2).

Peraturan Pemerintah Nomor 8 Tahun 2007 tentang Investasi Pemerintah. (n.d.). Retrieved from https://jdih.kemenkeu.go.id

Peraturan Presiden Republik Indonesia Nomor 10 Tahun 2021 tentang Bidang Usaha Penanaman Modal. (n.d.). Retrieved from https://jdih.setkab.go.id

Pradja, J. S. (2011), Ekonomi Syariah. Bandung: Pustaka Setia Presiden Republik Indonesia. (2007). *UNDANG UNDANG REPUBLIK INDONESIA NOMOR 25 TAHUN 2007.* https://ojk.go.id/id/regulasi/regulasi-terkait-lainnya/Pages/undang-undang-nomor-25-tahun-2007-tentang-penanaman-modal.aspx#:~:text=Mengatur%20ketentuan%20mengenai%20kebijakan%20dasar,serta%20mempercepat%20peningkatan%20penanaman%20modal

Presiden Republik Indonesia. (2024). *Undang-undang Nomor 59 Tahun 2024.* https://jdih.bappenas.go.id/peraturan/detailperaturan/3919/undang-undang-nomor-59-tahun-2024

RAS, H., & Suroso, J. T. (2020), Kepastian Hukum Dalam Hukum Investasi di Indonesia Melalui Omnibus Law. JIMEA Jurnal Ilmiah MEA (Manajemen, Ekonomi, dan Akuntansi), 4(1).

Sitepu, N. I. (2016), Perilaku Bisnis Muhammad SAW Sebagai Entrepreneur Dalam Filsafat Ekonomi Islam. Jurnal Human Falah, 3(1).

Sulistiawati, R. (2012), Pengaruh Investasi Terhadap Pertumbuhan Ekonomi dan Penyerapan Tenaga Kerja Serta Kesejahteraan Masyarakat di Provinsi di Indonesia. Jurnal Ekonomi Bisnis dan Kewirausahaan, 3(1), 29-50.

Undang-Undang Republik Indonesia Nomor 25 Tahun 2007 tentang Penanaman Modal. (n.d.). Retrieved from https://jdih.kemenkeu.go.id

Yohani. (2019), Pengaruh Investor Asing Terhadap Pengembangan Masyarakat Lokal di Indonesia. Jurnal Fiat Justicia, 5(1).

Chapter 7 Integrated Model of Islamic Digital Banking for Financial Inclusion Based on MAQASID Al-Shariah

Muhammad Ridhwan Ab. Aziz
Universiti Sains Islam Malaysia, Malaysia

ABSTRACT

The advancement of the current technology has totally changed the banking and financial services. Financial institution has been urged to react to the changes in order to provide a better service and product to the customers as well as to the underserved people. Throughout the development of digital banking, it will help many people to access the banking services in improving their socio-economic. However, the model of Shariah compliant digital banking is compulsory in order to achieve Maqasid al-Shariah for financial inclusion. The objective of this study is aimed to develop integrated model of Islamic digital banking based on Maqasid al-Shariah for financial Inclusion. Research methodology that has been applied is qualitative approach in which this research is conducted verification model with the experts. The selection of the experts is based on digital banking field and Shariah background. A general finding shows that, the integrated model is viable to be implemented in line with the current development of digital era.

DOI: 10.4018/979-8-3693-5653-1.ch007

INTRODUCTION

Banks around the world have operated in a highly competitive, frantic, and ever-changing market. Islamic banking and finance is the one of a sector that has contributed to economic development in Malaysia and worldwide. The model of Islamic banking is one of the rapid growing subsectors, and it has attracted the attention of both traditionalists and progressives in the field of Islamic finance. Islamic banking acts as alternative for conventional banking system that offered to the Muslim community. This banking system had offered justice and fairness in dealings as it prohibited the element of interest (riba), ambiguity (gharar), and gambling (maysir) as well as other prohibited element such as pork, liquor, and pornography in the transaction. This is in contrast to the conventional banking system, which allows what is forbidden in Islam in order to achieve sole profitability.

Islamic banks have been urged to reacts to the proliferation of information and communication technology in order to serve a better service to the community in the digitally fast-paced world. It is difficult to envision a world without the internet and mobile devices in the present day. They have introduced a great deal of disruption to virtually every aspect of business and have become fundamental to our way of life. The financial services industry is not exempt from the impact of the digital revolution, which is altering how consumers access financial products and services. Innovative technologies such as blockchain, the internet of things (IoTs), artificial intelligence (AI), and robotics have reached a stage of development where they can cause a disruption in the banking and finance industry. This includes both the conventional finance industry and the Islamic finance industry (Hassnian Ali, 2019).

Banks have no choice but to become digital due to the characteristics of digital environments, and they must eventually eliminate the divide between the physical and digital environments (Gill, 2016). In order to Islamic bank to respond to the digitalization mainstream, the development of Shariah compliant digital banking had been supported by Bank Negara Malaysia with issuing license for the IFI to offer digital banking services in Malaysia but it is necessarily to the applicant to meet requirement as standardized by BNM in which they required to provide the banking service to the underserved community (BNM, 2022).

The incorporation of financial inclusion is a significant component that must be incorporated into the development of digital banking. This is because the World Bank stated that if a country can pioneer an effort to enhance financial inclusion in developing nations, it will assist the country in alleviating poverty in developing and rising economies (World Bank, 2018). Apart from that, the model of digital banking based on Maqasid al-Shariah is important to the community as Maqasid al-Shariah serves to bring benefit to the community instead of harm. Maqasid al-Shariah is

Shariah objective that aimed to preserve the five elements including preservation of religion, mind, wealth, lineage and oneself.

Islamic digital banking is viewed as beneficial to the ummah because it offers Islamic banking and financial products that comply with Shariah law. It also facilitates extended financial inclusion beyond the current geographical reach of physical businesses. As a consequence, the physical distance between a consumer and a physical bank branch is becoming less significant throughout the era of Islamic digital banking. Therefore, it suggests that Islamic digital banking can make it easier for rural and urban Muslims to appreciate Islamic banking products from a social and economic standpoint (Ridhwan Ab Aziz M, 2021).

Furthermore, the progress of Islamic digital banking enables the marketing and promoting of halal products to non-Muslims in Malaysia, as halal discourse is recognisable to both Muslims and non-Muslims (Ibrahim, 2021). Therefore, this study is aimed to investigate on how integrated model of Islamic digital banking is in accordance with Maqasid al-Shariah for financial inclusion. Throughout this study, it will provide a better integrated model to practitioner and give better comprehension about digital knowledge to the unbanked society in order to adopt the digital banking platform henceforward.

LITERATURE REVIEW

There are a lot of study that had be done related to the development of digital banking and many experts and researchers had come out with various understanding of definition and concept of digital banking. In general, the term "digital banking" relate to the combination of online banking with traditional banking. It offers traditional banking services, but they can be accessed via a website or a mobile programme instead of a physical location. Digital banking makes it possible to perform a variety of banking transactions, such as opening a bank account, transferring funds, making remote payments, and setting up direct deposits, all without having to physically visit a location of the bank. Every single transaction that takes place in a digital bank is completed instantly and involves a significant amount of financial management, security, and adaptability on the part of the user (Santander, 2020).

According to Oanh Thi (2020), digital banking is a method of conducting business that makes use of a technological framework to facilitate connections and transactions between customers and financial institutions. It is not necessary for customers to physically attend a bank branch in order to complete a transaction, nor is it necessary for financial institutions to meet with customers in order to accomplish this task. By utilising digital banking, financial institutions may very well be able to provide additional services to their clientele while simultaneously lowering the costs associated with mailing out statements and conducting in-branch business with clients. Consumers have a growing desire for digital banking to have the same level of interactivity as social media.

Moreover, many study also mentioned that electronic devices such as the telephone, the internet, and mobile devices have all emerged as significant digital banking service channels, making them crucial to the continued existence of banks due to the numerous advantages they provide, such as the ability to receive services at any time and from any location (Sundarraj, 2005; Daniel, 1999; Mols, 2001). According to Mbama (2018), the introduction of digital banking channels such as telephone banking (t-banking), internet banking (e-banking), and mobile banking (m-banking) has revolutionised the way that customers can utilise the services. Digital banking also has given banks the ability to provide multi-channel services, which has altered the way in which they interact with customers digitally (Payne, 2017; Cortiñas, 2010).

Apart from that, the implementation of digital banking must be based on Maqasid al-Shariah. According to Imam al-Ghazali (1058–111 CE), the objective of Shariah is to promote the well-being of all mankind, which includes preserving their faith, ego, intellect, posterity and wealth. Anything that assures the protection of these five principles serves the societal interest and is therefore valuable. Imam al-Ghazali further categorised Maqasid al-Shariah into three groups: The essentials or necessities (*daruriyyat*), the requirements (*hajiyyat*), and the supplementary items (*tahsiniyyat*) (M.S. Abdul Rasool, 2020). Al-Shatibi (2004) defines Maqasid al-Shariah as achieving good, welfare, advantage, and benefits and preventing evil, harm, and loss of creatures.

Maqasid al-Shariah is based on the concept that all Shariah injunctions and commandments are directed towards protecting people from harm (*Daf' al-Mafasid)* and bringing benefit to all people (*Jalb al-Masalih*). As a consequence, the outcomes of all Islamic rule should be directly related to and consistent with these goals (IBFIM, 2020). The prior research recommended that the wealth is commonly regarded as being beneficial to the human. In order to maintain one's property, one must take precautions to ensure that it is safe from devastation and is not distributed to other people in a manner that is unethical or coercive (*hifz al-Mal*) (Yazid Ahmad & Ibnor Azli Ibrahim, 2006).

In Malaysia, the component of the objective of Shariah should be utilized to the growth of digital banking for the community advantages. It is also mentioned in previous research that it would appear that the use of digital platforms that allow for cashless financial interactions can lessen the likelihood of theft occurring (Liang, 2021). Firdaus (2018) demonstrated that users do not need to carry around a large amount of currency and may even make precise payments without the need to save coins or cash back when they use digital platforms like E-wallets. Because of this, using an electronic wallet is not only easy but also quite comfortable and convenient. The previous study found that digital banking not only provides a higher level of security, but also a lower risk of the manipulation or theft of checks. This means that customers do not need to carry around large amounts of cash because they have the option of paying with credit or with debit cards, or through online wallets, which is a much safer option. Digital banking also improves the consistency of cash flows and increases the rate at which cash can be moved (North, 2018).

According to North (2018), digital banking has benefited both customers and banks in terms of time constraints, as it eliminates the need for customers to travel to a bank to conduct transactions. They are not required to wait in endless lines only to be directed to a separate counter to complete their transaction. Online services enable customers to conduct transactions from the convenience of their homes, offices, or vehicles, without having to wait for an extended period. Given that several services required lengthy waiting times. Even the act of redeeming a check required time. However, instantaneous digital banking eliminates time constraints (North, 2018).

The implementation of Islamic digital banking should combine with the purpose of achieving financial inclusion. The term of financial inclusion can be defined in numerous ways. In other words, the imperative of financial inclusion necessitates that some individuals and businesses be denied access to financial services. According to Howard Thomas (2019), financial inclusion is a process that provides simple access, availability, and active use of the formal financial system for all members of an economy, society, and practitioner. Individuals and businesses are considered financially included in a society when they not only have access to and prompt availability of financial services, but also the knowledge and willingness to utilise them. Furthermore, according to Srivastava (2019), those who are presently incapable of using financial services can be considered excluded from the financial system. Financial inclusion is defined as making it possible for these individuals to access financial services at an affordable price.

Meanwhile, according to Buckley and Malady (2014), adoption of digital financial services is essential to expanding people's access to financial services and should be considered as an integral part of any viable financial solution. Implementing digital banking is an important step towards attaining financial inclusion. This is made possible by the increased opportunity to create banking alternatives outside of the network of bank branches and ATMs (Md. Nur Alam Siddik, 2014). In an endeavour to increase financial inclusion among the unbanked, an increasing number of nations are capitalising on digital banking alternatives (Srivastava, 2019).

In addition, George Okella (2019) realises that the unbanked society, especially in unpopulated areas of emerging country, can benefit greatly from the widespread usage of digital banking services using new technology like mobile phones. This is because there is some evidence that digital banking can reduce fees for customers and financial institutions alike. The fees typically associated with getting payments and saving money through bank accounts can be minimised with the help of digital banking services. Additionally, digital banking can expand the availability of low-cost, easy-to-use, and safe banking options for the underprivileged in emerging countries (Kikulwe, 2014).

METHODOLOGY

This study applies a qualitative research to scrutinize the opinion of experts on Islamic digital banking based on Maqasid al-Shariah for achieving financial inclusion and eventually an integrated model of Islamic Digital Banking will be developed. Interviews with subject matter experts are a common approach taken in observational social research. Numerous subfields of practical social research, including policy and implementation research, industrial sociology, research on elites and usage, and research on usage, all make use of it. The expert knowledge and experience of the individual being interviewed is what of primary interest in the interview (cf. Bohnsack et al, 2003).

Ethnography served as the basis for the design of the research, which aimed to investigate the comprehension and social interactions that are typical of a particular group (Reeves, 2008). The experts who have prior experience in the fields of digital banking, technology, financial inclusion and Shariah will serve as the focus of the sample population for this research. The technique of purposeful sampling was selected in order to achieve an in-depth understanding of digital banking services and generate new knowledge (Palinkas, 2005). There are four experts in their respective fields who were chosen based on their expertise comprising of two digital banking experts and two Shariah experts.

CONCEPTUAL FRAMEWORK

In general, digital banking is a banking service that fulfilled digitally without necessarily need the customer to come to the branch in order to use banking service. In simple terms, a digital bank is a bank that conducts its business entirely online and makes accessible to its customers the same kinds of services that were formerly available only at physical bank branches. The concept of digital banking refers to the practise of digitising all traditional banking products, procedures, and activities in order to better service customers through online channels. The traditional financial services that can be accessed on mobile phones, computers, and other smart devices around the clock and without the requirement of a customer's physical presence in a bank branch (Mbama & Cajetan, 2018). According to Sathye (1999), customers have been urged by the worldwide banking and financial service industry to make use of banking services via computerised platforms, which the business has made available to them. To improve overall productivity, this step has been taken.

According to Mastura Razali et. al. (2021), the idea of "maslahah" (benefits) plays a significant role in Islamic jurisprudence, particularly in regard to digital platforms. This is due to the significance of ensuring the well-being of humans and avoiding harm to one's own life. According to Narcisa Roxana (2020), digital banking has promoted social and financial inclusion to the community. It has also given a major impact on the quality of the socio-economic life of the population, by providing more sensitive and transparent governance in line with Maqasid al-Shariah framework.

INTEGRATED MODEL OF ISLAMIC DIGITAL BANKING

Figure 1. Integrated model of Islamic digital banking

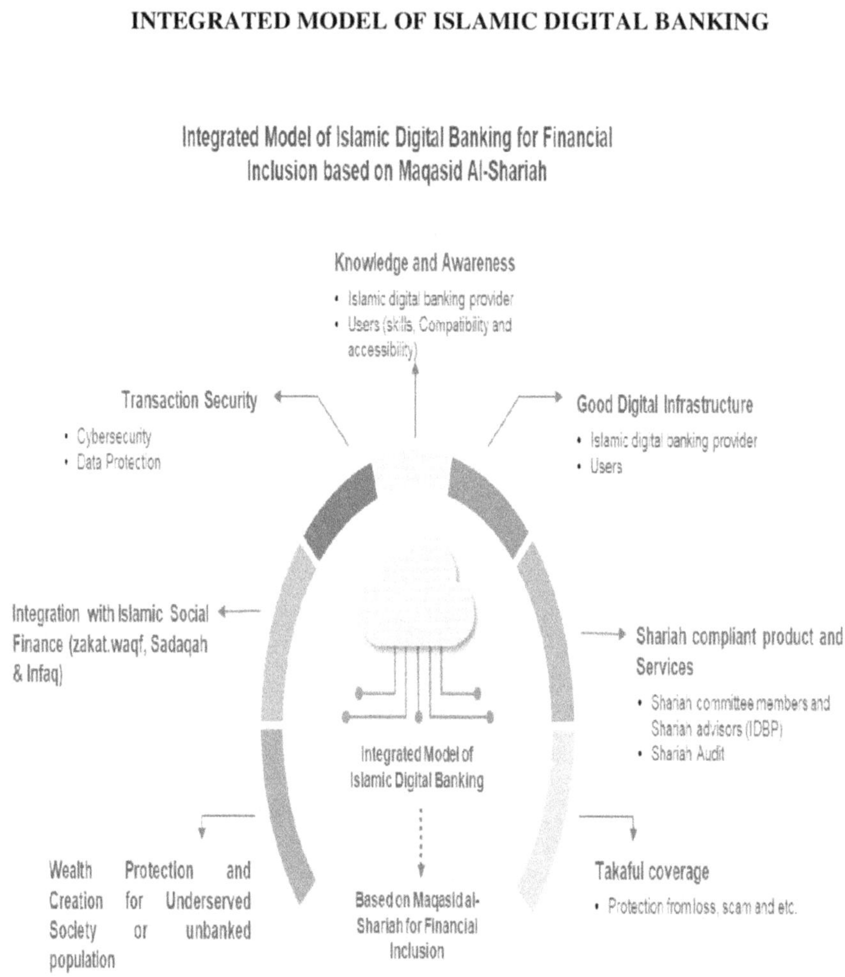

Based on Figure 1, the proposed integrated model of Islamic Digital Banking consists of: 1) Knowledge and Awareness, 2) Transaction Security, 3) Good Digital Infrastructure, 4) Integration with Islamic Social Finance, 5) Shariah Compliant Product and Services, 6) Wealth Protection and Creation for Underserved Society, and 7) Takaful Coverage. Below are the details explanation on the proposed and developed integrated model of Islamic Digital Banking (Figure 1).

The Knowledge and Awareness of Islamic Digital Banking (Protection Of Mind)

It would be difficult for people in the community to take advantage of any new technology if they lack of the comprehension and information required of that technology. This fact has been backed up by Van Hove and Dubus (2019), who pointed out that the community's lack of knowledge and awareness regarding specific aspects of digital banking is a barrier that prevents digital banking from being able to facilitate the community's access to banking products. This barrier was cited as the reason why digital banking is unable to do so. Digital banking provider must need to look out the way on how to educate the customers to acquire awareness on the adoption of Shariah compliant digital banking service.

According to the research conducted by Shanmugapriya and A. S. Lakshmirani (2021), the vast majority of respondents are at least somewhat familiar with various aspects of digital finance. In terms of the frequency of usage for the benefits, the time savings come out to be the major benefit followed by easy processing, inexpensive, and easy fund transfer, bill payment, and various mobile apps. The most preferred choice is digital banking services, followed by ATMs, internet banking, mobile banking, and various mobile apps. For the benefits, the time savings come out to be the most important benefit. A number of the respondents are customers of a variety of financial institutions, and a number of those customers have taken advantage of the digital banking services offered by those financial institutions. People can be made more conscious of the benefits of digital banking technologies and the fact that they will use digital banking in the future. According to the findings of a study that was carried out by Bhatt and Bhatt (2016), a lack of knowledge is one of the primary barriers that prevents customers from readily accepting mobile banking services. The awareness and knowledge of digital banking is significant to the community in order to be in line with elements of Maqasid al-Shariah in preserving one's mind.

Transaction Security on Digital Banking (Protection Of Wealth)

Digital banking has always placed a significant emphasis on security. According to Casaló et. al. (Casaló, 2007) website security, privacy, and reputation have a direct and substantial effect on consumer trust and commitment in online financial services transactions. According to Bhatt and Bhatt (2016), security concerns were cited as a major reason for consumer resistance to mobile banking services. The banks make every effort to persuade customers that their data and transactions are secure (Sharma, 2011). Online banking has been observed to be influenced by security and privacy (Hernandez, 2017; Chen, 2007; Sathye, 1999; Hamlet, 2000).

Digital banks have a significant competitive advantage in terms of security and customer protection compared to other financial service providers. These characteristics are incorporated from the start into a secure IT infrastructure and prevent both data misuse and data selling to other parties (G. Prisco, 2015). In addition to the dependability of cash flows and the swiftness of cash movement, digital banking provides a higher level of security and reduces the risk of check fraud or theft. Thus, customers no longer need to carry a large amount of cash with them because they can pay by credit card, debit card, or online wallet (North, 2018). So, it implies that digital banking can provide wealth protection to the customers this is in accordance with the Maqasid al-Shariah.

Good Digital Infrastructure (Protection Of Wealth)

Customers have new possibilities to conduct transactions using electronic mode, which are made available to them through the website of the bank (Wigand, 2007). According to Floh and Treiblmaier (2006), the quality of a website has a significant influence on the degree to which a customer is satisfied with the service they receive and the level of confidence they have in the business.

According to Hollins-Kirk (2022), for digital banking to be successful, a reliable and high-quality communications network is required. Because underserved communities are more likely to be located in rural areas, expanding access to and availability of digital connectedness in these regions is a prerequisite for achieving financial inclusion through the use of digital banking. In Malaysia, 96.9% of households in metropolitan areas have access to the internet, while only 89.2% of households in rural areas do. The urban-rural access gap is wider in terms of access to computers, with 91% of urban households having access to a computer, compared to 76.3% of rural homes. On the other hand, there is almost no difference in terms of access to mobile phones, with 99% of households in both urban and rural areas having one. Even though there is a gap in ICT access between urban and rural areas, the overall low levels of financial inclusion indicate that the urban-rural divide in connectivity may not be the primary barrier to financial inclusion. Instead, the issue may be a disparity between metropolitan and rural areas in terms of digital and/or financial literacy, competency, and experience.

In order to increase financial inclusion through digital banking, there is a need for improvements in both the affordability of devices and digital literacy, particularly in rural regions (Hollins-Kirk, 2022). Increasing access to digital banking requires improving internet infrastructure, particularly in rural areas and designing inclusive digital financial systems. Availability of good digital infrastructure will ensure digital banking transaction will be conducted in justice and fairness manner for all parties in accordance with the Maqasid al-Shariah.

Integration With Islamic Social Finance (Protection Of Wealth)

The introduction of blockchain technology has provided a glimmer of hope for the strengthening of social financing products and institutions in the contemporary Islamic finance industry. It possesses a number of desirable characteristics that are naturally required by all parties involved in establishing the trustworthiness of such products and institutions (Habib, 2021). Fintech has the potential to offer a comprehensive solution to the entire zakat value chain, which includes the collection, disbursement, and intermediation of funds for the purpose of improving beneficiary selection (Yahaya, 2019; Utami, 2020).

In addition, Syed et. al. (2020) proposes employing an integrated Artificial Intelligence (AI) and Natural Language Processing (NLP) based on Islamic FinTech Model incorporating zakat and qard al-hasan to mitigate the effects of the COVID-19 pandemic on SMEs and individuals. Using AI and NLP, they presented the following three modules for implementing the zakat-qard al-hasan model on a web-based platform: The first module is responsible for generating and processing data provided by beneficiaries. AI and NLP will aid in the collection of vital information that will significantly aid zakat-qard alhasan representatives in validating the request. The second method will aid the lender in generating a list of potential beneficiaries. AI and NLP will aid in the verification and recommendation of eligible beneficiaries; the third module maintains transaction records and provides communication functionality. Through this integration, it can help to realise the wealth protection to the society, which is in line with the Maqasid al-Shariah.

Shariah Compliant Product and Services (Protection Of Religion)

In accordance with the Shariah, Islamic banks provide Muslims with the means to meet their fundamental monetary requirements, allowing Muslims to take advantage of banking services. The Shariah, which is the Islamic code of law governing financial transactions, is closely followed by Islamic banking. The laws are derived from the holy book known as the Quran as well as Hadits, in addition to other important secondary sources, such as Ijma' and Qiyas. In accordance with the guidelines of Shariah, the form of financing ought to be based on a profit-and-loss sharing basis (Raza, 2019).

The three most important principles are riba, gharar, and maysir, and all financial transactions must be free from these three elements in order for them to be a valid transaction according to the given texts and the Prophet Muhammad's (PBUH) practices. Further investigation reveals that Shariah law also forbids commercial transactions that have elements like unfairness (Ghubn), harshness (Ikrah), error (Ghala'), deceit (Taghrir), and deception (Jahalah). Islamic banks must have a firm grasp of these challenges in order to apply Shariah risk management in an efficient manner (Hassan, 2016).

In Islamic banks, the process of making a new product is broken down into three main steps: coming up with and accepting an idea, turning a concept into a product, and putting the product on the market. To make sure that contracts and business operations are in line with Islamic law and meet Shariah requirements, more units and processes are needed. Shariah bodies usually consist of an internal Shariah department or unit and an outside Shariah Supervisory Board (SSB). Shariah jurists and scholars make up the SSB. They meet regularly to make sure that Shariah requirements are met in general and to approve new products in particular. In other words, the SSB's main job is to make sure that Islamic finance stays "Islamic" (Habib Ahmed, 2014).

In the phase after a product has been released, it is important to make sure that it follows the approved Shariah procedures and processes. The Islamic bank's internal Shariah department or unit should also do an internal Shariah audit of how its products are made. One job of the Shariah audit is to make sure that the processes are carried out in line with the approved plans. Shariah requirements related to operational issues are overseen by an in-house Shariah department or unit, but the SSB must be aware of the problems and fix them when necessary. Shariah audits may be hard to do in smaller banks because they do not have enough resources, but larger banks have enough resources to do Shariah audits to find non-compliance. If the audit finds problems with the way transactions are handled that make them invalid from a Shariah point of view, the money from those transactions has to be taken out of the bank's income and given to charity (Habib Ahmed, 2014). So, throughout Shariah compliant product and services assurance in the digital banking, it will help Muslim community to enjoy *Halal* (permissible) product and service and indirectly preserve the purity of Islam, which is in accordance with the Maqasid al-Shariah.

Wealth Creation for Underserved Society or Unbanked Population (Protection Of Lineage)

In the Islamic financial system, Muslim scholars have a variety of opinions regarding how wealth is created. They argue on the basis of two premises (Chapra, 1983; Afar, 1994; Nyazee, 2000). To begin, Islamic banking is subject to the regulations of the monetary authorities, and as a result, it cannot be held accountable for the production of new wealth. Second, Islamic banking provides legitimate Shariah-compliant products and services. The vast majority of Shariah scholars and economists disagree with this viewpoint and hold that it is forbidden to create wealth under the current financial system since doing so would require unethically consuming the wealth of other people (Khaf, 2011).

There has been a tremendous shift in the financial environment with the advent of mobile banking, internet banking, ATMs, and agency banking, all of which make money transfers and payments more convenient, less expensive, and accessible to people from all walks of life. Clients of banks may now get their hands on fundamental banking services, in which small enterprises function as offshoots of banks (Musau, 2013). The three primary indicators of financial inclusion identified by Allen et. al. (2012) are the presence of a bank, the ease of using that bank, and the frequency with which the bank is utilised. While considering the availability of banks, factors like market saturation and the existence of branch locations should be taken into account. One major barrier to financial inclusion is the sheer distance that separates people from the nearest bank branch.

According to Suri and Jack (2016), the number of households in Kenya led by women who had access to digital banking services saw an increase in their savings of more than a fifth. They were able to build their businesses with this assistance, which resulted in a 22% drop in extreme poverty. This evidence has been argued by Leo Van Hove and Antoine Dubus (2019), in which M-PESA is actually promoting financial inclusion. However, their finding found that in the early stages of the adoption of M-PESA; poor, non-educated, and female are excluded, and M-PESA lacked access to the "poorest of the poor" because of certain barriers such as a lack of knowledge related to the use of cell phones among women in Kenya.

According to Ram A. Cnaan et. al. (2012), it is possible that having access to affordable financing may make it possible for the poor to engage in economic activities (such as taking out loans for small businesses) and to take advantage of growth possibilities, both of which are important for achieving financial independence. This is the case because having access to affordable financing may make it possible for the poor to take out loans for small businesses. It is regarded a crucial precursor for achieving rapid economic growth, as well as for reducing income disparity and helping to alleviate poverty. So, it implies that, through digital banking it can help the community to sustain their economy development while at the same time allow the wealth creation for underserved population in order to help their next generation excluded from poverty crisis, which is perfectly in line with the Maqasid al-Shariah.

Takaful Coverage (Protection Of Life)

Digital banking ecosystems socially create financial inclusion (Diana Kangwa, 2021). Takaful is an Islamic form of insurance that adheres to Shariah rules (Bahari, 2021). The key to digital banking conforming to Maqasid al-Shariah is the incorporation of wealth and life protection products like Takaful. By incorporating a wealth and life protection model like Takaful, Muslims will have a Shariah-compliant option for protecting their wealth and life. Takaful is one of the means through which the Islamic financial system pursues its goals and objectives. Among the objectives of takaful are instilling a sense of social responsibility and encouraging collaboration among society. Takaful also strives to safeguard lives and improve the flow of wealth (Furqani, 2012).

According to Muhammad Ashfaq and Najeeb Zada (2020), the combination of Fintech and microtakaful can facilitate widespread financial inclusion. Moreover, this combination offers additional advantages, including innovation, formalisation of the economy, cost and time efficiency, and consumer protection. These obstacles include, among others, privacy concerns, data protection challenges, fraud and cyber risks, and special regulatory challenges that would be encountered during the process of digital financial inclusion through microtakaful. This evidence implied that, by incorporating digital banking with takaful, it can help community to provide the protection from the perils and harm to themselves, which eventually may achieve the Maqasid al-Shariah.

CONCLUSION

In conclusion, due to the fact that the majority of people living in Malaysia are Muslims, Malaysia is obligated to establish a Islamic digital banking system that is in accordance with Shariah law. According to Allah's commands in the divine revelation known as the Quran, it is obligatory for Muslims to follow the Shariah legal code in every facet of their lives, including engaging in permissible business transactions and avoiding those that are forbidden. A general finding shows that the integrated model can be used in line with the advance grow of digital platform. With the help of the integrated model that has been developed, it is possible to assist the Islamic digital banking provider in developing a better platform as the intermediary to the customer, including the unbanked population, so that they can conduct and enjoy banking products and services at anytime and anywhere via their smart device that complied with Shariah and Maqasid al-Shariah. The unbanked population can be exposed to information about Islamic digital banking through this model, and they can gain a better grasp of the ecosystem surrounding Islamic digital banking. This will help them improve their standard of life as well as their socioeconomic situation when applying Islamic digital banking.

ACKNOWLEDGEMENTS

This research was funded by the Ministry of Higher Education of Malaysia (MOHE) under the Fundamental Research Grant Scheme (FRGS) with reference code: USIM/FRGS/FEM/KPT/50920.

REFERENCES

Afar, M. (1994). View and Assesment of Writings about Money in an Islamic Framework. King Abdulaziz University Islamic Economic Research Center., Retrieved March 1, 2023, from.

Habib Ahmed. (2014). Islamic Banking and Shari'ah Compliance: A Product Development Perspective. *Journal of Islamic Finance*(2), 015 – 029.

Allen, F. D.-K. (2012). *The Foundations of Financial Inclusion: Understanding Ownership and Use of Formal Accounts.* World Bank Policy Research Paper. Retrieved March 1, 2023

Alnsour, M. H. (2011). Internet banking and Jordanian corporate customers: Issues of security and trust. *Journal of Internet Banking and Commerce*, 16(1), 81–106.

Angel Dwi Satria, A. K. (2021). Development of Sharia Finance Digitalization Towards Inclusive Finance Within a Sharia Maqashid Framework (Case Study on PT Bank Syariah Indonesia's BSI Mobile Banking Product). *Journal of Islamic Business and Economic Review*, 4(2), 84–96.

Ascarya, A. (2021). The role of Islamic social finance during Covid-19 pandemic in Indonesia's economic recovery. *International Journal of Islamic and Middle Eastern Finance and Management*, 15(2), 386–405. DOI: 10.1108/IMEFM-07-2020-0351

Ashfaq, M. Z. (2020). *The Application of Fintech in Microtakaful as a Means of Digital Financial Inclusion: Insights from the GCC*. Palgrave Macmillan., DOI: 10.1007/978-3-030-49248-9_5

Bahari, S. A. (2021). The role of micro Takaful industry for the achievement of Islamic financial inclusion in Pakistan. *Middle East Journal of Management*, 8(2-3), 125–139.

Bhatt, A. a. (2016). Factors afecting customer's adoption of mobile banking services. *Journal of Internet Banking and Commerce*, 21(1), 161.

BNM. B. N. (2022, April 22). *Five successful applicants for the digital bank licences*. Retrieved June 20, 2022, from Bank Negara Malaysia (BNM): https://www.bnm .gov.my/-/digital-bank-5-licences

Brunier, F. D. (2015). *Transforming the Banking Branch*. Retrieved February 25, 2023, from Accenture: https://www.accenture.com/t20160321T 020410Z__w __/ in- en/_acnmedia/Accenture/Conversion-Assets/ DotCom/Documents/Global/PDF/ Strategy_7/Accenture-StrategyTran

Buvat, J. (2014). *Doing Business the Digital Way: How Capital One Fundamentally Disrupted the Financial Services Industry*. Capgemini Consulting. Retrieved February 20, 2023, from https://www.capgemini.com/wp-content/uploads/2017/07/ capital-one-doing-business-the-digital-way_0.pdf

Casaló, L. V., Flavián, C., & Guinalíu, M. (2007). The role of security, privacy, usability and reputation in the development of online banking. *Online Information Review*, 31(5), 583–603. DOI: 10.1108/14684520710832315

Chapra, U. (1983). Money and Banking in an Islamic Economy. *International Center for Research in Islamic Economics*, 145-186.

Chen, Y., & Barnes, S. (2007). Initial trust and online buyer behaviour. *Industrial Management & Data Systems*, 107(1), 21–36. DOI: 10.1108/02635570710719034

Diana Kangwa, J. T. (2021). The Social Production of Financial Inclusion of Generation Z in Digital Banking Ecosystems. *AABJ*, 15(3), 6–118. DOI: 10.14453/ aabfj.v15i3.6

Elbek Musaev &Muhammed Yousoof. (2015). A Review on Internet Banking Security and Privacy. *ICIT 2015 The 7th International Conference on Information Technology*, 1-5. DOI: 10.15849/icit.2015.0070

Floh, A., & Treiblmaier, H. (2006). What keeps the e-Banking customer loyal? A multigroup analysis of the moderating role of consumer characteristics on e-loyalty in the fnancial service industry. *SSRN*, 7(2), 97–110. DOI: 10.2139/ssrn.2585491

Furqani, S. A. (2012). The Objectives of Shariah (Maqasid Shariah) in Takaful: Highlighting the Noble Practice. *International Conference on Management, Economics & Finance Proceeding*, 910-918.

Gill, M. (2016). *The Digital Maturity Model*. Cambridge: Forrester Research. Retrieved February 25, 2023, from http://forrester.nitro-digital.com/pdf/Forrester-s %20Digital%20Maturity%20Model%204.0.pdf

Habib, A. U. (2021). FinTech-Based Islamic Social Financing Products: A Critical Evaluation. *Innovative Strategies for Implementing FinTech in Banking*, 67-82. DOI: 10.4018/978-1-7998-3257-7.ch004

Hamlet, C. a. (2000). Community banks go online. *ABA Banking Journal's 2000 white paper/banking on the internet,* 61–65.

Hassnian Ali, R. A. (2019). Fintech and Its Potential Impact on Islamic Banking and Finance Industry: A Case Study of Brunei Darussalam and Malaysia. *IJIEF: International Journal of Islamic Economics and Finance*, 2(1), 73–108. DOI: 10.18196/ijief.2116

Hernandez, J. (2017). Adoption of internet banking: Proposition and implementation of an integrated methodology approach. *International Journal of Bank Marketing*, 25(2), 72–88. DOI: 10.1108/02652320710728410

Hollins-Kirk, R. G. (2022). *Digital Banking and Financial Inclusion.* Kuala Lumpur: Khazanah Research Institute. Retrieved February 20, 2023, from https://www.krinstitute.org/assets/contentMS/img/template/editor/20220826%20Digital%20Banking%20Views%20pub.pdf

Ibrahim, M. Z. (2021). alāl linguistic meaning understanding among Non-Muslim in Malaysia. *Journal al-Irsyad, 6*(2), 697-705. DOI: 10.53840/alirsyad.v6i2.210

Jack & Suri. (2016, December). The long-run poverty and gender impacts of mobile money. *DEVELOPMENT ECONOMICS*, 1288-1292.

Karjaluoto, H. A., Shaikh, A. A., Leppäniemi, M., & Luomala, R. (2019). Examining consumers' usage intention of contactless payment systems. *International Journal of Bank Marketing*, 38(2), 332–351. DOI: 10.1108/IJBM-04-2019-0155

Khaf, M. (2011). The Fundamentals of Islamic Finance. ISRA., Retrieved March 2, 2023, from.

Lakshmirani, S. A. (2021). Study on customer awareness towards digital banking services. *Palarch's Journal Of Archaeology Of Egypt/Egyptology, 18*(1), 4599-4604.

Loh, H.-S. C. (2020, May). Physical Frictions and Digital Banking Adoption. *Behavioral & Experimental Economics eJournal*, 1-50. DOI: 10.2139/ssrn.3333636

Marous, J. (2013, March 18). *Migrating Banking Customers to Digital Channels.* Retrieved February 25, 2023, from The Financial Brand: https://thefinancialbrand.com/news/digital-banking/migrating-banking-customers-to-digital-37287/

Mastura Razali, N. M. (2021). Maqasid Shariah HIFZ MAL in E-Wallet Application. *ISLĀMIYYĀT*, 113 - 120. doi:DOI: 10.17576

Mbama & Cajetan. (2018, October 8). Digital banking services, customer experience and financial performance in UK banks. *Journal of Research in Interactive Marketing*, •••, 432–451.

Munshi, U. (2021). The role of Islamic crowdfunding in the new economy in Islamic Fintech. Routledge., Retrieved February 28, 2023, from.

Musau, S. M. (2013). An analysis of the utilization of agency banking on performance of selected banks in Nairobi County, Kenya. Kenyatta University., Retrieved March 2, 2023, from.

Narcisa Roxana Moşteanu, A. F. (2020). Digital Technologies Implementation within Financial and Banking System During Socio Distancing Restrictions – Back to the Future. [IJARET]. *International Journal of Advanced Research in Engineering and Technology*, 11(6), 307–315.

North, R. (2018, November 6). *THE ROLE OF DIGITAL BANKING IN INDIA – IMPORTANCE OF DIGITAL BANKING IN INDIA*. Retrieved from Entreprise Edges: https://www.enterpriseedges.com/role-of-digital-banking-india

Nyazee, I. A. (2000, 2023 March). *The Concept of Riba and Islamic Banking*. Retrieved 1, from Nyazee.com: http://www.nyazee.com/islbanks/riba/riba.html

Prisco, G. (2015, December 22). *Enigma, MIT Media Lab's Blockchain-based Encrypted Data Marketplace, to Launch Beta*. Retrieved February 22, 2023, from bitcoinmagazine: https://bitcoinmagazine.com/business/enigma-mit-media-lab-s-blockchain-based-encrypted-data-marketplace-to-launch-beta-1450810499

Rabbani, M. R., Bashar, A., Nawaz, N., Karim, S., Ali, M. A. M., Rahiman, H. U., & Alam, M. S. (2021). Exploring the role of Islamic fintech in combating the aftershocks of Covid-19: The open social innovation of the Islamic financial system. *Journal of Open Innovation*, 7(2), 136. DOI: 10.3390/joitmc7020136

Ram, A., & Cnaan, M. S. (2012). Financial Inclusion: Lessons From Rural South India. *Journal of Social Policy*, 41(1), 183–205. DOI: 10.1017/S0047279411000377

Raza, S. A., Shah, N., & Ali, M. (2019). Acceptance of mobile banking in Islamic banks: Evidence from modi fi ed UTAUT model. *Journal of Islamic Marketing*, 10(1), 357–376. DOI: 10.1108/JIMA-04-2017-0038

Ridhwan Ab Aziz M, &. Z. (2021). Islamic Digital Banking in the Light of Maqasid Shariah: A Review of Literatures. *Al-Qanatir: International Journal of Islamic Studies, 23*(2), 63-73. Retrieved from https://al-qanatir.com/aq/article/view/358

Sarel, D., & Marmorstein, H. (2002). Migrating customers to new distribution channels: The role of communication. *Journal of Financial Services Marketing*, 6(3), 254–266. DOI: 10.1057/palgrave.fsm.4770056

Sathye, M. (1999). Adoption of Internet banking by Australian consumers: An empirical investigation. *International Journal of Bank Marketing*, 17(7), 324–334. DOI: 10.1108/02652329910305689

Sathye, M. (1999). Adoption of Internet banking by Australian consumers: An empirical investigation. *International Journal of Bank Marketing*, 17(7), 324–334. DOI: 10.1108/02652329910305689

Shaikh, A. M., Alharthi, M. D., & Alamoudi, H. O. (2020). Examining key drivers of consumer experience with (non-financial) digital services-An exploratory study. *Journal of Retailing and Consumer Services*, 55, 1–10. DOI: 10.1016/j.jretconser.2020.102073

Sharma, , Al-Badi, A., Rana, N. P., & Al-Azizi, L. (2018). Mobile applications in government services (mG-App) from user's perspectives: A predictive modelling approach. *Government Information Quarterly*, 35(4), 557–568. DOI: 10.1016/j.giq.2018.07.002

Sharma, H. (2011). National Journal of Research in Management. *Bankers' perspectives on e-banking, 1*(1), 71–85.

Syed, M. H. (2020). An artificial intelligence and NLP based Islamic fintech model combining zakat and qardh-al-hasan for countering the adverse impact of COVID 19 on SMEs and individuals. *International Journal of Economics and Business Administration*, 3(2), 351–364. DOI: 10.35808/ijeba/466

Utami, P. S., Suryanto, T., Nasor, M., & Ghofur, R. A. (2020). The effect digitalization zakat payment against potential of zakat acceptance in national Amil zakat agency. *Iqtishadia*, 13(2), 216–223. DOI: 10.21043/iqtishadia.v13i2.7809

Van Hove, L., & Dubus, A. (2019). M-PESA and Financial Inclusion in Kenya: Of Paying. *Sustainability (Basel)*, 11(3), 1–26. DOI: 10.3390/su11030568

Van Hove, L., & Dubus, A. (2019). M-PESA and Financial Inclusion in Kenya: Of Paying Comes Saving? *Sustainability (Basel)*, 11(3), 1–26. DOI: 10.3390/su11030568

Waite, K., & Harrison, T. (2002). Consumer expectations of online information provided by bank websites. *Journal of Financial Services Marketing*, 6(4), 309–322. DOI: 10.1057/palgrave.fsm.4770061

Wigand, S. S. (2007). Key dimensions of e-commerce service quality and its relationships to satisfaction and loyalty. *Proceedings of the 20th Bled Electronic Commerce Conference*, 1-15. Retrieved from https://www.researchgate.net/publication/228867485_Key_dimensions_of_e-commerce_service_quality_and_its_relationships_to_satisfaction_and_loyalty

World Bank. (2018, April 19). *Financial Inclusion on the Rise, But Gaps Remain, Global Findex Database Shows*. Retrieved from THE WORLD BANK: https://www.worldbank.org/en/news/press-release/2018/04/19/financial-inclusion-on-the-rise-but-gaps-remain-global-findex-database-shows

Yahaya, M. H. (2019). Factors affecting the acceptance of financial technology among asnaf for the distribution of zakat in Selangor-A study using UTAUT. *Journal of Islamic Finance*, 8, 35–46. https://journals.iium.edu.my/iiibf-journal/index.php/jif/article/view/345

Chapter 8
Exploring Public Perceptions of Sharia Securities Crowdfunding:
A Case Study From Indonesia

Johan Arifin
Universitas Islam Negeri Walisongo Semarang, Indonesia

Nasrul Fahmi Zaki Fuadi
https://orcid.org/0000-0001-5176-632X
Universitas Islam Negeri Walisongo Semarang, Indonesia

Refi Agustina
Universitas Islam Negeri Walisongo Semarang, Indonesia

Chantika Khoirunnisa
Universitas Islam Negeri Walisongo Semarang, Indonesia

Reza Putri Maharani
Universitas Islam Negeri Walisongo Semarang, Indonesia

ABSTRACT

This research aims to assess public attitudes towards a novel investing approach known as Islamic securities crowdsourcing, drawing on established context. Researchers employed the Unified Theory of Acceptance and Use of Technology (UTAUT) methodology to maintain this viewpoint. This research is based on the integrated UTAUT. The data were analyzed using multiple linear regression models in SPSS. The primary findings indicate that Performance Expectancy, Social Influence, and Facilitating Conditions strongly influence an individual's inclination to invest in secu-

DOI: 10.4018/979-8-3693-5653-1.ch008

rities crowdsourcing. Effort Expectancy does not significantly influence the decision to invest in stocks crowdsourcing. The results indicate that cooperation between the government and securities crowdfunding institutions is essential for establishing a well-organized investment environment and enhancing sharia financial literacy. This study enhances sharia financial literacy in securities crowdfunding and offers an overview of these institutions in the advancement of securities crowdfunding.

INTRODUCTION

The progress of humanity in terms of technology has been characterized by a series of waves of invention, each of which has significantly changed the way we live, work, and interact with our environment (Ngafifi, 2014). Industry 5.0 is a leading concept in the current revolution, utilizing sophisticated technologies like the Internet of Things (IoT), artificial intelligence (AI), and robotics to improve human well-being and efficiency in everyday life (Perpustakaan, 2022). In 2021, the European Commission officially acknowledged Industry 5.0 as a deliberate attempt to guide technical advancements towards sustainable and human-centered results (Xu et al., 2021).

Indonesia, like to other countries, is currently facing the problems and opportunities brought about by digitalization, placing itself at the center of this technological revolution (Harahap et al., 2018). Indonesia's economic growth strategy has identified the digital economy as a crucial element, defined by widespread connectivity and the smooth movement of data (Manik & Sukadana, 2020). Facilitated by the widespread use of mobile technology and internet-connected devices, this digital ecosystem enables a wide range of economic activities, including e-commerce transactions and digital payments (Kagramanto & Serfiyani, 2019).

An essential aspect of this digital revolution is the notion of crowdfunding, an innovative method of acquiring finance that utilizes online platforms to request funds from a wide range of investors (Willems, 2013). Crowdfunding has revolutionized the way entrepreneurs and innovators can access financing by providing them with unprecedented flexibility and accessibility. This has resulted to a surge in startup development and creativity (Fund, 2012). Furthermore, the emergence of crowdfunding aligns with a wider transition towards digital-centric financial markets, which has been expedited by the disruptive impact of the COVID-19 pandemic (Oktavian & Maika, 2020).

The origins of capital markets in Indonesia may be traced back to the colonial era, highlighting the lasting importance of financial systems in creating the country's economic environment (Bursa Efek Indonesia, 2022). Although Indonesia has a rich historical past, the introduction of digital technology has brought about a new era of financial innovation. One notable aspect of this is the rise of crowdfunding in Indonesia's digital economy (Febriaty, 2019). Despite the existence of regulatory frameworks like Regulation Number 57/POJK.04/2020, which aim to offer legal safeguards for crowdfunding transactions, there is still a widespread lack of awareness and comprehension among the Indonesian population regarding the advantages and consequences of crowdfunding (Wicaksana & Rachman, 2018).

In navigating the landscape of Sharia-compliant crowdfunding securities in Indonesia, attention must be paid to the legal and regulatory framework governing these financial instruments. Academics like Noor (2022) and Nelly et al. (2022) have highlighted the importance of customized legislation to foster confidence and guarantee safety in the Sharia-compliant crowdfunding industry. In addition, Nelly et al. (2022) emphasizes the prospective economic advantages that Sharia crowd-funding can offer to enterprises and the overall economy. Nevertheless, Noor (2022) and Muhammad & Yuningsih (2020) express apprehensions about the absence of precise legislation governing Sharia debt-based crowdfunding, highlighting potential hazards for consumers. These observations emphasize the necessity of strong regulatory measures and systems to protect consumers in the Sharia-compliant crowdfunding securities business in Indonesia. These observations align with the broader demand for clear regulations and control, as mentioned by Noor (2022) and Muhammad & Yuningsih (2020).

In light of this situation, the rise of Sharia-compliant crowdfunding securities is a noteworthy advancement in Indonesia's financial environment. Sharia-compliant crowdfunding, based on Islamic concepts of ethical finance and social responsibility, provides a distinct chance to harmonize financial activities with religious values (Kurniasih, 2022). However, there is a significant lack of public knowledge and comprehension regarding the growing industry of Sharia-compliant funding, despite its potential benefits. This research seeks to investigate public perceptions of a novel investment strategy called sharia securities crowdfunding, building upon the provided background. In order to ascertain this perspective, researchers employed the Unified Theory of Acceptance and Use of Technology (UTAUT) methodology.

The paper is structured as follows. Section 2 reviews related literature and presents hypothesis development. Section 3 describes the data and methodology. The results are discussed in Section 4, and the conclusion and recommendations are in Section 5.

LITERATURE REVIEW

Securities Crowdfunding

Crowdfunding is a phrase that originates from the broader concept of "crowdsourcing," which refers to the utilization of the collective intelligence of a big group of persons to create ideas, opinions, and solutions for furthering company activities. Crowdfunding is a continuous online approach of raising funds, typically using incentives, in order to support a particular cause (Belleflamme et al., 2014). The book "The Crowdfunding Bible" by Steinberg (2012) provides a concise definition of crowdfunding as the act of seeking financial contributions or investments from the general public in order to get the initial cash required for a new business venture. Entrepreneurs and small business owners might circumvent financiers and investors by utilizing this approach, wherein they immediately present their ideas to regular internet users, who possess the capacity to offer financial support (Naldi & Muljaningsih, 2022).

The emergence of crowdfunding aligns with the expansion of digital communities, giving rise to certain apprehensions. Green (2014) states that the rise of digital communities has allowed more people to find and participate in their communities, causing significant changes to traditional crowdfunding approaches. The expectation is that this trend will continue to develop (Abdillah & Danial, 2015). Crowdfunding, as per the Oxford Dictionary, refers to the method of funding a project or business endeavor by collecting monetary contributions from a large number of persons, each making a relatively small donation, typically facilitated through online platforms. Crowdfunding is the process of gathering funds from a large number of individuals to back a certain project or initiative (OxfordDictinoary, 2022).

Crowdfunding is a direct derivative of the crowdsourcing concept. Crowdsourcing, as defined by Jeff Howe, is the process of delegating a task that would normally be done by personnel within a company to a wide group of individuals via the internet (Whitla, 2009). Crowdfunding is the practice of collecting money from several persons using online platforms, with the purpose of using the funds for either business endeavors or charity contributions (Athief, 2019). Crowdfunding was established with the purpose of providing financial loans specifically for the creative economy. This model exemplifies a method of obtaining financing from several persons through social media platforms, with the objective of providing capital solutions for startups and small and medium-sized organizations (SMEs). The main goal is to obtain financial resources through contributions and investments (Boudreau et al., 2021).

Crowdfunding can be categorized as a charitable method of generating funds, as it entails making contributions without expecting any financial gains in return. Alternatively, the creator provides incentives to donors, such as acknowledgments, exclusive experiences, or tangible objects. Once a donation system is put in place, creditors take on the role of donors, determined by their willingness and capacity to contribute (Permana & Rahayuni, 2023). The crowdfunding concept exhibits similarities to the Amil Department's method of gathering zakat. However, zakat is specifically related to religious problems and does not allocate funding for entrepreneurial endeavors that target profitability (Nugraheni, 2020).

Securities crowdfunding is an online way of selling securities that enables new companies to acquire capital at a reduced expense. It also democratizes the market for financing high-risk startups (Schwartz, 2013). The anticipated impact of this development on securities law and capital markets is twofold: firstly, it will enable startup companies to access capital through peer networks and the internet, and secondly, it will provide investors with limited financial resources the opportunity to participate in investments that were previously exclusive to wealthy individuals (Schwartz, 2013). Nevertheless, there are apprehensions over the possibility of aggressive acquisitions of companies that offer shares through crowdfunding (Schwartz, 2013). Furthermore, the expansion of secondary markets for securities crowdfunding remains constrained, resulting in post-offering dynamics that resemble those of private equity transactions (Vismara, 2022). Securities crowdfunding has novel prospects for enterprises and investors, although it necessitates the resolution of regulatory and market development obstacles.

Equity crowdfunding, or securities crowdfunding, is a way for firms to raise funds from many individuals, usually online, in exchange for equity shares (Lee, 2019; Utama & Putra Ganda, 2022) Crowdfunding became popular as an alternative to traditional financing for startups and small firms that may not qualify for an IPO. Equity crowdfunding has risks and challenges. Regulations are needed to reduce systemic risks and protect investors against fraud, herding, insolvency, and shareholder equity dilution (Lee, 2019). Though these concerns remain, equity crowdsourcing has been proved to benefit early-stage enterprises and allow investors to make ethical investments that improve society (Ahmad Mohamad et al., 2021; Schwienbacher, 2021). Equity crowdfunding has expanded entrepreneurial finance but also introduced risks and regulations. Platforms and regulators must assure sharia compliance in Islamic markets and investor protections (X. Li, 2016; Marwa et al., 2024). As the practice expands, elements like securities allocation systems, crowdfunding firms, and crowdfunding campaign success drivers shape it (Caputo et al., 2022; Hornuf & Schwienbacher, 2018; Smirnova et al., 2021).

The existing body of research on securities crowdfunding demonstrates a range of elements that impact the outcome of crowdfunding campaigns and the behavior of investors. Zakhlebin & Horvát (2019) proposes that the diversity of investment decisions and past accomplishments may have an impact on investor retention on crowdfunding platforms, especially for rookie investors compared to experienced investors. Lukkarinen et al. (2016) suggests that in equity crowdfunding, the conventional investment choice criteria employed by venture capitalists or business angels are of lesser significance, whereas campaign characteristics and the utilization of networks have a more prominent impact.

In addition, Wu et al. (2023) examines the dynamics of syndicate formation on equity crowdfunding platforms. The study emphasizes a relationship that follows an inverted U-shaped pattern between the similarity of the leader and backers and the possibility of co-investment. This relationship differs from the patterns observed in typical venture capital syndicates. Wallmeroth (2019) indicates that the crowd is not uniform, since a tiny subset of individuals makes significantly larger contributions to the raised capital.

The study conducted by Hornuf et al. (2022) highlights the significance of investor motives. It reveals that investors with a focus on sustainability tend to invest higher sums of money and are more responsive to defaults compared to regular crowd investors. The study conducted by Venturelli et al. (2019) examines gender dynamics and reveals that there is no significant relationship between the success of a campaign and the gender of the person leading it. However, the study does highlight a similarity impact in investment decisions made by female investors.

Cross-border investments have been identified as a significant field of interest, as emphasized by Maula & Lukkarinen (2019, 2022). These studies underscore the significance of international investor attention and the shared nationality between companies and investors in attracting such investments. Lastly, Ndou et al. (2022) and Lukkarinen (2020) examine the determinants of investor decision-making and the function of platforms in mitigating information asymmetries, respectively.

The Unified Theory of Acceptance and Use of Technology (UTAUT)

The Unified Theory of Acceptance and Use of Technology (UTAUT) is a highly regarded framework for forecasting the acceptance and use of technology. Taiwo & Downe (2013) performed a meta-analysis of 37 studies, which demonstrated a strong association between performance expectancy and behavioral intention. However, the analysis also indicated that the relationships between effort expectancy, social influence, and behavioral intention were less strong. Likewise, the relationships between facilitating conditions, behavioral intention, and usage behavior were also shown to be lacking in strength. Van Schaik (2009) utilized the UTAUT framework to examine the acceptance of prescribed and user-selected platforms on higher education student websites, yielding successful insights. In addition, Or & Chapman (2021) extended the UTAUT model in the context of educational technology acceptance by integrating additional components such as usability, learnability, and attitude. These studies emphasize the crucial importance of performance expectancy in predicting technology acceptance and recommend future research to strengthen other relational features within the model.

The Unified Theory of Acceptance and Use of Technology (UTAUT), developed by Venkatesh et al. (2003), explains the process of accepting and utilizing information technology (IT). The theory seeks to define the criteria or variables that influence the acceptability of IT among users. The initial set of eight criteria for assessing IT adoption was subjected to scrutiny, categorized based on commonalities, and consolidated into four basic criteria. This resulted in the formation of the Unified Theory of adoption and Use of Technology (UTAUT) as proposed by Ardi Hamzah (2010).

After conducting an examination, UTAUT produced an evaluation that nearly matched the eight previous benchmarks used to measure the acceptance of IT and user intention (Fuadi et al., 2020). The UTAUT model consists of four components that directly impact behavioral intention and usage behavior: performance expectancy, effort expectancy, social influence, and facilitating factors. In addition, Ajzen (1991) states that there are four moderators - gender, age, voluntariness, and experience - that help regulate the impact of conceptions on behavioral intention and usage behavior.

The Unified Theory of Acceptance and Use of Technology (UTAUT) is a concept that aims to clarify the factors that influence the usage and acceptance of technology. The UTAUT model, as proposed by Venkatesh et al. (2003), states that performance expectations, commercial expectations, and social influence have a major impact on the level of interest in using a system and the subsequent behavior of using it. Furthermore, the model takes into account variables such as gender, age, experience, and the voluntary nature of usage. The concept focuses on four main elements that influence an individual's intention to use a technology, as well as up to four additional aspects that affect the link between these main factors.

Figure 1. UTAUT model

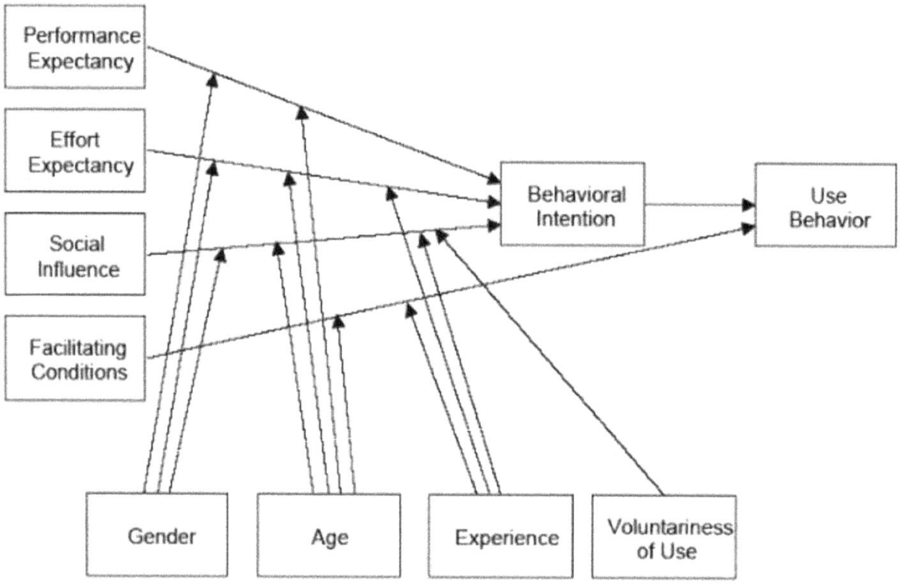

Performance expectancy (PE)

Performance expectation refers to the belief that utilizing a system would lead to improvements in job performance (Venkatesh et al., 2003). In the realm of social crowdfunding, the act of donating funds might be swayed by the motivation to avoid criticism or receive admiration and acknowledgment from others, in order to foster social engagement (Wong et al., 2018). Donating to social crowdfunding can evoke a sense of personal gratification, leading to an enhancement of one's self-esteem in their surroundings. Moreover, this sense of self-satisfaction significantly enhances their inclination to engage. PE is defined by scholars as the degree to which social crowdfunding donors perceive that utilizing the crowdfunding platform to contribute funds will result in personal gratification, social engagement, social acknowledgment, and personal accomplishment (Wong et al., 2018). Given the information provided, the hypothesis developed by the researcher is:

H1: Performance Expectancy has a significant positive effect on investment intentions through securities crowdfunding.

Effort expectancy (EE)

Effort expectancy refers to the perceived level of ease with which an individual can use a system (Venkatesh et al., 2003). Three constructs derived from established models of electronic engineering (EE) are perceived ease of use (Technology Acceptance Model/TAM2), complexity (Multiple Perspectives on Computer Use/MPCU), and ease of use (Information Display Theory/IDT). Studies indicate that the level of convenience in utilizing technology can greatly influence one's behavioral intentions (Wang et al., 2013). The researchers suggest that the user-friendly nature of the securities crowdfunding platform and the convenient investment process have a substantial and favorable impact on users' inclinations to invest via securities crowdfunding. Given the information provided, the researcher developed the subsequent hypothesis:

H2: Effort expectancy has a significant positive effect on investment intentions through securities crowdfunding

Social influence (SI)

Social influence refers to the degree to which an individual feels that influential individuals endorse the adoption of a new system (Venkatesh et al., 2003). Subjective norms in TRA, TAM2, TPB/DTPB, social variables in MPCU, and visuals in IDT all demonstrate SI as a direct driver of behavioral intention. Peer pressure can have influence on an individual's social responsibility and intention to donate in the realm of social crowdfunding (Y.-Z. Li et al., 2018). Hence, the Social Influence component is primarily characterized by a perception of social obligation and the impact of external individuals. The extent of individual charitable efforts is contingent upon the aggregate sum of gifts made by others (Y.-Z. Li et al., 2018). Given the information provided, the hypothesis we propose is:

H3: Social influence has a significant positive effect on investment intentions through securities crowdfunding

Facilitating conditions (FC)

Facilitating conditions refer to the degree to which an individual believes that the organizational and technical infrastructure is present to enable the utilization of the system (Venkatesh et al., 2003). This description demonstrates that this notion is implemented through three distinct constructs: perceived behavioral control (TPBI DTPB, C-TAM-TPB), enabling conditions (MPCU), and compatibility (IDT). Each of these factors is defined and measured to include elements of the technology and/or organizational environment that are designed to address and resolve usability challenges. Per the UTAUT model, the utilization of Internet information systems can be directly influenced by perceived behavioral control and extrinsic objective circumstances (Venkatesh et al., 2003). In the realm of social crowdfunding, the variety of information sources and various media portrayals of social crowdfunding endeavors, such as social media, frequently lead to heightened awareness and a desire to contribute financially to social crowdfunding initiatives (Gerber & Hui, 2013). The researcher formulated a hypothesis based on the provided description.

H4: Facilitating conditions have a significant positive effect on investment intentions through securities crowdfunding

Perception

Perception, as defined by The Big Indonesian Dictionary (KBBI), refers to the immediate acceptance or direct response to something, or the cognitive process through which individuals acquire knowledge about various things using their five senses. Perception is the cognitive process through which individuals receive, select, organize, and interpret information in order to construct a coherent understanding of the world (Morissan, 2015). Perception, as defined by the Indonesian Encyclopedia, is a cognitive process that generates a mental representation in an individual's mind, enabling them to identify an object by linking it to a specific memory. This process can occur through various senses, such as sight or touch, resulting in the realization of the mental image (Shadily, 1983).

The Dictionary of Theories defines perception as a fundamental process that integrates and unifies sensory input, encompassing physical, physiological, neurological, sensory, cognitive, and emotional behavioral components. Jon E. Roeckelein's Dictionary of Psychology, authored by Roeckelein et al. (2013).

Sugihartono et al. (2007) define perception as the cognitive capacity of the brain to interpret incoming stimuli through the human sense organs. The human perception encompasses various perspectives in the process of perceiving. Some individuals have positive or negative beliefs that can impact their observable human behavior.

Perception, as described by (Walgito, 1994), is the process by which an organism or individual organizes and interprets received stimuli in order to give them meaning. It is an integrated activity within the individual. Individuals can interpret stimuli in different ways based on their perception. The specific stimulus that triggers a response in an individual depends on their level of attention. persons possess unique emotions, cognitive capacities, and life experiences, which consequently lead to variations in their perception of stimuli. As a result, the outcomes of perception can differ among persons.

METHODOLOGY

This research methodology employs quantitative techniques. The research employed a data gathering methodology involving the use of a questionnaire or online survey administered through Google Form. Subsequently, the data collected from the survey was subjected to statistical analysis utilizing the Statistical Package for Social Science (SPSS) software version 20, thereby enhancing computational efficiency. The study population comprises individuals who meet the following criteria: 1) Both males and females, 2) Regular users of social media platforms, and 3) Possessing knowledge about crowdfunding activities. Due to the impracticality of testing the entire population, researchers rely on samples that represent a subset of the population for their research. In this study, sample collecting in Central Java using a random or probability sampling method. The respondents consisted of 100 students who have information regarding crowdfunding. Students belong to a generation that has a strong affinity for technology, including crowdfunding. The purpose of this study is to ensure that the participants are able to accurately depict the situation in Indonesia. Random sampling was chosen to ensure equal possibilities for the entire community. The research was conducted using the formula developed by Lemeshow et al. (1997), with a sample size of 100 respondents.

The research used the multiple linear regression method with SPSS statistical tools to test the four hypotheses put forth in this study. The goal of multiple regression, as stated by Sugiyono (2021), is to forecast the fluctuations of the dependent variable by manipulating the values of two or more independent variables acting as predictors.

RESULTS AND ANALYSIS

Table 1 displays the profiles of the responders. The majority of the participants fall are under the age of 25 and possess a relatively elevated level of education. Therefore, they are capable of demonstrating a relatively high degree of technological proficiency.

Table 1. Demographic characteristics

	Number of Samples	Number of Percentages
Gender		
Male	40	40%
Female	60	60%

continued on following page

Table 1. Continued

	Number of Samples	Number of Percentages
Age		
< 20	49	49%
20 – 25	48	48%
> 25	2	2%
Department		
Management	10	10%
Islamic economics	54	54%
Sharia Banking	22	22%
Sharia Accounting	15	15%

According to the observational data, there were 100 responses, with females outnumbering males by 60%. The majority of respondents belong to Generation Z and are under the age of 25. Approximately 54% of the participants are enrolled as students in the Islamic economics study program. Based on this data, it can be inferred that the respondents are individuals belonging to Generation Z, who possess a high level of familiarity with securities crowdfunding.

Validity and Reliability Test

The questionnaire underwent a validity and reliability test using SPSS 25 analysis. The test was conducted on a sample of 100 data points. The results, shown in Table 2's Pearson Correlation item-total correlation column, indicate that the validity test results for each question item have a value exceeding 0.3, thus confirming their validity. Furthermore, this strategy can be applied in further research.

Table 2. Validity and reliability test results

Item		Performance Expectancy	Effort Expectancy	Social Influence	Facilitating Condition	Intention to Invest
Performance expectancy	PE1	0,767				
	PE2	0,795				
	PE3	0,793				
	PE4	0,762				
	PE5	0,785				
	PE6	0,735				

continued on following page

Table 2. Continued

Item		Performance Expectancy	Effort Expectancy	Social Influence	Facilitating Condition	Intention to Invest
Effort Expectancy	PEU1		0,822			
	PEU2		0,846			
	PEU3		0,861			
	PEU4		0,781			
Social Influence	SI1			0,548		
	SI2			0,605		
	SI3			0,778		
	SI4			0,708		
	SI5			0,732		
	SI6			0,745		
	SI7			0,790		
	SI8			0,833		
Facilitating condition	FC1				0,531	
	FC2				0,473	
	FC3				0,779	
	FC4				0,775	
	FC5				0,794	
Intention to Invest	In1					0,627
	In2					0,669
	In3					0,459
	Cronbach's alpha	0,920	0,925	0,914	0,847	0,752
	r-Table	0,1339	0,1339	0,1339	0,1339	0,1339

The r table value is 0.1339 based on Table 2, derived from a sample of 100 respondents. An instrument value is considered legitimate if the calculated r value is greater than the r table value at the 5% significance level. All instruments in Table 1 have a r value greater than 0.1339, indicating that they pass the validity test. Reliability was assessed using the Cronbach's Alpha Technique. When the Cronbach's Alpha score exceeds 0.7, the respondents' questionnaire responses are deemed credible as a measuring tool. All research instruments in table 1 have Cronbach's alpha values greater than 0.7, indicating that they have passed the reliability test.

Classic Assumption Test

Classical assumption testing is necessary in multiple linear regression models to ascertain the absence of heteroscedasticity, multicollinearity, or autocorrelation in the regression estimation results. The research involved conducting tests to challenge the traditional assumptions made about the models, specifically focusing on normalcy, multicollinearity, and heteroscedasticity. An autocorrelation test is unnecessary for this research as the data utilized does not pertain to time-series data. The results of the classical assumption test analysis for the proposed model were conducted using SPSS 25.0.:

Table 3. Classic assumption test

Multicollinearity Test	**Tolerance**	**VIF**
Performance Expectancy **Effort Expectancy** **Social Influence** **Facilitating Condition**	0.078 0.086 0.052 0.361	2,576 2,723 2,870 3,215
Heteroscedasticity Test (Glejser test)	Sig. t-test	
Performance Expectancy **Effort Expectancy** **Social Influence** **Facilitating Condition**	0.078 0.086 0.052 0.361	
Durbin-Watson test	1.831	
Normality Test		
kolmogorov- Smirnov test	0,096	
Adj R Square	0.840	
N = 100		

The research data passes all the conditions for the classical assumption test, including the multicollinearity test, heteroscedasticity test, autocorrelation test, and normalcy test, as shown in table 3. The research yielded an adjusted R2 value of 0.840, indicating that the variables performance expectancy, effort expectancy, social impact, and facilitating conditions may account for 84% of the variance in the variable intention to invest. The remaining 16% of the variance is attributed to other factors.

A desirable independent variable in a multiple regression model exhibits a significant correlation with the dependent variable, while showing no correlation with other independent variables. The calculation of the Variation Inflation Factor (VIF) and TOL yields the tolerance test. If the tolerance (TOL) value is about 1, it indicates the absence of collinearity. Additionally, if the variance inflation factor

(VIF) value is less than 10, it confirms that the independent variable is not affected by multicollinearity.

The Performance Expectancy variable has a VIF value of 2.576, the Effort Expectancy variable has a VIF value of 2.723, the Social Influence variable has a VIF value of 2.870, and the Facilitating Conditions variable has a VIF value of 3.215, as indicated in Table 3. Therefore, there is no presence of multicollinearity among the independent variables, as all the variables are independent from each other. The VIF value is 2.576. The VIF value is below 10. The Tolerance values for the Performance Expectancy, Effort Expectancy, Social Influence, and Facilitating Conditions variables are 0.388, 0.367, 0.348, and 0.311, respectively. The Tolerance value for the three variables is around one, indicating the absence of multicollinearity among the independent variables.

Hypothesis Testing

Table 4. Hypothesis test

Independent variable			
Hypothesis test	**Coefficient**	**t value**	**Sign**
Performance Expectancy	0,251	9,793	0,000
Effort Expectancy	0,002	0,045	0,964
Social Influence	0,044	2,307	0,022
▪ Facilitating Condition	0,207	6,213	0,000

The t-test results in table 4 indicate that the hypotheses regarding Performance Expectancy, Social Influence, and Facilitating Conditions are all below 0.05, supporting these hypotheses. However, the hypothesis concerning the Effort Expectancy variable is above 0.05, leading to its rejection.

Performance expectation refers to the degree to which an individual perceives that utilizing a system will provide them with a competitive edge in their performance (Venkatesh et al., 2003). Various research have investigated the correlation between performance expectancy and investment intention. Sashikala & Chitramani (2018) discovered that behavioral factors have a considerable influence on both short and long-term investment intentions. Palacios-Gonzãlez & Chamorro-Mera (2018) found that socially responsible consuming habits, perception of personal gain, and assessment of the effectiveness of the action are important elements that affect the desire to spend in a socially responsible way. Lim et al. (2013) discovered that attitudes, subjective norms, perceived behavioral control, and risk inclination are important factors that can predict investing intentions. Lim et al. (2013) emphasized the influence of product knowledge, involvement, and perceived risk on investment intentions. These studies indicate that performance expectancy, a crucial element of the Technology Acceptance Model, has a substantial role in influencing investment intentions.

Effort Expectancy refers to the perceived ease of using a system. An accessible securities crowdfunding investment system will attract individuals to participate and contribute to charitable causes within the system. This will facilitate investors in participating in securities crowdfunding. Studies have consistently demonstrated that effort expectancy, which refers to the perceived ease of using a system, greatly impacts the intention to invest (Handoko et al., 2020; A. K. Mishra et al., 2023; Rahadjeng & Fiandari, 2020). Rahadjeng & Fiandari (2020) discovered that the anticipated reward and effectiveness of effort are key factors in deciding the level of mental effort and control distribution in investment choices. Mishra et al. (2023) confirmed that attitude, awareness, and investment decision involvement are key indicators of investment intention. Handoko et al. (2020) emphasized the significance of financial knowledge and self-efficacy in impacting the investment intentions of older pre-retirees. Effort Expectancy does not have a significant impact on a person's interest in investing through securities crowdfunding in this study, suggesting that its influence may differ based on the investment scenario.

Social influence refers to an individual's sense of the significance of something to others when they adopt a new system. Various factors impact individuals' decision to invest. (Fadila et al., 2020) discovered that the learning process, especially through monitoring stock prices, significantly influences students' investment intentions. Natsir & Arifin (2021) found that product expertise and social influence were important elements, but perceived risk did not operate as a mediator. Ummah et al. (2021) emphasized that purpose significantly influences investment decisions, while returns and technical improvements also have a direct and indirect impact. S. Mishra et al. (2022) highlighted the significance of attitude, awareness, and investment decision involvement in predicting investment intention, noting that perceived barriers and social media influence had a minor impact. This aligns with the results of the study, indicating that social influence plays a crucial role in shaping an individual's inclination towards participating in securities crowdsourcing.

Facilitating conditions refer to a person's belief in how much an organization's presence and technical infrastructure assist the use of a system. The UTAUT model suggests that the acceptance of behavioral control and extrinsic goal elements can directly influence the utilization of online information systems (Venkatesh et al., 2003). Various research have investigated the elements that impact investment intention. Narsaa et al. (2020) discovered that financial and non-financial data, along with market conditions, have a notable impact. Gainau (2020) emphasized the impact of job prospects and the significance of attitudes and perceived behavioral control. Salisa (2021) highlighted the significance of perceived behavioral control, financial literacy, and risk perception. Ummah et al. (2021) pinpointed the impact of intention on investing choices, especially concerning returns and technology improvements. These results indicate that a mix of financial, non-financial, and market-related factors, along with individual attitudes and perceived control, can greatly impact investing intention. Consistent with the research, it was found that Facilitating conditions greatly impact an individual's inclination to invest in securities crowdsourcing.

Multiple Regression Equation

Table 5. Multicollinearity test results

Coefficients[a]								
Model		**Unstandardized Coefficients**		**Standardized Coefficients**	**t**	**Sig.**	**Collinearity Statistics**	
		B	**Std. Error**	**Beta**			**Tol**	**VIF**
1	(Constant)	0,374	0,327		1,146	0,254		
	Performance Expectency	0,251	0,026	0,518	9,793	0,000	0,385	2,596
	Effort Expectency	0,002	0,039	0,002	0,045	0,964	0,366	2,730
	Social Influence	0,044	0,019	0,129	2,307	0,022	0,346	2,887
	Fasilitating Conditions	0,207	0,033	0,363	6,213	0,000	0,316	3,166

a. Dependent Variable: Intention to Invest

The following regression model is derived based on the data presented in Table 5.

$$\text{Intention} = \beta + \beta_1 X_1 + \beta_2 X_2 + \beta_3 X_3 + \beta_4 X_4 + e$$

$$\text{Intention} = 0.374 + 0.251\ PE + 0.002\ EE + 0.044\ SI + 0.207\ FC + e$$

The regression analysis results provide valuable insights into the relationship between various independent factors (Performance Expectancy, Effort Expectancy, Social Influence, and Facilitation Condition) and the dependent variable, intention to contribute through securities crowdfunding. With a constant coefficient of 0.374, it is observed that even in the absence of any independent factors, there is a projected increase of 0.374% in the likelihood of investing through securities crowdfunding. Individual coefficients further elucidate this relationship, such as the 0.251 coefficient for Performance Expectancy (X1), indicating a positive impact on intention to participate, and the 0.002 coefficient for Effort Expectancy (X2), suggesting a slight decrease in intention with increased effort expectancy. Additionally, the negative correlation between Social Influence (X3) and intention to invest, evidenced by a coefficient of 0.044, and the 0.207 coefficient for Facilitation Condition (X4), implying a decrease in desire with increased facilitation condition, contribute to a comprehensive understanding of the dynamics at play.

These coefficients shed light on the influence of each independent variable on the intention to invest in securities crowdfunding within the specified context. For instance, the positive or negative impact of changes in Performance Expectancy, Effort Expectancy, Social Influence, and Facilitation Condition on the intention to contribute through securities crowdfunding can be quantified based on these coefficients. Understanding these relationships is crucial for stakeholders in securities crowdfunding, enabling them to tailor strategies and interventions effectively to enhance investor participation and engagement. By comprehensively analyzing these coefficients, researchers and practitioners can develop targeted approaches to address factors influencing investor behavior in securities crowdfunding, ultimately fostering a more conducive environment for investment and financial growth.

CONCLUSION AND RECOMMENDATION

Based on an examination of the community's viewpoint on Sharia Securities Crowdfunding, it can be inferred that this method holds significant promise in enabling investment in line with sharia principles, promoting financial inclusivity, and bolstering the expansion of small enterprises. Nevertheless, it is imperative to comprehend and address the potential hazards, making financial literacy and effective oversight indispensable. Significance of this study illuminates the community's positive perspective on Sharia Securities Crowdfunding, emphasizing its ability to enable investment in line with Sharia principles, foster financial inclusion, and bolster the development of small businesses. The study highlights the importance of this funding approach in creating a more secure investment climate and promoting public welfare through an analysis of public attitudes. Furthermore, the focus on improving financial knowledge and efficient supervision highlights the significance of dealing with potential risks related to Sharia Securities Crowdfunding.

Although the study has positive potential, it admits specific constraints. Firstly, the study may not encompass the viewpoints of all demographic groups within the society, necessitating additional research to assure inclusiveness. Furthermore, the study highlights the significance of cooperation between governments, crowdfunding platforms, and Sharia organizations in creating a well-organized and reliable investment environment that adheres to Sharia principles. Stakeholders are advised to give priority to projects focused on improving financial awareness and developing strong monitoring systems to reduce risks related to Sharia Securities Crowdfunding.

Based on our data, it is evident that the public holds a favorable opinion on securities crowdfunding. This is due to its robust security system, which ensures a safer investment environment and contributes to public welfare. Enhancing financial literacy is essential to enhance public comprehension of Islamic crowdfunding investments in this scenario. In addition, collaboration among governments, crowdfunding platforms, and sharia institutions can facilitate the establishment of a structured and dependable investing environment that adheres to sharia norms. If executed effectively, Sharia Securities Crowdfunding has the capacity to emerge as a significant instrument in the advancement of sustainable Islamic finance.

In the future, research should focus on addressing numerous important aspects. Firstly, it is necessary to conduct longitudinal research in order to evaluate the long-term effects and durability of Sharia Securities Crowdfunding activities. Furthermore, conducting comparative research across various locations and demographic groups can offer useful insights into the differences in public views and the efficacy of regulatory regimes. Moreover, qualitative research techniques, including as interviews and focus groups, can provide more profound understanding of the motives and apprehensions of investors engaging in Sharia Securities Crowdfunding. Furthermore, the integration of viewpoints from finance, law, and Islamic studies in multidisciplinary research collaborations can enhance our comprehension of the complex processes that influence the development of Sharia Securities Crowdfunding.

REFERENCES

Abdillah, F., & Danial, E. (2015). Crowdfunding: Demokratisasi Akses Keuangan Dalam Mendukung Aksi Sosial Mahasiswa. *Jurnal Ilmiah Mimbar Demokrasi*, 15(1), 1–16. DOI: 10.21009/jimd.v15i1.9108

Ahmad Mohamad, K., Nor, R. M., & Kamely, A. A. (2021). Crowdfunding: New Form of Both Investment Opportunities and Source of Capital. In *Innovative Strategies for Implementing FinTech in Banking* (pp. 110–135). IGI Global. DOI: 10.4018/978-1-7998-3257-7.ch007

Ajzen, I. (1991). The theory of planned behavior. *Organizational Behavior and Human Decision Processes*, 50(2), 179–211. DOI: 10.1016/0749-5978(91)90020-T

Athief, F. H. N. (2019). Embedding Crowdfunding Structure in Islamic Venture Capital for SMEs Development. *Economica: Jurnal Ekonomi Islam*, 10(1), 1–28. DOI: 10.21580/economica.2019.10.1.3186

Belleflamme, P., Lambert, T., & Schwienbacher, A. (2014). Crowdfunding: Tapping the right crowd. *Journal of Business Venturing*, 29(5), 585–609. DOI: 10.1016/j.jbusvent.2013.07.003

Boudreau, K. J., Jeppesen, L. B., Reichstein, T., & Rullani, F. (2021). Crowdfunding as Donations to Entrepreneurial Firms. *Research Policy*, 50(7), 104264. DOI: 10.1016/j.respol.2021.104264

Bursa Efek Indonesia. (2022). *Sejarah dan Milestone Pasar Modal*. IDX Channel.

Caputo, A., Schiocchet, E., & Troise, C. (2022). Sustainable business models as successful drivers in equity crowdfunding. *Business Strategy and the Environment*, 31(7), 3509–3522. DOI: 10.1002/bse.3102

Fadila, D., Sastrawinata, H., Maulana, R., & Mariskha, Z. (2020). Impact of Learning, Socialization, and Financial Lifestyle of Students' Intention to Invest in Capital Market. *Proceedings of the 3rd Forum in Research, Science, and Technology (FIRST 2019)*. DOI: 10.2991/assehr.k.200407.038

Febriaty, H. (2019). Pengaruh Sistem Pembayaran Non Tunai Dalam Era Digital Terhadap Tingkat Pertumbuhan Ekonomi Indonesia. [Festival Riset Ilmiah Manajemen Dan Akuntansi]. *Prosiding FRIMA*, 6681(2), 307–313. DOI: 10.55916/frima.v0i2.47

Fuadi, N. F. Z., Farida, D., & Saadah, N. (2020, May 20). Empathy or Self-credibility? An Empirical Study of Intentions to Donate through Social Crowdfunding using the UTAUT Model. *Proceedings of the Proceedings of the 1st Conference on Islamic Finance and Technology, CIFET, 21 September, Sidoarjo, East Java, Indonesia*. DOI: 10.4108/eai.21-9-2019.2293953

Fund, C. M. (2012). Crowdfunding. In Publication, C. (Ed.), *A Canadian Context: Exploring The Potential Of Crowdfunding In The Creative Content Industries*.

Gainau, P. C. (2020). Have Students Comprehended Investment? *Journal of Accounting and Investment*, 21(3). Advance online publication. DOI: 10.18196/jai.2103162

Gerber, E. M., & Hui, J. (2013). Crowdfunding. *ACM Transactions on Computer-Human Interaction*, 20(6), 1–32. DOI: 10.1145/2530540

Green, C. H. (2014). *Banker's Guide to New Small Business Finance, + Website: Venture Deals, Crowdfunding, Private Equity, and Technology*. Wiley. https://books.google.co.id/books?id=rDIWBAAAQBAJ

Ardi Hamzah. (2010). *FAKTOR-FAKTOR PEMAKAI YANG MEMPENGARUHI MINAT PEMANFAATAN SISTEM INFORMASI*. 279–292.

Handoko, L., Nugroho, V. C., & Sembel, J. S. (2020). INTENTION TO INVEST IN FINANCIAL PRODUCT OF OLDER PRERETIREES WITH FINANCIAL SELF EFFICACY AS AN INTERVENING VARIABLE. *Ultima Management : Jurnal Ilmu Manajemen*, 12(1), 34–45. DOI: 10.31937/manajemen.v12i1.1539

Harahap, B. A., Paundralingga, A. Y., Cinditya, A., & Kusuma, M. (2018). Implikasi Makroekonomi dari Inovasi Digital: Studi Literatur. *Occasional Paper*, 1–50.

Hornuf, L., & Schwienbacher, A. (2018). Market mechanisms and funding dynamics in equity crowdfunding. *Journal of Corporate Finance*, 50, 556–574. DOI: 10.1016/j.jcorpfin.2017.08.009

Hornuf, L., Stenzhorn, E., & Vintis, T. (2022). Are sustainability-oriented investors different? Evidence from equity crowdfunding. *The Journal of Technology Transfer*, 47(6), 1662–1689. DOI: 10.1007/s10961-021-09896-9

Kagramanto, L. B., & Serfiyani, C. Y. (2019). The Principles of Contract in Donation Based Crowdfunding. *Yuridika*, 34(1), 78. DOI: 10.20473/ydk.v34i1.11801

Kurniasih, W. (2022). *Pengertian Modal: Sejarah, Jenis, Sumber, dan Manfaat*. Gramedia.

Lee, E. (2019). Equity crowdfunding in Hong Kong: Potential, challenges and investor protection. *Journal of Corporate Law Studies*, 19(2), 277–302. DOI: 10.1080/14735970.2017.1369235

Lemeshow, S. J, D. W. H., Klar, J., & K.Lwanga, S. (1997). *Besar Sampel dalam Penelitian Kesehatan*. Gajah Mada Uneversity Press.

Li, X. (2016). Status and Challenges of Equity Crowdfunding Development. *Proceedings of the 2016 International Conference on Economy, Management and Education Technology*. DOI: 10.2991/icemet-16.2016.338

Li, Y.-Z., He, T.-L., Song, Y.-R., Yang, Z., & Zhou, R.-T. (2018). Factors impacting donors' intention to donate to charitable crowd-funding projects in China: A UTAUT-based model. *Information Communication and Society*, 21(3), 404–415. DOI: 10.1080/1369118X.2017.1282530

Lim, K. L., Soutar, G. N., & Lee, J. A. (2013). Factors affecting investment intentions: A consumer behaviour perspective. *Journal of Financial Services Marketing*, 18(4), 301–315. DOI: 10.1057/fsm.2013.23

Lukkarinen, A. (2020). Equity Crowdfunding: Principles and Investor Behaviour. In *Advances in Crowdfunding* (pp. 93–118). Springer International Publishing. DOI: 10.1007/978-3-030-46309-0_5

Lukkarinen, A., Teich, J. E., Wallenius, H., & Wallenius, J. (2016). Success drivers of online equity crowdfunding campaigns. *Decision Support Systems*, 87, 26–38. DOI: 10.1016/j.dss.2016.04.006

Manik, N., & Sukadana, I. W. (2020). MEMAHAMI EKONOMI DIGITAL DI INDONESIA : STUDI KASUS MARKETPLACE. *E-Journal Ekonomi Pembangunan Universitas Udayana, 9 No.2*(Februari), 383–412.

Marwa, M. H. M., Al-Fatih, S., Hussain, M. A., & Haris, H. (2024). The Position and Role of the Sharia Supervisory Board in Ensuring Sharia Compliance Equity Crowdfunding in Indonesia. *Jurnal Hukum*, 39(2), 212. DOI: 10.26532/jh.v39i2.33330

Maula, M. V. J., & Lukkarinen, A. (2019). Attention Across Borders: Investor Attention as a Driver of Investment Choices in Cross-Border Equity Crowdfunding. SSRN *Electronic Journal*. DOI: 10.2139/ssrn.3487467

Maula, M. V. J., & Lukkarinen, A. (2022). Attention across borders: Investor attention as a driver of cross-border equity crowdfunding investments. *Strategic Entrepreneurship Journal*, 16(4), 699–734. DOI: 10.1002/sej.1424

Mishra, A. K., Bansal, R., Maurya, P. K., Kar, S. K., & Bakshi, P. K. (2023). Predicting the antecedents of consumers' intention toward purchase of mutual funds: A hybrid <scp>PLS-SEM-neural</scp> network approach. *International Journal of Consumer Studies*, 47(2), 563–587. DOI: 10.1111/ijcs.12850

Mishra, S., Aravind, S. M., Charpe, P., Ajlouni, S., ... (2022). Traditional rice-based fermented products: Insight into their probiotic diversity and probable health benefits. *Food Bioscience*. https://www.sciencedirect.com/science/article/pii/S2212429222005429

Morissan. (2015). *Periklanan : Komunikasi Pemasaran Terpadu* (4th ed.). Prenadamedia.

Muhammad, R., & Yuningsih, A. (2020). Shariah Compliance Analysis of Islamic Crowdfunding: Case Study of ethiscrowd.com. *IQTISHODUNA: Jurnal Ekonomi Islam*, 9(1), 75. DOI: 10.36835/iqtishoduna.v9i1.472

Naldi, G. A., & Muljaningsih, S. (2022). Pengaruh Motivasi, Persepsi Risiko, Pengetahuan terhadap Investasi pada UMKM melalui Platform Securities Crowdfunding. *Islamic Economic and Finance in Focus*, 1(1), 50–60. DOI: 10.21776/ieff.2022.01.1.05

Narsaa, I. M., Dian, N. P., & Handayani, R. (2020). An Experimental Study of the Effect of Financial and Non-Financial Information on Intention to Invest in the Bearish and Bullish Market. *International Journal of Innovation. Creativity and Change*, 11(11), 421–439.

Natsir, K., & Arifin, A. Z. (2021). The Effect of Product Knowledge and Influence of Society on Investment Intention of Stock Investors with Perceived Risk as Mediation. *Estudios de Economía Aplicada*, 39(12). Advance online publication. DOI: 10.25115/eea.v39i12.6022

Ndou, V., Scorrano, P., Mele, G., & Stefanizzi, P. (2022). Fundraising activities and digitalization: Defining risk indicators for evaluating equity crowdfunding campaigns. *Meditari Accountancy Research*, 30(4), 1169–1190. DOI: 10.1108/MEDAR-03-2021-1237

Nelly, R., Harianto, H., Abd.Majid, M. S., Marliyah, M., & Handayani, R. (2022). Studi Empiris Perkembangan Crowdfunding Syariah di Indonesia. *Al-Kharaj : Jurnal Ekonomi. Keuangan & Bisnis Syariah*, 4(5), 1283–1297. DOI: 10.47467/alkharaj.v4i5.926

Ngafifi, M. (2014). Kemajuan Teknologi Dan Pola Hidup Manusia Dalam Perspektif Sosial Budaya. *Jurnal Pembangunan Pendidikan: Fondasi Dan Aplikasi*, 2(1), 33–47. DOI: 10.21831/jppfa.v2i1.2616

Noor, A. (2022). THE LEGAL REGULATORY FRAMEWORK OF SHARIA SECURITIES CROWDFUNDING IN INDONESIA. *Masalah-Masalah Hukum*, 51(4), 433–444. DOI: 10.14710/mmh.51.4.2022.433-444

Nugraheni, N. (2020). Crowdfunding-based fiduciary warrant in providing capital loans for small and medium enterprises. *Hasanuddin Law Review*, 6(3), 224–231. DOI: 10.20956/halrev.v6i3.2201

Oktavian, R. D., & Maika, M. R. (2020). The Application of Utaut Model To the Crowdfunding Based Halal Tourism Capital Platform Innovation. *Laa Maisyir : Jurnal Ekonomi Islam*, 7(2), 188. DOI: 10.24252/lamaisyir.v7i2.16104

Or, C., & Chapman, E. (2021). An Extended Unified Theory of Acceptance and Use of Technology Model for Education Contexts. *Journal of Applied Learning & Teaching*, 4(2). Advance online publication. DOI: 10.37074/jalt.2021.4.2.7

OxfordDictinoary. (2022). *CrowdFunding*. Oxford Dictinoary.

Palacios-González, M. M., & Chamorro-Mera, A. (2018). Analysis of the predictive variables of the intention to invest in a socially responsible manner. *Journal of Cleaner Production*, 196, 469–477. DOI: 10.1016/j.jclepro.2018.06.066

Permana, G. P. L., & Rahayuni, D. A. B. (2023). Determinan Penggunaan Crowdfunding Berbasis Donasi. *Jurnal Aplikasi Akuntansi*, 7(2), 315–327. DOI: 10.29303/jaa.v7i2.211

Perpustakaan, J. I. (2022). *PENERAPAN INTERNET OF THINGS (IoT) DALAM UPAYA MEWUJUDKAN PERPUSTAKAAN DIGITAL DI ERA SOCIETY 5.0. 11*(1), 29–36.

Rahadjeng, E. R., & Fiandari, Y. R. (2020). THE EFFECT OF ATTITUDE, SUBJECTIVE NORMS AND CONTROL OF BEHAVIOR TOWARDS INTENTION IN SHARE INVESTMENT. *Manajemen Bisnis*, 10(2). Advance online publication. DOI: 10.22219/jmb.v10i2.13616

Roeckelein, J. E., Anwar, A., & Irawati, I. (2013). *Dictionary of Theories, Laws, and Concepts*. Kencana.

Salisa, N. R. (2021). Faktor yang Mempengaruhi Minat Investasi di Pasar Modal: Pendekatan Theory of Planned Behaviour (TPB). *Jurnal Akuntansi Indonesia*, 9(2), 182. DOI: 10.30659/jai.9.2.182-194

Sashikala, V., & Chitramani, P. (2018). The Impact of Behavioural Factors on Investment Intention of Equity Investors. *Asian Journal of Management*, 9(1), 183. DOI: 10.5958/2321-5763.2018.00028.8

Schwartz, A. A. (2013). Crowdfunding securities. *The Notre Dame Law Review*, 88(3), 1457–1490. https://www.scopus.com/inward/record.uri?eid=2-s2.0-84878133437&partnerID=40&md5=715516b683824cba2e6c244333febb57

Schwienbacher, A. (2021). Equity Crowdfunding and Capital Formation for Early-Stage Firms. In *The Palgrave Handbook of Technological Finance* (pp. 425–440). Springer International Publishing., DOI: 10.1007/978-3-030-65117-6_18

Shadily, H. (1983). *Ensiklopedia Indonesia* (staf penyunting redaksi Ensiklopedi Indonesia (ed.)). Ichtiar baru-Van Hoeve.

Smirnova, E., Platt, K., Lei, Y., & Sanacory, F. (2021). Pleasing the crowd: The determinants of securities crowdfunding success. *Review of Behavioral Finance*, 13(2), 165–183. DOI: 10.1108/RBF-07-2019-0096

Steinberg, S. (2012). *The Crowdfunding Bible: How to Raise Money for Any Startup, Video Game Or Project*. Lulu.com. https://books.google.co.id/books?id=MzBwvgEACAAJ

Sugihartono, N. S. R., & Harahap, F. (2007). *Pengantar Psikologi Umum* (1st, Cet.A ed.). UNY Press.

Sugiyono. (2021). Resensi Buku Metode Penelitian Kuantitatif Kualitatif dan R&D. In *Alfabeta* (3rd ed.).

Taiwo, A. A., & Downe, A. G. (2013). *THE THEORY OF USER ACCEPTANCE AND USE OF TECHNOLOGY (UTAUT) : A META-ANALYTIC REVIEW OF EMPIRICAL FINDINGS 1*. https://api.semanticscholar.org/CorpusID:15178994

Ummah, A., Ahsan, M., & Anas, A. (2021). Students' Investment Decisions with Intention as an Intervening Variable. *Equilibrium: Jurnal Ekonomi Syariah*, 9(1), 135. DOI: 10.21043/equilibrium.v9i1.9995

Utama, S. M., & Putra Ganda, R. A. (2022). ANALYSIS OF SHARIA CONFORMITY ASPECTS IN STOCK INVESTMENT BASED ON SECURITIES CROWDFUNDING. *Al-Muamalat: Jurnal Ekonomi Syariah*, 9(2), 62–73. DOI: 10.15575/am.v9i2.18857

Van Schaik, P. (2009). Unified Theory of Acceptance and Use for Websites Used by Students in Higher Education. *Journal of Educational Computing Research*, 40(2), 229–257. DOI: 10.2190/EC.40.2.e

Venkatesh, M., Morris, , Davis, , & Davis, . (2003). User Acceptance of Information Technology: Toward a Unified View. *Management Information Systems Quarterly*, 27(3), 425. DOI: 10.2307/30036540

Venturelli, V., Pedrazzoli, A., & Gualandri, E. (2019). *From Seeker Side to Investor Side: Gender Dynamics in UK Equity Crowdfunding Investments* (pp. 97–115). DOI: 10.1007/978-3-030-16295-5_4

Vismara, S. (2022). Expanding corporate finance perspectives to equity crowdfunding. *The Journal of Technology Transfer*, 47(6), 1629–1639. DOI: 10.1007/s10961-021-09903-z PMID: 34803218

Walgito, B. (1994). *Pengantar Psikologi Umum*. Andi Offset.

Wallmeroth, J. (2019). Investor behavior in equity crowdfunding. *Venture Capital*, 21(2–3), 273–300. DOI: 10.1080/13691066.2018.1457475

Wang, N., Shen, X.-L., & Sun, Y. (2013). Transition of electronic word-of-mouth services from web to mobile context: A trust transfer perspective. *Decision Support Systems*, 54(3), 1394–1403. DOI: 10.1016/j.dss.2012.12.015

Whitla, P. (2009). Crowdsourcing and Its Application in Marketing Activities. *Contemporary Management Research*, 5(1). Advance online publication. DOI: 10.7903/cmr.1145

Wicaksana, A., & Rachman, T. (2018). KESADARAN DAN PERSEPSI USAHA MIKRO DAN KECIL TERHADAP CROWDFUNDING SYARIAH. *Angewandte Chemie International Edition, 6(11), 951–952.*, *3*(1), 10–27.

Willems, W. (2013). *What characteristics of crowdfunding platforms influence the success rate ? July*, 70.

Wong, S.-L., Hsu, C.-C., & Chen, H.-S. (2018). To Buy or Not to Buy? Consumer Attitudes and Purchase Intentions for Suboptimal Food. *International Journal of Environmental Research and Public Health*, 15(7), 1431. DOI: 10.3390/ijerph15071431 PMID: 29986474

Wu, J., Liu, L., & Cao, Y. (2023). Understanding investor co-investment in a syndicate on equity crowdfunding platforms. *Industrial Management & Data Systems*, 123(5), 1599–1623. DOI: 10.1108/IMDS-09-2022-0538

Xu, X., Lu, Y., Vogel-Heuser, B., & Wang, L. (2021). Industry 4.0 and Industry 5.0—Inception, conception and perception. *Journal of Manufacturing Systems*, 61(September), 530–535. DOI: 10.1016/j.jmsy.2021.10.006

Zakhlebin, I., & Horvát, E.-Á. (2019). Investor Retention in Equity Crowdfunding. *Proceedings of the 10th ACM Conference on Web Science*, 343–351. DOI: 10.1145/3292522.3326037

Chapter 9
Unleashing the E-Wallet Enchantment:
A Journey Through Maqasid al-Shariah

Ahmad Azwan bin Meor Hashim
https://orcid.org/0009-0008-2738-8427
Universiti Sains Islam Malaysia, Malaysia

Muhammad Ridhwan Ab Aziz
Universiti Sains Islam Malaysia, Malaysia

Junaidah Abu Seman
Universiti Sains Islam Malaysia, Malaysia

ABSTRACT

Due to the increasing use of e-wallets, it is crucial to evaluate their compliance with Shariah to meet the needs of Muslim customers in line with Islamic principles. This chapter seeks to offer understanding of maqasid al-Shariah in the context of e-wallet usage and financial well-being. In connection with this, the development of financial technology will expand the capabilities and services of e-wallets beyond being just a basic payment tool. This expansion includes multiple funding sources, such as credit cards, buy now, pay later (BNPL), and short-term loans. These multi-sourcing fundings may trigger expenditure, aid, or impede financial well-being. Therefore, a user's spending behaviour can affect the e-wallet usage and their financial well-being. Understanding the results of this research would partly contribute to the general knowledge of Islamic finance and fintech, with the intention of developing Shariah-compliant digital financial solutions suited to the needs of Muslims all over the world.

DOI: 10.4018/979-8-3693-5653-1.ch009

INTRODUCTION

The increasing popularity and demand for digital technology led to the introduction of electronic wallets, which changed how financial transactions were done for people across the globe. The reinstatement of a landscape of personal finance and consumer spending behaviour saw wide acceptance in digital and electronic payment systems. On that note, in the opinion of Muslims, it is a valuable area worth investigating the influence e-wallets could have attached to the *maqasid al-Shariah*, which is guided by higher objectives of Islamic law.

Consumer finances have been revolutionised by the exponential expansion of financial technology (fintech) (Lim et al., 2022). According to McKinsey's 2023 Global Payments Report (Bionducci et al., 2023), cash usage declined by nearly four percentage points globally in 2022. Over the past five years, the growth rate for electronic transactions has roughly tripled the overall growth in payments revenue. The same payment trend can be seen in Malaysia. In 2022, electronic payment (e-payment) transactions grew by 31.5 per cent to 9.5 billion from 7.2 billion in 2021. Averaged across the whole country, each Malaysian could have made 291 e-payment transactions in 2022, indicating that cashless payment methods were gaining traction over cash-based (Fong, 2023).

Concurrently, e-wallets have gained significant traction as a preferred method for users to conduct digital transactions, shopping, and gain access to other financial services via mobile applications (Bionducci et al., 2023). In Malaysia, e-wallets have experienced tremendous expansion, where more than forty per cent of the populace utilises them for routine financial activities, according to Bank Negara Malaysia (BNM) Annual Report 2022 (BNM, 2023). With increased collaborations between e-money issuers (EMIs) and other financial service providers, customers can now access more financial products on e-wallet applications or platforms such as remittance, microinsurance, microfinancing and micro-investments (Fong, 2023). A recent report on global retail by fintech platform Adyen has shown that Malaysia is leading the world in e-wallet use, with 63 per cent of Malaysians using such payment options for their transactions (Adyen, 2024). The report – which drew its results from a survey of over 38,000 shoppers and 13,000 merchants across 26 markets – also noted that Malaysians are shifting away from physical wallets, with 55 per cent now relying on mobile-enabled solutions like QR Codes. The convenience of payment, together with the availability of various wallet funding methods, may influence consumer spending.

Spending behaviour is a key determinant of financial well-being (Fan & Henager, 2022; Kempson et al., 2017; M. Rahman et al., 2021; Sabri, Anthony, et al., 2023). Given the rise of e-wallets, an important question is how consumers' intention to continue using e-wallet financial services relates to their spending habits and financial well-being. Some research suggests that overspending and improper use of credit can negatively impact financial well-being (Xiao & Yao, 2022). However, few studies have examined associations between e-wallet use, spending behaviour, and financial well-being. Understanding these relationships can help policymakers and e-wallet providers promote responsible financial behaviours.

The Islamic financial business worldwide should recognise this innovative possibility in the financial sector, given the increasing number of digital and mobile banking users, especially in Malaysia. However, while revolutionising the financial industry into digital, fintech must adhere to Islamic objectives (*maqasid al-Shariah*). Islamic finance authorities assert that fintech is permissible and a benefit to humanity (*maslahah*). However, its efficacy is contingent upon how its consumers employ it. Fintech can be utilised for legitimate and beneficial purposes, as well as for executing illegal operations (Adam, 2021).

This chapter is structured to delve into the aspects of e-wallets and their impact on user's spending behaviour and financial well-being. At first, we examine the trends and advancements of e-wallet in Malaysia, emphasizing government regulations and incentives that have influenced adoption. We then explore the perspective from *Shariah* law, assessing how e-wallets align with principles of *maqasid al-Shariah*. The discussion extends to how mobile payments influence spending habits, considering how personal beliefs and Islamic guidelines influence choices. Additionally, we investigate the effects of e-wallet usage on well-being, analysing the link between spending behaviours and individual's financial well-being. Ultimately, we suggest a framework to grasp the connections between e-wallet use, spending behaviours, and financial well-being to contribute to creating *Shariah*-compliant digital financial solutions.

E-WALLETS TRENDS AND DEVELOPMENTS IN MALAYSIA

E-wallets have gained popularity as a mobile payment option thanks to advancements in technology, the rise in smartphone usage and their ease of use. The increasing prevalence of e-commerce and the shift towards transactions have fuelled the adoption of e-wallets, enabling users to make both online and offline payments effortlessly using their smartphones or physical cash or cards (Ramli & Hamzah, 2021; Ruldeviyani & Saraswati, 2023). The COVID-19 pandemic further accelerated this trend as people turned to payment methods to reduce contact (Shukur et al., 2022). E-wallets provide a comprehensive experience by integrating various financial services such as facilitating purchases, online shopping, bill payments, and both local and international fund transfers, while also offering cashbacks and discounts onto a unified platform (Teng & Khong, 2021).

Furthermore, the integration of security features such as encryption and blockchain technology has bolstered user confidence and reduced risks related to cybercrime (Kaur et al., 2018; Pachpande & Kamble, 2018). The ability to make payments through technologies like near-field communication (NFC), sound waves and radio frequency signals has also boosted their popularity by offering convenience and cost management options (David & Kathrine, 2019; Kanimozhi & Kamatchi, 2017). Moreover, the wide acceptance of e-wallets by both small retailers has established them as a common payment option (Ruopeng et al., 2015). Research indicates that factors such as tailored services, ease of use and perceived advantages play a role in influencing users' readiness to share details and embrace e-wallets.

The financial landscape of Malaysia is undergoing a significant transformation, driven by the rapid adoption of digital payment methods. Popular platforms like GrabPay, Boost and Touch 'n Go have become indispensable for their cashless and touch-free advantages during the pandemic period (Mat et al., 2022; Nair et al., 2023). This industry expansion is fuelled by backing and strategies aimed at transitioning Malaysia into a cashless society by 2050 and a prominent player in the economy by 2025 (Seng et al., 2023). E-wallets have also been incorporated into religious practices, such as zakat collection and distribution, enhancing transparency, accountability and effectiveness (Beik et al., 2021; Bella & Efendi, 2021; Nordin et al., 2023).

The VISA Consumer Payment Attitudes (CPA) 2023 report offers a look at the changing landscape, focusing on trends and consumer behaviours in Malaysia (VISA, 2024). An important discovery in the report is that 40% of consumers envision a completely cashless society by 2025. This positive outlook is backed by data showing that 75% of consumers successfully embraced cashless transactions in 2023, an increase from the previous year. Malaysians, on average, have adopted cashless methods for 11.3 days, signalling a shift in payment habits. The decline in cash usage among consumers is being driven by factors such as increased use of contactless payments, wider acceptance of cashless options, and concerns about safety. According to the report, over six out of ten Malaysian consumers utilize wallets for in-app purchases. The incorporation of payment features into applications has made transactions seamless, contributing to the rising popularity of mobile wallets.

Despite the increasing usage, challenges persist regarding acceptance rates among those with incomes and concerns about security and trust issues, particularly among university students (Abu Bakar, 2022; Izaidin, 2022). Influential factors affecting the adoption of e-wallets comprise how useful and easy they are to use, government backing, and promotional perks, all of which have an impact on user satisfaction and intention (Kamis et al., 2022; Kiew et al., 2022). The e-wallet market is expected to reach USD 20 billion by 2024, indicating a future for payments in Malaysia (Research & Markets, 2024). However, challenges such as readiness among merchants and connectivity issues during transactions need to be resolved to improve user acceptance and experience.

As of March 2024, there are currently 44 e-wallet providers in Malaysia. Notable platforms that are accessible include Touch 'n Go, Boost, GrabPay, Razer Pay, Fave, Lazada Wallet, ShopeePay, Maybanks MAE, and Air Asias BigPay. The primary e-wallets, like Touch 'n Go, Boost, GrabPay, and ShopeePay, offer an array of features, including ride-hailing services, food delivery options, money transfer capabilities, and other services. Refer to Table 1 for an overview of these features.

Table 1. Additional features offered by the top four e-wallets

Transportation	
buy public transport and flight[#] ticket. fuel[#] toll payment[1] car battery[#]	e-hailing[2] food delivery[2,#] parcel delivery[2,1#]
Financial Services	
investment[1] short-term loan[1,4] insurance (car, travel, home, wallet)	visa prepaid card[1,2] foreign exchange[1,#] buy now, pay later (BNPL)[2,3,4]
Bills	
utilities mobile services	international mobile prepaid[1]
Entertainments	
online game match[#] game top up[#] digital rewards movies[#]	leisure, tour and travel[#] spa, wellness & accommodation[#] online streaming[3,#]
Others	
online/offline store[#] donation car rental[#] vouchers, gifts	zakat (collection & disbursement)[3] car breakdown/service[1#] housekeeping & cleaning[1#]

Source: Author's compilations

Note

1 – Touch ‘n Go e-wallet 2 – GrabPay e-wallet

3 – Boost 4 – ShopeePay

- embedded third-party service

E-wallet issuers have put in much work to attract more customers. To differentiate themselves in the competitive e-wallet industry, issuers have introduced a wide range of promotions, discounts, cashback, and app features. E-wallets now offer their customers options for investments and short-term credit facilities (such as GO + and GOPinjam in Touch 'N Go), as well as cashless and contactless payment and money transfer options through QRPay. Previously, this was the only service offered. Although still in their infancy, these facilities will help increase interest in and use of electronic wallets. With the introduction of Buy Now Pay Later (BNPL) instalment payments within e-wallet apps, customers can now purchase products from online retailers that offer a deferred payment option without paying additional fees, as long as the payment is made on time. The underserved and unbanked group is usually served by the short-term loans and BNPL facilities offered by e-wallet issuers. On the other hand, the drawbacks need to be addressed, especially the way they encourage spending and increase leverage.

In terms of cross-border payments, the Touch 'n Go e-wallet can be used beyond Malaysia (Mainland China, to be specific). In addition, users can also make payments whenever the Alipay+ QR code is displayed in Japan, South Korea, Singapore, the United Kingdom, Italy, France, and Germany (Fintech News Malaysia, 2022). These features are facilitated by the fact that TnG e-wallet is a partnership between TNG Digital Sdn Bhd and Ant Group (China), which owns Alipay digital payment solution. Cross-border bilateral payments between Malaysia and other ASEAN nations have become a reality thanks to Bank Negara Malaysia and Payment Network Malaysia Sdn. Bhd. (PayNet) collaboration and participation in Project Nexus. According to the report, Malaysians can use DuitNow QRPay to make in-person payments by scanning the physical QR codes displayed by retailers and cross-border online purchases in the Philippines (coming soon), Thailand, Indonesia, and Singapore (which have gone live). Project Nexus, led by the Innovation Hub of the Bank for International Settlements (BIS), is closely related to the G20 Roadmap for Enhancing Cross-Border Payments initiative. Although there are now only a few participating banks (AmBank, CIMB Bank, Hong Leong Bank, Maybank, Public Bank, and UOB Bank) and e-wallet providers (Boost and TnG e-wallet), there will be more soon.

Malaysia has emerged as a major hub for Islamic fintech innovation, and embedded financial services built into e-commerce platforms (R. Hasan et al., 2020) . The country provides supportive regulatory infrastructure for offering digital financial products that adhere to religious customs, driving the development of *Shariah*-compliant BNPL plans, personal financing, and takaful products via e-wallet apps (Firmansyah & Anwar, 2019). Adoption of these embedded services has accelerated during COVID-19 as consumers shift online (Rabbani, 2022). Key players include e-wallets like Boost and Touch 'n Go, and Shopee integrating *Shariah*-compliant BNPL and micro-investment channels.

With the availability of credit cards as one of the primary funding channels for e-wallets and the extension of e-wallet functionalities beyond mobile payment to include BNPL and short-term personal financing, credit and self-control aspects might be included as antecedents in the present study. In addition, religious belief has a significant effect on our purchasing decisions and decision-making. Understanding the impact of consumer behaviour is, therefore, a crucial business discipline. Overall, the e-wallet industry in Malaysia is poised for continued growth, driven by technological advancements, supportive government policies, and changing consumer behaviours towards digital and contactless payments.

Government Regulation and Incentives in Boosting E-wallet Adoption

Government regulations play a pivotal role in shaping the e-wallet industry in Malaysia by providing the necessary framework and incentives to encourage adoption and ensure compliance with financial standards. The Malaysian government has actively promoted the use of e-wallets through initiatives like the E-Tunai Rakyat, e-Penjana, and eMADANI, which have significantly boosted e-wallet usage by offering financial incentives to users (MOF, 2024; K. S. Moorthy et al., 2022; Nair et al., 2023). Additionally, the Financial Sector Blueprint 2011-2020 by Bank Negara Malaysia (BNM) aims to transition the country towards a cashless society by increasing e-payments and eliminating cheques, further accelerating the adoption of e-wallets (Tenk et al., 2020; Wong & Mohamed, 2021).

Government support has been particularly crucial during the COVID-19 pandemic, as it has heightened the need for contactless transactions, thereby increasing the reliance on e-wallets (Ming & Jais, 2022; K. Moorthy et al., 2021). Moreover, the establishment of the Interoperable Credit Transfer Framework (ICTF) policy in 2018 has facilitated seamless transactions across different e-wallet platforms, enhancing user convenience and trust (Bee & Ying, 2021). Despite these efforts, challenges remain, such as ensuring *Shariah* compliance for e-wallets, which BNM has addressed by aligning e-wallet systems with the *wakalah* (agency) agreement, although some e-wallets still fall short of these standards (Noor & Yusoff, 2022). The government's role extends to addressing perceived risks and enhancing security measures, which are critical for user trust and adoption (Abdullah et al., 2020; N. L. A. Rahman et al., 2022). Overall, government regulations and support have been instrumental in driving the growth of the e-wallet industry in Malaysia, making it a key player in the country's digital economy transformation.

THE *SHARIAH* PERSPECTIVE OF E-WALLET

Shariah principles significantly influence the design and usage of e-wallets in countries like Indonesia and Malaysia by ensuring compliance with Islamic law, which emphasises ethical and interest-free financial transactions. E-wallets comply with *Shariah* principles in finance by adhering to specific Islamic contracts and ensuring that their operations do not involve elements prohibited in Islam, such as *riba* (usury), *gharar* (excessive uncertainty), and *maysir* (gambling) (Muchtar & Zubairin, 2022).

The initial development of fatwas on the application of FinTech was championed by Dewan Syariah Nasional, Majelis Ulama Indonesia, under which published *fatwas* (legal opinion or decree by an Islamic religious leader) in two areas: (117/DSNMUI/II/2018) information technology basis payment (DSN-MUI, 2018) and (116/DSN-MUI/IX/2017) electronic money (DSN-MUI, 2017). These have enabled a proper guideline for the first and only *Shariah*-compliant e-wallet in Indonesia and Southeast Asia, namely LinkAja Syariah, which was established in April 2020. The contract used in the *Shariah* e-wallet is a wadiah contract between the e-wallet provider and the owner of the funds. In addition, LinkAja Syariah services prioritises several basic principles, namely placing funds in cooperation with several Islamic banks and applying transaction procedures under *Shariah* principles, which can be accepted by all LinkAja merchants. At present, LinkAja Syariah services has collaborated with more than 242 institutions and ZISWAF (*zakat* - alms, *infaq* - disbursement, *sadaqah* - charity, and *waqf* - endowment) distribution institutions, more than 1,000 mosques, Islamic boarding schools, as well as several e-commerce and offline merchants' partners (LinkAja, 2020).

In Malaysia, the 117th convention of Muzakarah Majlis Kebangsaan Bagi Hal Ehwal Ugama Islam Malaysia (MKI), which took place from 25th to 29th August 2020, presented a perspective on the utilisation of e-wallets as per the *syarak* (*Shariah* or Islamic law). As a result, the Fatwa Committee for the states of Perak and Kedah adopted the regulation as a guideline for *Shariah* jurisdiction (*irsyad hukm*) for *fatwa* (Jabatan Mufti Negeri Kedah, 2020; Jabatan Mufti Negeri Perak, 2021). The MKI deems the utilisation of electronic wallets as *harus* (permissible) on the condition that the subsequent criteria are met (JAKIM, 2020):

1. It is mandatory to conduct digital transactions via an e-wallet operator that has received official approval and regulation from the relevant authority.
2. Users and operators must be well-informed on the proper utilisation of electronic wallets and be cognizant of their rights and obligations as parties to contracts.
3. It is recommended that the Operator pursue *Shariah* consulting services from a certified *Shariah* Advisor in order to comply with this transaction.

4. The Operator must explicitly communicate contractual terms and their ramifications to the User.
5. Provision of a refund mechanism in the event of account closure or bereavement involving funds belonging to the customer or the customer's heirs.
6. Encouragement to adopt *Shariah*-compliant electronic wallets by users.

Moreover, e-wallet operation in Malaysia is justified under e-money jurisdiction. A *Shariah*-compliant e-money contract is an agency contract (*wakalah*) in which the authorised issuer pays the merchant on the user's behalf (*wakil bi ad-dafi*). In compliance with Section 137 of the 2013 Islamic Financial Services Act (IFSA) 2013, funds must be placed in a *Shariah*-compliant escrow or deposit account. Technological advancements have facilitated the development of digital products that are both seamless and efficient. As technology is neutral and permissible, commercial transactions through modern means or devices of communication are allowed, subject to the following *fiqh* legal maxims:

1. The original state (of thing) is permissible.
2. The original rule in *muamalat* is permissibility unless there is an indication that prohibits it.
3. The original rule of a contract is mutual consent or agreement by both contracting parties. The consequence of a contract is based on (the rights and responsibilities) agreed upon in the contract.

According to the Policy Document on Electronic Money issued by Bank Negara Malaysia (BNM) on December 30, 2022, an e-money issuer (EMI) that issues *Shariah*-compliant e-money shall comply with the rulings of the Shariah Advisory Council of Bank Negara Malaysia (SAC) and relevant *Shariah* standards issued by BNM. These include the appointment of a *Shariah* advisor and an annual assessment of *Shariah* compliance (BNM, 2022). Moreover, all EMI must adhere to general regulations stated in the policy document, such as minimum capital funds for non-bank EMI, safeguarding of funds, fraud risk management, and account management, among others. This could be construed as a loan from the User to the authorised issuer (*qard*). Since the approved issuer functions as a payment channel for the merchant, the user should verify *Shariah's* compliance.

As a facilitator, technology is neutral from a *Shariah* standpoint, according to Adam (2021). Nevertheless, adherence to *Shariah* principles is a must for Fintech advancements in Islamic financial services, just as it is for any other financial product or service. In the realm of investment advice services, finance, and investments, fintech must be designed and constructed in accordance with the tenets of *Shariah*. For *Shariah*-compliant services-based Fintech solutions, including mobile payment, money transfer, and trading platforms, require minimal adjustment and are suitable for both conventional and Islamic finance.

Various studies indicate that factors like user-friendliness, practicality and social influence play a positive role in encouraging the adoption of *Shariah*-compliant e-wallets. On the other hand, perceived risk tends to have a negative impact on adoption rates, with little variation between Indonesian and Malaysian users (A. Alam & Saputro, 2022). The acceptance of *Shariah*-compliant e-wallets is also influenced by expectations regarding performance, ease of use, social influence and adherence to *Shariah* principles, especially among millennials in Malaysia (Bakri et al., 2023). The regulatory hurdles faced in overseeing Islamic Fintech services like e-wallets underscore the importance of clear regulations, a Shariah Supervisory Board and standardised governance practices for ensuring compliance (Muryanto, 2022). Moreover, ethical considerations in e-wallet transactions, such as avoiding gambling-related activities (*maysir*), uncertainties (*gharar*), usury (*riba*) and ensuring contract legitimacy are crucial for upholding Islamic business ethics (Minarni & Asnawi, 2022).

In Indonesia, the perceived usefulness of *riba*, trustworthiness concerns and understanding of *riba* significantly shape decisions regarding the use of *Shariah*-compliant e-wallets among users (Andriyaningtyas et al., 2021). The design of *Shariah* fintech apps should prioritise user friendliness and accessibility for users of all ages, meeting the needs of both younger and older individuals. It is important to ensure that the interface is easy to navigate while also aligning with *Shariah* principles (Hamsin et al., 2023). In general, *Shariah* principles play a significant role in influencing the regulations, user adoption and ethical aspects involved in crafting and utilising e-wallets within these regions.

Maqasid Al-Shariah and E-wallet

The purpose or objective of *Shariah* (*maqasid al-Shariah*), according to Imam al-Ghazali (Al-Ghazali & Hammad, 2017), is to promote the well-being of all people so as to preserve religion (*din*), life (*nafs*), intellect (*aql*), progeny or lineage (*nasl*), and wealth (*mal*). Adhering to these five principles is mandatory and will serve to preserve the public interest or *maslahah*. Any breach of these standards will lead to an increase in human exploitation and fraud. Since *maslahah* is the fundamental aim of Islamic law (Al-Shatibi, 2012), legislation is not created for its own sake but rather to serve the interests of humanity and prevent misfortunes (*mafsadah*) in this life and the Hereafter (Hidayatullah, 2023). As stated by Imam al-Shatibi (Al-Raysuni, 2006), the *Shariah* places human interests at the forefront of its priorities, which can be categorised into the following three hierarchical levels:

1. **Necessities** (*Daruriyyat*)

Things that are indispensable for forming and sustaining the five fundamental parts of humanity: religion, life, intellect, progeny, and wealth. This classification comprises subjects essential for safeguarding the elements mentioned above against potential harm (Khan & Ghifari, 1992), as well as those indispensable for attaining and sustaining the protection of these five elements (Al-Zarqa, 1984).

2. **Needs or Conveniences** (*Hajiyyat*)

Human needs that, while not critical for the survival of the five necessary elements, facilitate the smooth operation of human lives by eliminating obstacles and distress, such as automobiles, higher education, and economic activities. Insofar as it is possible to eliminate challenges or attain conveniences in life, Islam strongly advises providing such matters (Al Zarqa, 1982; Al-Zarqa, 1984; Mustafar & Borhan, 2013).

3. **Embellishments or Refinements** (*Tahsiniyyat*)

Complementary necessities that do not eliminate or alleviate difficulties but instead contribute to the overall happiness and pleasure of human existence, such as luxury products, gifts, and decorations. This category includes matters that exceed the boundaries of convenience, provided they are employed moderately (Al-Zarqa, 1984) and assigned the lowest priority, especially in cases where the first two categories still need to be fulfilled (Mustafar & Borhan, 2013).

The level of significance attributed to fintech goods differs across many facets; hence, it may be implausible to attempt to categorise them into a singular *maqasid al-Shariah* category (Daud & Salim, 2022). When all payment methods are widely accepted in metropolitan areas, electronic wallets may be considered *tahsiniyya*t. In contrast, using electronic wallets may be classified as *hajiyyat* in situations where shops providing essential goods accept only digital payments. In dire circumstances—when physical currency is no longer recognised as legal money in a nation—e-wallets can be considered *daruriyyat*. However, irrespective of the categorisation of e-wallets, according to *maqasid al-Shariah*, the essential e-wallet services and functionalities in Malaysia satisfy the stipulations and preferences outlined in *maqasid al-Shariah*.

E-wallets have transformed from mere payment platforms to super apps that incorporate various financial services, including investment, zakat, waqf, takaful, and financing options like personal loans and buy now, pay later (BNPL). E-wallet providers in Malaysia have implemented several digital functions and services, illustrated in Table 2, along with examples of how these contribute to the fulfilment of *maqasid al-Shariah*.

Table 2. Fulfilment of maqasid al-Shariah based on e-wallet functions and services

Maslahah	**Preservation and Protection of**	**E-wallet Functions and Services**
Daruriyyat	Religion	*Zakat* (alms), *sadaqah* (charity), and *waqf* (endowment).
	Life	Family and health takaful.
	Intellect	Savings, personal financing, and BNPL for education purpose.
	Progeny	Savings, personal financing, and BNPL for marriage purpose.
	Wealth	Investment and takaful protection for properties, and other valuable belongings.
Hajiyyat	Wealth	Personal financing, BNPL and savings for general needs, QRPay, DuitNow.
Tahsiniyyat	Wealth	Personal financing, BNPL and savings for vacation and luxuries.

Source: Adapted from (Daud & Salim, 2022) *with additional author's resource.*

E-wallets, as financial technology, are well in line with the principles of *maqasid al-Shariah*, specifically in safeguarding wealth (*hifz mal*) and providing benefits for users. Research shows that e-wallets enable simpler and more secure transactions, which are crucial for economic efficiency and safety (Alotaibi, 2022; Hafidh, 2022; Muamar et al., 2020). The adherence to the law is evident in e-wallets as they steer clear of *haram* elements (*Shariah* prohibited) while offering robust security measures to safeguard users' funds (Andriyaningtyas et al., 2021; Muamar & Alparisi, 2017). For example, all e-wallet apps in Malaysia adhere to *maqasid al-Shariah* by ensuring transaction security through verified PINs and codes. Moreover, the Malaysian government has implemented data privacy regulations to ensure that *Shariah*-compliant e-wallets adhere to legal standards and protect personal data, which is vital for fostering trust and security in digital transactions (Razali et al., 2021). However, challenges such as mishandling personal data and the need to enhance digital financial literacy remain pertinent, highlighting the importance of educating individuals and increasing awareness to mitigate risks (Hamsin et al., 2023).

Additionally, boosting the popularity of *Shariah*-compliant electronic wallets can be advanced through strategies such as providing points that can be converted into charitable donations, partnering with businesses, and utilizing social media for educational purposes (Nashirah et al., 2020). The advantages of using wallets, such as convenience in transactions and effectiveness, should be utilized to advocate for *maslahah* and promote financial inclusion, particularly for disadvantaged individuals, which aligns with the fundamental goal of *maqasid al-Shariah* (Aunurrochim

& Saharudin, 2021; Zustika & Fageh, 2022). By addressing these factors, e-wallet providers can ensure that their services not only adhere to Islamic law but also have a positive impact on the socio-economic welfare of their users. In essence, integrating e-wallets within the context of *maqasid al-Shariah* not only aids in safeguarding wealth but also fosters economic inclusivity and efficiency in line with the broader goals of Islamic finance (Ardiyanti et al., 2023).

MOBILE PAYMENTS AND SPENDING BEHAVIOUR

Spending behaviour refers to how people allocate their financial resources to purchase goods and services (Thaler, 1999). It is influenced by a complex interplay of internal and external factors, including demographics, income level, culture, emotions, self-control, social comparison, and cues in the environment (Dholakia et al., 2016; Haws et al., 2016; Rick et al., 2008; Soman & Cheema, 2011). Gaining insight into what drives consumer spending is important for policymakers seeking to stimulate certain sectors of the economy, financial institutions developing products and services, as well as individuals hoping to make sound financial decisions (Bernthal et al., 2005).

A robust body of research across disciplines like psychology, behavioural economics, marketing, sociology and neuroscience has explored various determinants of spending tendencies (Rick et al., 2008). For instance, income and wealth are correlated with higher spending capacity, but the relationship is not always linear (Friedline & West, 2016). Emotions experienced at the point of purchase can override rational calculations about the long-term impact, leading to impulsive buying and overspending (Dholakia et al., 2016). Social influences also pressure people to maintain lifestyle standards within a reference group, even by incurring debt (Schor, 1998).

Mobile payments have had an impact on how people spend money, making transactions easier and changing how consumers feel about spending. The ease and perceived advantages of using mobile payments have been discovered to boost purchases by reducing the "pain of paying" (discomfort of paying) and even generating a feeling of "pleasure of paying" (enjoyment in spending) as they streamline the process. This, consequently, increases the probability of buying both essential items (J. Xue & Lin, 2019). However, this ease of payment can also lead to excessive spending, especially among younger users who may turn to credit to maintain their spending habits (Mu & Lee, 2021; Park et al., 2022).

Additionally, according to liquidity constraint theory, differences in interest rates among consumers—reflecting varying levels of constraints—affect how people respond to economic stimulus measures (Kreiner et al., 2019). People with financial constraints tend to show more noticeable changes in their spending habits. Research on adults has shown that e-wallets can promote overspending through factors such as convenience, promotions, self-restraint challenges and the perception of having more funds than they actually do—an effect known as the illusion of liquidity (Aji & Adawiyah, 2021). This perceived abundance of funds influences the link between self-control and spending behaviour, leading e-wallet users to spend more. Furthermore, studies on the impact of changes in credit card payments reveal that altering these amounts can have a significant effect on how much consumers spend and their debt levels. This underscores the importance of constraints in shaping decision-making regarding money (Agarwal et al., 2023).

The perceived risks linked to using mobile payment methods can influence how people view their convenience and ease of use, which in turn affects their intentions and behaviours related to sustainable spending (Wang et al., 2022). Lifestyle choices and financial literacy also play roles; lifestyle indirectly affects spending habits through the frequency of mobile payment usage, while financial literacy does not show this indirect impact (Yuan & Jiang, 2023). Social aspects and trust are factors influencing the adoption of mobile payments; they can either encourage or discourage spending based on perceptions of credibility and social influence (Gosal & Linawati, 2018; Liu et al., 2019). Moreover, the shift from traditional to mobile payment methods is primarily driven by dissatisfaction with traditional ways and the perceived benefits of using mobile options. However, concerns about risks may impede this transition (Kamil & Istianingsih, 2020). Although mobile payments promote increased spending and smoother transactions overall, it is essential to manage them to avoid overspending and financial insecurity (Gohil et al., 2023).

Spending Behaviour According to *Maqasid Al-Shariah*

Spending behaviour based on *maqasid al-Shariah* emphasizes striking a balance between material and spiritual contentment, ensuring that consumption aligns with ethical values and societal well-being. It takes an approach that combines ethical, spiritual and material factors to promote the welfare of both individuals and society (Maharani & Hidayat, 2020). The *maqasid al-Shariah* framework guides consumers to prioritize their needs by safeguarding religion, life, intellect, lineage and wealth (Al-Ghazali & Hammad, 2017), reflecting a holistic decision-making process that considers social and spiritual aspects (N. N. A. Hasan et al., 2022; Muhammad & Hanapi, 2019). The *maqasid al-Shariah* framework urges Muslims to prioritize necessities and shun excess and wastefulness, diverging from the rationality concept that emphasizes personal material satisfaction above everything else. In terms, this suggests that Muslims should consume permissible (*halal*) products that are wholesome (*toyyib*) goods while steering clear of excessiveness (*israf*) and wastefulness (*tabzir*) practices (Bahri, 2014).

Moreover, Sustainable and Responsible Investment (SRI) practices resonate with the values of *maqasid al-Shariah* by emphasizing social and governance considerations. However, there is a need for alignment with *Shariah* principles on issues such as human rights and freedom of expression (Ghassan, 2016). The ethical framework of economics promotes responsible spending habits that strike a balance between maximizing utility and upholding moral standards (Darma, 2022). This mindful consumption behaviour plays a role in fostering both material prosperity and spiritual well-being while prioritizing societal welfare over individual gains (Azra et al., 2023; Sarwono, 2009).

The relationship between consumer spending and Islamic principles is a fascinating area of study, as the religious and cultural guidelines of Islam have a profound impact on how Muslims approach financial matters. In Islamic teachings, consumption is not merely an economic activity but is deeply intertwined with one's faith and adherence to moral and ethical standards (Gunawijaya, 2017; Hanapi, 2017).

One key concept in this context is the notion of "*wasatiyyah*-consumerism," which applies the principle of tawhid (the oneness of God) to the realm of consumption (Hanapi, 2017). Tawhid is a fundamental tenet of Islam, and the *wasatiyyah*-consumerism concept seeks to align consumer behaviour with this core belief. This approach emphasizes moderation, fairness, and benevolence in consumption, in contrast with the more materialistic and individualistic tendencies often associated with conventional consumerism (Muhammad & Hanapi, 2018).

The Quran provides clear guidance on the ethical dimensions of consumption, emphasizing the importance of moderation and restraint. Muslims are encouraged to avoid extravagance, wastefulness, and the pursuit of material wealth for its own sake, and instead focus on consumption that is aligned with the broader objectives of the Sharia, or Islamic law (Bukhari et al., 2021; Jafari & Süerdem, 2012). Furthermore, Islamic principles encourage consumers to be mindful of the societal impact of their spending habits. Muslims are called upon to consider the welfare of others, to engage in fair and transparent transactions, and to avoid any activities that may cause harm to individuals or the community (Shaikh et al., 2017).

Personal Values and Spending Behaviour

Personal values play a role in how people spend their money, influencing their attitudes, preferences, and decision-making processes. Research shows that values like self-transcendence, self-direction and hedonism are factors in understanding consumer behaviour because they are deeply ingrained in an individual's thoughts and beliefs (Sandhya & Nair, 2019; Vincent & Selvarani, 2013). For example, values such as caring for the environment and health can drive consumers to choose products over others, and price plays a part in this decision (Goldsmith et al., 2015). In the fashion industry, values like being fashion-forward and open to ideas are linked to spending on clothing items, demonstrating how personal values influence shopping habits (Nye & Hillyard, 2013). Moreover, materialism and impulsive buying behaviours driven by values can lead individuals into debt due to financial choices (O'Mahony & Hall, 2011). Body image perceptions and related values have an impact on food purchasing patterns among women who may adopt both healthy and unhealthy eating habits to meet their body image standards (Makkonen et al., 2019).

Their beliefs also impact the way people shop online. Factors such as excitement and modesty play a role in how much money they spend and whether they choose international online stores (Pražić, 2020). Additionally, values like kindness and global awareness are connected to eco-consumer habits, such as recycling and using harmful products (Ferraz et al., 2015). When it comes to shopping habits, values that prioritize others over oneself have a positive impact on consumers in Brazil and Canada. However, cultural differences might influence the strength of this connection (Lee & Cho, 2019). Lastly, individual principles like independence, enjoyment and self-improvement are closely linked to perceptions of purchasing. These perceptions then shape how people behave when shopping online (Jayawardhena, 2004). Therefore, personal beliefs play a role in shaping aspects of consumer spending behaviour across various fields and cultural settings.

E-WALLET & FINANCIAL WELL-BEING

Financial well-being is a multidimensional concept that reflects an individual's ability to meet current financial obligations, feel secure about their financial future, and make autonomous financial choices (Michael Collins & Urban, 2020). A solid financial footing means feeling confident about one's situation, being able to cover expenses, having the ability to handle unexpected events, making progress towards financial objectives, and having the flexibility to make decisions that enhance the quality of life (Netemeyer et al., 2018). Various factors influence financial well-being. Employment status and income levels are determinants of greater financial well-being linked to full-time employment and higher income levels (Fan & Henager, 2022; Mahdzan et al., 2019, 2023). Personal behaviours and knowledge also play a role; higher levels of literacy and positive money habits like budgeting, saving and investing are associated with better financial well-being (Henager & Wilmarth, 2018; Mayer et al., 2020; Netemeyer et al., 2018). Psychological aspects such as confidence, locus of control and social connections also impact an individual's well-being (Abdullah et al., 2019; Ghazali et al., 2020; She et al., 2021). Another research by Khumalo et al. (2012) and Sirgy (2021) suggest that demographic factors such as race, gender and relationship status play a role in determining an individual's financial well-being.

The use of e-wallets has an impact on financial well-being through aspects like convenience, spending behaviours and trust. E-wallets enable speedy transactions, thus reducing the need for contact – especially crucial during the COVID-19 era – leading to their increased adoption, as highlighted by Mourizka and Nisha (2023). This convenience is particularly attractive to Generation Z users, who mainly utilize e-wallets for buying food, clothes and transportation due to their ease-of-use nature and enticing promotions (Amadea & Indrawati, 2022; Mourizka & Nisha, 2023). Nevertheless, users' financial well-being can be affected by their income levels and spending habits. Higher incomes or larger sums kept in e-wallets may result in increased consumption levels, potentially impacting financial stability if not managed prudently (Nimansa & Kuruwitaarachchi, 2020; Subagiyo et al., 2022).

Trust and how well e-wallets fit into people's lifestyles are factors that influence the use of e-wallets. Trust plays a role in shaping users' attitudes and behaviours, according to studies by Anshari et al. (2021) and Ruldeviyani and Saraswati (2023). The perceived advantages and privacy controls also have an impact on users' willingness to share information, which is crucial for e-wallets to function properly. While e-wallets offer numerous benefits, their adoption in areas like Sri Lanka is restricted due to concerns about security and reliability. This highlights the need for developers to improve these aspects to attract more users, as emphasized by (Ikhsan et al., 2022). Furthermore, the use of alternative financial services (AFS), including e-wallets, has been associated with negative financial indicators like lower credit scores and lack of emergency funds, especially among lower-income individuals, according to Chen and Livermore (2020). Therefore, while e-wallets offer convenience and advantages, their impact on well-being is complex and can differ depending on income levels, spending behaviours, and trust in the technology.

SPENDING BEHAVIOUR AND FINANCIAL WELL-BEING

The way people spend their money has an impact on their financial situation, and this is influenced by different factors like personality traits, knowledge about finances and how they interact with others. Studies show that qualities like self-control and careful decision-making are important for forming money habits and financial well-being in adults, while things like self-esteem and optimism have a smaller effect (Aknin et al., 2018). For college students, how they budget, save money and handle credit cards can affect their health, with impulsive shopping habits having an impact on their finances (Hashmi et al., 2021). Being overly active on social media can lead to compulsive shopping, which can make young adults feel more stressed about money (Caprariello & Reis, 2021).

Spending money on others (prosocial spending) tends to bring happiness than spending it on oneself, especially when the intention is to benefit someone else (Bartholomae & Fox, 2021; Singh et al., 2015). Spending on experiences (experiential spending) over possessions when making purchases can also lead to overall well-being (Gutter & Copur, 2011). Understanding how to manage money is crucial for improving stability and making spending decisions more effective (She et al., 2021). People's habits and involvement in activities can be indicators of financial success than just looking at basic demographics (R. Xue et al., 2020). Young adults with low incomes tend to have better financial well-being when they have a good grasp of financial concepts and feel in control of their own choices, with their actions playing a key role (Zhang et al., 2018).

Moreover, the financial choices made by college students are influenced by their traits and family dynamics greatly impact their well-being, even though the effects of credit card use and student loans can vary (Sabri, Wahab, et al., 2023). Therefore, it is important to take into account the psychological, educational and behavioural aspects to improve financial well-being.

THE PROPOSED CONNECTION BETWEEN E-WALLET USE, SPENDING BEHAVIOUR AND FINANCIAL WELL-BEING

The way people spend money plays a role in how e-wallets affect financial well-being. Research indicates that e-wallets frequently contribute to increased spending, occasionally leading to excessive expenditure, given their convenience, promotional offers, and the perception of readily available funds. Consequently, adults may find themselves making impulsive financial choices (Jhonson & Tamara, 2023). This behaviour is crucial as it directly influences financial management and overall financial well-being. Studies have demonstrated that financial behaviour, such as spending habits, serves as a factor in the relationship between financial literacy, financial socialization (the key process of developing financial values, attitudes, knowledge, and behaviours that contribute to individuals' financial well-being), self-control, and financial well-being (Bangun & Kurniyati, 2022).

Moreover, digital financial literacy (DFL) has been proven to affect financial well-being through its influence on spending, saving, and investment habits. This indicates that enhancing financial education can assist in managing the spending inclinations linked to e-wallet usage (Nalurita et al., 2022). Attitudes towards finances and knowledge also contribute to shaping how people manage their money, including their spending habits, which are crucial for achieving financial stability (Mawaddah, 2022; Wijekoon et al., 2022).

Additionally, how a person manages their finances can affect how socioeconomic factors and personal characteristics influence their happiness. This indicates that enhancing our financial behaviours can enhance our well-being (Iramani & Lutfi, 2021). The connection between knowledge, attitudes toward money and economic welfare is also shaped by how we manage our finances, underscoring the significance of controlling our spending behaviours (Sabri, 2023). In essence, how we spend money is an element that links e-wallet usage to well-being. Efforts to enhance literacy and behaviour can have a positive impact on individuals' financial outcomes (Aji & Adawiyah, 2021).

The concept of *maqasid al-Shariah* is essential in comprehending spending patterns and financial wellness within a context. Islamic finance seeks to align spending choices with the principles of *maqasid al-Shariah* by emphasizing a balance between material and spiritual satisfaction (I. Alam et al., 2022; Muhammad & Hanapi, 2019). Islamic teachings encourage individuals to prioritize needs, additional requirements, comfort items and luxury goods while steering clear of expenses. This approach fosters holistic well-being (Nouman & Ullah, 2023).

In addition, the Islamic financial system, guided by *Shariah* principles, underscores the significance of both community welfare and money matters, underscoring how financial choices are linked to well-being and societal progress (Abdul Ghani et al., 2022; Gutter & Copur, 2011). By following *maqasid al-Shariah* in spending habits, individuals can attain prosperity while adhering to the moral principles outlined in Islamic teachings. These ideas are depicted in Figure 1 below.

Figure 1. The relationship of e-wallet use, financial well-being, spending behaviours and maqasid al-Shariah

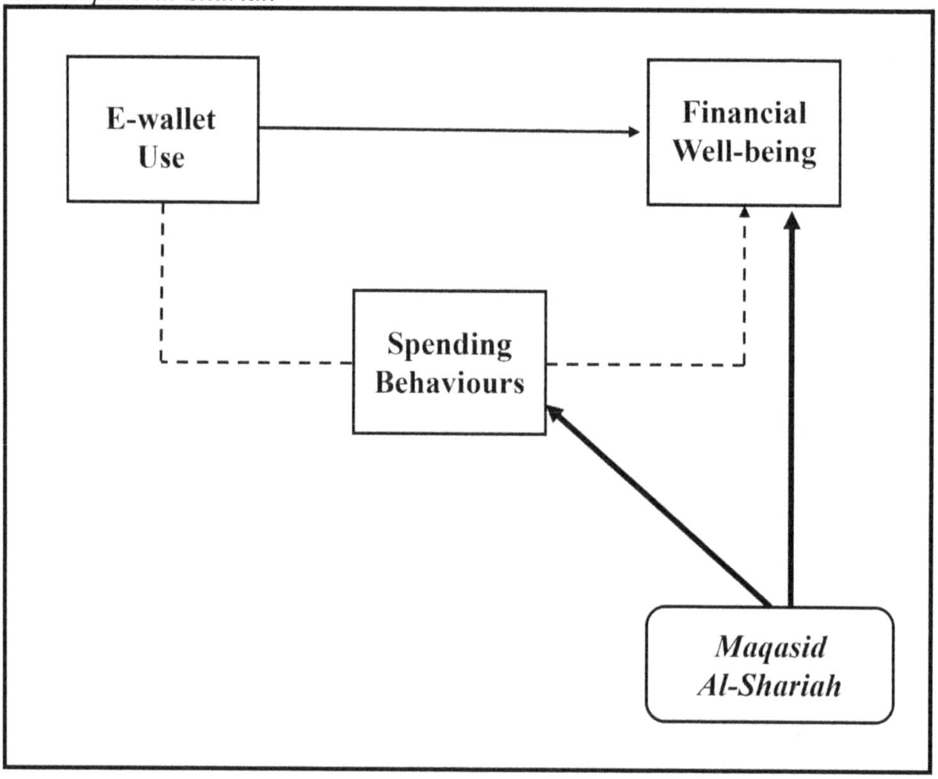

Figure 1 illustrates a framework that explains the connections between using e-wallets, spending behaviours, financial well-being, and *maqasid al-Shariah.* It shows that e-wallet usage directly affects how people spend money, emphasizing the influence of e-wallets on shaping spending behaviours. These spending habits impact well-being, highlighting the relationship between spending choices and individuals' overall financial well-being. Furthermore, the framework demonstrates how *maqasid al-Shariah* influences spending behaviours by ensuring that Islamic principles guide these actions to align with religious standards. This alignment also affects well-being by promoting stability through adherence to these principles. In addition, there is a correlation between using e-wallets and the financial well-being of spending patterns. This relationship indicates that utilizing e-wallets impacts an individual's financial well-being beyond how money is spent. This holistic model emphasizes the importance of considering both technology use and religious values in understanding and improving financial well-being among consumers.

CONCLUSION

The increasing use of e-wallets could have an impact on economic growth and development by promoting financial inclusion, making transactions more convenient, and boosting consumer spending. Research suggests that the rise of cashless payments through e-wallets can bring about developmental advantages like increased economic activity and better access to financial services (Andrew et al., 2021; Vachruddin et al., 2022). Moreover, embracing digital financial tools such as e-wallets can have a positive effect on real per capita income, public health, and education levels, underscoring the importance of technology infrastructure and digital payments in driving economic progress (Barthakur et al., 2022). Additionally, the advancement of e-wallets is viewed as a way to speed up economic growth, enhance inclusion, and break down geographical barriers for the benefit of businesses and society at large (Sirait et al., 2023).

Spending is in line with *maqasid al-Shariah*, which can lead to improved welfare, fairness, and economic equality (Arif & Mustaming, 2020; Goud et al., 2021; Zatadini & Syamsuri, 2018). The idea behind *maqasid al-Shariah* focuses on maximizing benefits while minimizing consequences in the realm of Islamic finance, where technology plays a role in promoting positive social change and reducing harm (Abdussalam & Shodiq, 2022). Scholars such as Imam al-Syatibi have underscored the significance of *maqasid al-Shariah* in policy-influencing areas like government spending, taxation and household expenses (Nouman & Ullah, 2023). By incorporating *maqasid al-Shariah* principles into spending decisions, governments and institutions can empower communities to enhance the quality of life and ensure that budget allocations cater to the welfare of society, ultimately leading to more effective and meaningful results.

REFERENCES

Abdul Ghani, N., Wan Chik, W., Mohd, Y., Abd. Wahab, M. A., & Mohd. Ghazalli, F. S. (2022). Social Deprivation and its Threats to Social Well-Being According to The Perspective of Maqasid. *International Journal of Academic Research in Business & Social Sciences*, 12(1). Advance online publication. DOI: 10.6007/IJARBSS/v12-i1/12261

Abdullah, N., Fazli, S. M., & Muhammad Arif, A. M. (2019). The Relationship between Attitude towards Money, Financial Literacy and Debt Management with Young Worker's Financial Well-being. *Pertanika Journal of Social Science & Humanities*, 27(1).

Abdullah, N., Redzuan, F., & Daud, N. A. (2020). E-wallet: Factors influencing user acceptance towards cashless society in Malaysia among public universities. *Indonesian Journal of Electrical Engineering and Computer Science*, 20(1), 67–74. DOI: 10.11591/ijeecs.v20.i1.pp67-74

Abdussalam, A., & Shodiq, A. (2022). Maqashid As-Syariah Perspektif Imam Al-Ghazali: Studi Lietrasi Maslahah Mursalah. *Moderasi: Journal of Islamic Studies*, 2(2), 139–159. DOI: 10.54471/moderasi.v2i2.32

Abu Bakar, F. M. (2022). E-wallet usage to pay zakat during Covid-19 pandemic among Malaysian's polytechnic lecturers. *International Journal of Islamic Economics and Finance Research, 5*(2 December), 57–79. DOI: 10.53840/ijiefer91

Adam, F. (2021). Fintech Versus I-Fintech: A Dichotomy. *Islamic FinTech: Insights and Solutions*, 19–35.

Adyen. (2024). *Adyen Index: Retail 2024 - Balancing customers experience and business efficiency*.

Agarwal, S., Hadzic, M., Song, C., & Yildirim, Y. (2023). Liquidity Constraints, Consumption, and Debt Repayment: Evidence from Macroprudential Policy in Turkey. *Review of Financial Studies*, 36(10), 3953–3998. Advance online publication. DOI: 10.1093/rfs/hhad024

Aji, H. M., & Adawiyah, W. R. (2021). How e-wallets encourage excessive spending behavior among young adult consumers? *Journal of Asia Business Studies*. Advance online publication. DOI: 10.1108/JABS-01-2021-0025

Aknin, L. B., Wiwad, D., & Hanniball, K. B. (2018). Buying well-being: Spending behavior and happiness. *Social and Personality Psychology Compass*, 12(5), e12386. Advance online publication. DOI: 10.1111/spc3.12386

Al-Ghazali, I., & Hammad, A. Z. M. (2017). *Al Mustasfa Min Ilm Al Usul - Imam Ghazali*. Repro Books Limited. https://books.google.com.my/books?id=rxQ7zQEACAAJ

Al-Raysuni, A. (2006). *Imam al-Shatibi's theory of the higher objectives and intents of Islamic law*. The Other Press.

Al-Shatibi, I. I. (2012). *The Reconciliation of the Fundamentals of Islamic Law: Al-Muwafaqat fi Usul al-Shari'a* (Vol. 1). UWA Publishing.

Al-Zarqa, M. (1984). *Ni ām al-Ta'mīn*. Haqīqatuh Wa Al-Ra'yu Al-Syar'i Fīh.

Al Zarqa, M. A. (1982). al Qiyam wa 'l Ma 'ayir al Islamiyyah fi Taqwim al Mashru 'at. *Islamic Values and Criteria in Project Evaluation), al Muslim al Mu 'asir, 3*, 85–105.

Alam, A., & Saputro, I. A. (2022). A qualitative analysis of user interface design on a sharia fintechapplication based on technology acceptance model (tam). [Technology Acceptance Model]. *Jurnal TAM*, 13(1), 9. DOI: 10.56327/jurnaltam.v13i1.1142

Alam, I., Haider, W. A., & Munir, A.Dr. Iftikhar AlamWaqas Ali Haider. (2022). Aspiring Maqasid al-Shariah and Socio-Economic Well-Being in Islamic Finance. [IRJIS]. *International Research Journal on Islamic Studies*, 4(1), 104–122. DOI: 10.54262/irjis.04.01.e07

Alotaibi, H. A. S. (2022). E-Wallet -A foundation applied study. *Journal of Human and Administrative Sciences*, 1–21. DOI: 10.56760/ZUFR5920

Amadea, A., & Indrawati, . (2022). The Influence of Perceived Usefulness, Perceived Ease of Use, Social Influence, Facilities Conditions, Lifestyle Compatibility, and Perceived Trust on Intention to Use E-wallet Dana. *International Journal of Business and Management*, 10(8). Advance online publication. DOI: 10.24940/theijbm/2022/v10/i8/BM2208-002

Andrew, J. V., Abdullah, N. S. W., Nordin, S., & Tan, K. E. (2021). *A Systematic Review of E-wallet Usage Intention: Integrating UTAUT2 with Perceived Security. 16*(1), 124–133. DOI: 10.24191/ji.v16i1.372

Andriyaningtyas, I., Adam, M., & Herianingrum, S. (2021). Penerimaan e-wallet Syariah LinkAja dalam rangka pengembangan ekonomi digital di Indonesia. [Jurnal Ekonomi Dan Keuangan]. *EKUITAS*, 5(4), 534–552. DOI: 10.24034/j25485024.y2021.v5.i4.4772

Anshari, M., Arine, M. A., Nurhidayah, N., Aziyah, H., & Salleh, H. (2021). Factors influencing individual in adopting eWallet. *Journal of Financial Services Marketing*, 26(1), 10–23. DOI: 10.1057/s41264-020-00079-5

Ardiyanti, D., Surwandono, S., Maharani, P. D., & Amalia, N. (2023). Human Security Identification in Maqoshid Sharia Concept as Implementation in Debt Trap of Digital Finance. *Afkaruna: Indonesian Interdisciplinary Journal of Islamic Studies*, 19(1), 123–132. DOI: 10.18196/afkaruna.v19i1.17136

Arif, F. M., & Mustaming, M. (2020). Regional Development Budget Based Maqasid Al Syari'ah: Realization Analysis of the Palopo City Budget. *PROCEEDING IAIN Batusangkar, 1*(2), 17–29. https://ejournal.uinmybatusangkar.ac.id/ojs/index.php/proceedings/article/view/1886/1552

Aunurrochim, M., & Saharudin, M. A. bin. (2021). *E-Wallet: A Study On Contracts Involved Within Its Operational Mechanism*. 1–16. DOI: 10.33102/jfatwa.vol26no1.382

Azra, A. M., Epriyanti, N., & Nuzula, Z. F. (2023). Analisis Perilaku Konsumen Muslim yang Melakukan Transaksi Real Money Trading. *Bandung Conference Series Sharia Economic Law*, 3(1). Advance online publication. DOI: 10.29313/bcssel.v3i1.5733

Bahri, S. A. (2014). Etika konsumsi dalam perspektif ekonomi islam. *Jurnal Studi Islamika*, 11(2), 347–370. DOI: 10.24239/jsi.v11i2.360.347-370

Bakri, M. H., Almansoori, K. K. S. M., & Azlan, N. A. S. B. M. (2023). Determinants intention usage of Islamic E-Wallet Among Millennials. *Global Business and Finance Review*, 28(1), 11–32. DOI: 10.17549/gbfr.2023.28.1.11

Bangun, B., & Kurniyati, N. N.Nany Noor Kurniyati. (2022). Role of financial behavior in mediation the influence of financial literacy and financial self efficacy on financial will being. *International Journal of Economics and Management Research*, 1(3), 166–176. DOI: 10.55606/ijemr.v1i3.54

Bank Negara Malaysia. (2023). *Bank Negara Malaysia Annual Report 2022*. https://www.bnm.gov.my/publications/ar2022

Barthakur, G., Rajkonwar, A. B., & Barua, P. (2022). Potential of an e-wallet: a study among the sellers in dibrugarh city, assam. *PARIPEX INDIAN JOURNAL OF RESEARCH*, 119–222. DOI: 10.36106/paripex/4508318

Bartholomae, S., & Fox, J. J. (2021). A Decade Review of Research on College Student Financial Behavior and Well-Being. *Journal of Family and Economic Issues*, 42(1), 154–177. DOI: 10.1007/s10834-021-09756-6

Bee, T. S., & Ying, K. Y. (2021). An examination of determinants for e-wallet adoption in Malaysia: A combined approach. *F1000 Research*, 10, 1155. DOI: 10.12688/f1000research.73402.1

Beik, I. S., Swandaru, R., & Rizkiningsih, P. (2021). Utilization of Digital Technology for Zakat Development. In Billah, M. M. (Ed.), *Islamic FinTech: Insights and Solutions* (Vol. 9, pp. 231–248). Springer International Publishing., DOI: 10.1007/978-3-030-45827-0_13

Bella, F. I., & Efendi, N. F. (2021). Strengthening the Islamic Digital Payment System Through Sharia Electronic Wallet (E-Wallet). *El Dinar: Jurnal Keuangan Dan Perbankan Syariah, 9*(2), 94–107. https://pdfs.semanticscholar.org/a823/158e1c37edd15e77202bb2bca9658e9de44b.pdf

Bernthal, M. J., Crockett, D., & Rose, R. L. (2005). Credit cards as lifestyle facilitators. *The Journal of Consumer Research*, 32(1), 130–145. DOI: 10.1086/429605

Bionducci, L., Botta, A., Bruno, P., Denecker, O., Gathinji, C., Nadeau, M.-C., & Sttanathan, B. (2023). *2023 McKinsey Global Payments Report.*

BNM. (2022). *Policy Document on Electronic Money (E-Money).* https://www.bnm.gov.my/documents/20124/943361/PD-eMoney-202302.pdf

Bukhari, S. F. H., Woodside, F. M., Hassan, R., Ali, O. M. S. H., Hussain, S., & Waqas, R. (2021). Intrinsic and extrinsic attributes that drive Muslim consumer purchase behavior. *Journal of Islamic Marketing*, 12(1), 70–94. DOI: 10.1108/JIMA-01-2018-0004

Caprariello, P. A., & Reis, H. T. (2021). "This one's on me!": Differential well-being effects of self-centered and recipient-centered motives for spending money on others. *Motivation and Emotion*, 45(6), 1–23. DOI: 10.1007/s11031-021-09907-0

Chen, Z., & Livermore, M. (2020). The Negative Association between Alternative Financial Services Usage and Financial Well-Being: Variations by Income. *Social Work Research*, 44(3), 183–195. DOI: 10.1093/swr/svaa009

Darma, S. (2022). Urgensi Maqashid Syariah Dalam Pengembangan Ekonomi. *Al Mashaadir*, 2(2), 44–53. DOI: 10.52029/jis.v2i2.58

Daud, A. H. M., & Salim, H. M. (2022). Digital finance and maqasid al-Shariah. *ACADEMIC PROGRAMMES*, 4, 28–33.

David, S., & Kathrine, J. W. (2019). An Investigative Report On Encryption Based Security Mechanisms For E-Wallets. *International Journal of Scientific & Technology Research*, 8(10), 1755–1769.

Dholakia, U., Tam, L., Yoon, S., & Wong, N. (2016). The ant and the grasshopper: Understanding personal saving orientation of consumers. *The Journal of Consumer Research*, 43(1), 134–155. DOI: 10.1093/jcr/ucw004

DSN-MUI. (2017). *Fatwa - Uang Elektronik Syariah*. https://drive.google.com/file/d/1KPAvhhziJ61Pt8EFxxTFfDPNmRHJoQDG/view?usp=sharing

DSN-MUI. (2018). Fatwa - Layanan Pembiayaan Berbasis Teknologi Informasi Berdasarkan Prinsip Syariah. In *Majelis Ulama Indonesia*. https://drive.google.com/file/d/1qCu2X6MTIFnYqK22eMx7uFL53AXBT9Vo/view?usp=sharing

Fan, L., & Henager, R. (2022). A Structural Determinants Framework for Financial Well-Being. *Journal of Family and Economic Issues*, 43(2), 415–428. DOI: 10.1007/s10834-021-09798-w PMID: 34548774

Ferraz, S. B., Romero, C. B. A., Nogami, V. K. da C., & Veloso, A. R. (2015). *Personal values and green purchase behaviour: a cross-cultural study between Brazil and Canada.*

Fintech News Malaysia. (2022, July 18). *Malaysia's Fintech Map 2022*. Https://Fintechnews.My/31945/Malaysia/Fintech-Report-Malaysia-2022/.

Firmansyah, E. A., & Anwar, M. (2019). Islamic financial technology (FINTECH): its challenges and prospect. *Achieving and Sustaining SDGs 2018 Conference: Harnessing the Power of Frontier Technology to Achieve the Sustainable Development Goals (ASSDG 2018)*, 52–58.

Fong, V. (2023). *Malaysia Fintech Report 2023*. https://fintechnews.my/malaysia-fintech-report-2023/

Friedline, T., & West, S. (2016). Young adults' race, wealth, and entrepreneurship. *Race and Social Problems*, 8(1), 42–63. DOI: 10.1007/s12552-016-9163-z

Ghassan, H. B. (2016). Fairness and Ethics in Spending. *Journal of Reviews on Global Economics*, 5, 281–287. DOI: 10.6000/1929-7092.2016.05.24

Ghazali, M. S., Alwi, S. F. S., Abd Aziz, N. N., & Hazudin, S. F. (2020). Pathway to Financial Well-being: A review on the role of psychological factors. *Environment-Behaviour Proceedings Journal*, 5(13), 55–61. DOI: 10.21834/e-bpj.v5i13.2063

Gohil, Prof. S., Vinchhi, K., & Yewale, N. (2023). A study on impact of mobile payment with special reference to youths. *EPRA International Journal of Economic and Business Review*, 32–35. DOI: 10.36713/epra12530

Goldsmith, R. E., Stith, M. T., & White, J. D. (2015). *An Empirical Study of the Relationship Between Personal Values and Innovative Purchasing Behavior.*, DOI: 10.1007/978-3-319-17055-8_17

Gosal, M. A., & Linawati, N. (2018, October 10). Pengaruh Intensitas Penggunaan Layanan Mobile Payment terhadap Spending Behavior. *Seminar Nasional Manajemen 3*. https://repository.petra.ac.id/id/eprint/18031

Goud, B., Uddin, T. A., & Fianto, B. A. (2021). Islamic fintech and ESG goals: Key considerations for fulfilling maqasid principles. In *Islamic Fintech* (pp. 16–35). DOI: 10.4324/9781003014614-2

Gunawijaya, R. (2017). Kebutuhan manusia dalam pandangan ekonomi kapitalis dan ekonomi Islam. *Jurnal Al-Maslahah, 13*(1), 131–150. https://www.academia.edu/download/103112520/495.pdf

Gutter, M. S., & Copur, Z. (2011). Financial Behaviors and Financial Well-Being of College Students: Evidence from a National Survey. *Journal of Family and Economic Issues*, 32(4), 699–714. DOI: 10.1007/s10834-011-9255-2

Hafidh, A. A. (2022). Tinjauan Maqashid Syariah Tentang E-Money. *Jurnal Ilmiah Ekonomi Islam*, 8(1), 140. DOI: 10.29040/jiei.v8i1.3946

Hamsin, M. K., Halim, A., Anggriawan, R., & Lutfiani, H. (2023). Sharia E-Wallet: The Issue of Sharia Compliance and Data Protection. *Jurnal Kajian Hukum Islam*, 17(1), 53–68. DOI: 10.24090/mnh.v17i1.7633

Hanapi, M. S. (2017). The Wasatiyyah-Consumerism Concept as an Equivalent to the Consumerism Phenomenon in Conventional Economy. *International Journal of Academic Research in Business & Social Sciences*, 7(12), 944–961. DOI: 10.6007/IJARBSS/v7-i12/3724

Hasan, N. N. A., Noor, K. M., Malik, A. A., & Ghani, Z. A. (2022). Maqasid Al-Shariah in Management: How it's Relevant to Non-muslims. In N. N. M. Shariff, M. A. Yakob, Z. S. Hamidi, Z. A. A. Aghwan, & N. Lateh (Eds.), *Selected Proceedings from the 1st International Conference on Contemporary Islamic Studies (ICIS 2021)* (pp. 83–91). Springer Nature Singapore.

Hasan, R., Hassan, M. K., & Aliyu, S. (2020). Fintech and Islamic finance: Literature review and research agenda. [IJIEF]. *International Journal of Islamic Economics and Finance*, 3(1), 75–94. DOI: 10.18196/ijief.2122

Hashmi, F., Aftab, H., Martins, J. M., Nuno Mata, M., Qureshi, H. A., Abreu, A., & Mata, P. N. (2021). The role of self-esteem, optimism, deliberative thinking and self-control in shaping the financial behavior and financial well-being of young adults. *PLoS One*, 16(9), e0256649. DOI: 10.1371/journal.pone.0256649 PMID: 34492043

Haws, K. L., Davis, S. W., & Dholakia, U. M. (2016). Control over what? Individual differences in general versus eating and spending self-control. *Journal of Public Policy & Marketing*, 35(1), 37–57. DOI: 10.1509/jppm.14.149

Henager, R., & Wilmarth, M. J. (2018). The relationship between student loan debt and financial wellness. *Family and Consumer Sciences Research Journal*, 46(4), 381–395. DOI: 10.1111/fcsr.12263

Ikhsan, R. B., Sari, C. L., Fernando, E., Wijaya, L., Bangapadang, S., & Sangkereng, I. (2022). The Rapid Adoption of E-wallet: An empirical study. *2022 10th International Conference on Cyber and IT Service Management, CITSM 2022*. DOI: 10.1109/CITSM56380.2022.9935931

Iramani, Rr., & Lutfi, L. (2021). *An integrated model of financial well-being: The role of financial behavior.* 7(3), 691–700. DOI: 10.5267/j.ac.2020.12.007

Izaidin, M. D. B. A. (2022). Touch n Go e-Wallet: The New Payment Style Existed when COVID-19 Hits. [IJAFAP]. *International Journal of Accounting & Finance in Asia Pasific*, 5(3), 107–116. DOI: 10.32535/ijafap.v5i3.1933

Jabatan Mufti Negeri Kedah. (2020, November 8). *Irsyad Al-Fatwa: Hukum Penggunaan E-wallet Menurut Perspektif Syarak*. Jawatankuasa Fatwa Negeri Kedah. https://ifatwa.kedah.gov.my/wp-content/uploads/2022/08/15-HUKUM-PENGGUNAAN-e-WALLET-MENURUT-PERSPEKTIF-SYARAK.pdf

Jabatan Mufti Negeri Perak. (2021, August 4). *Irsyad Hukum: Penggunaan E-wallet Mengikut Perspektif Syarak*. Jawatankuasa Fatwa Negeri Perak. https://mufti.perak.gov.my/images/isu_semasa/2021/sept/ewallet.pdf

Jafari, A., & Süerdem, A. (2012). An analysis of material consumption culture in the Muslim world. *Marketing Theory*, 12(1), 61–79. DOI: 10.1177/1470593111424184

JAKIM. (2020, August). *Penggunaan e-wallet mengikut perspektif syarak*. Majlis Kebangsaan Bagi Hal Ehwal Ugama Islam Malaysia (MKI) Kali Ke-117. https://i-fiqh.islam.gov.my/portal/view.php?id=16579

Jayawardhena, C. (2004). Personal values' influence on e-shopping attitude and behaviour. *Internet Research*, 14(2), 127–138. DOI: 10.1108/10662240410530844

Jhonson, B., & Tamara, D. (2023). Influence of digital financial literacy on financial well-being through spending, saving, and investment behavior in indonesia. *Journal of Business Studies and Management Review*, 6(2), 157–168. DOI: 10.22437/jbsmr.v6i2.24793

Kamil, I., & Istianingsih, I. (2020). *Spending Behavior as an Impact of Lifestyle and Financial Literation in the Intensity of use of Mobile Payment Services.*

Kamis, R., Ismail, S., & Rahman, N. H. A. (2022). Go Cashless: A Proposed Conceptual Framework for e-Wallet Acceptance. *International Journal of Academic Research in Business & Social Sciences*, 12(11). Advance online publication. DOI: 10.6007/IJARBSS/v12-i11/15264

Kanimozhi, G., & Kamatchi, K. S. (2017). Security Aspects of Mobile Based E Wallet. *International Journal on Recent and Innovation Trends in Computing and Communication*, 5(6). Advance online publication. DOI: 10.17762/IJRITCC.V5I6.931

Kaur, R., Li, Y., Iqbal, J., Gonzalez, H., & Stakhanova, N. (2018). A Security Assessment of HCE-NFC Enabled E-Wallet Banking Android Apps. *2018 IEEE 42nd Annual Computer Software and Applications Conference (COMPSAC), 02*, 492–497. DOI: 10.1109/COMPSAC.2018.10282

Kempson, E., Finney, A., & Poppe, C. (2017). *Financial well-being: a conceptual model and preliminary analysis.* https://www.fincap.org.uk/en/insights/financial-well-being-a-conceptual-model-and-preliminary-analysis

Khan, M. F., & Ghifari, N. M. (1992). Shatibi's objectives of Shariah and some implications for consumer theory. *Readings in Islamic Economic Thought: Selected Readings*, 176, 202.

Khumalo, I. P., Temane, Q. M., & Wissing, M. P. (2012). Socio-demographic variables, general psychological well-being and the mental health continuum in an African context. *Social Indicators Research*, 105(3), 419–442. DOI: 10.1007/s11205-010-9777-2

Kiew, J. P., Toh, E. T. L., Ngian, E. T., & Law, S. H. C. (2022). Perceived Trust, Convenience and Promotion For the Adoption of e-Wallet. *International Journal of Academic Research in Business & Social Sciences*, 12(9). Advance online publication. DOI: 10.6007/IJARBSS/v12-i9/14591

Kreiner, C. T., Lassen, D. D., & Leth-Petersen, S. (2019). Liquidity Constraint Tightness and Consumer Responses to Fiscal Stimulus Policy. *American Economic Journal. Economic Policy*, 11(1), 351–379. DOI: 10.1257/pol.20140313

Lee, J., & Cho, M. (2019). New insights into socially responsible consumers: The role of personal values. *International Journal of Consumer Studies*, 43(2), 123–133. DOI: 10.1111/ijcs.12491

Lim, X. J., Ngew, P., Cheah, J. H., Cham, T. H., & Liu, Y. (2022). Go digital: Can the money-gift function promote the use of e-wallet apps? *Internet Research*, 32(6), 1806–1831. Advance online publication. DOI: 10.1108/INTR-06-2021-0406

Liu, Z., Ben, S., & Zhang, R. (2019). Factors affecting consumers' mobile payment behavior: A meta-analysis. *Electronic Commerce Research*, 19(3), 575–601. DOI: 10.1007/s10660-019-09349-4

Maharani, D., & Hidayat, T. (2020). Rasionalitas Muslim : Perilaku Konsumsi dalam Prespektif Ekonomi Islam. *Jurnal Ilmiah Ekonomi Islam*, 6(3), 409–412. DOI: 10.29040/jiei.v6i3.1374

Mahdzan, N. S., Sabri, M. F., Husniyah, A. R., Magli, A. S., & Chowdhury, N. T. (2023). Digital financial services usage and subjective financial well-being: Evidence from low-income households in Malaysia. *International Journal of Bank Marketing*, 41(2), 395–427. DOI: 10.1108/IJBM-06-2022-0226

Mahdzan, N. S., Zainudin, R., Sukor, M. E., Zainir, F., & Wan Ahmad, W. M. (2019). Determinants of Subjective Financial Well-Being Across Three Different Household Income Groups in Malaysia. *Social Indicators Research*, 146(3), 699–726. DOI: 10.1007/s11205-019-02138-4

Makkonen, M., Frank, L., & Kemppainen, T. (2019).. . *The Effects of Individual Values on Online Shopping Spending*, 10, 969–994. Advance online publication. DOI: 10.18690/978-961-286-280-0.51

Mat, N., Abdullah, N. A., & Norazman, M. F. (2022). Penerimaan Aplikasi E-Wallet Pre-Covid-19 di Kalangan Penduduk di Lembah Klang. *MALIM: Jurnal Pengajian Umum Asia Tenggara*, 23(1), 21–30. DOI: 10.17576/malim-2022-2301-02

Mawaddah. (2022). The role of financial behavior in mediating the influence of socioeconomic characteristics and neurotic personality traits on financial satisfaction. *Cogent Business & Management, 9*(1). DOI: 10.1080/23311975.2022.2080152

Mayer, V. F., Machado, J. dos S., Marques, O., & Nunes, J. M. G. (2020). Mixed feelings?: Fluctuations in well-being during tourist travels. *Service Industries Journal*, 40(1–2), 158–180. DOI: 10.1080/02642069.2019.1600671

Michael Collins, J., & Urban, C. (2020). Measuring financial well-being over the lifecourse. *European Journal of Finance*, 26(4–5), 341–359. DOI: 10.1080/1351847X.2019.1682631

Minarni, & Asnawi, N. R. (2022). An Analysis of Islamic Business Ethics in E-Wallet in Indonesia with A Case Study of Go-Pay. *Journal of Islamic Economis Lariba, 8*(2), 341–356. DOI: 10.20885/jielariba.vol8.iss2.art13

Ming, K. L. Y., & Jais, M. (2022). Factors Affecting the Intention to Use E-Wallets during the COVID-19 Pandemic. *Gadjah Mada International Journal of Business*, 24(1), 82. DOI: 10.22146/gamaijb.64708

MOF. (2024, January 9). *eMADANI | Portal Manfaat*. Ministry of Finance Malaysia. https://manfaat.mof.gov.my/individu/emadani

Moorthy, K., Chiang, O. Y., Kamarudin, A. A., T'ing, L. C., Mei, C. Y., & Johanthan, S. (2021). Factors That Influence the Adoption of E-Wallets by the Malaysians. *International Journal of E-Adoption*, 13(2), 78–95. DOI: 10.4018/IJEA.2021070105

Moorthy, K. S., Ting, T. Y., Kamarudin, A. A., T'ing, L. C., & Johanthan, S. (2022). Impact of government incentive and social influence in the consumer adoption of e-wallets in malaysia. *ASIAN JOURNAL OF ECONOMICS AND FINANCE*, 4(4), 347–368. DOI: 10.47509/AJEF.2022.v04i04.01

Mourizka, A. V., & Nisha, N. (2023). Pola Konsumsi Generasi Z Pengguna E-Wallet di Kota Bandung. In N. Nurhayati (Ed.), *Bandung Conference Series: Economics Studies* (Vol. 3, Issue 1, pp. 45–54). UPT Publikasi Ilmiah, Universitas Islam Bandung. DOI: 10.29313/bcses.v3i1.5926

Mu, H.-L., & Lee, Y.-C. (2021). How Inclusive Digital Financial Services Impact User Behavior: A Case of Proximity Mobile Payment in Korea. *Sustainability (Basel)*, 13(17), 9567. DOI: 10.3390/su13179567

Muamar, A., & Alparisi, A. S. (2017). Electronic money (e-money) in maqashid al-sharia perspective. *Journal of Islamic Economics Lariba*, 3(2), 75–84. https://journal.uii.ac.id/JIELariba/article/download/9657/7821

Muamar, A., Samsudin, S., & Fitriyah, L. (2020). Dompet elektronik dalam transaksi pelanggan OVO menurut perspektif maqasid syari'ah. *Al-Mustashfa: Jurnal Penelitian Hukum Ekonomi Syariah*, 5(1), 92–105. DOI: 10.24235/jm.v5i1.6814

Muchtar, E. H., & Zubairin, A. (2022). Fintech syariah dalam perspektif hukum islam. *Jurnal Asy-Syukriyyah*, 23(1). Advance online publication. DOI: 10.36769/asy.v23i1.185

Muhammad, S. M., & Hanapi, M. S. (2018). The Principle of Wasatiyyah-Consumerism in Syama'il Muhammadiyyah: A Study of Al-Hadith Al-Mawdu 'iy. *International Journal of Academic Research in Business & Social Sciences*, 8(4). Advance online publication. DOI: 10.6007/IJARBSS/v8-i4/4049

Muhammad, S. M., & Hanapi, M. S. (2019). Consumerism Rationality Concept According To Maqasid Syariah. *International Journal of Academic Research in Business & Social Sciences*, 9(4), 79–88. DOI: 10.6007/IJARBSS/v9-i4/5820

Muryanto, Y. T. (2022). The urgency of sharia compliance regulations for Islamic Fintechs: A comparative study of Indonesia, Malaysia and the United Kingdom. *Journal of Financial Crime*. Advance online publication. DOI: 10.1108/JFC-05-2022-0099

Mustafar, M. Z., & Borhan, J. T. (2013). Muslim consumer behavior: Emphasis on ethics from Islamic perspective. *Middle East Journal of Scientific Research*, 18(9), 1301–1307.

Nair, S., Jayabalan, N., & Perumal, I. (2023). E-Wallet Usage Intention in Selangor, Malaysia. *Journal of Hunan University Natural Sciences*, 50(4). Advance online publication. DOI: 10.55463/issn.1674-2974.50.4.2

Nalurita, F., Leon, F. M., & Nisfiannoor, M. (2022). Financial Management Behavior for E-Wallet Users in Jabodetabek. *Business and Entrepreneurial Review*, 22(2), 229–250. DOI: 10.25105/ber.v22i2.13951

Nashirah, A. B., Rosbi, S., & Uzaki, K. (2020). E-Wallet Transactional Framework for Digital Economy: A Perspective from Islamic Financial Engineering. *International Journal of Management Science and Business Administration*, 6(3), 50–57. DOI: 10.18775/ijmsba.1849-5664-5419.2014.63.1005

Netemeyer, R. G., Warmath, D., Fernandes, D., & Lynch, J. G.Jr. (2018). How Am I Doing? Perceived Financial Well-Being, Its Potential Antecedents, and Its Relation to Overall Well-Being. *The Journal of Consumer Research*, 45(1), 68–89. DOI: 10.1093/jcr/ucx109

Nimansa, A. T., & Kuruwitaarachchi, N. (2020). A Study on Finding the Factors, Hindering the use of digital wallets among youth in Developing Countries. *Scholedge International Journal of Management & Development*, 7(6), 107–117. DOI: 10.19085/sijmd070602

Noor, K. A. M., & Yusoff, A. F. J. (2022). Issues in the Application of Wakalah (Agency) in E-wallet. *International Journal of Academic Research in Business & Social Sciences*, 12(11). Advance online publication. DOI: 10.6007/IJARBSS/v12-i11/15119

Nordin, N., Shahwan, S., Ibrahim, N., & Awang, N. (2023). Using E-Wallet in Collecting and Distributing Zakat in Malaysia. *International Journal of Business and Technology Management*, 5(1), 175–186. DOI: 10.55057/ijbtm.2023.5.1.16

Nouman, M., & Ullah, K. (2023). Maqasid Al Shari'ah and Financial Concern of Human Life. In Nouman, M., & Ullah, K. (Eds.), *Participatory Islamic Finance: Ideals, Contemporary Practices, and Innovations* (pp. 29–46). Springer Nature Singapore., DOI: 10.1007/978-981-19-9555-2_2

Nye, P., & Hillyard, C. (2013). Personal Financial Behavior: The Influence of Quantitative Literacy and Material Values. *Numeracy*, 6(1), 3. DOI: 10.5038/1936-4660.6.1.3

O'Mahony, B., & Hall, J. (2011). *Personal values, vanity, physical health, and perceived body image influences in food-purchasing and consumption decisions.*, DOI: 10.1007/978-0-387-92271-3_200

Pachpande, B. R., & Kamble, A. A. (2018). Study of E-wallet Awareness and its Usage in Mumbai. *Journal of Commerce and Management Thought*, 9(1), 33–45. DOI: 10.5958/0976-478X.2018.00004.6

Park, J., Velasco, C. M. B., & Spence, C. (2022). "Looking sharp": Price typeface influences awareness of spending in mobile payment. *Psychology and Marketing*, 39(6), 1170–1189. DOI: 10.1002/mar.21651

Pražić, I. T. (2020). Influence of personal values on consumer choice and intention to buy: a case of Croatian automobile market. In Bevanda, V. (Ed.), *Fourth International Scientific Conference on Recent Advances in Information Technology, Tourism, Economics, Management and Agriculture* (pp. 117–124). Association of Economists and Managers of the Balkans. DOI: 10.31410/ITEMA.S.P.2020.117

Rabbani, M. R. (2022). Fintech innovations, scope, challenges, and implications in Islamic Finance: A systematic analysis. *International Journal of Computing and Digital Systems*, 11(1), 1–28.

Rahman, M., Isa, C. R., Masud, M. M., Sarker, M., & Chowdhury, N. T. (2021). The role of financial behaviour, financial literacy, and financial stress in explaining the financial well-being of B40 group in Malaysia. *Future Business Journal*, 7(1), 1–18. DOI: 10.1186/s43093-021-00099-0

Rahman, N. L. A., Mutalib, H. A., Sabri, S. M., Annuar, N., Mutalib, S. K. M. S. A., & Rahman, Z. S. A. (2022). Factors Influencing E-Wallet Adoption among Adults During Covid-19 Pandemic in Malaysia: Extending The Tam Model. *International Journal of Academic Research in Business & Social Sciences*, 12(7). Advance online publication. DOI: 10.6007/IJARBSS/v12-i7/14327

Ramli, F. A. A., & Hamzah, M. I. (2021). Mobile payment and e-wallet adoption in emerging economies: A systematic literature review. *Journal of Emerging Economies and Islamic Research*, 9(2), 1. DOI: 10.24191/jeeir.v9i2.13617

Razali, M., Mohd, N., Hadigunawan, N., & Saidon, R. (2021). Maqasid shariah hifz mal in e-wallet application. *Islamiyyat: International Journal of Islamic Studies, 43*(1), 113–120. https://ejournal.ukm.my/islamiyyat/article/download/48498/11967

Research and Markets. (2024, February). *Malaysia Buy Now Pay Later Business and Investment Opportunities Databook - 75+ KPIs on BNPL Market Size, End-Use Sectors, Market Share, Product Analysis, Business Model, Demographics - Q1 2024 Update*. Research and Markets. https://www.researchandmarkets.com/reports/5305023/malaysia-buy-now-pay-later-business-and?utm_source=CI&utm_medium=PressRelease&utm_code=759g6p&utm_campaign=1941191+-+Malaysia+Buy+Now+Pay+Later+Business+and+Investment+Opportunities+Report+2024%3a+Market+to+Grow+by+17.5%25+to+Reach+%242.78+Billion+in+2024+-+Forecasts+to+2029&utm_exec=chdomspi

Rick, S. I., Cryder, C. E., & Loewenstein, G. (2008). Tightwads and spendthrifts. *The Journal of Consumer Research*, 34(6), 767–782. DOI: 10.1086/523285

Ruldeviyani, Y., & Saraswati, K. (2023). An Empirical Investigation of Factors Affecting Personal Information's Disclosure on Mobile Payment (E-Wallet) Platforms. *International Journal on Advanced Science, Engineering and Information Technology*, 13(3), 1031–1040. DOI: 10.18517/ijaseit.13.3.18054

Ruopeng, L., Weicheng, X., Xudong, W., & Huang, W. (2015). *Electronic wallet-based payment method and system.*

Sabri, M. F. (2023). Impact of financial behaviour on financial well-being: Evidence among young adults in Malaysia. *Journal of Financial Services Marketing*. Advance online publication. DOI: 10.1057/s41264-023-00234-8

Sabri, M. F., Anthony, M., Law, S. H., Rahim, H. A., Burhan, N. A. S., & Ithnin, M. (2023). Impact of financial behaviour on financial well-being: Evidence among young adults in Malaysia. *Journal of Financial Services Marketing*, •••, 1–20.

Sabri, M. F., Wahab, R., Mahdzan, N. S., Magli, A. S., Rahim, H., Suhaimi, S. S. A., & Nazuri, N. S. (2023). An enigma of Malaysia's low-income young adults: Mediation of financial behaviour on financial well-being and locus of control cohesion. *PLoS One*, 18(7), e0288204. Advance online publication. DOI: 10.1371/journal.pone.0288204 PMID: 37440508

Sandhya, G., & Nair, G. M. (2019). The influence of personal values on consumers purchase intention for organic products. *International Journal of Business Forecasting and Marketing Intelligence*, 5(4), 412. DOI: 10.1504/IJBFMI.2019.105339

Sarwono. (2009). *Analisis perilaku konsumen perspektif ekonomi islam. 8*(1). https://doi.org/DOI: 10.33061/INNOFARM.V8I1.225

Schor, J. (1998). Time, Labour and Consumption: Guest Editor's Introduction. *Time & Society*, 7(1), 119–127. DOI: 10.1177/0961463X98007001007

Seng, N. D., Ibrahim, N. F., Yin, L. S., & Maiyus, M. B. (2023). An Empirical Study on Acceptance of E-wallet among Malaysian University Students. *International Journal of Academic Research in Business & Social Sciences*, 13(1). Advance online publication. DOI: 10.6007/IJARBSS/v13-i1/15728

Shaikh, S. A., Ismail, M. A., Ismail, A. G., Shahimi, S., & Mohd. Shafiai, M. H. (2017). Towards an integrative framework for understanding Muslim consumption behaviour. *Humanomics*, 33(2), 133–149. DOI: 10.1108/H-01-2017-0005

She, L., Rasiah, R., Waheed, H., & Sharif, S. P. (2021). Excessive use of social networking sites and financial well-being among young adults: The mediating role of online compulsive buying. *Young Consumers*, 22(2), 272–289. DOI: 10.1108/YC-11-2020-1252

Shukur, M. H., Ismail, R. J., & Flaih, L. R. (2022). Empower E-wallets Payment System by using A Hybrid Approach of Online and Offline Services. *Cihan University-Erbil Scientific Journal*, 6(2), 23–27. DOI: 10.24086/cuesj.v6n2y2022.pp23-27

Singh, V. K., Bozkaya, B., & Pentland, A. (2015). Money walks: Implicit mobility behavior and financial well-being. *PLoS One*, 10(8), e0136628. DOI: 10.1371/journal.pone.0136628 PMID: 26317339

Sirait, H., Rosalina, S. S., & Sari, E. (2023). The Impact of Digital Innovation on Economic Growth. *International Journal of Professional Business Review*, 8(6), e01842–e01842. DOI: 10.26668/businessreview/2023.v8i6.1842

Sirgy, M. J. (2021). Effects of Demographic Factors on Wellbeing. In *The Psychology of Quality of Life: Wellbeing and Positive Mental Health* (pp. 129–154). Springer. DOI: 10.1007/978-3-030-71888-6_6

Soman, D., & Cheema, A. (2011). Earmarking and partitioning: Increasing saving by low-income households. *Journal of Marketing Research, 48*(SPL), S14–S22.

Subagiyo, G., Gustia, A., & Oktavian Syah, D. (2022). The Effect of E-wallet and Sales Promotion on Purchasing Decisions. *Best Journal of Administration and Management*, 1(1), 53–60. DOI: 10.56403/bejam.v1i1.30

Teng, S., & Khong, K. W. (2021). Examining actual consumer usage of E-wallet: A case study of big data analytics. *Computers in Human Behavior*, 121, 106778. https://doi.org/https://doi.org/10.1016/j.chb.2021.106778. DOI: 10.1016/j.chb.2021.106778

Tenk, M. T. T., Yew, H. C., & Heang, L. T. (2020). E-wallet adoption: A case in Malaysia. *International Journal of Research In Commerce and Management Studies*, 2(2), 216–233. https://ubipayroll.com/ijrcms/index.php/ijrcms/article/download/64/57

Thaler, R. H. (1999). Mental accounting matters. *Journal of Behavioral Decision Making*, 12(3), 183–206. DOI: 10.1002/(SICI)1099-0771(199909)12:3<183::AID-BDM318>3.0.CO;2-F

Vachruddin, V. P., Hamid, A., & Nasril, N. (2022). Development of e-wallet application "DASIGU" - based teaching factory. *Jurnal Pendidikan Vokasi*, 12(3). Advance online publication. DOI: 10.21831/jpv.v12i3.47417

Vincent, T. N., & Selvarani, D. C. (2013). Personal Values Approach for a Better Understanding of Consumer Behaviour. *International Journal of Innovative Research and Development*, 2(3), 509–517.

VISA. (2024). *VISA Consumer Payment Attitudes Study 2023*. https://www.visa.com.sg/dam/VCOM/regional/ap/singapore/global-elements/documents/visa-cpa-2023-report-smt-final.pdf

Wang, M., Ling, A., He, Y., Tan, Y., Zhang, L., Chang, Z., & Ma, Q. (2022). Pleasure of paying when using mobile payment: Evidence from EEG studies. *Frontiers in Psychology*, 13, 1004068. Advance online publication. DOI: 10.3389/fpsyg.2022.1004068 PMID: 36389456

Wijekoon, R., Sabri, M. F., Ahmad, N., & Rahim, H. (2022). Mediating Role of Financial Behavior between Financial Factors and Economic Well-being: Through the Lens of the Extended Family Resource Management Model. *International Journal of Academic Research in Business & Social Sciences*, 12(10). Advance online publication. DOI: 10.6007/IJARBSS/v12-i10/15194

Wong, C. Y., & Mohamed, M. I. P. (2021). Understanding The Factors That Influence Consumer Continuous Intention To Use E-Wallet In Malaysia. *Research in Management of Technology and Business, 2*(1), 561–576. https://publisher.uthm.edu.my/periodicals/index.php/rmtb/article/download/1938/717

Xiao, J. J., & Yao, R. (2022). Good debt, bad debt: Family debt portfolios and financial burdens. *International Journal of Bank Marketing*, 40(4), 659–678. DOI: 10.1108/IJBM-06-2021-0243

Xue, J., & Lin, L. (2019). Analysis of the Influence of Mobile Payment on Consumer Behavior. *2019 4th International Conference on Humanities Science and Society Development (ICHSSD 2019)*, 121–127. DOI: 10.2991/ichssd-19.2019.24

Xue, R., Gepp, A., O'Neill, T. J., Stern, S., & Vanstone, B. J. (2020). Financial well-being amongst elderly Australians: The role of consumption patterns and financial literacy. *Accounting and Finance*, 60(4), 4361–4386. DOI: 10.1111/acfi.12545

Yuan, J., Jiang, S., & Mary Joy Dela Cruz, B. (2023). Toward the digital economy: Mobile payment affecting sustainable consumption behavior. *Innovative Marketing*, 19(1), 220–232. DOI: 10.21511/im.19(1).2023.19

Zatadini, N., & Syamsuri, S. (2018). Konsep Maqashid Syariah menurut Al-Syatibi dan kontribusinya dalam kebijakan fiskal. *AL-FALAH: Journal of Islamic Economics*, 3(2), 1–16. DOI: 10.29240/alfalah.v3i2.587

Zhang, W., Chen, M., Xie, Y., & Zhao, Z. (2018). Prosocial Spending and Subjective Well-Being: The Recipient Perspective. *Journal of Happiness Studies*, 19(8), 2267–2281. DOI: 10.1007/s10902-017-9918-2

Zustika, A. F., & Fageh, A. (2022). Analisis Dompet Digital "Link Aja Syariah" dari Perspektif Maslahah Mursalah. *Islamic Economics Journal*, 8(1), 25. DOI: 10.21111/iej.v8i1.6279

Chapter 10
Empirical Study on Relationship Between Macro Economic Variables and Non-Performing Assets in Private Banks

Priyanshi Verma
Christ University, India

ABSTRACT

The research aims at analyzing the correlation between the accumulation of Non-Performing Assets (NPAs) in the private sector banks (ICICI, HDFC, Kotak Mahindra, Federal, Axis Bank) and the economic development of the Indian economy. An analysis of the correlation between NPAs of various private sector banks with annual Gross Domestic Product (GDP), Interest rates, Inflation rates, Unemployment rates. The purpose of this study is to investigate the relationship between various economic variables and the increase in NPA, particularly during a period when the economy is recovering from the COVID-19-induced stagnation in economic activities leading to an increase in inflation rates.

DOI: 10.4018/979-8-3693-5653-1.ch010

INTRODUCTION

The banking sector plays an essential role in India's economic growth and development. Banks are shifting capital from surplus to deficit and enabling productive investments and consumption. Sound and resilient banking systems are essential to financial stability and sustainable economic growth.

However, one of the biggest challenges facing Indian banks is the problem of bad loans or NPAs. Loans or advances in a non-performing or near-performing condition are classified as NPAs. If the borrower does not pay the interest or principal over a period of more than 90 days, the loan is considered not to be viable. The NPA crisis in India has been going on for a long time.

The NPAs crisis in India has been ongoing for quite some time now. According to RBI data, the ratio of Gross Non-Performing Loans (NPLs) as a proportion of Total Advances of the scheduled commercial banks stood at 11.2% in the fiscal year 2017-18. High levels of NPLs have a major impact on banks' profitability, asset value, capital position, and liquidity. NPLs limit banks' ability to generate income through lending activities, reduce banks' net worth, and limit their ability to use deployed capital for new lending. The government, regulatory authorities, and banks have all worked together to reduce the NPL ratio to around 5% by 2022, but the legacy of NPLs continues to be a major challenge in the Indian banking system.

NPAs are a lag indicator for the overall health of the economy and the business. The build-up of NPAs is influenced by a variety of factors, including but not limited to, bank-specific issues (e.g. bad credit assessment and monitoring), sectoral issues arising from the cyclical nature of the industry, political paralysis, project delays and macro shocks. One of the most interesting relationships between macroeconomic factors (e.g., GDP growth, inflation rate, unemployment rate, and interest rate) and the build-up of bad loans in the banking system.

The macro-principle relationships are not only relevant to risk management and alerting systems, but also to policymaking. Strong economic growth increases debt service capacity and improves debt repayment capacity. On the other hand, weak economic growth lowers business cash flows and increases credit risk. Inflation affects borrowers' real income. Interest rates' dynamics influence loan availability. High unemployment increases the burden on individuals and households to repay their debts. The aim of this study is to empirically analyse the relationship between the number of non-performing loans from the Indian private banking sector from 2014-15 to 2018-19, as well as various macroeconomic indicators such as GDP, interest rates, inflation and unemployment. The study focuses on five major private sector banks, ICICI Bank, HDFC Bank, Kotak Mahindra Bank, Federal Bank and Axis Bank. This period is particularly important because it coincides with the current state of the Indian economy. The economic crisis after 2014 was the result of domestic policy uncertainty, external factors and the impact of structural reforms such as demonetization and the introduction of GST. After the high growth period of the mid-2000s, this recession in economic growth is likely to exacerbate bank NPAs. The second part of the analysis period from 2018 also captures the changing dynamics of the COVID-19 pandemic, which has had a devastating impact on economic growth, business and revenue prospects in various industries. The significance of this research cannot be overstated given the crucial role that private banks play in stimulating investment and consumption in the Indian economy. In 2021, private banks accounted for 36% of total bank credit disbursements and 30% of total bank deposits in Indian banking space. The resilience and prudential management of NPAs by private banks is not only crucial for maintaining financial stability but also for sustaining economic recovery in the post covid-19 climate of high inflation and tightening monetary conditions.

The main focus of the study is Firstly, To Examine the empirical correlation between the NPAs of the chosen private banks over the study period and the annual growth rate of GDP, interest rates, inflation rates, and unemployment rates over the study period. Secondly, To Analyze the dynamic relationship between these macroeconomic drivers and the rise in bad loans particularly during the economic slowdown caused by the COVID19 pandemic combined with rising inflation. Thirdly, To Identify potential causes of build-up in bad loans in the private banks and propose prudential measures to effectively manage and mitigate bad loans.

The empirical investigation shows that GDP growth is negatively correlated with net national accounts as the increase in economic activity improves the debt repayment capacity of the borrowers. However, higher interest rate, inflation rate and unemployment rate increase the debt repayment burden and are positively correlated with the net national accounts, according to empirical investigation. Econometric methods used in empirical analysis are correlation and regression based on aggregate data from the Reserve Bank of India (RBI) reports, bank financial statements, and other dependable secondary sources.

The findings of the study are expected to offer valuable insights into the complex relationship between macro prudential environment and asset quality in the banking industry. The findings can be used to inform policy makers to develop compensatory prudential measures; provide regulatory insight to reduce NPAs build-up in challenging macro environments; and equip banks with tools for proactive monitoring and risk mitigation.

The academic value of the study is that it complements the existing research on the factors that influence NPAs. In particular, the study concentrates on the macro-relationships in the private banking landscape in India over a short span of time. The Indian private banking landscape is characterized by cyclical peaks and busts.

LITERATURE REVIEW

Lenders and policymakers are quite concerned about the NPA situation. Numerous research has been conducted to pinpoint the elements responsible for the rise in measures put in place to lower NPAs. The following are the important reviews for this study:

Jimerrez, & Saurina (2006) found that the GDP growth rate, true loan cost, and lax lending conditions had the biggest effects on NPLs. The GDP growth rate is a crucial component on NPLs since it might affect borrows' capacity to repay their loans as a result of financial development. Strong GDP growth suggests that the economy as a whole is performing well, which may encourage increased business activity and greater personnel costs. As a result, the chance of NPLs is reduced because borrowers are more likely to have the assets necessary to repay their advances. The genuine loan charge, which affects the acquisition costs, is another significant factor in NPLs.

Dash, & Kabra (2010) found that two factors that lead to high NPAs are high loan cost and high certifiable solid trading scale, both of which increase the default risk and hence the NPAs. A high certifiable normal trading scale may lead to a decline in the real economy of the country, which may negatively impact the visibility of the business and increase the probability of credit default, leading to a higher NPAs.

Sofolis, & Eftychia (2011) used univariate regression to break out several variables related to the Greek financial system, such as growth, unemployment rate, and growth consumption. They found that these variables interacted with country-specific variables linked to the Greek emergency to affect the credit risk of the financial framework. This suggests that changes in any of these variables could affect the likelihood of Greek banks experiencing credit disasters or defaults.

Asari et al (2011) found that neither the loan fees nor the development had any effect on NPAs. Therefore, changes to these limits are unlikely to have a significant effect on the quantity of NPAs in the financial system.

Dimitrios, Angelos & Vasilios (2012) found that Macroeconomic variables such as actual GDP growth rate, unemployment rate, credit crediting rate, and public duty, had a significant effect on the proportion of NPLs. Real GDP improvement rate had a negative effect on NPL levels. An increase in the claimed GDP improvement rate could lead to a reduction in the amount of NPAs. The analysis showed that unemployment rate had a general effect on NPLs. An increase in unemployment rate could lead to an increase in NPLs.

Dimitrios, & Louzis (2012) examined the impact of macroeconomic conditions on NPAs Levels in the Spanish Banking Sector. The review examined the impact of Real GDP Growth Rate, Real Loan Charge, and Liberal Lending Conditions on

NPA Levels in the Spanish Financial Sector. The review concluded that the impact of Real GDP Growth Rate on NPA Levels was Negative.

Smir and Kmara (2013) Examined the effects of NPA on bank productivity and liquidly, as well dissiliency.

Rahman and Ahmad (2017) found that NPAs have a negative impact on the productivity and liquidity of the Indian banks. According to Gupta and jain (2016), NPAs have an adverse impact on Indian banks' monetary execution. According to Singh and sharmam (2018), on behalf of SBI, Provincial Banks of india (PNB) and Central bank of india (CBI), the situation of NPAs in the Indian banks was examined. According to the study, NPAs account for a significant share of the financial industry and are an inevitable burden on the sector.

Narula & Singh (2014) found that NPAs have a negative impact on banks' cash flow. NPAs reduce production, which can lead to insolvency. Banks have to set a provision for NPAs. NPAs can reduce banks' capital adequacy (VAT) percentage and reduce their lending capacity. It is necessary to reduce NPAs in order to improve banks' productivity. PNB's net profit has been impacted by NPAs, according to an assessment ordered by Goyal in 2016.

Ibrahim, & Thangavelu (2014) focused on the NPA of Booked Business Banks in India and highlighted the role of the financial sector in the development and improvement of the monetary framework in India. A strong economy requires a sound monetary base. NPAs have become India's top monetary concern because of their negative effect on the bank's performance and on the overall economy.

Shrialashetti, & Poojari (2016) found a reasonable correlation between an organization bank's net NPA and its net profit. As NPA increased, the bank's profit decreased accordingly. This implies that NPA's have a negative impact on the bank's overall financial strength. This highlights the need to manage and reduce NPA. There was no significant difference in NPA levels across locations./

Ombir and Bansal (2016) examined the effect of ownership designs on the NPA level. Contrary to the finding that public area banks have a higher NPA level than their private partners, the researchers found string regions with no evidence to back up the finding that public sector banks have higher NPA levels than their private partners.

Bhattarai (2017) found that NPLs have a negative impact on a bank’s profit as they require higher haircuts, which reduces the bank’s productivity. Bhattarai also noted that NPLs impacted the efficiency of banks in China.

Tiwari & Garg (2018) examined the impact of NPAs on the economy of India. The evaluation focused on the impact of increasing NPA rates on the trust and confidence of financial supporters, contributors and loan professionals. Tiwari also found that increasing NPAs may lead to an increase in credit loan fees, which would directly affect financial supporters who want to advance funds for foundations, contemporary activities and other purposes. The rising finance prices lead to a shortage of assets in the Indian economic sectors which can significantly affect the overall monetary development of the country.

Tejashwini & Ramani (2019) aimed to examine the performance of Bank of Baroda (a public sector bank), and HDFC (a private sector bank) during the three-year period 2017-2019. The purpose of the study is to evaluate the presentation of HDFC and the factors that influenced its exhibition. The study revealed that HDFC had more advances, shops and pay age limit than Bank of Baroda.

Mittal (2019) aimed to understand the effects of increasing NPAs on the Indian Banking industry and on the economy. The study revealed that the proportion of NPAs in India increased significantly over the past decade. The researchers noted that NPAs pose a major challenge for banks as a large proportion of the bank's resources becomes non-revenue generating, thus reducing the bank's productivity and its capacity to generate new loans.

Selvam & Premnath (2020) founds that NPAs are a major concern of the banking sector and have a negative impact on the performance of banks. Due to the COVID-19 pandemic, banks' NPAs have worsened further. In the current climate of low crop yields, unpredictable weather, limited access to credit and high interest rates for loans, the small and marginal farmers of the agriculture sector face many challenges in repaying their loans.

OBJECTIVES

To Analyze the relationship between NPAs of various private sector banks and the annual GDP, interest rate, inflation rate, and unemployment rate.

To examine the relationship between different economic elements and the increase in NPA, particularly during the period when the economy recovered from the lull caused by the pandemic and inflation rates increased.

To Identify the causes of the rise in NPAs in private sector banks and suggest remedial measures for NPA management.

HYPOTHESIS STATEMENTS

Table 1. Hypothesis statements

	Coefficients	Standard Error	t Stat	P-value	Lower 95%	Upper 95%	Lower 95.0%	Upper 95.0%
Intercept	65302.6	109193.6	0.598044	0.061051	-404519	535124.6	-404519	535124.6
GDP	-0.93029	15.60727	-0.05961	0.045789	- 68.0829	66.22236	- 68.0829	66.22236
Interest Rate	-3617.31	3918.109	-0.92323	0.025352	- 20475.6	13240.95	- 20475.6	13240.95
Inflation Rate	1761.189	2204.63	0.798859	0.038166	- 7724.57	11246.95	- 7724.57	11246.95
Unemployment Rate	-3172.94	3920.281	-0.80937	0.020329	- 20040.6	13694.67	- 20040.6	13694.67

H0- There is no significant relationship between NPA and GDP.

H1- There is a significant relationship between NPA and GDP.

For GDP, the P value is p=0.045789 and for NPA, p=0.05. Therefore, there is a strong correlation between the two. Therefore, the claim that NPA does not correlate with GDP is false. There is sufficient evidence to show a strong correlation between GDP and the NPA.

H0- There is no significant relationship between NPA and Borrowing costs

H1- There is significant relationship between NPA and Borrowing costs.

The correlation between loan fee and NPA is high. The difference between NPA and loan fee is less than 0.05 (p = 0.253). Therefore, the correlation between NPA and borrowing costs is high. There is enough evidence to support the hypothesis that there is a significant relationship between the level of NPA and financing cost. The alternative hypothesis is based on the strong correlation between NPA level and loan cost.

H0: There is no significant relationship between NPA and Expansion Rate.

H1: There is a significant relationship between NPA and Expansion Rate.

The p value of the expansion rate (p < 0.05) is p=0.0381. This means there is a significant relationship between the NPA and the expansion rate.

H0: There is no significant relationship between NPA and Unemployment Rate.

H1: There is a significant relationship between NPA and Unemployment Rate.

The p value for unemployment is p = p.0203 (p < 0.05). The correlation between NPA and unemployment rate is high.

RESEARCH METHODOLOGY

The study compiled data from five private banking banks in India for five years from 2014 to 2018. This period is especially important because it occurs during an unstable period in the Indian economy. The economic slowdown after 2014 was due to the combination of domestic political uncertainties, external factors, and structural reforms, such as the introduction of Goods and Services Tax (GST). The economic slowdown has probably exacerbated banks' problems with NPLs, after high credit growth in the early 2000s. The analysis also covers the second half of 2018 and the impact of COVID-19 on economic activity, business and income prospects in various sectors.

In recent years, there have been major economic events in the banking sector. Although my data may not always be the most accurate, they provide a comprehensive overview of the economic environment and the impact of these events on private banks' NPAs. I understand the limitations of the lack of more recent data and suggest that future research will focus on the developments following 2019 to improve our understanding. The data are compiled using tables and correlation coefficients. Data are regularly obtained from the RBI's website and other reports published by other banks and RBI. The purpose of this study is to analyze the relationship between different economic variables and the rise in NPAs, especially at a time when the economy emerges from the stagnation of economic activity caused by COVID-19 and inflation rates are increasing.

R Squared

R-squared efficacy, also known as Coefficient of assurance, is a fact metric. It measures the degree to which a dependent variable's variability is understood by a relapse model's free variable. R-squared efficacy ranges from 0 to 1. A value of 1 indicates that all variability within a dependent variable can be understood by a free variable. A value of 0 means that no variability can be understood.

Table 2. R squared

Multiple R	**0.8973**
R Square	0.805148
Adjusted R Square	0.415444
Standard Error	3060.842
Observations	7

Using an R-squared of 0.805148, the free variables in the relapse model contribute 80.51 percent to the dependent variable difference. A good R-squared indicates that the model fits the data well and the free variables predict the dependent variables well.

ANOVA

ANOVA, or Analysis of Variance, is a statistical test to determine whether a regression model has a significant effect (or not) on a dependent variable.

ANOVA allows to test the model to see if it can explain variation in the dependent variable. The test is called an F-Test. The F-Test tells you if the model can explain the variation in the dependent better than a chance effect.

An ANOVA is considered statistically significant when the p-value is less than 0.05 and at least one of the independent variables is strongly associated with or predicts the dependent variable.

Table 3. ANOVA

	Sum of Squares	df	Mean Square	F	Sig.
Regression	77425279	4	19356320	2.066051	0.035174
Residual	18737504	2	9368752		
Total	96162783	6			

The F value indicates if the independent variables affect the dependent variables significantly. If the F value is low, the false assumption that all of the regression coefficients in the model equal zero should be discarded. On the other hand, if the F value is high, it means that at least one independent variable has a significant impact on the dependent variable.

In Table 3, An F value of 0.035174 indicates that there is a low probability that the dependent variable and independent components of a single relapse model interact randomly.

Residual Plot and Line Fit Plot of all the Independent Variable

Table 4. Residual output

Observation	Predicted NPA	Residuals	Standard Residuals
1	5132.75	-1249.02	-0.70679
2	3941.96	3193.065	1.806872
3	5303.274	-2525.8	-1.42929
4	4414.595	454.3246	0.257091
5	4456.723	-420.113	-0.23773
6	9433.457	87.66295	0.049606
7	13609.2	459.8901	0.26024

Table 4 shows some observed values, their predicted values, and residuals (the difference between observed and predicted values). The residuals are normalized, i.e., they are reported as the standard deviation.

We can observe from the Table 4:

Since the estimated net present value for perception 1 is less than the observed value, the negative remainder means that the model undervalued the net present value for that impression.

For Perception 2, the residual is higher than the expected NPA due to the difference between the expected NPA and the observed NPA. This suggests that the model was wrong about the NPA for this impression.

For Perception 3, The expected NPA is a bit higher than the observed NPA, so there is a bit of NPA left over. This implies that the model was correct about the NPA of this perception but only marginally.

For Perception 4, The expected NPA is lower than the NPA observed, so the residual value is slightly negative. This suggests that the model miscalculated the NPA for this perception, but only slightly.

For Perception 5, predicted NPA is close to the observed NPA, so the residual value is low. This indicates that the model predicted the NPA from this perspective.

For Perception 6, The residual value is slightly higher than the expected NPA. This means that the model did not correctly estimate the NPA for this impression but only marginally.

In summary, the model appears to be reasonably accurate in predicting NPA. There is some potential for further refinement, particularly in the case of perception (1), (2), and (3), where residual values are relatively high. Further exploration is warranted to find examples or patterns in residual values and to determine if there are additional parameters that can be remembered to improve the model's accuracy.

PROBABILITY OUTPUT

Table 5. Probability output

Percentile	NPA
7.142857	2777.47
21.42857	3883.725
35.71429	4036.61
50	4868.92
64.28571	7135.025
78.57143	9521.12
92.85714	14069.09

Table 5 shows the percentiles and the corresponding NPA values. The NPA percentage ranges from 7.14% to 92.85% and the NPA value ranges from 2777,47 to 1406,09.

The higher the percentile, the higher the NPA value. This means that a higher proportion of banks have higher NPA levels. This is a sign of the challenges that banks are facing in terms of assessing the quality of their loan portfolio.

NPAs also increased dramatically from 50.29% to 64.1%. This shows that there are few banks with a very high NPA and may indicate some fundamental weakness in the credit structure of these institutions.

The highest NPA is 92.85%, indicating a relatively low number of banks with very high NPAs and indicating serious problems in the quality of their portfolio of advances requiring immediate attention from bank executives and supervisors.

In general, these data emphasize the importance of establishing strong loan portfolios and managing NPAs to maintain long-term financial stability and growth. It also emphasizes the need for administrative supervision and mediation in order to solve existing portfolio quality problems and avoid financial crises.

RESEARCH FINDINGS

The level of NPAs of private Indian Banks is heavily influenced by the macroeconomic environment.

GDP growth has a negative correlation with NPA, while inflation and unemployment rates have a positive correlation with NPA. Therefore, higher GDP growth rates will result in lower NPA levels.

The relationship between NPA and Interest rates is positively correlated with inflation and Unemployment rates.

Higher interest rates, higher inflation rates and higher unemployment rates will result in higher NPA levels.

SUGGESTIONS

1. Keep a close eye on macroeconomic indicators to predict changes in NPAs levels.
2. Improve risk management processes to mitigate the impact of macroeconomic events at the NPA level.
3. Take proactive steps to reduce your credit risk, including improving your credit scores and implementing credit monitoring programs
4. Improve Loan Portfolio Quality by Focusing on Credit Underwriting and Origination.
5. Keep a close eye on the performance of all banks and the banking industry at large to spot areas of weakness and areas of growth.

CONCLUSION

As a result of this analysis, it can be concluded that NPA is closely linked to macroeconomic indicators like the unemployment rate and GDP growth, as well as loan cost. Changes in these macroeconomic indicators can have a significant impact on the level of NPA in the financial system.

The unemployment rate protects against NPAs. A rise in unemployment can lead to more loan defaults. Growth in GDP can also affect NPAs. An increase in GDP can reduce the NPA, while an unchanged or declining GDP can increase the NPA.

NPAs may also be affected by loan expansion rates. High rates of loan expansion can increase NPAs, making it more difficult for borrowers to repay their loans. Financial costs have also had a major impact on NPAs. Higher loan fees may make it more difficult to repay the loan, leading to higher NPAs.

It is therefore important that the banking system monitors these macroeconomic drivers and takes the necessary measures to manage the NPA. Monitoring these drivers enables banks to adapt lending policies and find ways to reduce the impact of macroeconomic shocks on the NPA level.

REFERENCES

Asari, N., Lopes, A. B., & Saito, R. (2011). Interest rate, growth and non-performing assets: Evidence from Indian banking. *International Journal of Economics and Finance*. Advance online publication. DOI: 10.5539/ijef.v3n2p216

Bhattarai, K. (2017). Non-Performing Loans and Bank Productivity: Evidence from Nepalese Commercial Banks. *Journal of Business and Management*, •••, 10–22. DOI: 10.3126/jbm.v19i3.18315

Dash, R. K., & Kabra, G. (2010). Real wage variation and non-performing assets: evidence from Indian banks. International Journal of Social Economics, https://www.emerald.com/insight/content/doi/10.1108/03068291011091152/full/html

Dimitrios, D., Angelos, K., & Vasilios, P. (2012). Macroeconomic determinants of nonperforming loans: A panel data analysis of South Asian countries. International Journal of Economics and Financial Issues, https://www.econjournals.com/index.php/ijefi/article/view/59/12

Ibrahim, M., & Thangavelu, S. M. (2014). Non-performing assets in Indian booked business banks: A review. *Global Journal of Emerging Market Economies*, 6(1), 87–96. https://journals.sagepub.com/doi/abs/10.1177/0974910114534104. DOI: 10.1177/0974910114534104

Jiménez, G., & Saurina, J. (2006). Credit cycles, credit risk, and prudential regulation. International Journal of Central Banking, https://www.ijcb.org/journal/ijcb06q2a3.htm

Maheshwari, R., & Reddy, N. (2022). *Non-performing assets in Indian banking: causes and solutions*. International Journal of Management, Technology, and Social Sciences., DOI: 10.5281/zenodo.5728365

Mittal, P. (2019). *Non-performing Assets (NPAs) in Indian Banking Sector: Causes, Effects and Remedies. International Journal of Management, Technology, and Social Sciences*. IJMTS., DOI: 10.5281/zenodo.337895

Narula, R., & Singla, S. (2014). Non-performing assets (NPAs) and its impact on Indian banking sector. International Journal of Innovative Research and Developme-https://www.academia.edu/download/42963536/NON_PERFORMING_ASSETS_NPAs_AN D_ITS_IMPACT.pdf

Ombir, & Bansal. (2016). Non-performing Assets in Indian Banks: Trends and Determinants. Journal of Commerce and Accounting Research, Retrieved from https://www.semanticscholar.org/paper/Non performing-Assets-in-Indian-Banks%3ATrends-and-Ombir Bansal/34f170caae82aa7c1a390d1c7b444a182fac90d7

Samir, M., & Kamra, S. (2013). Non-performing assets of banks: an overview. Journal of Management Research. Retrieved from https://www.proquest.com/docview/1477975941

Selvam, R., & Premnath, N. G. (2020). Impact of Coronavirus on NPA and GDP of Indian Economy. Prabandhan: Indian Journal of Management, https://journal.prabandhan.co.in/index.php/pim/article/view/152602/85849

Shiralashetti, S. S., & Poojari, V. (2016). Non-Performing Assets (NPA): A study on its causes and impact on the profitability of the bank. International Journal of Applied Research, Retrieved from https://www.allresearchjournal.com/archives/2016/vol2issue10/PartH/2-10- 71-838.pdf

Sofolis, I., & Eftychia, N. (2011). Factors Influencing the Credit Risk of the Greek Financial System. International Journal of Economics and Financial Issues, Retrieved from 47 https://www.econjournals.com/index.php/ijefi/article/view/142/97

Tejashwini, R., & Ramani, R. (2019). A Comparative Study of the Performance of Public and Private Sector Banks in India. [IJITEE]. *International Journal of Innovative Technology and Exploring Engineering*, 8(9), 1027–1032. https://www.ijitee.org/wpcontent/uploads/papers/v8i9s/E11410582S19.pdf

Tiwari, A., & Garg, A. (2018). Impact of non-performing assets on the Indian economy. International Journal of Engineering Technology Science and Research, https://www.ijetsr.com/images/short_pdf/1538663848_8447.pdf

Chapter 11 Harnessing Sadaqa to Achieve Inclusivity and Progressiveness of Islamic Banking

Ahmad Yani Ismail
Universiti Islam Selangor, Malaysia

ABSTRACT

Sadaqa is a charitable donation encouraged by Islam. It is donated to the marginalized society or for community empowerment initiatives. The instrument can be deployed for inclusivity-motive projects. Empirical evidences on the programmes are well-documented. Islamic Banking Industry (IBI) has shown to be successful in the commercial sector but less pro-active in the welfare sector. The introduction of Sustainable Development Goals agenda and Value Based Intermediation (VBI) has inspired IBI to proactively embark on social empowerment initiatives positioning IBI in the inclusivity initiatives. Case study on Sadaqa House initiative by Bank Islam Malaysia Berhad showcasing how sadaqa can be harnessed and contribute to inclusivity programmes. Malaysia's Islamic Finance sector is progressive with a top-down agenda by the regulatory bodies. Bank Negara Malaysia's VBI, Malaysia International Islamic Finance Centre (MIFC) Leadership Council's Position Paper and other initiatives proof the progressiveness of IBI. This includes Sadaqa House's blended financing instruments.

DOI: 10.4018/979-8-3693-5653-1.ch011

INTRODUCTION

Sadaqa holds a central place in Islamic tradition, serving as a key form of voluntary charity. Unlike *zakat* and *waqf*, it offers flexibility in its application, making it distinct among Islamic social finance instruments. As an essential component of Islamic economics, Islamic banking has an important role to play in advancing social welfare. Through *sadaqa* and other social finance tools, Islamic banks have the opportunity to expand their focus beyond profit-maximization. Currently, one of the criticisms directed at the Islamic Banking Industry (IBI) is its limited engagement with sectors lacking creditworthiness. By utilizing *sadaqa*, IBI can actively contribute to underserved communities by providing alternative funding sources beyond traditional depositor funds. Using *sadaqa* as a funding model allows Islamic banks to enter the social welfare sector, an area often seen as higher-risk. This approach aligns with the *Maqasid Al-Shariah* (objectives of Shariah), fostering justice, welfare, and equality. Additionally, digitization amplifies the impact of this initiative, enhancing both the collection and distribution of *sadaqa* funds.

The chapter commences with brief discussion on *sadaqa* in general and its significance in IBI. Following recap on Islamic bank principles and objectives, the author deliberates on inclusivity and the role of IBI in promoting inclusivity. Insight on some challenges for the Islamic banking community in meeting the financial inclusivity target is presented. The chapter then delves into how *sadaqa* can promote inclusivity including some innovative approach in utilising *sadaqa*. As evidence for the significance role of *sadaqa*, case study on successful *sadaqa*-based initiatives by an Islamic bank is documented. Details on collection and distribution of Islamic social finance instruments can be efficient by leveraging on the technology are also discussed. Sections on how *sadaqa* addresses financial exclusion and progressive Islamic banks are included. Finally, the chapter ends with an analysis of how institutionalisation of *sadaqa* can revolutionarise Islamic bank's intermediary role.

Introduction to *Sadaqa* and Islamic Bank

The term "*sadaqa*" originates from the Arabic root word "*sadq*" or "*sidq*", which conveys the notions of truthfulness and sincerity (Hans Wehr, 1980). However, within the framework of Islamic jurisprudence, "*sadaqa*" is specifically defined as a charitable donation given to the needy with the intention of pleasing Allah SWT or seeking blessings from Him (al-Ahkam al-cadliyah. 2002). *Sadaqa* possesses distinct characteristics not found in other forms of philanthropy such as *zakat* and *waqf*, particularly in its flexibility. Unlike *zakat* and *waqf*, which are allocated solely for specific recipients and purposes, *sadaqa* funds can be distributed to beneficiaries without strict proportions or predefined recipients (Ruzian Markom et al., 2015).

One significant trait of *sadaqa* is that all community can receive *sadaqa*, Muslim and non-Muslim (Musafar Hameed et al., 2017) including the rich people (muftiwp, 2024). However, Mufti of Federal Territory's Office, Malaysia (2024) stress that priority should be given to the needy people.

In Islam, *sadaqa* serves as a complementary instrument to obligatory practices like *zakat* and *waqf* (Abdullah Jalil & Muhammad Muda, 2008). When *zakat* and *waqf* funds are insufficient, *sadaqa* funds can provide additional support. Furthermore, *sadaqa* funds can serve as emergency aid in times of distress or disaster, offering assistance beyond the scope of *zakat* and *waqf* (Ruzian Markom et al., 2015). In Al-Quran, the term *sadaqa* can be traced with the term , , and . The word is repeated 5 times, 7 times, and once. Besides the term *sadaqa*, Al-Quran also refers the word *infaq* as *sadaqa* and mentioned 60 places in Al-Quran. This proves that in Islam *sadaqa* is a good deed and every Muslim is encouraged to give *sadaqa*. Al-Quran and As-Sunnah stress the significance of regularly giving *sadaqa*, and Allah SWT has promised numerous benefits to those who engage in this practice. The reasons for giving *sadaqa* are profound and multifaceted. Firstly, it fulfills individual needs. The Prophet Muhammad SAW said, "Whoever fulfilled the needs of his brother, Allah will fulfill his needs" (Sahih Al-Bukhari). It is part of human nature to have needs in this world, and while we should plan, save, and strive to meet our future requirements, we must also recognize that it is ultimately Allah SWT who grants our wishes. Therefore, by helping others, we not only assist them but may also find our own needs fulfilled by Allah SWT.

Moreover, *sadaqa* alleviates difficulties and dispels misfortunes. The Prophet SAW advised, "Give *sadaqa* promptly, as it serves as a barrier against adversity" (Tirmidhi). In Islam, life is viewed as a trial, and one way Allah SWT tests our faith is through challenges. Thus, offering *sadaqa* during difficult times reflects strong faith and gratitude. It is through Allah SWT's infinite mercy that circumstances can change, as highlighted in Al-Quran: "Allah erases and confirms what He wills, and with Him is the Mother of the Book" (13:39). This suggests that by easing the struggles of others, our *sadaqa* can serve as a safeguard against calamities in our own lives, by the will of Allah SWT.

Additionally, *sadaqa* is viewed as an investment for both this world and the hereafter. In finance, investment is a means of accumulating wealth for future needs, and *sadaqa* is no different, with its dividends realized in the afterlife. Allah SWT states in Al-Quran, "Indeed, the men who practice charity and the women who practice charity, and they who have loaned Allah a goodly loan—it will be multiplied for them, and they will have a noble reward" (57:18). Thus, by giving *sadaqa*, we are essentially investing in our afterlife.

Sadaqa also serves to eliminate small sins. On the Day of Judgment, we will be accountable for all our actions, both good and bad. Since minor sins are inevitable, one way to expiate them is through *sadaqa*. The Prophet SAW said, "Charity extinguishes the sins like water extinguishes a fire" (Ibn Majah). By giving *sadaqa* sincerely and for the sake of Allah SWT, we can remove these small sins.

Furthermore, *sadaqa* helps to eliminate *riba* (usury), aligning with the objectives of Shariah. The prohibition of *riba* in Islam aims to protect wealth, as stated in Al-Quran: "God has permitted commerce, and has forbidden usury" (2: 275). This verse underscores the need to eliminate riba through its prohibition and allows for trade. In addition, Al-Quran states, "God condemns usury, and He blesses charities" (2: 276), indicating that *sadaqa* can flourish as Allah SWT will cause it to prosper. Both verses imply that *sadaqa* is an essential aspect of commercial transactions (*mu'amalah*), complementing permissible trade and the prohibition of *riba*.

In the context of this chapter, the role of *sadaqa* in elevating Islamic banking is significant and will be discussed in detail in the following paragraphs. *Sadaqa* embodies the Islamic principles of social justice, welfare, and equity, which are also central to *Maqasid Al-Shariah* (objectives of Shariah). By incorporating *sadaqa* into their operations, Islamic banks can fulfill these objectives by addressing social needs, supporting the disadvantaged and promoting fairness within the financial system.

Overview of Islamic Bank Principles and Objectives

At the heart of an Islamic bank lies adherence to Shariah requirements in its operations, offerings, products, and services, as stipulated in the Islamic Financial Services Act 2013 enacted by Bank Negara Malaysia (BNM) on March 22, 2013. Shariah, serving as the primary guiding principle, underscores the principles that Islamic banks should steer clear of in their operations, as outlined by the International Shari'ah Research Academy for Islamic Finance (ISRA) in 2023. These principles include avoiding *riba* (interest), *gharar* (uncertainty), and *maysir* (gambling). Additionally, according to ISRA (2023), Islamic banks must refrain from engaging in unethical practices such as manipulation, price exploitation, hoarding, and monopolizing, as well as abstain from involvement in impermissible business activities such as pornography, alcohol sales, and prostitution.

Islamic banking in Malaysia was introduced in 1983 with moral objectives as its compass (Noor Yakcop, 1981). In other words, its establishment is within the context of Islamic economics principles. Islamic economics promotes brotherhood, socio-economic justice, and the well-being of all by integrating values, ethics, market mechanisms, family structures, society, and, most importantly, good governance. Values and ethics are essential in any economic system. Their violation can cause substantial harm to a country's development (Musafar Hameed et al., 2024).

During the virtual launch of the World Bank Islamic Finance Reports on October 7, 2020, Abdul Rasheed Ghaffour, then Deputy Governor and now Governor of Bank Negara Malaysia, emphasized the importance of Islamic finance being value-driven and impact-focused to achieve the *Maqasid Shariah* (the objectives of Shariah) (World Bank, 2020, October 7, *Islamic finance reports*, retrieved from https://www.worldbank.org/en/events/2020/10/07/maximizing-islamic-finance-for-financial-inclusion). He noted that the core values of Islamic principles align with a vision of economic growth that is balanced, sustainable, and inclusive. Shariah advocates for a balance between wealth creation and wealth circulation, fostering fairness and *ihsan* (benevolence) to promote benefits and prevent harm.

Understanding Inclusivity in Islamic Bank

Inclusivity in the context of Islamic banking refers to the dedication to offering financial services and products that are accessible to all segments of society, while adhering to Shariah principles. All segments of community, including the poor and the marginalised, are able to participate in banking products and services (Musafar Hameed et al., 2024). They should be able to open accounts and enjoy financing from the bank. In other words, banking products and services are not exclusive to a group of people by way of their income and other requirements. By giving the same opportunities as other segment of society, they are able to actively participate in economic activities.

Inclusivity, financial, economy or social, is crucial for sustainable development because it guarantees that every segment of society can engage in and reap the benefits of economic growth, social advancement, and environmental stewardship (Musafar Hameed et al., 2024; Securities Commission Malaysia, 2024). Securities Commission Malaysia (2024) also highlighted that financial inclusion policy and initiatives are paramount for shared prosperity and reducing poverty.

Inclusivity contributes to sustainable development by fostering economic growth through broader participation, as access to education, employment, and financial services for all members of society, including marginalized groups, enhances overall economic productivity and innovation potential. It also helps reduce inequality by implementing inclusive economic policies that diminish income and wealth disparities, leading to a more equitable distribution of resources and opportunities. Additionally, inclusivity enhances stability, as economies with diverse participants are more resilient and capable of withstanding economic shocks due to a wider base of contributors.

Inclusivity also lead to sustainable development through social progress by ensuring that everyone has access to essential services such as healthcare, education, and housing, thereby enhancing overall well-being and quality of life. It empowers individuals by providing opportunities for all to participate in societal development, allowing them to contribute to and shape their communities. Furthermore, inclusive societies foster a sense of belonging and cooperation, which helps reduce social tensions and promotes harmony and peace.

Challenges to Achieving Inclusivity in Islamic Bank

Achieving inclusivity in Islamic banking involves overcoming several challenges that stem from structural, regulatory, cultural, and operational factors. One of the major challenges is the operationalising of Islamic banks' financing products using the mechanism of credit creation. Despite the implementation of Shariah Governance Policies aimed partly at ensuring that financing products comply with Shariah principles, the Islamic banking industry remains entangled in ongoing controversy surrounding its long-standing funding mechanisms which is largely benefiting the credit worthiness segment. Although the liquidity multiplication mechanism supports economic development, its potential negative impacts remain under scrutiny by concerned stakeholders.

The profit-maximisation focus within the Islamic banking industry has drawn criticism, as prioritising profits often restricts resources available to low-income groups. This emphasis on risk management and creditworthy clients limits banks' capacity to serve underserved populations. Expanding financial access to these groups would necessitate a structural shift towards incorporating social finance instruments like *zakat, waqf*, and microfinance. However, these tools typically fall outside the core banking model, making their integration complex. In countries like Malaysia, where *zakat* and *waqf* are managed by the respective State Islamic Religious Councils (SIRCs), it becomes challenging for Islamic banks to proactively offer financial solutions.

Another key challenge is the regulatory and legal frameworks. Islamic banks operate across various countries, each with its own set of regulations. Harmonizing these diverse legal systems to support inclusive practices is complex. Additionally, ensuring that all products and services strictly comply with Shariah principles while also meeting regulatory requirements is challenging, especially in non-Muslim majority countries where conventional banking norms predominate.

Financial literacy and awareness post hindrance to the development of the industry. Many potential customers, particularly in marginalized communities, have a limited understanding of Islamic banking principles and products. To address this, extensive educational campaigns are needed to raise awareness about the benefits and principles of Islamic banking.

Role of *Sadaqa* in Promoting Inclusivity

The Concept of Wealth Redistribution Through Sadaqa

Wealth distribution refers to how a nation's wealth is shared among its citizen (Francis, 2020). If a nation's wealth is distributed equally amongst its population, equal wealth distribution is reached. Wealth includes assets, income, property and other forms of wealth. Analyzing wealth distribution helps to understand economic inequality and the concentration of wealth within a community.

Under the present global economic system, wealthier core nations stand to benefit at the expense of poorer peripheral nations. This imbalance extends to internal divisions within countries. Wealth accumulation remains concentrated in a few corporations, echoing historical patterns despite globalization (Francis, 2020). Francis (2020) clarifies wealth remains concentrated in a few corporations despite globalization due to several factors. These include the monopolistic practices and market dominance of these corporations, the ability to exploit cheap labour and resources in developing countries, the unequal distribution of power and resources in the global economic system, and the structural barriers that prevent smaller businesses from competing on an equal footing.

In light of the aforementioned, *sadaqa* can play a significant role in addressing wealth imbalances within society. In Islam, *sadaqa* is a traditional method for ensuring that wealth is distributed from the affluent to those in need. According to Kunhibava et al., (2024), *sadaqa* can facilitate wealth redistribution across the community.

Sadaqa as a Tool for Poverty Alleviation and Social Welfare in Islamic Bank

Sadaqa, being a key component of Islamic social finance, directly target poverty alleviation (World Bank, 2017). In its Global Report on Islamic Finance 2016: A Catalyst for Shared Prosperity?, World Bank argued that *zakat* and *sadaqa* are inherently grounded in redistribution and philanthropy hence able to meet the fundamental needs of the extremely poor and establish a social safety net. The Bank, however, reminded that such objective can only be met with dedicated and correct policies to ensure the effective mobilization of the instruments, the efficient utilization and management of these resources, and their integration with microfinance to enhance inclusivity and affordability.

Sadaqa can also be utilized to foster economic development and social welfare. It can fund microfinance projects, educational initiatives, and other programs that support the poor and needy. (Bursa Academy, 2024). For example Teach for Malaysia, a Non-Governmental Organisation (NGO) affiliated with Malaysia's Ministry of

Higher Education, seeks donation for education related community projects. Islamic Relief Malaysia has established a crowdfunding platform to encourage public to give *sadaqa* to assist them in running Pusat Bimbingan Alternatif in Kajang providing holistic education program for refugee community.

As an institution rooted in social welfare, Islamic bank can play paramount role in assisting the less fortunate and shoulder the government's responsibility in reducing poverty as well as contributing to the welfare sector (Polyzos et al., 2022). Rosman et al., (2022)'s investigation concluded that Islamic Finance is based on the higher objective of Shariah hence the right establishment to contribute to the welfare sector. The growing social activities implemented by Islamic banks contribute to the institutionalisation of Islamic social finance within Islamic banking framework.

In Malaysia a number of Islamic banks are actively involved in Islamic social finance sector, individually and collectively. Prior to the emergence of Islamic social finance, Islamic banks' role in *sadaqa* only limited to registering savings account for NGOs or Foundations for the purpose of fund collection. Collectively, under the patronage of Association of Islamic Banking and Financial Institutions of Malaysia (AIBIM), nine Islamic banks work together under myWakaf initiatives. Among the initiatives include *waqf* of solar dome dryer for fishermen and farmers community (AIBIM myWaqaf), *waqf* housing (Bank Islam Malaysia Berhad), *waqaf* homestay (Bank Muamalat Malaysia Behad), Dana Waqaf Al-Bait (RHB Islamic Bank) and dialysis centre (Bank Rakyat Malaysia Berhad). In addition to the above, Islamic banks also have their own initiatives such as Sadaqa House (Bank Islam Malaysia Berhad), Jariah Fund (Bank Muamalat Malaysia Berhad), and Maybank Heart (Maybank).

Innovative Approaches to Utilizing *Sadaqa*

Zakat, Waqf, and other forms of Sadaqa: Traditional and contemporary practices

Both *zakat* and *waqf* have been long practiced in Islam since the beginning of Islam. Both are a form of *sadaqa* whereby money or assets or properties are given as a charity and no returns are expected except for the returns in the hereafter. However, both have distinct characteristics and purposes. They are also governed by different rules and regulations.

Being one of the pillars of Islam, *zakat* is an obligatory form of *sadaqa* (zakat.org, 2024) prescribed upon each and every Muslim *(fardhu ain)* who fulfills all the conditions of obligatory *zakat*. Only a proportion of the wealth and property is required to be paid (Pusat Pungutan Zakat-MAIWP, 2022). In Malaysia, the *zakat* is paid to respective State's zakat authorities who will distribute to the 8 asnaf (Masruki et al., 2021; Wazan, 2024). Different zakat authorities have different schemes under the 8 asnaf (Masruki et al., 2021). Among the schemes are monthly food assistance, chronic disease assistance, dialysis treatment assistance, children schooling assistance, residence rental assistance, higher education student assistance, *aidiladha* assistance, Ramadhan and Syawal assistance (MAIM, 2024), education scholarship, business capital assistance, medical assistance, flood victim assistance (LZS, 2024).

Waqf is another form of *sadaqa* (Laluddin et al., 2021). It is a type of endowment where a property or asset is donated to a charitable cause, and the income generated from it is used for charitable purposes (Olatubosun,2022). The *waqf* can also be in the form of cash provided that there is an element of perpetuity. Similar to *zakat*, in Malaysia' *waqf* is managed by individual State Islamic Religious Council (SIRC) (Abd. Malib et al., 2021). All *waqf* assets must be registered with respective SIRC. Abd. Malib et. al. (2021) also highlighted that the administration, distribution, maintenance and development of *waqf* properties is the responsibilities of each SRIC. Any party who wish to develop the *waqf* properties must obtain the consent of the SIRC (Abd. Malib et al., 2021).

Since *zakat* and *waqf* matters are under the jurisdiction of respective State's zakat authorities and SRIC, Islamic banks' roles in both instruments are limited to facilitating the collection of *zakat* and *waqf* (cash *waqf*) and paying business *zakat* to the state's zakat authorities. Islamic banks' active roles in *zakat* and *waqf* initiatives become apparent after BNM announced Value Based Intermediation project in 2017. The announcement was also timely with the Sustainable Development Goals (SDGs) agenda by the United Nations launched in 2015 (UN, 2024). These have motivated Islamic banks in Malaysia to play active roles in *zakat*, *waqf*, *sadaqa* and other forms of instruments.

For example, through myWakaf initiative 6 Islamic banks have participated in the initiative. MyWakaf is a collaborative effort to standardize the *Waqf* Fund initiative action plan in partnership with SIRC. This initiative aims to develop the potential of *waqf* and strengthen the economy of the ummah in Malaysia. Currently, ten Islamic banks are involved in implementing *waqf* initiatives: Affin Islamic Bank Berhad, Bank Islam Malaysia Berhad, Bank Muamalat Malaysia Berhad, Bank Rakyat, Bank Simpanan Nasional, CIMB Islamic Bank Berhad, Hong Leong Islamic Bank Berhad, Maybank Islamic Berhad, MBSB Bank Berhad, and RHB Islamic Malaysia Berhad (myWakaf, 2024).

The active leading roles played by the above Islamic banks have led to various modern *waqf* initiatives. The contemporary *waqf* projects include *waqf* housing (Bank Islam Malaysia Berhad), *waqf* homestay (Bank Muamalat Malaysia Behad), Dana Waqaf Al-Bait (RHB Islamic Bank) and dialysis centre (Bank Rakyat Malaysia Berhad). In addition to the above, Islamic banks also have their own initiatives such as Sadaqa House (Bank Islam Malaysia Berhad), Jariah Fund (Bank Muamalat Malaysia Berhad), and Maybank Heart (Maybank).

Impact and Outcomes

Table 1. The amount of sadaqa fund disbursed

Change makers	Remarks	Collected	No. of recipient
Bangkit Revolving Fund	For underbanked micro-entrepreneurs	RM7,759,920.00 (2021 - 2023)	551 micro-entrepreneurs
Institut Jantung Negara Foundation (IJNF)	Focus on paediatric patients from underprivileged families	RM1,574,876.01 (2018 - 2023)	203 paediatric patients
Brain For Future (BFF)	Focus on alleviating poverty by offering financial aid to underprivileged university students	RM379,516.00 (2020 - 2022)	244 students
Buku Jalanan Chow Kit (BJCK)	To provide equal education opportunities to children in the Chow Kit catchment area	RM 462,182.75 (2020 - 2023)	348 children
Yayasan Sultanah Bahiyah (YSB)	Supports women entrepreneurs	RM 124,765.79 (2018 - 2023)	37 women entrepreneurs
University Teknologi Malaysia (UTM)	To provide renewable energy solar systems for Orang Asli community and other underserved populations in rural areas of Malaysia.	RM394,000 (2019 - 2022)	57 households
MyVista	To manufacture 3D-printed prosthetic hands and arms at a reduced cost particularly targeting physically disabled children from economically disadvantaged families.	RM75,888 (2019 - 2023)	10 children
Pertubuhan Kegiatan Dakwah Islamiah Sekolah-Sekolah Malaysia (PEKDIS)	To solidify *dakwah* activities among Islamic studies teachers nationwide and run *dakwah* activities in the schools at all levels.	RM537,314.68 (2021-2023)	9296 students (32 schools)
Mercy Mission Malaysia	A special project aimed at providing financial assistance to combat malnutrition among primary school children hailing from *asnaf fakir* and *miskin* backgrounds.	RM367,200 (2020-2023)	556 *asnaf* families

(Musafar Hameed et al., 2024):

As shown in the above, the Sadaqa House projects by Bank Islam Malaysia Berhad (BIMB) have resulted in significant impact and outcomes, especially in relation to Value-Based Intermediation (VBI). Cross referring to VBI principles, the Sadaqa House initiative prove to be an effective model for how Islamic banks can extend their role in social finance and community development.

The disbursed funds under Sadaqa House have primarily supported projects that address pressing social needs, including healthcare, education, and poverty alleviation. By channeling resources into impactful, community-driven projects, Sadaqa House contributes to the well-being of underserved communities, directly embodying VBI's goal of creating meaningful socio-economic impact. These funds have empowered low-income groups with access to healthcare services, educational support, and essential resources, promoting inclusivity and social welfare.

The Sadaqa House initiative reinforces the use of Islamic social finance tools, such *as sadaqa, waqf*, and *zakat*, in supporting welfare-oriented projects. Through these mechanisms, Sadaqa House addresses the gaps left by conventional banking products, which often focus on commercial sectors. By leveraging *sadaqa* funds, the initiative supports sectors traditionally overlooked in profit-driven banking, demonstrating how Islamic finance can go beyond commercial interests to address welfare and inclusivity goals central to VBI.

Sadaqa House utilises innovative funding mechanisms, such as crowdfunding and digital platforms, to collect and disburse funds efficiently. This technological integration not only broadens the reach of Islamic social finance but also aligns with VBI's call for innovation and adaptability. The approach demonstrates how Islamic banks can adopt digital solutions to expand their social finance efforts and reach a broader segment of donors and beneficiaries.

Sadaqa House projects contribute to Malaysia's Sustainable Development Goals (SDGs), such as reducing poverty and ensuring access to essential services, which align closely with VBI objectives. By supporting sustainable development, the initiative underscores VBI's holistic vision of a financial system that serves societal needs and promotes long-term welfare. The outcomes of Sadaqa House reflect the broader aspirations of VBI, showcasing the potential for Islamic banks to be catalysts for sustainable socio-economic development.

The success of the Sadaqa House initiative has enhanced the reputation of Islamic banking in the social finance sector. As a pioneering project, it positions BIMB as a leader in Islamic social finance, setting an example for other Islamic financial institutions to follow. This aligns with VBI's goal of redefining the role of Islamic banks, showing that they can contribute to social good while maintaining sound financial practices.

Sadaqa House has strengthened BIMB's relationship with various stakeholders, including communities, regulators, and the general public. By transparently managing and disbursing *sadaqa* funds, BIMB has built trust with donors and beneficiaries alike. This engagement aligns with VBI's emphasis on accountability, ethics, and stakeholder trust, demonstrating that Islamic banks can operate as trustworthy intermediaries for social finance.

Bank Islam's Sadaqa House represents a successful model of how Islamic banks can leverage charitable contributions to drive social change. By focusing on transparency, sustainability, and impactful projects, Sadaqa House not only fulfils the spiritual and social obligations of *sadaqa* but also enhances the bank's role in community development. This case study underscores the potential of *sadaqa*-

based initiatives in Islamic banking to create lasting social benefits and economic empowerment for the *ummah*.

Interestingly, Sadaqa House Bank Islam is one of the initiatives that differ from other Islamic social finance initiatives since it is implemented as a banking product/ services and the bank fully responsible in collecting and distributing the fund. This initiative is unique in terms of implementation where it became as one of the main offerings of BIMB.

Leveraging Technology for Efficient Social Finance (*zakat, waqaf, sadaqa*) Collection and Distribution

The adoption of technology in the Islamic social finance sector in Malaysia is addressed in two sections. The first section examines how State Islamic Religious Councils (SIRCs) utilize technology to manage Islamic social finance instruments, including *zakat, waqf,* and various forms of *sadaqa*. The second section focuses on the application of relevant technologies by Islamic banks and financial institutions within the Islamic social finance segment.

The advancement of technologies has motivated SIRCs to adopt them in an effort to better manage the traditional Islamic social finance namely *zakat* and *waqf*. This is further encouraged by the offering of relevant technologies by the technology companies tailor to the niche of the SIRCs especially relating to *zakat* and *waqf*. Research by Nordin, Shahwan, & Ibrahim, (2021) found Selangor Zakat Collection Centre (Pusat Pungutan Zakat, PPZ) has utilised six (6) e-wallet in apps feature for *zakat* in e-wallet. They are Boost, Tulus, Shopee, GoPayz, MAE and The Noor (as of August 2023). These e-wallets are in addition to online payment. Similarly, the acceptance of online transactions by zakat authorities enables *zakat* payers to individually calculate *zakat* amount. They can also make *zakat* payment via online and track the payment without going to zakat collection centres (Ahmad et al., 2014). Zakat authority of Selangor, Lembaga Zakat Selangor (LZS), has equipped employers with an online *zakat* deduction system called e-employers system for employers to deduct employees' salaries for *zakat* instead of cheques payments (Selangorkini, 2016). To facilitate *zakat* payment by individuals, LZS also installed 'Cashless ATM' at their selected branches (Selangorkini, 2016). Via the ATM, *zakat* payers can pay *zakat* using debit cards unlike bringing cash previously.

In addition to the above, numerous research conducted on the possibility of using technology on *zakat*. The employment of blockchain technology is expected to ease the process of applying for *zakat* by the asnaf (Nazeri & Mohd Nor, 2023). They also claimed that the technology result in the smooth and efficient *zakat* distribution. Similalry, Artificial intelligence (AI) and blockchain technologies are perceived to be improving efficiencies in the donors' experience (Nor Paizin et al., 2022). The finding is congruent with Al Azizah & Choirin (2018)'s study regarding financial technology vis-a-vis *zakat* distribution in Indonesia and concluded that the technology used has improved the *zakat* collection significantly.

In the case of *waqf*, the adoption of technology can be seen in the payment system of cash *waqf*. In general the payment of cash *waqf* can be in several ways; walk-in at respective SIRCs counter, on-line payment via each SIRC's web portal, monthly auto debit to SIRCs' account, check or bank draft or salary deduction (JAWHAR, 2024).

In addition to the technology adopted by the SIRCs, various technological tools and models proposed by past researchers. Mohd Danuri (2019) suggested a conceptual design of *waqf* management system using crowdfunding for *Mutawalli*. The system focuses more on the collection of *waqf* from the Wakaf Donor and monitored by the *waqf* committee. Wan Mohd Sidik & Ahmad (2021) proposed a Geographical Information System (GIS) to visually display *waqf* land in cadastral maps. Cadastral maps present detailed information about land within a certain area. These maps are crucial for understanding the property boundaries, sizes, and uses. They serve as a vital tool for governments, land surveyors, property developers, and individuals interested in land ownership and use. Such precise land information is crucial in enhancing systematic planning and management of *waqf* land.

The above are some of the technological adoption by some SIRCs. Motivated by the global movement in social finance by the banking and finance industry, Malaysian Islamic Banking and Finance fraternity has increased their roles in actively involved in *zakat*, *waqf*, *sadaqa* and other instruments hence birthing to the term Islamic Social Finance. The motivation is also propelled by the announcement of Value Based Intermediation strategic paper by BNM. The move supports Malaysia's government Sustainable Development Goals initiative.

As an industry that is technological savvy, Islamic banks integrate technological advancement with Islamic social finance. Bank Islam's Sadaqa House, for example utilise crowdfunding platform, Boost e-wallet, internet banking fund transfer and QR code as contribution channels (Bank Islam, 2024). Bank Muamalat's Jariah Fund also employs Financial Process Exchange (FPX), an internet based payment gateway, for fund collection channel (jariahfund.muamalat.com.my, 2024). Maybank Heart, a Maybank's arm of social finance, invites public to donate via its e-wallet called MAE as well as MaybankHeart's crowdfunding platform (Maybank, 2024).

In addition to the above technologies implemented by SIRCs and Islamic banks in *zakat*, *waqf* and *sadaqa*, fintech companies also offer their fintech products tailor to *zakat*, *waqf* and *sadaqa*. Fintech Systems Sdn Bhd has developed and launched e*Zakat* portal for people to pay *zakat* e*Zakat* is an online digital platform for *zakat*, *sadaqa*, Infaq and other wealth management services (e*Zakat*, 2024). Tulus Digital developed an Islamic social fintech platform called Tulus application providing a channel for *Zakat* Fitrah (a type of *zakat*) payments in nine Malaysian states during

Ramadan. Additionally the application provides services facilitating *Zakat*, *Waqf*, Infaq and *Sadaqa* payment services.

Addressing Financial Exclusion through *Sadaqa*

Strategies for Increasing Access to Financial Services Through Sadaqa

Financial exclusion is a term to describe certain segment of population, due to financial status (Persaud & Thaffe (2023), is unable to participate or access to financial products and services offered by financial institution including banking institutions (Carbó et al., 2005). Due to regulatory requirement which sets certain requirements resulting in this segment unable to open accounts or apply for bank's loan or financing (Demirgüç-Kunt et al., 2020). They are excluded from the radar of banking products and services.

Demirgüç-Kunt et al. (2020) argued that increasing financial inclusion among the society promotes positive countries developmental goals including decreasing poverty and income inequality (Demir et al., 2020), improved healthy population, healthcare and education system (Kabakova & Plaksenkov, 2018) hence meeting several sustainability goals (Adegbite & Machethe, 2020).

In view of the above, achieving greater financial inclusion has been one of the main government's target in developing countries. Numerous policies are established and financial resources are allocated in an attempt to encourage the marginalised groups to have access to the financial services and products (Beck et al., 2007). In June 2023, BNM has launched its second Financial Inclusion Framework (2023–2026) aiming to resolve several barriers and challenges (BNM, 2024). It delineates seven policy objectives aimed at addressing existing gaps and accelerating progress in financial inclusion, while also presenting four strategic enablers designed to facilitate the effective implementation of the framework.

The above Financial Inclusion Framework (2023 – 2026) is in addition to the 2017 Value Based Intermediation strategic paper which serves the same goal of promoting financial inclusivity (AIBIM, 2024). Through VBI initiatives, Islamic banks in Malaysia seek public donations and disburse them to the marginalised groups. Bank Islam Malaysia Berhad (BIMB) via its Sadaqa House initiatives, encourages public and corporate bodies to contribute to Sadaqa House platform to be disbursed to the social enterprise as well as the underserved such as single mothers, *zakat* recipients and small micro entrepreneurs. Under Micro iTekad BangKIT financing initiative, the Bank aims to provide financing to unbankable or under bankable micro entrepreneurs to expand their business (Bank Islam, 2024). Maybank Hearts' initiative offers Person with Disabilities (PwD) to be on board under Maybank Work

Placement Programme for PwDs (Maybank, 2024). Other Islamic Banks namely CIMB Islamic Bank and Bank Muamalat also involved in iTEKAD project (CIMB, 2024). Both banks' iTEKAD target the asnaf and B40 income groups by offering seed capital to empower them to achieve financial resilience, generate sustainable income, and contribute to the community.

Collaborative Efforts Between Islamic Financial Institutions and Social Enterprises

As explained in the previous paragraphs, the introduction of VBI by BNM has served as catalyst for Islamic banking institutions to embark on social finance projects. As financial intermediary, Islamic banks' role is to facilitate funds from the surplus units to be channelled to the deficit sectors who need fund for expansion of their activities. In the context of social finance, they also play the role as the intermediary between the donors and the community who are in need of the fund.

A social enterprise in Malaysia is a legally registered organization that operates with a clear purpose. It employs a financially sustainable business model to tackle social and/or environmental issues, striving to create positive impacts for its beneficiaries and contribute to the economy (kuskop, 2024). It is well-known that one of the most contentious issues with social enterprises is the ability to secure funding to run their activities and to stay sustainable (Rajah et al., 2022). Hence, the collaboration with Islamic banking institutions bridges the gap of funding requirement. Islamic banking institutions, being the intermediary, rely on the social enterprise expertise in the community related projects.

Bank Islam's Sadaqa House, for example, works closely with social enterprises diligently identified for community works. The social enterprises identified, called change makers, include Brain For Future (BFF), Buku Jalanan Chow Kit (BJCK) and MyVista. The bank also collaborates with Foundations and Non-Profit Organisations who run community works such as Institut Jantung Negara Foundation (IJNF), Yayasan Sultanah Bahiyah (YSB), Pertubuhan Kegiatan Dakwah Islamiah Sekolah-Sekolah Malaysia (PEKDIS), OrphanCare Foundation, Pertubuhan Kebajikan Anak Yatim Malaysia (PEYATIM) and Youth Empowerment Foundation Malaysia (Musafar Hameed et al., 2024).

Maybank Group, under its crowd-funding platform called Maybank Hearts, together with NGOs embarked on various community programmes in collaboration with Persatuan Aktivis Sahabat Alam, the bank provides community training and establishes farms and nurseries for the Orang Asli communities in the Titiwangsa Forest Complex. Each contribution directly empowers the Orang Asli communities, enhancing their food security, climate resilience, and economic growth. Other NGOs are Cancer Research Malaysia (CRMY) and Women's Aid Organisation (WAO) (Maybankheart, 2024).

Bank Muamalat Malaysia Berhad's social welfare crowdfunding platform called Jariah Fund works closely with Malaysian Association for the Blind to seek public fund to purchase reflexology chairs. Other NGOS include The National Autism Society of Malaysia, Yayasan Ikhlas, Yayasan Muslimin and Yayasan Sejahtera (Jariahfund, 2024).

Collaborations among all concerned establishments have become one of the key success factors in making impact on community related projects. All parties concerned include the Islamic banking institutions, Islamic banking association, social enterprises, NGOs and Foundations. Association of Islamic Banking and Finance Malaysia (AIBIM) acts as secretariat for all Islamic banks in Malaysia in the initiatives to assist the needy groups financially. AIBIM is an association for all Islamic Banks in Malaysia. Under AIBIM, ten (10) Islamic banks work together in a community empowerment project, called myWakaf, to install solar dome dryer to enable fishermen and farmers to dry their products, such as salted fish and dried fruits, regardless of weather conditions. The banks are Affin Islamic Bank, Bank Islam Malaysia Berhad, Bank Muamalat Malaysia Berhad, Bank Rakyat, Bank Simpanan Nasional, CIMB Islamic Bank, Hong Leong Islamic Bank, Maybank Islamic, MBB Bank and RHB Islamic Bank (myWakaf, 2024).

Promoting Progressiveness in Islamic Bank

Generally "progressive" means favouring or promoting progress, change, or improvement. Etymonline dictionary refers progressive as characterized by advancement, going forward, moving onward (etymoline, 2024). Progressiveness in Islamic banks can be described as an industry that continuously strive for progress, change and improve.

The progressiveness of Islamic banks can be analysed in two aspects namely the regulatory initiatives and the players' efforts. The former consists of Value Based Intermediation (VBI) project, digitalization drive and Islah (Reform) through Islamic Finance agenda. The later consists of the industry players individual efforts. Presented below are the details of the progressive hallmarks by the regulators.

Value Based Intermediation (VBI)

Value-Based Intermediation (VBI) is a strategic framework introduced by BNM on 20th July 2017 to enhance the role and impact of Islamic finance. VBI aims to position Islamic finance as a key driver of positive change within the financial system, promoting a network economy founded on shared values of integrity, inclusivity, and sustainability (Bank Negara Malaysia, 2019).

As a top down approached, Malaysian IBI is encouraged to implement practices, conduct, and offerings that create positive and sustainable impacts on the economy, community, and environment, while still ensuring financial returns for shareholders (BNM, 2019). VBI is a progressive effort by the regulator with aiming at uplifting the industry's strategic direction to embrace intermediation role based on value beyond profit maximisation paradigm without compromising return to shareholders (Ismail et al., 2020).

Digitisation of Islamic Banking

The progressiveness of banking industry, including Islamic banking, is also evidenced by the proactive move by BNM in facilitating the industry's appetite for digitalisation. In 2016, BNM established an internal Fintech Working Group and launched a regulatory Fintech Sandbox (Bank Negara Malaysia, 2020). This sandbox enables fintech solutions to be tested in a live environment under regulatory supervision. In 2020, the Central Bank of Malaysia issued a Know Your Customer (KYC) policy document, allowing account openings and related transactions to be conducted digitally without requiring customers to be physically present at the bank. E-KYC is crucial for overcoming barriers to digital banking development. This represents a significant step towards creating a virtual banking framework (Fintech News, 2020) and in April 2022, BNM announced five successful applicants for the digital bank licences including two (2) Islamic banks digital licenses.

In view of the above, Islamic banks have announced their move in offering digital banking products and services. Maybank, for example, announced a cashless payment solution using Quick Response (QR) code and strategic partnership with Grab to accelerate the acceptance and usage of cashless payment. Centre of Digital Experience Division of Bank Islam Malaysia Berhad has formed partnerships with Mambu, Experian and Pod to develop new digital banking product offerings (Fintech News, 2021).

Bank Muamalat Malaysia has entered into a multi-year partnership with Google Cloud in 2024 to leverage its technology in infrastructure, data analytics, security, and generative Artificial Intelligence (AI). This collaboration aims to deliver more personalized and accessible banking services (Fintech News, 2024). The above are examples of selected Malaysian Islamic banks' digitalisation initiative. In short, all of Islamic banks in Malaysia have uniquely embraced digitalisation project.

Islah (Reform) through Islamic Finance

On May 2024, Malaysia International Islamic Finance Centre (MIFC) Leadership Council (MLC) has launched a Position Paper titled 'Establishing *Islah* (Reform) through Islamic Finance'. This paper outlines the collective efforts and strategic changes within the industry aimed at driving positive societal transformation through Islamic finance (BNM, 2024).

Established in 2022, the Malaysia International Islamic Financial Centre (MIFC) Leadership Council (MLC) is a collaborative initiative between BNM and the SC and aims to drive the next phase of growth for Islamic finance in Malaysia. Comprising distinguished members in Islamic Finance industry, the Council plays a crucial role in offering thought leadership and developing strategies to reinforce Malaysia's leading position in Islamic finance (MIFCLC, 2024).

The paper outlines 7 principles for change, emphasizing inclusivity, sustainability, and ethical practices. It also presents 10 key shifts under the "*Hijrah* to *Islah*" concept, designed to drive positive societal transformation through Islamic finance. Additionally, the report details 5 key thrusts for co-creating the future of Islamic finance and identify 10 MLC Key Focus Areas (MKFAs) and 18 MLC Impact Projects (MIPs) to guide industry transformation. The ten MKFAs outlined by MIFCLC (2024) include several key initiatives aimed at enhancing the effectiveness and reach of the Islamic finance sector. First, there is a focus on advancing the MIFC international agenda, which seeks to enhance the global standing of Islamic finance. Another important initiative involves unlocking philanthropic capital to better serve communities in need. Additionally, there is a strong emphasis on unlocking equity risk capital, which is essential for fostering growth and innovation.

Efforts to strengthen *waqf* and zakat systems are also prioritized, recognizing their vital roles in community welfare and economic support. The MKFAs further aim to elevate knowledge, capacity building, and institutional development to ensure that stakeholders are well-equipped to navigate the evolving financial landscape. Strengthening takaful is another objective, promoting the principles of mutual assistance and protection.

Moreover, there is a concerted effort to elevate inclusivity and entrepreneurship, fostering opportunities for marginalized groups. The agenda also emphasizes the importance of sustainability, aiming to promote environmentally and socially responsible financial practices. Finally, accelerating the adoption of digital innovation and technology is crucial for enhancing efficiency and accessibility within the Islamic finance sector.

The above are top-down approach as the initiatives are initiated by Bank Negara Malaysia (BNM) and Securities Commission Malaysia (SC) as well as regulatory-led initiative. They announced the projects and facilitate the progressive-related programmes. The banks are encouraged to embark on their own progressive-related projects as long as they meet the objective of the above initiatives. It is voluntary for the banks to implement programmes suitable to their individual niche.

Sadaqa House Bank Islam: Revolutionising Islamic Bank's Intermediary Role

Case studies of successful Sadaqa-based initiatives in Islamic bank: The Case of Bank Islam's Sadaqa House

Overview of Bank Islam Malaysia Berhad

Bank Islam Malaysia Berhad introduced the Sadaqa House initiative as a groundbreaking effort to channel sadaqa towards impactful social and community development projects. This case study examines the initiative's successful implementation and outcomes, emphasising its innovative approach, significant projects, and broader implications for Islamic banking and social finance. Following the success of Tabung Haji in enabling Malaysian Muslims to perform Hajj in Makkah, alongside growing calls from the Muslim community for an interest-free bank, the government established the National Steering Committee on Islamic Banking (NSC) to explore creating an Islamic bank (Kitamura, 2020). Based on the NSC's recommendations, BIMB was founded, with Abdul Halim Ismail appointed as its first Managing Director in 1983 (Kitamura, 2020).

BIMB was established as a bank that offers modern banking facilities similar to its conventional counter parts but without elements prohibited in Islam. With a capital RM 80 million, the bank offers various products including savings accounts and financing products based on Shariah contracts such as Qard al-Hassan, Murabahah and Bay' bithaman ajil (Muhammed, 2013). With 40 years of tremendous experience in Islamic banking products, BIMB has recorded RM66.8 billion (unaudited) financing amounts disbursed compared to RM64.9 billion in the previous year (The Edge Malaysia, 2024). The bank's net profit for 2023 recorded a 12.5% increase with RM553.1 million.

Introduction to the Concept of Sadaqa House

Mooted by Dato' Ab Halim Ismail, the first and former Managing Director of Bank Islam Malaysia Berhad, Sadaqa House is proposed as a platform for an Islamic bank to play an important role to actively serving the welfare sector (Musafar Hameed et al., 2017). After 4 years of research, in collaboration with International Research Centre of Islamic Economics and Finance-Selangor Islamic University,

BIMB introduced Sadaqa House in 2018 as a banking services in the form of a charity crowdfunding platform to facilitate voluntary charitable donations (*sadaqa*) from individuals and corporate donors (Bank Islam, 2024). The initiative aims to address social issues and improve the quality of life for the underprivileged through sustainable and impactful projects. It leverages BIMB's extensive network and expertise in Islamic finance to ensure transparency, accountability, and effectiveness in the use of *sadaqa* funds (Bank Islam, 2024).

In his speech, after being awarded the Royal Award for Islamic Finance 2014, he noticed Islamic banks in Malaysia have played significant role in commercial sector but lacking in the welfare sector. He saw IBI has responded well to the financial requirements and demand of government and private sectors. Unfortunately the Islamic banking circles have not made active efforts in offering products and services required and suited the social welfare sector. He then urged Islamic banks to start looking at the welfare sector and proposed Sadaqa House as a platform for Islamic banks to serve the needy people (Musafar Hameed et al., 2017). The scenario exhibited IBI belongs to only the elites and financially viable. Hence SDG's initiatives present a challenge for the IBI to embark on initiatives fulfilling the requirement of the sidelined community. A true Islamic bank should serve all segments of society including the marginalized.

Implementation Strategy

The journey from idea to the implementation is full of challenges as the industry is commercial in nature and welfare sector is commercially not viable and risky. Supported by the originator of the Sadaqa House himself and the involvement of senior staff of BIMB as well as researchers from International Research Centre of Islamic Economics and Finance (IRCIEF), the multidisciplinary team diligently examined the implementation of Sadaqa House within the Islamic banking framework. Malaysia's dual judiciary system necessitates the research team to investigate whether or not the term *sadaqa* can be used by an Islamic bank in Malaysia as any Islamic related affairs must obtain necessary approvals from respective SIRC. Additionally, the team scrutinised all relevant acts pertaining to IBI, Companies Act and income tax regulation. As Islamic banks involve Shariah matters, aspect of Shariah on *sadaqa* is also investigated.

After two phases of research spanning over 4 years, another challenge is to get approval from the bank's Board of Directors. To obtain the approvals, justifications were presented including the return expected to the bank. With the support of the bank's management team, necessary approvals were obtained.

Even though the *sadaqa* fund does not requires regulatory framework-installed committees approvals and monitoring, in the spirit of proper governance of public funds, the bank necessitates the Sadaqa House funds to be subject to various committees; Board Committees, Management Committees, and Executive. The Board Committees consist of Shariah Supervisory Council, Board Strategic Review Committee, Board of Directors, Board Audit Management Committee, and Board Risk Committee. Three committees are established at the Management level: Management Committee, Sadaqa House & Zakat Committee and Management Risk Control Committee. Executive level consists of the Centre of Social Finance and Internal Audit Division is executive levels establishments (Musafar Hameed, 2024).

The operational model and how it works

Figure 1. Structure model of Sadaqa House Bank Islam 2018 (Sadaqa House Impact Report 2020)

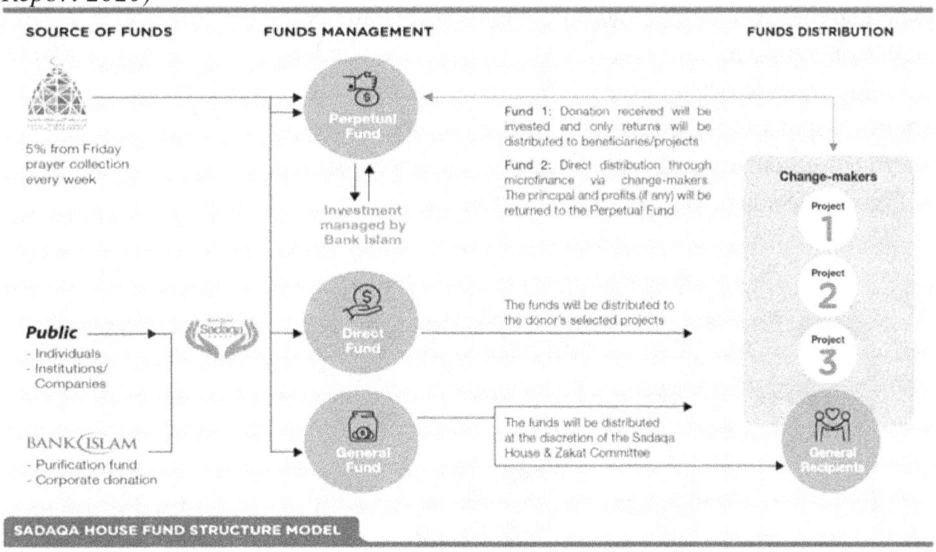

During the first year operation of Sadaqa House in the uncharted waters, BIMB has to strategically plan the structure of Sadaqa House operation model including selective in identifying sectors of focus as well as the beneficiaries. This careful approach undertaken to ensure the model is accepted by the donors and the beneficiaries selected bring impact. The selective approach is paramount as other IBI players choose to adopt “wait and see” point of view.

As presented in Figure 1, BIMB structures the implementation model into; source of funds, fund management, and fund distribution. The bank seeks *sadaqa* fund from weekly Friday prayers' collection (5% from the total collection), public (individuals, companies and corporates) and its own purification fund as well as corporate donations (Sadaqa House Impact Report 2020).

In managing the collected funds, BIMB assigned them into three types of funds: perpetual fund, direct fund, and general fund. Adopting sustainable perspective, part of collection from perpetual fund will be invested and managed by BIMB, disbursing the proceeds to the beneficiaries or projects. Another part of the pool in perpetual fund is distributed directly to social enterprises (termed as change makers) through microfinance instruments, with the principals and profits returning to the perpetual fund (Musafar Hameed et al., 2024).

As for the direct fund, donors are also given options to choose the beneficiary of their choices diligently identified by BIMB. To cater for other forms of *sadaqa* recipients to be identified by the Sadaqa House and Zakat Committee, collection in general fund is used.

The promising performance of the early years operationalising of Sadaqa House plus fund injection by internal fund, inspired the bank to further enhance its Sadaqa House operation model. In 2021, BIMB expanded Sadaqa House operationalizing model to include new source of fund incorporating *wakalah zakat* and Corporate Social Responsibility funds. The bank also enhanced type of recipients to include micro entrepreneurs and orphanage. The enhanced Sadaqa House model is shown in Figure 2 (Sadaqa House Impact Report 2022).

Figure 2. Structure model of Sadaqa House 2022 (Sadaqa House Impact Report 2022)

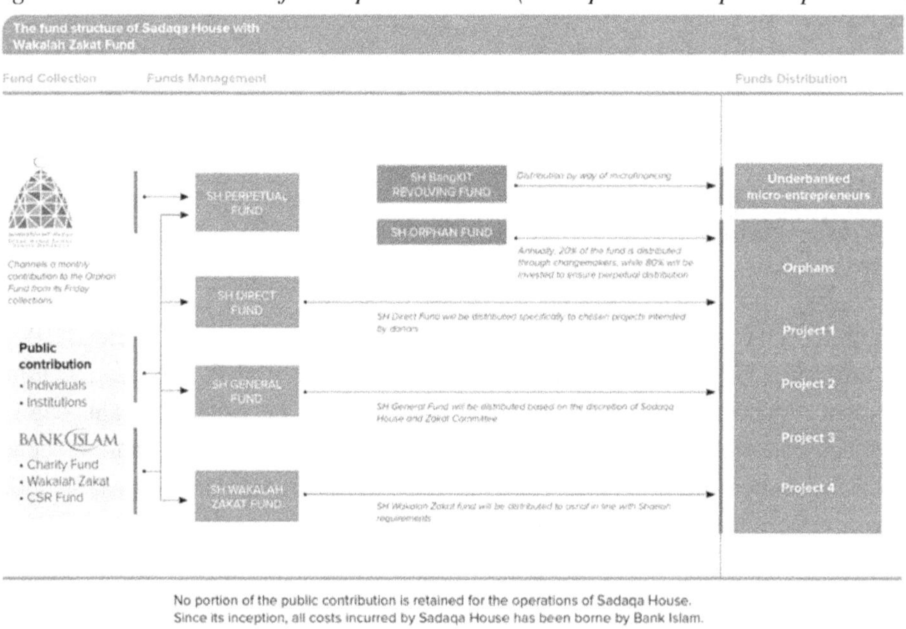

Notably, while Shariah permits the bank to levy charges, BIMB has covered all operational costs of Sadaqa House from day one. Accordingly, the entire fund collected is disbursed to the beneficiaries as per the model structured. Such move by BIMB indicates that the bank has truly implemented Sadaqa House initiatives purely in the spirit of Islamic economy philosophical foundation of the wellbeing of the society defying profit maximization paradigm embedded in conventional economy.

Sadaqa House's Focus Sector

As discussed in the previous paragraph, the focus sectors identified is crucial to the success of the initiatives. The failure of this industry's pioneer effort may discourage other players in venturing into this project. In this respect the bank choose orphanage, micro entrepreneurs, community empowerment, healthcare, education and environment to embark on as shown in Figure 3 (Musafar Hameed et al., 2024).

Figure 3. Focus sector of Sadaqa House (Prospectus Sadaqa House Orphan Fund)

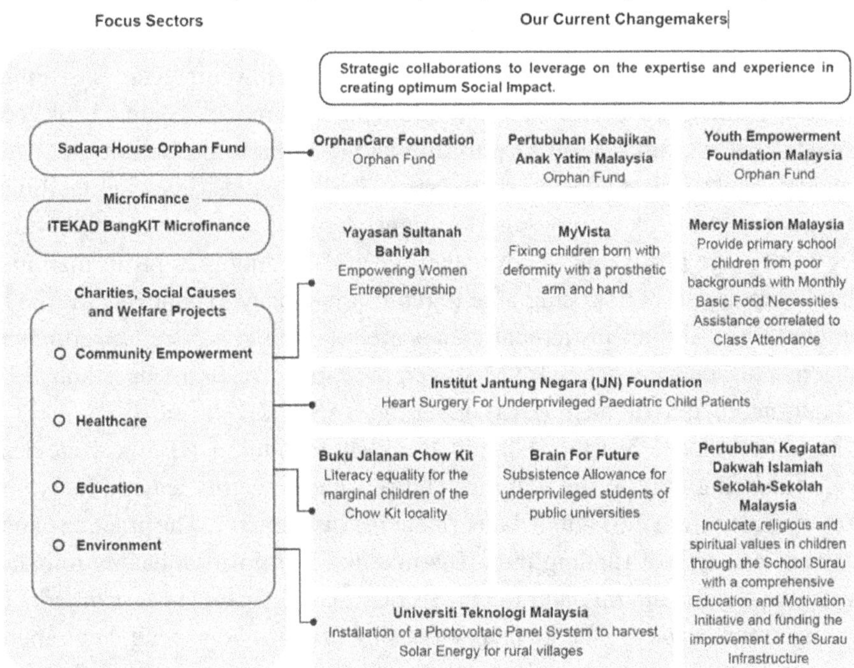

Under the normal modus operandi of social impact program, Islamic banking role is solely on opening of saving accounts for the NGOs and Foundations seeking *sadaqa* fund from the public and other sectors. Islamic banking players have no direct role in assisting the needy. The NGOs or Foundations will distribute the pooled fund to the marginalized society. Islamic banks do not directly involved in the community projects or measure the impact of the projects. Under this modus operandi, the real impacts of the donation are invincible and the impacts cannot be measured. Hence transparency and accountability are questionable.

With the above in mind, BIMB decided to take a ground breaking approach by collaborating with the NGOs or Foundations they called the change makers. The funds are disbursed to the change makers who then distribute to the recipients. Additionally, the bank closely monitors the progress of the projects and request consistent report from the identified NGOs and Foundations. From the data gathered, the bank prepares yearly impact reports and made accessible for the public to scrutinize. Hence, elements of transparency and accountability are properly governed. At the same time, the bank also needs to report to BNM.

Revolutionizing Islamic Bank's Intermediary Role

As deliberated in the previous paragraph, BIMB through its Sadaqa House inventiveness has successfully proven that Islamic bank is able to provide a *qardh al hassan* loan to borrowers or give financing at profit rate lower than the Base Financing Rate or market rate. Under normal modern banking model, Islamic banks act as intermediary using funds from surplus unit and loan out to the deficit unit. Under this model, banks utilise depositors' money to be lent out as financing facilities to the borrowers. As banks are required to return depositors' money with dividend, banks will charge profit rate to cover their cost of lending plus profit margin. As the banks are at risk of not being able to return the money to depositors if the borrowers fail to fulfil their instalment, banks are required to adhere to rigorous risk management framework set by BNM as well the capital requirement established by Bank International Settlement (BIS) under the BASEL III standard.

The above model restricts Islamic Banking Institution (IBI)'s strategies to provide financing only to the viability and profitable sectors leaving the welfare sectors excluded from the Islamic bank financing instruments. The practice of using deposits as a source of funding puts IBIs in a difficult position having to balance between the cost of funding and the profit rate for the financing instrument. This financing model leads to Islamic banks focusing primarily on specific commercial sectors while neglecting the welfare sectors, thereby straying from their original purpose as a moral compass grounded in the principles of Islamic economics, such as inclusivity.

The initial five years (2018 – 2023) phase of its introduction as banking product and service, Bank Islam's Sadaqa House has successfully collected RM33,262,896.96 and a total of RM13,090,246.58 has been disbursed benefiting numerous segment of population including *asnaf*, orphans, marginalised groups and Orang Aslis (Musafar Hameed et al., 2024). The balance is retained as a designated amount to sustain the perpetual fund. Such tremendous performance is an indication that Islamic banks can play a significant role in promoting inclusivity, complementing both the government sector and the welfare sector, contributing significantly to the realization of socio-economic justice. Furthermore, the initiatives undertaken by Sadaqa House align with the Maqasid al-Shariah and objectives of VBI as well contribute to the attainment of Sustainable Development Goals.

The significant contribution by Sadaqa House has motivated the bank to progress further with reimagining the Bank's intermediary role. Before the introduction of Sadaqa House, the first VBI initiative implemented by BIMB, the bank's role was confined to credit-based intermediation, as illustrated in Figure 4 below. Today, the Sadaqa House initiative has expanded to encompass investment accounts and Islamic social finance funding, as depicted in the figure below (Musafar Hameed et al., 2024).

Figure 4. VBI Initiative by BIMB (Bank Islam, 2024)

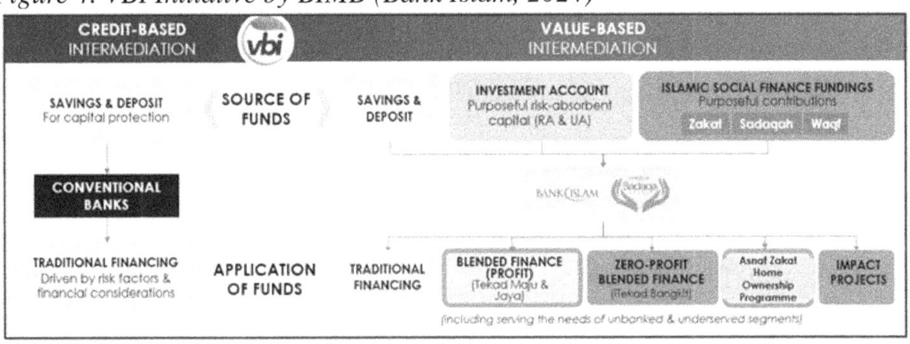

As seen in Figure 4, the latest expansion of Bank Islam's Sadaqa House model, incorporate the combination of credit-based intermediation and VBI. Traditionally, conventional banks and Islamic Banks rely on savings and deposits as source of fund for loan and financing products. This funding model, as explained earlier, restrict banks' lending and financing strategies as the banks are regulated by the robust risk management mechanism. With new source of fund namely *sadaqa*, *zakat*, *waqf* and social impact investment plus the existing savings and deposits fund, BIMB is able to offer traditional financing, blended financing products (with minimal profit) and zero-profit blended financing facilities.

Traditional financing products are the usual banking financing products such as personal financing, trade financing, business financing, car financing and home financing. As traditional financing offerings utilize savings and deposits, existing strict regulatory risk management framework is applied. On the contrary, blended finance with profit element and zero profit blended finance employ *sadaqa*, social impact investment, *zakat*, cash *waqf* and microfinance (Musafar Hameed et al., 2024). Examples of blended financing offerings include iTekad BangKIT and iTekad Maju. Details of the financing products are discussed below.

iTekad BangKIT Financing

The iTEKAD BangKIT Micro Financing Program is a program that provides affordable micro financing to segments of society that are less able and are not eligible to apply for normal banking financing facilities but need working capital and/or financing for capital expenditures. It aims at financing micro-entrepreneurs who have not yet qualified for banking financing for the purpose of working capital (including Takaful contribution - optional) and or Capital expenditure. The financing is based on the *qard* contract where the loan repayment amount is equal to the amount borrowed without any element of profit. The financing amount is from RM5,000 to RM20,000 with repayment tenure from 6 to 36 months and no collateral or guarantor required. However, the bank necessitates the approved borrowers to register for business development training program conducted by the bank's appointed implementing partner (Bank Islam, 2024).

Mikro iTEKAD Maju Financing

The iTEKAD Maju Micro Financing Program is a social finance initiative designed to provide financial support to B40 (low income group) micro-entrepreneurs and *asnaf* who have experienced income loss due to the COVID-19 pandemic and aspire to develop their businesses that generate sustainable income. The potential borrowers can apply working capital financing from RM10,000 to RM50,000 with payback period between 1 to 5 years. At 4.00% per annum profit rate, the facility applies *tawarruq* contract and collateral or guarantor are not required. Similar to iTekad BangKIT financing program, the successful applicants must participate in training and monitoring program (Bank Islam, 2024). In the initial phase of iTEKAD, BIMB partnered with the Majlis Agama Islam Wilayah Persekutuan (MAIWP) and SME Corporation Malaysia.

The above proposition of using *sadaqa* fund, instead of depositors' money, for financing products is congruent with Malaysia International Islamic Financial Centre (MIFC) Leadership Council (MLC)'s proposed transformation for Islamic Finance Industry (IFI) announced in May 2024 as stated in Shift number 3 as below:

"A shift to deepen and broaden the Islamic financial instruments spectrum (2): broaden and deepen philanthropic capital. This includes the continued improvement and unlocking of existing channels of zakat, waqf, sadaqah and qard hasan under the Islamic social finance system, but to also channel new ideas and practices to include more efficient market-making mechanisms, to harness and combine with conventional." (MIFC Leadership Council, 2024, page 25)

The use of *sadaqa* collection to fund financing instruments offered by Islamic Banking Institution is a revolutionary step as it contradicts with the traditional method of funding. It will also acts as one of the solutions to the controversial money creation issue that has been debated for decades among the financial circles. Under the fractional reserve banking system, the traditional funding mechanism as practiced by the global banking industry utilising deposits results in money being made to exists and multiplied.

The MLC emphasizes the importance of investigating various areas to transform the Islamic finance industry (MIFC Leadership Council, 2024, p. 25). This includes a shift towards a deeper understanding and connection between Islamic finance and Islamic economics, as well as other related fields. Such a shift entails closely examining foundational economic concepts, including the functions and creation of money, the establishment of a just and equitable society, and the development of a civilizational society. Research topics are expected to encompass the nature, role, and function of money; the creation of money, including fiat currency; the fractional reserve banking system; the shadow banking system; and aspects of production, consumption, and distribution.

The above new funding mechanism employing *sadaqa* fund allows the bank, as presented above, to serve the underbanked as well as the unbankable leading to them to be more visible in the welfare sector as well as being inclusive and contribute to Islamic economy. *Sadaqa* instrument, and other philanthropic sources, as funding source revolutionise bank's intermediary role.

CONCLUSION

The blended financing model that incorporates funds from *sadaqa, zakat, waqf*, and microfinance, initially designed for the unbankable, under bankable and underserved segments, has the potential to be expanded to encompass additional segments and ultimately reach all demographics as long as there is adequate funding available. With this model, banks are not restricted by the risk management framework.

However, banks can continue applying the same risk management framework as guidelines to ensure all risks are mitigated.

The model also releases IBIs from the constraints of balancing acts between the excess units and deficit units of the economy. Financing innovations, collaborative efforts and community empowerment are the key words for the new funding model giving IBIs freedom to structure financing instruments with minimal financing charge. Even though the new funding mechanism falls outside of the risk management regime, existing governance of Islamic bank can be applied to ensure proper management of the public funds as well as its sustainability. Eventually, the model contributes to assisting the government's effort in economically elevating the welfare sector hence inclusivity and Sustainable Development Goals.

The employment of *sadaqa* fund, in addition to the present deposits, to fund the financing instruments is a progressive step for Islamic banking to move forward. A case of Sadaqa House by Bank Islam Malaysia Berhad proves the model is successful and reliable to be expanded to other Islamic banks. Innovation financing instruments blending *sadaqa* fund with zakat fund as financing products allow the bank to structure financing instruments for the unbankable sector. More innovative financing products can be structured utilising Islamic social finance instruments, traditional and modern. The *sadaqa* from the public is collected through fintech platform such as crowdfunding and existing bank's digital platform.

Currently, Sadaqa House Bank Islam operates as part of the group's Social Inclusion Division. The division can further be expanded to become a digital entity on its own using solely sadaqa fund as financing instruments instead of depositors' money. With such funding mechanism, the bank would be able to offer *qard hassan* loan to selected financing seekers. The success of the present Sadaqa House is achieved without tax exemption element. The success can be further elevated with tax exemption element encouraging the donors to donate to the Sadaqa House platform.

The present Sadaqa House's impact to the unbankable group is achieved without challenges. The obstacles include having to convince the support from the Board of Directors and Management. The employees involve in the community projects and managing the collected public fund must have a correct mind-set and willing to provide extra effort in empowering the community engaged. Harnessing *sadaqa*, empirically proven to be an emergent force for inclusive and progressive Islamic Banking.

REFERENCES

Abd. Malib, M., Nordin, R., Nordin, M.N., Mustafa, M. S., Izzat, M. & Arif, M. A. (2021). The Role Of The State Islamic Religious Council (Sirc) In Strengthening Thewaqf Management In Malaysia: An Overview And Recommendations. *Türk Fizyoterapi ve Rehabilitasyon Dergisi/Turkish Journal of Physiotherapy and Rehabilitation.* 32. 4872-4880.

Adegbite, O. O., & Machethe, C. L. (2020). Bridging the financial inclusion gender gap in smallholder agriculture in Nigeria: An untapped potential for sustainable development. *World Development*, 127, 127. DOI: 10.1016/j.worlddev.2019.104755

Ahmad, N. N., Tarmidi, M., Ridzwan, I. U., Hamid, M. A., & Roni, R. A. (2014). The application of unified theory of acceptance and use of technology (UTAUT) for predicting the usage of e-zakat online system. *International Journal of Scientific Research*, 3(4), 63–67.

AIBIM. (2024) Retrieved from https://aibim.com/

al-Ahkam al-cadliyah (2002)

Al Azizah, U. S., & Choirin, M. (2018). Financial innovation on zakat distribution and economic growth. In International Conference of Zakat 2018 Proceedings (ISSN: 2655-6251). Paper presented at International Conference of Zakat 2018, 15-16 November, Universitas Gadjah Mada, Yogyakarta, Indonesia. UN. (2024) Retrieved from https://sdgs.un.org/goals

Bank Islam. (2024). Retrieved from https://www.bankislam.com/corporate-info/social-finance-bank-islam/pembiayaan-mikro-bangkit/

Bank Negara Malaysia. (2020). Retrieved from https://www.bnm.gov.my/web/guest/-/sandbox-pd24

Beck, T., Demirguc-Kunt, A., & Peria, M. S. M. (2007). Reaching out: Access to and use of banking services across countries. *Journal of Financial Economics*, 85(1), 234–266. DOI: 10.1016/j.jfineco.2006.07.002

BNM. (2019). Retrieved from efaidnbmnnnibpcajpcglclefindmkaj/https://www.bnm.gov.my/documents/20124/761679/VBIAF_Final+guidance+1.11.2019.pdf

BNM. (2024). Retrieved from https://www.bnm.gov.my/financial-inclusion-data-for-malaysia

Bouakkaz, N. (2022). Using blockchain technology to revolutionize Waqf: The Finterra Waqf Chain model. *Journal of Economics and Sustainable Development*, 50(1), 136–841.

Carbó, S., Edward P. M. Gardener, Philip Molyneux (2005). Financial Exclusion. Palgrave Macmillan Studies in Banking and Financial Institutions (SBFI)

CIMB. (2024). Retrieved from https://www.cimb.com/en/newsroom/2021/itekad-2-0-introduced-to-extend-support-for-the-asnaf-and-b40-communities.html

Demir, A., Pesqué-Cela, V., Altunbas, Y., & Murinde, V. (2020). Fintech, financial inclusion, and income inequality: A quantile regression approach. *The European Journal of Finance*. eZakat (2024). Retrieved from https://ezakat.com/#/

Demirgüç-Kunt, A., Klapper, L., Singer, D., Ansar, S., & Hess, J. (2020). The global findex database 2017: Measuring financial inclusion and opportunities to expand access to and use of financial services. *The World Bank Economic Review*, 34(Supplement_1), S2–S8. DOI: 10.1093/wber/lhz013

(•••). E-zakat online system. *International Journal of Scientific Research*, 3(4), 63–67.

Fintech News. (2020) Retrieved from https://fintechnews.my/23063/digital-banking-news-malaysia/bank-negara-malaysia-issues-updated-virtual-banking-draft/

Fintech News. (2021). Retrieved from https://fintechnews.my/26417/digital-banking-news-malaysia/bank-islam-gears-up-a-fully-digital-bank-by-inking-partnerships-with-mambu-experian-and-pod/

Fintech News. (2024). Retrieved from https://fintechnews.my/44259/digital-transformation/bank-muamalat-to-launch-digital-islamic-super-app-powered-by-backbase/

Francis, M. (2020). Global structures of inequality and unequal distribution of wealth. In Leal Filho, W., Azul, A., Brandli, L., Özuyar, P., & Wall, T. (Eds.), *Decent work and economic growth. Encyclopedia of the UN Sustainable Development Goals*. Springer. DOI: 10.1007/978-3-319-71058-7_10-2

International Shari'ah Research Academy for Islamic Finance. (2023). *Islamic financial system: Principles and operation*. INCEIF University.

Islamic Financial Services Act. (2013).

Ismail, A. Y., Musafar Hameed, L. B., Mohamad Suhaimi, A. F., & Jamaludin, N. I. (2020). Value-based intermediation and interconnection of sustainable development goals in Islamic banking framework. *International Journal of Islamic Economics and Finance Research*, 3(1).

Abdullah Jalil, & Muhammad Muda. (2008). Pengurusan dana sedekah secara sistematik: Analisa peranan institusi kerajaan dan swasta. USIM: Fakulti Ekonomi dan Muamalat.

Jariahfund (2024). Retrieved from https://jariahfund.muamalat.com.my/

JAWHAR. (2024). Retrieved from https://www.jawhar.gov.my/en/zakat-and-general -source-mal/

(2018)... *Journal of Business Research*, 89(C), 198–205.

Kabakova, O. & Plaksenkov, E. (2018). Analysis of factors affecting financial inclusion: Ecosystem view

Kitamura, H. (2020). Who pioneered Islamic banking in Malaysia? The background of the pioneers of Bank Islam Malaysia Berhad. *Contemporary Islam*, 14(1), 75–93. DOI: 10.1007/s11562-019-00443-w

Kunhibava, S., Muneeza, A., Khalid, M. B., Mustapha, Z., & Sen, T. M. (2024). Sadaqah, zakat, and qard

Kuskop (2024). Retrieved from https://www.kuskop.gov.my/PerusahaanSosial/ index-BI.php

Laluddin, Haneef, Mohammad & Rahman, M. P. (2021). Revisiting the

LZS. (2024) Retrieved from https://www.zakatselangor.com.my/lzspeduli/

MAIM. (2024) Retrieved from https://maim.gov.my/index.php/ms/lagi-berita/majlis -pengagihan-bantuan-ramadhan-syawal-kepada-asnaf-maim-di-dun-bukit-katil-dan -dun-pantai-kundor

Markom, R., Zakaria, M. R., & Asma, H. A. H. (2015). Kerangka perundangan rumah sedekah sebagai institusi perbankan: Satu tinjauan. In Proceeding of Seminar Sadaqa House 2015 (29 Oktober 2015, Menara Bank Islam Kuala Lumpur, Malaysia).

Rosnia Masruki, Maliah Sulaiman, & Hafiz-Majdi Ab. Majid. (2021). Innovative zakat distribution practices of Malaysian state zakat institutions and their socio-economic impact during the COVID-19 pandemic. *International Journal of Innovation, Creativity and Change*, 15(9). Rosman, Redzuan, Mokhtar, Engku, Engku Ali & Mustafa

Rosnia Masruki, Maliah Sulaiman, & Hafiz-Majdi Ab. Majid. (2021). Innovative zakat distribution practices of Malaysian state zakat institutions and their socio-economic impact during the COVID-19 pandemic. *International Journal of Innovation, Creativity and Change*, 15(9).

Maybank (2024). Retrieved from https://www.maybankfoundation.com/index.php/our-impact/maybank-heart

Maybankheart (2024). Retrieved from https://www.maybankfoundation.com/index.php/our-impact/maybank-heart

MIFC Leadership Position Paper. (2024).

Mohamad Isa Abd Jalil. (2020). Issues and challenges of waqf practice in Malaysia: A review. *Labuan E-Journal Of Muamalat And Society*, 14.

Mohammed, O. (2022). Islamic social finance and sustainable development goals: Issues and challenges. *Journal of Islamic Finance*, 11(2), 56–67.

Mohd Danuri, M. S. N. (2019). Empowering People: 4th Industrial Revolution and Us', 6th International Research Management and Innovation Conference (IRMIC) 2019, KUIS.

Mohd Shahrul, N. M. D., Khirulnizam, A. R., & Che Wan Shamsul Bahri, C. W. A. (2019). Proposed conceptual design of Waqf management system. *Malaysian Journal of Information and Communication Technology*, 4(2).

Mohd Sidik, W., & Ahmad, Z. (2021). Application of GIS (Geographical Information System) in The Management of Waqf Lands in Selangor. *International Journal of Academic Research in Business & Social Sciences*, 11(11). Advance online publication. DOI: 10.6007/IJARBSS/v11-i11/11651

Mufti of Federal Territory's Office. Malaysia (2024). Retrieved from https://muftiwp.gov.my/en/artikel/al-kafi-li-al-fatawi/3740-al-kafi-1397-the-ruling-of-giving-sadaqah-donation-to-the-rich

Muhammed, D. D. J. (2013). Introduction to history of Islamic banking in Malaysia. *Humanomics*, 29(2), 80–87. DOI: 10.1108/08288661311319157

Musafar Hameed, L. B., Chik, M. N., & Mohamad Suhaimi, A. F. (2017). *Sadaqa House: Its viability in the Islamic banking framework*. Penerbit KUIS.

Musafar Hameed, L. B., Muneeza, A., Mohd Dasar, M. H., Ismail, A. Y., & Mohamad Suhaimi, A. F. (2024). *Sadaqa house: Inspiring 'Adl and Ihsan in the realm of Islamic banking. Penerbit UIS & International Research Centre of Islamic Economics and Finance*. IRCIEF.

myWakaf (2024) Retrieved from https://www.mywakaf.com.my/

Naoual, B. (2022). Using blockchain technology to revolutionize Waqf: The Finterra Waqf Chain model.

Nazeri, A. N. N.SHIFA MOHD NOR. (2023). The Implementation Of Blockchain Technology In The Zakat Management System: A Conceptual Research. *Journal of Information Systems and Digital Technologies*, 5(2), 287–300. DOI: 10.31436/jisdt.v5i2.419

Nik Mohd Saiful W. Mohd Sidik, & Zaid Ahmad. (2021). Application of GIS (Geographical Information System)

Nor Mohamed Yakcop. (1981). Islamic banking in Malaysia: An early document 1981.

Nordin, N., Shahwan, S., & Ibrahim, N. (2021). E-wallet as a new approach in zakat collection and distribution: Exploring the experience of zakat and e-wallet providers in Malaysia. In The International Islamic Economic System Conference – The 9th I-iECONS 2021 (pp. 364–371). *Journal of Economics and Sustainable Development*, 50(1), 136–841.

Nordin, N., Shahwan, S., & Ibrahim, N. (2021). E-wallet as a new approach in zakat collection and distribution: Exploring the experience of zakat and e-wallet providers in Malaysia. In The International Islamic Economic System Conference – The 9th I-iECONS 2021 (pp. 364–371).

Nurul'ain M., Mastura R., Muhammad Hasif Y., & Zainur Nadiyah Baharuddin. (2024). The roles of Islamic financial technology (FINTECH) in fostering financial inclusion in Malaysia. *Management and Accounting Review*, 23(1), April 2024.

Olatubosun, A. A. (2022). Resource mobilization and financial performance of Islamic cooperative societies in southwestern Nigeria. *International Journal of Umranic Studies*.

Nor Paizin, Muhsin & Som, Hairullfazli & Hj. Ismail, Mokthar & Saadan, Mohd. (2022). Innovation and Technology Optimization for Increasing The Collection and Distribution of Zakat in Malaysia. Presented at 6th MUZAKARAH FIQH AND INTERNATIONAL FIQH CONFERENCE (MFIFC) 2022At: Kolej Universiti Islam Antarabangsa Selangor, KUIS

Persaud, A., & Thaffe, W. (2023). The state of financial inclusion research on developing countries. *Transnational Corporations Review*, 15(4), 22–34. DOI: 10.1016/j.tncr.2023.08.002

Polyzos, E., Samitas, A., & Syriopoulos, K. (2022). Islamic banking, efficiency and societal welfare: A machine learning, agent-based study. *International Journal of Islamic and Middle Eastern Finance and Management*, 16(4), 777–801. DOI: 10.1108/IMEFM-04-2022-0144

Pusat Pungutan Zakat-MAIWP. (2022). Zakat and Islamic social finance: The way forward.

Rajah, N., Amran, A., & Cheah, J. (2022). Determinants that enhance resilience and performance of social enterprises in Malaysia: A conceptual framework. *Journal of Governance and Integrity*, 5(3), 297–307. DOI: 10.15282/jgi.5.3.2022.8981

Sadaqa House Impact Report (2020)

Sadaqa House Impact Report (2022)

Selangor, Z. (2022). Types of general assistance. Zakat Selangor. System) in the management of Waqf lands in Selangor. *International Journal of Academic Research in Business & Social Sciences*, 11(11).

https://www.worldbank.org/en/events/2020/10/07/maximizing-islamic-finance-for-financial-inclusion

https://muftiwp.gov.my/ms/artikel/bayan-linnas/3560-bayan-linnas-siri-ke-194-konsep-sedekah-jariah-menjana-kesatuan-ummah

Selangorkini (2016) Retrieved from https://arkib.selangorkini.my/2018/01/lzs-perkenal-cashless-atm-mudah-urusan-zakat/

The Edge Malaysia. (2024). Retrieved from https://theedgemalaysia.com/node/704947

(2021).. . *Thought*, 20(December).

Wazan (2024) Retrieved from https://wazan.upm.edu.my/

Wehr, H. (1980). *A Dictionary of Modern Written Arabic* (4th ed.). Spoken Language Services.

zakat.org. (2024). Retrieved from https://www.zakat.org/what-is-the-difference-between-sadaqa-and-zakat/

Chapter 12
Waqf-Driven Inclusive Prosperity Exploring the Intersection of Islamic Finance, Fintech, and Sustainable Development Goals

Mohd Asyraf bin Yusof
Universiti Teknologi MARA, Malaysia

ABSTRACT

Waqf-driven Inclusive Prosperity: Exploring the Intersection of Islamic Finance, Fintech, and Sustainable Development Goals (SDGs) examines how fintech innovations and AI-driven tools are advancing waqf management to foster inclusive economic growth and support the SDGs. The chapter explores the Waqf Analytics Platform for predictive analytics, resource optimization, and impact assessment, alongside fintech advancements such as AI-based fundraising, smart contracts, and digital platforms. It addresses challenges like data privacy, Shariah compliance, and implementation costs, and identifies future research opportunities, including Shariah-compliant AI algorithms and AI blockchain integration. The chapter offers insights into how these technologies can drive waqf initiatives and contribute to sustainable development.

DOI: 10.4018/979-8-3693-5653-1.ch012

INTRODUCTION

Inclusive prosperity, a concept deeply ingrained in the principles of Islamic finance, extends economic benefits and opportunities to all segments of society (Barom, 2012). Within the Islamic economic framework, ensures that wealth circulates widely, and benefits are not concentrated among a select few. This aligns with Islamic finance's core tenets, which emphasize social justice, equitable distribution of wealth, and financial inclusion. By promoting risk-sharing and prohibiting exploitative practices, Islamic finance aims to establish a fair and balanced economic system where prosperity is shared among all members of society.

Waqf, an Islamic endowment established for charitable and social purposes, has historically played a pivotal role in fostering inclusive economic growth. Originating in the early days of Islam, waqf has been instrumental in supporting various social welfare activities, such as education, healthcare, and infrastructure development (Mohammad Abdullah, 2020). By dedicating assets or funds for the public good, waqf ensures a continuous flow of resources to address societal needs. This mechanism alleviates poverty and empowers communities by providing essential services and opportunities for economic advancement.

The potential of waqf to drive inclusive prosperity is further amplified when integrated with modern financial technologies (fintech). Fintech innovations offer new avenues for managing, distributing, and expanding waqf assets, making them more efficient and transparent. Blockchain technology, for example, can ensure the integrity and traceability of waqf funds, while digital platforms can facilitate wider participation in waqf contributions and projects (Zariff & Yusoff, 2024). These advancements can democratize the waqf system, allowing more individuals to contribute to and benefit from its initiatives, thus broadening the scope of inclusive prosperity.

In the context of SDGs, waqf holds the potential to serve as a potent instrument for the attainment of targets such as poverty eradication, ensuring quality education, and fostering sustainable cities and communities (Ascarya, 2022; Umar, 2020). Through the strategic alignment of waqf initiatives with SDGs, stakeholders can optimize the social and economic impact of waqf assets (Ibrahim et al., 2022). This alignment not only addresses immediate community needs but also contributes to sustained, long-term development. Integration of waqf with Islamic finance and fintech presents a comprehensive approach to fostering inclusive prosperity, providing a model that other financial systems can emulate to engender a more just and equitable world.

Nevertheless, despite the rich historical underpinnings and significant potential of waqf in promoting social welfare and economic development, the contemporary Islamic finance sector underutilizes its full capacity (Muneer & Khan, 2022). This is due to various challenges facing traditional waqf practices, including a lack of transparency, ineffective management, and limited public participation. The resolution of these issues is crucial for enabling waqf to effectively contribute to inclusive prosperity and sustainable development.

Furthermore, the integration of modern financial technologies (fintech) with waqf management is still in its nascent stages. While fintech offers promising solutions to enhance the efficiency and transparency of waqf operations, its adoption is currently constrained by regulatory, technological, and infrastructural obstacles. This discrepancy between traditional waqf practices and modern fintech innovations restricts the extent of waqf's impact on economic inclusion and sustainable development (Ascarya, 2022).

Additionally, there is a clear necessity for the strategic alignment of waqf initiatives with the SDGs to maximize their social and economic impact (Ibrahim et al., 2022). Without a well-defined framework for this alignment, waqf projects may not comprehensively address the urgent global challenges of poverty, inequality, and environmental sustainability.

Addressing these challenges necessitates a comprehensive understanding of the convergence of waqf, Islamic finance, fintech, and SDGs (Hai et al., 2022). This exploration is vital for unlocking the potential of waqf to drive inclusive prosperity and contribute to a more equitable and sustainable world.

This paper seeks to provide a thorough examination of the concept of waqf-driven inclusive prosperity within Islamic finance and its potential to stimulate fair economic growth. This includes defining inclusive prosperity within the context of Islamic finance and underscoring its fundamental principles of social justice, equitable wealth distribution, and financial inclusion. By delving into these principles, the intention is to illustrate how Islamic finance inherently promotes an equitable economic system that benefits all members of society.

Moreover, the paper aims to offer an overview of waqf, tracing its historical roots and analysing its role in supporting various social welfare activities and economic development. This analysis will explore the integration of fintech with waqf, showcasing how modern financial technologies can enhance the efficiency, transparency, and accessibility of waqf management and distribution. Additionally, it will address the alignment of waqf with SDGs to maximize social and economic impact, serving both immediate community needs and long-term development goals. Overall, the objective is to provide a comprehensive understanding of how waqf can propel inclusive prosperity and contribute to a more just and equitable world.

WAQF AND ITS ROLE IN ECONOMIC DEVELOPMENT

Waqf, a traditional Islamic endowment, has played a significant role in economic development and social welfare across various Muslim societies throughout history. Its potential to drive inclusive prosperity and foster economic growth remains highly relevant today. Numerous case studies highlight the success of waqf-driven projects, showcasing how this institution can be effectively leveraged to achieve substantial social and economic benefits (Ascarya, 2022; H. A. Hassan, 2019; Tahiri Jouti, 2019).

One notable example is the waqf-based healthcare system in the Ottoman Empire, where numerous hospitals (darüşşifas) were established through waqf endowments. These hospitals provided free medical services to the public, significantly improving healthcare accessibility and outcomes (Raja Adnan et al., 2021). Similarly, in modern times, the Waqf Al-Quds Endowment in Malaysia has been instrumental in funding educational institutions, scholarships, and research centres, thereby enhancing educational opportunities and fostering intellectual development within the community (Sani et al., 2022; Wan Kamal Mujani & Noor Inayah Yaakub, 2017).

The impact of waqf on poverty alleviation and community development is profound. By dedicating assets and resources to public welfare, waqf initiatives create a sustainable flow of benefits that directly address the needs of underserved populations. For instance, the waqf-driven housing projects in Indonesia have provided affordable housing to low-income families, improving their living conditions and economic stability. In another case, the waqf-based microfinance programs in Bangladesh have empowered marginalized communities by providing them with access to capital, enabling them to start small businesses and achieve financial independence (Umar, 2020).

These examples underscore the transformative potential of waqf in driving economic development and fostering inclusive prosperity. By addressing fundamental social needs such as healthcare, education, housing, and financial inclusion, waqf initiatives contribute to the overall well-being of communities and help bridge the gap between rich and poor. Moreover, the integration of modern financial technologies with waqf management can further enhance its efficiency, transparency, and reach, amplifying its impact on poverty alleviation and community development. Through strategic alignment with SDGs, waqf has the potential to be a powerful tool in creating a more equitable and sustainable world (H. A. Hassan, 2019; Muneer & Khan, 2022).

While waqf has historically played a crucial role in economic development and social welfare, its contemporary application faces significant challenges that hinder its potential to drive inclusive prosperity effectively. One of the critical issues is the inefficient management of waqf assets, often due to outdated administrative practices and lack of transparency. Many waqf properties are underutilized or mismanaged, leading to a loss of potential benefits that could otherwise be directed towards community development and poverty alleviation (Ascarya & Sakti, 2022; Umar, 2020).

Case studies of successful waqf-driven projects, such as the Ottoman healthcare system and modern educational endowments in Malaysia, demonstrate the immense potential of waqf. However, these successes are often not the norm but exceptions, highlighting a gap in the widespread implementation of effective waqf management practices. The Ottoman example, while historically significant, may not directly translate to contemporary contexts due to differences in legal, social, and economic environments. Similarly, while Malaysia's educational waqf has achieved notable success, replicating such models requires substantial institutional support and regulatory frameworks that may not be available in other regions (Usman & Ab Rahman, 2023).

The impact of waqf on poverty alleviation and community development is undeniable, as evidenced by initiatives like housing projects in Indonesia and microfinance programs in Bangladesh. However, these projects also face challenges related to sustainability and scalability. Waqf-based housing projects, while providing immediate relief, often struggle with long-term maintenance and expansion due to limited funding and bureaucratic hurdles. Microfinance programs, although beneficial, can sometimes lead to over-indebtedness among borrowers if not managed carefully, thereby exacerbating rather than alleviating poverty (Haneef et al., 2015).

Another critical aspect is the integration of fintech in waqf management, which promises enhanced efficiency and transparency. While fintech offers innovative solutions, its adoption is not without challenges. Regulatory barriers, technological infrastructure, and the digital divide can impede the effective implementation of fintech in waqf management. Moreover, the ethical considerations surrounding the use of technology in managing religious endowments must be carefully navigated to maintain trust and legitimacy among stakeholders (Ascarya & Sakti, 2022).

Furthermore, aligning waqf initiatives with SDGs requires a strategic approach that balances immediate community needs with long-term objectives. This alignment is often complicated by the diverse interpretations of Islamic law across different regions, which can affect the implementation and regulation of waqf projects. Additionally, there is a need for comprehensive impact assessment frameworks to measure the social and economic outcomes of waqf initiatives accurately, ensuring they contribute meaningfully to the SDGs (Abdul-Yakeen et al., 2014).

INTEGRATION OF FINTECH IN WAQF MANAGEMENT

The integration of fintech into waqf management represents a transformative opportunity to modernize and enhance the effectiveness of this ancient institution. Two key fintech innovations—blockchain technology and digital platforms—are at the forefront of this evolution, offering novel solutions for managing waqf assets, increasing transparency, and expanding access to waqf resources. This critical discussion explores how these technologies can address current challenges in waqf management and their potential to reshape the future of waqf practices (Chang & Wang, 2023).

On the other hand, Artificial Intelligence (AI) is a technology that enables machines to mimic human intelligence by performing tasks such as learning, reasoning, and problem-solving. The core components of AI include machine learning, which allows systems to learn from data and improve over time, and natural language processing, which helps machines understand and interact with human language. AI has made significant advancements in various sectors, such as finance and healthcare, by analyzing vast datasets to uncover patterns, predict future trends, and optimize decision-making. These capabilities have opened up new possibilities for using AI in waqf management, where data-driven insights can improve transparency, accountability, and operational efficiency (Alawiye & Keerio, 2023).

In the context of waqf management, AI offers several advantages by automating administrative tasks and enhancing resource allocation. For example, AI algorithms can be used to monitor waqf funds and track the progress of waqf projects in real-time, providing valuable insights into how resources are utilized. Predictive analytics, a subset of AI, can forecast future funding requirements for ongoing waqf initiatives, helping institutions allocate funds more effectively and prioritize projects based on potential social impact. By harnessing these capabilities, AI can transform traditional waqf practices, making them more adaptive to changing circumstances and better aligned with modern financial practices (Farag et al., 2024).

A Waqf Analytics Platform leverages AI to support data-driven decision-making and streamline various aspects of waqf operations. This platform can incorporate machine learning models to analyze historical data on donations and project outcomes, helping predict trends and optimize future waqf activities. Additionally, AI-powered tools such as chatbots can facilitate donor engagement by providing instant information about donation options, project updates, and other inquiries, thus improving user experience. These capabilities not only enhance operational efficiency but also build trust among stakeholders by ensuring that waqf institutions can provide transparent and timely reporting (O. Abdullah et al., 2022).

Despite the benefits, implementing AI in waqf management comes with challenges. Data privacy and security are critical concerns, as waqf institutions must ensure that sensitive information is protected from unauthorized access. There is also a need for adequate technological infrastructure to support AI applications, which may be limited in some regions. Moreover, the adoption of AI should be aligned with Shariah principles, requiring collaboration with Islamic scholars to ensure ethical use of technology. Addressing these challenges is essential for maximizing the potential of AI in waqf and ensuring that its use adheres to both legal and religious guidelines (Usman & Rahman, 2021).

The Role of Blockchain and Smart Contracts in Modern Waqf Management

Blockchain technology represents a revolutionary tool in waqf management by addressing issues related to transparency, accountability, and efficiency. Traditionally, waqf institutions have faced challenges such as mismanagement, limited transparency, and inefficient fund allocation. Blockchain's decentralized and immutable nature ensures that every waqf transaction is recorded on a public ledger accessible to all stakeholders. This visibility helps prevent fund misuse by providing a clear and unalterable record of how waqf assets are allocated and utilized. The ability to trace these records back to their origin significantly enhances donor confidence and supports compliance with Shariah principles (Anwar et al., 2024).

Smart contracts further bolster the capabilities of blockchain technology for waqf management. These are self-executing contracts where the terms are embedded in code, automatically enforcing agreements when specific conditions are met. For example, a smart contract could be used to distribute waqf funds for scholarships only when the recipient meets predefined criteria, such as maintaining a certain grade point average. This automation reduces administrative burdens and minimizes the potential for human error, ensuring that waqf resources are allocated efficiently and according to the donor's intent. Additionally, smart contracts can lower costs associated with managing waqf funds by eliminating intermediaries (Mutmainah et al., 2021).

Digital platforms complement blockchain and smart contracts by expanding the fundraising and distribution reach of waqf institutions. Platforms like Global Sadaqah have made it easier for global donors to contribute to waqf projects, fostering inclusivity in charitable giving. These platforms allow for small and large contributions alike, democratizing the process of waqf donations. They also enable real-time updates on project statuses, which enhances transparency and keeps donors informed about the impact of their contributions. This digital approach aligns well with modern financial practices while adhering to the traditional principles of waqf (Eldersevi & Muhammad, 2021).

Despite the benefits, the integration of fintech in waqf management is not without its challenges. One major issue is the need for appropriate regulatory frameworks to accommodate digital waqf solutions like blockchain and smart contracts. In many jurisdictions, legal recognition of digital records and automated contracts is still in its infancy, which may complicate the adoption of these technologies for waqf management. Additionally, there is a need to ensure that fintech solutions align with Islamic financial principles, which may require close collaboration between technology developers and Shariah scholars to address ethical and compliance issues (Ibrahim, 2023).

Technological infrastructure also poses a challenge for fintech adoption in waqf management, especially in regions where access to reliable internet and digital payment systems is limited. For fintech solutions to be effective, waqf institutions must invest in digital literacy and infrastructure improvements to ensure that potential donors and administrators can effectively utilize these technologies. Bridging the digital divide will be essential for the widespread adoption of blockchain and other fintech innovations in waqf (Zakariyah et al., 2023).

A relevant case study in Indonesia demonstrates the potential of blockchain for cash waqf management. By using blockchain, Indonesian waqf institutions have improved transparency and accountability in the distribution of funds, particularly for educational purposes. This approach not only complies with Shariah requirements but also boosts donor confidence by providing a traceable and auditable system for waqf transactions. The success of this implementation highlights the possibilities for expanding blockchain-based waqf solutions across other regions facing similar challenges in waqf management (Mutmainah et al., 2021).

Digital Platforms for Waqf Fundraising and Distribution

Digital platforms play a crucial role in modernizing waqf fundraising and distribution processes. These platforms facilitate online donations, expand the reach of waqf initiatives, and engage a broader audience of potential contributors. For example, crowdfunding platforms and mobile apps dedicated to waqf enable individuals to make small contributions, which can accumulate to support significant waqf projects. This democratization of the donation process allows for greater public participation and can lead to a more diverse and sustainable funding base for waqf initiatives (Fanani et al., 2021).

Moreover, digital platforms offer innovative solutions for the efficient distribution of waqf resources. By providing features such as real-time tracking of donations, transparent reporting mechanisms, and online management tools, these platforms enhance the efficiency and accountability of waqf operations. For instance, platforms like WaqfLink and GoFundMe provide infrastructure for collecting donations and managing funds, which can be used to support a wide range of waqf projects, from building schools to funding healthcare services. However, the effectiveness of these platforms depends on the quality of their design, the ease of use for diverse populations, and the ability to maintain user trust through secure and transparent operations (Fanani et al., 2021).

Additionally, the transparency features of digital platforms, such as real-time tracking of donations and detailed project updates, boost accountability and donor trust. These tools allow stakeholders to monitor the use of funds and ensure that they are allocated effectively, addressing common concerns about the misuse of waqf resources. Platforms like WaqfLink provide the necessary infrastructure to track project progress, thereby enhancing confidence among donors and improving the overall governance of waqf institutions (Fanani et al., 2021).

Integrating fintech solutions into digital waqf platforms further streamlines the management of donations and fund distribution. By incorporating mobile payment systems, e-wallets, and automated donation features, waqf institutions can facilitate seamless and recurring contributions. This technological integration ensures a steady flow of funds for long-term projects, such as scholarships or social welfare programs, while also reducing administrative burdens through automated processes (Fanani et al., 2021).

However, the effectiveness of these platforms relies heavily on user-friendly design, accessibility, and robust security measures. Ensuring that the platforms are easy to navigate for individuals with different levels of digital literacy is crucial for maximizing participation. Furthermore, implementing strong data protection protocols is essential to maintain donor privacy and secure financial transactions, thereby upholding the integrity of waqf operations (Faturohman et al., 2020).

Challenges and Opportunities in Fintech Integration

The integration of fintech in waqf management presents both opportunities and challenges. On the one hand, fintech solutions offer the potential to increase efficiency, transparency, and accessibility in waqf management. On the other hand, these technologies face obstacles such as regulatory hurdles, technological gaps, and resistance to change from traditional institutions. For example, the legal frameworks governing waqf may need to be updated to accommodate blockchain records and smart contracts, while community stakeholders may require education and trust-building efforts to embrace digital platforms (Dorfleitner et al., 2021).

Despite these challenges, the opportunities presented by fintech innovations are substantial. By addressing issues such as fund mismanagement, enhancing fundraising efforts, and ensuring transparent distribution, fintech can significantly improve the effectiveness of waqf management. Moving forward, a strategic approach that combines technological advancements with regulatory support, community engagement, and rigorous impact assessment will be essential for realising the full potential of fintech in waqf management (Chang & Wang, 2023).

Integrating fintech into waqf management presents both significant challenges and promising opportunities. One major challenge is navigating the regulatory landscape, as existing legal frameworks often struggle to keep pace with technological advancements like blockchain and smart contracts. This can create uncertainties around the enforceability of digital agreements and compliance with Islamic financial principles. Additionally, regulations differ across jurisdictions, complicating the management of cross-border waqf projects. Addressing these regulatory hurdles requires close collaboration between waqf institutions, fintech developers, and Islamic scholars to ensure that solutions align with both legal and Shariah standards (Ali, Hassnian, Hazik Mohamed, Hadia Saqib Hashmi, 2019).

Technological infrastructure is another barrier, especially in regions where access to reliable internet and digital payment systems is limited. The digital divide poses a challenge for both donors and waqf managers, particularly in developing countries where smaller institutions may lack the resources to implement fintech solutions effectively. To overcome this, there needs to be investment in digital literacy programs, training for waqf managers, and improvements in the underlying infrastructure to support digital waqf platforms (Wresch & Fraser, 2011).

On the other hand, fintech offers opportunities to facilitate cross-border waqf initiatives by providing secure and efficient ways to manage international donations. Blockchain technology, for instance, allows waqf institutions to transparently record and track donations across different jurisdictions, making it suitable for global waqf projects, such as humanitarian aid or international educational scholarships. Additionally, digital payment systems can simplify currency conversions, allowing for seamless contributions from donors around the world (Ali, Hassnian, Hazik Mohamed, Hadia Saqib Hashmi, 2019).

Lastly, fintech can promote financial inclusion by enabling underserved populations to participate in waqf initiatives. Mobile payment platforms and e-wallets make it possible for people without traditional bank accounts to contribute to waqf projects. This democratizes the donation process and helps waqf institutions gather significant resources through micro-donations. By making waqf more accessible to a broader audience, fintech has the potential to significantly increase the social impact of waqf initiatives (Alshater et al., 2022; Dorfleitner et al., 2021).

ALIGNING WAQF WITH SDGS

The alignment of waqf with the United Nations SDGs represents a powerful opportunity to leverage traditional Islamic endowments for global development efforts. With its historical role in social welfare and community support, Waqf has the potential to address various SDGs through strategic initiatives and innovative approaches. This discussion explores how waqf can contribute to specific SDGs and outlines strategies for leveraging waqf assets to advance sustainable development (M. Abdullah, 2018).

How Waqf Can Contribute to Specific SDGs

Waqf can be instrumental in advancing several SDGs due to its flexible and charitable nature. One of the most direct contributions is to SDG 1: No Poverty. By allocating waqf assets for community development projects, such as funding local businesses, providing microloans, or supporting vocational training, waqf initiatives can help uplift economically disadvantaged communities. For example, waqf-based microfinance programs in Bangladesh have successfully empowered small entrepreneurs, providing them with the capital needed to start and expand businesses, directly contributing to poverty reduction (Ibrahim et al., 2022).

Similarly, waqf can significantly impact SDG 2: Zero Hunger through the establishment of food banks, agricultural projects, and community kitchens. Historical examples include the waqf-funded agricultural lands used to support food security in the Ottoman Empire. In contemporary contexts, waqf can be used to create food distribution networks, support sustainable agriculture, and fund nutritional programs for vulnerable populations. For instance, the Waqf Al-Falah Foundation in Indonesia has been involved in various food security initiatives, including the establishment of community farms and food banks (Karimah et al., 2023).

Waqf also plays a crucial role in SDG 4: Quality Education. By funding educational institutions, scholarships, and research grants, waqf can enhance access to quality education for underserved communities. The establishment of waqf-funded schools and universities has historically provided educational opportunities in many Muslim-majority countries. Modern examples include the Al-Qasimia University in Sharjah, UAE, which was established through waqf to provide high-quality education and promote academic excellence (Rusydiana, 2024).

Another important contribution is to SDG 6: Clean Water and Sanitation. Waqf can be used to fund clean water projects, sanitation facilities, and hygiene education programs. For example, the Islamic Development Bank's Waqf for Clean Water project has supported the construction of wells and water purification systems in various countries, improving access to clean water for communities in need (Hisyam & Marwini, 2024).

Strategies for Leveraging Waqf Assets for Sustainable Development

To maximize the impact of waqf in achieving the SDGs, several strategic approaches can be employed. First, developing targeted waqf initiatives that align with specific SDGs is essential. This involves identifying key areas where waqf resources can address pressing global challenges and designing projects that are both impactful and sustainable. For example, waqf funds can be allocated to establish educational institutions in regions with high illiteracy rates or to support innovative agricultural practices in areas facing food shortages (A. Hassan, 2010).

Second, partnerships and collaborations play a crucial role in amplifying the impact of waqf initiatives. Engaging with governmental agencies, non-governmental organizations, and international development institutions can enhance the reach and effectiveness of waqf projects. For instance, partnerships with organizations like UNICEF or the World Food Programme can help align waqf projects with global development efforts and leverage additional resources and expertise (Listiana et al., 2021).

Third, embracing innovative financial models such as SIBs and blended finance approaches can enhance the effectiveness of waqf assets. These models combine waqf funding with investments from the private sector and philanthropic foundations to support large-scale development projects. An example is the use of waqf funds to create SIBs for education or health initiatives, where returns are reinvested into further waqf projects (Md. Shahedur Rahaman Chowdhury, 2011).

Fourth, improving transparency and accountability in waqf management is vital for building trust and ensuring the effective use of resources. Implementing modern financial technologies such as blockchain for transparent reporting and monitoring of waqf activities can address issues of mismanagement and enhance stakeholder confidence. For instance, blockchain can be used to create a transparent ledger for tracking donations and expenditures related to waqf-funded projects (Suyatno & Pakkana, 2024).

Finally, conducting rigorous impact assessments of waqf projects is necessary to measure their effectiveness and inform future strategies. Developing frameworks for evaluating the social and economic outcomes of waqf initiatives ensures that they are achieving their intended goals and provides insights for improving future efforts. For example, impact assessment tools can be used to evaluate the success of educational programs funded by waqf and identify best practices for scaling up successful models (Meeran et al., 2023).

MODERNISING WAQF: FINANCIAL INNOVATION AND INTEGRATION MODELS

The concept of waqf, a longstanding Islamic endowment system, has evolved over centuries to address various social and economic needs (Ramli & Jalil, 2015). In recent years, innovative waqf models that combine traditional waqf practices with contemporary financial instruments and public-private partnerships have emerged as powerful tools for fostering inclusive prosperity. This discussion explores hybrid waqf models that integrate modern financial instruments and examines the role of public-private partnerships in enhancing the impact of waqf-driven initiatives.

Hybrid Models Combining Waqf with Contemporary Financial Instruments

Hybrid waqf models represent a creative fusion of traditional waqf practices with modern financial instruments to maximize the impact of waqf assets and promote inclusive prosperity. One prominent example is the waqf-based social impact bonds (SIBs) model (Fauziah et al., 2019). SIBs are financial instruments that use private investment to fund social programs, with returns based on the achievement of specific social outcomes. By combining waqf assets with SIBs, stakeholders can create innovative funding mechanisms for social initiatives. For instance, waqf funds can be used as the initial capital for a social impact bond aimed at reducing homelessness or improving educational outcomes. If the program meets its performance targets, investors receive returns, and the waqf funds are reinvested into further community development projects.

Another effective hybrid model is the waqf-based venture philanthropy approach. Venture philanthropy applies investment principles to philanthropic endeavours, focusing on achieving measurable social impact alongside financial sustainability (Hambali & Aisyah, 2021). In this model, waqf assets are invested in high-impact social enterprises or start-ups that address pressing community needs. For example, waqf funds can support the growth of a social enterprise that provides affordable healthcare solutions or renewable energy technologies to underserved communities. This approach not only generates social benefits but also creates opportunities for financial returns that can be reinvested into additional waqf projects.

The waqf-linked crowdfunding model is another innovative approach that leverages digital platforms to attract a wide range of donors for specific waqf projects. Crowdfunding platforms facilitate small donations from many people, which can be pooled to fund significant social initiatives. By integrating waqf principles with crowdfunding, organizations can engage a broader audience in supporting causes such as building schools, funding medical research, or establishing community development programs (Abidullah Khan et al., 2023). This model democratizes the funding process and expands the reach of waqf initiatives beyond traditional donor bases.

Public-Private Partnerships in Waqf-Driven Initiatives

Public-private partnerships (PPPs) offer a collaborative framework for combining resources, expertise, and networks from both the public and private sectors to achieve common social goals. In the context of waqf, PPPs can enhance the effectiveness and reach of waqf-driven initiatives through various strategies (H. Noho, 2023).

One notable example is the waqf-public sector collaboration model, where government agencies partner with waqf institutions to address societal challenges. For instance, a local government might work with a waqf organization to develop affordable housing projects for low-income families (H. Noho, 2023). The government provides regulatory support and infrastructure, while the waqf institution supplies funding and project management expertise. This collaboration ensures that resources are used efficiently and that the projects align with both public policy objectives and waqf principles.

Another effective model is the waqf-private sector investment approach, where private companies invest in waqf projects as part of their corporate social responsibility (CSR) initiatives. This partnership benefits from the private sector's financial resources and innovation capabilities, while waqf institutions provide the strategic vision and community focus. For example, a corporation might invest in a waqf-managed educational institution or healthcare facility as part of its CSR program. This model leverages private sector efficiency and expertise to support waqf projects and achieve social impact (Suwandari & Suratkon, 2022).

The waqf-philanthropy and non-governmental organizations (NGO) collaboration model involves partnerships between waqf institutions and NGOs to implement and scale social programs. NGOs bring experience in community development and grassroots engagement, while waqf institutions provide funding and strategic oversight. An example is a partnership where a waqf institution funds an NGO-led initiative to provide vocational training for unemployed youth. This collaboration enhances the effectiveness of the initiative and ensures that it meets the needs of the target communities (Supiyan, 2023).

Challenges and Opportunities in Innovative Waqf Models

While innovative waqf models offer significant opportunities for enhancing the impact of waqf initiatives, they also face challenges that need to be addressed. One major challenge is ensuring regulatory compliance and alignment with Islamic legal principles. Hybrid models that combine waqf with contemporary financial instruments must navigate complex legal frameworks and ensure that all financial practices adhere to Shariah principles (Islam, 2015).

Another challenge is building trust among stakeholders. Successful implementation of these models requires cooperation among diverse entities, including public institutions, private investors, and community organizations. Establishing and maintaining trust among these stakeholders is crucial for the success of waqf-driven projects (M. Ahmad, 2019).

Despite these challenges, the potential for innovative waqf models to drive inclusive prosperity is substantial. By leveraging modern financial instruments and fostering effective partnerships, these models can address a wide range of social and economic issues. Moving forward, a focus on strategic planning, regulatory alignment, and stakeholder engagement will be essential for realizing the full potential of these innovative approaches (Uluyol et al., 2021).

CHALLENGES AND OPPORTUNITIES IN MODERN WAQF IMPLEMENTATION

Modern waqf implementation faces a range of challenges and opportunities that can significantly impact its effectiveness as a tool for social and economic development. Understanding these challenges and seizing the opportunities for international collaboration is crucial for advancing the role of waqf in contemporary society. This section explores the legal and regulatory obstacles encountered in different jurisdictions and highlights the potential for scaling waqf through international collaboration.

Legal and Regulatory Challenges in Different Jurisdictions

One of the primary challenges in modern waqf implementation is navigating the complex legal and regulatory frameworks that govern waqf institutions across different jurisdictions (Syamsuri et al., 2021). These challenges can vary widely depending on the legal systems and administrative practices in each country.

In many jurisdictions, the legal status of waqf is ambiguous or fragmented. For instance, in countries where waqf is not fully recognized as a distinct legal entity, waqf institutions may face difficulties in securing legal standing or enforcing their rights. In some regions, waqf is subject to outdated regulations that do not reflect contemporary needs or practices, leading to inefficiencies and limitations in waqf management (Sano & Kassim, 2021). For example, in some countries, waqf regulations may be based on historical frameworks that do not accommodate modern financial instruments or innovative waqf models.

Regulatory compliance also presents significant challenges. Waqf institutions must adhere to both local regulations and Islamic legal principles, which can create conflicts and complications. In some jurisdictions, the overlap between Shariah law and national legal systems can lead to legal ambiguities, making it difficult for waqf institutions to navigate legal requirements and ensure compliance with both Shariah and secular regulations (Azganin et al., 2021).

Furthermore, there is often a lack of standardized regulations for waqf management. Different countries have varying requirements for the establishment, governance, and auditing of waqf institutions. This lack of standardization can hinder the development of best practices and create barriers to international collaboration (Abu Talib et al., 2020). For example, the procedures for establishing a waqf, the roles and responsibilities of waqf trustees, and the reporting requirements for waqf funds can differ significantly between countries, complicating efforts to harmonize waqf practices across borders.

Another challenge is ineffective oversight and accountability mechanisms for waqf institutions. In many jurisdictions, the regulatory frameworks for waqf lack robust mechanisms for ensuring transparency, accountability, and effective management. Weak oversight can lead to issues such as mismanagement of waqf assets, lack of proper financial reporting, and inadequate protection of the rights of beneficiaries (Arshad et al., 2018).

Opportunities for Scaling Waqf Through International Collaboration

Despite these challenges, there are significant opportunities for scaling waqf through international collaboration. By leveraging global networks and sharing best practices, waqf institutions can enhance their impact and expand their reach (Azrai Azaimi Ambrose et al., 2018; Raja Adnan et al., 2021; Razak, 2020).

One major opportunity is the development of international partnerships to share knowledge and resources. Collaborative efforts between waqf institutions, NGOs, and international development agencies can facilitate the exchange of best practices, innovative models, and technical expertise. For instance, international conferences and workshops on waqf can bring together scholars, practitioners, and policymakers to discuss effective strategies for waqf management and explore opportunities for collaborative projects (A. U. Ahmad et al., 2010).

Cross-border waqf initiatives offer another avenue for scaling waqf's impact. By establishing waqf projects that span multiple countries, institutions can address global challenges and create synergies between different regions (Saiti et al., 2021). For example, cross-border waqf initiatives could focus on issues such as climate change, international education programs, or global health challenges. Such initiatives can benefit from diverse perspectives and resources, leading to more comprehensive and effective solutions.

Global standardization efforts represent a significant opportunity for improving waqf practices. Developing international standards for waqf management, governance, and financial reporting can help harmonize practices across different jurisdictions (Saiti et al., 2021). Organizations like the International Waqf Forum and the Islamic Development Bank have already started to work towards standardizing waqf practices and promoting the adoption of best practices globally. These efforts can lead to more consistent and effective waqf management practices worldwide.

Technological innovations offer new opportunities for enhancing waqf operations and expanding its reach. Advances in technology, such as blockchain for transparency and digital platforms for fundraising, can be utilized to overcome some of the legal and regulatory challenges faced by waqf institutions (Zakariyah et al., 2023). For example, blockchain technology can provide a transparent and immutable ledger for tracking waqf transactions, improving accountability and trust among stakeholders (Mutmainah et al., 2021).

Capacity building through international training programs and resources is another key opportunity. By investing in the development of skills and knowledge among waqf managers, trustees, and staff, institutions can improve their effectiveness and better address the challenges they face. International training programs, online courses, and knowledge-sharing platforms can support the professional development of individuals involved in waqf management (Vika Annisa Qurrata et al., 2021).

Examples of Successful International Collaboration and Technological Integration

Several successful examples illustrate how international collaboration and technological innovations can enhance waqf initiatives. For instance, the Global Waqf Fund, a collaborative effort between various waqf institutions and international donors, has supported numerous projects across different countries, including educational programs in Africa and healthcare initiatives in Asia. This fund demonstrates how pooling resources and expertise from multiple sources can lead to impactful outcomes (Saiti et al., 2021, 2021).

Another example is the Blockchain for Waqf initiative, which explores the use of blockchain technology to create transparent and efficient waqf management systems. Pilot projects in countries like Malaysia and Indonesia have shown how blockchain can improve financial transparency and enhance trust among donors and beneficiaries (Ibrahim, 2023; Muchlis Gazali et al., 2019; Mutmainah et al., 2021).

FUTURE DIRECTIONS FOR WAQF IN THE DIGITAL AGE

The digital age presents unprecedented opportunities and challenges for the evolution of waqf as a tool for social and economic development. Emerging technologies and innovative trends are reshaping the landscape of waqf management and operations, offering new avenues for enhancing its impact. This section explores these emerging trends and technologies and identifies potential areas for future research and development in the field of waqf and fintech.

Emerging Trends and Technologies Shaping the Future of Waqf

One of the most significant trends in the digital age is the integration of blockchain technology into waqf management. Blockchain offers a transparent, secure, and decentralized platform for managing waqf assets and transactions (Muchlis Gazali et al., 2019). By creating immutable records of waqf transactions, blockchain technology can enhance transparency and accountability in waqf management. For example, the use of blockchain can facilitate real-time tracking of waqf donations, expenditures, and project outcomes, ensuring that funds are used effectively, and beneficiaries' rights are protected. Several pilot projects and platforms, such as WaqfChain, are exploring blockchain applications in waqf to provide transparent reporting and efficient management of waqf assets (Ibrahim, 2023).

Another emerging trend is the use of artificial intelligence (AI) and machine learning for predictive analytics and decision-making in waqf management. AI algorithms can analyze large datasets to identify trends, predict future needs, and optimize the allocation of waqf resources. For instance, machine learning models can predict the long-term sustainability of waqf investments, assess the impact of waqf projects, and recommend strategies for improving waqf management. The application of AI in waqf could also extend to automated financial reporting, risk assessment, and the development of personalized donation platforms (Alawiye & Keerio, 2023).

The rise of digital platforms and mobile applications for waqf fundraising and management represents another key trend. These platforms enable waqf institutions to reach a broader audience, streamline fundraising efforts, and engage with donors in new ways. Platforms such as LaunchGood and GoFundMe can be adapted for waqf purposes to create campaigns for specific projects, manage donations, and provide updates to donors (Wang et al., 2022). Mobile apps can offer features such as donor engagement tools, project tracking, and virtual events to foster a stronger connection between waqf institutions and their supporters.

Crowdfunding and peer-to-peer (P2P) financing are also transforming how waqf projects are funded and managed. Crowdfunding platforms enable individuals to contribute to waqf projects from anywhere in the world, democratizing the donation process and expanding the reach of waqf initiatives. P2P financing models, which allow direct transactions between investors and project managers, offer new opportunities for waqf institutions to access funding and engage with a diverse range of stakeholders (A. U. Ahmad et al., 2010). Platforms like Kickstarter and Indiegogo can serve as models for developing specialised crowdfunding solutions for waqf.

Potential Areas for Research and Development in Waqf and Fintech

As waqf continues to evolve in the digital age, several key areas offer promising opportunities for research and development. These areas focus on exploring new technologies, developing innovative models, and addressing emerging challenges in the intersection of waqf and fintech (Rabbani et al., 2021).

One potential area for research is the development of Shariah-compliant fintech solutions for waqf management. Research could focus on creating financial products and services that align with Islamic principles while leveraging modern technologies. For example, studies could explore the development of Islamic fintech platforms for investment, savings, and donation that adhere to Shariah law and meet the needs of waqf institutions and their stakeholders (Hasif & Ahmad, 2019). This research would involve collaboration between scholars, fintech developers, and Shariah advisors to create solutions that are both innovative and compliant with Islamic jurisprudence.

Another important research area is the exploration of impact measurement and evaluation frameworks for waqf projects. Developing robust frameworks for assessing the social and economic impacts of waqf initiatives is crucial for ensuring that waqf funds are used effectively and that projects achieve their intended outcomes (Masruki & Shafii, 2013). Research could focus on creating metrics and methodologies for evaluating the success of waqf projects, including tools for measuring impact, tracking performance, and reporting results to stakeholders.

Integration of smart contracts into waqf management represents another exciting avenue for research and development (Umar et al., 2022). Smart contracts, which are self-executing agreements with the terms of the contract directly written into code, can automate various aspects of waqf management, including donation processing, fund distribution, and compliance monitoring. Research could explore the potential applications of smart contracts in waqf, such as automating administrative tasks, enforcing contractual obligations, and ensuring transparency in waqf transactions (Hambali & Aisyah, 2021).

The development of digital education and training programs for waqf management is also a promising area for future research. As waqf institutions increasingly adopt digital tools and technologies, there is a growing need for educational resources and training programs that equip waqf managers, trustees, and staff with the skills and knowledge they need to effectively utilize these tools (Ibrahim, 2023). Research could focus on creating online training modules, virtual workshops, and educational resources that address the needs of waqf professionals and support their development in the digital age.

Lastly, exploring the potential of big data and data analytics in waqf management offers significant opportunities for innovation. Research could investigate how big data can be used to gather insights from various sources, including donor behaviour, project performance, and community needs (Rusydiana, A. S., & Devi, 2014). This data-driven approach could lead to the development of advanced analytics tools for making informed decisions, improving strategic planning, and enhancing the effectiveness of waqf initiatives.

AI-Driven Waqf Management Tools

AI-driven waqf management tools are also emerging, such as the Waqf Analytics Platform, which uses machine learning algorithms to predict the outcomes of waqf projects and optimize resource allocation (Muneeza & Nadwi, 2019).

In the digital age, AI and machine learning have introduced transformative opportunities for waqf management, offering sophisticated tools that enhance decision-making, optimize resource allocation, and maximize the impact of waqf initiatives. One prominent example of this evolution is the Waqf Analytics Platform, which exemplifies how AI technologies are being utilized to address the complexities of waqf management (Alawiye & Keerio, 2023). This platform employs advanced machine learning algorithms to analyse historical data, predict future outcomes, and provide actionable insights for waqf administrators, representing a significant advancement in the field.

The Waqf Analytics Platform offers several key functionalities that demonstrate the potential of AI-driven tools in waqf management. First, it utilizes predictive analytics to forecast the outcomes of waqf projects based on historical data. By analysing past performance and identifying trends, the platform helps administrators make informed decisions about resource allocation and project planning. For example, predictive models can project the future success of an educational initiative by evaluating data from similar past projects. This forward-looking approach allows waqf institutions to allocate resources more effectively and anticipate potential challenges before they arise.

Another notable feature of the Waqf Analytics Platform is its ability to optimize resource allocation through sophisticated machine learning algorithms. These algorithms analyse various factors, such as donor behaviour, project needs, and financial constraints, to provide recommendations for the most effective distribution of waqf assets. For instance, the platform might suggest reallocating funds from less successful projects to those with higher potential for impact, thereby improving the overall efficiency of waqf resource management. This optimization ensures that waqf assets are used in ways that maximize their social and economic benefits.

The platform also facilitates impact assessment by offering tools for evaluating the outcomes of waqf projects against predefined metrics. Administrators can use these tools to measure the effectiveness of their initiatives, track performance, and identify areas for improvement. For example, impact assessment tools might evaluate a health clinic funded by waqf donations based on patient satisfaction and health outcomes, providing insights that guide future project development and management.

Additionally, the Waqf Analytics Platform enhances donor engagement through features that offer personalized updates on project progress and detailed impact reports (Ascarya & Sakti, 2022). These features help build transparency and trust between waqf institutions and their supporters by keeping donors informed about how their contributions are being used and the positive outcomes achieved. Engaging donors in this manner strengthens the relationship between waqf institutions and their supporters, fostering continued support for future initiatives.

Several innovative examples illustrate the growing application of AI in waqf management. AI-Based Fundraising Platforms such as GoFundMe and Launch Good are exploring AI-driven features to optimize fundraising efforts for waqf projects. These platforms employ predictive analytics to forecast campaign success, personalize donation recommendations, and automate donor engagement strategies (Muneeza & Nadwi, 2019; Wang et al., 2022). Similarly, smart contract platforms integrate AI with blockchain technology to automate waqf management processes. The Waqf Smart Contract Framework, for example, uses AI to create and manage self-executing contracts that handle donations, fund distribution, and compliance checks, streamlining administrative tasks and ensuring transparency.

Another notable example is the use of data analytics for project evaluation, where tools like Impact Measurement Software leverage AI to analyse data from waqf-funded projects. These tools assess project performance, measure social impact, and generate reports that inform future decision-making. Additionally, AI-driven training programs are being developed to enhance the technical skills of waqf managers, providing online courses, webinars, and interactive tools to support their professional development in the digital age (Musa, 2024).

Despite these promising advancements, there are significant challenges associated with the implementation of AI-driven waqf management tools. One major concern is data privacy and security, as the collection and analysis of sensitive data require robust measures to protect donor information and maintain trust. Additionally, ensuring that AI tools adhere to Shariah principles presents a challenge that necessitates ongoing collaboration between technologists and Shariah scholars to develop solutions that comply with Islamic financial ethics (Musa, 2024).

Implementation costs are another challenge, as developing and maintaining advanced AI technologies can be expensive. Waqf institutions may face difficulties in securing the necessary funding and resources for these innovations (A. U. Ahmad et al., 2010). Furthermore, the effective use of AI tools requires specialized technical expertise, which may necessitate investment in training and capacity building for waqf staff.

Looking to the future, there are several research and development directions for advancing AI-driven tools in waqf management (Zariff & Yusoff, 2024). One promising area is the development of Shariah-compliant AI algorithms, focusing on creating financial products and services that adhere to Islamic law while leveraging modern technologies. Another important direction is the exploration of more advanced predictive models for assessing waqf project outcomes, aiming to develop algorithms that incorporate a broader range of variables and provide more accurate forecasts.

Research can also explore the potential of integrating AI with blockchain technology to create comprehensive solutions for waqf management. Combining the transparency of blockchain with the predictive capabilities of AI could lead to innovative approaches for managing waqf assets and ensuring effective oversight (DinarStandard, 2022). Additionally, there is a need for developing digital training programs that offer online courses, webinars, and resources to build the technical skills required for utilizing AI-driven tools in waqf management.

Finally, cross-sector collaborations offer significant opportunities for driving innovation in waqf management. Future research can investigate how partnerships between waqf institutions, fintech companies, and academic researchers can foster new solutions and enhance the effectiveness of waqf initiatives (Md Zabri & Mohammed, 2018). By exploring these opportunities, the field of waqf management can continue to evolve and adapt to the challenges and possibilities of the digital age.

Examples of Innovations and Future Trends in Waqf

Several examples illustrate how emerging technologies and trends are shaping the future of waqf. The Islamic Development Bank's Waqf Hub is a notable initiative that uses digital platforms to connect waqf institutions, donors, and beneficiaries. The Waqf Hub provides a centralised platform for managing waqf projects, sharing best practices, and fostering collaboration among stakeholders (Daud & Azam, 2011).

Another example is the Waqf Foundation's use of blockchain technology to create a transparent and efficient waqf management system. The foundation's blockchain-based platform enables real-time tracking of waqf donations and expenditures, improving transparency and accountability (Ibrahim, 2023).

CONCLUSION

As we reach the end of this chapter on AI-driven waqf management tools, integrating AI and machine learning into waqf administration marks a significant advancement in Islamic finance. Tools such as the Waqf Analytics Platform exemplify how cutting-edge technologies can be harnessed to enhance the effectiveness and efficiency of waqf management. Through predictive analytics, resource optimization, impact assessment, and improved donor engagement, these AI-driven innovations offer new opportunities for waqf institutions to achieve their goals of social and economic development.

The discussion highlighted several critical functions of AI-driven tools. The use of predictive analytics allows waqf administrators to forecast project outcomes with greater accuracy, enabling proactive decision-making and strategic resource allocation. Resource optimization algorithms help ensure that waqf assets are used in the most impactful ways, addressing financial constraints and aligning resources with project needs. Impact assessment tools provide valuable insights into the effectiveness of waqf initiatives, fostering transparency and accountability. Additionally, donor engagement features improve communication and maintain trust between waqf institutions and their supporters, enhancing the overall support for waqf projects.

However, the implementation of AI-driven waqf management tools also presents notable challenges. Ensuring data privacy and security is paramount, as sensitive donor information must be protected from unauthorized access. Furthermore, developing solutions that are Shariah-compliant requires careful consideration of Islamic financial principles and ongoing collaboration between technologists and Shariah scholars. The costs associated with technology development and implementation can be substantial, posing a barrier for some waqf institutions. Additionally, the effective use of these tools necessitates specialized technical expertise, which may require significant investments in training and capacity building.

Looking ahead, there are promising future research and development directions for AI-driven waqf management. One such direction is the development of Shariah-compliant AI algorithms, which would ensure that technological advancements align with Islamic financial ethics. Another area for exploration is the creation of more advanced predictive models for waqf project outcomes, which could provide even more accurate forecasts and strategic insights. The potential for integrating AI with blockchain technology offers a fascinating avenue for future innovation, combining the transparency of blockchain with the predictive power of AI. Additionally, there is a need for digital training programs to equip waqf managers with the necessary skills to utilize these advanced tools effectively. Finally, fostering cross-sector collaborations between waqf institutions, fintech companies, and academic researchers could drive new solutions and enhance the impact of waqf initiatives on a global scale.

AI-driven tools such as the Waqf Analytics Platform represent a transformative shift in waqf management, offering new methodologies for enhancing decision-making processes, optimizing resource allocation, and improving donor relations. While there are challenges to be addressed, the opportunities for innovation and growth are significant. By embracing these technologies and pursuing further research and development, waqf institutions can enhance their management practices and advance their missions of fostering social and economic development in line with both traditional principles and contemporary needs.

REFERENCES

Abdul-Yakeen, M. A., Gatawa, N. M., Aliyu, C. U., & Ibrahim, M. O. (2014). Six-Rs of establishing a Waqf in Ilorin emirate economy. *International Journal of Development and Sustainability*, 3(7), 1438–1454. www.isdsnet.com/ijds

Abdullah, M. (2018). Waqf, Sustainable Development Goals (SDGs) and maqasid al-shariah. *International Journal of Social Economics*, 45(1), 158–172. DOI: 10.1108/IJSE-10-2016-0295

Abdullah, M. (2020). Islamic endowment (Waqf) in India: Towards poverty reduction of Muslims in the country. *Journal of Research in Emerging Markets*, 2(2), 48–60. DOI: 10.30585/jrems.v2i2.482

Abdullah, O., Abdullah, O., Shaharuddin, A., Wahid, M. A., & Harun, M. S. (2022). The Potentials and Challenges of Decision Support System for Islamic Banking and Finance. *European Journal of Islamic Finance*, 9(3), 21–29. DOI: 10.13135/2421-2172/6901-

Abu Talib, N. Y., Abdul Latiff, R., & Aman, A. (2020). An institutional perspective for research in waqf accounting and reporting: A case study of Terengganu state Islamic Religious Council in Malaysia. *Journal of Islamic Accounting and Business Research*, 11(2), 400–427. DOI: 10.1108/JIABR-11-2016-0132

Ahmad, A. U., Osmani, N. M., & Karim, M. F. (2010). Islamic finance in Australia: the potential problems and prospects : "25 Years of Islamic Banking and Finance in Brunei" View project. *International Conference The Tawhidi Epistemology: Zakat and Waqf Economy, November*. https://www.researchgate.net/publication/303698257

Ahmad, M. (2019). An empirical study of the challenges facing zakat and waqf institutions in Northern Nigeria. *ISRA International Journal of Islamic Finance*, 11(2), 338–356. DOI: 10.1108/IJIF-04-2018-0044

Alawiye, H. O., & Keerio, I. K. (2023). Towards Resolving Overlapped Distribution of Waqf Funds Through Artificial Intelligence: Focusing on Educational Waqf's Beneficiaries. *Al-Kashaf, December*. https://alkashaf.pk/index.php/Journal/article/view/56%0Ahttps://alkashaf.pk/index.php/Journal/article/download/56/66

Ali, Hassnian, Hazik Mohamed, Hadia Saqib Hashmi, and M. H. (2019). Global landscape of the Islamic Fintech: opportunities, challenges and future ahead. *COMSATS Journal of Islamic Finance, 4*(2).

Alshater, M. M., Saba, I., Supriani, I., & Rabbani, M. R. (2022). Fintech in islamic finance literature: A review. *Heliyon*, 8(9), e10385. DOI: 10.1016/j.heliyon.2022.e10385 PMID: 36060472

Anwar, I. F., Rahayu, S. B., Yusoff, Y., Faizah, N., & Lajin, M. (2024).. . *INTERNATIONAL JOURNAL OF TRENDS IN The Sustainability of Cash Waqf Using Blockchain Technology : a Conceptual Study*, 5(2), 70–82.

Arshad, R., Zain, N. M., Urus, S. T., & Chakir, A. (2018). Modelling Maqasid Waqf Performance Measures in Waqf Institutions. *Global Journal Al-Thaqafah*, 8(Special Issue), 157–169. DOI: 10.7187/GJATSI2018-11

Ascarya, A. (2022). The role of Islamic social finance during Covid-19 pandemic in Indonesia's economic recovery. *International Journal of Islamic and Middle Eastern Finance and Management*, 15(2), 386–405. DOI: 10.1108/IMEFM-07-2020-0351

Ascarya, A., & Sakti, A. (2022). Designing micro-fintech models for Islamic micro financial institutions in Indonesia. *International Journal of Islamic and Middle Eastern Finance and Management*, 15(2), 236–254. DOI: 10.1108/IMEFM-05-2020-0233

Azganin, H., Kassim, S., & Sa'ad, A. A. (2021). Proposed waqf crowdfunding models for small farmers and the required parameters for their application. *Islamic Economic Studies*, 29(1), 2–17. DOI: 10.1108/IES-01-2021-0006

Azrai Azaimi Ambrose, A. H., Gulam Hassan, M. A., & Hanafi, H. (2018). A proposed model for waqf financing public goods and mixed public goods in Malaysia. *International Journal of Islamic and Middle Eastern Finance and Management*, 11(3), 395–415. DOI: 10.1108/IMEFM-01-2017-0001

Barom, M. N. (2012). Conceptualising a unified normative framework of social responsibility in Islamic economics. *IIUM Research, Invention and Innovation Exhibition 2011, 2*(2), 329–363. http://irep.iium.edu.my/28105/

Chang, S. E., & Wang, M. H. (2023). Blockchain-Enabled Fintech Innovation: A Case of Reengineering Stock Trading Services. *IEEE Access : Practical Innovations, Open Solutions*, 11(December), 137125–137137. DOI: 10.1109/ACCESS.2023.3339570

Daud, M., & Azam, A.-R. N. (2011). Islamic Development Bank (IDB), Foreign Aid and the Challenges for Sustainable Development in Africa. *International Journal of Business and Social Science*, 2(4), 190–199. http://www.ijbssnet.com/journals/Vol._2_No._4%253B_March_2011/22.pdf

DinarStandard. (2022). State of the Global Islamic Economy Report 2021/2022. In *State of the Global Islamic Economy Report 2020/21*. https://haladinar.io/hdn/doc/report2018.pdf

Dorfleitner, G., Forcella, D., & Nguyen, Q. A. (2021). The digital transformation of microfinance institutions: an empirical analysis. *Journal of Applied Accounting Research*. DOI: 10.1108/JAAR-02-2021-0041

Eldersevi, S., & Muhammad, M. (2021). "Asnaf Care: A Case Study of the Malaysian-based Charity Crowdfunding Platform to Combat the Impact of COVID-19." *5th International Conference of Zakat,* 2020, 615–626.

Fanani, A., Kuncoro, A. W., Husni, A. B. M., & Wijayanti, E. A. (2021). The Contribution of Waqf on Poverty Alleviation through Digital Platforms: A Case of Indonesia. *Shirkah: Journal of Economics and Business*, 6(2), 246–261. DOI: 10.22515/shirkah.v6i2.386

Farag, S. A. S., Edris, M., Abubakar, Y. S., ... (2024). Using Maqasid Shariah to Utilize the Contemporary Waqf: Implementing Artificial Intelligence as an Example. *Kurdish…, 4883,* 2905–2923. https://kurdishstudies.net/menu-script/index.php/KS/article/view/1579%0Ahttps://kurdishstudies.net/menu-script/index.php/KS/article/download/1579/1141

Faturohman, T., Hassandi, I., & Yulianti, Y. (2020). User Acceptance of Online Waqf Applications: Evidence From Indonesia. *Journal of Islamic Monetary Economics and Finance*, 6(3), 503–530. DOI: 10.21098/jimf.v6i3.1117

Fauziah, N. N., Rabiah, E., Ali, A. E., Alvierra Binti Md Bashir, A., & Bacha, A. M. (2019). an Analysis of Cash Waqf Linked Sukuk for Socially Impactful Sustainable Projects in Indonesia. *Journal of Islamic Finance, 10*(1), 001–010.

Hai, A., Kassim, D. S., & Mohtesham, M. M. J. (2022). An Innovative Sukuk-Waqf for Islamic Microfinance Institutions: Integrating Maqasid Al-Shariah, SDGs and Waqf. *Tazkia Islamic Finance and Business Review*, 15(1), 19–39. DOI: 10.30993/tifbr.v15i1.251

Hambali, A., & Aisyah, S. N. (2021). Equity Crowdfunding based on Islamic Philanthropy: A Concept. *5th INTERNATIONAL CONFERENCE OF ZAKAT PROCEEDINGS*, 545–554.

Haneef, M. A., Pramanik, A. H., Mohammed, M. O., Bin Amin, M. F., & Muhammad, A. D. (2015). Integration of waqf-Islamic microfinance model for poverty reduction: The case of Bangladesh. *International Journal of Islamic and Middle Eastern Finance and Management*, 8(2), 246–270. DOI: 10.1108/IMEFM-03-2014-0029

Hasif, M., & Ahmad, K. (2019). Factors Affecting the Acceptance of Financial Technology among Asnaf for the Distribution of Zakat in Selangor- A Study Using UTAUT. *Journal of Islamic Finance*, 2117(Special Issue), 35–46.

Hassan, A. (2010). Management and Development of the Management and Development of the. *Seventh International Conference – The Tawhidi Epistemology: Zakat and Waqf Economy, Bangi 2010*, 309–328. DOI: 10.1017/CBO9781107415324.004

Hassan, H. A. (2019). Takaful models: Origin, progression and future. *Journal of Islamic Marketing*, 11(6), 1801–1819. Advance online publication. DOI: 10.1108/JIMA-04-2018-0078

Hisyam, M. I., & Marwini, . (2024). Waqf Implementation in Supporting SDGs-6 (Clean Water and Sanitation) at Salman Waqf Institution in Indonesia. *Islamic Social Finance*, 4(1). Advance online publication. DOI: 10.58968/isf.v4i1.481

Ibrahim, S. S. (2023). Potential Blockchain Applications in Waqf for Sustainability: A Middle East and Asia Perspective. *Islamiyyat*, 45(2), 47–64. DOI: 10.17576/islamiyyat-2023-4502-04

Ibrahim, S. S., Daud, D., Hidayah, K., Shaharuddin, A., & Al-Amin, A. A. M. (2022). Waqf integrated income generating model (WIIGM) for enhancing sustainable development goals (SDGS) in Malaysia: An evaluation of behavioural intention. *International Journal of Ethics and Systems*, 3. Advance online publication. DOI: 10.1108/IJOES-02-2022-0030

Islam, M. M. (2015). Cash Waqf: An Innovative Instrument for Development of Ummah. *Banglavision Reseach Journal*, 15(1), 117–124.

Karimah, D. A., Pamuncak, M. B., & Mubin, M. K. (2023). The Role of Waqf in Supporting Sustainable Development Goals: Linking theory and its practices. *Suhuf*, 35(2), 31–38. DOI: 10.23917/suhuf.v35i2.23018

Khan, A., Sukmana, R., & Mahmood, A.ABIDULLAH KHANRADITYA SUKMANAABID MAHMOOD. (2023). Islamic Social Finance Ecosystem and the Role of Crowdfunding: A Proposed Model. *Hamdard Islamicus*, 46(3), 91–111. DOI: 10.57144/hi.v46i3.876

Listiana, L., Fauziyyah, N. E., & Sukmana, R. (2021). Waqf for Food Security: A Critical Assessment from Existing Studies. In *Badan Wakaf Indonesia*.

Masruki, R., & Shafii, Z. (2013). The Development of Waqf Accounting in Enhancing Accountability. *Middle East Journal of Scientific Research*, 13, 1–6. DOI: 10.5829/idosi.mejsr.2013.13.1873

Md Zabri, M. Z., & Mohammed, M. O. (2018). Qualitative validation of a financially affordable Islamic home financing model. *ISRA International Journal of Islamic Finance*, 10(2), 143–161. DOI: 10.1108/IJIF-08-2017-0023

Meeran, M., Mohtesham, J., & Marwan, S. (2023). Social Impact Measurement of Waqf: Case Study of Waqf Organisations in Karnataka, India. *AZKA International Journal of Zakat & Social Finance.*, 4(2), 199–218.

Muchlis Gazali, H., Che Ismail, C. M. H., Gazali, H. M., & Che Ismail, C. M. H. (2019). A Conceptual Framework for Cash Waqf with Blockchain in Financing Education for the Islamic Religious School in Malaysia. *Journal of Islamic Sciences and Comparative Studies*, 3(1), 73–88.

Mujani, W. K., & Yaakub, N. I. (2017). Waqf for higher education in Malaysia: Overview on challenges. *European Journal of Multidisciplinary Studies*, 5(1), 455–461. DOI: 10.26417/ejms.v5i1.p455-461

Muneer, F., & Khan, F. (2022). Impact of Qard-al-Hasan (interest-free loan) program in reducing multidimensional poverty: an evidence from the southwest Bangladesh. *International Journal of Islamic and Middle Eastern Finance and Management.* DOI: 10.1108/IMEFM-03-2021-0101

Muneeza, A., & Nadwi, S. (2019). The Potential of Application of Technology-Based Innovations for Zakat Administration in India. *International Journal of Zakat*, 4(2), 87–100. DOI: 10.37706/ijaz.v4i2.191

Musa, S. (2024). Islamic Perspectives on Advancing Economy and Trade through AI and Industry Revolution 5.0: Towards Enhanced Prosperity in Malaysia. *International Journal of Contemporary …, March*, 0–30. https://ijci.abrarglobal.com/images/IJCI VOL. 2 ISSUE 1 MARCH 2024.pdf#page=118

Mutmainah, liyatul, Nurwahidin, & Huda, N. (2021). Waqf Blockchain in Indonesia: at A Glance. *Al Awqaf, 14*(1), 31–49.

Noho, H., M. D. (. (2023). Development of Waqf Objects through Public Private Partnership (PPP) as a Means of Infrastructure Development for the Public Interest. *QURU'. Journal of Family Law and Culture*, 1(1), 90–108. DOI: 10.59698/quru.v1i1.116

Qurrata, V. A., Yusida, E., Hussain, N. E., Merlinda, S., Purnamasari, V., & Seprillina, L. (2021). Effectiveness of cash waqf management in improving community welfare: Challenges and opportunities. *Review of Integrative Business & Economics Research*, 10(1), 342–359. http://buscompress.com/uploads/3/4/9/8/34980536/riber_10-s1_29_u20-086_342-359.pdf

Rabbani, M. R., Ali, M. A. M., Rahiman, H. U., Atif, M., Zulfikar, Z., & Naseem, Y. (2021). The response of islamic financial service to the covid-19 pandemic: The open social innovation of the financial system. *Journal of Open Innovation*, 7(1), 85. DOI: 10.3390/joitmc7010085

Raja Adnan, R. A. binti, Abdul Mutalib, M., & Ab Aziz, M. R. (2021). Factors necessary for effective corporate waqf management for Malaysian public healthcare. *ISRA International Journal of Islamic Finance*. DOI: 10.1108/IJIF-11-2019-0178

Ramli, A. M., & Jalil, A. (2015). *Model Perbankan Wakaf Korporat : Analisis Wakaf Selangor Muamalat. 42*(2014), 159–167.

Razak, S. H. A. (2020). Zakat and waqf as instrument of Islamic wealth in poverty alleviation and redistribution: Case of Malaysia. *The International Journal of Sociology and Social Policy*, 40(3–4), 249–266. DOI: 10.1108/IJSSP-11-2018-0208

Rusydiana, A. S. (2024). Alternative Waqf Model for SDG-4 (Quality Education). *The Economic Review of Pesantren*, 2(2). Advance online publication. DOI: 10.58968/erp.v2i2.370

Rusydiana, A. S., & Devi, A. (2014). Analysis of cash waqf fund management in Indonesia: an Analytic Network Process (ANP) method approach. *InInternational Conference on Islamic Finance (AICIF),* Yogyakarta. 1–20.

Saiti, B., Dembele, A., & Bulut, M. (2021). The global cash waqf: A tool against poverty in Muslim countries. *Qualitative Research in Financial Markets*, 13(3), 277–294. DOI: 10.1108/QRFM-05-2020-0085

Sani, A. A., Saidin, A., Abd Samad, K., Bustamam, K. S., Adanan, S. A., & Mamat, S. N. (2022). Modelling Waqf Performance and Governance for Public Universities in Malaysia. *International Journal of Academic Research in Business & Social Sciences*, 12(10), 2743–2754. DOI: 10.6007/IJARBSS/v12-i10/14951

Sano, M. A. A., & Kassim, S. (2021). Waqf governance in the Republic of Guinea: Legal framework, issues, challenges and way forward. *ISRA International Journal of Islamic Finance*, 13(2), 194–210. DOI: 10.1108/IJIF-03-2020-0064

Shahedur Rahaman Chowdhury, M.Md. Shahedur Rahaman Chowdhury. (2011). Economics of Cash WAQF management in Malaysia: A proposed Cash WAQF model for practitioners and future researchers. *African Journal of Business Management*, 5(30), 12155–12163. DOI: 10.5897/AJBM11.1810

Supiyan, M. Y. B. M. (2023). *Essays on the Demand for and Supply of Cash Waqfs in the Muslim World*. https://digital.lib.washington.edu/researchworks/handle/1773/50534%0Ahttps://digital.lib.washington.edu/researchworks/bitstream/handle/1773/50534/MohamedSupiyan_washington_0250E_25487.pdf?sequence=1

Suwandari, Y. D., & Suratkon, A. B. (2022). Investigating The Potential of Cash Waqf for Funding Public Infrastructure Through Public-Private Partnership. *Res Militaris*, 4(12), 1026–1035. https://www.ptonline.com/articles/how-to-get-better-mfi-results

Suyatno, & Pakkana, M. (2024). Management and Development of Productive Waqf for Islamic Boarding Schools in Kampar Regency. *Indonesian Interdisciplinary Journal of Sharia Economics (IIJSE), 7*(1), 395–422.

Syamsuri, S., Putri, E. R., Zein, A. R., & Handayani, R. (2021). Sukuk Waqf for the Development of Islamic Educational Institutions. *ISLAMICONOMIC: Jurnal Ekonomi Islam*, 12(1), 39–52. DOI: 10.32678/ijei.v12i1.267

Tahiri Jouti, A. (2019). An integrated approach for building sustainable Islamic social finance ecosystems. *ISRA International Journal of Islamic Finance*, 11(2), 246–266. DOI: 10.1108/IJIF-10-2018-0118

Uluyol, B., Secinaro, S., Calandra, D., & Lanzalonga, F. (2021). Mapping waqf research: A thirty-year bibliometric analysis. *Journal of Islamic Accounting and Business Research*, 12(5), 748–767. DOI: 10.1108/JIABR-01-2021-0031

Umar, U. H. (2020). The business financial inclusion benefits from an Islamic point of view: A qualitative inquiry. *Islamic Economic Studies*, 28(1), 83–100. DOI: 10.1108/IES-09-2019-0030

Umar, U. H., Baita, A. J., Haron, M. H., & Kabiru, S. H. (2022). The potential of Islamic social finance to alleviate poverty in the era of COVID-19: The moderating effect of ethical orientation. *International Journal of Islamic and Middle Eastern Finance and Management*, 15(2), 255–270. DOI: 10.1108/IMEFM-07-2020-0371

Usman, M., & Ab Rahman, A. (2023). Funding higher education through waqf: A lesson from Malaysia. *International Journal of Ethics and Systems*, 39(1), 107–125. DOI: 10.1108/IJOES-12-2021-0217

Usman, M., & Rahman, A. A. (2021). Financing Higher Education through Waqf in Pakistan: Issues and Challenges. *Jurnal Pengurusan*, 62, 159–172. DOI: 10.17576/pengurusan-2021-62-13

Wang, J., Luo, J., & Zhang, X. (2022). How COVID-19 Has Changed Crowdfunding: Evidence From GoFundMe. *Frontiers of Computer Science*, 4, 1–8. DOI: 10.3389/fcomp.2022.893338

Wresch, W., & Fraser, S. (2011). Persistent Barriers to E-commerce in Developing Countries. *Journal of Global Information Management*, 19(3), 30–44. DOI: 10.4018/jgim.2011070102

Zakariyah, H., Salaudeen, A. O., Othman, A. H. A., & Rosman, R. (2023). The determinants of financial technology adoption amongst Malaysian waqf institutions. *International Journal of Social Economics*, 50(9), 1302–1322. DOI: 10.1108/IJSE-04-2022-0264

Zariff, W., & Yusoff, W. (2024). Concept of Fintech and Financial Inclusion in the Light of Sharī ` ah. *Al-Basirah*, 14(1), 59–77.

Chapter 13
Enhancing Co-Creation in Waqf Institutions With Sharing Information Initiatives in the Digital Era

Fuadah Bte Johari
https://orcid.org/0000-0003-3264-0742
Universiti Sains Islam Malaysia, Malaysia

Hanim Misbah
Universiti Sains Islam Malaysia, Malaysia

Nurul Adilah Bte Hasbullah
Universiti Sains Islam Malaysia, Malaysia

Noraini Yusuff
Northern University of Malaysia, Malaysia

Nor Syahidah Ishak
Northern University of Malaysia, Malaysia

Siti Hajar Salwa Ahmad Musadik
Northern University of Malaysia, Malaysia

Siti Latifah Harun
Northern University of Malaysia, Malaysia

Azuan Ahmad
Universiti Sains Islam Malaysia, Malaysia

ABSTRACT

The digital age is transforming Waqf institutions, enabling new opportunities for cooperation and co-creation. This chapter explores how digital information-sharing initiatives promote co-creation by enhancing information exchange efficiency. By leveraging digital platforms and tools, Waqf institutions can foster collaboration

DOI: 10.4018/979-8-3693-5653-1.ch013

among stakeholders like donors, beneficiaries, and community members. This open information sharing improves engagement, accountability, and trust. The chapter, based on research from 2013-2023, covers digital tools, effective dissemination, and overcoming challenges, with case studies and some examples. It also identifies risks and provides solutions, highlighting future opportunities for Waqf institutions.

INTRODUCTION

In recent years, the concept of waqf co-creation has emerged as a transformative approach within the waqf sector, driven by the principles of collaboration and participation among stakeholders. Waqf institutions, traditionally focused on charitable endowments and community development, are increasingly embracing co-creation to foster innovation, inclusivity, and sustainability in their initiatives.

Waqf co-creation refers to the collaborative and participatory approach taken to develop and innovate waqf assets and initiatives within the waqf sector (Priyadi, Achiria, & Imron, 2023). It involves active engagement from multiple stakeholders, including waqf institutions, donors, beneficiaries, and the broader community. Through co-creation, these stakeholders collectively identify needs, co-develop solutions, and collaboratively implement projects that align with the values and objectives of waqf institutions.

The topic of enhancing waqf co-creation in the digital era is critically important as it represents a transformative shift towards inclusive and participatory governance within waqf institutions. By involving diverse stakeholders—including donors, beneficiaries, and the community—in decision-making and project implementation, co-creation ensures that waqf initiatives are aligned with genuine community needs and aspirations (Johari et al, 2022). This approach fosters transparency, accountability, and trust, enhancing the effectiveness and sustainability of waqf assets and initiatives (Misbah et al, 2022). Moreover, in the digital age, leveraging digital platforms and technologies enables broader stakeholder engagement and facilitates innovative solutions to contemporary socio-economic challenges, thereby positioning waqf institutions as dynamic agents of social change and community development ((Haron, Mat Nor, Johari, Misbah, & Shafii, 2023)

To fully realize the potential of waqf institutions in fostering social good, there is a critical need to embrace advancements in co-creation practices within the digital era. This research aims to articulate and address the following problem: How can waqf institutions leverage technology and cultivate a culture of collaboration and innovation to enhance their impact on community welfare and development? By exploring effective strategies for integrating digital tools and promoting knowledge sharing among stakeholders, this study seeks to illuminate pathways that can propel the waqf sector towards greater relevance, sustainability, and societal impact in the future.

The literature extensively explores various motivations for individuals to engage in waqf donations across different societal segments, encompassing factors such as awareness, promotion, acceptance, knowledge, income, social culture, and trust between the community and waqf institutions (Fauzi et al., 2019; Hadiyati, Gladys, & Iqbal, 2020; Ibrahim et al., 2020; Merlinda et al., 2021; Nasiri et al., 2019). Studies consistently highlight internal and external factors influencing donor behavior, rooted in the Theory of Planned Behavior (TPB), including attitude, subjective norms, perceived behavioral control, and prior conduct, which significantly impact donation intentions and repeat donations (Allah Pitchay et al., 2015; Azizi et al., 2019; Dennis et al., 2018; Osman et al., 2014; Sakti et al., 2016; Yusoff et al., 2018). External factors like trust in the organization, familiarity, and perceived effectiveness of waqf management also play crucial roles in donors' decisions (Kassim et al., 2019). The accountability and trustworthiness demonstrated by waqf managers strongly influence donor decisions, underscoring the importance of transparency and governance in waqf institutions. The collaboration and interdependence among donors, beneficiaries, and mutawallis emerge as pivotal factors in enhancing the effectiveness and sustainability of the waqf ecosystem, promoting community welfare and socio-economic benefits through informed, collaborative initiatives in the digital era.

The main purpose of this study is to investigate and promote the concept of co-creation in waqf institutions through effective information sharing initiatives in the digital era By fostering active participation and collaboration, this study aims to identify digital tools and platform for information sharing and case study, enhancing co-creation through information sharing, challenges and risk, overcoming challenges and solution proposal and future direction and opportunities. The significance of this study lies in its potential to shift waqf management from traditional top-down approaches to a more inclusive and community-driven model, thereby aligning waqf initiatives more closely with community needs and aspirations in the digital age. This approach not only strengthens trust and accountability within waqf institutions but also promotes greater socio-economic impact and lasting benefits for the community at large.

AN OVERVIEW OF WAQF

Definition of Waqf and the Significance of Waqf in Islamic Philanthropy

Waqf in Arabic, also known as "al-Awqaf" in plural, refers to the Islamic practice of endowing and dedicating property or a sum of money for religious, charitable, or community purposes (Laluddin, Haneef, Mohammad, & Rahman, 2021). The assets or funds donated as waqf are then managed and administered by waqf institutions for the benefit of the community. This perpetual endowment is considered a form of charitable giving in Islam and plays a crucial role in supporting various social, educational, and welfare activities. Waqf assets are intended to generate ongoing benefits and contribute to the betterment of society.

Waqf holds significant importance in Islamic philanthropy for several reasons. Firstly, it is a sustainable means of supporting charitable and community initiatives. Unlike traditional forms of charity that involve one-time donations, waqf assets generate ongoing benefits (Abdullah, 2018), ensuring continuous support for social, educational, and welfare activities. Secondly, the concept of waqf promotes inclusivity and social welfare by providing resources for the entire community (Abu Seman, Jamil, & Che Mohd Hashim, 2021) . This aligns with the principles of Islamic philanthropy, which emphasize the well-being of all members of society, particularly those in need. Moreover, waqf institutions play a vital role in addressing long-term societal challenges (Kamaruzaman & Ishak, 2023). By pooling resources and engaging in co-creation, these institutions can develop innovative solutions and initiatives that address persistent social issues, thereby contributing to the overall betterment of society. The collaborative nature of waqf institutions allows for the active involvement of stakeholders, fostering transparency and accountability in the management and distribution of waqf assets. This serves to build trust within the community and ensures that the resources are utilized in accordance with the values and objectives of Islamic philanthropy.

Co-Creation and Its Impact on Waqf Institutions

Co-creation in waqf institutions has a significant impact on their overall effectiveness and relevance in serving the community (Priyadi et al., 2023). By embracing a collaborative approach, waqf institutions can harness the collective wisdom and expertise of multiple stakeholders, leading to more inclusive and innovative solutions to societal challenges. One of the key impacts of co-creation is the enhanced responsiveness of waqf institutions to the evolving needs of the community. Through active engagement with beneficiaries, donors, and other stakeholders, these institutions can gain a deeper understanding of the specific needs and aspirations of the community, allowing them to tailor their initiatives and programs more effectively.

Furthermore, co-creation fosters a sense of ownership (Harwood & Garry, 2014) and empowerment among the community members. When stakeholders are involved in the decision-making processes and the development of initiatives, they are more likely to feel a sense of ownership and commitment to the success of the institution's endeavors. Moreover, the collaborative nature of co-creation promotes transparency and accountability (Ganapathy, Sippy, Sinha, & Adarkar, 2022) within institutions. When various stakeholders are involved in the planning and implementation of initiatives, there is greater scrutiny and oversight, leading to improved governance and management of waqf assets. Additionally, co-creation enhances the sustainability of institutions (Edelmann & Virkar, 2023) by encouraging continuous innovation and adaptation. By working closely with the community and other stakeholders, waqf institutions can identify new opportunities, leverage emerging technologies, and develop novel approaches to address longstanding societal challenges. Overall, co-creation transforms waqf institutions into dynamic and responsive entities that are deeply connected to the community they serve. As they continue to embrace this collaborative approach, waqf institutions are better positioned to fulfill their role as drivers of positive change and social welfare within the Islamic philanthropic framework.

The Digital Era and Its Impact on Waqf Institutions

The digital era has brought about significant changes in the way waqf institutions operate and engage with their stakeholders (Abdullah, 2018). The integration of digital technologies has not only transformed the internal processes of waqf institutions but has also reshaped interaction and engagement with donors, beneficiaries, and the community at large (Wildana & Imamia, 2022). With the advent of the internet and digital platforms, waqf institutions now have the opportunity to reach a wider audience and communicate more effectively. This has allowed them to raise awareness about their mission and projects, attract more donors, and establish stronger relationships with stakeholders. It has also facilitated the collection and management of waqf data, enabling more efficient tracking and evaluation of waqf assets and initiatives (Omar & Sanyinna, 2018)).

To recap, the digital era presents both opportunities and challenges for waqf institutions. Embracing digital technologies allows these institutions to enhance their efficiency, expand their reach, and foster collaboration, while also ensuring transparency, accountability, and adaptability in an increasingly interconnected world (Nahar, 2018)

. As waqf institutions continue to navigate the digital landscape, the principles of co-creation will be essential in leveraging technological advancements to drive positive change and sustainable impact within the waqf sector (Wildana & Imamia, 2022)

. Thus, this chapter will discuss further the role of information sharing in fostering collaboration and innovation, digital tool and platforms for information sharing, strategies for effective information dissemination, enhancing co-creation through information sharing, challenge, and risks, overcoming challenges and solution and future directions and opportunities.

THE ROLE OF INFORMATION SHARING IN FOSTERING COLLABORATION AND INNOVATION: A REVIEW (DR ADILAH)

Information sharing is crucial for fostering collaboration and innovation (Atkočiūnienė & Siudikienė, 2019; Panahifar, Byrne, Salam, & Heavey, 2018) in a variety of circumstances. It facilitates individuals and teams to exchange their ideas, knowledge, and expertise, resulting in a deeper understanding of complicated challenges and the development of innovative solutions (Kettunen, Teppola, & Partanen, 2019; Nonaka & Takeuchi, 1995). Effective information sharing also fosters a culture of transparency and trust, removes obstacles, encourages multidisciplinary approaches, and combines multiple viewpoints. It also provides access to broader resources, allowing users to obtain new ideas and challenge established assumptions (Baran & Woznyj, 2021). Sharing information not only helps stakeholders align around common goals, but it also helps find new opportunities and areas for development. Organizations may preserve a competitive advantage and adjust quickly to changes by remaining up to date on market trends, consumer needs, and technological improvements (Garrido-Moreno, Martín-Rojas, & García-Morales, 2024; Farida & Setiawan, 2022). This leads to the creation of new products, services, and procedures, which improves the organization's problem-solving abilities and innovation.

The digital revolution has fundamentally altered how information is exchanged and accessed, presenting both enormous benefits and considerable obstacles (Egodawele et al., 2022). It has democratized knowledge, enabled rapid and global distribution while broke down historical obstacles to information flow. However, the ease of access has made it impossible to distinguish true information from the constant influx of data, which is exacerbated by issues of misinformation, privacy concerns, and data security (Kumar & Shah, 2018). Individuals can become overwhelmed by the amount of information available, making it difficult to digest and use efficiently.

To navigate this landscape, information must be critically evaluated and verified. To maintain information accuracy, people must evaluate sources and adhere to tight verification processes (Svensson, 2015; Vaidya, 2012). Addressing the difficulties of the digital age entails combining the benefits of technology developments in information exchange with strong safeguards for accuracy, dependability, and confidentiality. Potential ways for addressing these difficulties include improving digital literacy, establishing verification tools, and cultivating a critical thinking culture (Trattner et al., 2021)

The digital era provides unprecedented prospects for global connectivity and collaboration, but it also requires everyone involved to take on more responsibility and participate more actively. By striking the appropriate balance between benefits and problems, we may fully exploit the digital era's potential to extend our collective knowledge and secure the trustworthiness of shared information.

Importance of Transparency and Accountability in Waqf Management

Transparency and accountability are critical in managing waqf assets, ensuring that they are handled appropriately and in line with the waqf's original objectives. These principles not only protect beneficiary interests, but they also build stakeholder trust by providing clear insights into waqf resource management and strategic usage. The internet age has improved the ability to transmit information, providing waqf organizations with new chances to exhibit transparency and engage more broadly with donors and the public, potentially increasing their reach and influence (Welch, Hinnant, & Moon, 2004).

However, the adoption of digital technologies raises concerns, notably about maintaining transparency and accountability (Matheus, Jansen, & Janowski, 2021). Algorithms and artificial intelligence can complicate decision-making processes, creating questions about accountability for technology-driven results. Furthermore, the rapid expansion of digital technologies necessitates continued attention to guarantee that these fundamental principles are not jeopardized.

Addressing these difficulties demands a collaborative approach to developing principles and rules that promote digital transparency and accountability in waqf management. By implementing such frameworks, waqf institutions can efficiently traverse the digital terrain, leveraging technology to improve governance while adhering to their ethical responsibilities. Finally, a balanced strategy is required to use digital innovations while guaranteeing transparent and accountable administration of waqf assets (Ismail, 2020), so retaining stakeholder trust and effectively serving the greater good.

RESEARCH METHODOLOGY

This chapter is based on the on-going academic research work and content analysis to get an overview of the enhancing co-creation in waqf institutions: sharing information initiatives in digital era. Therefore, the chapter is conceptual in nature and analytical method is being used to give account the role of information sharing, digital tools and platforms for information sharing, strategies for effective information dissemination, enhancing waqf co-creation through information sharing, challenge, and risk, overcoming challenges and solution and future direction and opportunities. Data and information are collected through libraries, recognized journals both local and international. In other words, it is conceptual analysis in which taken into consideration majorly previous research between year 2013 and 2023 with a few exceptions due to their necessity.

RESULTS AND DISCUSSION

Digital Tools and Platforms for Information Sharing and Case study

Digital tools and platforms for information sharing encompass a wide range of technologies and services designed to facilitate the exchange of data, knowledge, and ideas among individuals, organizations, and communities. These tools leverage the power of the internet and digital technology to overcome geographical barriers and enable seamless communication and collaboration.

Digital tools serve as platforms for information sharing by providing users with digital environments where they can create, exchange, and consume information. These platforms leverage technology to facilitate communication, collaboration, and knowledge dissemination across various contexts. Digital tools enable users to generate various types of content, including text, images, videos, and multimedia presentations. Content creation platforms such as word processors, graphic design software, and video editing tools empower individuals and organizations to produce high-quality content that can be shared online.

Social media platforms are one example of digital tools which serve as digital hubs for information sharing, allowing users to post updates, share links, photos, and videos, and engage with others through likes, comments, and shares. These platforms facilitate real-time communication and enable content to reach a broad audience quickly.

Advanced social media tools have transformed communication, content sharing, interaction, and collaboration globally (Ahmed, Ahmad, Ahmad and Zakaria, 2019). Social media platforms are now vital for knowledge sharing and communication in both personal and organizational contexts. This evolution has revolutionized how people exchange knowledge, communicate, and collaborate, particularly in workplace discussions. Social media encompasses various forms, including Social Networking (SNS) platforms, microblogs, image and video-sharing apps, and collaborative platforms. These tools serve as essential channels for connecting individuals with similar interests and facilitating the exchange of ideas.

In today's era, social media platforms have expanded their utility beyond personal use and are increasingly embraced by organizations as tools for sharing knowledge and facilitating communication. This adoption spans various sectors, with public institutions exploring how social media can enhance citizen awareness and government operations, while businesses utilize it to foster knowledge exchange and engage customers across different areas.

Similarly, higher education institutions leverage social media to stimulate learning initiatives (Balakrishnan and Gan, 2016, Kulakli and Mahony, 2014), and healthcare organizations employ internal social media tools to streamline the flow of work-related information within and between teams. Furthermore, since the 2010 Haiti earthquake, social media has become an essential channel for knowledge sharing within disaster management contexts. Overall, the profound impact of social media on our daily lives, work environments, learning methods, and social interactions is evident, enabling a seamless and continuous exchange of knowledge in the virtual realm.

Case Studies of Successful Information Sharing Initiatives in Waqf Institutions

Waqf institutions, which manage and administer charitable endowments in the Islamic world, have increasingly recognized the importance of leveraging digital tools and platforms for information sharing to enhance transparency, efficiency, and impact. Here are a few case studies on successful information sharing initiatives in Waqf institutions:

i. Yayasan Waqaf Malaysia

Yayasan Waqaf Malaysia (YWM) is a government-linked foundation in Malaysia dedicated to the development and management of Waqf properties and assets. It was established to promote the concept of Waqf and utilize Waqf assets for the benefit of society. YWM created an official website which consists of broadening knowledge on waqf for society. The platform provides stakeholders with access to comprehensive information about Waqf projects, funds, and beneficiaries, fostering transparency and engagement. By leveraging digital technology for information sharing and fundraising, YWM has mobilized resources more effectively to support charitable projects and initiatives aligned with its mission (Yayasan Waqaf Malaysia, 2021). Other digital tools linked with YWM's official website are YWM Facebook, YWM Instagram, YWM Youtube and YWM Twitter.

ii. Islamic Development Bank (IsDB) Waqf Fund Platform

IsDB launched the Waqf Fund Platform to promote innovative Waqf-based financing solutions for sustainable development projects. The platform serves as a hub for sharing knowledge, best practices, and resources related to Waqf finance and development projects. By facilitating information sharing among Waqf institutions, policymakers, and stakeholders, the platform has contributed to the development and implementation of impactful Waqf initiatives worldwide (Islamic Development Bank, 2023).

□ENHANCING CO-CREATION THROUGH INFORMATION SHARING

The aim of a Waqf institution is to improve how efficiently and effectively Waqf funds are collected and distributed to help those in need. Promoting a culture of co-creation through sharing information is suggested as a way to fill gaps in the organization's processes. Originating from services marketing theory, the concept of value co-creation emphasizes the crucial role of customer involvement in the design, creation, and delivery of services (Vargo and Lusch, 2004). Co-creation involves bringing together different groups, like scholars, charities, government agencies, communities, and technology experts, to work together on enhancing how waqf funds are managed and distributed. The objective is to use the combined knowledge and resources of these groups to make Waqf initiatives more impactful and sustainable.

Information sharing in Waqf co-creation can be done in various ways, such as through conferences, seminars, and online forums. Stakeholders exchange knowledge, best practices, and insights on Waqf collection, calculation, and distribution methodologies. They discuss the latest research findings, regulatory developments, and case studies related to Waqf administration and utilization. Through information sharing and experiences, other parties gained a thorough understanding of the various needs and challenges encountered by Waqf recipients. They also identified opportunities to improve Waqf distribution for better societal outcomes.

In terms of public engagement, Waqf co-creation with the public could be achieved by inviting or creating events related to public opinion, such as sharing information on social media. Encouraging the public to share their opinions regarding enhancing Waqf development and sustainability will facilitate improved Waqf performance.

Examples of Collaborative Projects and Initiatives Enabled by Information Sharing

In the business field, numerous collaborative projects have been undertaken, successfully creating a new paradigm in the business platform. This kind of collaboration could be achieved through various methods, such as open-source software development, crowdsourced mapping, citizen science, global health initiatives, educational resources, as well as policy development. For instance, Toyota had successfully created and implemented a collaborative approach through information sharing with their stakeholders such as suppliers, dealers, and other stakeholders to share information, identify opportunities for efficiency gains, and drive innovation across its global operations. The same goes for Petronas and Kumpulan Wang Persaraan Malaysia (KWAP) who collaborates with various stakeholders, including government agencies, industry partners, local communities, and NGOs, to develop and operate its oil and gas projects responsibly and with positive social impacts for KWAP. KWAP promotes sustainable and responsible investing by collaborating with organizations such as the Principles for Responsible Investment (PRI) and the Malaysian Sustainable Finance Initiative (MSFI) to exchange information, share best practices, and allocate resources effectively.

Impact of Co-Creation on the Sustainability and Effectiveness of Waqf Activities

A recent study in education reported that students become more active and positive in the learning process when collaborating with other students of different grades (Kasumi & Xhemaili, 2023). Previous collaborations in philanthropy have provided substantial evidence that working together strategically enhances the effectiveness and efficiency of charitable activities in the modern era (Selsky & Parker 2005). This suggests that Waqf co-creation has the potential to achieve social goals within a community where everyone is dedicated to giving and learning together in deep and meaningful ways, driving towards extraordinary results.

Subsequently, collaborative learning and the exchange of knowledge will undoubtedly aid in the development of Waqf institutions. Any development process requires full commitment from all parties involved. Therefore, to maximize the development and sustainability of Waqf institutions, information sharing, and knowledge transfer must be fully supported and enforced. Without strong enforcement, these efforts will not be completely successful.

CHALLENGES AND RISKS

The challenges and risks associated with information sharing in waqf institutions must be recognized and dealt with to enhance co-creation and achieve effective collaboration (Laallam et al., 2020). Through the utilization of digital technology, waqf institutions can surmount these challenges and risks by implementing strong data protection measures, establishing secure communication channels, and ensuring transparency in information management and sharing (Sulaiman & Jamil, 2014). This will foster trust among stakeholders and facilitate improved decision-making processes within waqf institutions. Moreover, the adoption of a shariah-based performance assessment system can bolster transparency and accountability in waqf institutions (Sulaiman & Jamil, 2014). The amalgamation of information security governance and shariah principles can significantly contribute to the effective management and allocation of zakat funds, ensuring enhanced reporting transparency and fostering greater trust within the Islamic community. By leveraging digital technology and embracing a shariah-based performance measurement system, waqf institutions can address information sharing challenges and risks, promote co-creation, and ultimately play a role in the long-term wealth generation of society (Fachrurrazy et al., 2022).

Digital Literacy and Access Disparity

In addition to the aforementioned strategies, it is imperative for individuals engaged in waqf institutions to cultivate digital literacy. Proficiency in utilizing digital tools and platforms is indispensable in the contemporary digital age. By enhancing digital literacy, stakeholders can adeptly navigate and leverage digital technologies for information sharing, governance, and financial management within waqf institutions (Shaikh et al., 2017). This will streamline processes and ensure secure and accurate dissemination of information. Furthermore, embracing digital literacy can empower stakeholders to make well-informed decisions and adapt to the evolving digital landscape, ultimately enhancing the overall effectiveness and co-creation within waqf institutions. Alongside developing digital literacy, prioritizing continuous learning and adaptation in the digital epoch is crucial for waqf institutions (Wildana & Imamia, 2022) (Antoniuk & Zasiadivko, 2023).

Moreover, nurturing a culture of perpetual enhancement and innovation within waqf institutions is of utmost importance. This can be accomplished by fostering open dialogue and knowledge exchange among stakeholders, cultivating a culture of continuous learning and adaptation to new technologies. By embracing an innovative culture, waqf institutions can lead the way in leveraging digital tools and platforms for co-creation and effective collaboration, thereby contributing to the advancement of their mission and the enduring prosperity of society (Salman et al., 2022). Through the utilization of advanced technologies such as blockchain, smart contracts, and secure databases, waqf institutions can enrich their information sharing endeavors (Wildana & Imamia, 2022).

To truly enhance co-creation in waqf institutions, emphasis should not only be placed on technological advancements but also on the human element of collaboration. Cultivating robust relationships and fostering trust among stakeholders through transparent communication, active involvement, and shared values is fundamental in establishing an environment conducive to co-creation. This human-centric approach, coupled with resilient digital infrastructure and governance, will bolster the groundwork for sustainable co-creation and information sharing in waqf institutions.

Access disparity is a notable concern that requires attention to guarantee that all parties involved in waqf institutions can take advantage of the progressions in digital technology. It is essential to acknowledge that not every individual may possess uniform access to digital resources and platforms, potentially leading to a disparity in information exchange and cooperation (Meyers et al., 2013). Measures need to be taken to bridge this access rift through strategies like providing education and materials to enhance digital literacy capabilities, ensuring affordable and widespread internet connectivity, and advocating for inclusivity in technological advancement and application (Resta et al., 2018) (Warschauer & Xu, 2018). Furthermore, it is imperative for waqf institutions to establish precise guidelines and benchmarks for information exchange in the digital age, encompassing the delineation of protocols for data confidentiality and protection, guaranteeing ethical technology utilization, and setting up frameworks for quality control and answerability.

By implementing these actions, waqf institutions can establish an inclusive and ethical digital sphere that fosters effective collaboration and information exchange among stakeholders while upholding the ethics and doctrines of waqf. Through embracing technology and digital resolutions, waqf institutions can effectively surmount internal obstacles and enhance cooperation with other establishments (Wildana & Imamia, 2022). Moreover, harnessing emerging technologies like blockchain and cryptocurrency can significantly boost the transparency and effectiveness of waqf operations.

To alleviate access inequality, waqf institutions should contemplate launching initiatives aimed at providing digital access and literacy to all involved parties. This could involve programs to distribute gadgets such as smartphones or tablets to those lacking access, along with offering educational schemes to ensure everyone is equipped with essential digital competencies. By tackling access inequality, waqf institutions can shape a more inclusive and cooperative environment, enabling all stakeholders to actively engage in co-creation and information sharing ventures (Abdullah, 2019) (Aldeen, 2021).

Trust and Security Concern

Trust is the cornerstone of any successful institution, and waqf institutions are no exception. Fostering trust among stakeholders is crucial for creating a collaborative and transparent environment that facilitates effective co-creation and information sharing. One way to cultivate trust is through open and honest communication. When stakeholders feel that their voices are heard and their concerns are addressed, they are more likely to trust the institution and actively engage in co-creation efforts (Shukor et al., 2018).

Moreover, building trust also entails promoting inclusivity and diversity within the institution. By embracing different perspectives, backgrounds, and experiences, waqf institutions can demonstrate their commitment to valuing and respecting all stakeholders. Creating an inclusive environment where every voice is valued and every individual feels welcomed can significantly contribute to building trust and enhancing collaboration (Abdullah, 2019).

While it is crucial to focus on technological advancements and creating an inclusive environment, it is equally important to address security concerns in the digital era. Waqf institutions must prioritize the safeguarding of sensitive information and data privacy to ensure the trust and confidence of their stakeholders (Alhalafi & Veeraraghavan, 2021). Implementing robust security measures such as data encryption, multi-factor authentication, and regular security audits can help protect the integrity and privacy of the information shared within the institution. Additionally, establishing clear protocols for data privacy and security, aligned with shariah principles, will contribute to building trust and confidence among stakeholders (Alharbi et al., 2021)

Moreover, educating staff on identifying and responding to cyber threats, along with fostering a culture of vigilance and responsibility in managing digital data, will enhance the overall security stance of the institution. By giving importance to security protocols while also embracing innovation and cooperation, waqf institutions can promote a secure environment for collaborative creation and information exchange in the digital age (Ayub, 2022) (Salman et al., 2022). To promote co-creation and facilitate information sharing in waqf institutions during the digital era, it is vital to prioritize the advancement of technological infrastructure and digital capabilities (Wildana & Imamia, 2022).

Resistance of Changes and Traditional Mindset

In addition to resisting changes that may jeopardize data security, waqf institutions must embrace a conventional mindset that aligns with the fundamental principles of the institution. This traditional approach involves upholding the values and ethical standards that have been fundamental to waqf practices for centuries. By amalgamating modern technological progress with traditional values, waqf institutions can ensure that the incorporation of new technologies and information sharing endeavors is in harmony with the principles of waqf. This necessitates a delicate equilibrium between innovation and adherence to the core values of the institution (Ayub, 2018).

By fostering a culture of transparency and accountability within waqf institutions, stakeholders can be confident that the information shared is precise, trustworthy, and in accordance with the principles of waqf and Shariah (Wildana & Imamia, 2022).

Furthermore, upholding a traditional mindset involves giving priority to human interaction and personal relationships as essential elements of co-creation and information exchange. While digital technology facilitates communication and cooperation, it is crucial not to underestimate the importance of face-to-face interactions and the human aspect in waqf initiatives.

Financial Constraint and Resources Limitations

Financial limitations can present a significant obstacle to the implementation of modern technological solutions and information sharing efforts in waqf institutions. Scarce financial resources might hinder the capacity to invest in advanced cybersecurity measures, training schemes, and the integration of new technologies. Consequently, waqf institutions may encounter challenges in effectively strengthening their defenses against cyber threats and upholding robust data security (Priyadi et al., 2022). To tackle this issue, collaborations and partnerships with other institutions, organizations, and stakeholders can be pursued (Wildana & Imamia, 2022). Through collaboration and resource sharing, waqf institutions can collectively address financial constraints and deploy technological solutions that enhance co-creation and information sharing.

Given financial restrictions, it is crucial for waqf institutions to explore cost-effective cybersecurity solutions and allocate investments based on the most critical security requirements. This might involve conducting a comprehensive evaluation of existing cybersecurity capabilities and pinpointing key areas that demand immediate attention and enhancement (Wildana & Imamia, 2022) (Salman et al., 2022).

Furthermore, the collaboration with organizations or entities specializing in the provision of cost-effective cybersecurity solutions and services can be advantageous for enhancing data protection and mitigating threats. Engaging with such partners enables waqf institutions to access expertise and resources that may otherwise be unattainable due to financial constraints. Additionally, optimizing the utilization of current security tools and incorporating open-source solutions can help alleviate some of the financial challenges associated with improving cybersecurity measures. (Ismail & Mohsin, 2013)(Ayub, 2018)

Despite financial limitations, waqf institutions have the opportunity to seek out alternative sources of funding, such as grants, sponsorships, or partnerships with philanthropic organizations that prioritize investments in cybersecurity and data protection. Through actively pursuing external support and financial opportunities, waqf institutions can surmount financial barriers and make significant progress in fortifying their cybersecurity stance.

□OVERCOMING CHALLENGES AND SOLUTION PROPOSAL

Sharing information initiatives in enhancing co - creation among waqf stakeholder seen an important effort to become more accessible and efficient. However, there are certain issues and problem as have been discussed in the previous section including digital literacy and access disparity, trust and security concern, resistance of changes and traditional mindset and financial constraint and resources limitations. In addressing these issues, several solutions proposed to overcome the challenges. This chapter explores critical aspects of co creation in waqf institutions focusing on addressing concerns regarding privacy, security, and data integrity, strategies for managing misinformation and maintaining trust and legal and regulatory considerations in information sharing within Waqf institutions.

Addressing Concerns Regarding Privacy, Security, and Data Integrity

In addressing concerns regarding privacy, security, and data integrity in sharing information in enhancing waqf co-creation. Waqf institution manage confidential and sensitive personal dan waqf financial data. Some of the data considered to be sensitive personal data. On the other hand, waqf institution should only request and collect the data related to the waqf transactions and avoid any unnecessary information to reduce the risk of data security and protection. Any unnecessary details from the donor beyond what is required by the waqf institutions will expose to the risk of data privacy and data integrity. Data anonymization could be an important approach to protect donors' identities that involves removing personally identifiable information (PII) from dataset. Waqf institutions can use aggregated data to show the important information and general patterns without disclosing the details if the donors or beneficiaries.

Strategies for Managing Misinformation and Maintaining Trust

To ensure all the strategies practically work, waqf institutions could follow several approaches. Waf institution can conduct a privacy impact assessment for each waqf transaction or waqf project. In digital era, managing misinformation can undermine trust in waqf institution and prevent any co-creation element. Therefore, establish internal data analysis team to verify any information before dissemination and also remove any false information which may appear in the system.

Trust also played an important element in having an effective co-creation in waqf institutions. Waqf stakeholder engagement in decision making processes will keep open lines of communication. Besides that, waqf institution should share detailed and accurate information about waqf projects, financial reports and waqf impacts to build and maintain the trust among waqf stakeholder. Always seeking feedback from waqf stakeholder and responsiveness to all complaints and suggestions.

□Strategies for Effective Information Dissemination

In the advancement of technologies, Waqf co creation play an important role in strategizing the information dissemination. These includes content creation, multimedia content to convey information and targeting the right audience. These strategies in line with factors that contribute to the successful of the waqf information management system. Janom et al (2019) states that visibility, image, result demostrability and compatibility are among the vital elements to disseminate information effectively to targeted audience.

First, content creation strategies for engaging stakeholders. Variety of social media platform such as facebook, tik tok, Instagram, and tweeter should be used by waqf entity for content creation in attracting stakeholders in waqf co-create (Waters et al, (2009).

Second, utilizing multimedia content (videos, infographics, etc.) to convey information effectively (Irdale, S., Heinze, A., & Williams, M.J.,2024). The utilization of multimedia content, including videos, infographics, and other forms of digital media, has been increasingly popular among various organizations, including waqf institutions, to convey information effectively to their audiences. This trend is likely to continue as digital communication channels become more prevalent and accessible . However, the waqf co-creation or content is still lacking as multimedia content due less attractive. Therefore, academicians and waqf stakeholders should grab this opportunity to create more innovative waqf information and platform in social media content so that community engagement to the real waqf program could be improved.

Third, targeting diverse audiences and addressing their information needs. For example, initiatives such as creating friendly platforms to increase stakeholders' participation including beneficiaries, donors, scholars, community leaders, and relevant government agencies. Hassan and Siraj (2016) investigates the role of stakeholder engagement in waqf development in Bangladesh and discusses the challenges and opportunities associated with it. Lack of stakeholders' engagement especially administrative of waqf and mutawalli in disseminating waqf information to donors and society leads to many negative words towards waqf co creation. Therefore, waqf co-creation initiatives targeting diverse audiences play a crucial role in fostering collaboration, inclusivity, and community empowerment, ultimately enhancing the effectiveness and sustainability of waqf projects.

Legal and Regulatory Considerations in Information Sharing Within Waqf Institutions

In ensuring the privacy and confidential of the data, it is advised for all waqf institution to follow The Personal Data Protection Code of Practice in managing sensitive data under the Personal Data Protection Act 2010 (PDPA 2010). PDPA 2010 regulate the processing of personal data in commercial transaction and to provide for matters connected therewith and incidental thereto (Malaysia, P. D. P. (2017). PDPA 2010 also developed to as a protection to the matter related to personal information from being misused and manipulated (Yusoff, Z.M, 2011). This approach protects the interest of donors, beneficiaries and other waqf stakeholders. A special guideline and regulation related to sharing information in waqf institutions should be set by the waqf authorities and State Islamic Religius Council to ensure compliance and accountability.

By implementing robust strategies in this areas, waqf institution can leverage and increase collaboration and waqf co creation among stakeholders. Enhancing co creation in waqf institutions requires a multifaceted approach addressing privacy, security, data integrity, misinformation, trust and legal compliance.

FUTURE DIRECTIONS AND OPPORTUNITIES

The evolution of waqf has seen a transformative journey from its traditional roots to the digital era. As we navigate the complexities of the 21st century, the concept of digital waqf emerges as a pivotal innovation, harnessing modern technology to enhance its efficacy and reach. This section explores the future directions and opportunities of digital waqf, delving into how advancements in technology can revolutionize the management, transparency, and impact of waqf assets. By integrating blockchain, artificial intelligence, and other digital tools, digital waqf holds the potential to address contemporary challenges and foster sustainable development in Muslim communities worldwide.

Blockchain Technology

Blockchain technology is revolutionizing the management of Waqf assets by providing a decentralized and transparent ledger system. This technology ensures secure and immutable records of transactions, which enhances trust and accountability (Hassan & Ali, 2020). The implementation of blockchain can streamline the registration of Waqf properties, tracking donations, and disbursements, thereby minimizing the risks of fraud and mismanagement (Khan et al., 2021).

Fintech Technology

Research on the integration of financial technology (fintech) into waqf highlights its potential to enhance efficiency, transparency, and accessibility in waqf management and reporting. Kamaruddin *et al* (2022, 2023) explores fintech applications in waqf, emphasizing blockchain technology's role in creating a more transparent and efficient waqf market. The paper examines the challenges and prospects of waqf reporting practices in Malaysia, advocating for the adoption of fintech solutions to improve reporting accuracy and stakeholder trust.

Zaki Ahmad et al (2023) discusses the broader implications of fintech in Islamic finance, suggesting that fintech innovations can address current inefficiencies and enhance the overall impact of waqf institutions. These studies collectively underscore the transformative potential of fintech in modernizing waqf practices and expanding their socioeconomic contributions.

Artificial Intelligence

Artificial Intelligence (AI) is another pivotal trend influencing Waqf institutions. AI can optimize asset management by predicting maintenance needs, market trends, and investment opportunities (Siddiqi & Nisar, 2019). Moreover, AI-driven data analytics can help in identifying the most impactful areas for Waqf investments, ensuring that the resources are utilized in the most efficient manner (Iqbal & Mirakhor, 2021).

Internet of Things

The Internet of Things (IoT) connects physical devices to the internet, enabling real-time monitoring and management of Waqf assets. IoT devices can be used to oversee the condition of Waqf properties, ensuring timely maintenance and repairs (Ahmed et al., 2020). This technology enhances the ability of Waqf administrators to maintain the value and functionality of endowment assets, thereby ensuring their long-term sustainability.

Big Data Analytics

Big Data Analytics allows Waqf institutions to process vast amounts of data to gain insights into donor behaviors, asset performance, and beneficiary needs (Rahman & Zainuddin, 2021). By leveraging big data, Waqf institutions can make data-driven decisions that enhance their operational efficiency and impact.

Implications for Waqf Institutions

The integration of those technologies into Waqf institutions marks a significant shift in how these traditional Islamic endowments are managed and operated. This section delves into the profound implications of these technologies, examining how they can revolutionize the operational frameworks, improve stakeholder engagement, and align Waqf practices with modern governance standards.

Enhanced Transparency and Accountability

The integration of digital technologies, particularly blockchain, significantly enhances the transparency and accountability of Waqf institutions. Donors and stakeholders can track the utilization of funds and assets in real-time, fostering trust and encouraging more donations (Khan et al., 2021).

Improved Operational Efficiency

AI and Big Data Analytics enable Waqf institutions to optimize their operations. Predictive analytics can forecast maintenance needs, and investment analytics can identify profitable opportunities, ensuring that Waqf assets are managed effectively and sustainably (Siddiqi & Nisar, 2019).

Increased Engagement and Outreach

Digital platforms facilitate greater engagement with donors and beneficiaries. Online portals and mobile applications can simplify the donation process, provide updates on Waqf projects, and allow beneficiaries to apply for support more easily (Ahmed et al., 2020).

Sustainable Development

The strategic use of digital technologies can align Waqf initiatives with broader sustainable development goals. For instance, IoT-enabled monitoring can ensure that Waqf properties are environmentally sustainable, while AI-driven investments can focus on social impact projects (Iqbal & Mirakhor, 2021).

Potential for Blockchain Technology and Smart Contracts in Enhancing Transparency and Accountability

Blockchain technology and smart contracts are revolutionizing various sectors, including the management of Islamic endowments, known as Waqf. These digital innovations offer unprecedented levels of transparency and accountability, addressing long-standing challenges in the administration of Waqf assets. This section explores the potential of blockchain and smart contracts in enhancing transparency and accountability within Waqf institutions.

Transparency

Blockchain's transparency is one of its most significant advantages for Waqf institutions. All transactions recorded on a blockchain are visible to all participants, which means that donors and stakeholders can track the flow of funds and the management of assets in real-time (Hassan & Ali, 2020). This level of visibility can help build trust and confidence among donors, encouraging more contributions to Waqf projects.

Security

The security features of blockchain technology are crucial in preventing fraud and unauthorized alterations. Each transaction is encrypted and linked to the previous one, forming a chain that is virtually tamper-proof (Crosby et al., 2016). For Waqf institutions, this ensures that records of donations and asset transactions are protected against corruption and manipulation.

Automation and Efficiency

Smart contracts can automate various administrative tasks within Waqf institutions, such as disbursing funds to beneficiaries or paying for asset maintenance. This automation reduces the need for manual intervention, thus minimizing human error and operational costs (Khan et al., 2021).

Conditional Disbursements

One of the key benefits of smart contracts is their ability to enforce conditional disbursements. For instance, funds can be programmed to be released only when specific criteria are met, such as completion of a project milestone or verification of beneficiary eligibility (Buterin, 2014). This ensures that Waqf funds are used appropriately and efficiently, enhancing accountability.

Case Studies and Applications of Blockchain in Waqf

There are several case studies from around the world illustrate the application of blockchain technology in the Waqf process. These studies highlight how blockchain can enhance transparency, security, and efficiency in managing Waqf assets. By providing immutable records and streamlined processes, blockchain technology significantly improves trust and accountability in Waqf institutions.

Case Study: Waqf Property Management

In one implementation, blockchain and smart contracts were used to manage Waqf properties in Malaysia. The blockchain provided a transparent record of property transactions, while smart contracts automated rent collection and maintenance payments (Hassan et al., 2020). This system improved transparency for stakeholders and reduced administrative overhead.

The paper in Mohsin *et al* (2019) explores the innovative application of blockchain technology to enhance waqf management through crowdfunding. By leveraging the transparency, security, and efficiency of blockchain, the proposed model aims to create a dynamic waqf market that addresses contemporary challenges in waqf administration. The integration of crowdfunding allows for broader participation and funding opportunities, potentially leading to a more sustainable and impactful waqf system that benefits communities. This modern approach seeks to revitalize the traditional waqf system, making it more relevant and effective in today's digital age.

Case Study: World Food Program

Globally, blockchain is being explored for its potential to streamline charitable donations and asset management in various sectors. For example, the World Food Program has used blockchain to distribute aid more efficiently, demonstrating how the technology can enhance transparency and accountability in humanitarian efforts (WFP, 2017).

Opportunities for International Collaboration and Knowledge Exchange in Waqf Management

The landscape of Waqf management presents numerous opportunities for international collaboration and knowledge exchange, facilitating the sharing of best practices, innovations, and resources among Waqf institutions worldwide. This section explores the potential avenues for collaboration and exchange, emphasizing the benefits of cross-border partnerships in advancing Waqf management practices.

Cross-Border Research Collaborations

Collaborative research initiatives between Waqf institutions and academic institutions across different countries can contribute significantly to the development of innovative solutions and strategies in Waqf management. By pooling expertise and resources, researchers can address common challenges, explore new methodologies, and generate actionable insights to enhance the effectiveness of Waqf initiatives.

International Workshops and Conferences

Organizing international workshops and conferences focused on Waqf management provides a platform for practitioners, scholars, and policymakers to exchange knowledge, experiences, and perspectives. These events foster networking opportunities, facilitate discussions on emerging trends and challenges, and promote collaboration on research projects and capacity-building initiatives.

Joint Training and Capacity Building

Collaborative training programs and capacity-building initiatives can strengthen the skills and knowledge base of Waqf professionals and stakeholders across borders. By leveraging the expertise of international trainers and institutions, participants gain access to diverse perspectives, best practices, and practical tools to enhance their capabilities in Waqf administration, governance, and asset management.

□CONCLUSION

In today's interconnected world, information sharing plays a pivotal role in fostering collaboration and innovation. The advent of digital tools and platforms has revolutionized the way information is disseminated, allowing for more efficient and widespread access. Effective information dissemination strategies are crucial to maximize the benefits of these digital tools, ensuring that relevant information reaches the right stakeholders in a timely manner. Enhancing co-creation through information sharing is crucial, as it allows diverse teams to contribute unique perspectives and expertise, leading to innovative solutions. However, this process presents challenges and risks. In an era where digital innovation is reshaping industries globally, the waqf sector stands at a pivotal crossroads. The opportunity to harness digital tools and collaborative platforms to enhance our mission has never been greater. To fully realize the potential of waqf institutions in fostering social good, we must embrace these advancements and cultivate a culture of collaboration and innovation. By leveraging technology and sharing knowledge, we can significantly enhance the impact of waqf institutions. The future of the waqf sector depends on our collective efforts to innovate and collaborate. Thus, these findings critically contribute to waqf institutions to strategizing and improving waqf sustainability. Specifically of the waqf stakeholders sharing information for co-creation in Malaysia (WSIC-MY)

ACKNOWLEDGMENT

This research was funded by a matching grant between Universiti Sains Islam Malaysia (USIM) and Universiti Utara Malaysia (UUM) under code (USIM): USIM/MG/UUM/FEM/SEPADAN-K/72322 and code (UUM): 21386.

REFERENCES

Abdullah, M. (2018). Evolution in waqf jurisprudence and Islamic financial innovation. *Journal of Islamic Monetary Economics*, 4(1), 161–182. DOI: 10.21098/jimf.v4i1.920

Abdullah, M. (2018). Waqf, Sustainable Development Goals (SDGs) and maqasid al-shariah. *international Journal of Social Economics, 45*(1), 158-172. DOI: 10.1108/IJSE-10-2016-0295

Abdullah, M. (2019, July 8). Waqf and trust: the nature, structures and socio-economic impacts. Journal of Islamic accounting and business research (Online), 10(4), 512-527. DOI: 10.1108/JIABR-10-2016-0124

Abu Seman, J., Jamil, N. N., & Che Mohd Hashim, A. J. (2021). Development of integrated Islamic finance-based index of financial inclusion using zakat and cash waqf: A preliminary study in Malaysia. *The Journal of Muamalat Islamic Finance Research*, 18(2), 73–95. DOI: 10.33102/jmifr.v18i2.370

Ahmad, Z., Ahmed, M., & Mokal, M. N. (2023). Waqf Management Through Fintech in Malaysia. *Journal of Islamic Finance*, 12(2), 114–125. DOI: 10.31436/jif.v12i2.829

Ahmed, Y. A., Ahmad, M. N., Ahmad, N., & Zakaria, N. H. (2019). Social media for knowledge-sharing: A systematic literature review. *Telematics and Informatics*, 37, 72–112. DOI: 10.1016/j.tele.2018.01.015

Al-Rahma, F. A., Rahman, M. A., & Al-Mutawa, A. M. (2021). The role of artificial intelligence in enhancing Waqf management. *Journal of Islamic Economics and Finance*, 13(3), 104–118.

Aldeen, K. N. (2021, February 27). 40-Year Bibliometric Analysis Of Waqf: Its Current Status and Development, And Paths For Future Research. https://jimf-bi.org/index.php/JIMF/article/download/1308/842

Alhalafi, N., & Veeraraghavan, P. (2021, October 13). Cybersecurity Policy Framework in Saudi Arabia: Literature Review. https://www.frontiersin.org/articles/10.3389/fcomp.2021.736874/pdf

Alharbi, A. S., Halikias, G., Rajarajan, M., & Yamin, M. (2021, January 28). A review of effectiveness of Saudi E-government data security management. *International Journal of Information Technology : an Official Journal of Bharati Vidyapeeth's Institute of Computer Applications and Management*, 13(2), 573–579. DOI: 10.1007/s41870-021-00611-3

Alhogail, A. (2020, June 6). Enhancing information security best practices sharing in virtual knowledge communities. https://www.emerald.com/insight/content/doi/10.1108/VJIKMS-01-2020-0009/full/html

Allah Pitchay, A., Mydin Meera, A. K., & Saleem, M. (2015). Factors influencing the behavioral intentions of muslim employees to contribute to cash-waqf through salary deductions. *Journal of King Abdulaziz University: Islamic Economics*, 28(1), 57–90. DOI: 10.4197/Islec.28-1.3

Antoniuk, L., & Zasiadivko, V. (2023, April 24). DIGITAL LITERACY AND TECHNOLOGIES FOR EDUCATION: PRINCIPLES AND TOOLS. DOI: 10.36074/grail-of-science.14.04.2023.044

Atkočiūnienė, Z. O., & Siudikienė, D. (2019). Communication management in promoting knowledge and creativity in fostering innovations in the creative organization. *Creativity Studies*, 14(2), 549–576. DOI: 10.3846/cs.2021.15550

Ayub, M. (2018, December 1). Institutionalising 'Waqf ' for Realising the Shared Development Objective by Islamic Banks and Financial Institutions. Journal of Islamic business and management, 8(2). DOI: 10.26501/jibm/2018.0802-001

Azizi, N., Shukor, S., & Sabri, H. (2019). Determinants of Repeated Endowers' Donation Intention in Cash Waqf: A Case Study in Majlis Agama Islam dan Adat Melayu Perak (MAIPk). *Jurnal Manajemen Bisnis*, 10(2), 154–163. DOI: 10.18196/mb.10175

Balakrishnan, V., & Lay, G. C. (2016). Students' Learning Styles and Their Effects on the use of Social Media Technology for Learning. *Telematics and Informatics*, 33(3), 808–821. DOI: 10.1016/j.tele.2015.12.004

Banire, B., Al-Thani, D., & Yang, Y. (2021, July 1). Addressing Cyber Security Accessibility: A Qualitative Study. https://www.scienceopen.com/document_file/9e1391c1-8a9a-4706-87ea-50d428c193b3/ScienceOpen/W5.2%20Banire%20Al%20Thani%20Yang.pdf

Baran, B E., & Woznyj, H M. (2021). Managing VUCA. *Elsevier BV, 50*(2), 100787-100787. DOI: 10.1016/j.orgdyn.2020.100787

Beik, I S., Zaenal, M H., & Rizkiningsih, P. (2019, January 1). Waqf Led Halal Cryptocurrency Model. DOI: 10.1007/978-3-030-10749-9_18

Building Trust In Waqf Management — Implications Of Good Governance And Transparent Reporting. (2020, July 25). https://www.worldscientific.com/doi/10.1142/S0217590820420059

Buterin, V. (2014). "A Next-Generation Smart Contract and Decentralized Application Platform.", Ethereum White Paper.

Crosby, M., Pattanayak, P., Verma, S., & Kalyanaraman, V. (2016). Blockchain Technology: Beyond Bitcoin. *Applied Innovation Review*, 2, 6–19.

Dennis, D., Qoyum, A., & Sakti, M. P. (2018). Determinant of cash waqf nahdatul ulama (case of Muslim students in Indonesia). Madania. *Jurnal Kajian Keislaman*, 22(1), 19–32. DOI: 10.29300/madania.v22i1.886

Edelmann, N., & Virkar, S. (2023). The Impact of Sustainability on Co-Creation of Digital Public Services. *Administrative Sciences*, 13(2), 43. DOI: 10.3390/admsci13020043

Egodawele, M., Sedera, D., & Bui, V. (2022, January 1). A Systematic Review of Digital Transformation Literature (2013-2021) and the development of an overarching apriori model to guide future research. Cornell University.

Fachrurrazy, M., Siliwadi, D N., & Herlina, N. (2022, May 29). Potential for Digital-Based Productive Waqf Development (Case Study of Datuk Sulaiman ModernIslamic Boarding School and Muhammadiyah Boarding School) in Palopo City, South of Celebes. Al-Falah: journal of islamic economics (Online), 7(1), 141-141. DOI: 10.29240/alfalah.v7i1.3840

Farida, I., & Setiawan, D. (2022). Business strategies and competitive advantage: The role of performance and innovation. *Journal of Open Innovation*, 8(3), 1–16. DOI: 10.3390/joitmc8030163

Fauzi, M., Yahya, S., Hanaysha, J. R., Haron, M. S., & Zahrin, S. N. A. (2019). The impact of trust in cash waqf contribution: a case study of wakaf Selangor muamalat (WSM) service of bank Muamalat Malaysia Berhad (BMMB). International Journal of Business, Economics and Law, 18(2), 1-10. Retrieved from https://ijbel.com/wp-content/uploads/2019/05/KLIBEL-18_63.pdf

Ganapathy, S., Sippy, T., Sinha, V., & Adarkar, H. (2022). *Building the Foundations: Strengthening technical capacity in government*. Artha Global.

Garrido-Moreno, A., Martín-Rojas, R., & García-Morales, V. J. (2024). The key of innovation and organizational resilience in improving business performance: A mixed-methods approach. *International Journal of Information Management*, 77, 102777. Advance online publication. DOI: 10.1016/j.ijinfomgt.2024.102777

Hadiyati, P., Gladys, A. I., & Iqbal, M. (2020). Encourage Peopl e's Interest to Do Cash Waqf. *Islamiconomic: Jurnal Ekonomi Islam*, 11(2). Advance online publication. DOI: 10.32678/ijei.v11i2.192

Hakak, S., Kamsin, A., Khan, W. Z., Zakari, A., Imran, M., Ahmad, K., & Gilkar, G. A. (2020, June 14). Digital Hadith authentication: Recent advances, open challenges, and future directions. *Transactions on Emerging Telecommunications Technologies*, 33(6), e3977. Advance online publication. DOI: 10.1002/ett.3977

Haron, H., Mat Nor, F., Johari, F., Misbah, H., & Shafii, Z. (2023). Factors influencing the behavioural intention to accept benefidonor concept among stakeholders of Waqf. *Journal of Islamic Accounting and Business Research*, 14(8), 1344–1360. DOI: 10.1108/JIABR-06-2022-0146

Harwood, T., & Garry, T. (2014). Co-creation and ambiguous ownership within virtual communities: The case of the Machinima community. *Journal of Consumer Behaviour*, 13(2), 148–156. DOI: 10.1002/cb.1437

Hasan, R., & Siraj, S. A. (2016). Complexities of waqf development in Bangladesh. *Journal of Emerging Economies and Islamic Research*, 4(3), 1–10. DOI: 10.24191/jeeir.v4i3.9093

Hassan, R., & Ali, M. (2019). Big data analytics in Waqf institutions: Opportunities and challenges. *Journal of Islamic Philanthropy & Social Finance*, 7(2), 45–61.

Hassan, R., Rashid, N. R. N. A., & Akram, W. (2020). The Application of Blockchain Technology in Waqf Property Management in Malaysia. *International Journal of Islamic and Middle Eastern Finance and Management*, 13(4), 639–656.

Hassan, R., Rashid, N. R. N. A., & Akram, W. (2020). The Application of Blockchain Technology in Waqf Property Management in Malaysia. *International Journal of Islamic and Middle Eastern Finance and Management*, 13(4), 639–656.

Ibrahim, D., & Ibrahim, H. (2020, October 27). Governance, Location. *International Journal of Academic Research in Business & Social Sciences*, 10(10). Advance online publication. DOI: 10.6007/IJARBSS/v10-i10/7651

Ibrahim, E. N. M., Laila, N., & Mehad, S. (2016, August 12). Trust or distrust in the web-mediated information environment (W-MIE): A perspective of online Muslim users. https://www.emerald.com/insight/content/doi/10.1108/17410390910993527/full/html

Iredale, S., Heinze, A., & Williams, M. J. (2024). Engaging stakeholders with captivating content. In *Digital and Social Media Marketing*.Routledge (pp. 182-196)
Islamic Development Bank (2023). Islamic Finance Grant for Developing a Digital Awqaf Fund Management Platform- 2 Components. Retrieved at https://www.isdb.org/project-procurement/tenders/2023/gpn/islamic-finance-grant-developing-digital-awqaf-fund-management-platform-2, 30th May 2024.

Ismail, A. G., Shafiai, M. H. M., & Ahmad, M. A. (2022). Stakeholders' involvement in organisational governance structure of state islamic religious council. *UMRAN-International Journal of Islamic and Civilizational Studies*, 9(1), 23–35. DOI: 10.11113/umran2022.9n1.536

Ismail, M., & Mohsin, A. (2013, November 25). Financing through cash-waqf: a revitalization to finance different needs. https://www.emerald.com/insight/content/doi/10.1108/IMEFM-08-2013-0094/full/html

Ismail, W A W. (2020, January 31). Significance of Technology to Cash Waqf Collection [UTAUT]. *International Journal of Academic Research in Business & Social Sciences*, 11(1). Advance online publication. DOI: 10.6007/IJARBSS/v11-i1/8994

Janom, N., Izham, M. Z., Mansor, F. S., Aris, S. R. S., Bashah, N. S. K., & Arshad, N. H. (2019). Review on success factors of waqf information management system in Malaysia. *Indonesian Journal of Electrical Engineering and Computer Science*, 16(1), 412–419. DOI: 10.11591/ijeecs.v16.i1.pp412-419

Johari, F., Nor, F. M., Hamid, B. A., Zal, W. A., Ali, F., Misbah, H., & Shaharuddin, A. (2023). Enhancing Synergy in the Waqf Ecosystem in Malaysia: Promoting Increased Waqf Contributions among Beneficiaries, Donors, and Mutawalli. *International Journal of Economics Finance Studies*, 15(3), 76–107.

Kamaruddin, M.I.H., Hanefah, M.M. and Masruki, R., 2024. Challenges and prospects in waqf reporting practices in Malaysia. Journal of Financial Reporting and accounting, 22(3), pp.752-765.

Kamaruddin, M. I. H., Hanefah, M. M., Shaharuddin, A., Ayedh, A. M. A., & Othman, N. A. (2023). Development of Fintech in Islamic Social Finance in Malaysia. International Journal of Economics, Management and Accounting.

Karim, M. A., Rahman, H. A., & Abdullah, W. S. W. (2022). AI chatbots and their impact on donor engagement in Waqf institutions. *International Journal of Islamic and Middle Eastern Finance and Management*, 15(1), 80–95.

Kassim, M., Embi, N. A. C., Haron, R., & Ibrahim, K. (2019). Internal factors affecting continuous donations among cash waqf donors. *International Journal of Academic Research in Business & Social Sciences*, 9(9), 1304–1311. DOI: 10.6007/IJARBSS/v9-i9/6464

Kasumi, H., & Xhemaili, M. (2023). Student motivation and learning: The impact of collaborative learning in English as Foreign Language classes. *International Journal of Cognitive Research in Science. Engineering and Education*, 11(2), 301–309. DOI: 10.23947/2334-8496-2023-11-2-301-309

Kettunen, P., Teppola, S., & Partanen, J. (2019). Fostering continuous innovation with engaging IT-assisted transparent information sharing: a case study. In: Hyrynsalmi, S., Suoranta, M., Nguyen-Duc, A., Tyrväinen, P., & Abrahamsson, P. (eds). *Software Business*. ICSOB 2019. Lecture Notes in Business Information Processing, vol 370. Springer, Cham. DOI: 10.1007/978-3-030-33742-1_13

Khan, M., Nisar, Q. A., & Khattak, A. (2021). Blockchain Technology for Waqf Management: Challenges and Opportunities. *Journal of Islamic Accounting and Business Research*, 12(2), 219–235.

Kulakli, A., & Mahony, S. (2014). Knowledge Creation and Sharing with Web 2.0 Tools for Teaching and Learning Roles in So-called University 2.0. *Procedia: Social and Behavioral Sciences*, 150, 648–657. DOI: 10.1016/j.sbspro.2014.09.084

Kumar, S., & Shah, N. P. (2018). False information on web and social media: a survey. In *Social Media Analytics: Advances and Applications*. CRC Press. https://arxiv.org/abs/1804.08559

Laallam, A., Kassim, S., Ali, E R A E., & Saiti, B. (2020, March 30). Intellectual capital in non-profit organisations: lessons learnt for waqf institutions. DOI: 10.1108/IJIF-10-2018-0111

Laluddin, H., Haneef, S. S. S., Mohammad, M., & Rahman, M. (2021). Revisiting the concept of waqf: Its maintenance, issues and challenges.

Malaysia, P. D. P. (2017). Personal Data Protection Code of Practice (2017).

Matheus, R., Janssen, M., & Janowski, T. (2021). Design principles for creating digital transparency in government. *Government Information Quarterly*, 38(1), 1–18. DOI: 10.1016/j.giq.2020.101550

Merlinda, S., Qurrata, V. A., Yusida, E., Purnamasari, V., Seprillina, L., & Hussain, N. E. (2021). The role of cash waqf as a source of micro business financing for strengthening the local economy: A case study in Gunung Kawi District, Malang Regency. *Review of Integrative Business and Economics Research*, 10, 136–144. http://buscompress.com/uploads/3/4/9/8/34980536/riber_10-s1_15_u20-089_136-144.pdf

Meyers, E. M., Erickson, I., & Small, R. V. (2013, April 25). Digital literacy and informal learning environments: An introduction. *Learning, Media and Technology*, 38(4), 355–367. DOI: 10.1080/17439884.2013.783597

Misbah, H., Johari, F., Mat Nor, F., Haron, H., Shahwan, S., & Shafii, Z. (2022). Sustainable development, regional planning, and information management as an evolving theme in waqf research: A bibliometric analysis. *Sustainability (Basel)*, 14(21), 14126. DOI: 10.3390/su142114126

Mohsin, M. I. A., & Muneeza, A. (2019). Integrating waqf crowdfunding into the blockchain: A modern approach for creating a waqf market. In *Fintech in Islamic finance* (pp. 266–279). Routledge. DOI: 10.4324/9781351025584-17

Mollah, M. B., Azim, M. I., & Bhuiyan, A. B. (2018). Blockchain technology and its prospects in Islamic finance. *Journal of Islamic Finance*, 9(2), 51–60.

Nahar, H. S. (2018, January 9). Exploring Awqāf Governance. *Preliminary Evidence of Governance Practices and Disclosure of Two Malaysian Awqāf Institutions.*, 31(1), 139–150. DOI: 10.4197/islec.31-1.9

Nasiri, A., Noori, A., & Salleh, M. C. M. (2019). Acceptance and practices of cash WAQF among university's students. International Journal of Academic Research in Accounting. *Finance and Management Sciences*, 9(3), 38–48. DOI: 10.6007/IJARAFMS/v9-i3/6325

Nazli, M., & Yvonne, S. (2021, June 24). Relationship between Cultural Values, Sense of Community and Trust and the Effect of Trust in Workplace. https://doi.org//arXiv.2106.13347DOI: 10.48550

Nonaka, I., & Takeuchi, H. (1995). *The knowledge-creating company*. Oxford University Press. DOI: 10.1093/oso/9780195092691.001.0001

Omar, H. H., & Sanyinna, A. (2018). Administrative challenges of WAQF institution in the contemporary world: Future prospects.

Osman, A. F., Mohammed, M. O., & Amin, H. (2014). An Analysis Of Cash Waqf Participation Among Young Intellectuals. In *Seminar Waqf Iqlimi* (pp. 7–20). Universiti Sains Islam Malaysia. Retrieved from https://oarep.usim.edu.my/jspui/handle/123456789/11596

Panahifar, F., Byrne, P. J., Salam, M. A., & Heavey, C. (2018). Supply chain collaboration and firm's performance: The critical role of information sharing and trust. *Journal of Enterprise Information Management*, 31(3), 358–379. DOI: 10.1108/JEIM-08-2017-0114

Priyadi, U., Achiria, S., & Imron, M. A. (2023). *Digital-Based Nazhir Services for Co-Creation Value in Waqf Land Asset Management. International Journal of Management Research and Social Science.*

Priyadi, U., Achiria, S., Imron, M. A., & Zandi, G. R. (2022, December 27). Waqf management and accountability: Waqf land financing models for economic well-being. https://archive.aessweb.com/index.php/5002/article/download/4696/7423

Ramli, A., Fahmi, F. M., Darus, F., & Rasit, Z. A. (2019, March 15). Academic Research Publishing Group - ARPG. https://arpgweb.com/journal/7/special_issue/03-2019/1/&page=2

Resta, P., Laferrière, T., McLaughlin, R., & Kouraogo, A. (2018, January 1). Issues and Challenges Related to Digital Equity: An Overview. DOI: 10.1007/978-3-319-71054-9_67

Saeed, S., Altamimi, S. A., Alkayyal, N. A., Alshehri, E., & Alabbad, D. A. (2023, July 25). Digital Transformation and Cybersecurity Challenges for Businesses Resilience: Issues and Recommendations. *Sensors (Basel)*, 23(15), 6666–6666. DOI: 10.3390/s23156666 PMID: 37571451

Sakti, M. R. P., Thaker, H. M. T., Qoyum, A., & Qizam, I. (2016). Determinants of cash Waqf contribution in Klang Valley and Selangor: A SEM approach. *Journal of Islamic Monetary Economics and Finance*, 2(1), 111–144. DOI: 10.21098/jimf.v2i1.593

Salman, M., Mohamad, N A., & Sadique, M A. (2022, January 2). E-waqf implementation: A paradigm shift in Nigeria waqf system. Journal of Asian and African social science and humanities, 7(4), 41-53. DOI: 10.55327/jaash.v7i4.255

Selsky, J. W., & Parker, B. (2005). Cross-sector partnerships to address social issues: Challenges to theory and practice. *Journal of Management*, 31(6), 849–873. DOI: 10.1177/0149206305279601

Shaikh, S A., Ismail, A G., & Shafiai, M H M. (2017, July 10). Application of <i>waqf</i> for social and development finance. DOI: 10.1108/IJIF-07-2017-002

Shukor, S. A., Johari, F., Abd Wahab, K., Kefeli, Z., Ahmad, N., Alias, M. H., Rahman, A. A., Orip, N. M. M., Ibrahim, P., & Abu-Hussin, M. F. (2018). Trust on awqaf institutions: Evidence from Malaysia. *Journal of Islamic Marketing*.

Siddiqi, H. (2020). Blockchain applications in Islamic finance. *Islamic Finance Review*, 5(1), 32–45.

Sulaiman, H., & Jamil, N. (2014, November 1). Information security governance model to enhance zakat information management in Malaysian zakat institutions. DOI: 10.1109/ICIMU.2014.7066630

Svensson, J. (2015). *Promoting Social Change and Democracy through Information Technology*. IGI Global. DOI: 10.4018/978-1-4666-8502-4

The Impact of Internal Control System on the Accountability Practices in Waqf Institutions: Evidence from Al Rahma International Waqf. (2021, August 1). Research Journal of Finance and Accounting. DOI: 10.7176/RJFA/12-16-04

Trattner, C., Jannach, D., Motta, E., Meijer, I. C., Diakopoulos, N., Elahi, M., Opdahl, A. L., Tessem, B., Borch, N., Fjeld, M., Øvrelid, L., Smedt, K. D., & Moe, H. (2021, December 20). Responsible media technology and AI: Challenges and research directions. *AI and Ethics*, 2(4), 585–594. DOI: 10.1007/s43681-021-00126-4

Vaidya, J. (2012). Privacy in the context of digital government. *Proceedings of the 13th Annual International Conference on Digital Government Research* (pp. 302–303). https://doi.org/DOI: 10.1145/2307729.2307796

Vargo, S. L., & Lusch, R. F. (2004). Evolving to a new dominant logic in Marketing. *Journal of Marketing*, 68(1), 1–17. DOI: 10.1509/jmkg.68.1.1.24036

Warschauer, M., & Xu, Y. (2018, January 1). Technology and Equity in Education. DOI: 10.1007/978-3-319-71054-9_76

Waters, R. D., Burnett, E., Lamm, A., & Lucas, J. (2009). Engaging stakeholders through social networking: How nonprofit organizations are using Facebook. *Public Relations Review*, 35(2), 102–106. DOI: 10.1016/j.pubrev.2009.01.006

Welch, E. W., Hinnant, C. C., & Moon, M. J. (2004). Linking citizen satisfaction with e-government and trust in government. *Journal of Public Administration: Research and Theory*, 15(3), 371–391. DOI: 10.1093/jopart/mui021

Wildana, M D A., & Imamia, T L. (2022, May 19). Waqf in the 21st Century: The Implementation of Blockchain and Smart Contract Technology. DOI: 10.32535/jicp.v5i1.1774

Yayasan Waqaf Malaysia. (2021). Sejarah Perkembangan Wakaf. Retrieved from Portal Rasmi Yayasan Waqaf Malaysia (ywm.gov.my), 30th May 2024.

Yusoff, R., Rahman, S. A., & Mohamed, W. N. W. (2018). Factors influencing the intention to perform cash waqf among Muslim staff at Universiti Teknologi MARA, Kelantan Campus. In International Conference on Islam and Global Issues. niversiti Teknologi Mara Cawangan Kelantan, Bukit Ilmu, Machang Kelantan. Retrieved from https://dspace.adu.ac.ae/handle/1/3374

Yusoff, Z. M. (2011). The Malaysian Personal Data Protection Act 2010: A Legislation Note. *NZJPIL*, 9, 119.

Compilation of References

Abaidoo, R., & Agyapong, E. K. (2022). Banking industry stability and investment dynamics. *Journal of Financial Regulation and Compliance*, 30(2), 215–239. DOI: 10.1108/JFRC-06-2021-0049

Abd Rahman, S., Yaakob, A., Fadzil, A., & Shaban, M. (2017). *Asset Distribution Among the Qualified Heirs Based on Islamic Inheritance Law*. Academy of Contemporary Islamic Studies.

Abd. Malib, M., Nordin, R., Nordin, M.N., Mustafa, M. S., Izzat, M. & Arif, M. A. (2021). The Role Of The State Islamic Religious Council (Sirc) In Strengthening Thewaqf Management In Malaysia: An Overview And Recommendations. *Türk Fizyoterapi ve Rehabilitasyon Dergisi/Turkish Journal of Physiotherapy and Rehabilitation.* 32. 4872-4880.

Abdillah, F., & Danial, E. (2015). Crowdfunding: Demokratisasi Akses Keuangan Dalam Mendukung Aksi Sosial Mahasiswa. *Jurnal Ilmiah Mimbar Demokrasi*, 15(1), 1–16. DOI: 10.21009/jimd.v15i1.9108

Abdul Ghani, N., Wan Chik, W., Mohd, Y., Abd. Wahab, M. A., & Mohd. Ghazalli, F. S. (2022). Social Deprivation and its Threats to Social Well-Being According to The Perspective of Maqasid. *International Journal of Academic Research in Business & Social Sciences*, 12(1). Advance online publication. DOI: 10.6007/IJARBSS/v12-i1/12261

Abdullah Jalil, & Muhammad Muda. (2008). Pengurusan dana sedekah secara sistematik: Analisa peranan institusi kerajaan dan swasta. USIM: Fakulti Ekonomi dan Muamalat.

Abdullah, A., Mohd Zaidi, N. S., & Asar, A. K. (2023). Digital Wellbeing: Does It Matter in Malaysian Education? In *Industry Forward and Technology Transformation in Business and Entrepreneurship* (pp. 753-762).

Abdullah, M. (2019, July 8). Waqf and trust: the nature, structures and socio-economic impacts. Journal of Islamic accounting and business research (Online), 10(4), 512-527. DOI: 10.1108/JIABR-10-2016-0124

Abdullah, O., Shaharuddin, A., Wahid, M. A., & Harun, M. S. (2022). Artificial Intelligence (AI) Application In Islamic Finance: A Review Of Business Use Cases. In *The Seminar Antarabangsa Islam dan Sains (SAIS 2022).*

Abdullah, M. (2018). Evolution in waqf jurisprudence and Islamic financial innovation. *Journal of Islamic Monetary Economics*, 4(1), 161–182. DOI: 10.21098/jimf.v4i1.920

Abdullah, M. (2018). Waqf, Sustainable Development Goals (SDGs) and maqasid al-shariah. *International Journal of Social Economics*, 45(1), 158–172. DOI: 10.1108/IJSE-10-2016-0295

Abdullah, M. (2020). Islamic endowment (Waqf) in India: Towards poverty reduction of Muslims in the country. *Journal of Research in Emerging Markets*, 2(2), 48–60. DOI: 10.30585/jrems.v2i2.482

Abdullah, M. M. I., Fariddudin, S. N. F. M., Muhamad, N. H. N., & Awang, A. B. (2021). Islamic estate planning in the industrial revolution 4.0 era: Issues and challenges. *Journal of Emerging Economies and Islamic Research*, 9(2), 40–56. DOI: 10.24191/jeeir.v9i2.12413

Abdullah, N., Fazli, S. M., & Muhammad Arif, A. M. (2019). The Relationship between Attitude towards Money, Financial Literacy and Debt Management with Young Worker's Financial Well-being. *Pertanika Journal of Social Science & Humanities*, 27(1).

Abdullah, N., Redzuan, F., & Daud, N. A. (2020). E-wallet: Factors influencing user acceptance towards cashless society in Malaysia among public universities. *Indonesian Journal of Electrical Engineering and Computer Science*, 20(1), 67–74. DOI: 10.11591/ijeecs.v20.i1.pp67-74

Abdullah, O., Abdullah, O., Shaharuddin, A., Wahid, M. A., & Harun, M. S. (2022). The Potentials and Challenges of Decision Support System for Islamic Banking and Finance. *European Journal of Islamic Finance*, 9(3), 21–29. DOI: 10.13135/2421-2172/6901-

Abdul-Yakeen, M. A., Gatawa, N. M., Aliyu, C. U., & Ibrahim, M. O. (2014). Six-Rs of establishing a Waqf in Ilorin emirate economy. *International Journal of Development and Sustainability*, 3(7), 1438–1454. www.isdsnet.com/ijds

Abdussalam, A., & Shodiq, A. (2022). Maqashid As-Syariah Perspektif Imam Al-Ghazali: Studi Lietrasi Maslahah Mursalah. *Moderasi: Journal of Islamic Studies*, 2(2), 139–159. DOI: 10.54471/moderasi.v2i2.32

Abu Bakar, F. M. (2022). E-wallet usage to pay zakat during Covid-19 pandemic among Malaysian's polytechnic lecturers. *International Journal of Islamic Economics and Finance Research, 5*(2 December), 57–79. DOI: 10.53840/ijiefer91

Abu Dawud. (1992). *Sunan Abu Dawud*. https://www.alkhoirot.org/2018/04/terjemah-sunan-abu-dawud.html#english

Abu Seman, J., Jamil, N. N., & Che Mohd Hashim, A. J.Junaidah Abu SemanNurul Nazlia JamilAzreen Jihan Che Mohd Hashim. (2021). Development of integrated Islamic finance-based index of financial inclusion using zakat and cash waqf: A preliminary study in Malaysia. *The Journal of Muamalat Islamic Finance Research*, 18(2), 73–95. DOI: 10.33102/jmifr.v18i2.370

Abu Talib, N. Y., Abdul Latiff, R., & Aman, A. (2020). An institutional perspective for research in waqf accounting and reporting: A case study of Terengganu state Islamic Religious Council in Malaysia. *Journal of Islamic Accounting and Business Research*, 11(2), 400–427. DOI: 10.1108/JIABR-11-2016-0132

Adam, F. (2021). Fintech Versus I-Fintech: A Dichotomy. *Islamic FinTech: Insights and Solutions*, 19–35.

Adegbite, O. O., & Machethe, C. L. (2020). Bridging the financial inclusion gender gap in smallholder agriculture in Nigeria: An untapped potential for sustainable development. *World Development*, 127, 127. DOI: 10.1016/j.worlddev.2019.104755

Adyen. (2024). *Adyen Index: Retail 2024 - Balancing customers experience and business efficiency.*

Adzis, A. A., Bakar, J. A., & Shahar, H. K. (2017). Factors influencing young adults' debt in Malaysia. *The Journal of Business and Retail Management Research*, 12(1), 76–85. DOI: 10.24052/JBRMR/V12IS01/FIYADIM

Afar, M. (1994). View and Assesment of Writings about Money in an Islamic Framework. King Abdulaziz University Islamic Economic Research Center., Retrieved March 1, 2023, from.

Afiqah, F. & Sabit, M. T. (2021). A Proposal for A Single Tribunal of Estate Distribution. *Jurnal Teknologi (Sciences & Engineering)*, 75(10), 1–16.

Agarwal, S., Hadzic, M., Song, C., & Yildirim, Y. (2023). Liquidity Constraints, Consumption, and Debt Repayment: Evidence from Macroprudential Policy in Turkey. *Review of Financial Studies*, 36(10), 3953–3998. Advance online publication. DOI: 10.1093/rfs/hhad024

Ahmad Mohamad, K., Nor, R. M., & Kamely, A. A. (2021). Crowdfunding: New Form of Both Investment Opportunities and Source of Capital. In *Innovative Strategies for Implementing FinTech in Banking* (pp. 110–135). IGI Global. DOI: 10.4018/978-1-7998-3257-7.ch007

Ahmad, A. U., Osmani, N. M., & Karim, M. F. (2010). Islamic finance in Australia: the potential problems and prospects : "25 Years of Islamic Banking and Finance in Brunei" View project. *International Conference The Tawhidi Epistemology: Zakat and Waqf Economy, November*. https://www.researchgate.net/publication/303698257

Ahmadij. (2016), Islam Kaffah: Tinjauan Tafsir QS Al Baqarah: 208. Jurnal Syariati, 2(2).

Ahmad, M. (2019). An empirical study of the challenges facing zakat and waqf institutions in Northern Nigeria. *ISRA International Journal of Islamic Finance*, 11(2), 338–356. DOI: 10.1108/IJIF-04-2018-0044

Ahmad, N. N., Tarmidi, M., Ridzwan, I. U., Hamid, M. A., & Roni, R. A. (2014). The application of unified theory of acceptance and use of technology (UTAUT) for predicting the usage of e-zakat online system. *International Journal of Scientific Research*, 3(4), 63–67.

Ahmad, Z., Ahmed, M., & Mokal, M. N. (2023). Waqf Management Through Fintech in Malaysia. *Journal of Islamic Finance*, 12(2), 114–125. DOI: 10.31436/jif.v12i2.829

Ahmed, E., & Mustafa, A.Esra Ahmed Abdulhalim Mustafa. (2023). The Thirst for Islamic Knowledge in the Digital Era. *Digital Muslim Review*, 1(1), 54–67. DOI: 10.32678/dmr.v1i1.12

Ahmed, Y. A., Ahmad, M. N., Ahmad, N., & Zakaria, N. H. (2019). Social media for knowledge-sharing: A systematic literature review. *Telematics and Informatics*, 37, 72–112. DOI: 10.1016/j.tele.2018.01.015

Ahmetoğulları, K. (2023). The role of digitalisation in the financial performance of the participation banking sector. In Yücel, R., Ayyıldız, Y., & Er, H. (Eds.), *Innovations Brought by Digitalisation to the Finance Sector*. Özgür Yayın Dağıtım. (In Turkish)

AIBIM. (2024) Retrieved from https://aibim.com/

Aji, H. M., & Adawiyah, W. R. (2021). How e-wallets encourage excessive spending behavior among young adult consumers? *Journal of Asia Business Studies*. Advance online publication. DOI: 10.1108/JABS-01-2021-0025

Ajzen, I. (1991). The theory of planned behavior. *Organizational Behavior and Human Decision Processes*, 50(2), 179–211. DOI: 10.1016/0749-5978(91)90020-T

Akiyoshi, F. (2019). Effects of separating commercial and investment banking: Evidence from the dissolution of a joint venture investment bank. *Journal of Financial Economics*, 134(3), 703–714. DOI: 10.1016/j.jfineco.2019.05.004

Aknin, L. B., Wiwad, D., & Hanniball, K. B. (2018). Buying well-being: Spending behavior and happiness. *Social and Personality Psychology Compass*, 12(5), e12386. Advance online publication. DOI: 10.1111/spc3.12386

Aktepe, İ. E. (2014). *Participation banking with questions*. TKBB.

Al Azizah, U. S., & Choirin, M. (2018). Financial innovation on zakat distribution and economic growth. In International Conference of Zakat 2018 Proceedings (ISSN: 2655-6251). Paper presented at International Conference of Zakat 2018, 15-16 November, Universitas Gadjah Mada, Yogyakarta, Indonesia. UN. (2024) Retrieved from https://sdgs.un.org/goals

Al Quran dan Terjemahannya. (n.d.). Departemen Agama Republik Indonesia.

Al Zarqa, M. A. (1982). al Qiyam wa 'l Ma 'ayir al Islamiyyah fi Taqwim al Mashru 'at. *Islamic Values and Criteria in Project Evaluation), al Muslim al Mu 'asir, 3*, 85–105.

al-Ahkam al-cadliyah (2002)

AlAjmi, K., Deodoro, J., Farias, A., Iskender, E. S., Mirestean, A. T., & Ravikumar, R. (2021). Powering the Digital Economy.

Alam, N., & Nazim, S. (2021). Fintech, digital currency and the future of Islamic finance. *Cham: Springer International Publishing, 257*.

Alam, N., Gupta, L., Zameni, A., Alam, N., Gupta, L., & Zameni, A. (2019). Challenges and success factors for Islamic fintech. *Fintech and Islamic Finance: Digitalization, Development and Disruption*, 159-173.

Alam, N., Gupta, L., Zameni, A., Alam, N., Gupta, L., & Zameni, A. (2019). Cryptocurrency and Islamic finance. *Fintech and Islamic Finance: Digitalization, Development and Disruption*, 99-118.

Alam, N., Gupta, L., Zameni, A., Alam, N., Gupta, L., & Zameni, A. (2019). Emergence of Shariah-Tech and Its Landscape. *Fintech and Islamic Finance: Digitalization, Development and Disruption*, 63-79.

Alam, A., & Saputro, I. A. (2022). A qualitative analysis of user interface design on a sharia fintechapplication based on technology acceptance model (tam). [Technology Acceptance Model]. *Jurnal TAM*, 13(1), 9. DOI: 10.56327/jurnaltam.v13i1.1142

Alam, I., Haider, W. A., & Munir, A.Dr. Iftikhar AlamWaqas Ali Haider. (2022). Aspiring Maqasid al-Shariah and Socio-Economic Well-Being in Islamic Finance. [IRJIS]. *International Research Journal on Islamic Studies*, 4(1), 104–122. DOI: 10.54262/irjis.04.01.e07

Alam, N., Gupta, L., & Zameni, A. (2019). Digitalization and disruption in the financial sector. In *Fintech and Islamic finance* (pp. 1–22). Palgrave Macmillan., DOI: 10.1007/978-3-030-24666-2_1

Alawiye, H. O., & Keerio, I. K. (2023). Towards Resolving Overlapped Distribution of Waqf Funds Through Artificial Intelligence: Focusing on Educational Waqf's Beneficiaries. *Al-Kashaf, December*. https://alkashaf.pk/index.php/Journal/article/view/56%0Ahttps://alkashaf.pk/index.php/Journal/article/download/56/66

Aldeen, K. N. (2021, February 27). 40-Year Bibliometric Analysis Of Waqf: Its Current Status and Development, And Paths For Future Research. https://jimf-bi.org/index.php/JIMF/article/download/1308/842

Al-Ghazali, I., & Hammad, A. Z. M. (2017). *Al Mustasfa Min Ilm Al Usul - Imam Ghazali*. Repro Books Limited. https://books.google.com.my/books?id=rxQ7zQEACAAJ

Alhalafi, N., & Veeraraghavan, P. (2021, October 13). Cybersecurity Policy Framework in Saudi Arabia: Literature Review. https://www.frontiersin.org/articles/10.3389/fcomp.2021.736874/pdf

Alharbi, A. S., Halikias, G., Rajarajan, M., & Yamin, M. (2021, January 28). A review of effectiveness of Saudi E-government data security management. *International Journal of Information Technology : an Official Journal of Bharati Vidyapeeth's Institute of Computer Applications and Management*, 13(2), 573–579. DOI: 10.1007/s41870-021-00611-3

Alhogail, A. (2020, June 6). Enhancing information security best practices sharing in virtual knowledge communities. https://www.emerald.com/insight/content/doi/10.1108/VJIKMS-01-2020-0009/full/html

Ali, Hassnian, Hazik Mohamed, Hadia Saqib Hashmi, and M. H. (2019). Global landscape of the Islamic Fintech: opportunities, challenges and future ahead. *COMSATS Journal of Islamic Finance, 4*(2).

Ali, M. D. (1993). Hukum Islam: Pengantar Ilmu Hukum dan Tata Hukum Islam di Indonesia. Jakarta: Raja Grafindo, h. 43

Ali, S., & Khan, M. (2023). *The role of AI in enhancing Islamic finance*. SpringerLink. Retrieved from https://link.springer.com/chapter/10.1007/978-3-031-13302-2_11

Ali, H., Abdullah, R., & Zaini, M. Z. (2019). Fintech and its potential impact on Islamic banking and finance industry: A case study of Brunei Darussalam and Malaysia. [IJIEF]. *International Journal of Islamic Economics and Finance*, 2(1), 73–108. DOI: 10.18196/ijief.2116

Aliyu, A., Abu Bakar, K., Matsuda, G., Darwish, T. S., Abdullah, A. H., Ismail, A. S., & Yaacob, A. C. (2020). Review of some existing shariah-compliant cryptocurrency. *Journal of Contempory Islamic Studies*, 6(1), 22–43.

Allah Pitchay, A., Mydin Meera, A. K., & Saleem, M. (2015). Factors influencing the behavioral intentions of muslim employees to contribute to cash-waqf through salary deductions. *Journal of King Abdulaziz University: Islamic Economics*, 28(1), 57–90. DOI: 10.4197/Islec.28-1.3

Allen, F. D.-K. (2012). *The Foundations of Financial Inclusion: Understanding Ownership and Use of Formal Accounts.* World Bank Policy Research Paper. Retrieved March 1, 2023

Alnsour, M. H. (2011). Internet banking and Jordanian corporate customers: Issues of security and trust. *Journal of Internet Banking and Commerce*, 16(1), 81–106.

Alotaibi, H. A. S. (2022). E-Wallet -A foundation applied study. *Journal of Human and Administrative Sciences*, 1–21. DOI: 10.56760/ZUFR5920

Al-Rahma, F. A., Rahman, M. A., & Al-Mutawa, A. M. (2021). The role of artificial intelligence in enhancing Waqf management. *Journal of Islamic Economics and Finance*, 13(3), 104–118.

Al-Raysuni, A. (2006). *Imam al-Shatibi's theory of the higher objectives and intents of Islamic law*. The Other Press.

Alshater, M. M., Saba, I., Supriani, I., & Rabbani, M. R. (2022). Fintech in islamic finance literature: A review. *Heliyon*, 8(9), e10385. DOI: 10.1016/j.heliyon.2022.e10385 PMID: 36060472

Al-Shatibi, I. I. (2012). *The Reconciliation of the Fundamentals of Islamic Law: Al-Muwafaqat fi Usul al-Shari'a* (Vol. 1). UWA Publishing.

Alt, R., Beck, R., & Smits, M. T. (2018). FinTech and the transformation of the financial industry. *Electronic Markets*, 28(3), 235–243. DOI: 10.1007/s12525-018-0310-9

Amadea, A., & Indrawati, . (2022). The Influence of Perceived Usefulness, Perceived Ease of Use, Social Influence, Facilities Conditions, Lifestyle Compatibility, and Perceived Trust on Intention to Use E-wallet Dana. *International Journal of Business and Management*, 10(8). Advance online publication. DOI: 10.24940/theijbm/2022/v10/i8/BM2208-002

Anam, K., & Qomariyah, I. (2020). *Asas-asas Hukum Islam dalam Hukum Modern*. Jurnal Al-Maqashidi.

Andrew, J. V., Abdullah, N. S. W., Nordin, S., & Tan, K. E. (2021). *A Systematic Review of E-wallet Usage Intention: Integrating UTAUT2 with Perceived Security. 16*(1), 124–133. DOI: 10.24191/ji.v16i1.372

Andrianto, F. (2020), Kepastian Hukum Dalam Politik Hukum di Indonesia. Administrative Law Governance Journal, 3(1).

Andriyaningtyas, I., Adam, M., & Herianingrum, S. (2021). Penerimaan e-wallet Syariah LinkAja dalam rangka pengembangan ekonomi digital di Indonesia. [Jurnal Ekonomi Dan Keuangan]. *EKUITAS*, 5(4), 534–552. DOI: 10.24034/j25485024.y2021.v5.i4.4772

Angel Dwi Satria, A. K. (2021). Development of Sharia Finance Digitalization Towards Inclusive Finance Within a Sharia Maqashid Framework (Case Study on PT Bank Syariah Indonesia's BSI Mobile Banking Product). *Journal of Islamic Business and Economic Review*, 4(2), 84–96.

Ansar, R., Chekima, B., Lada, S., Lim, M. F., & Bouteraa, M. (2023). Determinants of personal financial management practices among Malaysian youth. *Asian Economic and Financial Review*, 13(12), 996–1007. DOI: 10.55493/5002.v13i12.4931

Anshari, M., Arine, M. A., Nurhidayah, N., Aziyah, H., & Salleh, H. (2021). Factors influencing individual in adopting eWallet. *Journal of Financial Services Marketing*, 26(1), 10–23. DOI: 10.1057/s41264-020-00079-5

Antonio, M. S. (2010). *Bisnis dan Kewirausahaan, Ensiklopedia, Leadership & Manajemen Muhammad SAW "The Super Leader Super Manajer" Jilid 2*. Tazkia Publishing.

Antonio, M. S. (2017). *Muhammad SAW: The Super Leader Super Manager*. ProLM Centre & Tazkia Multimedia.

Antoniuk, L., & Zasiadivko, V. (2023, April 24). DIGITAL LITERACY AND TECHNOLOGIES FOR EDUCATION: PRINCIPLES AND TOOLS. DOI: 10.36074/grail-of-science.14.04.2023.044

Anuar, S. B., Azmi, F. A. M., & Sidek, S. N. S. (2022). Exploring the potential and suggesting a new conceptual framework of blockchain technology in estate distribution. *International Journal of Advanced Research in Technology and Innovation*, 4(1), 35–43.

Anwar, I. F., Rahayu, S. B., Yusoff, Y., Faizah, N., & Lajin, M. (2024).. . *INTERNATIONAL JOURNAL OF TRENDS IN The Sustainability of Cash Waqf Using Blockchain Technology : a Conceptual Study*, 5(2), 70–82.

Ardi Hamzah. (2010). *FAKTOR-FAKTOR PEMAKAI YANG MEMPENGARUHI MINAT PEMANFAATAN SISTEM INFORMASI*. 279–292.

Ardiyanti, D., Surwandono, S., Maharani, P. D., & Amalia, N. (2023). Human Security Identification in Maqoshid Sharia Concept as Implementation in Debt Trap of Digital Finance. *Afkaruna: Indonesian Interdisciplinary Journal of Islamic Studies*, 19(1), 123–132. DOI: 10.18196/afkaruna.v19i1.17136

Arif, F. M., & Mustaming, M. (2020). Regional Development Budget Based Maqasid Al Syari'ah: Realization Analysis of the Palopo City Budget. *PROCEEDING IAIN Batusangkar, 1*(2), 17–29. https://ejournal.uinmybatusangkar.ac.id/ojs/index.php/proceedings/article/view/1886/1552

Arifin, Z. (2009), Dasar-dasar Manajemen Bank Syariah. (Tangerang: Azkia Publisher, h. 56. Asari, M. I. (n.d.). (2022), Omnibus Law Untuk Menata Regulasi Penanaman Modal. Retrieved from https://rechtsvinding.bphn.go.id

Arshad, R., Zain, N. M., Urus, S. T., & Chakir, A. (2018). Modelling Maqasid Waqf Performance Measures in Waqf Institutions. *Global Journal Al-Thaqafah*, 8(Special Issue), 157–169. DOI: 10.7187/GJATSI2018-11

Asari, N., Lopes, A. B., & Saito, R. (2011). Interest rate, growth and non-performing assets: Evidence from Indian banking. *International Journal of Economics and Finance*. Advance online publication. DOI: 10.5539/ijef.v3n2p216

Ascarya, A. (2021). The role of Islamic social finance during Covid-19 pandemic in Indonesia's economic recovery. *International Journal of Islamic and Middle Eastern Finance and Management*, 15(2), 386–405. DOI: 10.1108/IMEFM-07-2020-0351

Ascarya, A., & Sakti, A. (2022). Designing micro-fintech models for Islamic micro financial institutions in Indonesia. *International Journal of Islamic and Middle Eastern Finance and Management*, 15(2), 236–254. DOI: 10.1108/IMEFM-05-2020-0233

Ashfaq, M. Z. (2020). *The Application of Fintech in Microtakaful as a Means of Digital Financial Inclusion: Insights from the GCC*. Palgrave Macmillan., DOI: 10.1007/978-3-030-49248-9_5

Aslam Haneef, M. (2018). Islamic Finance Education: Is There a Misallocation of Resources Between Curriculum and Academic Talent? *Islamic Banking and Finance Review*, 05(01), 58–67. DOI: 10.32350/ibfr.2018.05.04

Athief, F. H. N. (2019). Embedding Crowdfunding Structure in Islamic Venture Capital for SMEs Development. *Economica: Jurnal Ekonomi Islam*, 10(1), 1–28. DOI: 10.21580/economica.2019.10.1.3186

Atif, M., Hassan, M. K., Rabbani, M. R., & Khan, S. (2021). Islamic FinTech: The digital transformation bringing sustainability to Islamic finance. In *COVID-19 and Islamic social finance* (pp. 91-103). Routledge.

Atkočiūnienė, Z. O., & Siudikienė, D. (2019). Communication management in promoting knowledge and creativity in fostering innovations in the creative organization. *Creativity Studies*, 14(2), 549–576. DOI: 10.3846/cs.2021.15550

Aunurrochim, M., & Saharudin, M. A. bin. (2021). *E-Wallet: A Study On Contracts Involved Within Its Operational Mechanism*. 1–16. DOI: 10.33102/jfatwa.vol26no1.382

Ayedh, A., Echchabi, A., Battour, M., & Omar, M. (2021). Malaysian Muslim investors' behaviour towards the blockchain-based Bitcoin cryptocurrency market. *Journal of Islamic Marketing*, 12(4), 690–704. DOI: 10.1108/JIMA-04-2019-0081

Ayub, M. (2018, December 1). Institutionalising 'Waqf ' for Realising the Shared Development Objective by Islamic Banks and Financial Institutions. Journal of Islamic business and management, 8(2). DOI: 10.26501/jibm/2018.0802-001

Azganin, H., Kassim, S., & Sa'ad, A. A. (2021). Proposed waqf crowdfunding models for small farmers and the required parameters for their application. *Islamic Economic Studies*, 29(1), 2–17. DOI: 10.1108/IES-01-2021-0006

Aziz, A. B. M. R. (2022). Digital Transformation Through Islamic Digital Banking For Financial Inclusion. *Proceeding of International Conference on Science and Technology*, 12–19. https://doi.org/https://doi.org/10.36378/internationalconfe renceuniks.v0i0.2818

Azizah, S. N. (2023). The adoption of FinTech and the legal protection of the digital assets in Islamic/Sharia banking linked with economic development: A case of Indonesia. *The Journal of World Intellectual Property*, 26(1), 30–40. DOI: 10.1111/jwip.12257

Azizi, N., Shukor, S., & Sabri, H. (2019). Determinants of Repeated Endowers' Donation Intention in Cash Waqf: A Case Study in Majlis Agama Islam dan Adat Melayu Perak (MAIPk). *Jurnal Manajemen Bisnis*, 10(2), 154–163. DOI: 10.18196/mb.10175

Azra, A. M., Epriyanti, N., & Nuzula, Z. F. (2023). Analisis Perilaku Konsumen Muslim yang Melakukan Transaksi Real Money Trading. *Bandung Conference Series Sharia Economic Law*, 3(1). Advance online publication. DOI: 10.29313/bcssel.v3i1.5733

Azrai Azaimi Ambrose, A. H., Gulam Hassan, M. A., & Hanafi, H. (2018). A proposed model for waqf financing public goods and mixed public goods in Malaysia. *International Journal of Islamic and Middle Eastern Finance and Management*, 11(3), 395–415. DOI: 10.1108/IMEFM-01-2017-0001

Bahari, S. A. (2021). The role of micro Takaful industry for the achievement of Islamic financial inclusion in Pakistan. *Middle East Journal of Management*, 8(2-3), 125–139.

Bahri, S. A. (2014). Etika konsumsi dalam perspektif ekonomi islam. *Jurnal Studi Islamika*, 11(2), 347–370. DOI: 10.24239/jsi.v11i2.360.347-370

Bakri, M. H., Almansoori, K. K. S. M., & Azlan, N. A. S. B. M. (2023). Determinants intention usage of Islamic E-Wallet Among Millennials. *Global Business and Finance Review*, 28(1), 11–32. DOI: 10.17549/gbfr.2023.28.1.11

Balakrishnan, V., & Lay, G. C. (2016). Students' Learning Styles and Their Effects on the use of Social Media Technology for Learning. *Telematics and Informatics*, 33(3), 808–821. DOI: 10.1016/j.tele.2015.12.004

Bangun, B., & Kurniyati, N. N.Nany Noor Kurniyati. (2022). Role of financial behavior in mediation the influence of financial literacy and financial self efficacy on financial will being. *International Journal of Economics and Management Research*, 1(3), 166–176. DOI: 10.55606/ijemr.v1i3.54

Banire, B., Al-Thani, D., & Yang, Y. (2021, July 1). Addressing Cyber Security Accessibility: A Qualitative Study. https://www.scienceopen.com/document_file/9e1391c1-8a9a-4706-87ea-50d428c193b3/ScienceOpen/W5.2%20Banire%20Al%20Thani%20Yang.pdf

Bank Islam. (2024). Retrieved from https://www.bankislam.com/corporate-info/social-finance-bank-islam/pembiayaan-mikro-bangkit/

Bank Negara Malaysia (BNM). (2022). Financial Sector Blueprint 2022-2026. *The Central Bank of Malaysia*, 1–121. https://www.bnm.gov.my/documents/20124/5915429/fsb3_en_book.pdf%0Ahttps://www.bnm.gov.my/publications/fsb3

Bank Negara Malaysia. (2020). Retrieved from https://www.bnm.gov.my/web/guest/-/sandbox-pd24

Bank Negara Malaysia. (2023). *Bank Negara Malaysia Annual Report 2022*. https://www.bnm.gov.my/publications/ar2022

Banking Law. (2005). Law Number: 5411. https://www.mevzuat.gov.tr/mevzuatmetin/1.5.5411.pdf

Banna, H., Hassan, M. K., Ahmad, R., & Alam, M. R. (2022). Islamic banking stability amidst the COVID-19 pandemic: The role of digital financial inclusion. *International Journal of Islamic and Middle Eastern Finance and Management*, 15(2), 310–330. DOI: 10.1108/IMEFM-08-2020-0389

Baran, B E., & Woznyj, H M. (2021). Managing VUCA. *Elsevier BV, 50*(2), 100787-100787. DOI: 10.1016/j.orgdyn.2020.100787

Barom, M. N. (2012). Conceptualising a unified normative framework of social responsibility in Islamic economics. *IIUM Research, Invention and Innovation Exhibition 2011, 2*(2), 329–363. http://irep.iium.edu.my/28105/

Barthakur, G., Rajkonwar, A. B., & Barua, P. (2022). Potential of an e-wallet: a study among the sellers in dibrugarh city, assam. *PARIPEX INDIAN JOURNAL OF RESEARCH*, 119–222. DOI: 10.36106/paripex/4508318

Bartholomae, S., & Fox, J. J. (2021). A Decade Review of Research on College Student Financial Behavior and Well-Being. *Journal of Family and Economic Issues*, 42(1), 154–177. DOI: 10.1007/s10834-021-09756-6

Bashir, M. S. (2024). Globalization, Digitalization, and Financial Inclusion in Islamic Banking. In Globalization, Digitalization, and Financial Inclusion in Islamic Banking (p. 37). DOI: 10.4018/979-8-3693-4111-7.ch012

Bayrakdaroğlu, A. (2016). Development of electronic banking after the crisis. In Gündoğdu, A. (Ed.), *Fundamentals of Banking in the Light of Developments After the Global Crisis*. Nobel Publishing. (In Turkish)

Beck, T., Demirguc-Kunt, A., & Peria, M. S. M. (2007). Reaching out: Access to and use of banking services across countries. *Journal of Financial Economics*, 85(1), 234–266. DOI: 10.1016/j.jfineco.2006.07.002

Bee, T. S., & Ying, K. Y. (2021). An examination of determinants for e-wallet adoption in Malaysia: A combined approach. *F1000 Research*, 10, 1155. DOI: 10.12688/f1000research.73402.1

Beik, I S., Zaenal, M H., & Rizkiningsih, P. (2019, January 1). Waqf Led Halal Cryptocurrency Model. DOI: 10.1007/978-3-030-10749-9_18

Beik, I. S., & Arsyianti, L. D. (2021). Application of SCL, PBL, and MM In Teaching Islamic Economics And Finance. *Teaching and Research Methods for Islamic Economics and Finance*, 137–151. https://doi.org/http://dx.doi.org/10.4324/9781003252764-12

Beik, I. S., Swandaru, R., & Rizkiningsih, P. (2021). Utilization of Digital Technology for Zakat Development. In Billah, M. M. (Ed.), *Islamic FinTech: Insights and Solutions* (Vol. 9, pp. 231–248). Springer International Publishing., DOI: 10.1007/978-3-030-45827-0_13

Bella, F. I., & Efendi, N. F. (2021). Strengthening the Islamic Digital Payment System Through Sharia Electronic Wallet (E-Wallet). *El Dinar: Jurnal Keuangan Dan Perbankan Syariah, 9*(2), 94–107. https://pdfs.semanticscholar.org/a823/158e1c37edd15e77202bb2bca9658e9de44b.pdf

Belleflamme, P., Lambert, T., & Schwienbacher, A. (2014). Crowdfunding: Tapping the right crowd. *Journal of Business Venturing*, 29(5), 585–609. DOI: 10.1016/j.jbusvent.2013.07.003

Bernthal, M. J., Crockett, D., & Rose, R. L. (2005). Credit cards as lifestyle facilitators. *The Journal of Consumer Research*, 32(1), 130–145. DOI: 10.1086/429605

Beybur, M., & Çetinkaya, M. (2020). The impact of covid-19 pandemic on usage of digital banking products and services in Turkey. [In Turkish]. *International Journal of Western Black Sea Socialand Humanities Sciences*, 4(2), 148–163. DOI: 10.46452/baksoder.829078

Bhatia, A., Chandani, A., Divekar, R., Mehta, M., & Vijay, N. (2022). Digital innovation in wealth management landscape: The moderating role of robo advisors in behavioural biases and investment decision-making. *International Journal of Innovation Science*, 14(3/4), 693–712. DOI: 10.1108/IJIS-10-2020-0245

Bhatt, A. a. (2016). Factors afecting customer's adoption of mobile banking services. *Journal of Internet Banking and Commerce*, 21(1), 161.

Bhattarai, K. (2017). Non-Performing Loans and Bank Productivity: Evidence from Nepalese Commercial Banks. *Journal of Business and Management*, •••, 10–22. DOI: 10.3126/jbm.v19i3.18315

Bionducci, L., Botta, A., Bruno, P., Denecker, O., Gathinji, C., Nadeau, M.-C., & Sttanathan, B. (2023). *2023 McKinsey Global Payments Report.*

Biplob, H., & Abdullah, M. (2019). The importance of islamic financial literacy for muslims: a general review. *Islam & Civilisational Renewal, 10*(1).

BNM. (2019). Retrieved from efaidnbmnnnibpcajpcglclefindmkaj/https://www.bnm.gov.my/documents/20124/761679/VBIAF_Final+guidance+1.11.2019.pdf

BNM. (2022). *Policy Document on Electronic Money (E-Money).* https://www.bnm.gov.my/documents/20124/943361/PD-eMoney-202302.pdf

BNM. (2024). Retrieved from https://www.bnm.gov.my/financial-inclusion-data-for-malaysia

BNM. B. N. (2022, April 22). *Five successful applicants for the digital bank licences.* Retrieved June 20, 2022, from Bank Negara Malaysia (BNM): https://www.bnm.gov.my/-/digital-bank-5-licences

Bouakkaz, N. (2022). Using blockchain technology to revolutionize Waqf: The Finterra Waqf Chain model. *Journal of Economics and Sustainable Development*, 50(1), 136–841.

Boudreau, K. J., Jeppesen, L. B., Reichstein, T., & Rullani, F. (2021). Crowdfunding as Donations to Entrepreneurial Firms. *Research Policy*, 50(7), 104264. DOI: 10.1016/j.respol.2021.104264

BRSA. (2006). Banking Regulation and Supervision Agency. Regulation on Credit Transactions of Banks. https://www.resmigazete.gov.tr/eskiler/2006/11/20061101-13.htm

Brunier, F. D. (2015). *Transforming the Banking Branch.* Retrieved February 25, 2023, from Accenture: https://www.accenture.com/t20160321T 020410Z__w __/in- en/_acnmedia/Accenture/Conversion-Assets/ DotCom/Documents/Global/PDF/Strategy_7/Accenture-StrategyTran

Bughin, J., Hazan, E., Ramaswamy, S., Chui, M., Allas, T., Dahlström, P., Henke, N., & Trench, M. (2017). Artificial intelligence: The next digital frontier? McKinsey Global Institute. https://www.mckinsey.com/mgi

Building Trust In Waqf Management — Implications Of Good Governance And Transparent Reporting. (2020, July 25). https://www.worldscientific.com/doi/10.1142/S0217590820420059

Bukhari. (2024). *Shahih Bukhari*. http://103.44.149.34/elib/assets/buku/Shahih_bukhari_muslim.pdf

Bukhari, S. F. H., Woodside, F. M., Hassan, R., Ali, O. M. S. H., Hussain, S., & Waqas, R. (2021). Intrinsic and extrinsic attributes that drive Muslim consumer purchase behavior. *Journal of Islamic Marketing*, 12(1), 70–94. DOI: 10.1108/JIMA-01-2018-0004

Bursa Efek Indonesia. (2022). *Sejarah dan Milestone Pasar Modal*. IDX Channel.

Buterin, V. (2014). "A Next-Generation Smart Contract and Decentralized Application Platform.", Ethereum White Paper.

Buvat, J. (2014). *Doing Business the Digital Way: How Capital One Fundamentally Disrupted the Financial Services Industry*. Capgemini Consulting. Retrieved February 20, 2023, from https://www.capgemini.com/wp-content/uploads/2017/07/capital-one-doing-business-the-digital-way_0.pdf

Çalış, N. (2023). The effect of digital banking applications on profitability: An application on participation banking sector. In Dündar, Ö. (Ed.), *Theory, Practice and Current Debates in Economics and Administrative Sciences*. Gazi Bookshop. (In Turkish)

Caprariello, P. A., & Reis, H. T. (2021). "This one's on me!": Differential well-being effects of self-centered and recipient-centered motives for spending money on others. *Motivation and Emotion*, 45(6), 1–23. DOI: 10.1007/s11031-021-09907-0

Caputo, A., Schiocchet, E., & Troise, C. (2022). Sustainable business models as successful drivers in equity crowdfunding. *Business Strategy and the Environment*, 31(7), 3509–3522. DOI: 10.1002/bse.3102

Carbó, S., Edward P. M. Gardener, Philip Molyneux (2005). Financial Exclusion. Palgrave Macmillan Studies in Banking and Financial Institutions (SBFI)

Casaló, L. V., Flavián, C., & Guinalíu, M. (2007). The role of security, privacy, usability and reputation in the development of online banking. *Online Information Review*, 31(5), 583–603. DOI: 10.1108/14684520710832315

Central Bureau of Statistics. (2024, May 17). *Religion in Indonesia, 2024*. https://samarindakota.bps.go.id/id/statistics-table/1/MzI0IzE=/agama-di-indonesia-2024.html

Chang, S. E., & Wang, M. H. (2023). Blockchain-Enabled Fintech Innovation: A Case of Reengineering Stock Trading Services. *IEEE Access : Practical Innovations, Open Solutions*, 11(December), 137125–137137. DOI: 10.1109/ACCESS.2023.3339570

Chapra, U. (1983). Money and Banking in an Islamic Economy. *International Center for Research in Islamic Economics*, 145-186.

Chen, Y., & Barnes, S. (2007). Initial trust and online buyer behaviour. *Industrial Management & Data Systems*, 107(1), 21–36. DOI: 10.1108/02635570710719034

Chen, Z., & Livermore, M. (2020). The Negative Association between Alternative Financial Services Usage and Financial Well-Being: Variations by Income. *Social Work Research*, 44(3), 183–195. DOI: 10.1093/swr/svaa009

Chong, F. H. L. (2021). Enhancing trust through digital Islamic finance and blockchain technology. *Qualitative Research in Financial Markets*, 13(3), 328–341. DOI: 10.1108/QRFM-05-2020-0076

Choudhury, M. A., Hossain, M. S., & Mohammad, M. T. (2019). Islamic finance instruments for promoting long-run investment in the light of the well-being criterion (maslaha). *Journal of Islamic Accounting and Business Research*, 10(2), 315–339. DOI: 10.1108/JIABR-11-2016-0133

Christanti, N., & Mahastanti Ariany. (2011), Faktor-faktor Yang Dipertimbangkan Investor Dalam Melakukan Investasi. Jurnal Manajemen Teori dan Terapan Tahun, 4(3).

CIMB. (2024). Retrieved from https://www.cimb.com/en/newsroom/2021/itekad-2-0-introduced-to-extend-support-for-the-asnaf-and-b40-communities.html

Comiter, M. (2019). Attacking artificial intelligence. *Belfer Center Paper*, 8, 2019–08.

Cooper, B. R., Concilla, A., Albrecht, J. M., Bhukhan, A., Laughter, M. R., Anderson, J. B., Rundle, C. W., Mceldrew, E. C., & Presley, C. L. (2022). *Social Media as a Medium for Dermatologic Education*. 103–109. DOI: 10.1007/s13671-022-00359-4

Crosby, M., Pattanayak, P., Verma, S., & Kalyanaraman, V. (2016). Blockchain Technology: Beyond Bitcoin. *Applied Innovation Review*, 2, 6–19.

Çürük, S. (2013). The development of İslamic finance in Turkey, existing problems and recommendations. *Doctoral Thesis. Selçuk University Institute of Social Sciences, Department of Business Administration,* Konya (In Turkish).

Darma, S. (2022). Urgensi Maqashid Syariah Dalam Pengembangan Ekonomi. *Al Mashaadir*, 2(2), 44–53. DOI: 10.52029/jis.v2i2.58

Dash, R. K., & Kabra, G. (2010). Real wage variation and non-performing assets: evidence from Indian banks. International Journal of Social Economics, https://www.emerald.com/insight/content/doi/10.1108/03068291011091152/full/html

Daud, A. H. M., & Salim, H. M. (2022). Digital finance and maqasid al-Shariah. *ACADEMIC PROGRAMMES*, 4, 28–33.

Daud, M., & Azam, A.-R. N. (2011). Islamic Development Bank (IDB), Foreign Aid and the Challenges for Sustainable Development in Africa. *International Journal of Business and Social Science*, 2(4), 190–199. http://www.ijbssnet.com/journals/Vol._2_No._4%253B_March_2011/22.pdf

David, S., & Kathrine, J. W. (2019). An Investigative Report On Encryption Based Security Mechanisms For E-Wallets. *International Journal of Scientific & Technology Research*, 8(10), 1755–1769.

Dayyan, M., Prodi, M., Syariah, P., & Langsa, I. (2023). Analysis Sharia Financial Literacy of Kualasimpang City Community in The Digital Era. *Jurnal Ekonomi Syariah* [JESKaPe]. *Akuntansi Dan Perbankan*, 7(2), 134–146. DOI: 10.52490/jeskape.v7i2.1459

Delle Foglie, A., Panetta, I. C., Boukrami, E., & Vento, G. (2021). The impact of the Blockchain technology on the global Sukuk industry: Smart contracts and asset tokenisation. *Technology Analysis and Strategic Management*, •••, 1–15. DOI: 10.1080/09537325.2021.1939000

Demir, A., Pesqué-Cela, V., Altunbas, Y., & Murinde, V. (2020). Fintech, financial inclusion, and income inequality: A quantile regression approach. *The European Journal of Finance*. eZakat (2024). Retrieved from https://ezakat.com/#/

Demirgüç-Kunt, A., Klapper, L., Singer, D., Ansar, S., & Hess, J. (2020). The global findex database 2017: Measuring financial inclusion and opportunities to expand access to and use of financial services. *The World Bank Economic Review*, 34(Supplement_1), S2–S8. DOI: 10.1093/wber/lhz013

Denizbank, 2024. How Safe Is Your Data: Blockchain Technology https://www.denizbank.com/blog/dijital-dunya/verileriniz-ne-kadar-guvende-blockchain-teknolojisi-105489#:~:text=Farkl%C4%B1%20bloklar%C4%B1n%20bir%20araya%20gelmesinden,payla%C5%9F%C4%B1ml%C4%B1%20bir%20defter%20olarak%20d%C3%BC%C5%9F%C3%BCn%C3%BClebilir

Dennis, D., Qoyum, A., & Sakti, M. P. (2018). Determinant of cash waqf nahdatul ulama (case of Muslim students in Indonesia). Madania. *Jurnal Kajian Keislaman*, 22(1), 19–32. DOI: 10.29300/madania.v22i1.886

Department of Statistics Malaysia. (2021). *Ict Use and Access By Individuals and Households Survey Report 2021*. Issue April.

Dholakia, U., Tam, L., Yoon, S., & Wong, N. (2016). The ant and the grasshopper: Understanding personal saving orientation of consumers. *The Journal of Consumer Research*, 43(1), 134–155. DOI: 10.1093/jcr/ucw004

Diana Kangwa, J. T. (2021). The Social Production of Financial Inclusion of Generation Z in Digital Banking Ecosystems. *AABJ*, 15(3), 6–118. DOI: 10.14453/aabfj.v15i3.6

Dimitrios, D., Angelos, K., & Vasilios, P. (2012). Macroeconomic determinants of nonperforming loans: A panel data analysis of South Asian countries. International Journal of Economics and Financial Issues, https://www.econjournals.com/index.php/ijefi/article/view/59/12

DinarStandard. (2022). State of the Global Islamic Economy Report 2021/2022. In *State of the Global Islamic Economy Report 2020/21*. https://haladinar.io/hdn/doc/report2018.pdf

Djazuli, A. (2010), Kaidah-kaidah Fiqih: Kaidah Hukum Islam Dalam Menyelesaikan Masalah-masalah Yang Praktis, Jakarta: Kencana, h.10

Dorfleitner, G., Forcella, D., & Nguyen, Q. A. (2021). The digital transformation of microfinance institutions: an empirical analysis. *Journal of Applied Accounting Research*. DOI: 10.1108/JAAR-02-2021-0041

DSN-MUI. (2017). *Fatwa - Uang Elektronik Syariah*. https://drive.google.com/file/d/1KPAvhhziJ61Pt8EFxxTFfDPNmRHJoQDG/view?usp=sharing

DSN-MUI. (2018). Fatwa - Layanan Pembiayaan Berbasis Teknologi Informasi Berdasarkan Prinsip Syariah. In *Majelis Ulama Indonesia*. https://drive.google.com/file/d/1qCu2X6MTIFnYqK22eMx7uFL53AXBT9Vo/view?usp=sharing

Edelmann, N., & Virkar, S. (2023). The Impact of Sustainability on Co-Creation of Digital Public Services. *Administrative Sciences*, 13(2), 43. DOI: 10.3390/admsci13020043

Egodawele, M., Sedera, D., & Bui, V. (2022, January 1). A Systematic Review of Digital Transformation Literature (2013-2021) and the development of an overarching apriori model to guide future research. Cornell University.

Elbek Musaev &Muhammed Yousoof. (2015). A Review on Internet Banking Security and Privacy. *ICIT 2015 The 7th International Conference on Information Technology*, 1-5. DOI: 10.15849/icit.2015.0070

Eldersevi, S., & Muhammad, M. (2021). "Asnaf Care: A Case Study of the Malaysian-based Charity Crowdfunding Platform to Combat the Impact of COVID-19." *5th International Conference of Zakat,* 2020, 615–626.

Emiroğlu, O. (2019). Participation and the importance of the banking in Turkey. *Unpublished Master Thesis. Kastamonu University, Institute of Social Sciences, Department of Economics,* Kastamonu (In Turkish).

Emlak Participation. (2023). History of Emlak katılım https://www.emlakkatilim.com.tr/tr/hakkimizda/tarihce

Erba, D. M. F., & Nofrianto, N. (2022). Implementation of Maqashid Syariah in Sharia Business Transactions. *Al-Falah: Journal of Islamic Economics*, 7(1), 125–139. DOI: 10.29240/alfalah.v7i1.3703

Erić, D. (2022). Innovation and Fintech. In *Digitalization and the Future of Financial Services: Innovation and Impact of Digital Finance* (pp. 19–39). Springer International Publishing. DOI: 10.1007/978-3-031-11545-5_2

Fachrurrazy, M., Siliwadi, D N., & Herlina, N. (2022, May 29). Potential for Digital-Based Productive Waqf Development (Case Study of Datuk Sulaiman ModernIslamic Boarding School and Muhammadiyah Boarding School) in Palopo City, South of Celebes. Al-Falah: journal of islamic economics (Online), 7(1), 141-141. DOI: 10.29240/alfalah.v7i1.3840

Fadila, D., Sastrawinata, H., Maulana, R., & Mariskha, Z. (2020). Impact of Learning, Socialization, and Financial Lifestyle of Students' Intention to Invest in Capital Market. *Proceedings of the 3rd Forum in Research, Science, and Technology (FIRST 2019).* DOI: 10.2991/assehr.k.200407.038

Fahmi, M., Warman, A. B., & Hayati, R. F. (2023). Literasi Hukum Ekonomi Syariah di Era Digital dan Kontribusinya bagi Penguatan Ekonomi Syariah di Indonesia (Studi terhadap Platform Instagram). *Al-Huquq: Journal of Indonesian Islamic Economic Law, 5*(1), 20–43. https://ejournal.iainmadura.ac.id/index.php/alhuquq/article/view/5729

Fanani, A., Kuncoro, A. W., Husni, A. B. M., & Wijayanti, E. A. (2021). The Contribution of Waqf on Poverty Alleviation through Digital Platforms: A Case of Indonesia. *Shirkah: Journal of Economics and Business*, 6(2), 246–261. DOI: 10.22515/shirkah.v6i2.386

Fan, L., & Henager, R. (2022). A Structural Determinants Framework for Financial Well-Being. *Journal of Family and Economic Issues*, 43(2), 415–428. DOI: 10.1007/s10834-021-09798-w PMID: 34548774

Farag, S. A. S., Edris, M., Abubakar, Y. S., ... (2024). Using Maqasid Shariah to Utilize the Contemporary Waqf: Implementing Artificial Intelligence as an Example. *Kurdish ..., 4883*, 2905–2923. https://kurdishstudies.net/menu-script/index.php/KS/article/view/1579%0Ahttps://kurdishstudies.net/menu-script/index.php/KS/article/download/1579/1141

Fariana, A. (2017), Urgensi Fatwa MUI dalam Pembangunan Sistem Hukum Ekonomi Islam di Indonesia. Al Ihkam Jurnal Hukum & Pranata Sosial, 12(1).

Fariana, A. (2021), Legal Politics as a Catalyst in Forming Sharia Economic Legal System in the Indonesia's New Order and Reform Era. Ijtihad: Jurnal Wacana Hukum Islam dan Kemanusiaan, 21(2).

Farida, I., & Setiawan, D. (2022). Business strategies and competitive advantage: The role of performance and innovation. *Journal of Open Innovation*, 8(3), 1–16. DOI: 10.3390/joitmc8030163

Faturohman, T., Hassandi, I., & Yulianti, Y. (2020). User Acceptance of Online Waqf Applications: Evidence From Indonesia. *Journal of Islamic Monetary Economics and Finance*, 6(3), 503–530. DOI: 10.21098/jimf.v6i3.1117

Fatwa-Laman 11-DSN-MUI. (n.d.). Retrieved from https://dsnmui.or.id, diakses pada 5 April 2022

Fauzi, M., Yahya, S., Hanaysha, J. R., Haron, M. S., & Zahrin, S. N. A. (2019). The impact of trust in cash waqf contribution: a case study of wakaf Selangor muamalat (WSM) service of bank Muamalat Malaysia Berhad (BMMB). International Journal of Business, Economics and Law, 18(2), 1-10. Retrieved from https://ijbel.com/wp-content/uploads/2019/05/KLIBEL-18_63.pdf

Fauziah, N. N., Rabiah, E., Ali, A. E., Alvierra Binti Md Bashir, A., & Bacha, A. M. (2019). an Analysis of Cash Waqf Linked Sukuk for Socially Impactful Sustainable Projects in Indonesia. *Journal of Islamic Finance, 10*(1), 001–010.

Fazmi, F. (2019). Role of robo-advisors in Islamic financial institutions. Retrieved from https://journal.wahedinvest.com/role-of-robo-advisors-in-islamic-financial-institutions/

Febriaty, H. (2019). Pengaruh Sistem Pembayaran Non Tunai Dalam Era Digital Terhadap Tingkat Pertumbuhan Ekonomi Indonesia. [Festival Riset Ilmiah Manajemen Dan Akuntansi]. *Prosiding FRIMA*, 6681(2), 307–313. DOI: 10.55916/frima.v0i2.47

Ferraz, S. B., Romero, C. B. A., Nogami, V. K. da C., & Veloso, A. R. (2015). *Personal values and green purchase behaviour: a cross-cultural study between Brazil and Canada*.

Financial Education Network. (2019). *National Strategy for Financial Literacy 2019-2023*. Strategy.

Fintech News Malaysia. (2022, July 18). *Malaysia's Fintech Map 2022*. Https://Fintechnews.My/31945/Malaysia/Fintech-Report-Malaysia-2022/.

Fintech News. (2020) Retrieved from https://fintechnews.my/23063/digital-banking-news-malaysia/bank-negara-malaysia-issues-updated-virtual-banking-draft/

Fintech News. (2021). Retrieved from https://fintechnews.my/26417/digital-banking-news-malaysia/bank-islam-gears-up-a-fully-digital-bank-by-inking-partnerships-with-mambu-experian-and-pod/

Fintech News. (2024). Retrieved from https://fintechnews.my/44259/digital-transformation/bank-muamalat-to-launch-digital-islamic-super-app-powered-by-backbase/

Firmansyah, E. A., & Anwar, M. (2019). Islamic financial technology (FINTECH): its challenges and prospect. *Achieving and Sustaining SDGs 2018 Conference: Harnessing the Power of Frontier Technology to Achieve the Sustainable Development Goals (ASSDG 2018)*, 52–58.

Fitrianingsih. (n.d.). Investasi dalam Islam: Hukum, Prinsip dan Jenisnya. Retrieved from https://www.qoala.app/2021

Floh, A., & Treiblmaier, H. (2006). What keeps the e-Banking customer loyal? A multigroup analysis of the moderating role of consumer characteristics on e-loyalty in the fnancial service industry. *SSRN*, 7(2), 97–110. DOI: 10.2139/ssrn.2585491

Fokri, W. N. I. W. M., Ali, E. M. T. E., Nordin, N., Chik, W. M. Y. W., Aziz, S. A., & Jusoh, A. J. M. (2021). The Unclaimed Inheritance Issues: A Solution Using Blockchain Technology. *Psychology (Savannah, Ga.)*, 58(1), 4709–4717. DOI: 10.17762/pae.v58i1.1630

Fong, V. (2023). *Malaysia Fintech Report 2023*. https://fintechnews.my/malaysia-fintech-report-2023/

Francis, M. (2020). Global structures of inequality and unequal distribution of wealth. In Leal Filho, W., Azul, A., Brandli, L., Özuyar, P., & Wall, T. (Eds.), *Decent work and economic growth. Encyclopedia of the UN Sustainable Development Goals*. Springer. DOI: 10.1007/978-3-319-71058-7_10-2

Friedline, T., & West, S. (2016). Young adults' race, wealth, and entrepreneurship. *Race and Social Problems*, 8(1), 42–63. DOI: 10.1007/s12552-016-9163-z

Fuadi, N. F. Z., Farida, D., & Saadah, N. (2020, May 20). Empathy or Self-credibility? An Empirical Study of Intentions to Donate through Social Crowdfunding using the UTAUT Model. *Proceedings of the Proceedings of the 1st Conference on Islamic Finance and Technology, CIFET, 21 September, Sidoarjo, East Java, Indonesia.* DOI: 10.4108/eai.21-9-2019.2293953

Fund, C. M. (2012). Crowdfunding. In Publication, C. (Ed.), *A Canadian Context: Exploring The Potential Of Crowdfunding In The Creative Content Industries*.

Furqani, S. A. (2012). The Objectives of Shariah (Maqasid Shariah) in Takaful: Highlighting the Noble Practice. *International Conference on Management, Economics & Finance Proceeding*, 910-918.

Gainau, P. C. (2020). Have Students Comprehended Investment? *Journal of Accounting and Investment*, 21(3). Advance online publication. DOI: 10.18196/jai.2103162

Ganapathy, S., Sippy, T., Sinha, V., & Adarkar, H. (2022). *Building the Foundations: Strengthening technical capacity in government*. Artha Global.

Garanti, B. B. V. A. (2020). The new hero of the financial sector: Artificial intelligence_https://www.garantibbva.com.tr/blog/yapay-zeka

Garanti, B. B. V. A. (2024). Possible Dangers in Digital Banking_https://www.garantibbva.com.tr/dijital-bankacilik/olasi-tehlikeler

Garrido-Moreno, A., Martín-Rojas, R., & García-Morales, V. J. (2024). The key of innovation and organizational resilience in improving business performance: A mixed-methods approach. *International Journal of Information Management*, 77, 102777. Advance online publication. DOI: 10.1016/j.ijinfomgt.2024.102777

Gazali, H. M., Jumadi, J., Ramlan, N. R., Abd Rahmat, N., Uzair, S. N. H. M., & Mohid, A. N. (2020). Application of artificial intelligence (AI) in islamic investments. *Journal of Islamic Finance*, 9(2), 70–77.

Gerber, E. M., & Hui, J. (2013). Crowdfunding. *ACM Transactions on Computer-Human Interaction*, 20(6), 1–32. DOI: 10.1145/2530540

Ghassan, H. B. (2016). Fairness and Ethics in Spending. *Journal of Reviews on Global Economics*, 5, 281–287. DOI: 10.6000/1929-7092.2016.05.24

Ghazali, M. S., Alwi, S. F. S., Abd Aziz, N. N., & Hazudin, S. F. (2020). Pathway to Financial Well-being: A review on the role of psychological factors. *Environment-Behaviour Proceedings Journal*, 5(13), 55–61. DOI: 10.21834/e-bpj.v5i13.2063

Ghode, D. J., Jain, R., Soni, G., Singh, S. K., & Yadav, V. (2020). Architecture to enhance transparency in supply chain management using blockchain technology. *Procedia Manufacturing*, 51, 1614–1620. DOI: 10.1016/j.promfg.2020.10.225

Gill, M. (2016). *The Digital Maturity Model.* Cambridge: Forrester Research. Retrieved February 25, 2023, from http://forrester.nitro-digital.com/pdf/Forrester-s%20Digital%20Maturity%20Model%204.0.pdf

Glavina, S. G., & Asmiatullin, R. R. (2023). Digital Currencies: Opportunities in Islamic Finance. Scientific and Educational Areas Under Modern Challenges, 128–135. DOI: 10.21661/r-560136

Global Digital Insight. (2022). *Digital 2022*. https://datareportal.com/reports/digital-2022-malaysia

Global Islamic Finance Report. (2017). *Islamic Finance in the Digital Age*, 282–290.

Goel, I. (2024). Financial Education and Digitalisation: Analysis of Avenues. *Sachetas*, 3(1), 17–25. DOI: 10.55955/310003

Gohil, Prof. S., Vinchhi, K., & Yewale, N. (2023). A study on impact of mobile payment with special reference to youths. *EPRA International Journal of Economic and Business Review*, 32–35. DOI: 10.36713/epra12530

Gökalp, M. F. ve Güngör, T. (1993*). Economic structure of Islamic society, Istanbul: Fey Foundation Publications(In Turkish).*

Golden, W., & Cordie, L. (2022). Digital Financial Literacy. *Adult Literacy Education: The International Journal of Literacy, Language, and Numeracy*, 4(3), 20–26. DOI: 10.35847/WGolden.LCordie.4.3.20

Goldsmith, R. E., Stith, M. T., & White, J. D. (2015). *An Empirical Study of the Relationship Between Personal Values and Innovative Purchasing Behavior.*, DOI: 10.1007/978-3-319-17055-8_17

Gosal, M. A., & Linawati, N. (2018, October 10). Pengaruh Intensitas Penggunaan Layanan Mobile Payment terhadap Spending Behavior. *Seminar Nasional Manajemen 3.* https://repository.petra.ac.id/id/eprint/18031

Goud, B., Uddin, T. A., & Fianto, B. A. (2021). Islamic fintech and ESG goals: Key considerations for fulfilling maqasid principles. In *Islamic Fintech* (pp. 16–35). DOI: 10.4324/9781003014614-2

Green, C. H. (2014). *Banker's Guide to New Small Business Finance, + Website: Venture Deals, Crowdfunding, Private Equity, and Technology*. Wiley. https://books.google.co.id/books?id=rDIWBAAAQBAJ

Griffiths, P. D. R. (2021). Fintech and its historical perspective. *The Palgrave Handbook of FinTech and Blockchain*, 19-50.

Gulrez, T. (2021). Strategic assessment of Islamic Fintech in GCC countries. *Fintech, digital currency and the future of Islamic finance: Strategic, regulatory and adoption issues in the Gulf Cooperation Council*, 223-241.

Gün, M. (2020). The path to fintech development research on Islamic finance in Turkey. In *Impact of Financial Technology (FinTech) on Islamic Finance and Financial Stability* (pp. 65-96). IGI Global.

Gunawan, M. R., Qurratu'ayuni Mustafa, M., Salsabil, N. Z., & Gunawan, M. R. (2020). The Effect of Social Media Content and Personal Background Performance on Financial Planning Awareness of Generation Z Muslim. *Ekonomi Islam Indonesia*, 2(2). Advance online publication. DOI: 10.58968/eii.v2i2.50

Gunawijaya, R. (2017). Kebutuhan manusia dalam pandangan ekonomi kapitalis dan ekonomi Islam. *Jurnal Al-Maslahah, 13*(1), 131–150. https://www.academia.edu/download/103112520/495.pdf

Gutter, M. S., & Copur, Z. (2011). Financial Behaviors and Financial Well-Being of College Students: Evidence from a National Survey. *Journal of Family and Economic Issues*, 32(4), 699–714. DOI: 10.1007/s10834-011-9255-2

Habib Ahmed. (2014). Islamic Banking and Shari'ah Compliance: A Product Development Perspective. *Journal of Islamic Finance*(2), 015 – 029.

Habib, A. U. (2021). FinTech-Based Islamic Social Financing Products: A Critical Evaluation. *Innovative Strategies for Implementing FinTech in Banking*, 67-82. DOI: 10.4018/978-1-7998-3257-7.ch004

Hadiyati, P., Gladys, A. I., & Iqbal, M. (2020). Encourage Peopl e's Interest to Do Cash Waqf. *Islamiconomic: Jurnal Ekonomi Islam*, 11(2). Advance online publication. DOI: 10.32678/ijei.v11i2.192

Hafidh, A. A. (2022). Tinjauan Maqashid Syariah Tentang E-Money. *Jurnal Ilmiah Ekonomi Islam*, 8(1), 140. DOI: 10.29040/jiei.v8i1.3946

Hai, A., Kassim, D. S., & Mohtesham, M. M. J. (2022). An Innovative Sukuk-Waqf for Islamic Microfinance Institutions: Integrating Maqasid Al-Shariah, SDGs and Waqf. *Tazkia Islamic Finance and Business Review*, 15(1), 19–39. DOI: 10.30993/tifbr.v15i1.251

Hakak, S., Kamsin, A., Khan, W. Z., Zakari, A., Imran, M., Ahmad, K., & Gilkar, G. A. (2020, June 14). Digital Hadith authentication: Recent advances, open challenges, and future directions. *Transactions on Emerging Telecommunications Technologies*, 33(6), e3977. Advance online publication. DOI: 10.1002/ett.3977

Hambali, A., & Aisyah, S. N. (2021). Equity Crowdfunding based on Islamic Philanthropy: A Concept. *5th INTERNATIONAL CONFERENCE OF ZAKAT PROCEEDINGS*, 545–554.

Hamlet, C. a. (2000). Community banks go online. *ABA Banking Journal's 2000 white paper/banking on the internet,* 61–65.

Hamsin, M. K., Halim, A., Anggriawan, R., & Lutfiani, H. (2023). Sharia E-Wallet: The Issue of Sharia Compliance and Data Protection. *Al-Manahij: Jurnal Kajian Hukum Islam*, 17(1), 53–68. DOI: 10.24090/mnh.v17i1.7633

Hanapi, M. S. (2017). The Wasatiyyah-Consumerism Concept as an Equivalent to the Consumerism Phenomenon in Conventional Economy. *International Journal of Academic Research in Business & Social Sciences*, 7(12), 944–961. DOI: 10.6007/IJARBSS/v7-i12/3724

Handoko, L., Nugroho, V. C., & Sembel, J. S. (2020). INTENTION TO INVEST IN FINANCIAL PRODUCT OF OLDER PRERETIREES WITH FINANCIAL SELF EFFICACY AS AN INTERVENING VARIABLE. *Ultima Management : Jurnal Ilmu Manajemen*, 12(1), 34–45. DOI: 10.31937/manajemen.v12i1.1539

Haneef, M. A., Pramanik, A. H., Mohammed, M. O., Bin Amin, M. F., & Muhammad, A. D. (2015). Integration of waqf-Islamic microfinance model for poverty reduction: The case of Bangladesh. *International Journal of Islamic and Middle Eastern Finance and Management*, 8(2), 246–270. DOI: 10.1108/IMEFM-03-2014-0029

Harahap, B. A., Paundralingga, A. Y., Cinditya, A., & Kusuma, M. (2018). Implikasi Makroekonomi dari Inovasi Digital: Studi Literatur. *Occasional Paper*, 1–50.

Harahap, M. A., & Harahap, I. (2023). Measuring Muslim Welfare: A Falah-Based Index. *Jurnal Ekonomi dan Keuangan Islam, 12*(2), 478-499. https://doi.org/DOI: 10.22373/share.v12i2.19191

Haridan, N. M., Hassan, A. F. S., Shah, S. M., & Mustafa, H. (2023). Financial innovation in Islamic banks: Evidence on the interaction between Shariah board and FinTech. *Journal of Islamic Accounting and Business Research*, 14(6), 911–930. DOI: 10.1108/JIABR-11-2022-0305

Harjono, A. (1968). *Hukum Islam: Keluasan dan Keadilannya*. Bulan Bintang.

Haron, H., Mat Nor, F., Johari, F., Misbah, H., & Shafii, Z. (2023). Factors influencing the behavioural intention to accept benefidonor concept among stakeholders of Waqf. *Journal of Islamic Accounting and Business Research*, 14(8), 1344–1360. DOI: 10.1108/JIABR-06-2022-0146

Harwood, T., & Garry, T. (2014). Co-creation and ambiguous ownership within virtual communities: The case of the Machinima community. *Journal of Consumer Behaviour*, 13(2), 148–156. DOI: 10.1002/cb.1437

Hasan, N. N. A., Noor, K. M., Malik, A. A., & Ghani, Z. A. (2022). Maqasid Al-Shariah in Management: How it's Relevant to Non-muslims. In N. N. M. Shariff, M. A. Yakob, Z. S. Hamidi, Z. A. A. Aghwan, & N. Lateh (Eds.), *Selected Proceedings from the 1st International Conference on Contemporary Islamic Studies (ICIS 2021)* (pp. 83–91). Springer Nature Singapore.

Hasan, R., Hassan, M. K., & Aliyu, S. (2020). Fintech and Islamic finance: Literature review and research agenda. [IJIEF]. *International Journal of Islamic Economics and Finance*, 3(1), 75–94. DOI: 10.18196/ijief.2122

Hasan, R., & Siraj, S. A. (2016). Complexities of waqf development in Bangladesh. *Journal of Emerging Economies and Islamic Research*, 4(3), 1–10. DOI: 10.24191/jeeir.v4i3.9093

Hashmi, F., Aftab, H., Martins, J. M., Nuno Mata, M., Qureshi, H. A., Abreu, A., & Mata, P. N. (2021). The role of self-esteem, optimism, deliberative thinking and self-control in shaping the financial behavior and financial well-being of young adults. *PLoS One*, 16(9), e0256649. DOI: 10.1371/journal.pone.0256649 PMID: 34492043

Hasif, M., & Ahmad, K. (2019). Factors Affecting the Acceptance of Financial Technology among Asnaf for the Distribution of Zakat in Selangor- A Study Using UTAUT. *Journal of Islamic Finance*, 2117(Special Issue), 35–46.

Hassan, M. K., Jreisat, A., Rabbani, M. R., & Al-Mohamed, S. (2022). Islamic fintech and Bahrain: an opportunity for global financial services. *Fintech in Islamic financial institutions: Scope, challenges, and implications in Islamic finance*, 65-87.

Hassan, M. K., Muneeza, A., & Khan, A. (2021). Pandemic crisis, digitalization and social responsibility: an emerging role of Islamic economics and finance. *Islamic Finance and Sustainable Development: A Sustainable Economic Framework for Muslim and Non-Muslim Countries*, 35-53.

Hassan, R. (2023). *Digital finance literacy programs and their impact on financial inclusion. Journal of Islamic Accounting and Business Research.* Retrieved from https://www.emerald.com/insight/content/doi/10.1108/JIABR-03-2023-0092/full/html

Hassan, A. (2010). Management and Development of the Management and Development of the. *Seventh International Conference – The Tawhidi Epistemology: Zakat and Waqf Economy, Bangi 2010*, 309–328. DOI: 10.1017/CBO9781107415324.004

Hassan, H. A. (2019). Takaful models: Origin, progression and future. *Journal of Islamic Marketing*, 11(6), 1801–1819. Advance online publication. DOI: 10.1108/JIMA-04-2018-0078

Hassan, M. K., Zulfikar, Z., Rabbani, M. R., & Atif, M. (2022). Fintech trends: Industry 4.0, Islamic fintech, and its digital transformation. In *FinTech in Islamic Financial Institutions: Scope, Challenges, and Implications in Islamic Finance* (pp. 113–130). Springer International Publishing. DOI: 10.1007/978-3-031-14941-2_6

Hassan, R., & Ali, M. (2019). Big data analytics in Waqf institutions: Opportunities and challenges. *Journal of Islamic Philanthropy & Social Finance*, 7(2), 45–61.

Hassan, R., Rashid, N. R. N. A., & Akram, W. (2020). The Application of Blockchain Technology in Waqf Property Management in Malaysia. *International Journal of Islamic and Middle Eastern Finance and Management*, 13(4), 639–656.

Haws, K. L., Davis, S. W., & Dholakia, U. M. (2016). Control over what? Individual differences in general versus eating and spending self-control. *Journal of Public Policy & Marketing*, 35(1), 37–57. DOI: 10.1509/jppm.14.149

Hayat Finans. (2024a). About us https://www.hayatfinans.com.tr/hakkimizda

Hayat Finans. (2024b). Advantages and disadvantages of mobile banking applications https://www.hayatfinans.com.tr/mobil-bankacilik-uygulamalarinin-avantajlari-ve-dezavantajlari

Hazıroğlu, T. (2004). *Private financial institutions or participation banking*. Yeni Şafak. (In Turkish)

Hazıroğlu, T. (2016). The emergence and conceptual importance of the participation banking idea in Turkey. [İEFD]. *Journal of Islamic Economics and Finance*, 2(1), 119–132. https://dergipark.org.tr/tr/pub/jief/issue/24515/259788

Hegre, H., Petrova, K., & Uexkull, N. V. (2020). Synergies and Trade-Offs in Reaching the Sustainable Development Goals. *Sustainability (Basel)*, 12(8729), 1–24. DOI: 10.3390/su12208729

Henager, R., & Wilmarth, M. J. (2018). The relationship between student loan debt and financial wellness. *Family and Consumer Sciences Research Journal*, 46(4), 381–395. DOI: 10.1111/fcsr.12263

Hernandez, J. (2017). Adoption of internet banking: Proposition and implementation of an integrated methodology approach. *International Journal of Bank Marketing*, 25(2), 72–88. DOI: 10.1108/02652320710728410

Hew, J. J., Wong, L. W., Tan, G. W. H., Ooi, K. B., & Lin, B. (2020). The blockchain-based Halal traceability systems: A hype or reality? *Supply Chain Management*, 25(6), 863–879. DOI: 10.1108/SCM-01-2020-0044

Hishamudin, M. Z., Kamarudin, N. S., & Abdul Hadi, N. (2024). Formal and Informal Digital Platform for Islamic Financial Education. *Semarak International Journal of Islamic Studies and Culture*, 2(1), 18–28. DOI: 10.37934/sijisc.2.1.1828

Hishamudin, M. Z., Kamarudin, N. S., Hadi, N. A., & Ahmad, A. (2025). Intention to Use Digital Platforms for Islamic Financial Education in Malaysia: Structural Equation Model. *Journal of Advanced Research in Applied Sciences and Engineering Technology*, 49(1), 298–311. DOI: 10.37934/araset.49.1.298311

Hisyam, M. I., & Marwini, . (2024). Waqf Implementation in Supporting SDGs-6 (Clean Water and Sanitation) at Salman Waqf Institution in Indonesia. *Islamic Social Finance*, 4(1). Advance online publication. DOI: 10.58968/isf.v4i1.481

Hollins-Kirk, R. G. (2022). *Digital Banking and Financial Inclusion.* Kuala Lumpur: Khazanah Research Institute. Retrieved February 20, 2023, from https://www.krinstitute.org/assets/contentMS/img/template/editor/20220826%20Digital%20Banking%20Views%20pub.pdf

Hornuf, L., & Schwienbacher, A. (2018). Market mechanisms and funding dynamics in equity crowdfunding. *Journal of Corporate Finance*, 50, 556–574. DOI: 10.1016/j.jcorpfin.2017.08.009

Hornuf, L., Stenzhorn, E., & Vintis, T. (2022). Are sustainability-oriented investors different? Evidence from equity crowdfunding. *The Journal of Technology Transfer*, 47(6), 1662–1689. DOI: 10.1007/s10961-021-09896-9

https://muftiwp.gov.my/ms/artikel/bayan-linnas/3560-bayan-linnas-siri-ke-194-konsep-sedekah-jariah-menjana-kesatuan-ummah

https://www.worldbank.org/en/events/2020/10/07/maximizing-islamic-finance-for-financial-inclusion

Humphrey, C. (2019). 'Minilateral'development banks: What the rise of Africa's trade and development bank says about multilateral governance. *Development and Change*, 50(1), 164–190. DOI: 10.1111/dech.12467

Ibrahim, E. N. M., Laila, N., & Mehad, S. (2016, August 12). Trust or distrust in the web-mediated information environment (W-MIE): A perspective of online Muslim users. https://www.emerald.com/insight/content/doi/10.1108/17410390910993527/full/html

Ibrahim, M. Z. (2021). alāl linguistic meaning understanding among Non-Muslim in Malaysia. *Journal al-Irsyad, 6*(2), 697-705. DOI: 10.53840/alirsyad.v6i2.210

Ibrahim, D., & Ibrahim, H. (2020, October 27). Governance, Location. *International Journal of Academic Research in Business & Social Sciences*, 10(10). Advance online publication. DOI: 10.6007/IJARBSS/v10-i10/7651

Ibrahim, M., & Thangavelu, S. M. (2014). Non-performing assets in Indian booked business banks: A review. *Global Journal of Emerging Market Economies*, 6(1), 87–96. https://journals.sagepub.com/doi/abs/10.1177/0974910114534104. DOI: 10.1177/0974910114534104

Ibrahim, N., Ismail, M. N., Sapian, S. M., Ramli, A. M., & Shazali, K. H. I. (2024b). Navigating The Implications for Heirs: An Analysis of The Amendment to The Small Estate Act (Distribution) 1955. *Ulum Alamiyyah.*, 36(2), 118–126. DOI: 10.33102/uij.vol36no02.590

Ibrahim, N., Shazali, K. H. I., & Rusgianto, S. (2024a). A Systematic Literature Review of Islamic Inheritance in Malaysia. *Islāmiyyāt: International Journal of Islamic Studies*, 46(1), 113–131. DOI: 10.17576/islamiyyat-2024-4601-09

Ibrahim, S. S. (2023). Potential Blockchain Applications in Waqf for Sustainability: A Middle East and Asia Perspective. *Islamiyyat*, 45(2), 47–64. DOI: 10.17576/islamiyyat-2023-4502-04

Ibrahim, S. S., Daud, D., Hidayah, K., Shaharuddin, A., & Al-Amin, A. A. M. (2022). Waqf integrated income generating model (WIIGM) for enhancing sustainable development goals (SDGS) in Malaysia: An evaluation of behavioural intention. *International Journal of Ethics and Systems*, 3. Advance online publication. DOI: 10.1108/IJOES-02-2022-0030

IFC. 2017. Digital Financial Services: Challenges and Opportunities for Emerging Market Banks, International Finance Corporation, World Bank Group._https://openknowledge.worldbank.org/server/api/core/bitstreams/f10918de-9755-58ac-9350-1cc944dfb94f/content

Ikhsan, R. B., Sari, C. L., Fernando, E., Wijaya, L., Bangapadang, S., & Sangkereng, I. (2022). The Rapid Adoption of E-wallet: An empirical study. *2022 10th International Conference on Cyber and IT Service Management, CITSM 2022*. DOI: 10.1109/CITSM56380.2022.9935931

Ikhwan, N. (2022), Makalah di dalam webinar series 22 Fakultas Ekonomi dan Bisnis Perbanas Institute bekerjasama dengan kementrian BKPM

Impact, E. (2020). *Islamic fintech: Reaching a new generation*. Retrieved from https://impact.economist.com/perspectives/sites/default/files/eiu-diedc_article_2_26th_april_2020_0.pdf

Indonesia Stock Exchange. (2019). *Surat Berharga Syariah Negara*. https://idxislamic.idx.co.id/edukasi-pasar-modal-syariah/sukuk-negara/

International Shari'ah Research Academy for Islamic Finance. (2023). *Islamic financial system: Principles and operation*. INCEIF University.

Iramani, Rr., & Lutfi, L. (2021). *An integrated model of financial well-being: The role of financial behavior.* *7*(3), 691–700. DOI: 10.5267/j.ac.2020.12.007

Iredale, S., Heinze, A., & Williams, M. J. (2024). Engaging stakeholders with captivating content. In *Digital and Social Media Marketing*.Routledge (pp. 182-196) Islamic Development Bank (2023). Islamic Finance Grant for Developing a Digital Awqaf Fund Management Platform- 2 Components. Retrieved at https://www.isdb.org/project-procurement/tenders/2023/gpn/islamic-finance-grant-developing-digital-awqaf-fund-management-platform-2, 30th May 2024.

İsbank. 2024a. World's Best Mobile Banking Application 'İşCep' https://www.isbank.com.tr/bankamizi-taniyin/dunyanin-en-iyi-mobil-bankacilik-uygulamasi-iscep

İsbank. 2024b. What is Big Data? https://www.isbank.com.tr/blog/big-data-buyuk-veri-nedir

Islamic Development Bank. (2019). *Country Youth Profile- Malaysia* (Issue February). https://www.jiasociety.org/content/10/6/148

Islamic Financial Services Act. (2013).

Islam, M. M. (2015). Cash Waqf: An Innovative Instrument for Development of Ummah. *Banglavision Reseach Journal*, 15(1), 117–124.

Ismail, M., & Mohsin, A. (2013, November 25). Financing through cash-waqf: a revitalization to finance different needs. https://www.emerald.com/insight/content/doi/10.1108/IMEFM-08-2013-0094/full/html

Ismail, A. G., Shafiai, M. H. M., & Ahmad, M. A. (2022). Stakeholders' involvement in organisational governance structure of state islamic religious council. *UMRAN-International Journal of Islamic and Civilizational Studies*, 9(1), 23–35. DOI: 10.11113/umran2022.9n1.536

Ismail, A. Y., Musafar Hameed, L. B., Mohamad Suhaimi, A. F., & Jamaludin, N. I. (2020). Value-based intermediation and interconnection of sustainable development goals in Islamic banking framework. *International Journal of Islamic Economics and Finance Research*, 3(1).

Ismail, W A W. (2020, January 31). Significance of Technology to Cash Waqf Collection [UTAUT]. *International Journal of Academic Research in Business & Social Sciences*, 11(1). Advance online publication. DOI: 10.6007/IJARBSS/v11-i1/8994

Ispriandina, A., & Sutisna, M. (2019). Faktor-Faktor Penerimaan Teknologi Yang Memengaruhi Intensi Kontinuitas Penggunaan Mobile Wallet Di Kota Bandung. *Prosiding Industrial Research Workshop and National Seminar, 10*(1), 1046–1055. https://jurnal.polban.ac.id/ojs-3.1.2/proceeding/article/view/1462

Izaidin, M. D. B. A. (2022). Touch n Go e-Wallet: The New Payment Style Existed when COVID-19 Hits. [IJAFAP]. *International Journal of Accounting & Finance in Asia Pasific*, 5(3), 107–116. DOI: 10.32535/ijafap.v5i3.1933

Jabatan Mufti Negeri Kedah. (2020, November 8). *Irsyad Al-Fatwa: Hukum Penggunaan E-wallet Menurut Perspektif Syarak*. Jawatankuasa Fatwa Negeri Kedah. https://ifatwa.kedah.gov.my/wp-content/uploads/2022/08/15-HUKUM-PENGGUNAAN-e-WALLET-MENURUT-PERSPEKTIF-SYARAK.pdf

Jabatan Mufti Negeri Perak. (2021, August 4). *Irsyad Hukum: Penggunaan E-wallet Mengikut Perspektif Syarak*. Jawatankuasa Fatwa Negeri Perak. https://mufti.perak.gov.my/images/isu_semasa/2021/sept/ewallet.pdf

Jack & Suri. (2016, December). The long-run poverty and gender impacts of mobile money. *DEVELOPMENT ECONOMICS*, 1288-1292.

Jafari, A., & Süerdem, A. (2012). An analysis of material consumption culture in the Muslim world. *Marketing Theory*, 12(1), 61–79. DOI: 10.1177/1470593111424184

JAKIM. (2020, August). *Penggunaan e-wallet mengikut perspektif syarak*. Majlis Kebangsaan Bagi Hal Ehwal Ugama Islam Malaysia (MKI) Kali Ke-117. https://i-fiqh.islam.gov.my/portal/view.php?id=16579

Jalal, A., Al Mubarak, M., & Durani, F. (2023). Financial technology (fintech). In *Artificial Intelligence and Transforming Digital Marketing* (pp. 525–536). Springer Nature Switzerland.

Janom, N., Izham, M. Z., Mansor, F. S., Aris, S. R. S., Bashah, N. S. K., & Arshad, N. H. (2019). Review on success factors of waqf information management system in Malaysia. *Indonesian Journal of Electrical Engineering and Computer Science*, 16(1), 412–419. DOI: 10.11591/ijeecs.v16.i1.pp412-419

Jariahfund (2024). Retrieved from https://jariahfund.muamalat.com.my/

Javaid, M., Haleem, A., Singh, R. P., Suman, R., & Khan, S. (2022). A review of Blockchain Technology applications for financial services. *BenchCouncil Transactions on Benchmarks. Standards and Evaluations*, 2(3), 100073.

Javed, M. M., Ayaz, M., & Kalim, R. (2022). Examining the influence of Maqāsid al-Sharīʿah orientation on financial performance of Islamic banks: Evidence from Pakistan. *Journal of Islamic Business and Management*, 12(2), 181–197. DOI: 10.26501/jibm/2022.1202-004

JAWHAR. (2024). Retrieved from https://www.jawhar.gov.my/en/zakat-and-general -source-mal/

Jayawardhena, C. (2004). Personal values' influence on e-shopping attitude and behaviour. *Internet Research*, 14(2), 127–138. DOI: 10.1108/10662240410530844

Jhonson, B., & Tamara, D. (2023). Influence of digital financial literacy on financial well-being through spending, saving, and investment behavior in indonesia. *Journal of Business Studies and Management Review*, 6(2), 157–168. DOI: 10.22437/jbsmr.v6i2.24793

Jiménez, G., & Saurina, J. (2006). Credit cycles, credit risk, and prudential regulation. International Journal of Central Banking, https://www.ijcb.org/journal/ijcb06q2a3.htm

Johari, F., Nor, F. M., Hamid, B. A., Zal, W. A., Ali, F., Misbah, H., & Shaharuddin, A. (2023). Enhancing Synergy in the Waqf Ecosystem in Malaysia: Promoting Increased Waqf Contributions among Beneficiaries, Donors, and Mutawalli. *International Journal of Economics Finance Studies*, 15(3), 76–107.

Jouti, A. T. (2021). Islamic fintech and financial inclusion. *Islamic FinTech: Insights and Solutions*, 209-229.

Juwana, H. (2006), Pidato di dalam Dies Natalis ke 56 Universitas Indonesia Kementerian Investasi / BKPM. (2024). *Siaran Pers*. https://bkpm.go.id/id/info/siaran-pers/rosan-realisasi-investasi-terus-bertumbuh-indonesia-konsisten-jalankan-hilirisasi

Kabakova, O. & Plaksenkov, E. (2018). Analysis of factors affecting financial inclusion: Ecosystem view

Kaçmaz, A. (2009). *The development of participation banks in the Turkish banking sector between 2005-2008. Unpublished Master's Project*. Fatih University, Institute of Social Sciences. (In Turkish)

Kadir, J. M. A., Shoukat, A., Naghavi, N., & Jamaluddin, A. A. (2021). The Saving Behavior in Emerging Country: The Role of Financial Knowledge, Peer Influence and Parent Socialization. *Pakistan Business Review, 22*(4). https://jmsnew.iobmresearch.com/index.php/pbr/article/view/396

Kagramanto, L. B., & Serfiyani, C. Y. (2019). The Principles of Contract in Donation Based Crowdfunding. *Yuridika*, 34(1), 78. DOI: 10.20473/ydk.v34i1.11801

Kallenos, T. L., Milidonis, A., Nishiotis, G. P., & Zenios, S. A. (2024). Financial Education and Spillover Effects. SSRN *Electronic Journal*. https://doi.org/DOI: 10.2139/SSRN.4094763

Kamaruddin, M.I.H., Hanefah, M.M. and Masruki, R., 2024. Challenges and prospects in waqf reporting practices in Malaysia. Journal of Financial Reporting and accounting, 22(3), pp.752-765.

Kamaruddin, M. I. H., Hanefah, M. M., Shaharuddin, A., Ayedh, A. M. A., & Othman, N. A. (2023). Development of Fintech in Islamic Social Finance in Malaysia. International Journal of Economics, Management and Accounting, pp.177-204.
Kamaruzaman, N. R., & Ishak [WAQF INSTITUTIONS: A SYSTEMATIC LITERATURE REVIEW ON GOVERNANCE, FINANCIAL MODELS, AND SOCIO-ECONOMIC IMPACT IN ISLAMIC SOCIAL FINANCE. *Advanced International Journal of Business, Entrepreneurship and SMES.*]. *Ms*, •••, I.

Kamarudin, M. K., Zaman, N., & Razak, R. M. (2019). Thematic Analysis on The Necessity of Hibah Law In Malaysia. *al-Qanatir*. *International Journal of Islamic Studies*, 16(1), 1–13.

Kamil, I., & Istianingsih, I. (2020). *Spending Behavior as an Impact of Lifestyle and Financial Literation in the Intensity of use of Mobile Payment Services*.

Kamis, R., Ismail, S., & Rahman, N. H. A. (2022). Go Cashless: A Proposed Conceptual Framework for e-Wallet Acceptance. *International Journal of Academic Research in Business & Social Sciences*, 12(11). Advance online publication. DOI: 10.6007/IJARBSS/v12-i11/15264

Kanapathipillai, K., Shari, A. N., Ajmain, M. F. B. M., & Rahman, N. S. B. A. (2023). Navigating The Digital Shift: How Acceptance Factors Shape Malaysia's Banking Evolution. *European Journal of Management and Marketing Studies*, 8(3). Advance online publication. DOI: 10.46827/ejmms.v8i3.1547

Kanimozhi, G., & Kamatchi, K. S. (2017). Security Aspects of Mobile Based E Wallet. *International Journal on Recent and Innovation Trends in Computing and Communication*, 5(6). Advance online publication. DOI: 10.17762/IJRITCC.V5I6.931

Karamitsos, I., Papadaki, M., & Al-Balghuti, N. B. (2018). Design of the Blockchain Smart, Contract: A Use Case for Real Estate. *Journal of Informative Security*, 2018(9), 177–190. DOI: 10.4236/jis.2018.93013

Karasoy, H. A., & Babaoğlu, P. (2021). Cyber security in Turkey: Legal and institutional infrastructure. Legislative (Yasama) [In Turkish]. *Journal*, (44), 123–155.

Karimah, D. A., Pamuncak, M. B., & Mubin, M. K. (2023). The Role of Waqf in Supporting Sustainable Development Goals: Linking theory and its practices. *Suhuf*, 35(2), 31–38. DOI: 10.23917/suhuf.v35i2.23018

Karim, M. A., Rahman, H. A., & Abdullah, W. S. W. (2022). AI chatbots and their impact on donor engagement in Waqf institutions. *International Journal of Islamic and Middle Eastern Finance and Management*, 15(1), 80–95.

Karimullah, S. S. (2023). The Application of Artificial Intelligence in Islamic Law Discovery. *Mutawasith: Jurnal Hukum Islam*, 6(2), 109–121.

Karjaluoto, H. A., Shaikh, A. A., Leppäniemi, M., & Luomala, R. (2019). Examining consumers' usage intention of contactless payment systems. *International Journal of Bank Marketing*, 38(2), 332–351. DOI: 10.1108/IJBM-04-2019-0155

Karyağdı Güngör, N. (2022). Effects of Digital Transformation on Efficiency in the Banking Sector: A Qualitative Study in the TRB2 Region. [In Turkish]. *Kahramanmaraş Sütçü İmam University Social Sciences Journal*, 19(2), 852–870. DOI: 10.33437/ksusbd.990218

Kassim, M., Embi, N. A. C., Haron, R., & Ibrahim, K. (2019). Internal factors affecting continuous donations among cash waqf donors. *International Journal of Academic Research in Business & Social Sciences*, 9(9), 1304–1311. DOI: 10.6007/IJARBSS/v9-i9/6464

Kasumi, H., & Xhemaili, M. (2023). Student motivation and learning: The impact of collaborative learning in English as Foreign Language classes. *International Journal of Cognitive Research in Science* [IJCRSEE]. *Engineering and Education*, 11(2), 301–309. DOI: 10.23947/2334-8496-2023-11-2-301-309

Katılımfinans. (2024). Digitalisation Highlights in the Turkish Participation Banking Sector https://katilimfinans.com.tr/finansal-raporlar/turk-katilim-bankaciligi-sektorunde-dijitallesmede-one-cikanlar-h14522.html

Kaur, R., Li, Y., Iqbal, J., Gonzalez, H., & Stakhanova, N. (2018). A Security Assessment of HCE-NFC Enabled E-Wallet Banking Android Apps. *2018 IEEE 42nd Annual Computer Software and Applications Conference (COMPSAC), 02*, 492–497. DOI: 10.1109/COMPSAC.2018.10282

Kementrian Keuangan Republik Indonesia. (n.d.). Proyeksi Pertumbuhan Ekonomi Indonesia 2022 dan 2023 kuat. Retrieved Maret 2022, from fiskal.kemenkeu.go.id/publikasi/siaran-pers-detil/364

Kempson, E., Finney, A., & Poppe, C. (2017). *Financial well-being: a conceptual model and preliminary analysis*. https://www.fincap.org.uk/en/insights/financial-well-being-a-conceptual-model-and-preliminary-analysis

Kettunen, P., Teppola, S., & Partanen, J. (2019). Fostering continuous innovation with engaging IT-assisted transparent information sharing: a case study. In: Hyrynsalmi, S., Suoranta, M., Nguyen-Duc, A., Tyrväinen, P., & Abrahamsson, P. (eds). *Software Business*. ICSOB 2019. Lecture Notes in Business Information Processing, vol 370. Springer, Cham. DOI: 10.1007/978-3-030-33742-1_13

Khaf, M. (2011). The Fundamentals of Islamic Finance. ISRA., Retrieved March 2, 2023, from.

Khalil, M., Khawaja, K. F., & Sarfraz, M. (2022). The adoption of blockchain technology in the financial sector during the era of fourth industrial revolution: A moderated mediated model. *Quality & Quantity*, 56(4), 2435–2452. DOI: 10.1007/s11135-021-01229-0

Khan, A., Hassan, M. K., Paltrinieri, A., Dreassi, A., & Bahoo, S. (2020). A bibliometric review of takaful literature. *International Review of Economics & Finance*, 69, 389–405. DOI: 10.1016/j.iref.2020.05.013

Khan, A., Sukmana, R., & Mahmood, A.ABIDULLAH KHANRADITYA SUKMANAABID MAHMOOD. (2023). Islamic Social Finance Ecosystem and the Role of Crowdfunding: A Proposed Model. *Hamdard Islamicus*, 46(3), 91–111. DOI: 10.57144/hi.v46i3.876

Khan, M. F., & Ghifari, N. M. (1992). Shatibi's objectives of Shariah and some implications for consumer theory. *Readings in Islamic Economic Thought: Selected Readings*, 176, 202.

Khan, M., Nisar, Q. A., & Khattak, A. (2021). Blockchain Technology for Waqf Management: Challenges and Opportunities. *Journal of Islamic Accounting and Business Research*, 12(2), 219–235.

Khan, S. N. (2023). The legality of cryptocurrency from an Islamic perspective: A research note. *Journal of Islamic Accounting and Business Research*, 14(2), 289–294. DOI: 10.1108/JIABR-02-2022-0041

Khatoon, A., Verma, P., Southernwood, J., Massey, B., & Corcoran, P. (2019). Blockchain in energy efficiency: Potential applications and benefits. *Energies*, 12(17), 3317. DOI: 10.3390/en12173317

Khumalo, I. P., Temane, Q. M., & Wissing, M. P. (2012). Socio-demographic variables, general psychological well-being and the mental health continuum in an African context. *Social Indicators Research*, 105(3), 419–442. DOI: 10.1007/s11205-010-9777-2

Kiew, J. P., Toh, E. T. L., Ngian, E. T., & Law, S. H. C. (2022). Perceived Trust, Convenience and Promotion For the Adoption of e-Wallet. *International Journal of Academic Research in Business & Social Sciences*, 12(9). Advance online publication. DOI: 10.6007/IJARBSS/v12-i9/14591

Kılıç, G., & Türkan, Y. (2023). The Emergence of Islamic Fintech and Its Applications. *International Journal of Islamic Economics and Finance Studies*, 9(2), 212–236.

Kitamura, H. (2020). Who pioneered Islamic banking in Malaysia? The background of the pioneers of Bank Islam Malaysia Berhad. *Contemporary Islam*, 14(1), 75–93. DOI: 10.1007/s11562-019-00443-w

Kreiner, C. T., Lassen, D. D., & Leth-Petersen, S. (2019). Liquidity Constraint Tightness and Consumer Responses to Fiscal Stimulus Policy. *American Economic Journal. Economic Policy*, 11(1), 351–379. DOI: 10.1257/pol.20140313

Kulakli, A., & Mahony, S. (2014). Knowledge Creation and Sharing with Web 2.0 Tools for Teaching and Learning Roles in So-called University 2.0. *Procedia: Social and Behavioral Sciences*, 150, 648–657. DOI: 10.1016/j.sbspro.2014.09.084

Kumar, S., & Shah, N. P. (2018). False information on web and social media: a survey. In *Social Media Analytics: Advances and Applications*. CRC Press. https://arxiv.org/abs/1804.08559

Kunhibava, S., Muneeza, A., Khalid, M. B., Mustapha, Z., & Sen, T. M. (2024). Sadaqah, zakat, and qard

Kurniasih, W. (2022). *Pengertian Modal: Sejarah, Jenis, Sumber, dan Manfaat*. Gramedia.

Kuskop (2024). Retrieved from https://www.kuskop.gov.my/PerusahaanSosial/index-BI.php

Kusuma, K., Sheela, P., Panigrahi, R. R., & Shaikh, Z. H. (2024). Blockchain Technology and Islamic Finance: A Decade of Growth Trends. *Fintech Applications in Islamic Finance: AI, Machine Learning, and Blockchain Techniques*, 59-79.

Kuveyttürk. 2024. How Will the Internet of Things Change Our Lives? https://www.kuveytturk.com.tr/blog/teknoloji/nesnelerin-interneti-hayatimizi-nasil-degistirecek

Laallam, A., Kassim, S., Ali, E R A E., & Saiti, B. (2020, March 30). Intellectual capital in non-profit organisations: lessons learnt for waqf institutions. DOI: 10.1108/IJIF-10-2018-0111

Lakshmirani, S. A. (2021). Study on customer awareness towards digital banking services. *Palarch's Journal Of Archaeology Of Egypt/Egyptology, 18*(1), 4599-4604.

Laluddin, H., Haneef, S. S. S., Mohammad, M., & Rahman, M. P. J. I. J. o. I. T. (2021). Revisiting the concept of waqf: Its maintenance, issues and challenges. *20*, 53-64.

Laluddin, Haneef, Mohammad & Rahman, M. P. (2021). Revisiting the

Lee, E. (2019). Equity crowdfunding in Hong Kong: Potential, challenges and investor protection. *Journal of Corporate Law Studies*, 19(2), 277–302. DOI: 10.1080/14735970.2017.1369235

Lee, J., & Cho, M. (2019). New insights into socially responsible consumers: The role of personal values. *International Journal of Consumer Studies*, 43(2), 123–133. DOI: 10.1111/ijcs.12491

Lemeshow, S. J, D. W. H., Klar, J., & K.Lwanga, S. (1997). *Besar Sampel dalam Penelitian Kesehatan*. Gajah Mada Uneversity Press.

Lim, K. L., Soutar, G. N., & Lee, J. A. (2013). Factors affecting investment intentions: A consumer behaviour perspective. *Journal of Financial Services Marketing*, 18(4), 301–315. DOI: 10.1057/fsm.2013.23

Lim, X. J., Ngew, P., Cheah, J. H., Cham, T. H., & Liu, Y. (2022). Go digital: Can the money-gift function promote the use of e-wallet apps? *Internet Research*, 32(6), 1806–1831. Advance online publication. DOI: 10.1108/INTR-06-2021-0406

Listiana, L., Fauziyyah, N. E., & Sukmana, R. (2021). Waqf for Food Security: A Critical Assessment from Existing Studies. In *Badan Wakaf Indonesia*.

Liu, E. X. (2021). Stay Competitive in the Digital Age: The Future of Banks, IMF Working Paper, WP/21/46. https://www.imf.org/-/media/Files/Publications/WP/2021/English/wpiea2021046-print-pdf.ashx

Liu, Z., Ben, S., & Zhang, R. (2019). Factors affecting consumers' mobile payment behavior: A meta-analysis. *Electronic Commerce Research*, 19(3), 575–601. DOI: 10.1007/s10660-019-09349-4

Li, X. (2016). Status and Challenges of Equity Crowdfunding Development. *Proceedings of the 2016 International Conference on Economy, Management and Education Technology*. DOI: 10.2991/icemet-16.2016.338

Li, Y.-Z., He, T.-L., Song, Y.-R., Yang, Z., & Zhou, R.-T. (2018). Factors impacting donors' intention to donate to charitable crowd-funding projects in China: A UTAUT-based model. *Information Communication and Society*, 21(3), 404–415. DOI: 10.1080/1369118X.2017.1282530

Locatelli, R., Schena, C., & Tanda, A. (2021). A historical perspective on disruptive technologies. *Disruptive Technology in Banking and Finance: An International Perspective on FinTech*, 9-45.

Loh, A. M., Peong, K. K. P., & Peong, K. K. P. (2019). Determinants of Personal Financial Literacy among Young Adults in Malaysian Accounting Firms. *GATR Global Journal of Business Social Sciences Review*, 7(1), 8–19. DOI: 10.35609/gjbssr.2019.7.1(2)

Loh, H.-S. C. (2020, May). Physical Frictions and Digital Banking Adoption. *Behavioral & Experimental Economics eJournal*, 1-50. DOI: 10.2139/ssrn.3333636

LSEG. (2023). *Islamic Finance Development Report 2023: Navigating Uncertainty*. London Stock Exchange Group. (accessed 25 October 2024) https://solutions.lseg.com/IslamicFinance_ICD_LSEG

Lukkarinen, A. (2020). Equity Crowdfunding: Principles and Investor Behaviour. In *Advances in Crowdfunding* (pp. 93–118). Springer International Publishing. DOI: 10.1007/978-3-030-46309-0_5

Lukkarinen, A., Teich, J. E., Wallenius, H., & Wallenius, J. (2016). Success drivers of online equity crowdfunding campaigns. *Decision Support Systems*, 87, 26–38. DOI: 10.1016/j.dss.2016.04.006

Lutfi, L., & Prihatiningrum, V. (2023). Social Media, Islamic Financial Literacy, and Islamic Banking Product Ownership: A Moderating Model. *EL DINAR: Jurnal Keuangan Dan Perbankan Syariah*, 11(1), 35–58. DOI: 10.18860/ed.v11i1.17803

Lyons, A., & Kass-Hanna, J. (2021). A Multidimensional Approach to Defining and Measuring Financial Literacy in the Digital Age. SSRN *Electronic Journal*. DOI: 10.4324/9781003025221-7

LZS. (2024) Retrieved from https://www.zakatselangor.com.my/lzspeduli/

Maharani, D., & Hidayat, T. (2020). Rasionalitas Muslim : Perilaku Konsumsi dalam Prespektif Ekonomi Islam. *Jurnal Ilmiah Ekonomi Islam*, 6(3), 409–412. DOI: 10.29040/jiei.v6i3.1374

Mahdzan, N. S., Sabri, M. F., Husniyah, A. R., Magli, A. S., & Chowdhury, N. T. (2023). Digital financial services usage and subjective financial well-being: Evidence from low-income households in Malaysia. *International Journal of Bank Marketing*, 41(2), 395–427. DOI: 10.1108/IJBM-06-2022-0226

Mahdzan, N. S., Zainudin, R., Sukor, M. E., Zainir, F., & Wan Ahmad, W. M. (2019). Determinants of Subjective Financial Well-Being Across Three Different Household Income Groups in Malaysia. *Social Indicators Research*, 146(3), 699–726. DOI: 10.1007/s11205-019-02138-4

Maheshwari, R., & Reddy, N. (2022). *Non-performing assets in Indian banking: causes and solutions*. International Journal of Management, Technology, and Social Sciences., DOI: 10.5281/zenodo.5728365

MAIM. (2024) Retrieved from https://maim.gov.my/index.php/ms/lagi-berita/majlis-pengagihan-bantuan-ramadhan-syawal-kepada-asnaf-maim-di-dun-bukit-katil-dan-dun-pantai-kundor

Makkonen, M., Frank, L., & Kemppainen, T. (2019).. . *The Effects of Individual Values on Online Shopping Spending*, 10, 969–994. Advance online publication. DOI: 10.18690/978-961-286-280-0.51

Malaysia, P. D. P. (2017). Personal Data Protection Code of Practice (2017).

Malaysian Communications and Multimedia Commission. (2020). *Internet Users Survey*. https://www.mcmc.gov.my/skmmgovmy/media/General/pdf/IUS-2020-Report.pdf

Malaysian Communications and Multimedia Commission. (2022). Internet users survey. In *Malaysian Communications And Multimedia Commission*. https://www.mcmc.gov.my/skmmgovmy/media/General/pdf/Internet-Users-Survey-2018-(Infographic).pdf

Manik, N., & Sukadana, I. W. (2020). MEMAHAMI EKONOMI DIGITAL DI INDONESIA : STUDI KASUS MARKETPLACE. *E-Journal Ekonomi Pembangunan Universitas Udayana, 9 No.2*(Februari), 383–412.

Mardani. (2014), Hukum Bisnis Syariah. Jakarta: Prenada Media

Markom, R., Zakaria, M. R., & Asma, H. A. H. (2015). Kerangka perundangan rumah sedekah sebagai institusi perbankan: Satu tinjauan. In Proceeding of Seminar Sadaqa House 2015 (29 Oktober 2015, Menara Bank Islam Kuala Lumpur, Malaysia).

Marous, J. (2013, March 18). *Migrating Banking Customers to Digital Channels*. Retrieved February 25, 2023, from The Financial Brand: https://thefinancialbrand.com/news/digital-banking/migrating-banking-customers-to-digital-37287/

Marwa, M. H. M., Al-Fatih, S., Hussain, M. A., & Haris, H. (2024). The Position and Role of the Sharia Supervisory Board in Ensuring Sharia Compliance Equity Crowdfunding in Indonesia. *Jurnal Hukum*, 39(2), 212. DOI: 10.26532/jh.v39i2.33330

Masruki, R., & Shafii, Z. (2013). The Development of Waqf Accounting in Enhancing Accountability. *Middle East Journal of Scientific Research*, 13, 1–6. DOI: 10.5829/idosi.mejsr.2013.13.1873

Mastura Razali, N. M. (2021). Maqasid Shariah HIFZ MAL in E-Wallet Application. *ISLĀMIYYĀT*, 113 - 120. doi:DOI: 10.17576

Mat Rahim, S. R., Mohamad, Z. Z., Abu Bakar, J., Mohsin, F. H., & Md Isa, N. (2018). Artificial Intelligence, Smart Contract And Islamic Finance. *Asian Social Science*, 14(2), 145–154. DOI: 10.5539/ass.v14n2p145

Matheus, R., Janssen, M., & Janowski, T. (2021). Design principles for creating digital transparency in government. *Government Information Quarterly*, 38(1), 1–18. DOI: 10.1016/j.giq.2020.101550

Mat, N., Abdullah, N. A., & Norazman, M. F. (2022). Penerimaan Aplikasi E-Wallet Pre-Covid-19 di Kalangan Penduduk di Lembah Klang. *MALIM: Jurnal Pengajian Umum Asia Tenggara*, 23(1), 21–30. DOI: 10.17576/malim-2022-2301-02

Maula, M. V. J., & Lukkarinen, A. (2019). Attention Across Borders: Investor Attention as a Driver of Investment Choices in Cross-Border Equity Crowdfunding. SSRN *Electronic Journal*. DOI: 10.2139/ssrn.3487467

Maula, M. V. J., & Lukkarinen, A. (2022). Attention across borders: Investor attention as a driver of cross-border equity crowdfunding investments. *Strategic Entrepreneurship Journal*, 16(4), 699–734. DOI: 10.1002/sej.1424

Mawaddah. (2022). The role of financial behavior in mediating the influence of socioeconomic characteristics and neurotic personality traits on financial satisfaction. *Cogent Business & Management, 9*(1). DOI: 10.1080/23311975.2022.2080152

Maybank (2024). Retrieved from https://www.maybankfoundation.com/index.php/our-impact/maybank-heart

Maybankheart (2024). Retrieved from https://www.maybankfoundation.com/index.php/our-impact/maybank-heart

Mayer, V. F., Machado, J. dos S., Marques, O., & Nunes, J. M. G. (2020). Mixed feelings?: Fluctuations in well-being during tourist travels. *Service Industries Journal*, 40(1–2), 158–180. DOI: 10.1080/02642069.2019.1600671

Mbama & Cajetan. (2018, October 8). Digital banking services, customer experience and financial performance in UK banks. *Journal of Research in Interactive Marketing*, •••, 432–451.

Md Zabri, M. Z., & Mohammed, M. O. (2018). Qualitative validation of a financially affordable Islamic home financing model. *ISRA International Journal of Islamic Finance*, 10(2), 143–161. DOI: 10.1108/IJIF-08-2017-0023

Meeran, M., Mohtesham, J., & Marwan, S. (2023). Social Impact Measurement of Waqf: Case Study of Waqf Organisations in Karnataka, India. *AZKA International Journal of Zakat & Social Finance.*, 4(2), 199–218.

Merlinda, S., Qurrata, V. A., Yusida, E., Purnamasari, V., Seprillina, L., & Hussain, N. E. (2021). The role of cash waqf as a source of micro business financing for strengthening the local economy: A case study in Gunung Kawi District, Malang Regency. *Review of Integrative Business and Economics Research*, 10, 136–144. http://buscompress.com/uploads/3/4/9/8/34980536/riber_10-s1_15_u20-089_136-144.pdf

Mertokusumo, S. (1993), Bab-bab tentang Penemuan Hukum. Bandung: Citra Aditya Bakti Ministry of Religion of Republic of Indonesia. (2022). *Al Quran Al Kareem*. https://quran.kemenag.go.id/

Meyers, E. M., Erickson, I., & Small, R. V. (2013, April 25). Digital literacy and informal learning environments: An introduction. *Learning, Media and Technology*, 38(4), 355–367. DOI: 10.1080/17439884.2013.783597

Michael Collins, J., & Urban, C. (2020). Measuring financial well-being over the lifecourse. *European Journal of Finance*, 26(4–5), 341–359. DOI: 10.1080/1351847X.2019.1682631

MIFC Leadership Position Paper. (2024).

Minarni, & Asnawi, N. R. (2022). An Analysis of Islamic Business Ethics in E-Wallet in Indonesia with A Case Study of Go-Pay. *Journal of Islamic Economis Lariba, 8*(2), 341–356. DOI: 10.20885/jielariba.vol8.iss2.art13

Ming, K. L. Y., & Jais, M. (2022). Factors Affecting the Intention to Use E-Wallets during the COVID-19 Pandemic. *Gadjah Mada International Journal of Business*, 24(1), 82. DOI: 10.22146/gamaijb.64708

Misbah, H., Johari, F., Mat Nor, F., Haron, H., Shahwan, S., & Shafii, Z. (2022). Sustainable development, regional planning, and information management as an evolving theme in waqf research: A bibliometric analysis. *Sustainability (Basel)*, 14(21), 14126. DOI: 10.3390/su142114126

Mishra, D. M. K. (2019). Financial Literacy and Education for Improving Financial Skills. SSRN *Electronic Journal*. https://doi.org/DOI: 10.2139/SSRN.3488670

Mishra, S., Aravind, S. M., Charpe, P., Ajlouni, S., ... (2022). Traditional rice-based fermented products: Insight into their probiotic diversity and probable health benefits. *Food Bioscience*. https://www.sciencedirect.com/science/article/pii/S2212429222005429

Mishra, A. K., Bansal, R., Maurya, P. K., Kar, S. K., & Bakshi, P. K. (2023). Predicting the antecedents of consumers' intention toward purchase of mutual funds: A hybrid <scp>PLS-SEM-neural</scp> network approach. *International Journal of Consumer Studies*, 47(2), 563–587. DOI: 10.1111/ijcs.12850

Mittal, P. (2019). *Non-performing Assets (NPAs) in Indian Banking Sector: Causes, Effects and Remedies. International Journal of Management, Technology, and Social Sciences*. IJMTS., DOI: 10.5281/zenodo.337895

MOF. (2024, January 9). *eMADANI | Portal Manfaat*. Ministry of Finance Malaysia. https://manfaat.mof.gov.my/individu/emadani

Mohamad Isa Abd Jalil. (2020). Issues and challenges of waqf practice in Malaysia: A review. *Labuan E-Journal Of Muamalat And Society*, 14.

Mohamed, H. (2017). Smart contracts in Islamic economic transactions. Retrieved from https://www.linkedin.com/pulse/smart-contracts-islamic-economic-transactions-hazik-mohamed/

Mohamed, N. A. (2017). Financial socialization: A cornerstone for young employees' financial well-being. *Reports on Economics and Finance*, 3, 15–35. DOI: 10.12988/ref.2017.711

Mohammed Esmail Alekam, J., & Salniza, Md. S., & Sanuri, Mohd. M. (. (2018). The Effect of Family, Peer, Behavior, Saving and Spending Behavior on Financial Literacy among Young Generations. *International Journal of Organizational Leadership*, 7(3), 309–323. DOI: 10.33844/ijol.2018.60258

Mohammed, O. (2022). Islamic social finance and sustainable development goals: Issues and challenges. *Journal of Islamic Finance*, 11(2), 56–67.

Mohanta, B. K., Panda, S. S., & Jena, D. (2018). *An Overview of Smart Contract and Use cases in Blockchain Technology. 9th ICCCNT 2018. July 10-12*. Bengluru.

Mohd Danuri, M. S. N. (2019). Empowering People: 4th Industrial Revolution and Us', 6th International Research Management and Innovation Conference (IRMIC) 2019, KUIS.

Mohd Nor, S., Abdul-Majid, M., & Esrati, S. N. (2021). The role of blockchain technology in enhancing Islamic social finance: the case of Zakah management in Malaysia. *foresight, 23*(5), 509-527.

Mohd Shahrul, N. M. D., Khirulnizam, A. R., & Che Wan Shamsul Bahri, C. W. A. (2019). Proposed conceptual design of Waqf management system. *Malaysian Journal of Information and Communication Technology*, 4(2).

Mohd Sidik, W., & Ahmad, Z. (2021). Application of GIS (Geographical Information System) in The Management of Waqf Lands in Selangor. *International Journal of Academic Research in Business & Social Sciences*, 11(11). Advance online publication. DOI: 10.6007/IJARBSS/v11-i11/11651

Mohd, K. B. (2019). The Integrity of Fintech In Information Security From Islamic Perspective. *Editorial board, 61*.

Mohsin, M. I. A., Ahmad, R., & Chan, W. M. (2022). Exploring Digitalization of Malaysian Banking and Fintech Companies' Services from the Customer's Perspective. *International Journal of Management and Applied Research*, 9(2), 140–160. DOI: 10.18646/2056.92.22-007

Molla, A., & Biru, A. (2023). The evolution of the Fintech entrepreneurial ecosystem in Africa: An exploratory study and model for future development. *Technological Forecasting and Social Change*, 186, 122123. DOI: 10.1016/j.techfore.2022.122123

Mollah, M. B., Azim, M. I., & Bhuiyan, A. B. (2018). Blockchain technology and its prospects in Islamic finance. *Journal of Islamic Finance*, 9(2), 51–60.

Moorthy, K. S., Ting, T. Y., Kamarudin, A. A., T'ing, L. C., & Johanthan, S. (2022). Impact of government incentive and social influence in the consumer adoption of e-wallets in malaysia. *ASIAN JOURNAL OF ECONOMICS AND FINANCE*, 4(4), 347–368. DOI: 10.47509/AJEF.2022.v04i04.01

Moorthy, K., Chiang, O. Y., Kamarudin, A. A., T'ing, L. C., Mei, C. Y., & Johanthan, S. (2021). Factors That Influence the Adoption of E-Wallets by the Malaysians. *International Journal of E-Adoption*, 13(2), 78–95. DOI: 10.4018/IJEA.2021070105

Morgan, P., Huang, B., & Trinh, L. Q. (2019). The Need to Promote Digital Financial Literacy for the Digital Age. In *The Future of Work and Education for the Digital Age. In Realizing Education for All in the Digital Age*. https://www.adb.org/sites/default/files/publication/503706/adbi-realizing-education-all-digital-age.pdf#page=56

Morissan. (2015). *Periklanan : Komunikasi Pemasaran Terpadu* (4th ed.). Prenadamedia.

Mourizka, A. V., & Nisha, N. (2023). Pola Konsumsi Generasi Z Pengguna E-Wallet di Kota Bandung. In N. Nurhayati (Ed.), *Bandung Conference Series: Economics Studies* (Vol. 3, Issue 1, pp. 45–54). UPT Publikasi Ilmiah, Universitas Islam Bandung. DOI: 10.29313/bcses.v3i1.5926

Muamar, A., & Alparisi, A. S. (2017). Electronic money (e-money) in maqashid al-sharia perspective. *Journal of Islamic Economics Lariba*, 3(2), 75–84. https://journal.uii.ac.id/JIELariba/article/download/9657/7821

Muamar, A., Samsudin, S., & Fitriyah, L. (2020). Dompet elektronik dalam transaksi pelanggan OVO menurut perspektif maqasid syari'ah. *Al-Mustashfa: Jurnal Penelitian Hukum Ekonomi Syariah*, 5(1), 92–105. DOI: 10.24235/jm.v5i1.6814

Muchlis Gazali, H., Che Ismail, C. M. H., Gazali, H. M., & Che Ismail, C. M. H. (2019). A Conceptual Framework for Cash Waqf with Blockchain in Financing Education for the Islamic Religious School in Malaysia. *Journal of Islamic Sciences and Comparative Studies*, 3(1), 73–88.

Muchtar, E. H., & Zubairin, A. (2022). Fintech syariah dalam perspektif hukum islam. *Jurnal Asy-Syukriyyah*, 23(1). Advance online publication. DOI: 10.36769/asy.v23i1.185

Mufti of Federal Territory's Office. Malaysia (2024). Retrieved from https://muftiwp.gov.my/en/artikel/al-kafi-li-al-fatawi/3740-al-kafi-1397-the-ruling-of-giving-sadaqah-donation-to-the-rich

Mu, H.-L., & Lee, Y.-C. (2021). How Inclusive Digital Financial Services Impact User Behavior: A Case of Proximity Mobile Payment in Korea. *Sustainability (Basel)*, 13(17), 9567. DOI: 10.3390/su13179567

Muhammad, A. M., Basha, M. B., & AlHafidh, G. (2024). Use of emerging social media platforms in reshaping the UAE Islamic banks' promotional strategies. *Journal of Islamic Marketing*, 15(2), 338–360. DOI: 10.1108/JIMA-01-2022-0015

Muhammad, R., & Yuningsih, A. (2020). Shariah Compliance Analysis of Islamic Crowdfunding: Case Study of ethiscrowd.com. *IQTISHODUNA: Jurnal Ekonomi Islam*, 9(1), 75. DOI: 10.36835/iqtishoduna.v9i1.472

Muhammad, S. M., & Hanapi, M. S. (2018). The Principle of Wasatiyyah-Consumerism in Syama'il Muhammadiyyah: A Study of Al-Hadith Al-Mawdu 'iy. *International Journal of Academic Research in Business & Social Sciences*, 8(4). Advance online publication. DOI: 10.6007/IJARBSS/v8-i4/4049

Muhammad, S. M., & Hanapi, M. S. (2019). Consumerism Rationality Concept According To Maqasid Syariah. *International Journal of Academic Research in Business & Social Sciences*, 9(4), 79–88. DOI: 10.6007/IJARBSS/v9-i4/5820

Muhammed, D. D. J. (2013). Introduction to history of Islamic banking in Malaysia. *Humanomics*, 29(2), 80–87. DOI: 10.1108/08288661311319157

Mujani, W. K., & Yaakub, N. I. (2017). Waqf for higher education in Malaysia: Overview on challenges. *European Journal of Multidisciplinary Studies*, 5(1), 455–461. DOI: 10.26417/ejms.v5i1.p455-461

Mukhopadhyay, M. (2018). *Ethereum Smart Contract Development*. Packt Publishing Ltd.

Muneer, F., & Khan, F. (2022). Impact of Qard-al-Hasan (interest-free loan) program in reducing multidimensional poverty: an evidence from the southwest Bangladesh. *International Journal of Islamic and Middle Eastern Finance and Management*. DOI: 10.1108/IMEFM-03-2021-0101

Muneeza, A., & Nadwi, S. (2019). The Potential of Application of Technology-Based Innovations for Zakat Administration in India. *International Journal of Zakat*, 4(2), 87–100. DOI: 10.37706/ijaz.v4i2.191

Munshi, U. (2021). The role of Islamic crowdfunding in the new economy in Islamic Fintech. Routledge., Retrieved February 28, 2023, from.

Murugiah, L., Ismail, R., Taib, H. M., Applanaidu, S. D., & Long, M. N. H. B. H. (2023). Children's understanding of financial literacy and parents' choice of financial knowledge learning methods in Malaysia. *MethodsX*, 11, 102383. Advance online publication. DOI: 10.1016/j.mex.2023.102383 PMID: 37767158

Muryanto, Y. T. (2022). The urgency of sharia compliance regulations for Islamic Fintechs: A comparative study of Indonesia, Malaysia and the United Kingdom. *Journal of Financial Crime*. Advance online publication. DOI: 10.1108/JFC-05-2022-0099

Muryanto, Y. T., Kharisma, D. B., & Ciptorukmi Nugraheni, A. S. (2022). Prospects and challenges of Islamic fintech in Indonesia: A legal viewpoint. *International Journal of Law and Management*, 64(2), 239–252. DOI: 10.1108/IJLMA-07-2021-0162

Musa, S. (2024). Islamic Perspectives on Advancing Economy and Trade through AI and Industry Revolution 5.0: Towards Enhanced Prosperity in Malaysia. *International Journal of Contemporary ..., March*, 0–30. https://ijci.abrarglobal.com/images/IJCI VOL. 2 ISSUE 1 MARCH 2024.pdf#page=118

Musafar Hameed, L. B., Chik, M. N., & Mohamad Suhaimi, A. F. (2017). *Sadaqa House: Its viability in the Islamic banking framework*. Penerbit KUIS.

Musafar Hameed, L. B., Muneeza, A., Mohd Dasar, M. H., Ismail, A. Y., & Mohamad Suhaimi, A. F. (2024). *Sadaqa house: Inspiring 'Adl and Ihsan in the realm of Islamic banking. Penerbit UIS & International Research Centre of Islamic Economics and Finance*. IRCIEF.

Musau, S. M. (2013). An analysis of the utilization of agency banking on performance of selected banks in Nairobi County, Kenya. Kenyatta University., Retrieved March 2, 2023, from.

Mustafar, M. Z., & Borhan, J. T. (2013). Muslim consumer behavior: Emphasis on ethics from Islamic perspective. *Middle East Journal of Scientific Research*, 18(9), 1301–1307.

Mutmainah, liyatul, Nurwahidin, & Huda, N. (2021). Waqf Blockchain in Indonesia: at A Glance. *Al Awqaf, 14*(1), 31–49.

myWakaf (2024) Retrieved from https://www.mywakaf.com.my/

Nacar, Y. (2007). *Participation banks and financial solutions*. Istanbul Chamber of Commerce.

Nafed, H. H. M. (2009) *Web Based Expert System for i-Faraid.* Masters thesis, Universiti Utara Malaysia.

Nagimova, A. (2022). Islamic Fintech: Digitalization of Global Islamic Finance. *World Economy and International Relations*, 66(5), 50–58. DOI: 10.20542/0131-2227-2022-66-5-50-58

Nahar, H. S. (2018, January 9). Exploring Awqāf Governance. *Preliminary Evidence of Governance Practices and Disclosure of Two Malaysian Awqāf Institutions.*, 31(1), 139–150. DOI: 10.4197/islec.31-1.9

Nair, S., Jayabalan, N., & Perumal, I. (2023). E-Wallet Usage Intention in Selangor, Malaysia. *Journal of Hunan University Natural Sciences*, 50(4). Advance online publication. DOI: 10.55463/issn.1674-2974.50.4.2

Naldi, G. A., & Muljaningsih, S. (2022). Pengaruh Motivasi, Persepsi Risiko, Pengetahuan terhadap Investasi pada UMKM melalui Platform Securities Crowdfunding. *Islamic Economic and Finance in Focus*, 1(1), 50–60. DOI: 10.21776/ieff.2022.01.1.05

Nalurita, F., Leon, F. M., & Nisfiannoor, M. (2022). Financial Management Behavior for E-Wallet Users in Jabodetabek. *Business and Entrepreneurial Review*, 22(2), 229–250. DOI: 10.25105/ber.v22i2.13951

Naoual, B. (2022). Using blockchain technology to revolutionize Waqf: The Finterra Waqf Chain model.

Narcisa Roxana Moşteanu, A. F. (2020). Digital Technologies Implementation within Financial and Banking System During Socio Distancing Restrictions – Back to the Future. [IJARET]. *International Journal of Advanced Research in Engineering and Technology*, 11(6), 307–315.

Narsaa, I. M., Dian, N. P., & Handayani, R. (2020). An Experimental Study of the Effect of Financial and Non-Financial Information on Intention to Invest in the Bearish and Bullish Market. *International Journal of Innovation. Creativity and Change*, 11(11), 421–439.

Narula, R., & Singla, S. (2014). Non-performing assets (NPAs) and its impact on Indian banking sector. International Journal of Innovative Research and Developme-https://www.academia.edu/download/42963536/NON_PERFORMING_ASSETS_NPAs_AN D_ITS_IMPACT.pdf

Nashirah, A. B., Rosbi, S., & Uzaki, K. (2020). E-Wallet Transactional Framework for Digital Economy: A Perspective from Islamic Financial Engineering. *International Journal of Management Science and Business Administration*, 6(3), 50–57. DOI: 10.18775/ijmsba.1849-5664-5419.2014.63.1005

Nasiri, A., Noori, A., & Salleh, M. C. M. (2019). Acceptance and practices of cash WAQF among university's students. International Journal of Academic Research in Accounting. *Finance and Management Sciences*, 9(3), 38–48. DOI: 10.6007/IJARAFMS/v9-i3/6325

Nasrul, M. A. D., Manaf, Z. I. A., Syafril, S., & Fathurrohman, M. (2021). An Overview of the Inheritance Legal System in Malaysia and Indonesia: Issues Faced by Both Countries. *Journal of Shariah Law Research*, 6(2), 181–200.

Nasrul, M. A., Mohd Alam Shah, N. A., Abdul Hak, N., & Halim, A. H. (2022). Administration Of Estates: Resolution Of Disputes In Achieving Sustainability Among The Deceased's Family. *IIUM Law Journal*, 30(2), 253–279. DOI: 10.31436/iiumlj.v30i2.711

National Sharia Council - Indonesian Ulema Council. (2024). *Fatwa DSN-MUI*. DSN-MUI.

Natsir, K., & Arifin, A. Z. (2021). The Effect of Product Knowledge and Influence of Society on Investment Intention of Stock Investors with Perceived Risk as Mediation. *Estudios de Economía Aplicada*, 39(12). Advance online publication. DOI: 10.25115/eea.v39i12.6022

Nazarov, I. I., & Dhiraj, N. S. (2019). A conceptual understanding and significance of takaful (Islamic insurance): History, concept, models and products. *International Journal for Innovation Education and Research*, 7(4), 280–298. DOI: 10.31686/ijier.vol7.iss4.1408

Nazeri, A. N. N.SHIFA MOHD NOR. (2023). The Implementation Of Blockchain Technology In The Zakat Management System: A Conceptual Research. *Journal of Information Systems and Digital Technologies*, 5(2), 287–300. DOI: 10.31436/jisdt.v5i2.419

Nazli, M., & Yvonne, S. (2021, June 24). Relationship between Cultural Values, Sense of Community and Trust and the Effect of Trust in Workplace. https://doi.org//arXiv.2106.13347DOI: 10.48550

Ndou, V., Scorrano, P., Mele, G., & Stefanizzi, P. (2022). Fundraising activities and digitalization: Defining risk indicators for evaluating equity crowdfunding campaigns. *Meditari Accountancy Research*, 30(4), 1169–1190. DOI: 10.1108/MEDAR-03-2021-1237

Negara Malaysia, B. (2019). *Commission Malaysia, S.* National Strategy for Financial Literacy.

Nelly, R., Harianto, H., Abd.Majid, M. S., Marliyah, M., & Handayani, R. (2022). Studi Empiris Perkembangan Crowdfunding Syariah di Indonesia. *Al-Kharaj : Jurnal Ekonomi. Keuangan & Bisnis Syariah*, 4(5), 1283–1297. DOI: 10.47467/alkharaj.v4i5.926

Netemeyer, R. G., Warmath, D., Fernandes, D., & Lynch, J. G.Jr. (2018). How Am I Doing? Perceived Financial Well-Being, Its Potential Antecedents, and Its Relation to Overall Well-Being. *The Journal of Consumer Research*, 45(1), 68–89. DOI: 10.1093/jcr/ucx109

Ngafifi, M. (2014). Kemajuan Teknologi Dan Pola Hidup Manusia Dalam Perspektif Sosial Budaya. *Jurnal Pembangunan Pendidikan: Fondasi Dan Aplikasi*, 2(1), 33–47. DOI: 10.21831/jppfa.v2i1.2616

Nienhaus, V. (2019). Blockchain technologies and the prospects of smart contracts in Islamic finance. In *Fintech in Islamic Finance* (pp. 183–210). Routledge. DOI: 10.4324/9781351025584-13

Nik Mohd Saiful W. Mohd Sidik, & Zaid Ahmad. (2021). Application of GIS (Geographical Information System)

Nikolopoulou, K. (2023). Digital Education in the Post-Covid Era: Challenges and Opportunities to Explore. *IFIP Advances in Information and Communication Technology, 685 AICT*, 3–14. DOI: 10.1007/978-3-031-43393-1_1

Nimansa, A. T., & Kuruwitaarachchi, N. (2020). A Study on Finding the Factors, Hindering the use of digital wallets among youth in Developing Countries. *Scholedge International Journal of Management & Development*, 7(6), 107–117. DOI: 10.19085/sijmd070602

Noho, H., M. D. (. (2023). Development of Waqf Objects through Public Private Partnership (PPP) as a Means of Infrastructure Development for the Public Interest. *QURU'. Journal of Family Law and Culture*, 1(1), 90–108. DOI: 10.59698/quru.v1i1.116

Nonaka, I., & Takeuchi, H. (1995). *The knowledge-creating company*. Oxford University Press. DOI: 10.1093/oso/9780195092691.001.0001

Noor, A. (2022). THE LEGAL REGULATORY FRAMEWORK OF SHARIA SECURITIES CROWDFUNDING IN INDONESIA. *Masalah-Masalah Hukum*, 51(4), 433–444. DOI: 10.14710/mmh.51.4.2022.433-444

Noordin, N., Shuib, A., Zainol, M., Azam, M., & Mohamed Adil, M. (2012). Review On Issues And Challenges In Islamic Inheritance Distribution In Malaysia. *OIDA International Journal of Sustainable Development*, 3, 27–38.

Noor, K. A. M., & Yusoff, A. F. J. (2022). Issues in the Application of Wakalah (Agency) in E-wallet. *International Journal of Academic Research in Business & Social Sciences*, 12(11). Advance online publication. DOI: 10.6007/IJARBSS/v12-i11/15119

Nor Mohamed Yakcop. (1981). Islamic banking in Malaysia: An early document 1981.

Nor Paizin, Muhsin & Som, Hairullfazli & Hj. Ismail, Mokthar & Saadan, Mohd. (2022). Innovation and Technology Optimization for Increasing The Collection and Distribution of Zakat in Malaysia. Presented at 6th MUZAKARAH FIQH AND INTERNATIONAL FIQH CONFERENCE (MFIFC) 2022At: Kolej Universiti Islam Antarabangsa Selangor, KUIS

Nordin, N., Shahwan, S., & Ibrahim, N. (2021). E-wallet as a new approach in zakat collection and distribution: Exploring the experience of zakat and e-wallet providers in Malaysia. In The International Islamic Economic System Conference – The 9th I-iECONS 2021 (pp. 364–371).

Nordin, N., Shahwan, S., & Ibrahim, N. (2021). E-wallet as a new approach in zakat collection and distribution: Exploring the experience of zakat and e-wallet providers in Malaysia. In The International Islamic Economic System Conference – The 9th I-iECONS 2021 (pp. 364–371). *Journal of Economics and Sustainable Development*, 50(1), 136–841.

Nordin, N., Shahwan, S., Ibrahim, N., & Awang, N. (2023). Using E-Wallet in Collecting and Distributing Zakat in Malaysia. *International Journal of Business and Technology Management*, 5(1), 175–186. DOI: 10.55057/ijbtm.2023.5.1.16

Nordin, S., & Ahmad, M. A. (2023). The internet of things and Islamic estate planning in the forth industry revolution (4ir) in Malaysia: Issues and challenges. [GBSE]. *Journal of Global Business and Social Entrepreneurship*, 9(27), 43–63.

North, R. (2018, November 6). *THE ROLE OF DIGITAL BANKING IN INDIA – IMPORTANCE OF DIGITAL BANKING IN INDIA*. Retrieved from Entreprise Edges: https://www.enterpriseedges.com/role-of-digital-banking-india

Nouman, M., & Ullah, K. (2023). Maqasid Al Shari'ah and Financial Concern of Human Life. In Nouman, M., & Ullah, K. (Eds.), *Participatory Islamic Finance: Ideals, Contemporary Practices, and Innovations* (pp. 29–46). Springer Nature Singapore., DOI: 10.1007/978-981-19-9555-2_2

Nugraheni, N. (2020). Crowdfunding-based fiduciary warrant in providing capital loans for small and medium enterprises. *Hasanuddin Law Review*, 6(3), 224–231. DOI: 10.20956/halrev.v6i3.2201

Nugroho, L., Hidayah, N., & Badawi, A. (2018). The Islamic Banking Asset Quality: Does Financing Segmentation Matter? (Indonesia Evidence). *Mediterranean Journal of Social Sciences*, 9(5), 235–245. DOI: 10.2478/mjss-2018-0154

Nurul'ain M., Mastura R., Muhammad Hasif Y., & Zainur Nadiyah Baharuddin. (2024). The roles of Islamic financial technology (FINTECH) in fostering financial inclusion in Malaysia. *Management and Accounting Review*, 23(1), April 2024.

Nusaibah, umu. (2023). Digitalisasi Ekonomi Syariah di Kalangan Generasi Z Untuk Peningkatan Literasi Keuangan Syariah (Studi Kasus Mbanking BSI). *Musyarakah: Journal of Sharia Economic (MJSE), 12*(1), 12–22. DOI: 10.24269/mjse.v12i1.6695

Nyazee, I. A. (2000, 2023 March). *The Concept of Riba and Islamic Banking*. Retrieved 1, from Nyazee.com: http://www.nyazee.com/islbanks/riba/riba.html

Nye, P., & Hillyard, C. (2013). Personal Financial Behavior: The Influence of Quantitative Literacy and Material Values. *Numeracy*, 6(1), 3. DOI: 10.5038/1936-4660.6.1.3

O'Mahony, B., & Hall, J. (2011). *Personal values, vanity, physical health, and perceived body image influences in food-purchasing and consumption decisions.*, DOI: 10.1007/978-0-387-92271-3_200

Obaidullah, M. (2021). Promise of IRSHAD: The Intelligent Robo Shariah Advisor. IBFNet. https://conference.ibfnet.ie/2021/03/03/promise-of-irshad-the-intelligent-robo-shariah advisor/

Oktavian, R. D., & Maika, M. R. (2020). The Application of Utaut Model To the Crowdfunding Based Halal Tourism Capital Platform Innovation. *Laa Maisyir : Jurnal Ekonomi Islam*, 7(2), 188. DOI: 10.24252/lamaisyir.v7i2.16104

Olatubosun, A. A. (2022). Resource mobilization and financial performance of Islamic cooperative societies in southwestern Nigeria. *International Journal of Umranic Studies*.

Omar, H. H., & Sanyinna, A. Y. J. T. J. o. S. S. R. (2018). Administrative challenges of WAQF institution in the contemporary world: Future prospects. 294-299: 296.

Omar, I. A., Jayaraman, R., Salah, K., Simsekler, M. C. E., Yaqoob, I., & Ellahham, S. (2020). Ensuring protocol compliance and data transparency in clinical trials using Blockchain smart contracts. *BMC Medical Research Methodology*, 20(1), 1–17. DOI: 10.1186/s12874-020-01109-5 PMID: 32894068

Ombir, & Bansal. (2016). Non-performing Assets in Indian Banks: Trends and Determinants. Journal of Commerce and Accounting Research, Retrieved from https://www.semanticscholar.org/paper/Non performing-Assets-in-Indian-Banks%3ATrends-and-Ombir Bansal/34f170caae82aa7c1a390d1c7b444a182fac90d7

Or, C., & Chapman, E. (2021). An Extended Unified Theory of Acceptance and Use of Technology Model for Education Contexts. *Journal of Applied Learning & Teaching*, 4(2). Advance online publication. DOI: 10.37074/jalt.2021.4.2.7

Oseni, U. A., & Ali, S. N. (2019). Fintech in Islamic finance. In *Fintech in Islamic finance* (pp. 3–14). Routledge. DOI: 10.4324/9781351025584-1

Osman, A. F., Mohammed, M. O., & Amin, H. (2014). An Analysis Of Cash Waqf Participation Among Young Intellectuals. In *Seminar Waqf Iqlimi* (pp. 7–20). Universiti Sains Islam Malaysia., Retrieved from https://oarep.usim.edu.my/jspui/handle/123456789/11596

OxfordDictinoary. (2022). *CrowdFunding*. Oxford Dictinoary.

Özsoy, İ. (1999). *Special finance institutions*. Asya Finans Institution Publication.

Özulucan, A., & Deran, A. (2009). The Comparison of Participation Banking and Traditional Banking on the Perspective of Banking Services and Accounting Applications. [In Turkish]. *Mustafa Kemal University Journal of Social Sciences Institute*, 6(11), 85–108.

Özulucan, A., & Özdemir, S. F. (2010). *Participation Banking*. Türkmen Kitabevi.

Pachpande, B. R., & Kamble, A. A. (2018). Study of E-wallet Awareness and its Usage in Mumbai. *Journal of Commerce and Management Thought*, 9(1), 33–45. DOI: 10.5958/0976-478X.2018.00004.6

Pal, A., Tiwari, C. K., & Behl, A. (2021). Blockchain technology in financial services: A comprehensive review of the literature. *Journal of Global Operations and Strategic Sourcing*, 14(1), 61–80. DOI: 10.1108/JGOSS-07-2020-0039

Palacios-González, M. M., & Chamorro-Mera, A. (2018). Analysis of the predictive variables of the intention to invest in a socially responsible manner. *Journal of Cleaner Production*, 196, 469–477. DOI: 10.1016/j.jclepro.2018.06.066

Palmié, M., Wincent, J., Parida, V., & Caglar, U. (2020). The evolution of the financial technology ecosystem: An introduction and agenda for future research on disruptive innovations in ecosystems. *Technological Forecasting and Social Change*, 151, 119779. DOI: 10.1016/j.techfore.2019.119779

Panahifar, F., Byrne, P. J., Salam, M. A., & Heavey, C. (2018). Supply chain collaboration and firm's performance: The critical role of information sharing and trust. *Journal of Enterprise Information Management*, 31(3), 358–379. DOI: 10.1108/JEIM-08-2017-0114

Pardede, M. (2023). DILEMA REFORMASI REGULASI HUKUM INVESTASI DALAM SISTEM HUKUM SIPIL DALAM PERSPEKTIF JAMINAN KEPASTIAN HUKUM PENANAMAN MODAL (Suatu Upaya Peningkatan Iklim Daya Saing dan Jaminan Kepastian Hukum Penanaman Modal). *Jurnal Penelitian Hukum De Jure*, 23(2), 231. DOI: 10.30641/dejure.2023.V23.231-244

Pardiansyah, E. (2017), Investasi dalam Perspektif Ekonomi Islam. Economica: Jurnal Bisnis dan Ekonomi Islam, 8(2).

Park, J., Velasco, C. M. B., & Spence, C. (2022). "Looking sharp": Price typeface influences awareness of spending in mobile payment. *Psychology and Marketing*, 39(6), 1170–1189. DOI: 10.1002/mar.21651

Peraturan Pemerintah Nomor 8 Tahun 2007 tentang Investasi Pemerintah. (n.d.). Retrieved from https://jdih.kemenkeu.go.id

Peraturan Presiden Republik Indonesia Nomor 10 Tahun 2021 tentang Bidang Usaha Penanaman Modal. (n.d.). Retrieved from https://jdih.setkab.go.id

Permana, G. P. L., & Rahayuni, D. A. B. (2023). Determinan Penggunaan Crowdfunding Berbasis Donasi. *Jurnal Aplikasi Akuntansi*, 7(2), 315–327. DOI: 10.29303/jaa.v7i2.211

Perpustakaan, J. I. (2022). *PENERAPAN INTERNET OF THINGS (IoT) DALAM UPAYA MEWUJUDKAN PERPUSTAKAAN DIGITAL DI ERA SOCIETY 5.0. 11*(1), 29–36.

Persaud, A., & Thaffe, W. (2023). The state of financial inclusion research on developing countries. *Transnational Corporations Review*, 15(4), 22–34. DOI: 10.1016/j.tncr.2023.08.002

Petry, N. M. (2002). A comparison of young, middle-aged, and older adult treatment-seeking pathological gamblers. *The Gerontologist*, 42(1), 92–99. DOI: 10.1093/geront/42.1.92 PMID: 11815703

Polyviou, A., Velanas, P., & Soldatos, J. (2019, October). Blockchain technology: financial sector applications beyond cryptocurrencies. In *Proceedings* (Vol. 28, No. 1, p. 7). MDPI. DOI: 10.3390/proceedings2019028007

Polyzos, E., Samitas, A., & Syriopoulos, K. (2022). Islamic banking, efficiency and societal welfare: A machine learning, agent-based study. *International Journal of Islamic and Middle Eastern Finance and Management*, 16(4), 777–801. DOI: 10.1108/IMEFM-04-2022-0144

Pradja, J. S. (2011), Ekonomi Syariah. Bandung: Pustaka Setia Presiden Republik Indonesia. (2007). *UNDANG UNDANG REPUBLIK INDONESIA NOMOR 25 TAHUN 2007*. https://ojk.go.id/id/regulasi/regulasi-terkait-lainnya/Pages/undang-undang-nomor-25-tahun-2007-tentang-penanaman-modal.aspx#:~:text=Mengatur%20ketentuan%20mengenai%20kebijakan%20dasar,serta%20mempercepat%20peningkatan%20penanaman%20modal

Pratiwi, R. E., Meirani, N., Khumairah, K., Saharan, M. S., & Hassan, H. E. (2023). Crowdfunding: As an Alternative to Islamic Funding. *Journal of Business Studies and Management Review*, 6(2), 109–117. DOI: 10.22437/jbsmr.v6i2.24535

Pražić, I. T. (2020). Influence of personal values on consumer choice and intention to buy: a case of Croatian automobile market. In Bevanda, V. (Ed.), *Fourth International Scientific Conference on Recent Advances in Information Technology, Tourism, Economics, Management and Agriculture* (pp. 117–124). Association of Economists and Managers of the Balkans. DOI: 10.31410/ITEMA.S.P.2020.117

Presiden Republik Indonesia. (2024). *Undang-undang Nomor 59 Tahun 2024*. https://jdih.bappenas.go.id/peraturan/detailperaturan/3919/undang-undang-nomor-59-tahun-2024

Prisco, G. (2015, December 22). *Enigma, MIT Media Lab's Blockchain-based Encrypted Data Marketplace, to Launch Beta*. Retrieved February 22, 2023, from bitcoinmagazine: https://bitcoinmagazine.com/business/enigma-mit-media-lab-s-blockchain-based-encrypted-data-marketplace-to-launch-beta-1450810499

Priyadi, U., Achiria, S., Imron, M. A., & Zandi, G. R. (2022, December 27). Waqf management and accountability: Waqf land financing models for economic well-being. https://archive.aessweb.com/index.php/5002/article/download/4696/7423

Priyadi, U., Achiria, S., & Imron, M. A. (2023). *Digital-Based Nazhir Services for Co-Creation Value in Waqf Land Asset Management. International Journal of Management Research and Social Science*. IJMRSS.

Pusat Pungutan Zakat-MAIWP. (2022). Zakat and Islamic social finance: The way forward.

Qadri, H. M.-D., & Malik, F. A. (2024). Emergence of Islamic Digital Economy. In Islamic Finance in the Modern Era (p. 14). DOI: 10.4324/9781003366751-2

Qudah, H., Malahim, S., Airout, R., Alomari, M., Hamour, A. A., & Alqudah, M. (2023). Islamic finance in the era of financial technology: A bibliometric review of future trends. *International Journal of Financial Studies*, 11(2), 76. DOI: 10.3390/ijfs11020076

Qurrata, V. A., Yusida, E., Hussain, N. E., Merlinda, S., Purnamasari, V., & Seprillina, L. (2021). Effectiveness of cash waqf management in improving community welfare: Challenges and opportunities. *Review of Integrative Business & Economics Research*, 10(1), 342–359. http://buscompress.com/uploads/3/4/9/8/34980536/riber_10-s1_29_u20-086_342-359.pdf

Rabbani, M. R., Abdulla, Y., Basahr, A., Khan, S., & Moh'd Ali, M. A. (2020, November). Embracing of Fintech in Islamic Finance in the post COVID era. In *2020 international conference on decision aid sciences and application (DASA)* (pp. 1230-1234). IEEE. DOI: 10.1109/DASA51403.2020.9317196

Rabbani, M. R., Hassan, M. K., Hudaefi, F. A., & Shaikh, Z. H. (2022). Islamic finance and cryptocurrency: a systematic review. *FinTech in Islamic Financial Institutions: Scope, Challenges, and Implications in Islamic Finance*, 279-306.

Rabbani, M. R. (2022). Fintech innovations, scope, challenges, and implications in Islamic Finance: A systematic analysis. *International Journal of Computing and Digital Systems*, 11(1), 1–28.

Rabbani, M. R., Ali, M. A. M., Rahiman, H. U., Atif, M., Zulfikar, Z., & Naseem, Y. (2021). The response of islamic financial service to the covid-19 pandemic: The open social innovation of the financial system. *Journal of Open Innovation*, 7(1), 85. DOI: 10.3390/joitmc7010085

Rabbani, M. R., Bashar, A., Nawaz, N., Karim, S., Ali, M. A. M., Rahiman, H. U., & Alam, M. S. (2021). Exploring the role of islamic fintech in combating the aftershocks of covid-19: The open social innovation of the islamic financial system. *Journal of Open Innovation*, 7(2), 136. DOI: 10.3390/joitmc7020136

Rachmat Riski, T., Sulistianingsih, H., Ekonomi Dan Bisnis, F., & Dharma Andalas, U. (2024). Literasi Keuangan, Media Sosial dan Perilaku investasi Instrument Keuangan Syariah Generasi Muda dikota Padang. *Jurnal Ekonomi Dan Bisnis Dharma Andalas*, 26(1), 176–189. DOI: 10.47233/jebd.v26i1.1244

Rahadjeng, E. R., & Fiandari, Y. R. (2020). THE EFFECT OF ATTITUDE, SUBJECTIVE NORMS AND CONTROL OF BEHAVIOR TOWARDS INTENTION IN SHARE INVESTMENT. *Manajemen Bisnis*, 10(2). Advance online publication. DOI: 10.22219/jmb.v10i2.13616

Rahim, N. F., Bakri, M. H., & Yahaya, S. N. (2019). Fintech and Shariah principles in smart contracts. In *FinTech as a disruptive technology for financial institutions* (pp. 207–220). IGI Global. DOI: 10.4018/978-1-5225-7805-5.ch009

Rahman, A. (2019). Opportunities and threats of Shariah-compliant robo advisory. the case of Wahed Invest. Retrieved October 15, 2019, from, https://www.grin.com/document/540407

Rahman, M., Isa, C. R., Masud, M. M., Sarker, M., & Chowdhury, N. T. (2021). The role of financial behaviour, financial literacy, and financial stress in explaining the financial well-being of B40 group in Malaysia. *Future Business Journal*, 7(1), 1–18. DOI: 10.1186/s43093-021-00099-0

Rahman, N. L. A., Mutalib, H. A., Sabri, S. M., Annuar, N., Mutalib, S. K. M. S. A., & Rahman, Z. S. A. (2022). Factors Influencing E-Wallet Adoption among Adults During Covid-19 Pandemic in Malaysia: Extending The Tam Model. *International Journal of Academic Research in Business & Social Sciences*, 12(7). Advance online publication. DOI: 10.6007/IJARBSS/v12-i7/14327

Raja Adnan, R. A. binti, Abdul Mutalib, M., & Ab Aziz, M. R. (2021). Factors necessary for effective corporate waqf management for Malaysian public healthcare. *ISRA International Journal of Islamic Finance*. DOI: 10.1108/IJIF-11-2019-0178

Rajah, N., Amran, A., & Cheah, J. (2022). Determinants that enhance resilience and performance of social enterprises in Malaysia: A conceptual framework. *Journal of Governance and Integrity*, 5(3), 297–307. DOI: 10.15282/jgi.5.3.2022.8981

Ram, A., & Cnaan, M. S. (2012). Financial Inclusion: Lessons From Rural South India. *Journal of Social Policy*, 41(1), 183–205. DOI: 10.1017/S0047279411000377

Ramli, A. M., & Jalil, A. (2015). *Model Perbankan Wakaf Korporat : Analisis Wakaf Selangor Muamalat. 42*(2014), 159–167.

Ramli, A., Fahmi, F. M., Darus, F., & Rasit, Z. A. (2019, March 15). Academic Research Publishing Group - ARPG. https://arpgweb.com/journal/7/special_issue/03-2019/1/&page=2

Ramli, F. A. A., & Hamzah, M. I. (2021). Mobile payment and e-wallet adoption in emerging economies: A systematic literature review. *Journal of Emerging Economies and Islamic Research*, 9(2), 1. DOI: 10.24191/jeeir.v9i2.13617

RAS, H., & Suroso, J. T. (2020), Kepastian Hukum Dalam Hukum Investasi di Indonesia Melalui Omnibus Law. JIMEA Jurnal Ilmiah MEA (Manajemen, Ekonomi, dan Akuntansi), 4(1).

Rashwan, A. R. M. S., & Kassem, Z. A. E. A. (2021). The role of digital transformation in increasing the efficiency of banks' performance to enhance competitive advantage. In *The big data-driven digital economy: Artificial and computational intelligence* (pp. 325–335). Springer International Publishing. DOI: 10.1007/978-3-030-73057-4_25

Razak, S. H. A. (2020). Zakat and waqf as instrument of Islamic wealth in poverty alleviation and redistribution: Case of Malaysia. *The International Journal of Sociology and Social Policy*, 40(3–4), 249–266. DOI: 10.1108/IJSSP-11-2018-0208

Razali, M., Mohd, N., Hadigunawan, N., & Saidon, R. (2021). Maqasid shariah hifz mal in e-wallet application. *Islamiyyat: International Journal of Islamic Studies, 43*(1), 113–120. https://ejournal.ukm.my/islamiyyat/article/download/48498/11967

Raza, S. A., Shah, N., & Ali, M. (2019). Acceptance of mobile banking in Islamic banks: Evidence from modi fi ed UTAUT model. *Journal of Islamic Marketing*, 10(1), 357–376. DOI: 10.1108/JIMA-04-2017-0038

Research and Markets. (2024, February). *Malaysia Buy Now Pay Later Business and Investment Opportunities Databook - 75+ KPIs on BNPL Market Size, End-Use Sectors, Market Share, Product Analysis, Business Model, Demographics - Q1 2024 Update*. Research and Markets. https://www.researchandmarkets.com/reports/5305023/malaysia-buy-now-pay-later-business-and?utm_source=CI&utm_medium=PressRelease&utm_code=759g6p&utm_campaign=1941191+-+Malaysia+Buy+Now+Pay+Later+Business+and+Investment+Opportunities+Report+2024%3a+Market+to+Grow+by+17.5%25+to+Reach+%242.78+Billion+in+2024+-+Forecasts+to+2029&utm_exec=chdomspi

Resta, P., Laferrière, T., McLaughlin, R., & Kouraogo, A. (2018, January 1). Issues and Challenges Related to Digital Equity: An Overview. DOI: 10.1007/978-3-319-71054-9_67

Rick, S. I., Cryder, C. E., & Loewenstein, G. (2008). Tightwads and spendthrifts. *The Journal of Consumer Research*, 34(6), 767–782. DOI: 10.1086/523285

Ridhwan Ab Aziz M, &. Z. (2021). Islamic Digital Banking in the Light of Maqasid Shariah: A Review of Literatures. *Al-Qanatir: International Journal of Islamic Studies, 23*(2), 63-73. Retrieved from https://al-qanatir.com/aq/article/view/358

Roeckelein, J. E., Anwar, A., & Irawati, I. (2013). *Dictionary of Theories, Laws, and Concepts*. Kencana.

Rosnia Masruki, Maliah Sulaiman, & Hafiz-Majdi Ab. Majid. (2021). Innovative zakat distribution practices of Malaysian state zakat institutions and their socio-economic impact during the COVID-19 pandemic. *International Journal of Innovation, Creativity and Change*, 15(9).

Rosnia Masruki, Maliah Sulaiman, & Hafiz-Majdi Ab. Majid. (2021). Innovative zakat distribution practices of Malaysian state zakat institutions and their socio-economic impact during the COVID-19 pandemic. *International Journal of Innovation, Creativity and Change*, 15(9). Rosman, Redzuan, Mokhtar, Engku, Engku Ali & Mustafa

Ruldeviyani, Y., & Saraswati, K. (2023). An Empirical Investigation of Factors Affecting Personal Information's Disclosure on Mobile Payment (E-Wallet) Platforms. *International Journal on Advanced Science, Engineering and Information Technology*, 13(3), 1031–1040. DOI: 10.18517/ijaseit.13.3.18054

Ruopeng, L., Weicheng, X., Xudong, W., & Huang, W. (2015). *Electronic wallet-based payment method and system.*

Rusydiana, A. S. (2024). Alternative Waqf Model for SDG-4 (Quality Education). *The Economic Review of Pesantren*, 2(2). Advance online publication. DOI: 10.58968/erp.v2i2.370

Rusydiana, A. S., & Devi, A. (2014). Analysis of cash waqf fund management in Indonesia: an Analytic Network Process (ANP) method approach. *InInternational Conference on Islamic Finance (AICIF),* Yogyakarta. 1–20.

Saad, M. S. M., & Rasli, R. M. (2022). Web Based Expert System in Area & Land Value Calculation and Faraid Distribution. *International Journal of Artificial Intelligence*, 9(2), 83–89. DOI: 10.36079/lamintang.ijai-0902.468

Sabah, 2023. Türkiye becomes world's most cyber targeted region in 2023 https://www.dailysabah.com/turkiye/turkiye-becomes-worlds-most-cyber-targeted-region-in-2023/news

Saba, I., Kouser, R., & Chaudhry, I. S. (2019).. . *Fintech and Islamic Finance-challenges and Opportunities.*, 5(4), 581–590. DOI: 10.26710/reads.v5i4.887

Sabri, M. F., Anthony, M., Law, S. H., Rahim, H. A., Burhan, N. A. S., & Ithnin, M. (2023). Impact of financial behaviour on financial well-being: Evidence among young adults in Malaysia. *Journal of Financial Services Marketing*, 0123456789. Advance online publication. DOI: 10.1057/s41264-023-00234-8

Sabri, M. F., Wahab, R., Mahdzan, N. S., Magli, A. S., Rahim, H., Suhaimi, S. S. A., & Nazuri, N. S. (2023). An enigma of Malaysia's low-income young adults: Mediation of financial behaviour on financial well-being and locus of control cohesion. *PLoS One*, 18(7), e0288204. Advance online publication. DOI: 10.1371/journal.pone.0288204 PMID: 37440508

Sadaqa House Impact Report (2020)

Sadaqa House Impact Report (2022)

Saeed, S., Altamimi, S. A., Alkayyal, N. A., Alshehri, E., & Alabbad, D. A. (2023, July 25). Digital Transformation and Cybersecurity Challenges for Businesses Resilience: Issues and Recommendations. *Sensors (Basel)*, 23(15), 6666–6666. DOI: 10.3390/s23156666 PMID: 37571451

Safina, Mohd Ali. (2021). Information Sharing and Search System to Ease Estate Distribution in Malaysia.

Sahabuddin, M., Ahmad, A. U. F., & Islam, M. A. (2023). Emergence of Islamic Finance in the Fourth Industrial Revolution and COVID-19 Post-Pandemic Era. In *Islamic Finance, FinTech, and the Road to Sustainability: Reframing the Approach in the Post-Pandemic Era* (pp. 123–141). Springer International Publishing. DOI: 10.1007/978-3-031-13302-2_6

Sahabuddin, M., Sakib, M. N., Rahman, M. M., Jibir, A., Fahlevi, M., Aljuaid, M., & Grabowska, S. (2023). The evolution of FinTech in scientific research: A bibliometric analysis. *Sustainability (Basel)*, 15(9), 7176. DOI: 10.3390/su15097176

Saiti, B., Dembele, A., & Bulut, M. (2021). The global cash waqf: A tool against poverty in Muslim countries. *Qualitative Research in Financial Markets*, 13(3), 277–294. DOI: 10.1108/QRFM-05-2020-0085

Sakti, M. R. P., Thaker, H. M. T., Qoyum, A., & Qizam, I. (2016). Determinants of cash Waqf contribution in Klang Valley and Selangor: A SEM approach. *Journal of Islamic Monetary Economics and Finance*, 2(1), 111–144. DOI: 10.21098/jimf.v2i1.593

Salisa, N. R. (2021). Faktor yang Mempengaruhi Minat Investasi di Pasar Modal: Pendekatan Theory of Planned Behaviour (TPB). *Jurnal Akuntansi Indonesia*, 9(2), 182. DOI: 10.30659/jai.9.2.182-194

Salman, M., Mohamad, N A., & Sadique, M A. (2022, January 2). E-WAQF IMPLEMENTATION: A PARADIGM SHIFT IN NIGERIA WAQF SYSTEM. Journal of Asian and African social science and humanities, 7(4), 41-53. DOI: 10.55327/jaash.v7i4.255

Salman, M., Mohamad, N. A., & Sadique, M. A. (2022, January 2). E-WAQF IMPLEMENTATION: A PARADIGM SHIFT IN NIGERIA WAQF SYSTEM. https://aarcentre.com/ojs3/index.php/jaash/article/download/255/529

Samir, M., & Kamra, S. (2013). Non-performing assets of banks: an overview. Journal of Management Research. Retrieved from https://www.proquest.com/docview/1477975941

Sandhya, G., & Nair, G. M. (2019). The influence of personal values on consumers purchase intention for organic products. *International Journal of Business Forecasting and Marketing Intelligence*, 5(4), 412. DOI: 10.1504/IJBFMI.2019.105339

Sani, A. A., Saidin, A., Abd Samad, K., Bustamam, K. S., Adanan, S. A., & Mamat, S. N. (2022). Modelling Waqf Performance and Governance for Public Universities in Malaysia. *International Journal of Academic Research in Business & Social Sciences*, 12(10), 2743–2754. DOI: 10.6007/IJARBSS/v12-i10/14951

Sano, M. A. A., & Kassim, S. (2021). Waqf governance in the Republic of Guinea: Legal framework, issues, challenges and way forward. *ISRA International Journal of Islamic Finance*, 13(2), 194–210. DOI: 10.1108/IJIF-03-2020-0064

Saputra, K. D., Rahmaastri, D. A., Setiawan, K., Suryani, D., & Purnama, Y. (2019). Mobile financial management application using google cloud vision API. *Procedia Computer Science*, 157, 596–604. DOI: 10.1016/j.procs.2019.09.019

Sarel, D., & Marmorstein, H. (2002). Migrating customers to new distribution channels: The role of communication. *Journal of Financial Services Marketing*, 6(3), 254–266. DOI: 10.1057/palgrave.fsm.4770056

Sarıdoğan, H. Ö. (2020). The factors affecting the performance of the partipacition banks: A dynamic panel data analysis in the context of the global crisis. [In Turkish]. *Bartın University Journal of Economics and Administrative Sciences*, 11(21), 148–167.

Sarwono. (2009). *Analisis perilaku konsumen perspektif ekonomi islam. 8*(1). https://doi.org/DOI: 10.33061/INNOFARM.V8I1.225

Sashikala, V., & Chitramani, P. (2018). The Impact of Behavioural Factors on Investment Intention of Equity Investors. *Asian Journal of Management*, 9(1), 183. DOI: 10.5958/2321-5763.2018.00028.8

Sathye, M. (1999). Adoption of Internet banking by Australian consumers: An empirical investigation. *International Journal of Bank Marketing*, 17(7), 324–334. DOI: 10.1108/02652329910305689

Sato, S. N., Condes Moreno, E., Rubio-Zarapuz, A., Dalamitros, A. A., Yañez-Sepulveda, R., Tornero-Aguilera, J. F., & Clemente-Suárez, V. J. (2023). Navigating the New Normal: Adapting Online and Distance Learning in the Post-Pandemic Era. *Education Sciences 2024, Vol. 14, Page 19, 14*(1), 19. DOI: 10.3390/educsci14010019

Schor, J. (1998). Time, Labour and Consumption: Guest Editor's Introduction. *Time & Society*, 7(1), 119–127. DOI: 10.1177/0961463X98007001007

Schwartz, A. A. (2013). Crowdfunding securities. *The Notre Dame Law Review*, 88(3), 1457–1490. https://www.scopus.com/inward/record.uri?eid=2-s2.0-84878133437&partnerID=40&md5=715516b683824cba2e6c244333febb57

Schwienbacher, A. (2021). Equity Crowdfunding and Capital Formation for Early-Stage Firms. In *The Palgrave Handbook of Technological Finance* (pp. 425–440). Springer International Publishing., DOI: 10.1007/978-3-030-65117-6_18

Sconti, A. (2022). Digital vs. in-person financial education: What works best for Generation Z? *Journal of Economic Behavior & Organization*, 194, 300–318. DOI: 10.1016/j.jebo.2021.12.001

Selangorkini (2016) Retrieved from https://arkib.selangorkini.my/2018/01/lzs-perkenal-cashless-atm-mudah-urusan-zakat/

Selangor, Z. (2022). Types of general assistance. Zakat Selangor. System) in the management of Waqf lands in Selangor. *International Journal of Academic Research in Business & Social Sciences*, 11(11).

Selsky, J. W., & Parker, B. (2005). Cross-sector partnerships to address social issues: Challenges to theory and practice. *Journal of Management*, 31(6), 849–873. DOI: 10.1177/0149206305279601

Selvam, R., & Premnath, N. G. (2020). Impact of Coronavirus on NPA and GDP of Indian Economy. Prabandhan: Indian Journal of Management, https://journal.prabandhan.co.in/index.php/pim/article/view/152602/85849

Seng, N. D., Ibrahim, N. F., Yin, L. S., & Maiyus, M. B. (2023). An Empirical Study on Acceptance of E-wallet among Malaysian University Students. *International Journal of Academic Research in Business & Social Sciences*, 13(1). Advance online publication. DOI: 10.6007/IJARBSS/v13-i1/15728

Shadily, H. (1983). *Ensiklopedia Indonesia* (staf penyunting redaksi Ensiklopedi Indonesia (ed.)). Ichtiar baru-Van Hoeve.

Shafie, F., Yusoff, W., Zahari, W., Abdullah, S., & al-Edrus, S. M. D. (2014). Islamic real estate management: Review on issues and challenges in managing inheritance property in Malaysia. Paper presented at the 7th International Real Estate Research Symposium 2014 (7th IRERS). Retrieved from https://www.inspen.gov.my/

Shafie, F., Yusoff, W., Zahari, W., & al-Edrus, S. M. D. (2016). *Factors of Failure and Delay in Islamic Inheritance Distribution in Malaysia, Conference IPERS*. INSPEN.

Shahedur Rahaman Chowdhury, M.Md. Shahedur Rahaman Chowdhury. (2011). Economics of Cash WAQF management in Malaysia: A proposed Cash WAQF model for practitioners and future researchers. *African Journal of Business Management*, 5(30), 12155–12163. DOI: 10.5897/AJBM11.1810

Shah, H. S., & Susilo, A. (2022). E-Commerce on the Study of Maslahah Mursalah (A Review from an Islamic Economic Perspective). *Tasharruf: Journal Economics and Business of Islam*, 7(1), 17–28. DOI: 10.30984/tjebi.v7i1.1944

Shaikh, I M., Qureshi, M A., Noordin, K., Shaikh, J M., Khan, A., & Shahbaz, M S. (2020). Acceptance of Islamic financial technology (FinTech) banking services by Malaysian users: an extension of technology acceptance model. Emerald Publishing Limited, 22(3), 367-383. https://doi.org/DOI: 10.1108/FS-12-2019-0105

Shaikh, S A., Ismail, A G., & Shafiai, M H M. (2017, July 10). Application of <i>waqf</i> for social and development finance. DOI: 10.1108/IJIF-07-2017-002

Shaikh, A. M., Alharthi, M. D., & Alamoudi, H. O. (2020). Examining key drivers of consumer experience with (non-financial) digital services-An exploratory study. *Journal of Retailing and Consumer Services*, 55, 1–10. DOI: 10.1016/j.jretconser.2020.102073

Shaikh, S. A., Ismail, M. A., Ismail, A. G., Shahimi, S., & Mohd. Shafiai, M. H. (2017). Towards an integrative framework for understanding Muslim consumption behaviour. *Humanomics*, 33(2), 133–149. DOI: 10.1108/H-01-2017-0005

Shaikh, Z. H., Sarea, A., & Irfan, M. (2021, September). Islamic banking strategies in the world of Fintech: success story of Bahrain. In *The International Conference On Global Economic Revolutions* (pp. 97-104). Cham: Springer International Publishing.

Sharizan, S., Redzuan, N. H., & Rosman, R. B. (2021). Issues and Challenges of Financial Inclusion Among Low-Income Earners In Rural Areas of Malaysia. *Turkish Journalof Islamic Economics, 8*(Special Issue), 278–299. https://www.tujise.org/content/6-issues/16-special-issue-06-2021/5-a2376/tuj2376.pdf

Sharma, H. (2011). National Journal of Research in Management. *Bankers' perspectives on e-banking, 1*(1), 71–85.

Sharma, , Al-Badi, A., Rana, N. P., & Al-Azizi, L. (2018). Mobile applications in government services (mG-App) from user's perspectives: A predictive modelling approach. *Government Information Quarterly*, 35(4), 557–568. DOI: 10.1016/j.giq.2018.07.002

Shehadeh, M., Almajali, D., Abu-AlSondos, I. A., Alkhwaldi, A. F., & Al-Gasaymeh, A. S. (2023, March). Digital transformation and its impact on operational efficiency and competitive advantage in Islamic banks. In *2023 International Conference on Business Analytics for Technology and Security (ICBATS)* (pp. 1-6). IEEE. DOI: 10.1109/ICBATS57792.2023.10111266

She, L., Rasiah, R., Waheed, H., & Sharif, S. P. (2021). Excessive use of social networking sites and financial well-being among young adults: The mediating role of online compulsive buying. *Young Consumers*, 22(2), 272–289. DOI: 10.1108/YC-11-2020-1252

Shiralashetti, S. S., & Poojari, V. (2016). Non-Performing Assets (NPA): A study on its causes and impact on the profitability of the bank. International Journal of Applied Research, Retrieved from https://www.allresearchjournal.com/archives/2016/vol2issue10/PartH/2-10- 71-838.pdf

Shofawati, A. (2023). The Role of Islamic Fintech in Indonesia to Improve Financial Inclusion for Resolving SDGs. In *Artificial Intelligence, Fintech, and Financial Inclusion* (pp. 112-134). CRC Press. DOI: 10.1201/9781003125204-8

Shukor, S. A., Johari, F., Abd Wahab, K., Kefeli, Z., Ahmad, N., Alias, M. H., Rahman, A. A., Orip, N. M. M., Ibrahim, P., & Abu-Hussin, M. F. (2018). Trust on awqaf institutions: Evidence from Malaysia. *Journal of Islamic Marketing*.

Shukur, M. H., Ismail, R. J., & Flaih, L. R. (2022). Empower E-wallets Payment System by using A Hybrid Approach of Online and Offline Services. *Cihan University-Erbil Scientific Journal*, 6(2), 23–27. DOI: 10.24086/cuesj.v6n2y2022.pp23-27

Siddiqi, H. (2020). Blockchain applications in Islamic finance. *Islamic Finance Review*, 5(1), 32–45.

Singh, V. K., Bozkaya, B., & Pentland, A. (2015). Money walks: Implicit mobility behavior and financial well-being. *PLoS One*, 10(8), e0136628. DOI: 10.1371/journal.pone.0136628 PMID: 26317339

Sirait, H., Rosalina, S. S., & Sari, E. (2023). The Impact of Digital Innovation on Economic Growth. *International Journal of Professional Business Review*, 8(6), e01842–e01842. DOI: 10.26668/businessreview/2023.v8i6.1842

Sirgy, M. J. (2021). Effects of Demographic Factors on Wellbeing. In *The Psychology of Quality of Life: Wellbeing and Positive Mental Health* (pp. 129–154). Springer. DOI: 10.1007/978-3-030-71888-6_6

Sitepu, N. I. (2016), Perilaku Bisnis Muhammad SAW Sebagai Entrepreneur Dalam Filsafat Ekonomi Islam. Jurnal Human Falah, 3(1).

Smirnova, E., Platt, K., Lei, Y., & Sanacory, F. (2021). Pleasing the crowd: The determinants of securities crowdfunding success. *Review of Behavioral Finance*, 13(2), 165–183. DOI: 10.1108/RBF-07-2019-0096

Sofolis, I., & Eftychia, N. (2011). Factors Influencing the Credit Risk of the Greek Financial System. International Journal of Economics and Financial Issues, Retrieved from 47 https://www.econjournals.com/index.php/ijefi/article/view/142/97

Soman, D., & Cheema, A. (2011). Earmarking and partitioning: Increasing saving by low-income households. *Journal of Marketing Research, 48*(SPL), S14–S22.

Srivastava, U., & Gopalkrishnan, S. (2015). Impact of big data analytics on banking sector: Learning for Indian banks. *Procedia Computer Science*, 50, 643–652. DOI: 10.1016/j.procs.2015.04.098

Standard, D. (2022). Global Islamic Fintech Report 2023. In *Global Islamic Fintech Report*. https://cdn.salaamgateway.com/special-coverage/islamic-fintech-2021/Global-Islamic-Fintech-Report-2021-Executive-Summary.pdf

Statista, 2023. Distribution of cyberattacks across worldwide industries in 2023 https://www.statista.com/statistics/1315805/cyber-attacks-top-industries-worldwide/

Steinberg, S. (2012). *The Crowdfunding Bible: How to Raise Money for Any Startup, Video Game Or Project*. Lulu.com. https://books.google.co.id/books?id=MzBwvgEACAAJ

Subagiyo, G., Gustia, A., & Oktavian Syah, D. (2022). The Effect of E-wallet and Sales Promotion on Purchasing Decisions. *Best Journal of Administration and Management*, 1(1), 53–60. DOI: 10.56403/bejam.v1i1.30

Sugihartono, N. S. R., & Harahap, F. (2007). *Pengantar Psikologi Umum* (1st, Cet.A ed.). UNY Press.

Sugiyono. (2021). Resensi Buku Metode Penelitian Kuantitatif Kualitatif dan R&D. In *Alfabeta* (3rd ed.).

Sulaiman, H., & Jamil, N. (2014, November 1). Information security governance model to enhance zakat information management in Malaysian zakat institutions. DOI: 10.1109/ICIMU.2014.7066630

Sulistiawati, R. (2012), Pengaruh Investasi Terhadap Pertumbuhan Ekonomi dan Penyerapan Tenaga Kerja Serta Kesejahteraan Masyarakat di Provinsi di Indonesia. Jurnal Ekonomi Bisnis dan Kewirausahaan, 3(1), 29-50.

Sulong, J. (2011). *Pembaharuan Undang-undang Pentadbiran Pusaka Islam*. Penerbit Universiti Sains Malaysia.

Sümer, G. & ONAN, F. (2015). Emergence of participation banking in the world,developing period of participation banking in Turkey and difference versus conventional banking sector. [In Turkish]. *Gazi University Journal of Faculty of Economics and Administrative Sciences*, 17(3), 296–308.

Supiyan, M. Y. B. M. (2023). *Essays on the Demand for and Supply of Cash Waqfs in the Muslim World*. https://digital.lib.washington.edu/researchworks/handle/1773/50534%0Ahttps://digital.lib.washington.edu/researchworks/bitstream/handle/1773/50534/MohamedSupiyan_washington_0250E_25487.pdf?sequence=1

Suryono, R. R., Budi, I., & Purwandari, B. (2020). Challenges and trends of financial technology (Fintech): A systematic literature review. *Information (Basel)*, 11(12), 590. DOI: 10.3390/info11120590

Susilawati, S., & Chakim, A. Hambali, Muh., Islamy, M. I., & Rahmaniah, A. (2021). *The urgency of digital literacy for generation z in improving learning of islamic religious education*. https://digitalcommons.unl.edu/libphilprac/5143/?utm_source=digitalcommons.unl.edu%2Flibphilprac%2F5143&utm_medium=PDF&utm_campaign=PDFCoverPages

Suwandari, Y. D., & Suratkon, A. B. (2022). Investigating The Potential of Cash Waqf for Funding Public Infrastructure Through Public-Private Partnership. *Res Militaris*, 4(12), 1026–1035. https://www.ptonline.com/articles/how-to-get-better-mfi-results

Suyatno, & Pakkana, M. (2024). Management and Development of Productive Waqf for Islamic Boarding Schools in Kampar Regency. *Indonesian Interdisciplinary Journal of Sharia Economics (IIJSE), 7*(1), 395–422.

Svensson, J. (2015). *Promoting Social Change and Democracy through Information Technology*. IGI Global., DOI: 10.4018/978-1-4666-8502-4

Syamsuri, S., Putri, E. R., Zein, A. R., & Handayani, R. (2021). Sukuk Waqf for the Development of Islamic Educational Institutions. *ISLAMICONOMIC: Jurnal Ekonomi Islam*, 12(1), 39–52. DOI: 10.32678/ijei.v12i1.267

Syarif, S. (2020). Building plurality and unity for various religions in the digital era: Establishing Islamic values for Indonesian students. *Journal of Social Studies Education Research*, 11(2), 111–119. https://www.learntechlib.org/p/217571/

Syed, M. H. (2020). An artificial intelligence and NLP based Islamic fintech model combining zakat and qardh-al-hasan for countering the adverse impact of COVID 19 on SMEs and individuals. *International Journal of Economics and Business Administration*, 3(2), 351–364. DOI: 10.35808/ijeba/466

Tahiri Jouti, A. (2019). An integrated approach for building sustainable Islamic social finance ecosystems. *ISRA International Journal of Islamic Finance*, 11(2), 246–266. DOI: 10.1108/IJIF-10-2018-0118

Taiwo, A. A., & Downe, A. G. (2013). *THE THEORY OF USER ACCEPTANCE AND USE OF TECHNOLOGY (UTAUT) : A META-ANALYTIC REVIEW OF EMPIRICAL FINDINGS 1*. https://api.semanticscholar.org/CorpusID:15178994

Takan, M. (2002). *Banking theory, practice and method*. Nobel Kitabevi. (In Turkish)

Tariq, M. U. (2024). Revolutionizing health data management with blockchain technology: Enhancing security and efficiency in a digital era. In *Emerging Technologies for Health Literacy and Medical Practice* (pp. 153–175). IGI Global. DOI: 10.4018/979-8-3693-1214-8.ch008

TBB. (2022). Digital Journeys of Banks and Studies of the Banks Association of Turkey https://www.tbb.org.tr/Content/Upload/tos/Dijital%20Yolculuk.pdf

TBB. (2023). Digital, Internet and Mobile Banking Statistics, March 2023, Banks Association of Turkey https://www.tbb.org.tr/Content/Upload/istatistikiraporlar/ekler/4057/Dijital-Internet-Mobil_Bankacilik_Istatistikleri-Mart_2023.pdf

Tejashwini, R., & Ramani, R. (2019). A Comparative Study of the Performance of Public and Private Sector Banks in India. [IJITEE]. *International Journal of Innovative Technology and Exploring Engineering*, 8(9), 1027–1032. https://www.ijitee.org/wpcontent/uploads/papers/v8i9s/E11410582S19.pdf

Tekin, Z. (2020). Innovative and digital solutions in participation banking: A model proposal for Turkey, Turkish Studies-Economics, Finance, Politics. https://www.researchgate.net/profile/Zeliha-Tekin/publication/344467452_Katilim_Bankaciliginda_Inovatif_ve_Dijital_Cozumler_Turkiye_Icin_Bir_Model_Onerisi_Innovative_and_Digital_Solutions_in_Participation_Banking_A_Model_Proposal_for_Turkey/links/5f7a1f9ea6fdcc00865723d7/Katilim-Bankaciliginda-Inovatif-ve-Dijital-Coezuemler-Tuerkiye-Icin-Bir-Model-Oenerisi-Innovative-and-Digital-Solutions-in-Participation-Banking-A-Model-Proposal-for-Turkey.pdf

Teng, S., & Khong, K. W. (2021). Examining actual consumer usage of E-wallet: A case study of big data analytics. *Computers in Human Behavior*, 121, 106778. https://doi.org/https://doi.org/10.1016/j.chb.2021.106778. DOI: 10.1016/j.chb.2021.106778

Tenk, M. T. T., Yew, H. C., & Heang, L. T. (2020). E-wallet adoption: A case in Malaysia. *International Journal of Research In Commerce and Management Studies*, 2(2), 216–233. https://ubipayroll.com/ijrcms/index.php/ijrcms/article/download/64/57

Thaker, M. A. B. M. T., Khaliq, A. B., Thaker, H. B. M. T., Amin, M. F. B., & Pitchay, A. B. A. (2022). The potential role of fintech and digital currency for islamic green financing: toward an integrated model. In *Green digital finance and sustainable development goals* (pp. 287–308). Springer Nature Singapore. DOI: 10.1007/978-981-19-2662-4_14

Thaler, R. H. (1999). Mental accounting matters. *Journal of Behavioral Decision Making*, 12(3), 183–206. DOI: 10.1002/(SICI)1099-0771(199909)12:3<183::AID-BDM318>3.0.CO;2-F

The Edge Malaysia. (2024). Retrieved from https://theedgemalaysia.com/node/704947

The Impact of Internal Control System on the Accountability Practices in Waqf Institutions: Evidence from Al Rahma International Waqf. (2021, August 1). Research Journal of Finance and Accounting. DOI: 10.7176/RJFA/12-16-04

Tiwari, A., & Garg, A. (2018). Impact of non-performing assets on the Indian economy. International Journal of Engineering Technology Science and Research, https://www.ijetsr.com/images/short_pdf/1538663848_8447.pdf

TKBB. (2021). Participation Banking Digital. *Research Reports (Montgomery)*, 2021, •••. https://yonetim.tkbb.org.tr/upload/KATILIM%20BANKACILI%C4%9EI%20D%C4%B0J%C4%B0TAL%20ARA%C5%9ETIRMA%20RAPORU%202021.pdf

TKBB. (2024). Banking and Sector Information Participation Banks Association of Turkey https://www.tkbb.org.tr/veripetegi

Tlemsani, I., Zaman, A., Hashim, M. M., & Matthews, R. (2023). Digitalization and sustainable development goals in emerging Islamic economies. *Journal of Islamic Accounting and Business Research*. Advance online publication. DOI: 10.1108/JIABR-03-2023-0092

Tok, A. (2006). Fund collection and utilisation transactions of participation banks and classical banking transactions in Turkish law. *Published Master Thesis*. Marmara University, Institute of Social Sciences, Department of Law, Istanbul (In Turkish).

Tokiran, N. S., Hussin, N., & Shahibi, M. S. (2021). Challenges in Implementation of Digital Culture Environment among Rural Community in Malaysia: An Overview. *Journal of Asian Scientific Research*, 11(3), 25–33. DOI: 10.18488/journal.2.2021.113.25.33

TOM BANK. (2024). About Us. https://www.tombank.com.tr/index.html

Trattner, C., Jannach, D., Motta, E., Meijer, I. C., Diakopoulos, N., Elahi, M., Opdahl, A. L., Tessem, B., Borch, N., Fjeld, M., Øvrelid, L., Smedt, K. D., & Moe, H. (2021, December 20). Responsible media technology and AI: Challenges and research directions. *AI and Ethics*, 2(4), 585–594. DOI: 10.1007/s43681-021-00126-4

Trimulato, N., Nafis, M. C., & Amalia, E. (2022). The role of Sharia fintech in supporting the Sustainable Development Goals (SDGs) program. *Jurnal Ilmiah Ekonomi Islam*, 8(1), 251–259. DOI: 10.29040/jiei.v8i1.3911

TSDG. (2016). TÜSİAD, Samsung Türkiye, Deloitte Türkiye, GFK Türkiye, "CEO Perspective on Digital Change in Turkey" https://www2.deloitte.com/content/dam/Deloitte/tr/Documents/technologymedia-telecommunications/turkiyedeki-dijital-degisime-CEO-bakisi.pdf

Uluyol, B., Secinaro, S., Calandra, D., & Lanzalonga, F. (2021). Mapping waqf research: A thirty-year bibliometric analysis. *Journal of Islamic Accounting and Business Research*, 12(5), 748–767. DOI: 10.1108/JIABR-01-2021-0031

Umar, U. H. (2020). The business financial inclusion benefits from an Islamic point of view: A qualitative inquiry. *Islamic Economic Studies*, 28(1), 83–100. DOI: 10.1108/IES-09-2019-0030

Umar, U. H., Baita, A. J., Haron, M. H., & Kabiru, S. H. (2022). The potential of Islamic social finance to alleviate poverty in the era of COVID-19: The moderating effect of ethical orientation. *International Journal of Islamic and Middle Eastern Finance and Management*, 15(2), 255–270. DOI: 10.1108/IMEFM-07-2020-0371

Ummah, A., Ahsan, M., & Anas, A. (2021). Students' Investment Decisions with Intention as an Intervening Variable. *Equilibrium: Jurnal Ekonomi Syariah*, 9(1), 135. DOI: 10.21043/equilibrium.v9i1.9995

Unal, I. M., & Aysan, A. F. (2022). Fintech, digitalization, and blockchain in Islamic finance: Retrospective investigation. *FinTech*, 1(4), 388–398. DOI: 10.3390/fintech1040029

Undang-Undang Republik Indonesia Nomor 25 Tahun 2007 tentang Penanaman Modal. (n.d.). Retrieved from https://jdih.kemenkeu.go.id

United Nations. (2015). *The UN Sustainable Development Goals.* United Nations. Available at (accessed 25 October 2024): https://www.un.org/sustainabledevelopment/summit/

Usman, M., & Ab Rahman, A. (2023). Funding higher education through waqf: A lesson from Malaysia. *International Journal of Ethics and Systems*, 39(1), 107–125. DOI: 10.1108/IJOES-12-2021-0217

Usman, M., & Rahman, A. A. (2021). Financing Higher Education through Waqf in Pakistan: Issues and Challenges. *Jurnal Pengurusan*, 62, 159–172. DOI: 10.17576/pengurusan-2021-62-13

Ustaömer, K., & Bakırtaş, T. (2019). Case of Digitalization in Turkish Banking Sector. *Journal of Economy* [In Turkish]. *Business and Management*, 3(1), 1–24.

Utama, S. M., & Putra Ganda, R. A. (2022). ANALYSIS OF SHARIA CONFORMITY ASPECTS IN STOCK INVESTMENT BASED ON SECURITIES CROWDFUNDING. *Al-Muamalat: Jurnal Ekonomi Syariah*, 9(2), 62–73. DOI: 10.15575/am.v9i2.18857

Utami, P. S., Suryanto, T., Nasor, M., & Ghofur, R. A. (2020). The effect digitalization zakat payment against potential of zakat acceptance in national Amil zakat agency. *Iqtishadia*, 13(2), 216–223. DOI: 10.21043/iqtishadia.v13i2.7809

Vachruddin, V. P., Hamid, A., & Nasril, N. (2022). Development of e-wallet application "DASIGU" - based teaching factory. *Jurnal Pendidikan Vokasi*, 12(3). Advance online publication. DOI: 10.21831/jpv.v12i3.47417

Vaidya, J. (2012). Privacy in the context of digital government. *Proceedings of the 13th Annual International Conference on Digital Government Research* (pp. 302–303). https://doi.org/DOI: 10.1145/2307729.2307796

Vakıf Participation. (2023). Know Vakıf Katılım. https://www.vakifkatilim.com.tr/tr/hakkimizda

Van Hove, L., & Dubus, A. (2019). M-PESA and Financial Inclusion in Kenya: Of Paying. *Sustainability (Basel)*, 11(3), 1–26. DOI: 10.3390/su11030568

Van Schaik, P. (2009). Unified Theory of Acceptance and Use for Websites Used by Students in Higher Education. *Journal of Educational Computing Research*, 40(2), 229–257. DOI: 10.2190/EC.40.2.e

Vargo, S. L., & Lusch, R. F. (2004). Evolving to a new dominant logic in Marketing. *Journal of Marketing*, 68(1), 1–17. DOI: 10.1509/jmkg.68.1.1.24036

Venkatesh, M., Morris, , Davis, , & Davis, . (2003). User Acceptance of Information Technology: Toward a Unified View. *Management Information Systems Quarterly*, 27(3), 425. DOI: 10.2307/30036540

Venturelli, V., Pedrazzoli, A., & Gualandri, E. (2019). *From Seeker Side to Investor Side: Gender Dynamics in UK Equity Crowdfunding Investments* (pp. 97–115). DOI: 10.1007/978-3-030-16295-5_4

Vierescu, E. M., & Toader, C. I. (2023). The Impact of Digitalisation and Cyber Risks on the Banking Sector, *The 6th International Conference on Economics and Social Sciences Geopolitical Perspectives and Technological Challenges for Sustainable Growth in the 21st Century,* June 15-16, 2023, Bucharest University of Economic Studies, Romania.

Vincent, T. N., & Selvarani, D. C. (2013). Personal Values Approach for a Better Understanding of Consumer Behaviour. *International Journal of Innovative Research and Development*, 2(3), 509–517.

VISA. (2024). *VISA Consumer Payment Attitudes Study 2023.* https://www.visa.com.sg/dam/VCOM/regional/ap/singapore/global-elements/documents/visa-cpa-2023-report-smt-final.pdf

Vismara, S. (2022). Expanding corporate finance perspectives to equity crowdfunding. *The Journal of Technology Transfer*, 47(6), 1629–1639. DOI: 10.1007/s10961-021-09903-z PMID: 34803218

Waite, K., & Harrison, T. (2002). Consumer expectations of online information provided by bank websites. *Journal of Financial Services Marketing*, 6(4), 309–322. DOI: 10.1057/palgrave.fsm.4770061

Wajis, N. R. N. (2018). Mutalib, LA. Rahman, AA. Sahid, MM. Saleh, NSSN, Rusli, MHM. Ali, MM. Rab, MAA. Gunardi, S.Tagoranao, MS. Saleh, MAM. Hanafo, LHH. & Ahmad, AS. (2018) Harta Tidak Dituntut: Punca dan Kaedah Penyelesaiannya. *Malaysian Journal of Syariah and Law*, 7(June), 129–141. DOI: 10.12816/0051395

Walgito, B. (1994). *Pengantar Psikologi Umum*. Andi Offset.

Wallmeroth, J. (2019). Investor behavior in equity crowdfunding. *Venture Capital*, 21(2–3), 273–300. DOI: 10.1080/13691066.2018.1457475

Wang, J., Luo, J., & Zhang, X. (2022). How COVID-19 Has Changed Crowdfunding: Evidence From GoFundMe. *Frontiers of Computer Science*, 4, 1–8. DOI: 10.3389/fcomp.2022.893338

Wang, M., Ling, A., He, Y., Tan, Y., Zhang, L., Chang, Z., & Ma, Q. (2022). Pleasure of paying when using mobile payment: Evidence from EEG studies. *Frontiers in Psychology*, 13, 1004068. Advance online publication. DOI: 10.3389/fpsyg.2022.1004068 PMID: 36389456

Wang, N., Shen, X.-L., & Sun, Y. (2013). Transition of electronic word-of-mouth services from web to mobile context: A trust transfer perspective. *Decision Support Systems*, 54(3), 1394–1403. DOI: 10.1016/j.dss.2012.12.015

Warschauer, M., & Xu, Y. (2018, January 1). Technology and Equity in Education. DOI: 10.1007/978-3-319-71054-9_76

Waters, R. D., Burnett, E., Lamm, A., & Lucas, J. (2009). Engaging stakeholders through social networking: How nonprofit organizations are using Facebook. *Public Relations Review*, 35(2), 102–106. DOI: 10.1016/j.pubrev.2009.01.006

Wazan (2024) Retrieved from https://wazan.upm.edu.my/

WB. 2023. World Bank Data_https://data.worldbank.org/

Wehr, H. (1980). *A Dictionary of Modern Written Arabic* (4th ed.). Spoken Language Services.

Welch, E. W., Hinnant, C. C., & Moon, M. J. (2004). Linking citizen satisfaction with e-government and trust in government. *Journal of Public Administration: Research and Theory*, 15(3), 371–391. DOI: 10.1093/jopart/mui021

Whitla, P. (2009). Crowdsourcing and Its Application in Marketing Activities. *Contemporary Management Research*, 5(1). Advance online publication. DOI: 10.7903/cmr.1145

Wicaksana, A., & Rachman, T. (2018). KESADARAN DAN PERSEPSI USAHA MIKRO DAN KECIL TERHADAP CROWDFUNDING SYARIAH. *Angewandte Chemie International Edition, 6(11), 951–952., 3*(1), 10–27.

Wigand, S. S. (2007). Key dimensions of e-commerce service quality and its relationships to satisfaction and loyalty. *Proceedings of the 20th Bled Electronic Commerce Conference*, 1-15. Retrieved from https://www.researchgate.net/publication/228867485_Key_dimensions_of_e-commerce_service_quality_and_its_relationships_to_satisfaction_and_loyalty

Wijekoon, R., Sabri, M. F., Ahmad, N., & Rahim, H. (2022). Mediating Role of Financial Behavior between Financial Factors and Economic Well-being: Through the Lens of the Extended Family Resource Management Model. *International Journal of Academic Research in Business & Social Sciences*, 12(10). Advance online publication. DOI: 10.6007/IJARBSS/v12-i10/15194

Wildana, M D A., & Imamia, T L. (2022, May 19). Waqf in the 21st Century: The Implementation of Blockchain and Smart Contract Technology. DOI: 10.32535/jicp.v5i1.1774

Willems, W. (2013). *What characteristics of crowdfunding platforms influence the success rate ? July*, 70.

Wong, C. Y., & Mohamed, M. I. P. (2021). Understanding The Factors That Influence Consumer Continuous Intention To Use E-Wallet In Malaysia. *Research in Management of Technology and Business, 2*(1), 561–576. https://publisher.uthm.edu.my/periodicals/index.php/rmtb/article/download/1938/717

Wong, S.-L., Hsu, C.-C., & Chen, H.-S. (2018). To Buy or Not to Buy? Consumer Attitudes and Purchase Intentions for Suboptimal Food. *International Journal of Environmental Research and Public Health*, 15(7), 1431. DOI: 10.3390/ijerph15071431 PMID: 29986474

World Bank. (2018, April 19). *Financial Inclusion on the Rise, But Gaps Remain, Global Findex Database Shows*. Retrieved from THE WORLD BANK: https://www.worldbank.org/en/news/press-release/2018/04/19/financial-inclusion-on-the-rise-but-gaps-remain-global-findex-database-shows

Wresch, W., & Fraser, S. (2011). Persistent Barriers to E-commerce in Developing Countries. *Journal of Global Information Management*, 19(3), 30–44. DOI: 10.4018/jgim.2011070102

Wu, J., Liu, L., & Cao, Y. (2023). Understanding investor co-investment in a syndicate on equity crowdfunding platforms. *Industrial Management & Data Systems*, 123(5), 1599–1623. DOI: 10.1108/IMDS-09-2022-0538

Xiao, J. J., & Yao, R. (2022). Good debt, bad debt: Family debt portfolios and financial burdens. *International Journal of Bank Marketing*, 40(4), 659–678. DOI: 10.1108/IJBM-06-2021-0243

Xue, J., & Lin, L. (2019). Analysis of the Influence of Mobile Payment on Consumer Behavior. *2019 4th International Conference on Humanities Science and Society Development (ICHSSD 2019)*, 121–127. DOI: 10.2991/ichssd-19.2019.24

Xue, R., Gepp, A., O'Neill, T. J., Stern, S., & Vanstone, B. J. (2020). Financial well-being amongst elderly Australians: The role of consumption patterns and financial literacy. *Accounting and Finance*, 60(4), 4361–4386. DOI: 10.1111/acfi.12545

Xu, X., Lu, Y., Vogel-Heuser, B., & Wang, L. (2021). Industry 4.0 and Industry 5.0—Inception, conception and perception. *Journal of Manufacturing Systems*, 61(September), 530–535. DOI: 10.1016/j.jmsy.2021.10.006

Yahaya, M. H. (2019). Factors affecting the acceptance of financial technology among asnaf for the distribution of zakat in Selangor-A study using UTAUT. *Journal of Islamic Finance*, 8, 35–46. https://journals.iium.edu.my/iiibf-journal/index.php/jif/article/view/345

Yahya, F., Wilson, S., Sochos, A., Talib, A. T., Singh, S. S. D., Khiri, M. J. A., & Khan, A. (2021). Parent-Child Attachment and Romantic Relationship among Young Adults in Malaysia. [TURCOMAT]. *Turkish Journal of Computer and Mathematics Education*, 12(5), 1343–1352. DOI: 10.17762/turcomat.v12i5.2026

Yasini, S., & Yasini, M. (2019). Current trends and future impacts of fintech in Islamic finance. In *FinTech in Islamic Finance* (pp. 327–335). Routledge. DOI: 10.4324/9781351025584-20

Yayasan Waqaf Malaysia. (2021). Sejarah Perkembangan Wakaf. Retrieved from Portal Rasmi Yayasan Waqaf Malaysia (ywm.gov.my), 30th May 2024.

Yıldırım, S., & Yıldırım, D. Ç. (2022). Digital transformation and adaptation in Islamic banking sector: A case of Turkey. [In Turkish]. *Journal of Kapanalti Accounting Finance Economics*, (1), 73–84.

Yohani. (2019), Pengaruh Investor Asing Terhadap Pengembangan Masyarakat Lokal di Indonesia. Jurnal Fiat Justicia, 5(1).

Yuan, J., Jiang, S., & Mary Joy Dela Cruz, B. (2023). Toward the digital economy: Mobile payment affecting sustainable consumption behavior. *Innovative Marketing*, 19(1), 220–232. DOI: 10.21511/im.19(1).2023.19

Yudaruddin, R. (2023). Financial technology and performance in Islamic and conventional banks. *Journal of Islamic Accounting and Business Research*, 14(1), 100–116. DOI: 10.1108/JIABR-03-2022-0070

Yunus, S. M., Kamaruddin, Z., & Embong, R. (2017). Towards banking jurisprudence: Understanding Islamic banking products in Malaysia. *International Journal of Academic Research in Business & Social Sciences*, 7(8), 215–228. DOI: 10.6007/IJARBSS/v7-i8/3223

Yunus, S. M., Kamaruddin, Z., & Embong, R. (2018). The Concept of Islamic Banking from the Islamic Worldview. *International Journal of Academic Research in Business & Social Sciences*, 8(11). Advance online publication. DOI: 10.6007/IJARBSS/v8-i11/4928

Yurttadur, M. (2021). The effects of the covid 19 pandemic on the profitability of participation banks. [In Turkish]. *Nevşehir Hacı Bektaş Veli University Journal of ISS*, 11(4), 2285–2297. DOI: 10.30783/nevsosbilen.1009126

Yusoff, R., Rahman, S. A., & Mohamed, W. N. W. (2018). Factors influencing the intention to perform cash waqf among Muslim staff at Universiti Teknologi MARA, Kelantan Campus. In International Conference on Islam and Global Issues. niversiti Teknologi Mara Cawangan Kelantan, Bukit Ilmu, Machang Kelantan. Retrieved from https://dspace.adu.ac.ae/handle/1/3374

Yusoff, Z. M. (2011). The Malaysian Personal Data Protection Act 2010: A Legislation Note. *NZJPIL*, 9, 119.

Yu, T., Lin, Z., & Tang, Q. (2018). Blockchain: The introduction and its application in financial accounting. *Journal of Corporate Accounting & Finance*, 29(4), 37–47. DOI: 10.1002/jcaf.22365

Zabir, A. (2018). Pengaruh Pemanfaatan Teknologi Pembelajaran Terhadap Motivasi Belajar Siswa SMPN 1 Lanrisang Kabupaten Pinrang. *Jurnal Azhari, 1*(1), 1–10. https://eprints.unm.ac.id/id/eprint/9823

Zain, N. R. M., Mahadi, N. F., & Noor, A. M. (2019). *The potential in reviving waqf through crowdfunding technology: the case study. Al-Shajarah: Journal of the International Institute of Islamic Thought and Civilization.* ISTAC.

Zakariyah, H., Salaudeen, A. O., Othman, A. H. A., & Rosman, R. (2023). The determinants of financial technology adoption amongst Malaysian waqf institutions. *International Journal of Social Economics*, 50(9), 1302–1322. DOI: 10.1108/IJSE-04-2022-0264

zakat.org. (2024). Retrieved from https://www.zakat.org/what-is-the-difference-between-sadaqa-and-zakat/

Zakhlebin, I., & Horvát, E.-Á. (2019). Investor Retention in Equity Crowdfunding. *Proceedings of the 10th ACM Conference on Web Science*, 343–351. DOI: 10.1145/3292522.3326037

Zariff, W., & Yusoff, W. (2024). Concept of Fintech and Financial Inclusion in the Light of Sharī ` ah. *Al-Basirah*, 14(1), 59–77.

Zatadini, N., & Syamsuri, S. (2018). Konsep Maqashid Syariah menurut Al-Syatibi dan kontribusinya dalam kebijakan fiskal. *AL-FALAH: Journal of Islamic Economics*, 3(2), 1–16. DOI: 10.29240/alfalah.v3i2.587

Zdravkova, K., & Basnarkov, L. (Eds.). (2022). *ICT Innovations 2022. Reshaping the Future Towards a New Normal. 1740.* DOI: 10.1007/978-3-031-22792-9

Zhang, W., Chen, M., Xie, Y., & Zhao, Z. (2018). Prosocial Spending and Subjective Well-Being: The Recipient Perspective. *Journal of Happiness Studies*, 19(8), 2267–2281. DOI: 10.1007/s10902-017-9918-2

Ziraat Participation. (2023). Ziraat Participation Corporate Information.https://www.ziraatkatilim.com.tr/bizi-taniyin/kurumsal-bilgiler/ziraat-katilim-hakkinda

Ziraat, (2024). Open Banking https://www.ziraatbank.com.tr/tr/dijital-bankacilik/acik-bankacilik#:~:text=A%C3%A7%C4%B1k%20Bankac%C4%B1l%C4%B1k%20Nedir%3F,i%C5%9F%20modeline%20A%C3%A7%C4%B1k%20Bankac%C4%B1l%C4%B1k%20denilmektedir

Zulkafli, B. N. A., & Ahmad, M. Y. (2016). Constraints and Solutions of Delayed Management of Muslim Immovable Property Management in Malaysia. *Islamiyyat-The International Journal of Islamic Studies*, 38(1), 53–63.

Zustika, A. F., & Fageh, A. (2022). Analisis Dompet Digital "Link Aja Syariah" dari Perspektif Maslahah Mursalah. *Islamic Economics Journal*, 8(1), 25. DOI: 10.21111/iej.v8i1.6279

About the Contributors

Muhammad Ridhwan Ab. Aziz, a Professor of Islamic Banking and Finance at the Faculty of Economics and Muamalat, Universiti Sains Islam Malaysia (USIM). He received his Bachelor Degree of Business Administration (Hons.) in 2001, Master Degree in Islamic Studies, specializing in Islamic Banking in 2008 and Doctorate in Islamic Banking in 2011 from University of Malaya. He is an Assessor for academic program accreditation of Malaysian Qualification Agency (MQA) in the field of Islamic banking and Islamic finance. He is also a Shariah Committee Member for Export-Import Bank of Malaysia Berhad (EXIM Bank) and Citibank Berhad (Malaysia), Internal Shariah Advisory Board for Citibank N.A. Labuan Branch, Shariah Supervisory Board Member for Shuaa Funds OEIC ICC Limited in United Arab Emirates as well as an Arbitrator (Hakam) for Negeri Sembilan Syariah Judiciary Department.

Fuadah Johari is an Associate Professor and Deputy Dean of Research and Innovation at the Faculty of Economics and Muamalat, Universiti Sains Islam Malaysia (USIM). In 2011, she obtained her PhD from the University of Malaya, a Master of Shariah (Hons) in Shariah and Economics in 2004 and a Bachelor of Shariah (Hons) in Shariah and Economics in 1999 from the same university. She is a Fellow Researcher at the Islamic Finance and Wealth Management Institute (IFWMI), and obtained certified Islamic Financial Planner (IFP) by the Islamic Banking and Financial Institutes of Malaysia (IBFIM). She is also a Editorial Board of the Journal of Muamalat and Islamic Finance Research (JMIFR), and several editorial journals at national and international levels. Her academic interests include Islamic Social Finance, focusing on Ijtima'i Economics (Zakat, Wakaf, and Baitulmal), Poverty Alleviation, and Islamic Business.

Ahmad Rafiki is an Assistant Professor and as the Dean of Faculty of Economics and Business, Universitas Medan Area (UMA). He was with University College of Bahrain in the Department of Business Administration as Assistant Professor and as Research Associate in the Mizan Research Centre, Faculty of Leadership and Management, Universiti Sains lslam Malaysia (USIM). He obtained his BBA degree with a major of Marketing from MARA University of Technology and Masters in Management from International Islamic University of Malaysia. In March 2014, he awarded Doctor of Philosophy from Universiti Sains Islam Malaysia (USIM). He is holding Certified Islamic Marketing Associate (CIMA) from the International Islamic Marketing Association (IIMA). He has published many chapters of books/ authored books and articles related to Islamic management, entrepreneurship, SMEs, leadership and halal industry by International publishers such as IBA-MacMillan, IGI Global, Emerald Publishing (Journal of Islamic Marketing, Asian Journal of Accounting Research, Journal of Investment Compliance, PSU Research Review, RAUSP Management Journal, International Journal of Organizational Analysis, Journal of Advance in Management Research, Enterprising Communities: People and Places in the Global Economy), Springer, Routledge etc. He also became the editorial advisory board and reviewer in reputable publishers of Emerald (Journal of Islamic Marketing, International Journal of Islamic and Middle Eastern Finance and Management) and Elsevier. He has presented academic papers in various international seminars/conferences such as in Indonesia, Malaysia, United Kingdom and Turkey. He won as the Outstanding Reviewer of Literati Awards 2020 by Emerald Publishing.

***

Junaidah Abu Seman is a Senior Lecturer at the Faculty of Economics and Muamalat, Universiti Sains Islam Malaysia (USIM). She earned her Doctor of Philosophy degree in Finance from the University of Salford (2017). She has extensively written on Islamic banking, finance, takaful, and business management across seminar papers, journal articles, and case studies. Also, she was an Evaluator for the FAA Programme Accreditation (FPA) under the Finance Accreditation Agency (FAA). Furthermore, she's a lifetime member of the Malaysian Muamalat Association (MMA) and a member of the International Council of Islamic Finance Educators (ICIFE). Her research interests encompass inclusive finance, Islamic banking and finance, and takaful. Contact her at junaidah@usim.edu.my.

Refi Agustina is a student of Universitas Islam Negeri Walisongo Semarang.

Johan Arifin, S.Ag., M.M., is a faculty member at UIN Walisongo Semarang specializing in Islamic Economics and Business. As the Secretary of LP2M, he is actively involved in research and community service to enhance societal well-being. His academic focus includes syariah management and the application of

Total Quality Management (TQM) in Islamic financial institutions, aiming to improve operational efficiency while maintaining ethical leadership and good governance. Arifin teaches courses that integrate syariah principles into modern business practices and contributes to the development of academic curricula that blend Islamic economic theory with practical application. His work emphasizes the competitive edge of syariah-compliant organizations and promotes ethical business practices grounded in Islamic values.

Nasrul Fahmi Zaki Fuadi is a respected academic at the Faculty of Islamic Economics and Business at UIN Walisongo Semarang. His work focuses on Islamic finance, economics, and social issues, with a particular emphasis on sustainable financial practices and halal markets. Fuadi's research includes the impact of zakat literacy, religiosity, and income on zakat payments, as well as developing sustainable Hajj funds using innovative cash waqf models. He has co-authored studies on Islamic banking, exploring factors influencing customers' decisions to switch from conventional to Islamic banks. Fuadi also examines the role of Islamic financial instruments like waqf in economic development. As editor-in-chief of Economica: Jurnal Ekonomi Islam, he plays a key role in advancing Islamic finance research.

Muhammad Zikry Hishamudin is Sales Consultant at RHB Bank where he excels in leveraging his expertise to drive sales initiatives and foster client relationship for Islamic product. Concurrently, he is pursuing a Master's degree in Economic and Muamalat Administration at Universiti Sains Islam Malaysia, focusing on advancing his knowledge in economic principles and the administration of Islamic financial practices. His academic journey began with the successful completion of a Bachelor of Economics (Honours) in Islamic Finance from Universiti Pendidikan Sultan Idris, underscoring his deep-rooted understanding of the principles and applications of Islamic finance within the economic landscape.

Khairatun Hisan is currently a senior lecturer at the Faculty of Business, UNITAR International University. She obtained her Master from International Centre for Education in Islamic Finance (INCEIF). Her main research interests include Islamic wealth management funded by the industry and Ministry of Education.

Nur Shuhada Kamarudin, PhD (Finance) from the University of Salford, UK, is currently a lecturer at the Faculty of Economics and Muamalat. She also holds a professional certificate as an Islamic Financial Planner (IFP). Dr. Nur Shuhada has been invited as a speaker at various community and organizational training programs, where she shares her expertise in Islamic financial planning, wealth management, entrepreneurship, including digital entrepreneurship. Her research interests include personal finance management, Islamic financial planning, business, entrepreneurship, digital entrepreneurship, and Halal tourism. Currently, she is leading and involved in several research grants and also supervises postgraduate students. Additionally, Dr. Nur Shuhada actively presents her research findings at local and international conferences.

Chantika Khoirunnisa is a student of Universitas Islam Negeri Walisongo Semarang.

Reza Maharani is a student of Universitas Islam Negeri Walisongo Semarang.

Yasemin Tekiner is graduate student and Hatice Işıl Alkan is Associate Professor in the field of Economics in Turkey. Hatice Işıl Alkan works for Ondokuz Mayıs University (Economics Department), Turkey.

Muhammad Zarunnaim Haji Wahab serves as a lecturer in finance and banking at the Faculty of Business Management, UiTM Kedah. With expertise in Islamic Finance and Banking, his doctoral research centered on the Environment, Social, and Governance (ESG) concept. Demonstrating proficiency in research and publication, Dr. Muhammad Zarunnaim has authored numerous journal articles indexed in prestigious databases such as WoS, Scopus, and Mycite. He actively contributes to other publications like Majalah Dewan Bahasa dan Pustaka and FBM Insights, alongside his role as a reviewer for various Scopus journals. He also actively involved in several research grants from national, industrial and international matching grant.

Index

G

I

L

M

N

P

S

T

U

www.ingramcontent.com/pod-product-compliance
Lightning Source LLC
LaVergne TN
LVHW080347011026
849161LV00009B/2220